Windows 8 and Windows Phone 8 Game Development

Adam Dawes

Apress®

Windows 8 and Windows Phone 8 Game Development

ISBN-13 (pbk): 978-1-4302-5836-0

ISBN-13 (electronic): 978-1-4302-5837-7

President and Publisher: Paul Manning
Lead Editor: Ewan Buckingham
Technical Reviewer: Don Sorcinelli
Editorial Board: Steve Anglin, Mark Beckner, Ewan Buckingham, Gary Cornell, Louise Corrigan, Morgan Ertel, Jonathan Gennick, Jonathan Hassell, Robert Hutchinson, Michelle Lowman, James Markham, Matthew Moodie, Jeff Olson, Jeffrey Pepper, Douglas Pundick, Ben Renow-Clarke, Dominic Shakeshaft, Gwenan Spearing, Matt Wade, Tom Welsh
Coordinating Editor: Anamika Panchoo
Copy Editor: Ann Dickson
Compositor: SPi Global
Indexer: SPi Global
Artist: SPi Global
Cover Designer: Anna Ishchenko

Distributed to the book trade worldwide by Springer Science+Business Media New York, 233 Spring Street, 6th Floor, New York, NY 10013. Phone 1-800-SPRINGER, fax (201) 348-4505, e-mail orders-ny@springer-sbm.com, or visit www.springeronline.com. Apress Media, LLC is a California LLC and the sole member (owner) is Springer Science + Business Media Finance Inc (SSBM Finance Inc). SSBM Finance Inc is a Delaware corporation.

For information on translations, please e-mail rights@apress.com, or visit www.apress.com.

Apress and friends of ED books may be purchased in bulk for academic, corporate, or promotional use. eBook versions and licenses are also available for most titles. For more information, reference our Special Bulk Sales–eBook Licensing web page at www.apress.com/bulk-sales.

Any source code or other supplementary materials referenced by the author in this text is available to readers at www.apress.com. For detailed information about how to locate your book's source code, go to www.apress.com/source-code/.

For Ritu and Kieran

Contents at a Glance

Contents

About the Author

Adam Dawes is a software developer and systems architect working at a cutting-edge, online service development company.

He has been a compulsive programmer since the age of four, when he was first introduced to a monochrome Commodore PET. The love affair has continued through three subsequent decades, flourishing through the days of the 8-bit dinosaurs to today's era of multicore processors and pocket supercomputers.

A constant throughout all of this has been Adam's fondness for computer games. From the very first time *Nightmare Park* displayed its devious maze of pathways in green symbols back in 1980, he has been a games player across a variety of genres and styles. These days, he spends his spare time playing the latest 3-D titles on his PC and enjoying some of the classics in his stand-up arcade machine or sit-in cockpit driving cabinet. Creating his own games has always been a hobby and while he has no plans to become part of the professional games industry, Adam has a lot of fun developing his own titles nonetheless.

Adam lives with his wife, Ritu, and son, Kieran, in the southeast of England. His web site can be found at www.adamdawes.com (and all of his finished projects can be downloaded from here), and he can be e-mailed at adam@adamdawes.com or found on Twitter @AdamDawes575. He would particularly like to see the results of your own game development projects.

About the Technical Reviewer

Don Sorcinelli has been involved in the planning, development, and deployment of enterprise applications for over 20 years. His involvement in these projects expanded to include mobile device platforms in the late 1990s. He is currently involved in the planning and deployment of mobile-device management solutions for Tangoe, Inc. in Waltham, MA.

Don has regularly presented on Windows Mobile and Windows Phone development, deployment, and usage topics at regional and national conferences and user groups for more than a decade. He also was a co-manager of the Boston/New England Window Mobile (and eventually Windows Phone) User and Developer Groups for 11 years. As a result of these efforts, Don was awarded Microsoft Most Valuable Professional ("MVP") status for his work in the community around Windows Phone from 2005 through 2011.

Acknowledgments

I must start by thanking my parents for all of the opportunities they gave me when I was growing up and for encouraging my computer habit from a very young age.

Thank you to everyone at Apress for their assistance in getting this book written and delivered, in particular to Ewan Buckingham for getting the project underway and supporting it throughout, to Anamika Panchoo for her tireless assistance and encouragement, and to Ann Dickson for making the book much more readable than it would otherwise have been.

I owe thanks too to Don Sorcinelli for his invaluable input throughout the whole book—it's always a pleasure Don! And thanks to Tom Spilman and the rest of the MonoGame dev team, too, without whom none of this would have been possible—you guys have done an awesome job.

And finally, of course, thanks without end to my wife, Ritu, and my son, Kieran, for their constant encouragement and for tolerating my shutting myself in my study and writing every evening and weekend—I'll be spending much more time with you both now, I promise!

Introduction

The Goal of This Book

The effect of mobile computing in recent years has been impossible to miss. Nearly everyone carries a smartphone with them every second of the day. The last few years have also seen an explosion in the popularity of tablet devices, offering many of the uses and benefits of a phone but with much more screen space and processing power.

With the latest iterations of its desktop and mobile operating systems, Microsoft has started its push to conquer these areas of technology. Alongside the established desktop operating system market, Windows 8 introduces an all-new, touch-screen-orientated user interface that is fast and responsive on the desktop and on tablet devices alike. Windows Phone 8 continues to improve upon Microsoft's phone operating system, offering a smooth and powerful experience on both high- and low-specification devices.

Writing games for mobile devices offers huge potential. It is very easy for people to "pick up and play" a game on their mobile device because they always have it in their pocket or bag. Whether users are progressing through a sprawling role-playing game while riding on a train or they simply want a few minutes of casual diversion while waiting for an appointment, they can turn to mobile gaming. With Windows 8 on the desktop, too, even greater numbers of users are available.

One thing that didn't make the jump from Windows Phone 7 to Windows Phone 8, and was never available at all for Windows 8 app development, is the popular XNA gaming framework. Fortunately, an existing open source project named MonoGame was able to step in to fill this void, continuing to offer a powerful and easy-to-learn game development framework that can be used by .NET developers, with no need to get involved with C++ or DirectX. MonoGame is almost entirely compatible with XNA, so existing knowledge and code can be transferred from XNA to MonoGame with a little effort.

This book aims to bring you the knowledge and techniques that you will need to create your own games for computers and devices running the Windows 8 and Windows Phone 8 operating systems. Starting with the basics of the platforms and their development environment and progressing to advanced topics such as 3-D graphics, it will guide you step-by-step toward creating a simple and manageable environment into which you can write your own games and distribute them to the world for fun or profit. Example projects are provided to demonstrate all of the techniques discussed, and they are ideal as a basis for experimentation.

Who This Book Is For

This book is written for those users who are already familiar with programming one of the two main managed Visual Studio languages, C# or Visual Basic.NET. It is assumed that you already have a grasp of the fundamentals of programming and are familiar with using the environment for PC-based application development. This is not an introduction to programming or to Visual Studio itself.

You will, however, be given a complete guide to setting up the development environment for Windows 8 and Windows Phone 8 application programming, to getting your first programs to compile, and to interactively debugging your games as they run within the various development environments available—on a local desktop PC, a tablet device, or the Windows Simulator for Windows 8 app development—and for Windows Phone development on either the Windows Phone emulator included with the phone's free software development kit, or on a real device.

From there, you will be shown in detail how to set up and use MonoGame for your own creations, covering 2-D and 3-D graphics, user input, sound effects and music, and much more.

In order to develop your games, you will need to use the Visual Studio 2012 development environment. If you already have Visual Studio 2012, you can add the required development tools into your existing environment. If you do not have it, you can download the various Visual Studio 2012 Express editions for both Windows 8 and Windows Phone 8 development free of charge from Microsoft's web site.

While most of the projects in the book can be developed using just the provided software testing tools, it is recommended that you also have access to real devices to test your games if possible—a phone for Windows Phone development or a Windows 8 tablet of some description for Windows 8 development.

The examples in this book are all written using C#. Developers who are more familiar with VB.NET should find that the language code and concepts translate over to C# fairly easily, so this should not present too much of a barrier to entry.

Chapter Overview

The following overview provides a brief description of each chapter. The chapters tend to build on one another, so it is recommended that you read them in sequence to avoid knowledge gaps in later chapters.

Chapter 1 introduces Windows 8 and Windows Phone 8 development and explores how to use the Visual Studio 2012 development environment to create games and applications for each one. This chapter also explains how to set up simple .NET projects running against the various testing environments and real devices, explores debugging techniques, and discusses the various options for code development across the two operating systems.

Chapter 2 dives into MonoGame, exploring in detail the structure of MonoGame projects, the approach to displaying and updating graphics, how sprites can be used to create complex 2-D graphics output, and how to work with fonts and text.

Chapter 3 takes the concepts explored so far and builds them into a simple reusable game framework that simplifies many of the tedious elements of setting up a game project. This allows you to focus on the game itself rather than getting weighed down with object management. This chapter also introduces an example game project named *Cosmic Rocks*, which will bring together many of the techniques covered.

Chapter 4 covers the subject of user input. All sorts of input devices are available on Windows 8 and Windows Phone 8 devices, from touch screens, keyboards, and mice to gamepads and accelerometers. All of these are explored in detail to show how they can be used to allow your games to be controlled.

Chapter 5 turns up the volume and reveals the options for game audio. Covering simple sound effects to MP3 music playback, this chapter gives you everything you need to know about sound for your games.

Chapter 6 begins to explore rendering with vertices and matrices instead of using sprites. Matrix transformations are uncovered and explained so that graphics can be rotated, scaled, and translated, and concepts such as texture mapping, blending, and alpha effects in this environment are explored.

Chapter 7 lifts the MonoGame feature set up into the third dimension, explaining how to create 3-D game worlds. Subjects covered include perspective and orthographic projections, the depth buffer, and lighting so that your scenes really come to life.

Chapter 8 continues the exploration of MonoGame in the third dimension and introduces a number of useful new rendering features. These include importing 3-D objects from third-party modeling packages, moving and manipulating the camera within a game world, creating particle effects, creating background imagery with sky boxes, applying fog to a 3-D scene, and using MonoGame's Effect objects to add new features and capabilities to your game.

Chapter 9 provides some useful reusable components that may be used in any game. A framework for managing multiple game modes to simplify switching between menu screens and game play sections, a simple mechanism for loading and saving user settings, and a high score table implementation are provided to allow you to focus on writing your game rather than having to reinvent these features yourself.

Chapter 10 exposes the application life cycle and provides techniques for handling the window size changing. These are essential topics that you will need to come to grips with so that your game can live side-by-side with other applications that the user chooses to open.

Chapter 11 takes a brief diversion away from MonoGame and begins to explore the XAML user interface features available to Windows 8 and Windows Phone 8. While not specifically geared around games, XAML has a lot of functionality that can be used in your game to simplify the task of creating user interfaces. This chapter introduces the environment and explores how it is used.

Chapter 12 takes a more detailed look at the controls that are available for use in XAML pages. It also explores topics such as XAML page layout options, page navigation, and device orientation.

Chapter 13 brings MonoGame and XAML together at last, demonstrating how both of these frameworks can be used in the same project, separately or both on screen at once.

Chapter 14 sets up shop inside the Windows Store and the Windows Phone Store. These are the outlets that you need to use to distribute your games to the rest of the world and perhaps make some money from them, too. The chapter contains a guide to the Store submission requirements as well as tips on testing your game, managing application versions, creating trial versions, and more.

CHAPTER 1

■ ■ ■

Getting Started

Developing games for Windows 8 and Windows Phone 8 can be a hugely enjoyable and rewarding way to spend your time. With a little effort and determination, you can create wonderful, enjoyable games that you can put in your pocket and spread to audiences around the world at the same time.

Microsoft's latest versions of its operating systems provide some rather different environments from the versions that came before them. In Windows 8, the design of the operating system has been adapted to suit both desktop and touch-screen operation. Windows Phone is radically different to Microsoft's earlier Windows Mobile platform. While these two systems look and function differently in a number of ways, they have begun to converge into a more consistent set of programming commands and libraries to make developing applications across the two a much easier task than in the past.

There is one key element of Windows 8 and Windows Phone 8 that has stayed essentially the same as the platforms that preceded them: the use of the .NET programming environment to create games and applications. This brings with it some exceedingly powerful and flexible programming languages and one of the best available development environments.

The development platform for Microsoft's mobile devices has advanced substantially over the last decade. During the early years of the original Windows Mobile/Pocket PC operating system, programming involved using the suite of eMbedded Visual tools. They came supporting two different languages: eMbedded Visual Basic and eMbedded Visual C++.

eMbedded Visual Basic was based on the same technologies as Visual Basic for Applications (VBA). It was similar in a number of ways to Visual Basic 6 (VB6), the desktop version of VB that was current at the time, but had many shortcomings such as the lack of strongly typed variables and poor object orientation features. Programs were written using a stand-alone integrated development environment (IDE), which had its own peculiarities and different ways of working from VB6.

eMbedded Visual C++ presented more of a challenge because of differences not only in the IDE but also in the code. Although established C++ programmers would no doubt have managed to pick up this language without too many problems, those who were less versed in the intricacies of C++ would have found that the amount of new information they needed to learn might be a significant barrier to entry.

All this changed with the release of Visual Studio .NET, and then later the versions of the .NET Framework that are built to target Windows 8 and Windows Phone 8 application development. These .NET versions provide class libraries that are parallel to the desktop .NET Framework. While not completely identical to their desktop equivalents, a substantial set of identical functionality does exist, and any programmer who is comfortable developing C# or VB .NET applications for Windows will be instantly at home developing for Windows 8 and Windows Phone.

Windows 8 and Windows Phone 8 development uses the very latest Visual Studio 2012. The IDE has made advances in a number of ways since that of the earlier versions of Visual Studio, but best of all, Microsoft has chosen to release "Express" versions of Visual Studio that support development completely free of charge. Although there are charges and fees involved in some areas of development and in distribution of finished applications (as we will see later in this book when we discuss this subject in more detail), these are generally fairly modest and do not create the barriers to entry that having to purchase the full versions of Visual Studio presented in the past.

The development environment also integrates into the full (Professional, Premium, or Ultimate) versions of Visual Studio seamlessly if you have such a version already installed.

On Windows Phone 8, all applications are delivered through the Windows Phone Store (previously known as the Marketplace). The Store is operated by Microsoft, and it provides a lot of very useful features. These features include an extremely simple installation mechanism with no need to worry about the installation of runtime frameworks, support for trial versions of applications, automatic update notifications, and protection against piracy.

Windows 8 also installs applications through its own Windows Store, which operates in an extremely similar way. The desktop is also available on Windows 8, however, and for computers running the "full" versions of the operating system (Windows 8, Windows 8 Pro, or Windows 8 Enterprise, but not Windows RT, the cut-down version of the operating system intended for tablet devices such as Microsoft's Surface), it is possible to download and install applications without using the Windows Store. For the purposes of this book, we will only be considering Windows Store applications. These applications will work on all versions of Windows 8, including Windows RT.

A major advantage of developing using Visual Studio is that the exact same IDE is used as for any other Windows development you may undertake. There is no need to learn the details or keyboard shortcuts of a new IDE; instead, you will be working within the environment you are already used to, which includes all your user interface tweaks and preferences changes. Developing an application for Windows 8 or Windows Phone 8 is simply a question of creating a different project type.

Programming within Visual Studio also means that the Windows Phone developer can take advantage of the maturity of its development environment. Microsoft has spent many years improving the user interfaces and functionality of Visual Studio, and countless versions and releases have cumulated in an extremely powerful and user-friendly studio for application design, development, and debugging. All this is at your disposal when developing your games and applications.

The Framework also retains much of the power of its desktop cousin, including extensive object orientation features, strong variable typing, generics, flexible collections, and powerful XML processing functions.

In this chapter, we will take a closer look at the .NET Framework, at setting up and using Visual Studio, and at creating your first simple Windows Phone application. We will also examine some of the options that are available for game development.

A Closer Look at Visual Studio Development for Windows 8 and Windows Phone 8

Let's start by taking a look at the versions of Visual Studio that we can use for developing software for these operating systems.

The free versions of Visual Studio are available as a number of "Express" installations. The two versions we are interested in are Visual Studio Express 2012 for Windows 8 and Visual Studio Express 2012 for Windows Phone. These can be installed individually or together, depending on your requirements.

Alternatively the "full" paid versions of Visual Studio 2012 can be used, in which case the Windows 8 and Windows Phone 8 development options will be integrated into your existing IDE.

Development does have system requirements that necessitate a reasonably modern PC. For Windows 8 development, your computer will need to be running Windows 8 Pro; for Windows Phone 8 development, you will need a 64-bit installation of Windows 8 Pro. Windows Phone development generally uses the Windows Phone Emulator a lot, too. In order for this to work, you will need to have a processor that supports hardware-assisted virtualization (this will need to be enabled in your PC's BIOS settings), Second Level Address Translation (SLAT), and hardware-based Data Execution Prevention (DEP). Without these, you will only be able to test your applications by running them on a physical device. You can find full details about these hardware requirements and how to configure them on Microsoft's web site at http://tinyurl.com/wp8emulator.

There is no support for developing for Windows 8 or Windows Phone 8 in earlier versions of Visual Studio. The good news is that Visual Studio 2012 will install side by side with earlier versions of Visual Studio without causing any problems.

Language Choices

.NET development offers the choice of a number of different languages. Three "managed" languages are supported: C#, VB, and C++. Both platforms also now support development with unmanaged C++ and also with JavaScript/ HTML. These latter options provide a lot of new options in terms of cross-platform application development.

In this book, we will focus on C# for all of our samples and example code. If you are familiar with any of these other languages, you should find that both reading and writing C# will come naturally with a little practice.

IDE Features

As would be expected from Visual Studio, a number of very useful features are available to help develop and debug Windows Phone applications.

Simulators and Emulators

Visual Studio offers a number of options to help test and debug your programs on a variety of devices. Although it is strongly advised to use a real device regularly during your application development process to ensure that everything works properly on actual hardware, being able to use these test environments for general coding and testing is extremely useful.

For Windows 8 development, there are several options available. By default, your applications will simply run on your PC, just as they would if they were finished applications downloaded from the store. Most of the time, this is the way that you will execute them.

In order to know how your app will work on other devices, however, the simulator can be used as an alternative target for execution. The simulator runs in a window and pretends to be a separate device. This allows you to try out your application in a number of different resolutions and also to simulate both mouse and touch input. A screenshot of the Windows 8 simulator is shown in Figure 1-1.

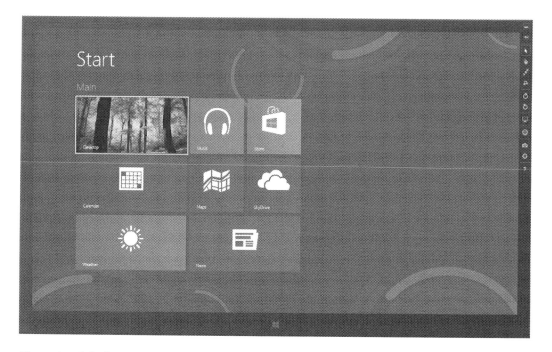

Figure 1-1. *Windows 8 simulator*

It should be noted that the simulator is actually running a virtual view of your own machine: any changes that you make inside the simulator will be made to your own PC as well, so be careful what you do!

For Windows Phone development, an emulator is provided inside which your applications can be executed. This emulator provides a full working implementation of a device, allowing you to test all aspects of integration between your app and other parts of the operating system. (This is a change from the emulator that was used for Windows Phone 7 development, which provided only a small subset of the functionality available on a real phone.)

The emulator offers access to a number of features of the device, including the ability to simulate networking, screen rotation, and touch-screen input using the mouse cursor. A screenshot of the emulator is shown in Figure 1-2.

Figure 1-2. *Windows Phone 8 emulator*

Whichever platform you are developing for, switching between these different deployment options is as simple as can be. All you need to do is select to the target environment in the Visual Studio toolbar and start your application—it will launch in the appropriate environment, ready for you to use.

When we fire up the simulator and emulator shortly, you'll see that it takes a few seconds for each to initialize itself. This delay can be frustrating when you are in a repeat modify/compile/test cycle, but both the simulator and emulator can be left running in the background when you stop your code from executing. They will then resume much more quickly the next time you begin a debug session.

Also note that the Windows Phone emulator does not retain its state when it is closed. Each time you restart it, all previous data will have been cleared and the emulated device will be reset to its default settings. In order to retain stored data from one execution to the next, it is important not to close the emulator window.

XAML Page Designer

A fully featured page designer is available to lay out windows and controls for use within your applications. The designer goes as far as to display an image of the device around the edge of your page to help visualize its appearance.

These pages are created using an XML-based markup language called XAML (pronounced "zammal"), which is an abbreviation for eXtensible Application Markup Language. Pages may be created and modified by using the visual designer or by editing the underlying XAML directly.

Visual Studio will display both the designer and the XAML editor as side-by-side panels within the IDE, as shown in Figure 1-3, and any change made to either will be immediately reflected in the corresponding panel. This provides a very flexible mechanism for page design, allowing each panel to work together to perform its actions more efficiently.

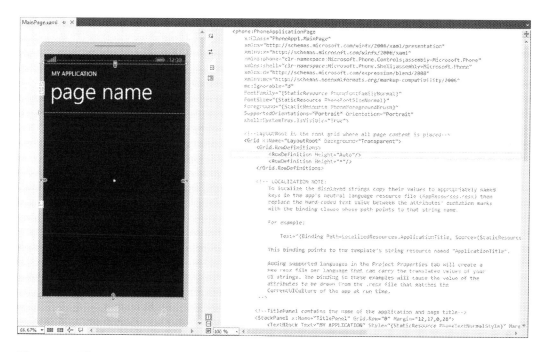

Figure 1-3. *The XAML page editor showing the designer and page source together for a Windows Phone app*

We won't be using XAML for actual game development in this book, but later on we will look in much more detail at how it can be used alongside other parts of our games in order to provide easy and functional user interfaces.

Breakpoints

Another extremely useful tool is Visual Studio's breakpoint feature. No doubt familiar to any desktop developer, breakpoints are fully supported for Windows 8 and Windows Phone development, and they can be used when running against the simulator, emulator, and a physical device. It can be extremely useful to break into your code, examine your variables, and step through the instructions while watching the results on a real device on the desk next to you.

Debug Output

Access to the Visual Studio Output window is available from applications running inside the IDE. Text can be written to the Output window at any time, allowing you to easily keep track of what your program is doing. Pairing this with the ability to have two independent screens (your PC screen and your device screen) makes this tool particularly powerful.

Windows 8 Devices

Windows 8 itself runs on a very diverse set of devices: desktop PCs, laptops with or without touch screens, and tablet devices. Some devices may be running the cut-down Windows RT, others the full versions of Windows 8. In order to maximize your potential audience, your applications will need to tolerate all of these environments and work seamlessly regardless of what conditions they find themselves running in.

Let's take a look at what we can expect.

Screen Hardware

PCs come with screens of all shapes, sizes, and resolutions. At the time of this writing, according to the "Steam Hardware and Software Survey," which is performed by the game company Valve, the most common desktop PC display resolution is 1920-by-1080 pixels (which is standard "full HD" resolution), used by 28 percent of users. While this may be a good default resolution to target, it does mean that 72 percent of users are not going to be using that resolution. (If you'd like to see up-to-date statistics on this and other areas of hardware, http://store.steampowered.com/hwsurvey contains the full survey results.)

When it comes to tablet devices, things are different once again. While the Surface Pro does use a 1920-by-1080 screen, the cut-down Surface RT's resolution is only 1366-by-768 pixels. Other tablets from other manufacturers could fall anywhere on this scale, and let's not forget that tablet devices can easily be switched between landscape and portrait orientations.

Clearly, knowing the resolution to use for your game is going to be a challenge!

Fortunately, there are some features of the game environment that we will be using that will come to our rescue here. We'll take a look at these later on. The important thing to bear in mind is that you have no idea what screen resolution you will be operating in, so you will need to test in a variety of resolutions inside the Windows 8 simulator.

Hardware Buttons

Once again, the identity of the physical buttons your users will have connected is going to be a complete unknown. At one end of the scale is the desktop PC, replete with keyboards and multibutton mice. At the other end is the tablet device, which has just one single button—the Windows button.

In order for your game to work across all these devices, you will have to cater for the simplest set of hardware buttons available, which is essentially none at all. (The Windows button cannot be intercepted by your application.) There are standard ways to deal with this that we will look at later on.

It should be noted, however, that if you can provide additional functionality for users who are using a desktop PC, they will more than likely appreciate it! Little touches such as supporting the Escape key to go backward can make all the difference to your users' experience.

Graphics Hardware

The range of graphics cards and their capabilities is, of course, huge. In terms of desktop PCs, all modern graphics cards are astoundingly powerful and will more than likely cope with whatever challenges you throw at them. Laptops and, in particular, tablet devices are likely to be less capable in this area.

In order to avoid any nasty surprises, try to test your games on lower-powered devices such as tablets as frequently as possible. If you find that you are pushing past the capabilities of the hardware, it's important to realize this as soon as possible to prevent significant reworking later on.

The simulator will not provide a realistic representation of performance on other devices as its performance will be based on that of your development PC, so there is no substitute for real devices in this instance.

Location and Orientation

Some devices will offer sensors to tell you which way up the device is being held and the location in the world where it is being used (using GPS or even via detection of local WiFi connections if GPS is not available, albeit with less accuracy). In certain environments, these are great for games. Orientation sensors can be used to implement steering wheels for driving games, for example, where tilting the device steers the car. Location sensors offer possibilities for "accentuated reality" games, where the real world and the game mix together to provide an additional layer of realism.

These sensors are unlikely to be available in anything other than tablet devices, however (tilting your desktop PC monitor is probably not going to catch on!), so if you decide to take advantage of one of these sensors, consider your alternatives for when they are not available.

Cooperation with the Device

Unlike desktop applications, Windows Store apps have a stricter set of requirements when it comes to their interactions with other parts of the device. They have limited access to the file system, can only use the managed .NET APIs, and have highly constrained multitasking capabilities.

Generally, when your app loses focus, Windows will allow it to keep running in the background for a short time. After a while, however, the app will be put to sleep and will no longer execute any code. It can be resumed at any time the user wishes, but it cannot perform updates while in this state.

For games, this does not often create too many problems, but do be aware that you have less power and control over the device than you may be used to on other operating systems.

Windows Phone Devices

One of the major changes that Microsoft made when first introducing Windows Phone, as compared with the previous Windows Mobile platform, concerns hardware requirements.

The huge diversity of hardware could provide quite a barrier for entry for Windows Mobile. Devices all had different screen resolutions, different hardware buttons, and a fairly substantial range of other internal hardware. Writing games and applications that worked across the entire set of devices could result in a considerable amount of additional effort, whereas saving time by not addressing all these platforms could exclude a significant proportion of the potential customer base from being able to use the application.

This was tackled head on in Windows Phone 7 by requiring a very rigid set of hardware requirements. As the operating system and technologies evolved, this started to become overly restrictive. As a result, with Windows Phone 8, these restrictions have been relaxed slightly. This does create some overheads that you will need to be aware of, but it still provides a solid and predictable platform to develop against.

Let's take a look at what we can expect.

Screen Hardware

To begin with, all Windows Phone 7 devices had exactly the same screen resolution: Wide VGA (WVGA) resolution (480 pixels across-by-800 pixels tall). This greatly simplified the task of ensuring that games and applications properly fit on the screen without having to stretch, shrink, or leave large areas of the screen unused.

As technology and competing devices marched forward, Windows Phone had to ensure that it kept up pace, so this is now just the minimum resolution. A number of devices currently use higher resolution screens (for example, the HTC 8x has a 720-by-1280 pixel screen, and the Nokia Lumia 920 uses a resolution of 768 by 1280). This results in some superb-looking devices, but it also means that you, the developer, will have to cater for all the possible displays that your game will need to run on. Fortunately, the emulator is able to run at all these resolutions, so you can see how your app responds without needing a fleet of different phones.

All Windows Phone devices have multitouch capacitive touch screens, with a minimum of four distinct points able to be tracked at once. This opens up some interesting possibilities for gaming, and we'll be looking at how to use multitouch in games later on in this book.

Just as with tablet devices running Windows 8, an important consideration when designing a game for the phone is that the screen orientation can be rotated into portrait or landscape orientation. Fortunately, Windows Phone has extremely good support for rotating between these orientations, so you can take advantage of whichever screen layout best suits your game.

Hardware Buttons

One of the details that Microsoft has been very strict about for devices running its new operating system is hardware buttons. All devices must have exactly three buttons on the front of the device: a Back button, a Windows button, and a Search button. Of these, only the Back button can actually be used by your application, and you must ensure that it is used for predictable navigation and nothing else. This is, of course, one button more than we can rely on when developing for Windows 8, so we can try to view this as a positive!

Having consistency over the available buttons is good for developers as it means that we don't have to worry about lots of combinations of control mechanisms. However, this limited set of buttons means that there will be no directional pad available, which is a pity because they are very useful as a game input device.

Instead, we can use the touch screen for input, and there are lots of clever and creative ways that this can be done from designing games that the user interacts with by touching objects on the screen, through virtual input pads that spring up wherever the user touches the display, to displaying movement buttons at the bottom of the screen for the user to press.

These rigid requirements don't rule out the possibility of a device manufacturer including a hardware keyboard with the device. A number of Windows Phone 7 devices featured such keyboards, though they don't seem to be available in the Windows Phone 8 world yet. The presence of a keyboard opens up the opportunities for the player to control your game, but clearly we need to avoid making this a necessity for your game so that it works on those devices that do not have one available.

Processors

The Windows Phone platform may not be at the absolute cutting edge when it comes to processors, but it is now commonly using dual-core processors in order to improve processing capability. The operating system has been tuned very well to run in the mobile environment, however, so it often outperforms more powerful competing devices in general use. For serious number crunching though, it may not be able to compete.

If your application is processor-intensive and you are testing it on a high-end device, it would be a good idea to find someone with a less powerful phone and get that person to verify that the performance is acceptable.

Graphics Hardware

All Windows Phone 8 devices contain dedicated graphics hardware and take advantage of this to provide hardware-accelerated 3-D graphics. This is extremely important for game development, of course, and it is one of the factors that make the platform viable for modern games.

The performance of the hardware is impressive considering its size, but there is no real comparison between it and the current top-end desktop graphics hardware. Be realistic about what you are going to ask it to do—though don't be afraid to experiment and see how far you can push it!

Location and Orientation

Also standard on all devices will be an accelerometer and a Global Positioning System (GPS) receiver.

The accelerometer can be very useful for game developers. It allows the device to detect which way up it is being held and can sense in detail any movement that results in the device being rotated. This provides an excellent input control mechanism, allowing players to influence what is happening on the screen by physically moving their phones.

Probably of less interest for gaming is the GPS functionality. When appropriate line-of-sight reception has been established with the GPS satellites, the device can detect where in the world it is located. This opens opportunities for making games that revolve around the player's whereabouts, but the scope for this in gaming may be limited.

Cooperation with the Device

Let's not forget an extremely important fact: your game is running on other people's phones and personal organizers. They will place more importance on tasks such as answering a phone call or responding to a calendar reminder alert than in continuing to play your game.

Running applications have limited control over what happens when other features of the device become active. An application that loses focus will be immediately placed into a suspended state, and no further processing is possible until it is reopened by the user.

In the original release of Windows Phone 7, games were terminated entirely when they lost focus and could only be restarted from scratch. If they wanted to maintain state so that the user could resume the game, they had to take care of handling the game state themselves. This could be a time-consuming and frustrating programming task.

Fortunately, this was hugely improved with a subsequent operating system update. This updated behavior is present in Windows Phone 8, too. Windows Phone is now able to automatically restore any recent app to exactly the state it was left in. Your app is notified when this happens; however, it can be useful to take advantage of this by, for example, automatically pausing when the game resumes to allow the user time to adjust to what is going on. People will appreciate small details such as these.

Using Visual Studio for Windows 8 and Windows Phone Development

Let's take a look now at the steps required to begin development of games and applications.

Installing Visual Studio

Installing Visual Studio for Windows Phone development is very easy. If you do not already have a full version of Visual Studio installed, you can visit www.microsoft.com/visualstudio/eng/products to download the Visual Studio 2012 Express editions. These are free, complete, and fully functional development environments that will provide all the tools needed for you to develop your games.

You will find editions for both Windows 8 and Windows Phone, so download whichever of these you need. For reasons we will cover later, however, it is important that the Windows Phone development environment is available, even if you are planning to develop only for Windows 8. Make sure that you do install that as well. The Express editions install as two separate applications, each of which enables you to target just the appropriate types of project.

When the Express versions of the product are first launched, they will prompt you to enter a registration product key. It is possible to continue without such a key for a period of 30 days, but after this, Visual Studio will stop working until such a key is entered. The keys can be obtained free of charge by clicking the Register online button and following the instructions that appear. You will need a Microsoft Live ID in order to complete this, and the registration process will guide you through creating one if necessary. Your Live ID will later be used for publishing your finished apps, so make sure you look after your account details carefully.

Following this, you may be prompted to obtain a developer license. This is also free and the process takes just a few seconds to complete. The developer license is valid for one year, after which time it will need to be renewed—Visual Studio will prompt you automatically to repeat these steps when needed.

If you already have a full version of Visual Studio 2012 installed (one of the Professional, Premium, or Ultimate editions), support for building Windows 8 apps (known as "Windows Store" applications) will already be available. In order to add support for Windows Phone development, use the same installer for Visual Studio Express for Windows Phone as detailed at the start of this section. The setup application will detect the presence of Visual Studio when it is launched, and it will download just the components that are required, based on your current system configuration.

Once the installation is complete, Visual Studio can be launched and the project types for Windows Store and Windows Phone projects will appear. Figure 1-4 shows the New Project window ready to create a new, empty Windows Store application for Windows 8. Figure 1-5 shows the same window preparing to create a new Windows Phone project.

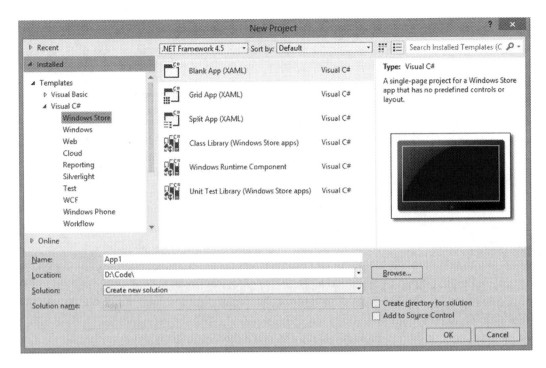

Figure 1-4. *Creating a new Windows Store project in Visual Studio 2012*

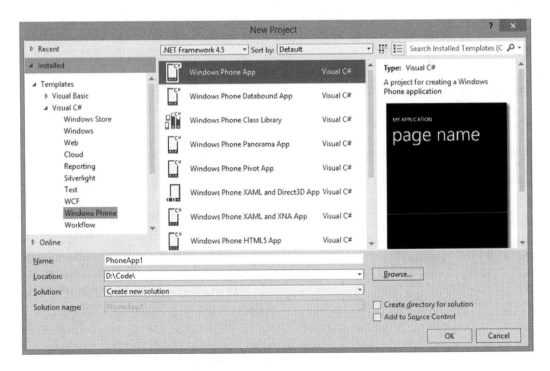

Figure 1-5. *Creating a new Windows Phone project in Visual Studio 2012*

▓ **Tip**   Visual Studio 2012 ships with two visual "themes" named Light and Dark, and it defaults to using the Dark theme. If you wish to switch between these two themes, you can do so via the Tools ➤ Options menu. The Color theme is the first item in the Environment ➤ General section of the Options window.

Once everything is installed as required, we are ready to begin. The following sections will guide you through creating your first project for Windows 8 and for Windows Phone. They will both follow essentially the same steps and end up with the same test project. Feel free to work through either or both of them, as needed. Much of the content is repeated for these sections so that they can each be read in isolation.

Creating a Windows Store Project

With tools all in place, it is time to create a simple Windows Store application for Windows 8 and take a look at how we can execute it. We will create a simple blank XAML application for this purpose.

To begin, select File ➤ New ➤ Project within Visual Studio, and choose the Visual C# item within the list of Installed Templates, followed by the Windows Store item. The panel to the right will display the available Windows Store templates that can be used to create a new project. Select the Blank App (XAML) item.

If you are using one of the full versions of Visual Studio, you will see that above the templates is a drop-down list that allows the .NET Framework version to be selected. For Windows Store development, we will always leave this set to .NET Framework 4.5. The Express editions of Visual Studio automatically select .NET 4.5.

At the bottom of the window, select a project directory and enter a project name (or accept the default name of App1 if you wish). Unless you have a particular preference for using separate directories for the solution and project files, uncheck the Create directory for solution check box to keep the directory structure a little tidier.

Once everything is ready, click the OK button to create the project. After a few seconds, the new project will open within the Visual Studio IDE.

Project Templates

A number of different templates are provided by Visual Studio for your new project, one of which we selected in the previous section. Each of these will result in a different initial project for you to start working on. The templates that you will most likely find useful are as follows:

- *Blank App (XAML)*: This is the default empty project template for creating XAML applications. If you are creating apps other than games, this is often the place you will begin. We will actually use a custom template for our games, which we will see in Chapter 2.

- *Grid App (XAML)*: This template creates another near-empty XAML project, but with some predefined user interface pages revolving around the XAML Grid control.

- *Split App (XAML)*: This is another near-empty XAML project template, this time with a different preset user interface design.

- *Class Library (Windows Store apps)*: If you need to create any separate Class Library projects (to build DLL files) for your Windows Store apps, use this project template to create them. The resulting project is essentially completely empty, but it is compatible with Windows Store projects and so ready for you to add your classes to.

It is not possible to change the project type once the project has been created. If you find that you need to change the project once you have started developing it, you will need to create a new project of the required type and copy in all of the existing code files.

Designing a Page

Now, we are ready to make some minor changes to your test application's default page. The page is named MainPage.xaml inside Solution Explorer, and you can double-click it to open it in the XAML page editor.

In the top section of the page editor window is the page designer and preview area. In the bottom half is the XAML code for the page. If you want, you can change the orientation of the divide by clicking the Horizontal Split or Vertical Split buttons at the bottom or right of the dividing bar between the two. The two parts can also be quickly swapped over by clicking the Swap Panes button, also located inside the divider. The designer panel also contains a useful zoom slider that allows you to focus more closely on the page design for detailed layout work, if required.

Initially, the page is a simple, empty, black page. For the purposes of this simple application, we will simply place a Button control onto the page and get it to display a message when clicked. The Button is added from the Toolbox exactly as it would be for a desktop application: click the Button icon in the Toolbox panel (expand the Common XAML Controls item if needed) and then draw it into the empty region in the center area of the page. The result can be seen in Figure 1-6.

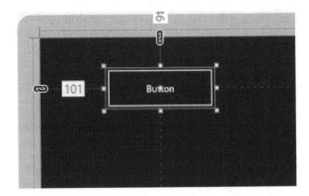

***Figure 1-6.** A button placed within the Windows Store app XAML page designer*

Once you have added your Button, take a look at its properties in the Properties window (see Figure 1-7). If you have created Silverlight applications in earlier versions of Visual Studio, you will probably recognize many of the available properties. If you have worked only with Windows Forms in the past, many of these properties might be unfamiliar, but there should also be some whose purpose is obvious. We'll look into more of these properties in greater detail in the XAML chapters later in this book.

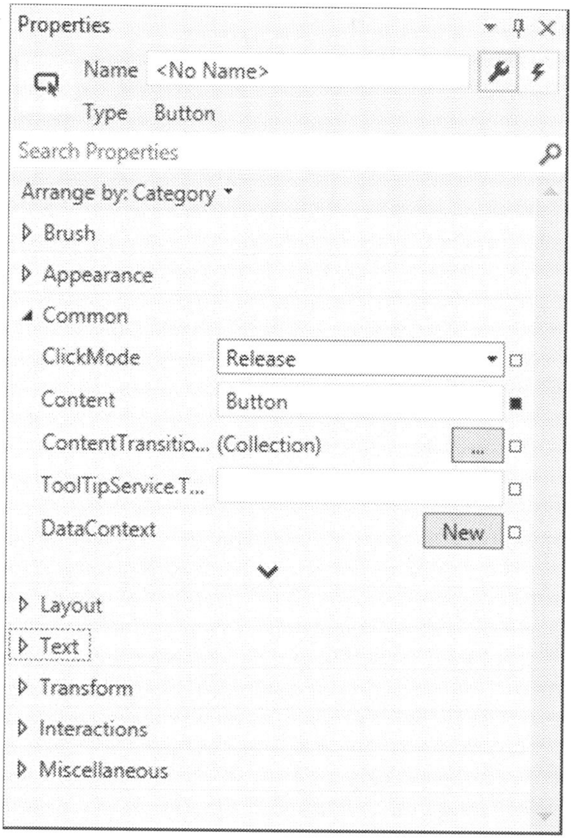

Figure 1-7. The Button's properties

▓ **Tip** If the Properties window is not open, it can be opened by selecting the View/Properties Window item from Visual Studio's main menus. Under the default key mappings, it can also be opened by pressing F4 on the keyboard.

Double-click the button to open the code designer and create the button's Click event handler. This will display the "code-behind" file for the page, which is where the C# code is developed. In Solution Explorer, you will see that the MainPage.xaml item has expanded to reveal MainPage.xaml.cs contained within. These two files are analogous to the form design and form code files that are present when working with Windows Forms.

The code within MainPage.xaml.cs should look just as you would expect when developing a desktop application. At this stage, it should be clear how much similarity there is within the Visual Studio IDE between desktop and Windows Store application development.

Complete the implementation of the Button_Click_1 procedure, as shown in Listing 1-1.

Listing 1-1. The Button_Click_1 procedure for the Windows Store app

```
private async void Button_Click_1(object sender, RoutedEventArgs e)
{
    MessageDialog msg = new MessageDialog("Welcome to your app!","Message");
    await msg.ShowAsync();
}
```

You may receive some compilation warnings after entering this. If you do, try checking the following:

- Note the async keyword that was added to the procedure declaration line. You will need to add this manually. This should resolve one of the errors.

- The MessageDialog class resides in a .NET namespace that we have not instructed the compiler to automatically use. To fix this, right-click the MessageDialog class name within your source code and then choose Resolve ➤ using Windows.UI.Popups; from the menu that appears. This will add the required using statement to the top of the source file and correct the other errors.

▓ **Note**   You may be unfamiliar with two of the keywords used here: async and await. These are both new to .NET 4.5 and are designed to simplify your code when operating time-consuming tasks that might otherwise cause the user interface to become unresponsive. We will look at these keywords in more detail later in the book.

Running the Application

We are now ready to compile and run the project. Press F5 or click the Run button in the Visual Studio toolbar to begin the process. After compilation (and assuming that there are no errors!), Visual Studio launches the application directly on your PC. As with all Windows Store applications, this will entirely take over the screen—this may be something of a surprise at first, but you will quickly get used to it!

Unsurprisingly, the app displays a black screen containing a button. Clicking the button will display the message dialog box shown in Figure 1-8.

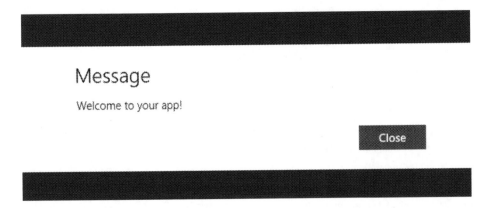

Figure 1-8. The test application in action

To stop the program, Alt-Tab back to the Desktop (or click the Desktop in the running apps panel by moving the mouse cursor to the very top-left of the screen) and click the Stop Debugging button in Visual Studio. The IDE will return to edit mode, and your program will close.

Running in the Simulator

Most of the time, the quickest and most efficient way to test and develop your app will be running it directly on your PC, but when you want to be able to see how it behaves on different devices (specifically, devices with different screen resolutions), the simulator is an excellent and straightforward way to achieve this.

To switch to using the simulator, click the drop-arrow on the Debug Target button on the toolbar and select Simulator, as shown in Figure 1-9. Then begin running your project as normal.

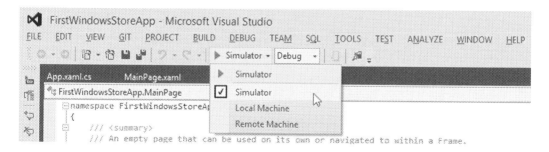

Figure 1-9. *Selecting to run the project against the simulator*

This time, instead of launching on your PC and taking over the whole display, the simulator application will launch on your desktop and the project will run inside it. You can then switch back and forth between the simulator and Visual Studio as much as you need to in order to debug and improve your project.

▓ **Caution** The simulator is actually a window into your own PC configuration (it is internally implemented as a specialized Remote Desktop session). Any changes that you make to the setup of the computer inside the simulator will also be made to your own PC, so be sure you know what you are doing before changing things!

On the right edge of the simulator window, a number of tools are displayed to help control the way the simulator works. These include a number of "input mode" buttons to control whether the simulator is simulating mouse or touch input. Among these are "pinch" and "rotate" modes, which simulate using two fingers at once. These can be operated by holding the left mouse button and rolling the mouse wheel. Clearly, this is not as intuitive and simple to use as an actual touch screen, but it is much better than nothing!

Another button allows the device resolution to be controlled, as shown in Figure 1-10. These options will immediately switch the simulator to the appropriate screen resolution without needing any kind of restart. This can sometimes prove quite confusing to your app, which may not expect such a change to be possible. If unusual behavior occurs following a resolution change, it is usually advisable to restart any running app

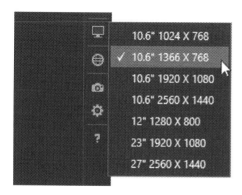

Figure 1-10. *Available simulator screen sizes and resolutions*

Some of these resolutions will be inconvenient or impossible to display on your PC monitor, so the simulated screen is automatically scaled to fit the size of the simulator window. On the larger resolutions, this will probably result in a loss of detail as the image will be shrunk to fit, so be aware that you may not be seeing the full display detail in these situations.

Running on an External Device

You will no doubt be pleased to hear that running your application on a separate device is no more difficult than running it on your PC or within the simulator, and it provides an extremely similar experience. This procedure works equally well for portable devices (tablets) and other desktop PCs. There are a few steps that you will need to go through before you can begin working with the device, however. Let's take a look at the details now.

Connecting the Device

First of all, you will need to ensure that the device you are going to work with is connected to the same network as your development PC. All remote-device interaction is carried out across the network rather than by connecting devices physically (with USB cables, for example).

If your target device is a portable device, ensure that its WiFi is enabled and connected to the appropriate network. If the device is another PC, ensure that it is part of the same Local Area Network as your development PC.

Installing the Remote Debugger

In order for your project to be able to launch on another device, that device must be running the Visual Studio Remote Debugger. This is a small, free application released alongside Visual Studio that you can install on the target device.

The installer for the Remote Debugger can be found on the Visual Studio download page: www.microsoft.com/visualstudio/downloads—search the page for "Remote Tools for Visual Studio 2012." There are three different versions of the installer available, one for each supported processor architecture (x86, x64, or ARM). If you wish to install this on a Windows RT device such as the Surface, you will need to launch the Desktop and then download to the device's disk in exactly the same way as you would on a normal desktop PC, then double-tap the downloaded file to begin the installation.

Once the debugger has been installed, you will find a new Remote Debugger icon on your Start menu. Select this to launch the debugger. The first time it launches, the debugger will display an Options window, as shown in Figure 1-11. These options can be left at their default settings. After clicking OK, the Remote Debugging Monitor will appear, showing content similar to that in Figure 1-12. When this appears, the device is ready to communicate with Visual Studio.

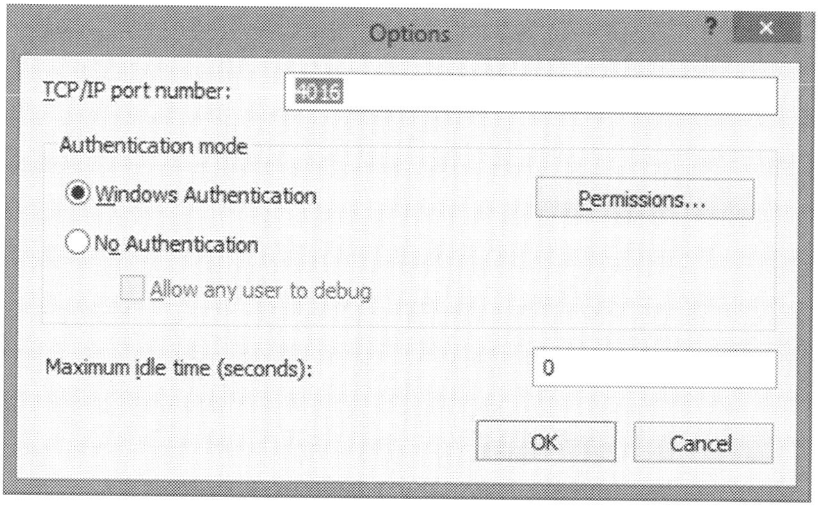

Figure 1-11. *The Remote Debugger Options window*

Figure 1-12. *The Remote Debugger Monitor window waiting for a connection from Visual Studio*

Deploying to the Device from Visual Studio

Now we are ready to deploy our project to the device from inside Visual Studio.

First, click the drop-arrow on the Debug Target button on the toolbar and select Remote Matching from the available targets. Visual Studio will display the Remote Debugger Connections window, as shown in Figure 1-13. Your configured remote device should appear in the device list (as "Europa" does in this illustration). Click the required device and then the Select button that appears next to it in order to specify the device against which to debug.

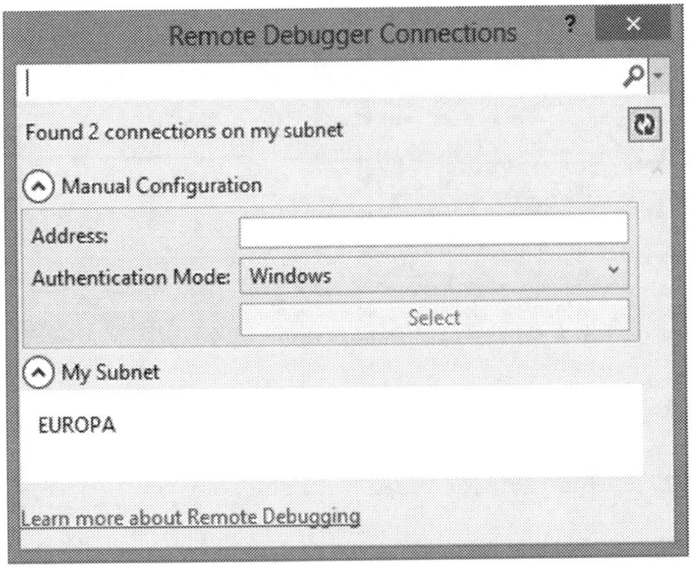

Figure 1-13. Selecting a remote device to use for debugging

▓ **Tip** Once you have selected a device, Visual Studio will save this selection as part of your Project configuration. If you wish to change to a different device later on, open the Project Properties window and select the Debug tab. Within the Start Options section, you will be able to select the appropriate target device within the Remote machine field.

At last, everything is configured and ready to run—start your project running and it will connect to and deploy your app to the target device. Well, almost. The very first time, you will need to obtain a developer license for the target machine. Just as with the license for your development machine, this is free and takes just a few seconds to obtain by following the prompts that appear to complete this step. Once this is done, your app should finally launch.

▓ **Note** For deployment to succeed, the device must be logged in, the screen must be on, and the lock screen must not be displayed. If these conditions are not met, a deployment error will occur, although Visual Studio usually provides good feedback about what the problem is to help you figure out how to proceed.

This sounds like quite a lot of work, but once the initial configuration has been completed, it's very easy to repeat later on: simply launch the Remote Debugger on the target machine, select Remote Machine as your debug target, and launch the project.

For tablet devices in particular, this is a delightful way to work: the tablet need not be tied down to your development machine with physical cables—it can simply sit on the desk next to you.

Apps that are deployed to target devices in this way will continue to be available even once the development machine and the Remote Debugger have been closed, so you can continue to use them just like any other app that you have installed.

Congratulations—you have written and deployed your first Windows Store application!

Creating a Windows Phone Project

Now it is time to create a simple Windows Phone application and take a look at how we interact with both the emulators and real devices. We will create a simple XAML project for this purpose.

To begin, select File ➤ New ➤ Project within Visual Studio, and choose the Visual C# item within the list of Installed Templates, followed by the Windows Phone item. The panel to the right will display the available Windows Phone templates that can be used to create a new project. Select the Windows Phone App item.

If you are using one of the full versions of Visual Studio, you will see that above the templates is a drop-down list that allows the .NET Framework version to be selected. For Windows Phone development, we will always leave this set to .NET Framework 4.5. The Express editions of Visual Studio automatically select .NET 4.5.

At the bottom of the window, select a project directory and enter a project name (or accept the default name of PhoneApp1 if you wish). Unless you have a particular preference for using separate directories for the solution and project files, uncheck the Create directory for solution check box to keep the directory structure a little tidier.

Once everything is ready, click the OK button to create the project. Another dialog box will appear prompting you to choose the target Windows Phone OS version: select Windows Phone OS 8.0 from the available options and click OK.

After a few seconds, the new project will open within the Visual Studio IDE.

Project Templates

Visual Studio provides a number of different templates for your new project. Each of these templates will result in a different initial project for you to start working on. The templates that you may find the most useful might include the following:

- *Windows Phone App*: This is the main project template for creating empty XAML applications. If you are creating apps other than games, this is often the place you will begin. We will actually use a custom template for our games, which we will see in Chapter 2.

- *Windows Phone DataBound/Panorama/Pivot App*: Each of these creates another near-empty Silverlight project, but a particular predefined user interface example is in place.

- *Windows Phone Class Library*: In order to create a class library that can be used by other Windows Phone projects, use this template. Such class libraries will be accessible from the games that we will be creating. The resulting project is essentially empty, ready for you to add your classes to.

It is not possible to change the project type once the project has been created. If you find that you need to change the project once you have started developing it, you will need to create a new project of the required type and copy in all of the existing code files.

Designing a Page

Now, we are ready to make some minor changes to your test application's default page. The page is named MainPage.xaml inside Solution Explorer and should open automatically when the project is created.

On the left half of the page editor window is the page designer and preview area. On the right half is the XAML code for the page. If you want, you can change the orientation of the divide by clicking the Horizontal Split or Vertical Split buttons at the bottom or right of the dividing bar between the two. The two parts can also be quickly swapped over by clicking the Swap Panes button, also located inside the divider. The designer panel also contains a useful zoom slider that allows you to focus more closely on the page design for detailed layout work, if required.

Initially, the page is a simple, empty, black page. For the purposes of this simple application, we will simply place a Button control onto the page and get it to display a message when clicked. The Button is added from the toolbox exactly as it would be for a desktop application: click the Button icon in the Toolbox panel (expand the Common Windows Phone Controls item if needed) and then draw it into the empty region in the center area of the page. The result can be seen in Figure 1-14.

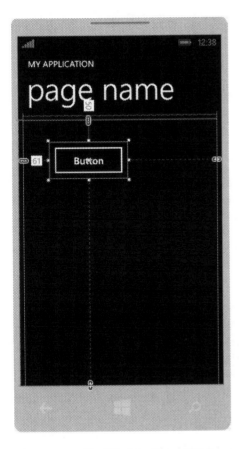

Figure 1-14. *The Windows Phone XAML page designer*

Once you have added your Button, take a look at its properties in the Properties window (this is pretty much the same as for the Windows Store project's Button properties, as shown back in Figure 1-7). If you are used to creating Silverlight applications in earlier versions of Visual Studio, you will probably recognize many of the available properties. If you have worked only with Windows Forms in the past, many of these properties might be unfamiliar, but there should also be some whose purpose is obvious. We'll look into many of these properties in greater detail in the XAML chapters later in this book.

Double-click the button to open the code designer and create the button's `Click` event handler. This will display the code-behind file for the page, which is where the C# code is developed. In Solution Explorer, you will see that the `MainPage.xaml` item has expanded to reveal `MainPage.xaml.cs` contained within. These two files are analogous to the form design and form code files that are present when working with Windows Forms.

The code within `MainPage.xaml.cs` should look just as you would expect when developing a desktop application. At this stage, it should be clear how much similarity there is within the Visual Studio IDE between desktop and Windows Phone (and Windows Store) application development.

Complete the implementation of the `Button_Click_1` procedure, as shown in Listing 1-2.

Listing 1-2. The Button_Click_1 procedure for the Windows Phone app

```
private void Button_Click_1(object sender, RoutedEventArgs e)
{
    MessageBox.Show("Welcome to your first app!", "Message", MessageBoxButton.OK);
}
```

Running in the Emulator

We are now ready to compile and run the project. Press F5 or click the Run button in the Visual Studio toolbar to begin the process. After compilation (and assuming that there are no errors!), Visual Studio launches the Windows Phone emulator. This can take a few seconds to open, so be patient while this task completes. Subsequent deployments to the emulator will go much more quickly if the emulator is already running, so try to get into the habit of leaving it open when you switch back to Visual Studio between debug runs.

Once this is all complete, your program will launch. Clicking the button will display the MessageBox, as you would expect (see Figure 1-15).

Figure 1-15. *The test application running in the Windows Phone emulator*

To stop the program, click the Stop Debugging button in Visual Studio. The IDE will return to edit mode, and your program will close on the emulator. The emulator will keep running, ready for any additional programs that you start.

Selecting an Emulator Image

Visual Studio actually ships with a number of different emulators, each representing a different device profile. Any one of these may be selected from the Debug Target drop-down in the Visual Studio toolbar. If you select an emulator image that is not already running, then it will launch. Otherwise, Visual Studio will reconnect to the existing running emulator image.

The emulator images that are available are as follows:

- *Emulator WVGA 512MB*: This emulates the lowest-spec device available for Windows Phone 8, both in terms of screen resolution and memory. The WVGA resolution is 480-by-800 pixels (the same resolution as used by all Windows Phone 7 devices). Most Windows Phone 8 devices have 1GB of RAM available, but some of the lower-cost devices have only 512MB available, as mirrored by this emulator image. This image therefore represents the "low-end" extreme of available devices, so you should ensure that your games run on this emulator without any display problems or crashes. For this reason, it can be useful to make this your standard development emulator so that problems can be detected as quickly as possible.

- *Emulator WVGA*: This image is the same as the WVGA 512MB image, except with the "standard" 1GB of RAM available.

- *Emulator WXGA*: This image keeps the standard 1GB of RAM but increases the screen resolution to 768-by-1280 pixels. This is the highest specification emulator image available. Consequently, it should represent the other extreme image against which to test. You will need to ensure that everything in your game scales correctly for display on this much higher-resolution display.

- *Emulator 720P*: This final image also has 1GB of RAM and uses a resolution of 720-by-1280 pixels—the standard 720p High Definition screen resolution.

Running on a Real Device

Switching your project across to run on a real phone is quick and painless and provides a very similar experience to running inside the emulator. One important difference between using a device and the emulator is that a device will give you a real indication of how fast your game is going to run. The emulator runs at the fastest speed it can, which is often much faster than on an actual phone.

There are a few steps that you will need to go through before you can begin working with the device, however. Let's take a look at the details now.

Registering the Device

Before you can deploy applications to a device, you must first have a Windows Phone developer account. These accounts are not free, though they are relatively inexpensive (currently priced at $99 per year, but this could change in the future). You will need this account before you can publish any of your finished games into the Windows Phone Marketplace anyway, so there is really no way to avoid this charge, even if you develop entirely on the emulator.

You can sign up for an account at the developer.windowsphone.com/join web page. You will be required to provide various pieces of information to Microsoft as part of this process and will receive notification messages telling you how to do this. The process might take a couple of days from start to finish. Besides providing your personal details, you will also be able to provide banking details so that you can be paid for applications that you create and sell in the Windows Phone Store.

Once your account is registered and active, the next step is to set the device up to connect to your PC. Unlike Windows 8 app development, Windows Phone apps are deployed from Visual Studio by connecting the phone to your PC via its USB connection. Plug the device in and allow Windows to set up its drivers. This should be a completely automatic process.

The next step is to register your device. This connects the device up to your developer account and allows Visual Studio to use it for deployment. To begin this process, launch the Windows Phone Developer Registration application, the main window of which can be seen in Figure 1-16. This application installed as part of the Windows Phone 8 SDK (or as part of Visual Studio Express for Windows Phone), and you should be able to find it in the Start menu. The application should connect to your phone and guide you through the registration process within a few seconds.

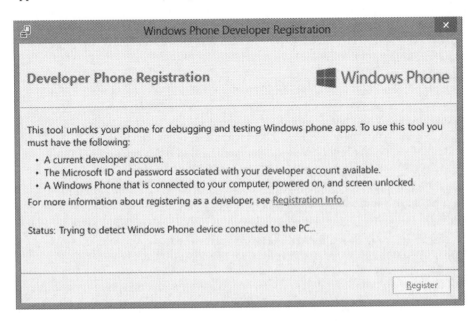

Figure 1-16. *The Windows Phone Developer Registration application*

▨ **Note**   If you have previously developed for Windows Phone 7, you may notice that there is no mention of launching the Zune software in this description. Zune is no longer needed when developing for Windows Phone 8; Visual Studio can now connect directly to the device on its own.

At this point, you are finally ready to begin working with your phone in Visual Studio. These steps only need to be performed once for each device that you use.

Deploying to the Device from Visual Studio

Now we are ready to deploy our project to the device from inside Visual Studio.

Once everything is ready, choose to deploy your application to the device rather than the emulator. This is done by dropping down the Debug Target combo box in the toolbar and selecting Device, as shown in Figure 1-17. When you next launch your project, Visual Studio will connect to the device and then install and launch the application executable.

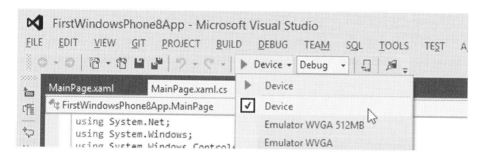

Figure 1-17. *Choosing to launch the application on a physical device*

▨ **Note**   For deployment to succeed, the phone must be switched on and the lock screen must not be displayed. If these conditions are not met, a deployment error will occur, although Visual Studio usually provides good feedback about what the problem is to help you figure out how to proceed.

Unsurprisingly, the project running on the phone looks and behaves just as it did in the emulator. Congratulations—you have written and deployed your first Windows Phone application!

Debugging

Now that you have a simple application written and working, let's take a closer look at some of the debugging features that are available.

The powerful debugging tools that can be used within the Visual Studio IDE make development systems from the past look extremely primitive in comparison. We can use all these tools for Windows 8 and Windows Phone development, making tracking down problems simple.

Breakpoints

First, try setting a breakpoint on the line of code containing the MessageDialog or MessageBox function call. Launch the program (on a real device, the simulator or the emulator), and click the button within the page. As you would expect, the breakpoint triggers just as it would on a desktop application.

From here, you can explore all the usual attributes of your application: the call stack, object property windows, visualizers, and immediate window commands. Everything is present and working.

The one useful feature that is not available, however, is "edit and continue." Unfortunately, code changes cannot be applied at runtime and will either need to be held back until the IDE returns to edit mode, or you will need to restart your application in order for the changes to have any effect.

Debug Output

At any stage within your application, you can display text in Visual Studio's Output window. This is done in just the same way as for a desktop application by using the System.Diagnostics.Debug object. To test this, add the code shown in Listing 1-3 to the beginning of your Button_Click_1 procedure.

Listing 1-3. Writing text to the Debug Output window

```
System.Diagnostics.Debug.WriteLine("Debug text");
```

Each time you click the button, you will now see your debug text appear within the IDE, as shown in Figure 1-18.

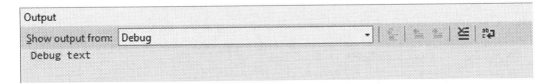

Figure 1-18. *Debug text appearing in the Debug Output window*

▓ **Tip** If the Output window is not displayed, it can be opened by selecting View/Output from Visual Studio's menu. If the Output window is open but no text is appearing, make sure that the "Show output from" combo box in the window toolbar is set to Debug, as shown in Figure 1-11.

Cross-Platform Development

This book's focus is on game development for both Windows 8 and Windows Phone 8. So far, the tiny example application that we have created has consisted of two separate and unrelated projects. If you intend to develop only for one of these platforms, there's probably little more to consider in this area. But, if you plan to develop for both, you will need to consider how to provide code that works across both of the platforms.

You may have already noticed that even with a trivial one-line application, the code is different between the two platforms. While it is true that the Windows 8 and Windows Phone product lines have become significantly closer together, they are sadly still some distance from one another.

This distance is reflected both in the way the devices operate (back button for Windows Phone, not for Windows 8; swiping gestures to control the environment for Windows 8, not for Windows Phone, and so on) and in their programming APIs.

The APIs are more consistent across platforms than in earlier versions of both Windows and Windows Phone, but there are still many differences that will need to be accounted for. In particular, the XAML language used to build user interfaces can differ fairly significantly between the two platforms.

Here are some of the options that are available for cross-platform development.

Building Entirely Separate Projects

The simplest solution to organize is to continue to use completely separate projects. The major advantage here is that you can customize each of the projects entirely for their target platform without having to worry about the effects on the other.

The disadvantage here is that you need to effectively code the application twice, once for each platform.

Using Shared Source Files

At the other end of the scale, you could set up your project so that it shares some or all of your source code files. This approach still requires the creation of a separate project for each platform, but these projects are configured to use the same source files—not copies of the same files, but rather the actual same files.

Such a set up can reduce the code duplication as common code can be created just once and be used by both projects. This configuration can become fragile, however. Changes made for one platform can end up adversely affecting the other. It can also become difficult to keep track of where your source files are actually physically located.

An example of two projects set up in this configuration can be found in the SharedSourceFiles folder within the source code that accompanies this book. The projects are essentially the same as those that we created earlier in this chapter, except that their button click handlers both call into a function named ShowMessage in the class named SharedClass. This code file has been created within the FirstWindowsStoreApp project's folder and then linked from the FirstWindowsPhoneApp project. The link was created by selecting to add an existing item to the Windows Phone project, browsing to and selecting the file, and then clicking the drop-down arrow on the Add Existing Item window's Add button and selecting Add As Link.

Of course, as we have already seen, the code required to display the message box is different between the two platforms, so we cannot simply create a single version of the function. Instead, we use conditional compilation to provide two versions of the same function: one for Windows Phone and one for Windows 8. Windows Phone projects will (by default) always have the WINDOWS_PHONE compiler constant defined, whereas Windows 8 applications will instead have NETFX_CORE defined. By checking for the presence or absence of these, we can create code that will compile only in one or the other project, as shown in Listing 1-4.

Listing 1-4. Using conditional compilation to create separate versions of code for each platform

```
    private const string MessageText = "Welcome to your app!";
    private const string MessageTitle = "Message";

#if WINDOWS_PHONE
    public void ShowMessage()
    {
        MessageBox.Show(MessageText, MessageTitle, MessageBoxButton.OK);
    }
#else
    public async Task ShowMessage()
    {
        MessageDialog msg = new MessageDialog(MessageText, MessageTitle);
        await msg.ShowAsync();
    }
#endif
```

In this particular example, none of the actual code is shared, only the string constants. For other projects that used APIs that are common between the two platforms, a much higher degree of code sharing could be achieved without having to repeat so much code.

Another similar approach to this is to move the shared source code files out into a separate class library. The class library would still need to be built around two separate project files (one for each platform) and would still require conditional compilation to control the code across the two platforms, but this keeps all the functional logic of the class library separate from the user interface. As we have already touched upon, the XAML requirements between the two platforms are not compatible, so it makes sense to keep these completely separate.

Choosing a Development Approach

You will need to decide for yourself which of these approaches works best for you. It is a very good idea to try setting up a couple of simple projects for yourself to identify the advantages and disadvantages of each.

In this book, we will use the first approach for all of the example projects, creating separate projects for each platform. As far as possible, we will keep the code the same between the duplicated projects, but this method will allow us to make any required changes to the functionality without having to worry about unexpected effects on the other platform.

As you will see, we will also build a "game framework" project, which is used by the majority of the examples that are used and can be used for your game projects too. This project is created using shared source files so that we can keep a consistent API and reuse as much code as possible.

Getting Help

Sooner or later, you will run into a development problem that you cannot solve on your own. A number of great resources can provide insight and inspiration to keep you moving. Here are some of them.

MSDN

As you would expect from one of Microsoft's products, comprehensive and detailed documentation is available for all aspects of the Windows 8 and Windows Phone development APIs. MSDN is an excellent source of help and is never farther away than a quick press of the F1 key.

Search Engines

The Web is, as ever, an indispensible fountain of information. When searching, try to accompany your search phrase with "windows 8," "windows store," or "windows rt" (including the quotation marks) when searching for Windows 8 content, or "windows phone" or "windows phone 8" for the phone.

Microsoft's Windows Phone Developer Center

The Developer Center can be found at the following URL:

```
http://dev.windowsphone.com/
```

In addition to your developer account dashboard, this site hosts a large variety of articles, development tips, frequently asked questions, and code samples. Of particular interest is the Community link, which leads to a number of very active message forums. There's a good chance that someone will be able to offer you some assistance.

Game Development

We've spent a lot of time discussing development in general, but we have not yet looked at game development. We will start preparing to actually write a game in Chapter 2, but let's conclude this overview of Windows 8 and Windows Phone software development by thinking about what types of games we can create and the technologies available to create them.

Suitable Games

Although the power of the graphics hardware in phone and tablet devices might not be approaching that of dedicated PC graphics cards, it is nonetheless very capable. With some effort and testing across real devices, impressive 3-D graphical displays should be well within your reach.

Not everything has to reach into the third dimension, however. Two-dimensional games can be extremely enjoyable and rewarding to play, too. We can do great things with the more laid-back game genres such as strategy, role-playing, and puzzle games. Well-crafted games such as these can become extremely popular because the immediate "switch-on-and-play" nature of portable devices is ideal for people who have only a few spare minutes to dedicate to gaming before real life gets in the way. This type of game is well suited to the phone and has a potentially large audience.

Board and card games are examples of other styles that are easily accessible to a wide audience, and they convert well to handheld devices. In particular, the ability to physically drag cards around the game with a finger leads to a satisfying feeling of involvement.

Novelty games have recently become popular on other platforms such as the iPhone, allowing users to create and distort photographs of their friends, to create sound effects in response to interactions with the device, and to perform a variety of other unusual things. If you have creative flair and imagination to spare, this could be an interesting area to explore!

Welcome to the World of Windows 8 and Windows Phone Development

This concludes our introduction to .NET development for Windows 8 and Windows Phone 8. We hope you are enthusiastic and excited about the opportunities of developing for these platforms.

Please spend a little time experimenting with the capabilities of the environment and the .NET libraries. We will look at some of the things we can do with .NET in more detail in the following chapters, but for now, do get comfortable with building and launching applications.

Have fun!

Summary

- Applications for Windows Store and Windows Phone applications can be developed in C#, VB, or C++. We will focus just on C# in this book.

- Visual Studio 2012 can be installed either as free stand-alone Express versions, or as an add-on for a "full" version (Professional, Premium, or Ultimate).

- A variety of different hardware configurations may be encountered, particularly for Windows 8 devices. Windows Phone devices tend to work within a narrower range of possible configurations.

- Windows Store applications can be developed and debugged on the local machine, in the simulator (allowing a variety of different screen resolutions to be tested), or on a remote device (either another desktop PC or a tablet device).

- Debugging on remote Windows 8 devices requires the Remote Debugger application to be installed and running. Debugging runs across the network without needing a direct wired connection between the development PC and the target device.

- Windows Phone applications can be developed and debugged in one of a number of emulators or on a physical device. Debugging on a device requires the device to be connected to the development PC with a USB cable.

- The same IDE features are available when debugging Windows 8 or Windows Phone applications as when building any other type of project, including full use of breakpoints and debugging commands.

- The APIs between Windows 8 and Windows Phone versions of .NET are not the same. Projects may be created independently with code manually copied between the two, or they can be set to use shared source code files.

CHAPTER 2

■ ■ ■

Getting Started with MonoGame

For the next few chapters, we will look at MonoGame, discover what it is and where it came from, explore its environment, and learn all we need to know to use it for displaying graphics, reading user input, and playing music and sound effects.

In this chapter, we will focus on some of the fundamental mechanics of MonoGame and drawing graphics in 2-D. These are important even if you wish to focus on 3-D games because the underlying program structure is identical. Even in 3-D applications, you are likely to want to use some 2-D graphics as well to present status information or text to the user, so it is important to have a good understanding of MonoGame's capabilities in this area. We'll look at how these principles begin to build into a proper game in Chapter 3.

What Is MonoGame?

Let's begin with a quick history lesson.

In the world of desktop development, DirectX has, for many years, been the Microsoft graphical API. It is very powerful with excellent support for all sorts of 2-D and 3-D graphical effects and, when paired with a capable graphics card, can produce breathtaking scenes and animations.

For many generations of DirectX, the API was really accessible only by developing in C or C++. All the library information was made available to these languages and, although it was theoretically possible to access them from Visual Basic 6 and later from the .NET languages, it was a significant amount of work to actually do so.

With the introduction of DirectX 9 in 2002, Microsoft provided a set of .NET libraries known as Managed DirectX (MDX). This finally gave a proper supported interface for .NET developers to use to access the DirectX features.

Before MDX was established, however, Microsoft changed direction and released a replacement set of technologies called XNA (it officially stands for "XNA's Not Acronymed," in case you were curious—I expect you wish you hadn't asked now!). XNA also offered a fully managed interface, available from any .NET language, and wrapped around DirectX functionality. It offered cross-platform development, initially supporting Windows and the Xbox 360, and then being extended to provide support for Windows Phone 7, too.

You have probably noticed that the whole of the previous paragraph referred to XNA in the past tense. This is because, unfortunately, with the arrival of Windows 8 and Windows Phone 8, XNA is no longer supported. It is still possible to use XNA to create Windows Phone 7 games (which will run on Windows Phone 8 devices but cannot take advantage of any new Windows Phone 8 APIs), but Windows Store and Windows Phone 8 games cannot be created using XNA.

The replacement technology provided by Microsoft is just DirectX, accessible once again from C++. This takes away the ability for C# and VB programmers to create games with a high=performance graphics library, and it also makes it extremely difficult for developers of older XNA games to upgrade on to these two new platforms. In my opinion, this is a huge shame.

Other developers were also unhappy with this situation and two existing open-source projects took action in order to provide an alternative.

The first of these projects is SharpDX (`www.sharpdx.org`). SharpDX provides a wrapper around the DirectX API, written in C#. This allows access to the DirectX functionality from C# (and VB), without having to code in C++.

The second project is MonoGame (www.monogame.net). MonoGame had been set up initially to help developers with porting their XNA games over to other existing platforms such as Android, iOS, Linux, and Mac OS X. Suddenly MonoGame found itself in a position where it could actually enable developers to keep their games working on Microsoft's own operating systems, Windows 8 and Windows Phone 8.

Support was added to MonoGame to support these new versions of Microsoft's operating systems, so now we can continue to take advantage of this for future development. This is a fantastic option for porting existing XNA games on to the new operating system versions, and also for new game development. XNA has a powerful and relatively simple set of APIs that are ideal for both beginning and experienced developers and MonoGame allows us to continue to use this functionality.

In order to maintain maximum compatibility with the real XNA project, all of the MonoGame classes are contained within a namespace of Microsoft.XNA. This may be confusing at first, but just remember that this is actually all MonoGame's code.

That's enough of the history lesson; let's move on and get some coding underway.

Installing MonoGame

First of all, we need to download and install MonoGame so that its libraries and project templates are available for us to use. The installer includes everything that is needed to get up and running, including SharpDX. The download can be found on the MonoGame web site: www.monogame.net.

▓ **Important** At the time of writing, MonoGame is stable and finished for Windows 8 with only one or two small exceptions, but it is still under development for Windows Phone. The v3.0 release contains a number of significant omissions and problems for Windows Phone game development. Most of these are resolved in later updates to the MonoGame source code, but there has not as yet been a new installer created containing these fixes. Whichever platform you are using, please visit http://tinyurl.com/monogameinstall for updated installation instructions before you start working with MonoGame. You will be able to download information and patches from here to get MonoGame working.

Download the "MonoGame Installer for Visual Studio" and launch it (it's probably best to close any running instances of Visual Studio first). The setup process will run and will begin to install the DLLs and project templates required for MonoGame on to your computer. You can keep the default installation options, though you may wish to unselect the Visual Studio 2010 Templates option unless you think that it may be of use elsewhere. After setup is complete, the installation application will close.

Now you can launch Visual Studio, and select to create a new project. Click on the Visual C# item in the templates tree and you should find that three new project templates have appeared. (If they're not there, don't panic! Just keep reading—we'll address this problem in a moment.) The new templates can be seen in Figure 2-1.

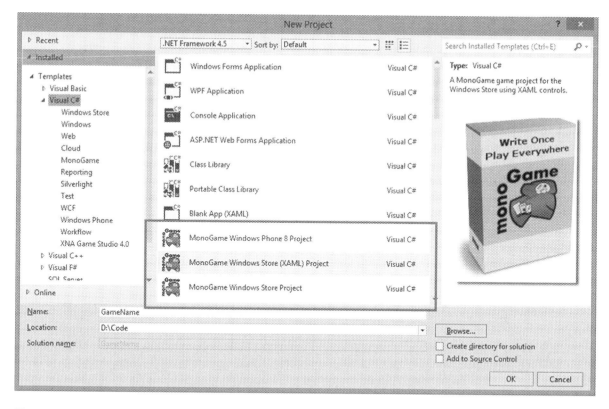

Figure 2-1. *Project templates installed by MonoGame*

If you find that the templates don't appear, this is possibly due to a known issue with the current MonoGame installer. To help work around this problem, the templates are also included with the downloadable content that accompanies this chapter. You can install them by carrying out the following steps:

1. Locate the My Documents/Visual Studio 2012/Templates/Project Templates/Visual C# directory on your computer.

2. Create a subdirectory within here named MonoGame.

3. Into this directory, copy the project template zip files from this chapter's Chapter2/MonoGameTemplates/ directory.

4. Open Visual Studio and select to create a new project. The templates should now appear within the template list.

With everything ready to go, let's create some very simple MonoGame projects.

Creating a MonoGame Project

We'll start by walking through the process for Windows 8 and for Windows Phone separately. After having done that, we can look at some things that can be done with MonoGame that are developed in just the same way for both platforms.

Creating a MonoGame Project for Windows 8

The construction of an empty Windows 8 MonoGame project is as easy as can be: Select to create a new project, choose the `MonoGame Windows Store (XAML) Project` template, choose a location and a name for your project, and click the OK button. Visual Studio will open the project ready for you to develop. You can also find the source code for this empty project in this chapter's accompanying source code, in the `Chapter2/Windows8/FirstProject_Win8` folder.

You can run the project straight away by pressing F5. The project will compile and launch, and it will then show you an empty blue screen. This is, in fact, a particular shade of blue called "cornflower blue." Empty XNA projects have always used this color as a positive indicator that the project is working, as opposed to a black screen, which could simply mean that the app has crashed and that nothing is being drawn to the screen at all. This tradition has, of course, been adopted by MonoGame, too.

You can return to Visual Studio and stop debugging to terminate the running code, just as with any other Windows 8 project. If you wish to try deploying the project to the simulator or another device (including a Windows RT device), you can do so just by changing the debug target, exactly as you did with the test projects that we created in Chapter 1.

Creating a MonoGame Project for Windows Phone

Creating MonoGame projects for Windows Phone is very nearly as simple as for Windows 8, but unfortunately there is one small annoyance that we will need to deal with in this environment. We will come to that in a moment, however. First of all, select to create a new project and select to use the `MonoGame Windows Phone 8 Project` template. Select a location and enter a project name, and then click OK to open the new project. The source code for this empty project can also be found in the accompanying source code in the `Chapter2/WindowsPhone8/FirstProject_WP8` folder.

Initially, the project is configured to run on a physical device. Change the debug target so that it instead is set to use the WVGA Emulator, and then press F5 to launch the project. At this point, you would reasonably expect the emulator to open and the project to start executing within it. Unfortunately, this is not what happens. Instead, an error message appears:

```
Deployment failed because an app with target platform ARM cannot be deployed to Emulator WVGA. If
the target platform is win32/ x86, select an emulator. If the target platform is ARM, select Device.
```

Unfortunately, it is not possible to switch the project between running on a physical device (which expects the project to be compiled for an ARM processor) and the emulator (which instead requires x86 code) without making a small configuration change to the project. This is something of a nuisance. Even though the change is trivial to make, it is still a pain to have to keep making it each time you want to switch between the two environments.

The reason that this is necessary in the first place is due to an omission in the Windows Phone 8 implementation of .NET. Normally, projects for Windows Phone are set to run on "Any CPU." This allows Visual Studio to create program code that will run on both ARM and x86 devices without requiring any modifications. One of the .NET classes required by SharpDX in order to access the DirectX libraries is missing from Windows Phone 8, however, and so to work around this, a C++ library had to be created instead. C++ does not support "Any CPU" compilation and, hence, this option is not available in any projects using SharpDX either.

Should this be resolved in the future, SharpDX and MonoGame will both be updated to support "Any CPU." Once that happens, these steps will no longer be necessary. In the meantime, however, you can use the following steps to switch between the two configurations.

If your project is currently configured to run in the ARM configuration, you can switch to x86 mode as follows. First of all, select Build ➤ Configuration Manager from the Visual Studio menu. This will display the Configuration Manager window, as shown in Figure 2-2, which initially displays your project as being configured for the ARM platform.

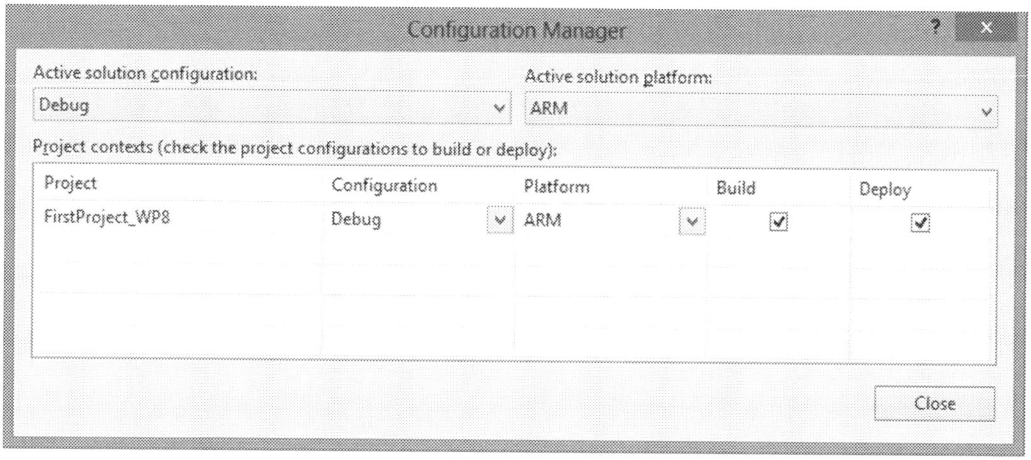

Figure 2-2. *The Configuration Manager window for a Windows Phone 8 project currently targeting the ARM platform*

You can switch across to the x86 platform by dropping open the `Active solution platform` combobox at the top-right of the window and switching it to x86. You will see that the `Platform` column within the table beneath updates automatically to target x86, too.

Close the Configuration Manager window now and make sure that the debug target is still set to use the emulator. Launch the project again and this time you will see that it does successfully open within the emulator, displaying the empty cornflower blue screen just as the Windows 8 project did.

To switch back to the ARM configuration for running on an actual phone, open the Configuration Manager window again and swap back to the ARM platform. Make sure that the debug target is set to `Device` and that your phone is connected to the PC. Now when you launch, the project should successfully open on the phone.

In fact, each configuration remembers the debug target that it last used, so Visual Studio will automatically switch to using one of the emulators when you switch to the x86 platform and to using a device when you switch back to the ARM platform. This means that once you get in the habit of using this approach to move between the two environments, it's not actually too painful.

Adding Some Content

Now let's put something on the screen other than just a solid color. The steps in this section can be applied to both the Windows 8 and the Windows Phone versions of the project. You will find the finished project in the `Sprites_Win8` and `Sprites_WP8` folders of the source code accompanying this chapter.

We will start by displaying a graphic file "sprite" on the screen and by moving it around to show a simple animation.

▓ **Note**   The use of the word *sprite* dates back to the old 8-bit computers of the 1970s and 1980s, whose graphical capabilities were generally limited to moving only small 2-D graphics around the screen. These graphics were given the name *sprite* in reference to their ability to make lively movements, as compared with background images that were usually static. Hardware capabilities are, of course, a world away in modern computer graphics, but the term has stuck around as a way of referring to moving 2-D graphical images. We'll be looking at how sprites can be used in MonoGame in much more detail later in this chapter.

Adding the Sprite Graphic to the Project

In order for MonoGame to be able to display our graphics, we need to load the image into memory. This is achieved using a special type of project known as a "Content" project. The content project compiles our graphics (and also other game resources such as sound effects) into a format that MonoGame can easily use. We will look at the reason for having a Content project later on in this section.

However, before we get there, we have to explore a limitation of the MonoGame engine: It does not currently have any support for building the content or for hosting the Content project. At the time of writing, development is underway to add support for this to MonoGame, but until such time as that is complete, we have to take advantage of a slightly messy workaround.

The workaround is to use XNA itself (actual genuine XNA, not MonoGame) to host and compile the Content project for us. Once it has done this, we can simply copy the compiled content files from the XNA project and paste them into our MonoGame project. Let's take a look at how to achieve this.

The first step is to create another new project. You may wish to open a second instance of Visual Studio for this to avoid having to keep reloading projects. If you are using the Express editions, you will need to use Visual Studio Express for Windows Phone in order to create the required project. In the New Project window, select the `Visual C#/XNA Game Studio 4.0` item in the project templates tree, and then pick the `Windows Phone Game (4.0)` template, as shown in Figure 2-3. Click OK to create the new XNA game solution.

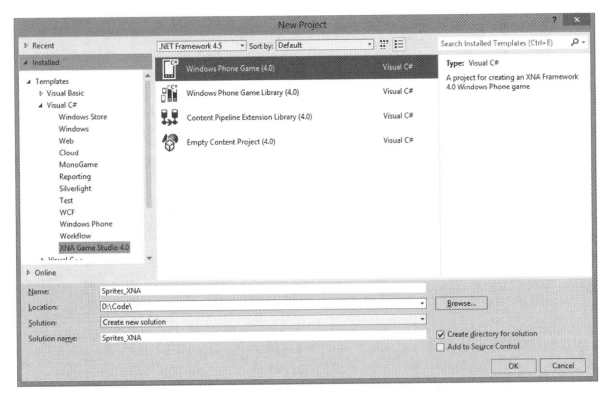

Figure 2-3. *Creating a new empty XNA game project to build our content*

The resulting solution contains two separate projects, as shown in Figure 2-4. The first project, named `Sprites_XNA` here, is a game project built around XNA, just as the projects we created earlier are based around MonoGame. The second project, named `Sprites_XNAContent` here, is the Content project that we are going to use.

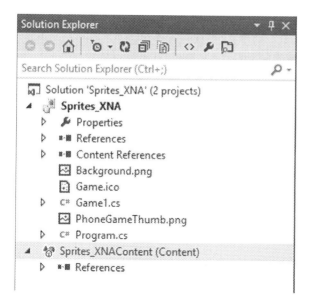

Figure 2-4. *The default projects in a new XNA Windows Phone Game solution*

> ▓ **Note** The game project that appears within the solution can also be compiled and launched, and it will run on both the Windows Phone emulator and on a real device. Remember that XNA is only able to target Windows Phone 7, however, so even if you are developing just for Windows Phone, you will be unable to access any of the new features of the Windows Phone 8 platform. We will be using this type of project only for its abilities to compile resource, not for actual development.

To add a graphic file, right-click the main `Sprites_XNAContent` node in Solution Explorer and select Add ➤ Existing Item from the pop-up menu that appears, as shown in Figure 2-5.

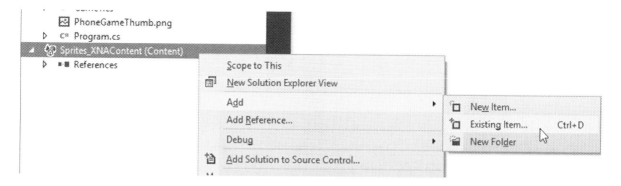

Figure 2-5. *Adding an existing item to the Content project*

In the file browser window that appears, choose a graphic file that you wish to display on the screen. Try to pick something that is not too large—perhaps stick to an upper limit of 256 x 256 pixels for the time being. If you want to use the mouse graphic that is shown in the following example, you can find it in the `Graphics` folder of the source code that accompanies this chapter with the filename `Mouse.png`.

▓ **Tip**   Visual Studio will automatically copy any content files that you select into the Content project's directory, if they are not already present there. This means that there is no need to manually copy files into this folder before selecting them, nor is there a need to keep the files in their selected locations on your hard drive after they have been added.

Once this has been done, the graphic file will appear within the Content project inside Solution Explorer, as shown in Figure 2-6.

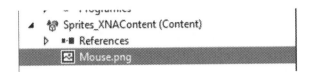

Figure 2-6. *The Content project with a graphic file added*

Now we are ready to compile the content into a form that can be used by MonoGame. Select Build ➤ Build Solution from the Visual Studio menu; the Output window should indicate after a few seconds that the build was successful. The content file has been compiled, but we're not quite done yet. We now need to transfer it across to our MonoGame project so that it can use it.

You will be able to find the compiled content file by browsing to the folder containing the XNA project (named `Sprites_XNA` in our example) and looking from there into the `bin/Windows Phone/Debug/Content` folder. Here you will find a file named, in this case, `Mouse.xnb`. This is the compiled file that we need to transfer across to the MonoGame project (all compiled resource files will use the `.xnb` file extension). Select to copy the file.

Now browse to your MonoGame project (in our examples, this is one of either the `Sprites_Win8` or `Sprites_WP8` projects) and locate the folder containing the main source files. Create a new folder here named `Content` and paste the `Mouse.xnb` file into it.

Finally, return to your project in Visual Studio. At the top of Solution Explorer, click the Show All Files button in its toolbar. This will cause the Content folder to appear within Solution Explorer's list of files. This can be seen in Figure 2-7.

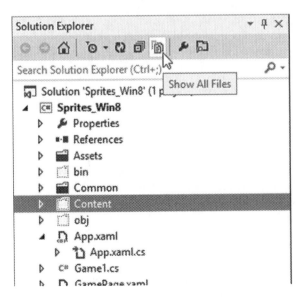

Figure 2-7. *Using the Show All Files button to display the Content folder*

To complete the final steps, expand the Content folder to reveal the Mouse.xnb file inside. Right-click Mouse.xnb and select Include In Project from the menu that appears. Now, with the Mouse.xnb file selected, update its properties so that Build Action is set to Content and Copy to Output Directory is set to Copy if newer. This completes the steps needed to add the graphic file to the game project. You can de-select the Show All Files button now to return Solution Explorer to its default view.

Clearly, this is quite a bit of work to simply add a graphic file to the project. Fortunately it is quicker to update graphics files if they are modified. This involves simply copying the .xnb file from the XNA project's Content directory to our own game project's Content directory. Each time a new file is added, however, all of these steps will need to be repeated.

For your reference, the following is a quick summary of the steps required:

1. Add the graphic resource to the XNA Content project and compile.

2. Locate the resulting .xnb file in the XNA project's bin/Windows Phone/debug/Content directory.

3. Copy the file to a Content directory within your own MonoGame project's main source code directory.

4. Use Show All Files to locate the .xnb file inside Solution Explorer, and select to include it in the project.

5. Set the .xnb file's properties to have a Build Action of Content and Copy to Output Directory set to Copy if newer.

6. Switch off Show All Files once the .xnb file has been added.

Displaying the Graphic

With our graphic in place, we can now amend the code to display it on the screen. This is very simple and consists only of modifications to Game1.cs, so make sure that it is open in the code editor. The required code is identical for both Windows 8 and Windows Phone.

First of all, we need to add a class-level object into which our graphic image will be stored. The object type for this is Texture2D, so we declare it, as shown in Listing 2-1, just below the existing _spriteBatch declaration.

Listing 2-1. Declaring the Texture2D object for the graphic

```
private Texture2D _spriteTexture;
```

■ **Note**   As a naming convention in this book, private class fields will be prefixed with an underscore. All fields will be defined as being private, with internal or public properties added to access them if is required from other classes.

The next step required is to load the graphic into the variable that we have created. This is performed in the class's LoadContent procedure, which you'll find about halfway through the source code. In addition to the existing code, we load the texture by calling the Content.Load function, as shown in Listing 2-2.

Listing 2-2. Loading the graphic file into the Texture2D object

```
/// <summary>
/// LoadContent will be called once per game and is the place to load
/// all of your content.
/// </summary>
protected override void LoadContent()
```

```
{
    // Create a new SpriteBatch, which can be used to draw textures.
    _spriteBatch = new SpriteBatch(GraphicsDevice);

    // TODO: use this.Content to load your game content here
    _spriteTexture = Content.Load<Texture2D>("Mouse");
}
```

The Content.Load function uses .NET's *generics* feature to allow us to specify its return type. In this case, we want it to return a Texture2D object, so we specify this type in the angle brackets in the function call. We then pass a parameter to identify which content item is to be loaded, in this case it is Mouse. Note that this doesn't exactly match the file name that we added to the Content project—when loading content the .xnb file extension is omitted.

The project is now set to load the graphic, so the final step is to display it on the screen. This is achieved by adding a few new lines of code to the Draw function at the bottom of the source listing. The modified function is shown in Listing 2-3.

Listing 2-3. Drawing the graphic file to the screen

```
/// <summary>
/// This is called when the game should draw itself.
/// </summary>
/// <param name="gameTime">Provides a snapshot of timing values.</param>
protected override void Draw(GameTime gameTime)
{
    // Clear the background
    GraphicsDevice.Clear(Color.CornflowerBlue);

    // Set the position for the sprite
    Vector2 position = new Vector2(100, 100);

    // Begin a sprite batch
    _spriteBatch.Begin();
    // Draw the sprite
    _spriteBatch.Draw(_spriteTexture, position, Color.White);
    // End the sprite batch
    _spriteBatch.End();

    // Let the base class do its work
    base.Draw(gameTime);
}
```

We first declare a position for the graphic using a Vector2 structure. This structure is very important in MonoGame and we'll look at it in more detail later on. Then we use the _spriteBatch object that the initial project template code created for us to begin drawing a series of graphics to the screen. The _spriteBatch object is then used once again to actually draw the graphic, specifying which graphic we wish to draw, the position to draw it at, and the color to draw. The color is specified as white in this case; we will look at the behavior of this parameter shortly. Once the image is drawn, we call the _spriteBatch.End method to tell MonoGame that we have finished drawing.

You may also notice the call to GraphicsDevice.Clear in this listing, passing in the parameter Color.CornflowerBlue. It is this line of code that is responsible for the blue background when the project is running. You can change this color to anything you wish if you tire of the default color.

Once the code has been added to your project, run it. If all is well, you should see your graphic presented on the screen. The project can be seen running in Windows Phone in Figure 2-8.

Figure 2-8. *Displaying the sprite on the screen*

This is obviously a trivial example (although we will build on it), but it hopefully demonstrates the tiny amount of code required to get a graphic to display on the screen.

Moving the Graphic

Static images aren't too interesting, so let's make the graphic move. At the moment, we are specifying its position within the Draw procedure by passing a Vector2 structure initialized with the values 100 and 100. These two values are the x and y positions at which the graphic will be drawn and represent its top-left corner. This position is known as a *coordinate*.

When coordinates are written down, they are enclosed within parentheses inside which the two values are placed, separated by a comma. The first value is the x coordinate (the horizontal position of the sprite), and the second is the y coordinate (the vertical position). For example, (20, 50) represents a coordinate with an x position of 20 and a y position of 50.

The coordinate system used by MonoGame sprites starts from (0, 0) at the top-left corner of the screen. It then extends across the screen's width and height so that the point at the bottom-right corner of the screen is (GraphicsDevice.Viewport.Width - 1, GraphicsDevice.Viewport.Height - 1). All sprite coordinates are measured in pixels.

To make the sprite move, we just need to remember its coordinate from one draw to the next and modify its values so that the sprite's position changes. We can do this very easily. First, we will declare another class-level variable to store the sprite position, as shown in Listing 2-4.

Listing 2-4. Declaring a variable to hold the position of the sprite

```
private Vector2 _spritePosition;
```

Next, we need to provide an initial position for the graphic. The default uninitialized Vector2 object has a coordinate of (0, 0), corresponding to the top-left corner of the screen. We will continue to use the coordinate (100, 100) as our initial position. We have a couple of options for setting it, one of which is to specify the position as part of the variable declaration from Listing 2-4. It may be useful to be able to reset the position later on, however, so we will create a new procedure called ResetGame and set the coordinate here, as shown in Listing 2-5.

Listing 2-5. Setting the initial position for the sprite

```
/// <summary>
/// Reset the game to its default state
/// </summary>
private void ResetGame()
{
    // Set the initial smiley position
    _spritePosition = new Vector2(100, 100);
}
```

To get this code to run, we will call the ResetGame procedure from the existing Initialize procedure that was generated automatically when the project was created. The modified procedure is shown in Listing 2-6.

Listing 2-6. Calling the ResetGame procedure

```
/// <summary>
/// Allows the game to perform any initialization it needs to before starting to run.
/// This is where it can query for any required services and load any non-graphic
/// related content.  Calling base.Initialize will enumerate through any components
/// and initialize them as well.
/// </summary>
protected override void Initialize()
{
    // Reset the game
    ResetGame();

    base.Initialize();
}
```

The Draw code now needs to be modified to use the new position variable. This is achieved by removing the Vector2 position variable and, instead, using the _spritePosition variable, as shown in Listing 2-7.

Listing 2-7. Drawing the sprite from the class-level variable

```
// Draw the sprite
_spriteBatch.Draw(_spriteTexture, _spritePosition, Color.White);
```

Finally, we need to change the position stored in the _spritePosition variable so that the graphic actually moves. Although it would be easy to do this in the Draw code, this wouldn't be the appropriate place to make this change; the Draw function should be entirely focused on the drawing operation alone and not on updating the game variables. Instead, we use the Update procedure, which once again was added when the project was created, to make these variable changes. Listing 2-8 shows a simple Update implementation that moves the sprite toward the bottom of the screen and resets its position back to the top once the bottom is reached.

Listing 2-8. The update procedure, modified to update our graphic position

```
/// <summary>
/// Allows the game to run logic such as updating the world,
/// checking for collisions, gathering input, and playing audio.
/// </summary>
/// <param name="gameTime">Provides a snapshot of timing values.</param>
protected override void Update(GameTime gameTime)
```

```
{
    // Update the game state
    _spritePosition.Y += 5;
    if (_spritePosition.Y >= GraphicsDevice.Viewport.Height) _spritePosition.Y = 0;

    base.Update(gameTime);
}
```

If you now run the project again, you should find that the graphic moves smoothly down the screen, wrapping back around to the top after it leaves the bottom edge.

This implementation causes the sprite to "jump" back to the top each time, rather than smoothly emerging from the top of the screen. The reason for this is that we set its y coordinate back to zero, at which position the sprite is fully visible. To position the sprite to appear above the top of the screen, we can give it a negative coordinate. As this coordinate increases toward zero, the sprite will gradually begin to appear within the visible area of the screen.

We could guess at what negative value to use, but we actually want to use the negative sprite height for this. Setting such a position will initially position the sprite so that its bottom edge is exactly at the top of the screen, which is just where we want it. The width and height of the sprite can be easily read from the Texture2D object in order to allow us to do this. The Update code that modifies the sprite position in this way can be seen in Listing 2-9.

Listing 2-9. Updating the sprite reset code so that it reappears smoothly at the top of the screen

```
protected override void Update(GameTime gameTime)
{
    // Update the game state
    _spritePosition.Y += 5;
    if (_spritePosition.Y >= GraphicsDevice.Viewport.Height)
                                   _spritePosition.Y = -_spriteTexture.Height;

    base.Update(gameTime);
}
```

The separation of updating the game and drawing the game is something that you will see across all our MonoGame samples and is something you should try to stick to in your own projects. There is nothing physically stopping you from updating the game variables in the Draw function (nor, in fact, from drawing in the Update function), but both to enable readability and to ensure that your game works in the way MonoGame expects, it is strongly advised to keep the appropriate functionality in each of these two procedures.

Examining the Projects in More Detail

Before we press on with making further modifications to the code, let's take a quick step back and look a little more closely at the projects and their contents. As you have already seen, the game itself is created in one project, but we also need to use a second XNA Content project to build our games resources (graphics so far, but this will also be used for music, sound effects, and 3-D models as we progress through the later chapters). Before we get to the reason for the Content project, let's look in a little more detail at the main game projects.

The Windows 8 MonoGame Project

An example of the files present in a new Windows 8 MonoGame project, taken here from the Sprites_Win8 project used earlier in this chapter, can be seen in Figure 2-9.

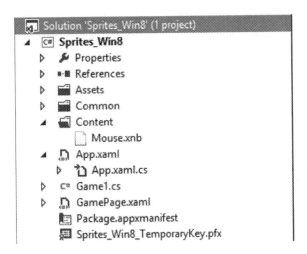

Figure 2-9. *The default files contained within a new Windows 8 MonoGame project*

The Properties and References sections of the project will no doubt be familiar from other projects you have worked on in the past, and they serve exactly the same purpose as for those projects, too. The rest of the items within the project deserve a little more explanation, however, so let's take a look at each of them.

First is the Assets folder, which contains all of the images that are needed for your app when it is not actually running. These include the splash screen logo, the logo that is shown on the app's tile in the Start menu, and the logo to display in the Windows Store after publication. We will look at all of those in more detail when we discuss how to prepare a game for publication in Chapter 14.

The Common folder contains a single file, StandardStyles.xaml. This file contains a large amount of XAML code that defines the default appearance of many aspects of the XAML user interface. This can be ignored for the time being. We'll cover some aspects of this when we examine XAML in the later chapters of this book.

The Content folder is next. This is one that we created ourselves to hold our game content files, so its purpose should already be understood.

Finally, we get to the game project's code files. The first of these is App.xaml and the code-behind file App.xaml.cs (if you can't see this, expand the App.xaml node within Solution Explorer's file tree to reveal it). App.xaml itself is essentially empty by default, but the App.xaml.cs file contains a number of pre-created functions. These serve as the entry point for your game; the App constructor function will be the first code to run, followed closely by the OnLaunched function.

▓ **Note** You can use the App class functions to initialize project-wide data should you need to though, generally, it is better to use your game class for this in order to keep all the game-related logic and variables contained in the same location.

The game class is, in fact, the next class within the project, named Game1.cs by default. Derived from Microsoft.Xna.Framework.Game (which is actually a MonoGame class, don't forget!), this is the main class around which all of the functionality of your game will revolve. As we have already touched upon, the main default functions within the class are the constructor, LoadContent, Update, and Draw. You can (and probably should) rename this class to whatever you wish, but each MonoGame project should contain only one such game class.

The final code file is a XAML page named GamePage.xaml. If you examine the XAML code, you will see that it contains no visible user interface content. We can, however, add content to this for display to the user, and we will see how to do that later in the book. The code behind this file is stored in GamePage.xaml.cs. This consists purely of a class constructor function that creates and initializes an instance of the Game1 class. Should you rename Game1, you will need to ensure that the new name is reflected in this piece of code, too.

The last two files are special files used for the Windows 8 environment. The first, `Package.appxmanifest`, contains all sorts of meta-data about your project: its name, description, supported screen orientations, and more. This is all presented in a custom user interface display, as you will see if you double-click the file to open it. Once again, we will look at this in much more detail in Chapter 14.

The final file, the `TemporaryKey.pfx` file, is a binary data file that contains no human-readable content of value. All Windows Store applications that are deployed to Windows 8 devices require a signed "key" to indicate that they are genuine. Upon publication of your app to the Windows Store, a final key will be generated for your app by Microsoft, but in order to allow you to deploy the app during development, this temporary key will be created. You should leave this alone to avoid causing problems working with your project. Modifying or damaging the certificate will break your project and may be tricky to track down and fix, so be careful to look after this file.

The Windows Phone MonoGame Project

When working with a project for Windows Phone, the set of files within the project is slightly different. An example of these files from the `Sprites_WP8` project is shown in Figure 2-10.

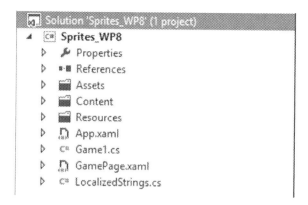

Figure 2-10. *The default files contained within a new Windows Phone MonoGame project*

Many of these are the same as with the Windows 8 project, detailed in the previous section. `Properties`, `References`, and `Content` are identical in purpose, as is `Assets` (though the graphics files required for Windows Phone apps are different from those used by Windows 8).

`Resources` and `LocalizedStrings.cs` both contain content allowing your app to be customized for localization into multiple languages. This can be a very useful thing to consider for your game, but it is not something that we will be covering in this book. If you'd like to learn more, you can visit `http://tinyurl.com/LocalizingWPApps`, where you will find an MSDN article covering the subject in more detail.

This leaves three further files: `App.xaml`, `Game1.cs`, and `GamePage.xaml`. The main code for your game will be placed into `Game1.cs`, just as with the Windows 8 project, and the good news is that a lot of the code will be absolutely identical for both of the platforms. The MonoGame libraries that the game is based upon are essentially the same in both cases, so a substantial amount of code can be reused without needing to change anything.

The remaining two files, `App.xaml` and `GamePage.xaml`, serve the exact same purposes as in the Windows 8 project.

The Content Project

Finally, there is the XNA Content project. This project, which is initially empty, has the sole purpose of containing and compiling all the external data files (graphics, sound files, 3-D models, and so on) that you wish to use within your game.

MonoGame uses the compiled output from this project in exactly the same way that XNA itself does, so we need to keep this project around to build the compiled .xnb files. So, why is this created as a separate project? The main reasons that are relevant to us when using them with MonoGame are the following:

- The main reason is for performance. Our test projects have a single graphic file, but full games can contain dozens of content files. Each time the project is compiled, all these files need to be processed by MonoGame in order to put them into a form that it can use. The content tends to be modified fairly infrequently, but the program code is modified in virtually every build. Putting the content into a separate project means that the processing of this content need only be performed each time the content actually changes, speeding up compile time for all the rest of the compilations.

- If you have content that you wish to share between multiple games (a company logo, for example), it can be placed into a separate Content project and referenced by each of the game projects. Changes made to this Content project will then be reflected in all the games.

The way in which the game accesses the content is very simple. In the Game1 constructor of the game projects we have been working on, you will find the line of code shown in Listing 2-10.

Listing 2-10. Setting the RootDirectory property of the Content object

```
Content.RootDirectory = "Content";
```

The value of "Content" that is set corresponds to the folder within your project into which the compiled .xnb files have been placed. Should you wish to use a different folder for these resources, you will need to remember to update the code that sets the RootDirectory property to reference this alternative location, too.

Within the properties of each item added to the XNA Content project is one named Asset Name, as shown in Figure 2-11. This controls the name of the resulting file that is produced when the Content project is compiled: Each item's name will be set to be the asset name ("Mouse," in this case), with the .xnb file extension.

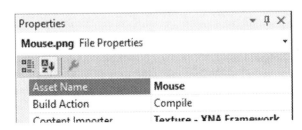

Figure 2-11. *The Asset Name property for a file within the XNA Content project*

When loading these content items into a MonoGame project, you can then refer to them just by specifying their asset name, as we have seen already. If you wish to divide your assets into groups (perhaps by type, graphics, sounds, music, and so on), you can create subdirectories within your game project's Content folder. When you place assets into these folders, you can access them either by setting the RootDirectory to include the subdirectory name or by including the directory name when calling the Content.Load function. Listing 2-11 shows an example of loading a resource from a Graphics subdirectory.

Listing 2-11. Loading content from a subdirectory

```
_myTexture = Content.Load<Texture2D>("Graphics/Frog");
```

Sharing Graphic Resources between Windows 8 and Windows Phone

As you will have noticed if you ran both the Windows 8 and the Windows Phone 8 versions of the Sprites project, the sprites are by default rendered at their actual size. The mouse image used in the project has a size of 256x256 pixels. When running on Windows Phone, this fills half the width of the screen. While running in Windows 8 with its much higher screen resolution, the image appears much smaller. If you are planning to develop your game for both platforms, this is clearly a situation that will need to be managed.

There are various techniques we can use to deal with this, some of which we will look at later on. However, one such approach is to provide different graphic images for each of the two platforms, with larger graphics files for Windows 8 and smaller files for Windows Phone. The simplest way to achieve this is just to create two separate XNA Content projects, one for each set of graphics.

Using smaller graphics for the phone can also help keep the performance of your game as high as possible. Moving large graphics images around in memory takes time and can slow the game down if this becomes too intensive. On the lower hardware capabilities of the phone, this can become very noticeable. Smaller images consume less memory and therefore allow more sprites to be processed in the game before any kind of performance problems occur.

▓ **Tip**   For the reasons discussed above, be sure to optimize your graphics files for the platform you are running them on. When catering for a phone screen, reduce the size of the original graphic files rather than using large graphics and scaling them in your game.

Sprites in Detail

You have now seen how easy it is to draw a simple graphic to the screen, but sprites have a few more tricks in store. Let's examine some of the other properties and abilities of MonoGame sprites.

Supported Graphic Formats

We have a choice of graphic file format to use when loading images for use within our games. Some are distinctly better than others. Here is a summary of the main formats that can be used:

- *PNG* (Portable Network Graphics) files, as used for the mouse sprite in the previous example, are the most recently developed graphic file format supported by MonoGame. They can store graphics using the full 24-bit color palette and are additionally able to support alpha (transparency) information. They compress their content to reduce the size of the graphic file. This compression is *lossless*, so no degradation of the image occurs as a result. For nonphotographic images, this is the file format that I recommend.

- *JPG* (a contraction of *JPEG*, the Joint Photographic Experts Group that developed the format) files revolutionized the Web and have been an enabling technology in a range of other areas, too, such as digital cameras. The format's strength is its ability to compress images to file sizes that are dramatically smaller than their uncompressed originals, far more so than the PNG format is able to offer. The problem with this, however, is that JPG uses a *lossy* compression technique—after decompressing the image, you don't get back exactly what you started with. Compressed JPGs quickly start to exhibit graphical distortions and "noise." This is most strongly apparent with graphics that contain highly contrasting areas of color, such as those within a computer game often do. JPG files can be useful for reducing the size of photographic images, but they are not well suited to hand-drawn game graphics. Even with photographs, be careful not to compress the image to a point where distortion begins to appear.

- *BMP* (bitmap) files have a simple structure internally and are, therefore, easy for graphics libraries to interact with. One of the reasons for this simplicity is that they do not employ any form of compression at all. For this reason, BMP files can be huge in terms of file size compared with the other graphics formats that are available. BMP files do not offer any form of transparency. There are no compelling reasons to use BMP files, so please avoid using them wherever possible.

One familiar graphic format that you may notice is absent from the list is the *GIF* (Graphics Interchange Format) file. MonoGame does not support GIF files. This is not really much of a loss because PNG files can do almost everything that GIF files can do. They have better compression, support more colors (24-bit color as opposed to GIF's 8-bit color), and have proper alpha support. If you have a GIF file that you wish to use, convert it to a PNG file and use it in that format instead.

Scaling

In the earlier example, we drew the sprite at its original size. MonoGame can *scale* the sprite as we draw it, changing its size to make it smaller or larger. It can scale either *uniformly* (the sprite scales equally along the x and y axes) or *nonuniformly* (the x and y axes scale differently, stretching or squashing the image).

Using a Uniform Scaling Factor

There are several overloads of the SpriteBatch.Draw method that support scaling in various different ways. The first and simplest of these allows us to specify the amount of scaling that should be applied to the sprite. The sprite width and height is multiplied by the provided value to determine the finished size, so passing a value of 1 will leave the sprite size unchanged, 2 will double it, 0.5 will halve it, and so on.

▓ **Note**   Passing a scale value of 0 will cause the width and height to be multiplied by 0, with the result that your sprite will vanish completely. This is particularly important to remember when you aren't actually taking advantage of scaling but are using the other features of the Draw methods instead. Remember that to draw your sprite at its normal size, you need to pass 1 as the scale factor.

The version of Draw that we use to access this scale parameter takes quite a few more parameters than the version we used earlier, as shown in Listing 2-12.

Listing 2-12. Rendering a sprite with scaling

```
_spriteBatch.Draw(_spriteTexture, new Vector2(100, 100), null, Color.White, 0,
                            Vector2.Zero, 3.0f, SpriteEffects.None, 0.0f);
```

From left to right, the parameters are as follows:

- texture: a Texture2D graphic texture to render (as before).
- position: a Vector2 structure that identifies the position to render at (as before).
- sourceRectangle: a Rectangle structure that can be used to pick out an area of the sprite texture to render (we will look at this parameter in more detail in the Partial Image Rendering section in a moment). Passing null tells MonoGame to render the entire image.

- color: a Color with which to render (as before). We'll look at this parameter in the Tinting section coming up shortly.

- rotation: a float that identifies the rotation angle. This is explained further in the Rotation section shortly.

- origin: another Vector2 that identifies the image origin. We'll discuss this in a moment.

- scale: the scaling factor, passed as a float. At last! This is where we tell MonoGame how much to enlarge or shrink the image. The example here uses a value of 3.0, so the sprite will be displayed at three times its normal width and height.

- effect: one of a number of possible SpriteEffect values. These can be used to flip the rendered graphic horizontally or vertically, but we aren't using it at the moment so we just pass the value None.

- depth: a float value that we can use to help sort the sprites into order so that those at the front appear in front of those behind. We'll look at this in detail in the Layer Depth section coming in a few pages.

As you can see, this is quite a lot of extra data to specify, but as in this example call, it is easy to pass values that result in these parameters having no effect.

In addition to the scaling factor, the origin parameter also has an effect on scaling. Listing 2-12 shows this passed as Vector2.Zero, which produces a coordinate of (0, 0). The origin has two immediate effects: It specifies which point within the image is actually being specified by the position parameter, and it controls the point around which scaling takes place.

Let's begin with the first effect. When we discussed rendering sprites back in the example project, we saw that the position parameter set the top-left corner of the rendered sprite. If we use the origin parameter, this allows us to control the location within the image that is actually set by position. For example, if we set the origin to new Vector2(10, 20), the point 10 pixels across the image and 20 pixels down the image would appear exactly at the location specified by position.

This may not sound very useful, but it becomes more important when the second effect is considered because the origin point within the image also becomes the center of image scaling. As the image is scaled up or down, the origin point will stay in exactly the same place, while the rest of the image scales around it.

This can be seen in Figure 2-12, in which the dot indicates the origin of the differently scaled rectangular sprites. In the image on the left, the origin is set at (0, 0), so the sprites scale down and to the right. The middle image has the origin in the center of the rectangle, causing the sprite to keep the same center point as the rectangle is enlarged and reduced. The final image shows the origin at the bottom-right corner of the sprite, causing it to scale up and to the left. In all three images, the position parameter was passed as the same location.

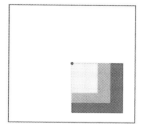 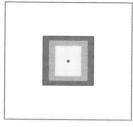 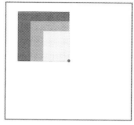

Figure 2-12. *Scaling with different origins*

It is also possible to scale with a negative factor, which will cause the image to be mirrored horizontally and vertically about the origin point.

Using a Nonuniform Scaling Factor

The Draw call in Listing 2-12 allows just a single value to be passed for the scaling factor, which means that it only supports uniform scaling. Nonuniform scaling is no harder to achieve, however. We just substitute a Vector2 structure in place of the float that we used before. The Vector2's x value will represent the scaling on the horizontal axis, and its y value will represent the scaling on the vertical axis.

An example nonuniform scale using this approach is shown in Listing 2-13. This listing doubles the width of the sprite and halves its height.

Listing 2-13. Rendering a sprite with nonuniform scaling

```
_spriteBatch.Draw(_spriteTexture, new Vector2(100, 100), null, Color.White, 0,
            Vector2.Zero, new Vector2(2.0f, 0.5f), SpriteEffects.None, 0.0f);
```

The origin parameter behaves in exactly the same way when using this approach as it did for uniform scaling.

Using a Destination Rectangle

The final method for scaling a sprite uses a slightly different approach. Instead of specifying the position, an origin, and a scale factor, we instead define the overall rectangle into which the sprite is to be rendered.

Listing 2-14 shows a call to the Draw method that scales a sprite in this way. The top-left corner of the rendered sprite is at the coordinate (50, 50), and it has a width of 300 pixels and a height of 500 pixels. This puts the bottom-right corner at the coordinate (350, 550).

Listing 2-14. Rendering a sprite to fill a defined rectangle

```
_spriteBatch.Draw(_spriteTexture, new Rectangle(50, 50, 300, 500), Color.White);
```

Exactly which of these scaling approaches works best for you will depend on the way in which you are using the sprite. Sometimes it is best to use a scaling factor (particularly if you want the sprite to grow or shrink in size as the game progresses), although other times a destination rectangle may be the easier approach. Make sure you consider all the options to avoid creating unnecessary work for yourself.

Rotation

Sprites also have the ability to be smoothly rotated to any angle you wish. The angle is specified by using either of the Draw calls shown in Listing 2-12 or 2-13, passing the angle for the appropriate parameter.

The angle is measured clockwise in radians, meaning that an angle of 0 is the right way up, PI / 2 is rotated one-quarter of the way around to the right, PI is upside down, and 3 PI / 2 is rotated three-quarters of the way around.

Personally, I find working in radians quite unnatural and I much prefer working in degrees. MonoGame is here to help with this because it offers a very useful class named MathHelper, which is full of static functions to assist with graphics-related mathematical functions. One such function is ToRadians, which converts the supplied degrees angle into radians. Using this with the Draw function's rotation parameter makes providing the angle much easier. Don't overlook that there is a small performance penalty for using this function, however, as the game will need to perform an additional calculation for each angle that it works with.

Just as with scaling, the point around which the image rotates can be controlled using the origin parameter. Set this to the center of the sprite image to rotate on the spot or provide a different origin for off-center rotation. The origin can be completely outside the sprite area if you wish.

Listing 2-15 shows a call to Draw that rotates a sprite by 45 degrees around its center. The center point is calculated by halving the Width and Height values from the sprite texture object. The output from this call can be seen in Figure 2-13.

Listing 2-15. Drawing a sprite rotated around its center

```
_spriteBatch.Draw(_spriteTexture, new Vector2(200, 200), null, Color.White,
            MathHelper.ToRadians(45),
            new Vector2(_spriteTexture.Width / 2, _spriteTexture.Height / 2),
            1.0f, SpriteEffects.None, 0.0f);
```

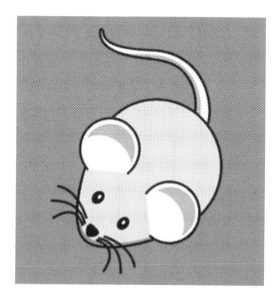

Figure 2-13. *Rotating a sprite*

Tinting

Throughout all the calls to Draw, we have passed through a Color parameter, and in each case it has been Color.White. We can pass different colors instead of white to tint the graphic that is being drawn. If we pass Color.Blue, the sprite will be shaded in blue, for example.

A very useful application of this feature is to allow a single graphic to be drawn in lots of different colors, without having to add all the different colored graphics individually into the Content project. If the source image is provided in grayscale, the tint can be used to display this in whatever color we want. You can see this in action in the TintedSprites_Win8 and TintedSprites_WP8 example projects, an image from which is shown in Figure 2-14 (this obviously looks better in color!).

Figure 2-14. *Tinted sprites*

To understand just how the tinting works (and what kind of results you can expect from it), we need to discuss how colors are represented in computer graphics.

In MonoGame, there are two ways that we can specify a color to use:

- Using one of the named color values from `Microsoft.Xna.Framework.Color`

- Specifying the individual levels of red, green, and blue that will make up the color

A large range of named colors is provided (approximately 140 in total), from standard colors such as `Black` and `Blue` to those with more extravagant names including the sublime `PapayaWhip` and the unmistakable `BlanchedAlmond`. This list of named colors is actually the full list of X11 colors, which also form the predefined named colors used for HTML and Cascading Style Sheets (CSS). For further information about these colors, see the Wikipedia page at `http://en.wikipedia.org/wiki/Web_colors`, where a list containing details and an example of each can be seen.

Alternatively, colors may be specified by providing the levels of red, green, and blue intensity (the additive primary colors) that are required to form the required color. Each of these is specified independently and ranges from 0 (no intensity) to 255 (full intensity). For example, creating a color with its red component set to 255 and its green and blue components set to 0 will result in a pure red. By varying the intensity of each color, all the available shades that the device is able to display can be created.

▒ **Note**   There are various different models in which colors can be specified. In printing, the most common model is the CMYK model. CMYK is an abbreviation for "cyan, magenta, yellow, and key-black." Cyan, magenta, and yellow are the primary *subtractive colors*—so named because when additional color is applied, they reduce the amount of light that is reflected and result in a darker color. The model that is most commonly used in computer devices is RGB, an abbreviation for "red, green, and blue." Red, green, and blue are the primary *additive colors*, which result in an increased amount of light when the colors are mixed together (so that, in fact, mixing all three results in white light). The .NET framework supports color specifications using the RGB model.

To create a color from red, green, and blue intensity levels, create a new Color structure and pass the intensity levels into its constructor. There are actually two ways in which the intensity levels can be specified: either as integer values from 0 to 255 as described, or as float values from 0 to 1. Exactly which of these approaches you prefer is up to you; they are functionally equivalent. Listing 2-16 shows an example of creating two identical Color structures, one using integer values and the other using floats.

Listing 2-16. Creating colors from red, green, and blue intensity levels

```
Color myColor1 = new Color(255, 128, 0);
Color myColor2 = new Color(1.0f, 0.5f, 0.0f);
```

Because we can specify 256 levels of each of the three color components, we can create colors from a total palette of 16,777,216 different colors (256 x 256 x 256 = 16,777,216). This is the same color depth as used on virtually all modern desktop PC displays. Because each of the three color components requires 8 bits of data (to store a value from 0 to 255), this is known as 24-bit color.

So, how does all this apply to tinting? In order to apply a tint, MonoGame first reads the color of each pixel from the image using the float representation, obtaining a value between 0 and 1 for each of the red, green, and blue components. It then obtains the tint color using the same float representation. The corresponding values for red, green, and blue are then multiplied together, and the resulting value is the color that is actually displayed on the screen.

Because the color white has RGB values of (1, 1, 1), the result of using white as a tint is that each pixel color component is multiplied by 1. In other words, it is not changed and the image is rendered untinted. If we used a tint color of black, which has RGB values (0, 0, 0), all the pixel color components would be multiplied by 0, resulting in the sprite appearing totally black. By using tint colors that have different levels of red, green, and blue—for example, orange has the RGB value (1, 0.5, 0)—we can cause the sprite to be tinted toward whatever color we wish.

Note that if the source image is not grayscale, however, it may not tint in the way you necessarily want. For example, if you have a sprite that consists of strips of red, green, and blue color and you tint it using a solid blue color, the areas of red and green will turn completely black (because the intensity levels for red and green in the blue tint are 0). This is why a grayscale image is often the best to use when tinting.

Partial Image Rendering

Sprites can draw just a subsection of their images, too. One of the main uses for this is for animation: Multiple animation frames can be placed into a single image, and then individual frames can be rendered to the screen in sequence to animate the sprite.

An example of how this can be used is in the AnimationFrames_Win8 and AnimationFrames_WP8 projects. Their Content folders each contain a single image, Radar.png, which can be seen in Figure 2-15.

Figure 2-15. *The frames of the radar animation placed into a single graphic file*

As this figure shows, there are eight individual images contained within the file. Each has exactly the same width (75 pixels), so we can draw any frame by locating its left edge and then drawing a section of the image that is 75 pixels wide. To find the edge, we take the animation frame number (from 0 to 7) and multiple it by the frame width (75 pixels). Frame 0 therefore has a left edge of 0 pixels, frame 1 a left edge of 75 pixels, frame 2 a left edge of 150 pixels, and so on.

Drawing a section of the image is easy and is achieved by passing a Rectangle structure to the sourceRectangle property of Draw. This defines the left and top corner of the rectangle within the source image, and also the width and height to copy. The code that performs the frame drawing in the AnimationFrames project is shown in Listing 2-17.

Listing 2-17. Rendering a sprite using a source rectangle

```
_spriteBatch.Draw(_radarTexture, new Vector2(100, 100),
                new Rectangle(_animationFrame * 75, 0, 75, 75), Color.White);
```

Although it is not shown in Listing 2-17, it is possible to combine the use of a source rectangle with scaling and rotation because all the versions of the Draw method that allow these operations to be specified also accept a sourceRectangle parameter. In fact, we have been passing this parameter in all the examples using these techniques, except that we passed null to indicate that we wanted the whole image to be drawn rather than a just subsection.

Layer Depth

If overlapping sprites are rendered using any of the code samples so far, each will be rendered in front of the sprites already on the screen. Sometimes you need to order the sprites in a particular way so that some sprites appear in front of other sprites.

MonoGame provides an easy way to implement this. Some of the Draw overloads accept a float parameter called layerDepth, and we can pass a value for this between 0 and 1 to control which sprites appear in front of others. A value of 0 puts the sprite right at the front, whereas a value of 1 puts it right at the back.

The only catch to this is that layerDepth processing is disabled by default. To enable it, we need to pass some additional parameters to the SpriteBatch.Begin call. The parameter that switches this on is the sortMode parameter, which we will set to SpriteSortMode.BackToFront. It instructs MonoGame to draw the objects at the back first and then work toward the front, allowing each sprite to draw over the top of the sprites behind. When this parameter is passed, Begin also requires a value for its blendState parameter; we will pass BlendState.AlphaBlend, which is the default for this property when the overload of Draw with no parameters is used.

Listing 2-18 shows this effect in operation. Although the sprites are drawn from left to right (which would normally result in the rightmost sprite appearing in the front), we are specifying layerDepth values that put the leftmost sprite in front and the rightmost sprite at the back. You can find the full code for this in the LayerDepth_Win8 and LayerDepth_WP8 example projects.

Listing 2-18. Drawing sprites with layerDepth sorting enabled

```
// Begin a sprite batch with BackToFront sorting enabled
_spriteBatch.Begin(SpriteSortMode.BackToFront, BlendState.AlphaBlend);
// Draw some sprites with different layerDepth values
_spriteBatch.Draw(_smileyTexture, new Vector2(100, 100), null, Color.White, 0.0f,
                        Vector2.Zero, 1.0f, SpriteEffects.None, 0.0f);
```

```
_spriteBatch.Draw(_smileyTexture, new Vector2(140, 100), null, Color.White, 0.0f,
                              Vector2.Zero, 1.0f, SpriteEffects.None, 0.5f);
_spriteBatch.Draw(_smileyTexture, new Vector2(180, 100), null, Color.White, 0.0f,
                              Vector2.Zero, 1.0f, SpriteEffects.None, 1.0f);
// End the sprite batch
_spriteBatch.End();
```

The end result is shown in Figure 2-16.

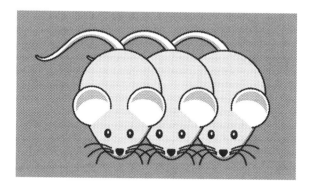

Figure 2-16. *Sprites rendered left-to-right with layerDepth sorting enabled*

Sprite Transparency

Sprites are always rectangular. The mouse texture we have been using, however, is an irregular shape. Why is it then that we don't end up with a rectangular box drawn around the edge of the sprite?

The reason is that we are using an image with transparency information. Without this, the sprite would be drawn completely to the edges of its draw rectangle. Figure 2-17 shows an example of drawing the mouse texture without any transparency. As you can see, it's not exactly the effect we want to achieve in most cases.

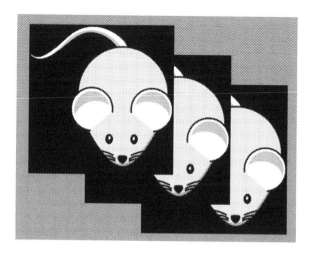

Figure 2-17. *Drawing the mouse sprite with no transparency information*

We have two techniques at our disposal for making transparent sections within our sprites: color keys and alpha channels. Let's take a look at each of these techniques. Examples of both techniques can be found within the `Transparency_Win8` and `Transparency_WP8` example projects, with the texture images themselves contained within the `Transparency_XNA` project.

▓ **Note**   JPEG images are not recommended for use with either of these transparency techniques. JPEG's lossy compression means that colors are not stored accurately enough for color key transparency, and the information required for alpha channels is not supported by JPEG images. If you wish to use transparency, you will need to stick with PNG image files instead.

Color Key Transparency

A color key provides the simplest mechanism for making areas of your sprite transparent, but it is less flexible than the alpha channel approach that we will discuss in a moment. A color key identifies a particular pixel color within your image that will be treated as transparent. Any and all pixels that exactly match the specified color will become completely transparent when your sprite is rendered, whereas all other pixels will be completely opaque.

By convention, the color *fuchsia* is by default used as the color key color. This has full intensity of red and blue and none of green and is, by any other name, purple. This has been chosen as it is a relatively infrequently used color within computer graphics.

The `ColorKey.png` image in the `Transparency_XNA` example's Content project is set up to use a color key. You can see the effect of this by running the `Transparency_Win8` and `Transparency_WP8` projects. As you will see when you run them, the sprite is drawn as if it were circular, and all the rest of the rectangular sprite area is left untouched when the sprite is drawn.

But why has MonoGame decided to use the color key? And how could we use a different color as the color key if we needed to use fuchsia in our graphic? The answer to these questions can be found in the Properties window for the `ColorKey.png` file within the XNA Content project. If you expand the `Content Processor` property, you will find that hiding inside are properties named `Color Key Enabled` and `Color Key Color`, as shown in Figure 2-18. These default to True and `255, 0, 255, 255`, respectively (the `Color Key Color` values represent the red, green, blue, and alpha values of the transparent color). If you wish to disable the color key or change the key color, modify these properties as required.

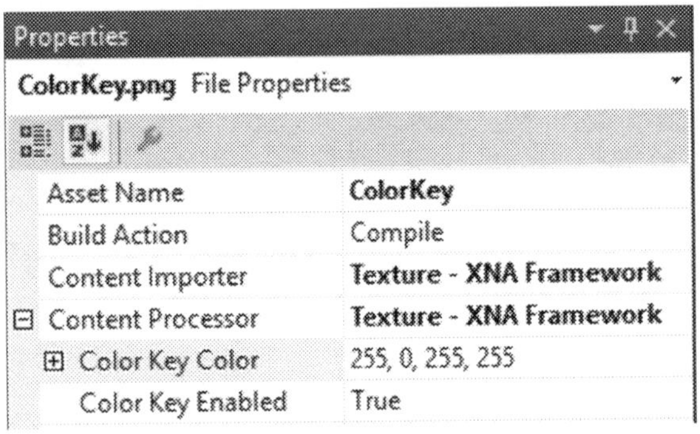

Properties	▾ ↕ ✕
ColorKey.png File Properties	▾
Asset Name	**ColorKey**
Build Action	Compile
Content Importer	**Texture - XNA Framework**
⊟ Content Processor	**Texture - XNA Framework**
⊞ Color Key Color	255, 0, 255, 255
Color Key Enabled	True

Figure 2-18. *The Color Key properties inside the XNA Content project*

Alpha Channel Transparency

Color key transparency is a quick and simple method, but it is binary: Pixels are either fully transparent or fully opaque. Sometimes we want more control than that, allowing individual pixels in the image to have different degrees of transparency. We can achieve this using an *alpha channel*.

As already discussed, each pixel color within an image is made from varying the intensity of red, green, and blue. PNG images are able to store one final additional value alongside each pixel: the alpha value. This also ranges from 0 to 255, where 0 represents a fully transparent pixel (which will actually be completely invisible when drawn to the screen) and 255 (which represents a fully opaque pixel). The values in between form a smooth gradation of transparency levels.

Although the end results of using an alpha channel are usually superior to those from color keyed graphics, the amount of effort required to set up the graphic can be much greater. For more information on how to use alpha channels in your graphics package of choice, please consult its documentation.

■ **Tip** Most well-featured graphics packages allow you to work on an image's alpha channel. If you are looking for a flexible and powerful image editor on a budget, try the freeware application Paint.NET. Visit the web site at `http://www.getpaint.net/` to download. Paint.NET has full alpha channel support, although it can take a while to get the hang of using it.

For images with alpha channels, there is no need to set up any properties within the Content project: MonoGame will automatically recognize and use the alpha data within the image. The `Transparency_Win8` and `Transparency_WP8` example projects also display two instances of a graphic with an alpha channel. The color data in the graphic is in fact completely white, but the alpha data contains a radial fade from opaque in the image center to fully transparent at the edges.

The project randomly changes the background color every few seconds. Note how the alpha channel images blend in with the background, taking on its color in their semitransparent regions. You can also see how the two overlapping images blend with one another rather than erasing the pixels of the sprite in the background, as shown in Figure 2-19.

Figure 2-19. *The overlapping alpha channel images, blending with the background and with each other*

■ **Tip** Alpha channels can be used when tinting sprites, too. Try changing the color of one of the alpha channel sprites from `Color.White` to `Color.Blue`, for example, and see how the sprites now appear when the project is run.

Alpha Tinting

Now that we have discussed alpha channels and transparency, we can revisit the sprite tinting feature that we discussed a few pages back.

You may recall that we could define a color for tinting by specifying the red, green, and blue intensity levels. But hold on—if PNG images can store alpha information as well as color information, can we use alpha values for tinting in order to vary the transparency of the entire sprite?

Well, yes, we can. A further overload of the Color constructor allows an alpha value to be specified alongside the red, green, and blue values. If we set our SpriteBatch object up in the appropriate way and pass the alpha value as something other than 255 (or 1.0f, if you prefer the float-based version), the sprite will be drawn semi-transparently. This can be used to smoothly fade objects in or out of the display, or to provide ghostly shadow effects in your games.

To use this effect, we first need to specify a different parameter when calling the SpriteBatch.Begin method. Pass the value of BlendState.NonPremultiplied for the blendState parameter. There are various methods that MonoGame uses to blend new graphics with those already on the screen, and this is the one that allows us to draw new sprites with varying levels of transparency.

Then it is simply a matter of providing an alpha level in your Color object: 0 for fully transparent; 255 for fully opaque. Listing 2-19 draws a series of sprite images that are fully transparent on the left to opaque on the right. The results are shown in Figure 2-20.

Listing 2-19. Drawing sprites with alpha tinting

```
// Begin a sprite batch with nonpremultiplied blending
_spriteBatch.Begin(SpriteSortMode.Deferred, BlendState.NonPremultiplied);
// Draw some sprites with different alpha tints
for (int i = 0; i < 20; i++)
{
    _spriteBatch.Draw(_spriteTexture, new Vector2(i * 20, 100),
                                    new Color(Color.White, i * 12));
}
// End the sprite batch
_spriteBatch.End();
```

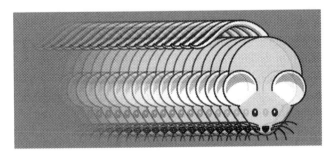

Figure 2-20. *Varying levels of alpha in the sprite color*

▓ **Note**   The code in listing 2-19 takes advantage of one of the overloads of the Color constructor, which allows an existing color to be specified as well as an alpha level. This allows us to create a new Color structure with a color of our choice (white, in this case) and any alpha level that we want to combine with it.

The example shown in Figure 2-20 can be found in the AlphaTinting_Win8 and AlphaTinting_WP8 projects in the accompanying download.

Useful Sprite Effects

Besides drawing individual graphics on the screen, there are various other useful effects that we can perform by using sprites. Let's take a look at a few of these effects: background images, fading to black, and fading between images.

Setting a Background Image

Games with solid color backgrounds can look a bit dull, but we can spice things up by drawing a single sprite that precisely fills the background of the game area. Because the sprite results in the entire screen being redrawn, there is no need for the Draw code to clear the graphics device, which saves a little bit of graphics processing time.

The background is then drawn by specifying a render rectangle rather than a sprite position and ensuring that the rectangle fills the entire screen. We can actually obtain such a rectangle from MonoGame very easily by querying the GraphicsDevice.Viewport.Bounds property. This returns a Rectangle structure that corresponds with the dimensions and position of the game window.

Provided that we draw the background first (or use a layerDepth value that ensures it appears behind everything else), this will draw the background texture to fill the screen and allow all our other graphics to appear on top. The code to achieve this is shown in Listing 2-20.

Listing 2-20. Using a sprite to create a background image

```
protected override void Draw(GameTime gameTime)
{
    // No need to clear as we are redrawing the entire screen with our background image
    //GraphicsDevice.Clear(Color.CornflowerBlue);

    // Begin the spriteBatch
    _spriteBatch.Begin();
    // Draw the background image
    _spriteBatch.Draw(_backgroundTexture, GraphicsDevice.Viewport.Bounds, Color.White);
    // Draw the sprite
    _spriteBatch.Draw(_spriteTexture, _spritePosition, Color.White);
    // End the spriteBatch
    _spriteBatch.End();

    base.Draw(gameTime);
}
```

This can be seen in action in the BackgroundImage_Win8 and BackgroundImage_WP8 example projects. Note that we use a JPEG image for the background because it is a photograph, which reduces the size of the compiled application—just make sure that the picture is of the same aspect ratio as the screen (portrait or landscape as appropriate) so that it isn't distorted when it is displayed. Figure 2-21 shows an area of output from this project.

Figure 2-21. *Rendering on top of a background image*

Fading to Black

A common and useful effect seen on TV and in films is the *fade to black,* which simply involves fading away everything on the screen to blackness. This is great for scene transitions because it allows the content of the entire screen to be updated without any jarring movement. It can add a layer of presentational sparkle to games, too, perhaps fading from the title screen into the game or fading between one level and the next.

We can implement a fade to black very easily by first drawing all the content on the screen and then rendering a full-screen sprite over the top, colored black and with variable alpha intensity. To fade to black, we start with an alpha value of 0 (transparent), at which point the sprite will be invisible, and fade to 255 (opaque), at which point the sprite will completely obscure everything on the screen. Once we reach this point, the rest of the scene can be changed in whatever way is appropriate and the alpha level faded back toward zero to fade the scene into visibility again.

Because the texture we need for the sprite is just a solid color, we can actually create the texture in code rather than having to add an image to the Content project. We can create a new texture by specifying the device on which we will render it (a reference to which is stored in the Game class's `GraphicsDevice` property) along with its width and height. We can create the texture with a width and height of just 1 pixel because MonoGame will happily stretch it to whatever size we want.

Perhaps surprisingly, we will tell MonoGame to make the texture's only pixel white rather than black because we can tint it black when we draw it. Setting the texture up this way means that we could also tint it any other color should we wish: fading to white, green, or powder blue as suits our game.

First then, let's look at the code that creates the texture, which can be seen in Listing 2-21. This is extracted from the project's `LoadContent` method. It creates the `Texture2D` object and then calls its `SetData` method to pass in the colors for the texture pixels. If the texture were larger, this would set a pixel for each provided array element, working horizontally across each row from left to right and then vertically from top to bottom. Our array has just a single element to match the pixels in the texture.

Listing 2-21. Creating the fader texture

```
// Create the texture for our fader sprite with a size of 1 x 1 pixel
_faderTexture = new Texture2D(GraphicsDevice, 1, 1);
// Create an array of colors for the texture -- just one color
// as the texture consists of only one pixel
```

```
Color[] faderColors = new Color[] {Color.White};
// Set the color data into the texture
_faderTexture.SetData<Color>(faderColors);
```

The texture is then used in the Draw method, as shown in Listing 2-22. In this example, we draw a number of sprites onto the background and then draw the fader in front. The alpha level for the fader is stored in a class variable named _faderAlpha, which is faded between 0 and 255 in the Update method.

Listing 2-22. Drawing the fader texture

```
protected override void Draw(GameTime gameTime)
{
    GraphicsDevice.Clear(Color.CornflowerBlue);

    // Begin the spriteBatch
    _spriteBatch.Begin(SpriteSortMode.Deferred, BlendState.NonPremultiplied);

    // Draw the sprite face sprites
    for (int i = 0; i < _spritePositions.Length; i++)
    {
        _spriteBatch.Draw(_spriteTexture, _spritePositions[i], Color.White);
    }

    // Draw the fader
    _spriteBatch.Draw(_faderTexture, GraphicsDevice.Viewport.Bounds,
                                    new Color(Color.Black, _faderAlpha));

    // End the spriteBatch
    _spriteBatch.End();

    base.Draw(gameTime);
}
```

Each time the fader reaches maximum opacity, the positions of the smiley faces are all updated, but we never see them move because they are always obscured when this takes place. For the full code and to see this running, take a look at the FadeToBlack_Win8 and FadeToBlack_WP8 example projects.

As an exercise, try changing the color with which the fader texture is drawn in the Draw function from Black to some other colors to see the effect that it has on the project.

Fading between Images

Similar to the fade to black effect is the fading between images effect. It is essentially the same technique, but it uses two sprites containing images rather than one sprite containing solid color. By using a series of images, slideshow effects can be set up, providing a very pleasant transition between each pair of images.

The effect can be seen in the FadeBetweenImages_Win8 and FadeBetweenImages_WP8 example projects. Although MonoGame provides a beautiful, smooth transition between the images, unfortunately a picture doesn't speak a thousand words in this case because it doesn't look very impressive at all on paper—it needs to be seen in motion.

We can take a quick look at the code, though. We set up an array of three different background textures and load them in the LoadContent method. To make the fade work, we store the index through the array of the current background image (which is the image that will be fading away) in the _backgroundImageIndex variable and the fader image (which is the image that will be fading into view) in the _faderImageIndex variable. These are initially given the values 0 and 1, respectively.

The Draw method, shown in Listing 2-23, should look very similar because it's just like the previous listing. Note that the tint color is now white rather than black so it shows in its normal colors.

Listing 2-23. Drawing the fading images

```
protected override void Draw(GameTime gameTime)
{
    // No need to clear as we are drawing a full-screen image
    //GraphicsDevice.Clear(Color.CornflowerBlue);

    // Begin the spriteBatch
    _spriteBatch.Begin(SpriteSortMode.Deferred, BlendState.NonPremultiplied);
    // Draw the background image
    _spriteBatch.Draw(_backgroundTextures[_backgroundImageIndex],
                      GraphicsDevice.Viewport.Bounds,
                      Color.White);
    // Draw the fader
    _spriteBatch.Draw(_backgroundTextures[_faderImageIndex],
                      GraphicsDevice.Viewport.Bounds,
                      new Color(Color.White, _faderAlpha));
    // End the spriteBatch
    _spriteBatch.End();

    base.Draw(gameTime);
}
```

The Update code simply increments the value of _faderAlpha, waiting for it to exceed 255. When this happens, it is reset back to 0, and both of the image index variables are incremented. We use the % modulus operator to automatically reset the index variables back to 0 once they reach the defined image count. The fade can, of course, be made faster by adding a greater value to _faderAlpha; to slow it down, the variable could be converted to a float and a fractional value added. The relevant part of the code is in Listing 2-24.

Listing 2-24. The Update code to fade between the series of images

```
// Increment the opacity of the fader
_faderAlpha += 1;
// Has it reached full opacity?
if (_faderAlpha > 255)
{
    // Yes, so reset to zero and move to the next pair of images
    _faderAlpha = 0;
    _backgroundImageIndex = (_backgroundImageIndex + 1) % IMAGE_COUNT;
    _faderImageIndex = (_faderImageIndex + 1) % IMAGE_COUNT;
}
```

Displaying Text

Most games need to display text while they are running, providing everything from the player's score to menus and game information pages.

There are two options available to use when developing games with MonoGame for Windows 8 and Windows Phone: to use MonoGame itself to draw the text, or to use the XAML user interface functionality. We'll look at how to do this with XAML in Chapters 11 through 13. In this section, we'll concentrate on how to display text with MonoGame.

There are some advantages of using MonoGame's text functionality, including the following:

- Easier integration into the rest of your game. You are using exactly the same code to display the text as you are to display the rest of your graphics, making it much easier to control fades, visibility, the order of overlapping text, and graphics, and so on.

- MonoGame's text functionality is much more portable between systems and will translate between Windows 8 and Windows Phone pretty much unmodified. The XAML code is not nearly as portable and will require its own implementation for each platform.

- XAML requires the fonts that you choose to use to be installed on the user's system, whereas fonts rendered by MonoGame are packaged into the game itself, removing the need for the user to have them installed.

MonoGame's mechanism for showing text on the screen is very easy to use, so let's take a look at what it can do and how we can use it.

Font Support

Fonts can cause all sorts of problems with regards to licensing. The vast majority of fonts that are included with Windows or can be downloaded from the Internet have license terms attached that prevent you from redistributing them in your own games.

Fortunately, Microsoft helped us out by licensing a number of fonts that can be used and distributed in MonoGame games without any threat of legal action, so these can be used in our MonoGame projects, too. We will, therefore, concentrate on how these particular fonts can be used in your games. All of the fonts detailed here will have been installed on your system as part of the XNA toolkit, which is provided with the Windows Phone SDK/Visual Studio Express for Windows Phone.

▦ **Note**   You can, of course, use any font you like in your game—just make sure that you don't breach any licensing terms and get yourself into trouble.

The provided fonts are summarized in Table 2-1.

Table 2-1. *Fonts Licensed for Use in Game Projects*

Name	Example	Variations
Andy	Windows Phone 7 Game Development	Bold
Jing Jing	WINDOWS PHONE 7 GAME DEVELOPMENT	Regular
Kootenay	Windows Phone 7 Game Development	Regular
Lindsey	Windows Phone 7 Game Development	Regular
Miramonte	Windows Phone 7 Game Development	Regular, Bold
Moire	Windows Phone 7 Game Development	Light, Regular, Bold, ExtraBold
Motorwerk	WINDOWS PHONE 7 GAME DEVELOPMENT	Regular
News Gothic	Windows Phone 7 Game Development	Regular, Bold
OCR A Extended	Windows Phone 7 Game Development	Regular
Pericles	WINDOWS PHONE 7 GAME DEVELOPMENT	Light, Regular
Pescadero	Windows Phone 7 Game Development	Regular, Bold
Quartz MS	Windows Phone 7 IENT	Regular
Segoe Keycaps	Game Development	Regular
Segoe Print	Windows Phone 7 Game Development	Regular, Bold
Segoe UI Mono	Windows Phone 7 Game Development	Regular, Bold
Wasco Sans	Windows Phone 7 Game Development	Regular, Italic, Bold, Bold Italic

As you can see, there are some diverse typefaces present. Note that some of them (Jing Jing, Motorwerk, Quartz MS) have no lowercase letters; they have display capitals instead. Pericles, on the other hand, uses small versions of its capital letters instead of lowercase letters.

The Variations column in Table 2-1 shows the different font variations that are fully supported within the fonts. We can choose to use any of the Regular, Bold, or Italic versions of the fonts, where they are available.

If you do want to use other fonts, you can easily do so, but please be careful that you have the appropriate permission first. There are freely licensed fonts around if you search for them on the Internet, but check the license terms carefully!

Creating SpriteFont Objects

Before we can display any text, we must first embed the font into our program. This is quickly and easily done, and it can generally be achieved with just a few mouse clicks.

Just like all the image resources we have been using, the font is first added into an XNA Content project. To add a font, right-click the main Content project node and select to Add a New Item. Select the SpriteFont template in the Add New Item window (under the Visual C# branch of the templates tree on the left of the window) and give the font a name. It's a good idea to name it after the font that you plan to use, as shown in Figure 2-22.

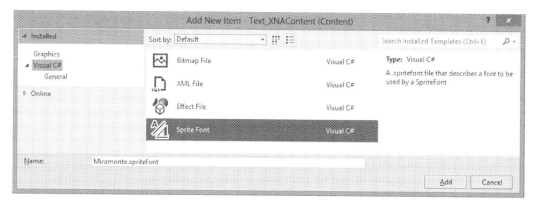

Figure 2-22. *Adding a spritefont file to an XNA Content project*

Once the font has been added, a `.spritefont` file will appear within Solution Explorer. This is an XML document that describes to the compiler the details of the font that is to be used. When the Content project compiles, it reads the font from disk and converts it into a bitmap image to embed in your project. It is this image of the font rather than the font itself that is therefore used by your program. The `.spritefont` file describes how this bitmap is to be constructed.

There isn't all that much within the file to change; the available items are as follows:

- `FontName` provides the name of the font to embed. Set it to one of the XNA licensed fonts mentioned in the previous section or to any other font installed in Windows that you are licensed to use.

- `Size` sets the size of the font to be used to generate the bitmap. If you choose a large value, a higher-quality bitmap will be generated, but it will require a lot more space and memory to process, which is particularly wasteful if the font doesn't need to be displayed in large sizes. Smaller values lower the resource requirements, but result in blocky text appearing if the font is rendered larger than its default size. You will need to find a balance between size and appearance when setting this. The size is specified in *points* rather than in pixels; due to the way points are handled by XNA and MonoGame, you can find the approximate pixel size by adding one-third to the point size. (A point size of 12 will result in a pixel size of 16 pixels.)

- `Spacing` sets the number of pixels that will be left as a horizontal gap between each rendered character. Increasing it above 0 can make the text look very spaced out, so use with caution.

- `UseKerning` controls whether font kerning is used. *Kerning* is the process whereby characters are moved closer together if it can be achieved without the characters colliding. For example, the letters "AV" can be positioned so that the boxes containing each letter overlap, without the letters themselves touching. Kerning generally produces much more natural-looking text, so it should usually be left enabled.

- `Style` allows the font style to be set to `Regular`, `Bold`, or `Italic`. For Wasco Sans' `Bold Italic` style, use the value `Bold, Italic`. For the other variations (`Light` or `ExtraBold`), suffix the variation to the font name (for example, `Moire ExtraBold`) and leave the `Style` element set to `Regular`. Fonts that do not show bold or italic variations in Table 2-1 can still be set to be bold or italicized by setting the `Style` element as required, but they will be programmatically converted into the requested version rather than using a design from the font definition itself, and so they might not look quite as good.

- CharacterRegions provides one or more ranges of characters to be included within the generated font bitmap. The smaller the number of characters, the smaller the resulting bitmap. If, for example, you knew that you would be including only uppercase letters in your game, you could omit the lowercase letters from the font and thus reduce the resource requirements. Multiple CharacterRegion elements can be included in the outer CharacterRegions element, if required.

- DefaultCharacter optionally provides a placeholder character that will be used any time a text string is printed that contains characters outside of the defined CharacterRegions. Without this, MonoGame will throw an exception if any such attempt to draw a string is made.

With the .spritefont file configured per your requirements, Visual Studio will automatically build the bitmap font each time the Content project is compiled.

Displaying Text

Our font is built so we are ready to print with it to the screen. This is straightforward and painless, and it involves first loading the font from its .xnb file, just as we did with our sprite textures. The first step is therefore to copy the .xnb file into your project's Content directory and add it into your project.

Once this is done, we can load the font into our game. This is achieved by once again calling the Content. Load method from within our game's LoadContent procedure, but indicating this time that we want it to return a SpriteFont object, as shown in Listing 2-25.

Listing 2-25. Loading the spritefont whose asset name is Miramonte

```
// Create a variable to hold the font
private SpriteFont _fontMiramonte;

/// <summary>
/// LoadContent will be called once per game and is the place to load
/// all of your content.
/// </summary>
protected override void LoadContent()
{
    // Create a new SpriteBatch, which can be used to draw textures.
    _spriteBatch = new SpriteBatch(GraphicsDevice);

    // Load the spritefont
    _fontMiramonte = Content.Load<SpriteFont>("Miramonte");
}
```

To print the text to the screen, we once again use the SpriteBatch object, calling its other method for drawing: DrawString. A number of overloads for this are available, but essentially they are all very similar. Some accept a String parameter, whereas others accept a StringBuilder; some expect parameters to control rotation and uniform scaling, and yet others allow nonuniform scaling.

The simplest version, which is shown in Listing 2-26, simply prints the text at the coordinate (100, 100) in white text.

Listing 2-26. Using DrawString to display text to the screen

```
_spriteBatch.Begin();
_spriteBatch.DrawString(_fontMiramonte, "Hello world", new Vector2(100, 100),
                                                        Color.White);

_spriteBatch.End();
```

The text appears on the screen just as you would expect (see Figure 2-23). The specified coordinate refers to the top-left corner of the displayed text.

Figure 2-23. *Displaying text on the screen using DrawString*

All the other features available to sprites are available to spritefonts too, allowing us to display text in different colors (including with variable alpha levels to allow text to fade in and out of view), rotated to different angles, or scaled to whatever size is required. The syntax for drawing text with these effects applied is essentially just the same as for drawing sprites.

We also have the ability to specify an origin for the text. When we drew sprites, we could easily identify the width and height of the sprite by querying the Width and Height properties of the Texture2D object used to provide the sprite image. But for text, the size will be different for every string we draw depending on the number of characters present in the string being displayed.

To overcome this, the SpriteFont object provides a very useful function called MeasureString. Passed the text to be displayed, it returns a Vector2 structure with the required text width stored in its X property and the text height in its Y property. This allows us to easily determine the dimensions of the rendered string, and this value can be used as the basis of calculating DrawString Origin parameter. Finding the center point is especially easy because the Vector2 can be multiplied or divided by a scalar value, resulting in its X and Y values each being multiplied or divided by the provided value. The center point can thus be obtained by simply dividing the result from MeasureString by 2.

▒ **Tip**   MonoGame can include line breaks within strings, both when drawing and measuring. Insert them into a string in C# using the \n character sequence.

Listing 2-27 shows an extract from the Text_Win8 and Text_WP8 example projects that does something a little more exciting-looking than the simple "Hello world" text. It measures a text string so that it can determine its center point and then uses it to draw a series of text strings to the same position on the screen, with each string a little larger, further rotated, and more faded than the last.

Listing 2-27. *A text-based graphical effect using rotation, scaling, and alpha blending*

```
// Calculate the size of the text
textString = "Text in MonoGame!";
textsize = _fontMiramonte.MeasureString(textString);
// Draw it lots of times
for (int i = 25; i >= 0; i--)
{
    // For the final iteration, use black text;
```

```
// otherwise use white text with gradually increasing alpha levels
if (i > 0)
{
    textcolor = new Color(Color.White, 255 - i * 10);
}
else
{
    textcolor = Color.Black;
}
// Draw our text with its origin at the middle of the screen and
// in the center of the text, rotated and scaled based on the
// iteration number.
_spriteBatch.DrawString(_fontMiramonte, textString, new Vector2(240, 400),
            textcolor, MathHelper.ToRadians (_angle * ((i + 5) * 0.1f)),
            textsize / 2, 1 + (i / 7.0f), SpriteEffects.None, 0);
}
```

The code actually loops backward so that the most faded/rotated/enlarged text is displayed first; each subsequent iteration then draws a more focused version on top of it. The color is finally set to black for the very last iteration to make the text easier to read.

The DrawString call may look a bit complex, but if we break it down, it's really very simple. We specify the spritefont to use, the text to write, and the position of the text origin, which is hard-coded at (240, 400) for simplicity in this example. After the color, we then provide the rotation angle, which is modified for each iteration so that each piece of text appears at a slightly different angle. The origin is specified next simply by passing the textsize value retrieved from MeasureString, divided by 2 so that we obtain its center point. Finally, we specify the scale, also set to change for each iteration, the SpriteEffects value (which can be used to flip text upside down or back to front), and the layer depth.

Once this is all put together, the output is as shown in Figure 2-24. This can also be seen in action in the example projects, which are yet more examples of effects that look much better in motion than in a static screenshot.

Figure 2-24. *Rotated, scaled, and alpha blended text*

Although the display of text is a basic requirement, MonoGame nevertheless provides a variety of options to make its display interesting and flexible.

Supporting Portrait and Landscape Orientations

All the examples that we have looked at in this chapter used the default device orientation for displaying their graphics—landscape for Windows 8 and portrait for Windows Phone. These are the orientations that the users are likely to be using for general purpose interaction with their devices, but you are not necessarily limited to just this one orientation.

If your game would benefit from orientations other than the default, this is easy to implement. Let's look at the options for supporting different orientations within your games. The Orientation_Win8 and Orientation_WP8 projects demonstrate these techniques in action.

Orientation in Windows 8 Projects

For Windows 8 apps, it is essential that landscape orientation be supported; otherwise, it won't work on desktop PCs and will fail certification when you submit to the Windows Store.

To use portrait orientation in a Windows 8 game, you simply need to tell MonoGame which orientations you wish to use in the game class constructor. The code to accomplish this, taken from the example project, can be seen in Listing 2-28.

Listing 2-28. Setting the supported orientations

```
public Game1()
{
    _graphics = new GraphicsDeviceManager(this);
    Content.RootDirectory = "Content";

    // Set the supported orientations
    _graphics.SupportedOrientations = DisplayOrientation.Portrait |
                    DisplayOrientation.LandscapeLeft |
                    DisplayOrientation.LandscapeRight;
}
```

With this property set, the game will automatically switch to portrait orientation when the device it is running on is physically rotated.

You can test this either on a physical tablet device or within the simulator. The simulator has two buttons in its toolbar that allow the simulated device to be rotated clockwise or counter-clockwise.

The example project displays the current window dimensions and the name of the current orientation. If you watch these while switching between resolutions, you'll find that they always update to show the appropriate values.

Orientation in Windows Phone Projects

Windows Phone games are less restricted and can be set to run in portrait only, landscape only, or a mixture of the two. However, at the time of writing, MonoGame isn't able to support both orientations within the same game—attempting to use both simultaneously results in the image being distorted when displayed in landscape mode. Hopefully this will be fixed in a future update to MonoGame. Each orientation works well in isolation, however.

The default orientation for MonoGame games is portrait mode, so nothing needs to be done at all to target this orientation.

To switch instead to a landscape orientation, there are two changes that need to be made. The first is to set MonoGame's SupportedOrientations property as shown in the Windows 8 example in Listing 2-28; however, make sure that just the LandscapeLeft and LandscapeRight options are included.

The second change is to the XAML of the project's GamePage.xaml file. Double-click the file to open it. Near the top of the file, you will find the line of code shown in Listing 2-29. This contains two instances of the value Portrait: The first sets the orientation with which the app actually executes, and the second with which the page designer shows the page.

Listing 2-29. The default XAML for a portrait-orientated page

```
SupportedOrientations="Portrait" Orientation="Portrait"
```

To complete the switch to landscape mode, change both instances of Portrait to Landscape. Now, when you run the project, you will find that the display is locked into landscape mode and that the window dimensions have updated to reflect this too—the width is greater than the height.

Note that if you switch the device over between being rotated to the left and to the right, it automatically rotates the screen content to match. The Current orientation display from the program will switch between LandscapeLeft and LandscapeRight as you do this. The game itself doesn't need to know anything about such a rotation because the screen size is absolutely unchanged.

Once support for both portrait and landscape orientations in MonoGame is fixed, this can be activated by setting the Page's SupportedOrientations XAML property to PortraitOrLandscape, and by adding DisplayOrientation.Portrait as one of the values passed to the _graphics.SupportedOrientations property in the game class constructor (as per Listing 2-28).

Detecting Orientation Changes

If you need to detect the orientation changing, the easiest way to do so is to subscribe to the game window's OrientationChanged event. This is fired each time the orientation changes, and the new orientation can be retrieved from the Window.CurrentOrientation property. The Orientation example projects use this event to display the new orientation to the debug window each time it changes.

Note that we will deal with a simple mechanism for responding to various window resize events including orientation changes later on in Chapter 10, in the section entitled Responding to the Game Window Resizing.

Experiment and Play with MonoGame

In this chapter, we have covered a lot of MonoGame's core capabilities for 2-D rendering. In the next chapter, we will build on these capabilities and start to develop a model for flexible game development.

Please feel free to spend some time experimenting with what you have learned so far. You already have lots of useful and flexible graphical techniques under your belt The more familiar and comfortable you can get with these, the better. Try out some of these effects and see what you can produce yourself!

Summary

- MonoGame is a rewritten implementation of Microsoft's XNA development framework, which is no longer being developed. It is available across a number of platforms, including Windows 8 and Windows Phone 8. The code required is very similar, if not identical, between the two platforms.

- Two project templates are provided with MonoGame to allow empty projects to be created for Windows 8 and for Windows Phone 8.

- MonoGame projects can be run on any device target, including the Windows 8 simulator, the Windows Phone emulator, and a Windows Phone device. When switching between Windows Phone emulator and device targets, the Configuration Manager window must be used to select either the ARM or x86 platform, as appropriate.

- Content such as graphics and fonts are added to a project by first compiling into a `.xnb` file in an actual XNA Content project and then adding to the MonoGame project. As standard, these are placed into a project folder named `Content`. The Build Action for such files must be set to `Content`, and the Copy to Output Directory setting to `Copy if newer`.

- Graphical content may be created from `.bmp`, `.png`, and `.jpg` files. The use of `.bmp` files should be avoided. For photographic images, `.jpg` files will offer much smaller files sizes and are probably the most appropriate. For other graphics, `.png` files may be the better choice as they support lossless compression, a full 24-bit color palette, and "alpha channel" transparency information.

- Content files are loaded into the MonoGame project using the `Content.Load` method.

- 2-D graphics may be rendered to the screen using a choice of position, scaling, rotation, tinting, and transparency. These graphics are known as "sprites."

- Subsections of images may be rendered by specifying a rectangular region within the source image.

- The ordering of sprites can be controlled using the `layerDepth` parameter of the `Draw` method. The `SpriteBatch` object must be instructed to observe this when its `Begin` method is called.

- Transparent areas of sprites may be controlled using either a simple color key, or a more flexible alpha channel contained within the sprite graphic.

- MonoGame can display text by using font files, created from a `spritefont` file within an XNA content project. Most of the options available for drawing sprites (position, rotation, color, transparency, and so on) can be applied when rendering text, too.

- Projects can be set to run in portrait or landscape orientation, or they can be set to support both. Windows 8 games must always include support for landscape orientation in order to be compliant with the Windows Store certification requirements. Windows Phone games can support either orientation.

CHAPTER 3

■ ■ ■

Creating a Game Framework

We have covered a lot of the technology foundations so far, and you have a good understanding of the functions required for displaying 2-D content to the screen. Now it is time to start organizing and structuring what you have learned.

It would be very easy to launch into our first game at this point, but instead of diving straight in, we will take a rather more deliberate approach.

In this chapter, we will begin the creation of a *game framework*, an object structure that we will build upon when writing games. The framework will be able to simplify the code that we write for each game, speeding up development time and allowing us to focus on the game rather than getting caught up in fiddly technical details. We can address all these details in the framework at one time—then we don't have to worry about them when we are developing.

Designing the Game Framework

MonoGame's Game class already provides a flexible engine for initializing and driving the game. What we will add to this is a flexible mechanism for managing the *game objects* that we want to display and manipulate inside the game.

The examples that we have been looking at have provided mechanisms for moving small numbers of sprites, but any real game needs to track significantly more objects than this. Instead of building all the objects into the game on an ad hoc basis, we will build the framework inside which the objects can be managed.

These objects will be used for all elements of the game that we need to draw. They will be the falling tiles in a game of *Tetris*; the ghosts, dots, and player in *Pac-Man*; and all the spaceships and bullets in *Space Invaders*. Objects will know various things about themselves (such as where they are on the screen) and will allow us to manage consistent and simple methods for moving and rendering efficiently. Providing this implementation for game objects is the primary area that we will address in the design and construction of the game framework within this chapter.

We will take advantage of the .NET object orientation features in the design of the framework. We will create an abstract base class that supports a core set of functions that will be generally useful in any of our game objects. We will then derive another abstract class from this and set up this derived class to provide support specifically for 2-D sprite-based game objects that we can create using the techniques in the previous chapter. In Chapter 6, we will derive another class for 3- D objects, allowing us to keep a significant part of the functionality and methodology that we have discussed and developed along the way.

All these classes will be placed into a separate class library project, which will allow us to reuse them between projects without having to reimplement them or share source files. Instead, we will just add a reference to the framework library, and its classes will be immediately available.

The game framework is implemented within two separate project files: GameFramework_Win8 and GameFramework_WP8. Both of these projects are located within the same GameFramework folder (you can find it in the download accompanying this chapter) and share the same source code files (but are, of course, set up to target each of the two platforms). The source code for this chapter is identical for both of the platforms; there is no need for any conditional compilation to be applied at this stage.

Let's take a look at the classes in the framework. You can find its code by opening the MultipleGameObjects_Win8 or MultipleGameObjects_WP8 projects from this chapter's example code.

▓ **Note**   The contents of the GameFramework project will continue to be developed throughout the following chapters of this book, too. You are free to modify and use this project for your own games in any capacity you wish, commercial or otherwise, though a mention of this book within your game would be appreciated if you are prepared to add one!

The GameObjectBase Class

The first class is the GameObjectBase class, an abstract class from which all our game object classes will ultimately be derived. The functionality within GameObjectBase is limited, but we can declare collections of game objects by using this class without initially needing to know any more details about which types of objects we are going to store.

In the class constructor, we take a GameHost object as a parameter. You might recall that the MonoGame games that we write all have their main class derived from the Game class. In our framework, we will derive a new class from the Game class so that we can supplement it with additional functionality—this new class is discussed shortly. We will store a reference to this GameHost object so that we can access both the native MonoGame functions and properties, and those added by the GameHost class itself. The constructor is shown in Listing 3-1.

Listing 3-1. The GameObjectBase class constructor

```
/// <summary>
/// Constructor for the object
/// </summary>
/// <param name="game">A reference to the MonoGame Game class inside which the object
/// resides</param>
public GameObjectBase(GameHost game)
{
    // Store a reference to the game
    Game = game;
}
```

In addition to the constructor, we define a single method, Update, which will be used to update the state of the object. It accepts a GameTime object as a parameter so that timing information can be extracted, just like the Update method in the main Game class. The function does nothing more than increment a variable, UpdateCount, so that we can tell how many updates have taken place; its code can be seen in Listing 3-2. Any derived classes that we create to represent objects within our games will override this function, however, so that they can perform the actual updates of their content.

Listing 3-2. The Update function

```
/// <summary>
/// Update the object state
/// </summary>
/// <param name="gameTime"></param>
public virtual void Update(GameTime gameTime)
{
    // Increment the UpdateCount
    UpdateCount += 1;
}
```

The SpriteObject Class

Derived from GameObjectBase is the SpriteObject class (see Figure 3-1). This is a concrete class (not abstract) in which we will add all the basic functionality that we might want to use to position and draw our sprites. In its basic form, the class is capable of maintaining a sprite's position, scaling, rotation, and origin, a texture for it to render with, a color to tint with, a source rectangle for partial texture rendering (if required), and a layer depth to help define the order in which the sprites should be rendered.

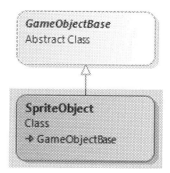

Figure 3-1. *The SpriteObject's position in the framework project*

It doesn't contain any object logic, however—it knows nothing about how to move or change any of its properties. This logic will be added by deriving further classes from SpriteObject, as we will see shortly. Such derived classes are generally what we will use when we build our games, but if a simple static sprite is all that is required, instances of SpriteObject can be created and added to the game.

Various different constructor overloads are provided to allow the calling code to easily set some of the common properties of the class. The signatures for each of these are shown in Listing 3-3 (the bodies of the functions are omitted for brevity because they are simply setting the provided parameter values into the class properties).

Listing 3-3. The available constructors for the SpriteObject class

```
public SpriteObject(Game game)
.
.
.


public SpriteObject(Game game, Vector2 position)
.
.
.


public SpriteObject(Game game, Vector2 position, Texture2D texture)
.
.
.
```

The class offers a lot of additional properties to allow us to control the position and appearance of the sprite, however, as follows:

- SpriteTexture stores a reference to a texture that can be used to render the sprite. The default implementation of the Draw method (which we will discuss in a moment) will use this texture to draw the sprite, though this behavior can be overridden if required.

- PositionX and PositionY store the sprite's position as float variables, whereas the Position property represents the same position as a Vector2. Any of them can be set or retrieved, though they update the same internal variables so setting PositionX or PositionY will have an immediate effect on the return value from Position, and vice versa. The reason they are stored as floats as well as a Vector2 is that Vector2 is a structure rather than a class, so when we read the Position property, we are actually given a copy of the underlying structure. This copy's properties cannot be modified, and Visual Studio will give an error if, for example, you attempt to assign a value to Position.X. So instead, we expose the individual coordinates for modification and interrogation and the Vector2 structure for passing into functions that expect a value of this type.

- OriginX, OriginY, and Origin store the sprite's origin coordinate, using a pair of floats and a Vector2 structure just as for the Position properties in the previous paragraph. The default origin is the coordinate (0, 0).

- Angle stores the angle of rotation in radians, defaulting to 0.

- ScaleX and ScaleY are float values that allow for uniform or non-uniform scaling to be applied to the sprite. In addition to this, the Scale property represents the same values as a Vector2 structure.

- SourceRect is a Rectangle structure with which we can define a subregion of the sprite's texture that is to be rendered. If the structure is "empty" (its values are all zero), this feature will be ignored, and the whole texture will be rendered. Its default state is to be empty.

- SpriteColor allows tinting and alpha levels to be applied to the sprite. It defaults to Color.White, with full intensity alpha.

- LayerDepth stores a float value that will be used for setting the rendering order of the sprite if the appropriate mode is set when calling the SpriteBatch.Begin method, as described in the previous chapter.

As you can see, the object allows virtually all the basic sprite states to be stored and maintained. Creating an instance of this class (or a class derived from it) allows a good deal of flexibility for displaying the sprite without needing any further variables to be defined. This greatly simplifies the repetitive code that we would otherwise need to write to store all this information.

In addition to storing the sprite state, we also add a virtual function called Draw. Just like the Draw method in the MonoGame main Game class, we expect a GameTime object as a parameter, but we also require a SpriteBatch object to be passed in. Because this class is dedicated entirely to drawing sprites, it makes sense to expect a SpriteBatch, and we need access to one so that we can call its Draw method to display our sprite to the screen.

The default behavior of the SpriteObject.Draw method is to draw the configured sprite to the screen. It can do this only if it has a valid SpriteTexture, so this is checked first. After that, one of two different calls is made to SpriteBatch.Draw, depending on whether a SourceRect has been specified. The code for the Draw function is shown in Listing 3-4.

Listing 3-4. The SpriteObject class Draw function

```
public virtual void Draw(GameTime gameTime, SpriteBatch spriteBatch)
{
    // Do we have a texture? If not then there is nothing to draw...
    if (SpriteTexture != null)
    {
        // Has a source rectangle been set?
        if (SourceRect.IsEmpty)
        {
            // No, so draw the entire sprite texture
            spriteBatch.Draw(SpriteTexture, Position, null, SpriteColor, Angle,
                                Origin, Scale, SpriteEffects.None, LayerDepth);
        }
        else
        {
            // Yes, so just draw the specified SourceRect
            spriteBatch.Draw(SpriteTexture, Position, SourceRect, SpriteColor, Angle,
                                Origin, Scale, SpriteEffects.None, LayerDepth);
        }
    }
}
```

Other classes that derive from SpriteObject can, of course, override the Draw method and supplement or entirely replace the default functionality as needed.

A final property present within the class can be used to help determine the area on the screen in which the sprite is being drawn. BoundingBox calculates this by looking at the sprite's position, its origin, the texture size, and the current scale. These are factored into a Rectangle structure that can then be used for simple collision checks, for example. The code for this function is shown in Listing 3-5.

Listing 3-5. Calculating the sprite's bounding box

```
public virtual Rectangle BoundingBox
{
    get
    {
        Rectangle result;
        Vector2 spritesize;

        if (SourceRect.IsEmpty)
        {
            // The size is that of the whole texture
            spritesize = new Vector2(SpriteTexture.Width, SpriteTexture.Height);
        }
        else
        {
            // The size is that of the rectangle
            spritesize = new Vector2(SourceRect.Width, SourceRect.Height);
        }
```

```
        // Build a rectangle whose position and size matches that of the sprite
        // (taking scaling into account for the size)
        result = new Rectangle((int)PositionX, (int)PositionY,
                        (int)(spritesize.X * ScaleX), (int)(spritesize.Y * ScaleY));

        // Offset the sprite by the origin
        result.Offset((int)(-OriginX * ScaleX), (int)(-OriginY * ScaleY));

        // Return the finished rectangle
        return result;
    }
}
```

The code first determines the size of the texture being displayed, which is the width and height of the whole texture, or the size defined by the SourceRect property if it has been set. It then creates its Rectangle structure by using the sprite position for the Left and Top values and the calculated texture size for its Width and Height. The texture size is scaled as appropriate to ensure that the resulting rectangle matches the size of the texture displayed on the screen.

The rectangle is then offset by the origin position. The further the origin moves toward the right, the further the sprite itself moves to the left, and so we subtract the origin position from the rectangle's top-left corner. Once again, this is scaled as appropriate.

The finished rectangle is then returned.

▓ **Caution**   This function works well for many sprite configurations, but those that have been rotated will not produce the expected results. The code does not take rotation into account, and so rotated sprites—and particularly those that are not square in shape—will protrude outside of the bounding box. If your sprites need more sophisticated bounding box calculation, this will need to be implemented in your derived game object classes. We will look at how some more sophisticated calculations can be added in Chapter 4, which covers User Input.

The TextObject Class

We have a simple way of representing a sprite, but it would be very useful to have a corresponding mechanism for representing text. We achieve this by creating the TextObject class. Because text shares many of the same features as sprites (a position, origin, color, rotation, scaling, and more), we derive TextObject from SpriteObject as shown in Figure 3-2, allowing us to take advantage of all the SpriteObject properties.

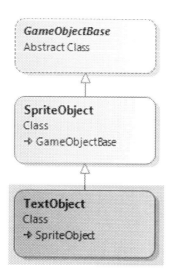

Figure 3-2. *The TextObject position in the framework project*

The constructors available to this class are more text-oriented and are shown in Listing 3-6.

Listing 3-6. The available constructors for the TextObject class

```
public TextObject(Game game)
  .
  .
  .

public TextObject(Game game, Vector2 position)
  .
  .
  .

public TextObject(Game game, Vector2 position, SpriteFont font)
  .
  .
  .

public TextObject(Game game, Vector2 position, SpriteFont font, String text)
  .
  .
  .

public TextObject(Game game, Vector2 position, SpriteFont font, String text,
                  TextAlignment horizontalAlignment, TextAlignment verticalAlignment)
  .
  .
  .
```

All the SpriteObject properties are relevant to TextObject except for SpriteTexture (we need a font instead of a texture) and SourceRect (which has no relevance to rendering text). We will ignore these and instead add a couple of new properties of our own:

- Font stores a reference to a SpriteFont object that will be used to render the text.

- Text stores a text string to be displayed.

- HorizontalAlignment and VerticalAlignment offer the creator of the object a simple way of automatically aligning the text around its position.

All four of these properties are backed by a private class variable rather than being autoimplemented using the { get; set; } syntax. This allows us to hook into their set code and perform some additional processing relating to text alignment, an example of which is shown in Listing 3-7.

Listing 3-7. The implementation of the Text property

```
public String Text
{
    get { return _text; }
    set
    {
        // Has the text changed from whatever we already have stored?
        if (_text != value)
        {
            // Yes, so store the new text and recalculate the origin if needed
            _text = value;
            CalculateAlignmentOrigin();
        }
    }
}
```

In each of the properties, if the code detects that a changed value has been provided, it calls into a function named CalculateAlignmentOrigin. This function examines the content of the HorizontalAlignment and VerticalAlignment properties, and if either is set to a value other than Manual, it automatically calculates a new Origin coordinate by calling the SpriteFont.MeasureString function (as detailed in the previous chapter). This allows the object creator to instruct the text to be left- or right-aligned, or for it to be centered (and the same options are available for vertical alignment, too). With the alignment properties set, this alignment will continue to be automatically applied whenever an update to the object is made. Alternatively, either or both of the alignment properties can be set to Manual (which is also their default), in which case the Origin coordinate can be set explicitly by the game.

Next, we have the Draw method. TextObject overrides it and replaces the SpriteObject implementation completely, rendering text rather than a texture. The implementation is very simple and is shown in Listing 3-8.

Listing 3-8. The TextObject Draw method

```
public override void Draw(GameTime gameTime, SpriteBatch spriteBatch)
{
    // Do we have a font? And some text? If not then there is nothing to draw...
    if (Font != null && !string.IsNullOrEmpty(Text))
    {
        // Draw the text
        spriteBatch.DrawString(Font, Text, Position, SpriteColor, Angle, Origin, Scale,
                                        SpriteEffects.None, LayerDepth);
    }
}
```

Finally, the class overrides the BoundingBox function to return a box calculated from the measured text size instead of from the texture size (because we don't use a texture in the TextObject class).

Just as with the SpriteObject class, the TextObject class gives us an easy-to-use mechanism for representing all the possible properties of a piece of text that is to be displayed within a game. Game-specific classes can derive from TextObject if they want to perform their own custom processing (they might override the Update method, for example, to change the content or positioning of the text), or alternatively an instance of TextObject might be directly instantiated if nothing else is required for display.

The GameHost Class

The next framework class is the GameHost class. This class holds collections of various objects that we will want to use in our games, specifically Dictionary objects containing textures and fonts, and a List of the actual game objects. The game objects are stored in a list containing objects of type GameObjectBase, which allows us to store within it the derived SpriteObject and TextObject game objects that we have so far discussed, as well as any game-specific classes that derive from any one of these.

The class also contains some simple methods that we can call to save having to write boilerplate functions in the main project's Game class.

The GameHost position within the framework is shown in Figure 3-3. It derives from the Microsoft.XNA. Framework.Game class (from which all MonoGame game projects must derive a single class). This means that in our game projects we can derive the main game class from GameFramework.GameHost instead of from Microsoft.XNA. Framework.Game. As a result, we get all the functionality of the MonoGame Game class as well as all the functionality added into GameHost.

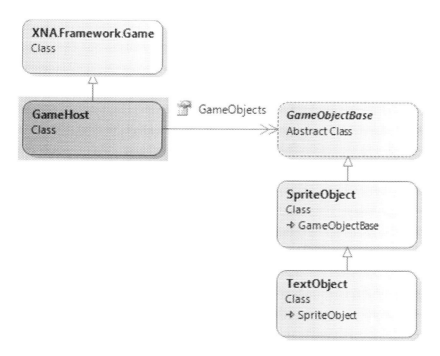

Figure 3-3. *The GameHost class position in the framework project*

The object collections are accessed by the following properties:

- Textures stores a dictionary of Texture2D objects. Any stored texture can be easily retrieved via its named dictionary key.

- Fonts performs the same function for SpriteFont objects.

- GameObjects is the list into which all the game's active objects will be placed. This is defined as a generic collection of GameObjectBase objects.

In many cases, we can add game objects to this GameObjects list and then simply allow them to carry out their own tasks until one encounters a circumstance that requires us to interact with it. For example, in an *Asteroids* game, we can simply set each asteroid object to move around the screen and then pretty much forget about the asteroids until one happens to collide with a bullet or the player's ship. When we detect that this has happened, we will process the asteroid as required. There is no reason to track the asteroids other than by having them present in the GameObjects list. We'll look at exactly this scenario in the Cosmic Rocks example project at the end of this chapter.

For other objects, however, we might need to be more proactive. The player's spaceship, for example, will need direct modification from the game so that it can respond to player input. To keep track of this, a separate reference to the game object will need to be stored in the game itself. The same applies for text objects whose values need to be updated (for the player score, for example).

Once the game is initialized and running, three additional methods are available to simplify the code in the main game class:

- UpdateAll loops through all the items in the GameObjects list and calls the Update method on each one. This function can be called from the main game class's Update method to keep everything moving forward.

- DrawSprites identifies all SpriteObject (and derived) objects in the GameObjects list and calls the Draw method of each. It requires an initialized SpriteBatch object to be passed in, and it is the calling code's responsibility to call its Begin and End methods. Keeping the call to Begin in the game class means that it can be given whatever parameters are appropriate for the sprite batch operation. A second overload draws only the sprites with a specified texture. This might be useful for some games, but it is provided for a particular reason that will be discussed in the "Benchmarking and Performance" section later in this chapter.

- DrawText identifies all TextObject (and derived) objects in the GameObjects list and calls the Draw method for them, just as DrawSprites does for SpriteObject game objects.

DrawSprites and DrawText are essentially provided for convenience and need not be used if additional functionality is required. If several sprite batches are needed with different parameters, for example, and the DrawSprites overload that separates the sprites by texture is not sufficiently flexible, the game class can simply implement its own custom version of this function.

The code within UpdateAll is more complex than a simple for each loop and it is worth some further exploration, so let's take a look at what it is doing. The reason for its complexity is that when .NET is iterating through a collection, GameObjects in this case, the collection is not allowed to be modified in any way. Attempting to add an object to or remove an object from the collection will result in an immediate exception because if the order of the objects is changed in any way, .NET cannot ensure that it hasn't skipped over or double-processed any of the objects.

A simple way in which we could have worked around this would be to call the collection's ToArray method and iterate over this instead of the collection, as shown in Listing 3-9.

Listing 3-9. A simple but flawed approach to iterating over the objects while still allowing collection modifications

```
foreach (GameObjectBase obj in GameObjects.ToArray())
{
    obj.Update(gameTime);
}
```

This appears to work very well and meets our objectives—all the objects are updated and each one can perform any modification to the collection that it wants. It has a flaw, however. Every time the loop is prepared, it creates another array of object pointers and, as a result, consumes a little extra memory. This might not sound important, but the method is being called 60 times per second and might be processing hundreds of objects. This quickly runs into noticeable amounts of memory being used: 60 updates per second with 100 objects requiring four bytes per object pointer results in 24,000 bytes allocated per second.

When memory is being allocated this quickly on portable devices, particularly phones, the garbage collection ends up triggering on a frequent basis. Each time this happens, the application briefly pauses while the process executes. This is not likely to be noticed in an e-mail or diary application, but in a fast running game it will really attract the user's attention in an unpleasant way.

We therefore want to try to minimize the amount of memory that is allocated within the game loop. To solve this within the GameHost, a private array of GameObjects is declared at class level, as shown in Listing 3-10. We will use this array over and over again, minimizing memory allocation as far as possible.

Listing 3-10. The class-level _objectArray variable

```
public class GameHost : Microsoft.Xna.Framework.Game
{

    //-----------------------------------------------------------------------------
    // Class variables

    private GameObjectBase[] _objectArray;

    [...]
}
```

This array initially starts off uninitialized. The UpdateAll function first checks for this state; when found, it creates the array with enough space to hold all the current known objects in the GameObjects collection, plus space for 20 percent more. Allowing a little extra space like this means that we don't need to reallocate the array every time a new object is added. If there are fewer than 20 objects in the game, it allocates a minimum of 20 to prevent reallocation each time a new object is added with low object numbers (adding 20 percent to four objects results in still only four objects after rounding).

If UpdateAll instead finds that the array has been previously created, it checks its capacity against the current game object count. If the object count fits within the array, it leaves the array alone. On the other hand, if the object count is now too large for the array, it reallocates the array by creating a new object collection, once again providing space for 20 percent more objects than are currently present.

This process ensures that the array starts at a reasonable size and increases in stages rather than one object at a time. The old arrays that are discarded will be garbage-collected in time, but they will be small in number so they won't waste large amounts of memory.

The opening section of UpdateAll that performs the steps discussed so far can be seen in Listing 3-11.

Listing 3-11. The beginning of the UpdateAll function, allocating space in the _objectArray variable

```
public virtual void UpdateAll(GameTime gameTime)
{
    int i;
    int objectCount;

    // First build our array of objects.
    // We will iterate across this rather than across the actual GameObjects
    // collection so that the collection can be modified by the game objects'
```

```
// Update code.
// First of all, do we have an array?
if (_objectArray == null)
{
    // No, so allocate it.
    // Allocate 20% more objects than we currently have, or 20 objects,
    // whichever is more
    _objectArray = new GameObjectBase[
                             (int)MathHelper.Max(20, GameObjects.Count * 1.2f) ];
}
else if (GameObjects.Count > _objectArray.Length)
{
    // The number of game objects has exceeded the array size.
    // Reallocate the array, adding 20% free space for further expansion.
    _objectArray = new GameObjectBase[(int)(GameObjects.Count * 1.2f)];
}
}
```

With the array created at an appropriate size, UpdateAll now populates it. This takes place for every update because we cannot tell at a high level whether the objects have been added to or removed from the GameObjects list (just checking the object count would not be sufficient as objects might have been removed and inserted in equal numbers). This might seem wasteful, but it is really just assigning object pointers and so is extremely quick to execute.

Another important thing we need to do with the array is to release any references we have to objects that have been removed from the GameObjects collection. Without doing this, our array could potentially keep references alive for extended periods within the elements past the end of our main object loop, even though nothing is actually using them any more. Releasing them ensures that their memory can be freed the next time garbage collection runs.

Removing these references is simply a matter of setting the array elements to null for all objects other than those in the GameObjects collection. As we are looping through the array to tell each object to update, it is easy to just continue looping to the end of the array, setting the elements that we are not using to null. This will release all the expired object references.

The array population section of UpdateAll is shown in Listing 3-12.

Listing 3-12. Copying the current game object references into _objectArray and removing expired object references

```
// Store the current object count for performance
objectCount = GameObjects.Count;

// Transfer the object references into the array
for (i = 0; i < _objectArray.Length; i++)
{
    // Is there an active object at this position in the GameObjects collection?
    if (i < objectCount)
    {
        // Yes, so copy it to the array
        _objectArray[i] = GameObjects[i];
    }
    else
    {
        // No, so clear any reference stored at this index position
        _objectArray[i] = null;
    }
}
```

With the array populated, we can now iterate through its objects and tell each one to update. The GameObjects collection is not being iterated, and so the objects are free to manipulate its items in any way they want without exceptions occurring.

We know how many objects we actually have to process because we already queried the GameObjects.Count property and stored it in the objectCount variable. Remember that we can't rely on the array length for this because we are allocating space for additional objects. The stored object count value has an additional use in the update loop. Because the GameObjects collection might be modified during the loop (which would affect the result returned by the Count property), we cannot rely on the value being stable while the updates are processing.

Once we know how many objects to process, it is then just a matter of calling the Update method for each. The remainder of the UpdateAll function is shown in Listing 3-13.

Listing 3-13. Updating the game objects

```
// Loop for each element within the array
for (i = 0; i < objectCount; i++)
{
    // Update the object at this array position
    _objectArray[i].Update(gameTime);
}
```

When the number of game objects is static, the array will persist without any reallocations from one update to the next. Each time the number of objects is allocated past the current maximum, a reallocation will occur, but the frequency of these reallocations will be reduced by the addition of the 20 percent buffer for additional objects. Once the game's operational maximum is reached, no further allocations will take place at all. The only overhead for all this is two simple loops through the array, one to copy references from the GameObjects collection, and the other to draw the objects and remove expired object references. In return, we gain complete flexibility to manipulate the set of objects from within each object's Update code.

The GameHelper Class

Finally, there is the GameHelper class, which is a place into which generally useful functions can be added (similar to MonoGame's own MathHelper class). The class is declared as static, so it cannot be instantiated.

For the moment, the class just contains a number of functions relating to random numbers. It hosts an instance of a Random object and exposes several overloads of a function called RandomNext, each of which returns a random number. There are two reasons for having these functions:

- They provide our game code with immediate access to random numbers (a common requirement for game development) without needing to instantiate its own Random instance.

- They add some useful overloads that return random float values, either between zero and a specified upper limit, or between an arbitrary lower and upper limit. They can be extremely useful when randomizing game objects because such objects use float variables for nearly all their properties.

We will add further functionality to this class (and indeed to the whole framework) as we progress through the following chapters.

Using the Game Framework

The MultipleGameObjects_Win8 and MultipleGameObjects_WP8 example projects show a simple demonstration of using the game framework to display a number of moving sprites on the screen with minimal code required in the game project itself.

The project creates a number of colored box objects that move toward the bottom of the screen while rotating, a number of colored ball objects that bounce around the screen (and squash against the edges when they hit), and a text object that displays a message in the middle of the screen. An image of the project running on Windows Phone can be seen in Figure 3-4.

Figure 3-4. *The results of the MultipleGameObjects_WP8 example project*

Let's take a look at how the project has been put together.

Referencing the GameFramework Project

Before the game framework classes can be accessed, we need to add a reference to the GameFramework project from the main game project. Assuming that the GameFramework project is already part of the current Solution, this is simply a matter of right-clicking the main game project node in Solution Explorer, selecting Add Reference, choosing Solution/Projects in the left panel of the Reference Manager window, and then picking the GameFramework project from the list of projects. (See in Figure 3-5.) This image shows the reference being added for a Windows Phone project, but the process is identical for Windows 8.

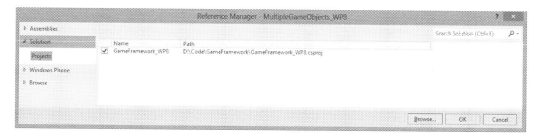

Figure 3-5. *Adding a reference to the GameFramework project*

If the GameFramework project is not a part of your solution, you can either add it or add a reference to GameFramework.dll by using the Browse tab in the Add Reference window (which can also be seen at the bottom of the tabs on the left in Figure 3-5).

Setting Inheritance for the Main Game Class

We already know that a MonoGame game project must contain exactly one class that derives from Microsoft.Xna. Framework.Game, and by default the MonoGame project templates create new game projects with one such class present (named Game1 to begin with).

In order to use the game framework, we must change the inheritance of this class so that it instead derives from GameFramework.GameHost, as shown in Listing 3-14.

Listing 3-14. The declaration of a game class using the game framework

```
/// <summary>
/// This is the main type for your game
/// </summary>
public class MultipleObjectsGame : GameFramework.GameHost
{
```

Creating Derived SpriteObject classes

Now that we are set up to use the game framework, we can start writing code to use it. In the MultipleGameObjects example, there are two classes that derive from the game framework's SpriteObject: BoxObject and BallObject. Each of these contains all the logic required for that object to update and draw itself.

The BoxObject Class

BoxObject is the more straightforward of the two derived object classes. Its constructor is shown in Listing 3-15.

Listing 3-15. The constructor for the BoxObject class

```
internal BoxObject(MultipleObjectsGame game, Texture2D texture)
    : base(game, Vector2.Zero, texture)
{
    // Store a strongly-typed reference to the game
    _game = game;
```

```
    // Set a random position
    PositionX = GameHelper.RandomNext(0, _game.GraphicsDevice.Viewport.Bounds.Width);
    PositionY = GameHelper.RandomNext(0, _game.GraphicsDevice.Viewport.Bounds.Height);

    // Set the origin
    Origin = new Vector2(texture.Width, texture.Height) / 2;

    // Set a random color
    SpriteColor = new Color(GameHelper.RandomNext(0, 256),
                    GameHelper.RandomNext(0, 256), GameHelper.RandomNext(0, 256));

    // Set a random movement speed for the box
    _moveSpeed = GameHelper.RandomNext(2.0f) + 2;

    // Set a random rotation speed for the box
    _rotateSpeed = GameHelper.RandomNext(-5.0f, 5.0f);
}
```

It accepts parameters that are relevant for the box, namely a reference to the MultipleGameObjects game class and the texture to display in the box. After storing the game class reference, the constructor randomizes the object ready for display on the screen.

This process consists of setting random values for the PositionX, PositionY, and SpriteColor properties (all of which are provided by the SpriteObject base class). It also sets the Origin property to be at the center of the sprite, calculated by halving the width and height of the provided texture.

Once the base class properties have been set, the constructor code also generates random values for its own class-specific variables. These values are _moveSpeed, a variable that controls how fast the box moves, and _rotateSpeed, which controls how fast it rotates. These values will be used each time the sprite updates and will be added to the PositionY and Angle properties, respectively. The GameHelper class is used to generate random float values for both of these. Note that the rotation speed can be either positive or negative, which means that the box can rotate either clockwise or counterclockwise.

Along with the functionality inherited from the SpriteObject class, this is already sufficient to display the colored box in a random position, but it won't yet move in any way. Movement is implemented by overriding the Update method, as shown in Listing 3-16.

Listing 3-16. The Update method for the BoxObject class

```
public override void Update(GameTime gameTime)
{
    // Allow the base class to do any work it needs
    base.Update(gameTime);

    // Update the position of the box
    PositionY += _moveSpeed;
    // If we pass the bottom of the window, reset back to the top
    if (BoundingBox.Top > _game.GraphicsDevice.Viewport.Bounds.Bottom)
    {
        PositionY = -SpriteTexture.Height;
    }

    // Rotate the box
    Angle += MathHelper.ToRadians(_rotateSpeed);
}
```

This is all very simple—the movement speed is first added to the PositionY property to update the sprite position. The position is then checked to see whether the sprite has passed the bottom of the screen. This is the case if its BoundingBox.Top is below the bottom of the window, at which point the sprite's position is reset back to the top. It is set so that its position is actually above the top of the screen so that it doesn't "pop" into view.

The Angle property is then updated according to the rotation speed. Note that we use the MathHelper.ToRadians function when rotating, which means that the _rotateSpeed variable is storing degrees rather than radians. It doesn't really matter which unit you use, but you should stick to the same unit throughout all of your game to avoid confusion.

Note that there is no need for any other code within the class, including any to perform drawing, because the SpriteObject base class provides all of this. All the class needs to concern itself with is the simple task of moving itself.

The BallObject Class

The BallObject implementation is slightly more complex, but only slightly. Instead of simply moving down the screen, the balls need to bounce off the screen edges, obey gravity (or an approximation thereof), and "wobble" when they hit the edges of the screen, as if they were made of rubber.

To make the ball move in this way, we need to store the direction in which it is moving (its velocity). In order to know an object's velocity, we need to know both the direction in which it is moving and the speed with which it is traveling. There are two methods in which we can describe an object's velocity: either by storing its direction (as an angle from 0 to 360 degrees) and its speed of movement in that direction, or by storing its speed as a value along each of the x and y axes.

The first of these methods provides for a simulation of movement that is closer to how things move in reality, and, in many scenarios, this will be an appropriate system to use. In fact, we'll use this approach for the player spaceship in our "Cosmic Rocks" example at the end of this chapter.

For the sake of simplicity in our example, however, we will use the second method because it's a little easier to manage. This method simply tracks the x and y distance that we want to move the object each time it updates. To bounce an object off the side of the screen, we can simply negate the speed in that particular axis. If we are adding a value of 5 to the x position and we hit the right side of the screen, we then start subtracting 5 to move to the left again. Subtracting 5 is the same as adding –5, so changing the x speed from 5 to –5 will reverse the direction on that axis. Exactly the same function applies to the y axis. The calculation is illustrated in Figure 3-6.

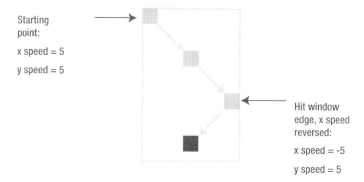

Figure 3-6. *The motion of a bouncing sprite, as controlled using x and y axis speeds*

Just as with the box class, we implement all this inside the derived game object. We use several class-level variables to support this:

- _xadd and _yadd keep track of the ball's velocity in the two axes of movement.

- _wobble tracks the amount that the ball is wobbling (where zero is not at all, and greater values indicate higher wobble levels).

The _xadd variable is set in the constructor along with some of the inherited sprite properties, as shown in Listing 3-17. The _yadd and _wobble variables are left with their default values of 0; they will be modified in the Update method, as we will see in a moment.

Listing 3-17. The constructor for the BallObject class

```
internal BallObject(MultipleObjectsGame game, Texture2D texture)
    : base(game, Vector2.Zero, texture)
{
    // Store a strongly-typed reference to the game
    _game = game;

    // Set a random position
    PositionX = GameHelper.RandomNext(0, _game.GraphicsDevice.Viewport.Bounds.Width);
    PositionY = GameHelper.RandomNext(0, _game.GraphicsDevice.Viewport.Bounds.Height);

    // Set the origin
    Origin = new Vector2(texture.Width, texture.Height) / 2;

    // Set a random color
    SpriteColor = new Color(GameHelper.RandomNext(0, 256),
                    GameHelper.RandomNext(0, 256), GameHelper.RandomNext(0, 256));

    // Set a horizontal movement speed for the box
    _xadd = GameHelper.RandomNext(-5.0f, 5.0f);
}
```

As with the box, the rest of the class code is contained within the Update method. To make the ball move, we first add the velocity in each axis to the corresponding position, detecting collisions with the left, right, and bottom edges of the screen as described at the start of this section. The beginning of the Update method, which handles these changes, is shown in Listing 3-18.

Listing 3-18. Part of the ball's Update method: moving the ball and bouncing from the screen edges

```
public override void Update(GameTime gameTime)
{
    // Allow the base class to do any work it needs
    base.Update(gameTime);

    // Update the position of the ball
    PositionX += _xadd;
    PositionY += _yadd;

    // If we reach the side of the window, reverse the x velocity so that the ball
    // bounces back
```

```
    if (PositionX < OriginX)
    {
        // Reset back to the left edge
        PositionX = OriginX;
        // Reverse the x velocity
        _xadd = -_xadd;
        // Add to the wobble
        _wobble += Math.Abs(_xadd);
    }
    if (PositionX > _game.GraphicsDevice.Viewport.Bounds.Width - OriginX)
    {
        // Reset back to the right edge
        PositionX = _game.GraphicsDevice.Viewport.Bounds.Width - OriginX;
        // Reverse the x velocity
        _xadd = -_xadd;
        // Add to the wobble
        _wobble += Math.Abs(_xadd);
    }

    // If we reach the bottom of the window, reverse the y velocity so that the ball
    // bounces upwards
    if (PositionY >= _game.GraphicsDevice.Viewport.Bounds.Bottom - OriginY)
    {
        // Reset back to the bottom of the window
        PositionY = _game.GraphicsDevice.Viewport.Bounds.Bottom - OriginY;
        // Reverse the y-velocity
        _yadd = -_yadd; // +0.3f;
        // Add to the wobble
        _wobble += Math.Abs(_yadd);
    }
    else
    {
        // Increase the y velocity to simulate gravity
        _yadd += 0.3f;
    }
}
```

The ball's position is checked against the screen edges by taking the origin values into account because the origin is set to be at the center of the ball. If the OriginX value is 20, the ball has hit the left edge of the window if the PositionX value falls below 20. The same applies to the right edge, where its OriginX value is subtracted from the window width to determine the maximum permitted PositionX value, and to the bottom edge, where its OriginY is subtracted from the window's Bottom position.

If the ball hasn't hit the bottom edge, we add a small amount to the _yadd variable, as seen in the final line of code in Listing 3-18. This is the all-important update that simulates gravity. For every update, the ball moves downward a little more than it did in the previous update. If the ball is moving upward, this erodes its upward momentum until it eventually starts to fall downward again. Changing the amount that is added to _yadd each update will increase or decrease the intensity of the simulated gravity.

The remainder of the update code deals with the ball's wobble. As you can also see in Listing 3-18, the _wobble variable is increased each time the ball bounces by adding the corresponding velocity. This means that the harder the ball hits into the window edge, the more it wobbles. The Math.Abs function is used to ensure that the wobble value increases even if the velocity contains a negative value.

The wobble is implemented by updating the ball's scale properties. We use a sine wave to make the ball oscillate between being thinner and fatter than normal, and offset it so that when it is at its thinnest on the x axis it is also at its fattest on the y axis, and vice versa. This provides a pleasing rubbery visual effect.

Listing 3-19 shows the rest of the Update function, containing the wobble code. If the wobble level is zero, it ensures that the scaling is reset by assigning a unit vector to the Scale property. Otherwise, it uses the UpdateCount property from GameObjectBase as a mechanism for moving through the sine values. The WobbleSpeed constant controls how rapidly the ball oscillates, and WobbleIntensity controls how much it squashes the ball. Try altering these values and see the effect that it has on the balls.

Finally, the wobble level is gradually decreased with each update and checked to stop it from falling below 0 or getting too high (at which point it looks silly).

Listing 3-19. The remaining Update method code: making the ball wobble

```
// Is there any wobble?
if (_wobble == 0)
{
    // No, so reset the scale
    Scale = Vector2.One;
}
else
{
    const float WobbleSpeed = 20.0f;
    const float WobbleIntensity = 0.015f;

    // Yes, so calculate the scaling on the x and y axes
    ScaleX = (float)Math.Sin(MathHelper.ToRadians(UpdateCount * WobbleSpeed))
                            * _wobble * WobbleIntensity + 1;
    ScaleY = (float)Math.Sin(MathHelper.ToRadians(UpdateCount * WobbleSpeed + 180.0f))
                            * _wobble * WobbleIntensity + 1;

    // Reduce the wobble level
    _wobble -= 0.2f;
    // Don't allow the wobble to fall below zero or to rise too high
    if (_wobble < 0) _wobble = 0;
    if (_wobble > 50) _wobble = 50;
}
```

Adding Game Objects to the Game Host

Let's focus now on the game class, which is named MultipleObjectsGame in the example projects. Instead of deriving from Microsoft.Xna.Framework.Game, it instead derives from GameFramework.GameHost, so it picks up all the functionality that the GameHost class offers.

In LoadContent, the textures and fonts are loaded in the same way as in the previous examples, but this time they are added into the appropriate GameHost collections, as shown in Listing 3-20.

Listing 3-20. Loading game resources into the Host object

```
protected override void LoadContent()
{
    // Create a new SpriteBatch, which can be used to draw textures.
    _spriteBatch = new SpriteBatch(GraphicsDevice);
```

```
    // Load the object textures into the textures dictionary
    Textures.Add("Ball", this.Content.Load<Texture2D>("Ball"));
    Textures.Add("Box", this.Content.Load<Texture2D>("Box"));

    // Load fonts
    Fonts.Add("Kootenay", this.Content.Load<SpriteFont>("Kootenay"));

    // Reset the game
    ResetGame();
}
```

The final line of code in LoadContent calls into a new function named ResetGame, in which we create the objects that will do the work when the game is running. Its code is shown in Listing 3-21.

Listing 3-21. Resetting the game

```
private void ResetGame()
{
    TextObject message;

    // Remove any existing objects
    GameObjects.Clear();

    // Add 10 boxes and 10 balls
    for (int i = 0; i < 10; i++)
    {
        GameObjects.Add(new BoxObject(this, Textures["Box"]));
    }
    for (int i = 0; i < 10; i++)
    {
        GameObjects.Add(new BallObject(this, Textures["Ball"]));
    }

    // Add some text
    message = new TextObject(this, Fonts["Kootenay"],
                    new Vector2(GraphicsDevice.Viewport.Bounds.Width / 2,
                                        GraphicsDevice.Viewport.Height / 2),
                    "MonoGame Game Development",
                    TextObject.TextAlignment.Center, TextObject.TextAlignment.Center);
    message.SpriteColor = Color.DarkBlue;
    message.Scale = new Vector2(1.0f, 1.5f);
    GameObjects.Add(message);
}
```

ResetGame first removes any objects that might have been added to the game host earlier. Although this will never happen in our example because the game is reset only once, in a proper game this could be called each time the player runs out of lives in order to prepare a new game. To stop the previous game from leaving debris behind, we would need to remove those objects that the previous game had been using.

The game then loops to add ten boxes and ten balls to the game host. These are created using the derived BoxObject and BallObject game object classes that we have been discussing over the last few pages. It also adds a TextObject instance to display the writing in the middle of the screen. No custom functionality is needed for this object, so the TextObject class is instantiated directly.

All that is left is to implement the Update and Draw functions, both of which can be seen in Listing 3-22. As you can see, these are absolutely trivial, just telling the game host to perform the required updates and drawing.

Listing 3-22. Updating and drawing the game

```
protected override void Update(GameTime gameTime)
{
    // Update all the game objects
    UpdateAll(gameTime);

    base.Update(gameTime);
}

protected override void Draw(GameTime gameTime)
{
    GraphicsDevice.Clear(Color.Wheat);

    // Begin the spritebatch
    _spriteBatch.Begin();
    // Draw the sprites
    DrawSprites(gameTime, _spriteBatch);
    // Draw the text
    DrawText(gameTime, _spriteBatch);
    // End the spritebatch
    _spriteBatch.End();

    base.Draw(gameTime);
}
```

The small amount of code presented in this section is all that is needed to get the game example running. Please spend a little time getting comfortable with the general approach used here—the framework classes, the derived game object classes, and the code within the game class. We will build on these principles throughout the rest of the book, so it is important that you become comfortable with how they fit together.

The framework is very lightweight in nature, essentially just allowing us to easily organize and access the objects that we want to work with. It is deliberately unobtrusive and transparent so that it doesn't get in the way of your game code, allowing you instead to simply focus on the game rather than the mechanics of managing your objects.

Because of the code present in the GameHost.UpdateAll function for transferring the game object collection into an array for processing (as discussed in "The GameHost Class" earlier in this chapter), game objects can also add objects to the game during their Update calls. If, for example, a sprite detects that it has landed in water and wants to create a splash, it can add objects for the water droplets at the point at which its movement into the water is being processed, which makes for a much more readable project overall.

Removing Objects from the Game Host

We can now add objects to the game, but how do we remove them?

The game (in its Update method) has full access to the GameObjects collection within GameHost. If it determines that an object is no longer needed, it can simply remove the object from the list.

Just as game objects can add further objects in their Update method, they can also remove objects. If one object finds another object that is no longer required, it can simply remove the unwanted object from the collection and no further calls to the dropped object's Update or Draw method will be made. This includes the ability for an object to remove itself from the collection if it needs to.

Overriding Object Properties

The example derived game object classes that we have looked at all declared additional properties to define their custom behavior (the downward movement speed for the box, the x and y axis velocities, and wobble for the ball) and used them in their Update methods to set their properties to affect how they are drawn.

In many cases, this will be the most appropriate way to control the presentation of the object, but there is an alternative mechanism that in other cases might result in simpler code.

All the basic properties in the SpriteObject class are defined as being virtual. This covers the sprite's texture, position coordinates, origin coordinates, angle, scale values, source rectangle, color and layer depth, but it excludes the Vector2-typed properties (Position, Origin, and Scale) because they are just based around the underlying float values. By default, they simply store and return the provided value. Because they are virtual, however, the properties can be overridden in the derived classes and the way that they work can be modified.

For example, we could create a moon object that orbited a planet object and override its PositionX and PositionY properties to allow them to calculate their positions on demand, based on the position of the planet and its rotation angle instead of having to calculate this in the Update method. Overriding the properties in this way guarantees that the position is up-to-date and accurate, even if the planet's position has changed since the moon's last Update call.

This scenario is demonstrated in the OrbitingSprite_Win8 and OrbitingSprite_WP8 example projects, an image from which is shown in Figure 3-7. It defines two sprite object classes, PlanetObject and MoonObject, and then creates a couple of planet instances with some moons orbiting them. Just to demonstrate the flexibility of this environment, it also creates a moon that orbits around one of the other moons. This scenario might be physically unlikely in the real universe, but it works well for demonstration purposes!

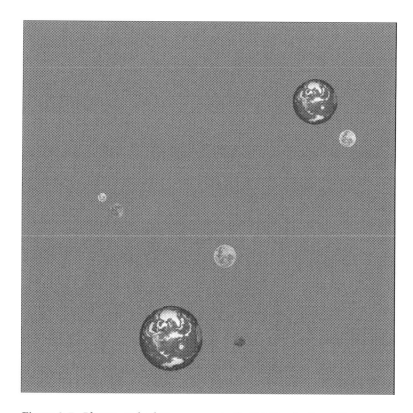

Figure 3-7. *Planets and orbiting moons in the OrbitingSprites_Win8 project*

Within `PlanetObject`, we just set up a simple horizontal bounce movement pattern so that the planets gradually move back and forth across the screen. (You have already seen code that is essentially identical in earlier parts of this chapter.)

`MoonObject` is where the interesting code resides. Its constructor includes parameters to define the moon's target object (around which it will orbit), its orbital speed, the distance at which it will orbit its target, and its size. The target object, speed, and distance are stored in variables defined for the moon, whereas the rest of the properties are passed through to the base class.

The moon class has no `Update` code at all. Instead, its movement relies on the position of the target object and on the `UpdateCount` property implemented within the `GameObjectBase` class. The position of the moon is calculated on demand when its `PositionX` and `PositionY` properties are queried. The implementation is shown in Listing 3-23.

Listing 3-23. The position property overrides for the moon object

```
/// <summary>
/// Calculate the x position of the moon
/// </summary>
public override float PositionX
{
    get
    {
        return _targetObject.PositionX + (float)Math.Sin(UpdateCount * _speed) * _distance;
    }
}


/// <summary>
/// Calculate the y position of the moon
/// </summary>
public override float PositionY
{
    get
    {
        return _targetObject.PositionY + (float)Math.Cos(UpdateCount * _speed) * _distance;
    }
}
```

The properties read the position of the target object and then use the `Sin` and `Cos` functions to return the positions of a circle that orbits this initial position. The `UpdateCount` value is multiplied by `_speed` variable to allow the moon to orbit at a defined rate, and the return values from `Sin` and `Cos` (which will always range between -1 and 1) are multiplied by the `_distance` variable to set the distance at which the moon is positioned from its target.

▓ **Note** As shown in Listing 3-23, it is quite possible to override just the `get` part of a property. Because the `PositionX` and `PositionY` properties in the `MoonObject` class make no use of the underlying value, we can simply ignore the `set` part and allow any attempts to access it to fall through to the base class.

`MoonObject`'s `Angle` property also uses the same technique, overriding the default behavior of the property to make each moon slowly rotate as it orbits around its target sprite.

The game objects are added to the game in the `ResetGame` function, as shown in Listing 3-24. First, a planet is instantiated and added to the `GameObjects` collection. A moon is then created and the corresponding planet is passed to it as its target object. This is then repeated for the second planet, which is given three moons. The last of those moons gets its own moon, too, because the moon can orbit any object—it doesn't matter whether it is a planet or another moon that it targets (and indeed, this moon-of-a-moon could itself be given a moon, and so on). With this object configuration in place, the simulation runs and produces this comparatively complex set of object movements with an extremely small amount of game code required.

Listing 3-24. Initializing the objects for the OrbitingSprites project

```
private void ResetGame()
{
    PlanetObject planet;
    MoonObject moon;

    // Add a planet...
    planet = new PlanetObject(this, new Vector2(150, 200),
                                    Textures["Planet"], 0.7f);
    GameObjects.Add(planet);
    // ...and give it a moon
    GameObjects.Add(new MoonObject(this, Textures["Moon"],
                                    planet, 0.02f, 60, 0.3f, Color.White));

    // Add another planet...
    planet = new PlanetObject(this, new Vector2(300, 500),
                                    Textures["Planet"], 1.0f);
    GameObjects.Add(planet);
    // ...and give it some moons
    GameObjects.Add(new MoonObject(this, Textures["Moon"],
                                    planet, 0.04f, 90, 0.2f, Color.OrangeRed));
    GameObjects.Add(new MoonObject(this, Textures["Moon"],
                                    planet, 0.025f,130, 0.4f, Color.PaleGreen));
    moon = new MoonObject(this, Textures["Moon"],
                                    planet, 0.01f, 180, 0.25f, Color.Silver);
    GameObjects.Add(moon);
    // Add a moon to the moon
    GameObjects.Add(new MoonObject(this, Textures["Moon"],
                                    moon, 0.1f, 25, 0.15f, Color.White));
}
```

Benchmarking and Performance

None of the example projects that we've used so far has created large volumes of objects, so their performance has all been very good, animating smoothly on the screen. Real games are likely to be much more complex and will result in substantially more objects being drawn during each update.

To allow us to monitor how the game is performing, it is very useful to use a *benchmark*. This is a measurement of how well the game is performing, and it allows us to see how many frames of animation are being displayed per second while the game is running.

MonoGame projects run by default at 60 frames per second, which is a speed that results in fast and smooth animation. In theory, this means that we will receive 60 calls to Update per second and 60 corresponding calls to Draw per second. This might well be the case with small numbers of objects in motion, but how about if there are thousands of them? Or tens of thousands? A benchmark will allow us to see exactly how the game performs under these conditions.

Another more important use for the benchmark is to allow us to spot unexpected low levels of performance and to provide us with an opportunity to identify and resolve them in order to improve the way that a game runs. We will look at an example of such a problem later in this section and see what can be done to resolve it.

Using the Frame Rate Counter

You have probably noticed through all of the Windows Phone projects that a little panel of numbers appeared along the right edge of the screen. This panel is a series of debug values known as the *frame rate counter*. These values are being enabled by the line of code in App.xaml.cs shown in Listing 3-25, and they result in a display as shown in Figure 3-8.

Listing 3-25. Switching on the Windows Phone frame rate counter

```
// Show graphics profiling information while debugging.
if (Debugger.IsAttached)
{
    // Display the current frame rate counters.
    Application.Current.Host.Settings.EnableFrameRateCounter = true;
}
```

Figure 3-8. A typical set of values from the frame rate counter

The very first of these figures, showing 59 in Figure 3-8, is the number of frames being displayed per second. Ideally, this value needs to be kept as close to 60 as possible. If the figure starts to fall, and particularly if it falls below 30, the display of graphics will become noticeably juddery and the feeling of smooth animation will be lost.

This is a very quick and easy way to check the frame rate within a Windows Phone project, but what about in Windows 8? The Windows 8 environment does have a frame rate counter, but due to the way that MonoGame interacts with the presentation of data on the screen, it is impossible to get the Windows 8 frame rate counter to actually appear.

To solve this for Windows 8, and also to provide a little more information for Windows Phone, we will now add our own benchmark object to the GameFramework project so that it can be added to your games while you are developing them.

The BenchmarkObject Class

To easily obtain frame rate information in any game, the BenchmarkObject class is added to the game framework. Because the task of this class is essentially to display some text (containing the benchmark information we are trying to obtain), it is derived from the TextObject class.

The class needs to be able to count the number of calls to Update and Draw that occur each second. On a periodic basis (approximately once per second is usually sufficient), we should determine exactly how much time has passed since our last measurement and how many updates and draws have taken place. The count of the updates and draws can then be divided by the elapsed time to calculate the count per second.

The GameObject base class already counts the number of updates in its UpdateCount property, so the benchmark class doesn't need to do that. It doesn't count the number of calls to Draw, however, so the benchmark class creates a class level variable named _drawCount and adds 1 to this each time its Draw method is called.

In order to tell how many calls have occurred since the last time the frame rate was calculated, the class also stores the previous draw and update counts. The newly elapsed counts can then be obtained by subtracting the last counts from the current counts. The class-level variables _lastDrawCount and _lastUpdateCount are defined for this purpose.

Finally, we need to know when the frame rate was last measured so that we can determine the time period during which the new updates and draws have occurred. This is stored in the class level _lastUpdateMilliseconds property. The full set of variables is shown in Listing 3-26.

Listing 3-26. The class level variables required by BenchmarkObject

```
//--------------------------------------------------------------------------------
// Class variables
private double _lastUpdateMilliseconds;
private int _drawCount;
private int _lastDrawCount;
private int _lastUpdateCount;
```

This gives us everything we need to measure the frame rate. First, the Draw method is overridden to increment the draw count. The frame rate calculation is then performed in the Update method, as shown in Listing 3-27.

Listing 3-27. The BenchmarkObject Update method

```
override void Update(GameTime gameTime)
{
    int newDrawCount;
    int newUpdateCount;
    double newElapsedTime;

    // Allow the base class to do its stuff
    base.Update(gameTime);

    // Has 1 second passed since we last updated the text?
    if (gameTime.TotalGameTime.TotalMilliseconds > _lastUpdateMilliseconds + 1000)
    {
        // Find how many frames have been drawn within the last second
        newDrawCount = _drawCount - _lastDrawCount;
        // Find how many updates have taken place within the last second
        newUpdateCount = UpdateCount - _lastUpdateCount;
        // Find out exactly how much time has passed
        newElapsedTime = gameTime.TotalGameTime.TotalMilliseconds -
                                                    _lastUpdateMilliseconds;

        // Build a message to display the details and set it into the Text property
        _strBuilder.Length = 0;
        _strBuilder.AppendLine("Object count: " + Game.GameObjects.Count.ToString());
        _strBuilder.AppendLine("Frames per second: " +
                    ((float)newDrawCount / newElapsedTime * 1000).ToString("0.0"));
        _strBuilder.AppendLine("Updates per second: " +
                    ((float)newUpdateCount / newElapsedTime * 1000).ToString("0.0"));
        Text = _strBuilder.ToString();
```

```
        // Update the counters for use the next time we calculate
        _lastUpdateMilliseconds = gameTime.TotalGameTime.TotalMilliseconds;
        _lastDrawCount = _drawCount;
        _lastUpdateCount = UpdateCount;
    }
}
```

The code refreshes the frame rate only once per second, detected by comparing the current total game time's elapsed milliseconds against the value stored in _lastUpdateMilliseconds. If a second has elapsed, the number of new calls to the Draw and Update methods is determined, the exact amount of time elapsed is calculated, and everything is built into a string for display onscreen. All the current values are then stored in the class variables for use the next time the frame rate is updated.

Using BenchmarkObject

BenchmarkObject can easily be used in any project by simply adding an instance of it to the GameObjects collection. Its constructor expects a font, position, and text color to be provided, but because it is derived from TextObject, it can also be scaled or rotated if needed.

■ **Tip** Don't forget to call DrawText() within your game's Update function; otherwise, the benchmark object will not be called to write its output to the screen.

The Benchmark_Win8 and Benchmark_WP8 example projects show this in action, and their output can be seen in Figure 3-9. The examples, which are based on the same game objects as in the OrbitingSprites examples from earlier in this chapter, are initially set to draw ten planets, each of which has a moon.

Figure 3-9. The text displayed by BenchmarkObject

As Figure 3-9 shows, there are 21 game objects (10 planets, 10 moons, and the benchmark object itself), and the game is achieving 60 drawn frames per second and 60 updates per second, which is exactly what we want to see.

Performance Considerations

Now that we can monitor the performance of our game on either platform, let's take a look at some of the things that can cause it to slow down and then determine some approaches to resolving these problems.

Texture Loading

What happens if we increase the number of planets significantly, perhaps to 1,000? An increase such as this is easily tested by modifying the PlanetCount constant at the top of the BenchmarkGame.cs source file. Give it a try and see what happens.

The result is a dramatic drop in the frames per second, as shown in Figure 3-10 (though this will depend upon your hardware—if you are running in Windows 8 on a desktop PC, you may need to increase a long way past 1,000 before the frame rate drops). In this case, running on a Surface RT device, the benchmark now displays a mere 3.9 frames drawn per second.

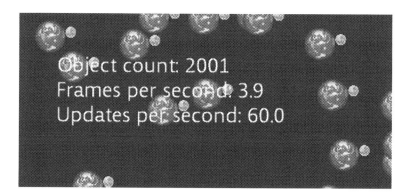

Figure 3-10. *The benchmark results with 1,000 planets*

░ **Note** This benchmark shows an important feature of the MonoGame engine. Although the frame rate has dropped all the way down to 3.9 frames per second, the rate at which updates occur still stays exactly as it was with just 10 planets—60 updates per second. This is because MonoGame is detecting that the game is running slowly due to the amount of time the sprites are taking to draw, and, as a result, it is calling the game's Draw method less frequently. It prioritizes calls to Update so that the game logic runs at a constant speed even though the rendering does not. This ensures that the game runs at the same speed across all devices and regardless of processor power being drained by other applications on the phone.

So, this large frame rate drop is disappointing, but perhaps that is all the device has the power to draw? There are a large number of sprites after all. In fact, the sprite count is not the only cause of the frame rate dropping. Another significant factor is the order in which the sprites are being drawn.

Each time MonoGame draws a sprite, it must pass the texture for the sprite to the graphics hardware ready for it to draw. Most of the information needed to draw a sprite will fit into just a few bytes of data (its position, rotation, scaling, and so on don't need very much memory to describe), but compared with the sprite location, the texture is comparatively huge. It is therefore in our interest to minimize the amount of texture information that is passed to the graphics hardware.

Once a texture has been loaded into the hardware, it can be used over and over again without needing to be reloaded, but when another texture is loaded, the original texture is discarded from its memory. If you recall, the way we set up the moons and planets in the game was by first adding a planet object and then adding the corresponding moon object. This means that planets and moons are alternating in the GameObjects collection. Every single sprite we draw needs a new texture to be loaded—first the planet texture, then the moon, then the planet again, right through to the end of the sprite batch. In total, we end up loading 2,000 textures in this configuration. No wonder the game slowed down.

There are various ways to address this problem. The first is to sort the objects in the GameObjects list so that they are ordered by texture. To try out this approach, modify the Benchmark project's ResetGame method so that it calls into AddPlanets_InBlocks instead of AddPlanets_Interleaved. (You'll see that both calls are present, with the second of the two calls commented out, so just swap the comment over to the first call instead.) This adds exactly the same number of objects (and the benchmark display will confirm this), but as 1,000 planets followed by 1,000 moons.

If you run this again, you should see that the frame rate has greatly increased. Running on the Surface RT again, the frame rate has increased from 3.9 frames per second to 19.7, an increase of over 400 percent. In this configuration, MonoGame has to load only two textures rather than 2,000, requiring just one load each of the planet texture and then the moon texture for each frame drawn.

▩ **Caution**   If you try this out on both the Windows Phone emulator and on a real phone, you will find that the device performance can vary greatly between the two. The same applies when comparing a Windows 8 desktop machine with that of a tablet device. Performance between different devices can vary greatly so it is important to performance test your game on real hardware as often as possible while you are developing in order to avoid unpleasant surprises later on.

In a real game, however, it is impractical to expect the objects to always be ordered by their textures. As objects are added and removed through the course of the game, the object collection will naturally become scrambled. To address this problem, we can take advantage of another feature in the GameFramework project.

The GameHost.DrawSprites method that we have been calling actually has another overload that allows a texture to be passed in as a parameter. When this version is used, only sprites that use the supplied texture will be drawn; all others will be completely ignored. This allows us to not only draw the sprites grouped by texture, but to also be in control of which textures are processed first.

If you look in the Draw function of the Benchmark project's BenchmarkGame class, you will see that there are two versions of the sprite batch code present: Version 1 is running and version 2 is commented out. Swap these over so that version 2 is used instead in order to see the new texture-based drawing in action. The frame rate should increase back to the same level as when the planets and moons were added in blocks, even though they were added in interleaved order.

However, this approach doesn't give quite the exact same rendering of the planets and the moons that we started with, in which each moon went in front of the planets defined earlier in the GameObjects list and behind any planets defined after. Now all of the moons appear in front of all the planets. In this case, we could replicate the original result using the sprites' LayerDepth properties, but some effects will be difficult to achieve when sprites are drawn on a per-texture basis. As a result, on occasion there may be no alternative but to repeatedly load the same textures into the graphics hardware. The important thing is to be aware of this performance bottleneck and to reduce or eliminate it wherever possible.

In most cases, the performance degradation will not be as significant as in this example. Use the BenchmarkObject to help you to identify drops in frame rate as soon as they occur so that you can focus your efforts to track them down as quickly as possible.

Creating and Destroying Objects

We have already briefly mentioned the .NET garbage collection feature, and you will probably be aware of it if you have developed using any of the .NET languages elsewhere. Once in a while, the .NET runtime will reach a trigger point that instructs it to search all its memory space, looking for objects that are no longer in use. They are marked as "unneeded," and then the remaining active objects are reorganized so that they use the system memory efficiently. This process stops memory from becoming fragmented and ensures that the application doesn't run out of space to create new objects.

This has many benefits for the developer, primarily by simplifying the creation of objects and removing any need to free up memory once those objects are no longer needed. The disadvantage is that when .NET does decide to perform a garbage collection operation, it can have a noticeable negative performance effect on your game. We therefore need to try to reduce the amount of garbage that we create as much as possible.

We already discussed an approach to this in the GameHost class's Update method earlier in this chapter. The number one rule is to try to avoid creating temporary object instances while the game is running. There will, of course, be instances where it is essential (all our game objects are object instances after all), but we should keep our eyes open for instances that can be avoided and eliminate them wherever possible.

Note Due to the way that .NET manages its memory, we need to worry about garbage collection only when using objects. A structure (struct) has its memory allocated in a different way that does not result in garbage being generated. It is therefore perfectly okay to create new Vector2, Rectangle, and Color structures, as well as any other struct-based data structure.

You will see examples of this efficient use of object allocation within the default content created when a new MonoGame project is created. The SpriteBatch object is declared at class level even though it is only used within the Draw method. Declaring it at class level means that it can be instantiated just once for the entire game run, whereas declaring it in Draw would result in a new object being created every time the sprites were drawn..

Using for and foreach Loops

The foreach syntax is extremely useful and, in many cases, faster to operate than a regular for loop when using collections because moving from one item to the next steps just one element forward through a linked list of objects. On the other hand, accessing collection object by index requires the whole of the collection to be traversed up to the point where the requested object is reached.

But in MonoGame games, there is a potential drawback with foreach loops, which means that they need a little extra consideration. These loops create an iterator object and use it to step through the collection items. For certain types of collection, when the loop finishes, the iterator object is discarded and ends up on the pile of objects ready for garbage collection. As discussed in the previous section, this process will increase the frequency of the garbage collection operation and cause the game performance to suffer.

The collection types that suffer this problem are all nongeneric collection types, and the generic Collection<T> object. For code inside your game loop (anywhere inside the Update or Draw methods), you should either avoid using these collection types or iterate through them with a for loop instead of a foreach loop. It is fine to use foreach for arrays and all other generic collection types, however.

Also, be aware that when you do use for loops, if you include a method or property call for the end condition of the loop, your compiled code will call into it for every iteration of the loop. It is, therefore, a good idea to read the collection size into a local variable prior to entering the loop and use it in your for loop instead. You can see this in the GameHost.Update method back in Listing 3-12; the GameObjects.Count value is read into a local variable, and the variable is used in the loop rather than the collection property.

An Example Game: Cosmic Rocks (Part 1)

At the end of this chapter and the next couple of chapters, we will start to build the material that we have covered into a simple game. The game, which is called *Cosmic Rocks*, is essentially an *Asteroids* clone.

In this chapter, we will cover the basic game design and implement the sprite processing into the game engine. We haven't yet discussed user input (which is covered in the next chapter), so the game won't be interactive yet, but you will see the beginnings of a playable game lurking at the end of this chapter.

All the code and resources for the game can be found in the `CosmicRocksPartI_Win8` and `CosmicRocksPartI_WP8` example projects.

In this section, we will focus on just some areas of code from within the example project to show how the areas that we've discussed in this chapter fit together into a finished project. Once you've read through the text here, please spend some time familiarizing yourself with the code within the project in order to gain a complete picture of how everything fits together. With the information presented here, everything should make sense without leaving any gaps or areas of confusion.

Designing the Game

The game design for *Cosmic Rocks* is pretty straightforward. The player will control a small spaceship that will initially be placed in the middle of the screen. Alongside the player's ship, there will be a number of cosmic space rocks that drift aimlessly across the screen. If one of these rocks makes contact with the player's ship, the ship explodes and the player loses a life. The player can shoot plasma bolts at the rocks, however. Shooting the initial rocks will cause them to divide into two smaller rocks. Shooting these rocks will cause them to divide once again into even smaller rocks. These smallest rocks can then be shot to completely destroy them.

Two control modes will be supported: touch control, or "button" control (in other words, using a keyboard or a gamepad). In touch mode, by tapping a point on the screen, the spaceship will turn to face that location and will fire a plasma bolt. By holding a point on the screen, the spaceship will thrust toward that point. It will continue to accelerate for as long as the touch point is held, after which it will gradually begin to slow down again.

In button control mode, control buttons will be provided to allow the ship to rotate, fire, and thrust across the screen.

The player's ship will be invulnerable for a brief period when it first enters play. The invulnerability will last until a point is reached in which no asteroids are within a small area around the ship to prevent it from being immediately destroyed as soon as it appears.

The edges of the screen wrap around, so anything moving off the left or right side of the screen will reappear on the opposite side, and the same for the top and bottom edges. This ensures that all objects remain in play no matter where they end up.

When all the rocks have been destroyed, the player will progress to the next level, which will contain one more cosmic rock than the previous level, ensuring that the difficulty steadily increases.

The game continues until the player has lost all his or her lives.

Creating the Graphics

If you are intending to create professional games, it is definitely advisable to ensure that you have someone on hand who can create professional-looking graphics (unless you have graphical talent as well as being a programmer!). I am no graphic artist, but I like to take advantage of materials around me and use them within my games whenever possible.

To this end, I created three images for my cosmic rocks by taking photographs of pebbles from my garden with a digital camera. With a little bit of a touch-up in a paint package, the photographs produced quite acceptable results. The rocks can be seen in Figure 3-11.

Figure 3-11. *A parade of cosmic rocks*

Note that these rocks are roughly circular in shape, which will help with collision detection in a moment.

The player's spaceship required a little more thought, but I eventually found a suitable object at the bottom of my son's toy box. The resulting ship image is shown in Figure 3-12.

Figure 3-12. *The rocks' nemesis: the player's spaceship*

With the graphics ready, they can be slotted into the game itself.

Creating the Game Objects

At this stage, the game object classes within the game are all very simple. We need a class for the rocks, another for the player's ship, one for handling explosions, and a fourth for each of the stars that will be displayed in the background to liven up the screen a little. Let's look at the content of each one.

The RockObject Class

The rocks have one aim in life: to drift in a single direction until they hit the player's ship or are blasted apart by a plasma bolt. In the examples we looked at earlier, we tracked movement by storing a value that was added to the objects' x and y coordinates each time the game was updated. For the rocks, we will use a variation of this approach.

We will store the direction in which the rock will move as a Vector2, in a class level variable named _direction. The movement direction is completely random, so we initialize both the variable's X and Y properties with a random value between -1 and 1. This will allow the rock to potentially move in any direction at all.

However, we want all the rocks to move at a consistent speed. One rock might emerge with a Vector2 containing the values (1, 1), whereas another might emerge with the values (0.01, 0.01). Clearly, the former will be moving much more quickly than the latter. To resolve this discrepancy, we can *normalize* the vector, which ensures that the length of the vector (the distance between the origin at (0, 0) and the position defined within the vector) is exactly 1. As a result, moving the rock as defined by the _direction vector will always result in the same movement speed, regardless of the angle in which the rock is moving. The code required to set up this vector, taken from the RockObject class's InitializeRock function, is shown in Listing 3-28.

Listing 3-28. Setting the rock's direction of movement

```
// Create a random direction for the rock. Ensure that it doesn't have zero
// as the direction on both the x and y axes
do
{
    _direction = new Vector2(GameHelper.RandomNext(-1.0f, 1.0f),
                             GameHelper.RandomNext(-1.0f, 1.0f));
} while (_direction == Vector2.Zero);

// Normalize the movement vector so that it is exactly 1 unit in length
_direction.Normalize();
```

The constructor sets a random position for the rock, sets its origin to its center, and then calls InitializeRock to set the rest of the rock properties. We separate these out from the constructor because when a rock is damaged and splits into two, we will reuse the existing instance for one of the two new rocks. This cuts down on the number of new objects that need to be created, helping reduce the garbage collection frequency.

In the constructor, we also take a parameter named generation, which helps us track how many more times the rock can split before it is finally destroyed. The initial rocks will be given the value 2 for this, and each time the rock is damaged the value will be decreased by 1. If this value is then found to still be zero or above, the rock will split into two smaller rocks; if it has fallen below zero, the rock will be completely destroyed instead.

InitializeRock sets all the operational parameters of the rock. It scales the rock as specified by the size parameter, generates a random rotation speed (which is purely cosmetic and has no actual effect on the game), and generates a random direction and speed for the rock to move. The speed is stored in the class level _moveSpeed variable.

To update the rock, all that is needed is for its rotation angle to be updated and its new position to be calculated. The position update is worth a little exploration because it demonstrates some useful features of the Vector2. The position is calculated as shown in Listing 3-29.

Listing 3-29. Updating the rock's position

```
// Update the position of the rock
Position += _direction * _moveSpeed;
```

As you can see, it multiplies the _direction vector by the movement speed and then adds this to the Position. This process looks simple enough, but don't forget that both Position and _direction are both Vector2 structures, not simple values. The reason we can do this is because Vector2 provides all sorts of additional functionality that is very useful for game programming.

When a vector is multiplied by a scalar value, such as when it is multiplied by the movement speed, all its elements will be individually multiplied by the value. For example, multiplying a vector of (5, 7) by 3 results in a new vector containing the values (15, 21).

Adding two vectors together results in a new vector in which the corresponding elements in each of the source vectors are added together. For example, adding the vector (5, 7) to the vector (3, 10) results in the vector (8, 17).

Both addition and multiplication can be performed with negative values and work exactly as you would expect. Vectors can also be subtracted from one another.

This very simple line of code therefore moves the rock in the direction and the speed that we have defined.

Once its position has been set, it is checked against the window boundaries to see whether it needs to wrap to the opposite side.

The rock's Draw code does nothing more than the base SpriteObject, so this method is not overridden within the RockObject class.

Finally, with this class is the DamageRock function, which will be called each time the rock is damaged. When the game code progresses a little further, we will call it when one of the player's bullets hits a rock. At the moment, however, the only thing that will cause this function to be called is a collision with the player's ship.

DamageRock first checks the generation value. If it is already 0, the rock has been destroyed and it is removed from the GameObjects list. Otherwise, the code splits the rock into two, which is done by reinitializing the current rock at a slightly smaller size (calculated by multiplying the current size by 0.7 for a 30-percent size reduction). The code then creates a second rock with exactly the same parameters, sets its position to match its own, and adds the new rock to the game.

The game adds five rocks to the GameObjects list in its ResetGame function. We don't need to do anything more to track their object references because we can loop through the object collection hunting for them. Because there could be many rock objects in play at once, this is the simplest way to manage them. Each rock gets a random texture from the three available, which is purely cosmetic and has no bearing on the behavior of the rock.

The SpaceshipObject Class

The player's spaceship is obviously a very important part of the game, but at this stage it is lacking some important functions; we haven't looked at how the user can interact with the device yet (this is coming up in the next chapter), so there is no way for us to control the ship. Instead, it is a bit of a sitting duck, motionless in the middle of the screen watching nervously as the huge lumps of rock hurtle past it.

We still have some interesting functionality to add, however. Even though the ship cannot move, it can still react to a collision with any rock that might happen to crash into it. This means we have to be able to determine whether a rock is touching the ship and, if one is, to explode in a fiery ball of destruction.

Let's deal with the collision detection first. This process is handled in the SpaceshipObject's HasCollided function, which returns a reference to any object that has collided with the ship, or null if no collision was detected. The only thing we need to worry about colliding with is a rock, so the code loops through all the game objects looking for objects that are of type RockObject. For each one found, the game performs some further checks to detect collisions.

The quickest but least accurate check is to see whether the bounding boxes of the ship and the rock intersect. If they do, there might possibly (but not necessarily) be a collision; if they do not, then the ship and the rock have definitely not collided. Figure 3-13 demonstrates some scenarios that this test might encounter.

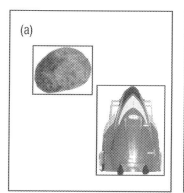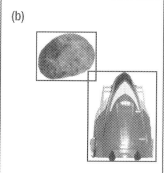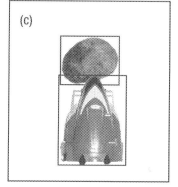

Figure 3-13. *Collision scenarios for the bounding box intersection check*

Figure 3-13(a) shows a scenario in which the bounding box can quickly and easily determine that the ship and rock have not collided. Their bounding boxes do not intersect, so it is impossible for the two to be touching each other.

Figure 3-13(b) and Figure 3-13(c) both pass the intersection check, although in (b) they are clearly not actually touching. If the bounding boxes do intersect, we need to perform an additional check to gain some additional accuracy. This more accurate check is a little more computationally expensive, so the simple bounding box check saves us from having to calculate it for the majority of the collision checks.

We can get a more accurate test by calculating the actual distance between the position of the rock and the position of the spaceship. This calculation will effectively place a circular collision region around the rock (all the space up to the distance we specify from the origin) and another circular region around the spaceship. Of course, neither of them are exactly circular so this won't be pixel perfect, but it will be good enough for our purposes here.

MonoGame gives us a nice easy mechanism for finding the distance between two points. To calculate this manually, we would need to use the Pythagorean theorem, but MonoGame saves us the effort of having to get out our old schoolbooks by providing the shared Vector2.Distance function. Passed two Vector2 structures, MonoGame calculates the distance between the two.

> ▨ **Tip** If you simply need to compare two distances to find out which is larger without actually needing to know what those distances are, use the `Vector2.DistanceSquared` function. This function performs the same Pythagorean calculation, but doesn't include the square-root operation at the end. It therefore produces a value that is useful only for comparison purposes, but that is much faster to calculate.

So, we can tell how far apart the two objects are, but how close must they get before they are treated as being in collision? If the distance is less than the radius of the collision circle of each of the objects added together, they have collided. The radius is calculated as the width of the texture divided by 2 and then multiplied by the scale of the object. The relationship between the object radii and the distance between them can be seen in Figure 3-14.

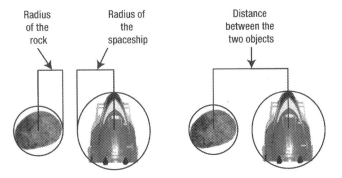

Figure 3-14. *The radius of each object and the distance between the two objects*

The distance check is illustrated in Figure 3-15, which shows the same three scenarios as before. In Figure 3-15(b), the sprites can now be seen not to be colliding, even though their bounding boxes overlap. In Figure 3-15 (c), the sprites are colliding because the distance between them has fallen below their combined radius values.

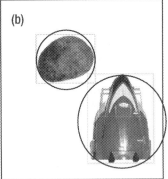
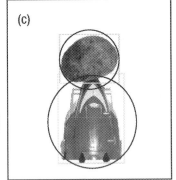

Figure 3-15. *Collision scenarios for the object distance check*

The `HasCollided` code that performs these checks is shown in Listing 3-30. Observe that all the checks we have discussed are performed. First, the bounding box intersection is checked using the `Rectangle.Intersects` function and then the sizes of the objects are compared to their distance as calculated by `Vector2.Distance`.

Wherever possible, values are calculated just once rather than repeatedly evaluated within the loop; examples of this are the spaceship bounding box (stored in shipBox) and the ship radius (stored in shipSize).

Listing 3-30. Checking for collisions between the player's ship and the rocks

```
internal SpriteObject HasCollided()
{
    SpriteObject spriteObj;
    Rectangle shipBox;
    float shipSize;
    float objectSize;
    float objectDistance;

    // Retrieve the ship's bounding rectangle.
    // Getting this just once reduces the workload as we will
    // be using it multiple times.
    shipBox = BoundingBox;

    // Calculate the distance from the center of the ship to the
    // edge of its bounding circle. This is the texture size
    // (we'll use the width) divided by two (as the origin is in
    // the middle) multiplied by the sprite scale.
    shipSize = SpriteTexture.Width / 2.0f * ScaleX;

    foreach (GameObjectBase gameObj in _game.GameObjects)
    {
        // Is this a space rock?
        if (gameObj is RockObject)
        {
            // It is... Does its bounding rectangle intersect with the spaceship?
            spriteObj = (SpriteObject)gameObj;
            if (spriteObj.BoundingBox.Intersects(shipBox))
            {
                // It does.. See if the distance is small enough for them to collide.
                // First calculate the size of the object
                objectSize = spriteObj.SpriteTexture.Width / 2.0f * spriteObj.ScaleX;
                // Find the distance between the two points
                objectDistance = Vector2.Distance(Position, spriteObj.Position);
                // Is this less than the combined object sizes?
                if (objectDistance < shipSize + objectSize)
                {
                    // Yes, so we have collided
                    return spriteObj;
                }
            }
        }
    }

    // The ship hasn't hit anything
    return null;
}
```

With the capability to detect whether the ship has hit a rock, the spaceship's Update method can ensure that such a collision receives an appropriate response. The method first determines whether the ship is already in the process of exploding. This will be the case when the ExplosionUpdateCount value is greater than zero. If so, the value is reduced by 1 so that the ship progresses toward resurrection on its next life.

If the ship is not currently exploding, the HasCollided function is used to check for collisions. If a RockObject is returned, its DamageRock method is called to break it into two (it hit something hard, after all, so it's only fair to expect that it would be damaged in the collision, too). The code then calls the Explode function to destroy the spaceship.

In Explode, we do two things: set the initial ExplosionUpdateCount value so that the ship is out of action for a small period of time and create a cloud of particles to represent the explosion within the game (the ParticleObject is described in the next section). When the game is finished, we will also decrease the player's remaining lives in this function.

This is all straightforward stuff, but we will need to add a lot of particle objects to the game (150 of them in this case) to display the explosion. They will be active only for a couple of seconds and will then no longer be required. This action will, of course, leave a large number of unused objects, which will then all be garbage-collected, and more will be added every time the player explodes. Is there a way that we could reduce these wasted objects?

The strategy that we will employ is to keep the expired particle objects alive and reuse them the next time an explosion takes place. When a particle's time runs out, instead of removing it from the GameObjects list, we simply set a flag, IsActive, to false to indicate that it is no longer needed. The next time we need some particles, we can hunt down all the inactive particles and reuse them, saving us from having to create any more. Only if insufficient inactive particles can be found will further objects be created.

This process is handled in the main game class's GetParticleObjects function, which is called from the spaceship's Explode method. It is passed the number of required particles, and it recycles and creates particle objects as required to ensure that the appropriate number of objects is returned.

A benchmark object is set up, ready for use within the project, but is commented out by default. If you enable it by uncommenting the line at the end of the ResetGame function, you will see that the object count increases the first time the player ship explodes, but the subsequent explosions require no further particles to be created.

The main game class creates a single instance of SpaceshipObject and stores the reference in its _playerShip class variable. Because the game will need to access this later on to apply the player's input to the game, we need to ensure that we can easily find this object. Keeping a separate reference for this single important object is faster than hunting through the GameObjects collection looking for it every time it needs to be interacted with.

The ParticleObject Class

Particles are just small fragments of material that will drift in space for some reason. They might be the debris from an explosion, a cloud of dust from a rock being split in half, or the exhaust emission from the player's ship once we have implemented thruster controls.

They all exhibit pretty much the same functionality, however—they move through space in a particular direction and gradually fade away to nothing and disappear.

The ParticleObject class has been created to handle each of these particles. It can be instantiated and set on its way and then forgotten about. Once it fades away to nothing, it will become inactive and wait to be recycled, as discussed in the previous section.

The class contains properties to keep track of its movement direction and speed, as we have seen in other classes. It also stores an inertia value, which is multiplied by the speed each time it updates. Setting this value to 1.0 results in no inertia at all; the particle will keep moving forever. Lower values will cause the particle to slow down as it moves. Don't set this value too low—a value of 0.9 already causes the particle to stop moving after a very short distance. Values between 0.9 and 1.0 are probably most useful.

The particles also track an Intensity, which is used as their SpriteColor alpha value, and an IntensityFadeAmount. The fade amount is subtracted from the intensity at each update, and once the intensity reaches zero, the particle is made inactive.

All the properties are set to their initial or randomized states in the ResetProperties method. This can be called either after a new instance is created or when an instance is being recycled to ensure that it is in a default state. The properties can then be updated as required for the task at hand.

The StarObject Class

The final class in the game so far is the StarObject, which is a very simple object that simply displays a star as a gently flickering dot. There is nothing too remarkable about this class, so we won't examine it in any more detail here.

Running the Game

Because all the objects know how to behave and how to react to significant events that take place, there is very little to do in the game class so far. The ResetGame function adds a number of stars, some rocks, and the player's ship to the game. The Draw function draws everything one texture at a time.

Although the game is not yet playable, it is still fun to watch the rocks crashing into the spaceship and to see the ship explode in a shower of particles. If you are patient enough, you will see that once a rock has divided in two twice, the remaining tiny rocks will disappear completely if they collide with the player, just as we need.

An image of the game is shown in Figure 3-16.

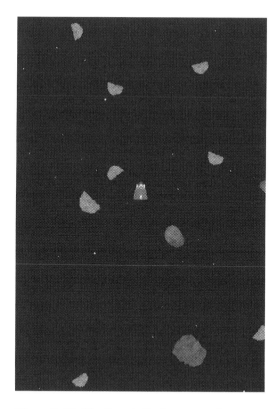

Figure 3-16. *The Cosmic Rocks game so far*

At the end of the next chapter, we will add interactivity into the game so that the player can shoot plasma bolts and move the spaceship around the screen.

Creating MonoGame Games

I hope that this chapter has given you an idea of the huge power and flexibility that we can obtain from MonoGame and from the game framework project that we have created. With very small amounts of code, you can create rich and complex environments with objects that behave in interesting ways and can interact with one another.

Feel free to play with what we have created so far and build some game projects of your own. With a little time, you should begin to feel very comfortable with creating new projects and getting your game objects to behave in whatever way you want.

In the next chapter, we will allow the player to get in touch with our game world by processing inputs to the device.

Summary

- In this book, we will build a GameFramework project to help manage some of the menial tasks of running a game. This will keep track of our content resources (graphics, fonts, and so on) and of game objects running within the game, and it will provide useful utility functions for us to call as we continue to develop it through the following chapters of this book. The GameFramework project can be used in your own game projects without restriction.

- The GameFramework project has been created as a set of shared source code files that are used by both Windows 8 and Windows Phone 8 project files.

- The GameFramework provides a simple object hierarchy to allow it to track the various types of objects that may be used in a game.

- Due to the way the GameFramework project loops through the game objects that have been added to its object collection, it is possible for any object to add or remove objects from the collection at any time without list synchronization exceptions being thrown.

- The approach used within the GameFramework for managing objects is for each object type to have its own class (usually derived from SpriteObject), and for these classes to provide all the logic needed to manage that type of object. This allows each object to fully manage its own behavior and life span autonomously, without the game itself having to tell each object what to do.

- SpriteObject provides built-in properties to manage each sprite's position, angle of rotation, scale, texture, color, and more. Many of these properties may be overridden in derived classes to provide customised behavior for different sprites.

- BenchmarkObject provides information about the number of objects in use as well as the number of frames and updates that take place each second. This can be a useful tool for monitoring and tracking down performance issues within your game.

- It is important not to switch between object textures more than necessary because doing so can significantly degrade performance. The GameFramework provides methods for specifying that objects should be drawn one texture at a time to help manage this potential issue.

- When game performance falls below the expected number of frames per second, MonoGame will prioritize calls to Update and will skip calls to Draw in order to keep the game logic running at the required speed.

- In order to avoid unnecessary garbage collection, objects should only be created when absolutely necessary. If possible, it is better to cache objects or re-use older object instances that are no longer needed than to create and dispose of objects on a frequent basis.

CHAPTER 4

User Input

We've given MonoGame plenty of opportunities to tell us what it is thinking. Now let's even things up and let it know what's going on inside our human brains. Input is, of course, an essential part of any game and will add interactivity and excitement to our projects.

The options that are available to us will vary from platform to platform and from device to device. In the Windows 8 world, your game may be running on a desktop PC with a keyboard, mouse, and gamepad, or it may be running on a tablet with a touch screen and no buttons to speak of whatsoever. If it is running on a phone, the environment is a little more predictable—all devices will have a touch screen and this will naturally form the primary input mechanism that we will use for gaming. With both table and phone touch input, the screens all support multitouch and are required to be able to track a minimum of four simultaneous touch points.

The only usable hardware button we can rely on on a Windows Phone device is the Back button. It will have other buttons available, such as the Windows button and the Search button, but we cannot do anything at all in response to these being pressed. In fact, we can expect our game to disappear from view when either of them is used.

On a Windows 8 tablet, there isn't even a Back button so, in order to replicate the functionality of the button, we will need to provide an onscreen icon to perform the same task. This is typically implemented as a left-facing arrow in the top-left corner of the screen, though you may choose to implement this however you wish if that doesn't suit the presentation of your game.

We do have some other inputs available to us, however. The most useful of them for gaming is the accelerometer, which allows us to work out exactly which way up the device is being held. This has lots of interesting uses for gaming. In this chapter, we'll examine these input mechanisms and explore how they can be used to control the games that you create.

Detecting Input Capabilities

When your game is working with user input, you may wish to be able to determine which input capabilities are actually available on your host device. This can have a bearing in the way you allow the user to interact with the game—perhaps, for example, the control mechanism may be slightly different if played with a mouse as compared to playing with a touch screen.

The .NET and MonoGame classes combined allow the input capabilities of the device to be queried with a fair degree of accuracy. The mechanisms for detecting these capabilities vary from one input type to the next, and they are also different on Windows 8 to Windows Phone. In order to flatten all of these inconsistencies, a new function is present in the GameFramework.GameHelper class named GetInputCapabilities.

The function returns an InputCapabilities data structure, inside which is a series of boolean properties covering each of the input methods that we are able to work with. These properties are as follows:

- IsAccelerometerPresent identifies whether the device has an accelerometer available. This will detect support as appropriate in both Windows 8 and Windows Phone.

- IsGamePadPresent identifies whether a compatible GamePad is connected to a Windows 8 system. GamePads are not supported in Windows Phone, so this will always return false in Windows Phone projects.

- `IsKeyboardPresent` identifies whether a keyboard is present on the device. This detects support as appropriate on both platforms, but note that it can produce some spurious results in Windows 8 (indicating that a keyboard is present when running on a Surface device with no keyboard connected, for example).

- `IsMousePresent` identifies the presence of a mouse. This will always return `false` on Windows Phone as mice are not supported.

- `IsTouchPresent` checks for the presence of a touch screen on both Windows 8 and Windows Phone.

You can see the function being used in the example projects `DeviceCapabilities_Win8` and `DeviceCapabilities_WP8`. These simple projects query the capabilities and then display the results on the screen. You can try running this across multiple devices to see the results, an example of which can be seen in Figure 4-1.

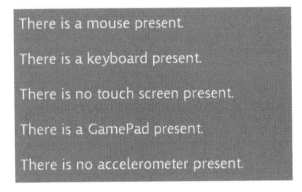

Figure 4-1. *Device capabilities from a Windows 8 desktop PC*

There are a couple of points worthy of note in the `GetInputCapabilities` function. First, the code uses *conditional compilation* for the first time so far in order to provide code that works consistently across both Windows 8 and Windows Phone, even though the internal implementation is entirely different. As the fragment of code from the function in Listing 4-1 shows, every single check between the two platforms is different, but from the point of view of code running outside the `GetInputCapabilities` function, the two appear to be identical.

Listing 4-1. Using conditional compilation to detect capabilities on Windows 8 and Windows Phone

```
#if WINDOWS_PHONE
    // Check for keyboard support
    _inputCaps.IsKeyboardPresent = Microsoft.Phone.Info.DeviceStatus.IsKeyboardPresent;
    // WP doesn't support mice
    _inputCaps.IsMousePresent = false;
    // WP always supports touch screens
    _inputCaps.IsTouchPresent = true;
    // Attempt to obtain an accelerometer object -- if this succeeds then the accelerometer
    // is present
    _inputCaps.IsAccelerometerPresent = (Accelerometer.GetDefault() != null);
    // WP doesn't support GamePads
    _inputCaps.IsGamePadPresent = false;
```

```
#else
    // Check the various device present values -- non-zero will indicate that the device is
    // present
    _inputCaps.IsKeyboardPresent =
                (new Windows.Devices.Input.KeyboardCapabilities()).KeyboardPresent != 0;
    _inputCaps.IsMousePresent =
                (new Windows.Devices.Input.MouseCapabilities()).MousePresent != 0;
    _inputCaps.IsTouchPresent =
                (new Windows.Devices.Input.TouchCapabilities()).TouchPresent != 0;
    // Attempt to obtain an accelerometer object -- if this succeeds then the accelerometer
    // is present
    _inputCaps.IsAccelerometerPresent = (Accelerometer.GetDefault() != null);
    // Check whether player one's gamepad is available. This isn't the full picture, but
    // will usually be indicative if a gamepad being connected.
    _inputCaps.IsGamePadPresent =
        Microsoft.Xna.Framework.Input.GamePad.GetCapabilities(PlayerIndex.One).IsConnected;
#endif
```

■ **Tip**   If you wish to use conditional compilation in your projects, you can use #if WINDOWS_PHONE (as shown in Listing 4-1) to set out a block of code that compiles only for Windows Phone, and #if NETFX_CORE to mark code that compiles only for Windows 8. You can see the definitions of these constants in the Conditional compilation symbols field of the Build tab inside the Project Properties window.

Another small point to note within the function is that it only ever actually builds and populates the structure once. This is to cut down the number of objects that are created if the function is called multiple times. Ideally, the calling code would only call GetInputCapabilities once and would then store the resulting data for future reference, but coding the function so that it only ever queries the capabilities once safeguards against external code calling in repeatedly and causing garbage collection issues as a result.

The only downside to caching the results in this way is that there is no mechanism to refresh them should, for example, the user plug in a gamepad after the game has started. To work around this, an optional parameter named forceRefresh is provided for the GetInputCapabilities function. Passing a value of true for this parameter will cause the code to request all of the input capabilities even if they were already determined during an earlier call. This can be a relatively time-consuming task to perform, however, so you should only refresh the capabilities once in a while (perhaps just once at the start of each game).

Now that we can tell which input methods are available to us, let's take a look through each one and discuss how each can be used in more detail.

Using the Touch Screen

All touch input from the screen is obtained using a class within MonoGame called TouchPanel. This provides two mechanisms with which input information can be obtained: raw touch point data and the Gestures API.

The raw touch point data provides a collection of all current input points on the screen ready to be interpreted in whichever way the program desires. Each touch point identifies whether its touch is new, moved, or released, and it allows its previous coordinate to be obtained if appropriate, but nothing more is provided. It is therefore up to the application to interpret this data and handle it as appropriate for the game.

The advantage of the touch point data is that it gives us the most flexible access to multitouch inputs. It also offers the most straightforward method for reading simple input if nothing more complex is required.

The Gestures API recognizes a series of types of input that the user might want to use, such as tap, double tap, or drag. By telling MonoGame which gestures we are interested in, it will look for these movement patterns and report back to us whatever it finds.

This greatly simplifies many types of input that would be more difficult to recognize and manage using the raw touch point data. The main disadvantage of using gestures is that they are primarily single-touch in nature (with the exception of the *pinch* gesture, which uses two touch points). If you need to be able to gain full access to multiple simultaneous input points, the raw touch point data might be more suitable.

Note that if you're developing for a desktop PC with a mouse rather than a touch screen, or you wish to be able to use the same code to read both touch input and mouse input, there's no need to worry! As we will see in a moment, all of the input mechanisms discussed in this section (apart from multitouch input) can be easily made to work with the mouse, too, so this section is still relevant.

Let's look at how each of these systems is used in detail.

▓ **Note**   At the time of writing, there is an unresolved issue in MonoGame regarding touch input on Windows Phone devices. The first time you touch the screen after launching your game from the Visual Studio IDE, the game will significantly slow down, dropping from 60 frames per second to sometimes just 1 or 2 frames. This only happens when debugging, and it will not affect your finished game, but it can be quite frustrating to work with. A quick way to restore the frame rate to normal when it slows down is to press the phone's Start button and then its Back button, navigating away from and then back to your game. After doing this, the frame rate should return to normal and no further problems should be encountered until the next time the game is launched from the IDE.

Reading Raw Touch Data

When reading the current touch points from the screen, we *poll* for information—we make a call out to the device and ask it for its current state.

This is in contrast with the way you might be used to obtaining data in desktop applications, which tends to be event driven—each time the operating system detects that something has happened, it queues up an event.

Event-driven systems tend not to "miss" any events, whereas polling systems can skip inputs if they happen too quickly. If the user taps the screen so quickly that the input state is not polled while the screen contact is made, the button press will be missed entirely.

The advantage of polling, however, is that it is fast, easy to use, and provides information at exactly the point where we need it. When you want to see if your player should shoot a rocket, you simply check to see if a screen location is currently being touched. This check can take place anywhere in your game code rather than having to be placed within an event handler.

To read the touch points, we simply call the TouchPanel.GetState function. It returns back a TouchCollection, inside which we will find a TouchLocation object for each touch point that is currently active. If the collection is empty, the user is not currently touching the screen. If multiple location objects are present, multiple touches are active simultaneously.

Listing 4-2 shows a simple piece of code in a game class's Update method that reads the current touch points and displays the number of touch points returned to the debug window.

Listing 4-2. Retrieving the current TouchPanel state

```
protected override void Update(GameTime gameTime)
{
    // Get the current screen touch points
    TouchCollection touches = TouchPanel.GetState();
```

```
    // Output the touch count to the debug window
    System.Diagnostics.Debug.WriteLine("Touch count: " + touches.Count.ToString());

    base.Update(gameTime);
}
```

Note that when running on Windows 8, the TouchPanel.GetState function will, by default, return *only* touch information, and it will ignore any clicks of the mouse. Fortunately, MonoGame has a trivial solution for this, which is to set the TouchPanel.EnableMouseTouchPoint property to true. This is set by default in all of the example projects that utilize touch in this chapter so that will all work on desktop PCs too.

When running on Windows Phone, the TouchPanel.GetState function will always return just the touch points, as there is no mouse to consider in this environment, and setting the EnableMouseTouchPoint property will have no effect.

When it comes to testing multitouch input, your best option is, of course, to run on a real touch-screen device. This is the only way to properly test how your app will respond to such input. For Windows 8 development, the Simulator offers a rudimentary simulation of multitouch but it is clearly not as as easy to manipulate the touch points as actually physically touching a screen.

When developing with the Windows Phone emulator, mouse clicks on the emulator will be translated into touches on the device's screen, but the emulator doesn't offer any kind of simulated multitouch input like the Windows 8 Simulator.

The Life and Times of a Touch Point

When the user touches the screen, we find a TouchLocation object in the collection returned by TouchPanel.GetState. Contained within this location object are the following properties:

- Id returns a unique identification value for this touch point. As long as the user maintains contact with the screen, location objects with the same Id value will continue to be sent to the application. Each time a new touch is established, a new Id value will be generated. This is very useful for multitouch input because it helps tell which point is which, but for single-touch input we can ignore it.

- Position is a Vector2 structure inside which the touch point coordinate is stored.

- State stores a value that helps us determine whether the touch point is new or has been released by the user.

Each time the touch data is obtained following a new touch point having been established, the State of that touch point will be set to the enumeration value TouchLocationState.Pressed. If you are interested only in when contact is established, check for this state in your location objects. This is the equivalent of a MouseDown event in a WinForms environment.

When the state is polled and a previously reported touch point is still active, its state will be set to Moved. Note that it doesn't matter whether the point actually *has* moved or not; this state simply means that this is an established touch point that is still present. You will see how we can determine whether it really has moved in a moment.

Finally, when the state is polled and a previously reported touch point has been released, it will be present within the touch collection for one final time with a state of Released. This will always be present once the touch point is released, so you can rely on the fact that every Pressed point will have a corresponding Released state. If the screen is tapped very quickly, it is entirely possible to see a point go straight from Pressed to Released without any Moved states in between.

Finding a Touch Point's Previous Location

For TouchLocation objects whose State is Moved, we can ask the for the point's previous location by calling its TryGetPreviousLocation method. This will return a Boolean value of true if a previous position is available, or false if it is not (which should be the case only if the State value is Pressed). The method also expects a TouchLocation to be passed as an output parameter, and into this the touch point's previous location will be placed.

Listing 4-3 shows a simple Update function that displays the state, current position, and previous position of the first detected touch point.

Listing 4-3. Retrieving a touch point's previous location

```
protected override void Update(GameTime gameTime)
{
    // Get the current screen touch points
    TouchCollection touches = TouchPanel.GetState();
    // Is there an active touch point?
    if (touches.Count >= 1)
    {
        // Read the previous location
        TouchLocation prevLocation;
        bool prevAvailable = touches[0].TryGetPreviousLocation(out prevLocation);
        // Output current and previous information to the debug window
        System.Diagnostics.Debug.WriteLine("Position: " + touches[0].Position.ToString()
                    + " Previous position: " + prevLocation.Position.ToString());
    }

    base.Update(gameTime);
}
```

Note that TryGetPreviousLocation gives back a TouchLocation object, not a Vector2, so we can interrogate its other properties, too. It gives access to its State property, which allows a touch point to tell whether it is receiving its first Move state (this will be the case if its previous location's state is Pressed). It is not possible to obtain additional historical information by further calling TryGetPreviousLocation on the previous location object—it will always return false.

If you want to experiment with this, take a look at the TouchPanelDemo_Win8 and TouchPanelDemo_WP8 example projects. These projects provide a simple TouchPanel display that places a circular object at the position of each detected touch point. It supports multitouch input and will display the first touch point in white, the second in red, the third in blue, and the fourth in green. Any additional touch points will display in gray. When the touch point is released, the circle will fade away into nothing.

All the while this is running, information about the first returned touch point will be written to the debug window. This includes the point's Id, State, Position, and previous Position. From this information, you will be able to see the sequence of State values that are returned, see the previous Position for each touch point, and observe the behavior of the previous Position for Pressed and Released touch points.

Touch Panel Capabilities

If you need to know how many simultaneous touch points are available, you can ask the TouchPanel for this information. Its GetCapabilities method returns a TouchPanelCapabilities object, from which the MaximumTouchCount property can be queried.

All Windows 8 and Windows Phone devices are required to support a minimum of four touch points, so anything you write should be able to rely on being able to read this many points at once. In practice, this number is probably quite sufficient for most games.

Working with Rotated Screens

It's very useful being able to read the touch-screen coordinate, but what happens if the game is running in a landscape orientation? Do we need to swap over the x and y coordinate values to find out where the touch point is relative to our game coordinates?

You will be pleased to find that the answer is no; MonoGame automatically takes care of this for us. We don't need to pay any attention at all to screen orientation because the touch coordinates will be translated into the same coordinate system that we are using for rendering. This is a very useful feature that greatly simplifies working with touch coordinates under all orientations.

Reading Input Using Touch Gestures

`TouchPanel.GetState` returns simple information about how the user is touching the screen; in many cases, this information will be perfectly sufficient for games that you might want to write. `TouchPanel` offers an alternative high-level way to read input, however, called *Gestures*.

The Gestures API recognizes a series of common movement types that the user might make when touching the screen and reports them back by telling you what type of movement has been detected as well as the relevant screen coordinates for the movement.

The recognized gestures are as follows:

- `Tap`: The user has briefly pressed and released contact with the screen.

- `DoubleTap`: The user has quickly tapped the screen twice in the same location.

- `Hold`: The user has made sustained contact with the same point on the screen for a short period of time.

- `VerticalDrag`: The user is holding contact with the screen and moving the touch point vertically.

- `HorizontalDrag`: The user is holding contact with the screen and moving the touch point horizontally.

- `FreeDrag`: The user is holding contact and moving the touch point around the screen in any direction.

- `DragComplete`: Indicates that a previous `VerticalDrag`, `HorizontalDrag`, or `FreeDrag` has concluded, and contact with the screen has been released.

- `Flick`: The user has moved a contact point across the screen and released contact while still moving.

- `Pinch`: Two simultaneous touch points have been established and moved on the screen.

- `PinchComplete`: Indicates that a previous `Pinch` has concluded, and contact with the screen has been released.

This list contains some very useful input mechanisms that your user will no doubt be familiar with. Using them saves a lot of effort tracking previous positions and touch points, allowing the gestures system to do all the work for us.

Just as with raw touch input, the Gestures API can also be easily persuaded to work with mouse input. This is achieved by setting the `TouchPanel.EnableMouseGestures` property to `true` before attempting to read any queued gestures. This property is set in all of the example projects in this chapter.

Let's look at the Gestures API and each of the supported gesture types in more detail and see exactly how they all work and how they can be used.

Enabling the Gestures

Before you can use gestures, you must tell MonoGame which of the gestures you are interested in being notified about. It is potentially able to track all of them at once, but it is likely that certain gestures are going to be unwanted in any given situation. Enabling only those gestures that you need improves the performance of the gesture recognition engine and also reduces the chance that an intended gesture will be misinterpreted as something else.

All the gestures are disabled by default. Attempting to read gesture information in this state will result in an exception.

To enable the appropriate gestures, use a boolean "or" operation to combine the required values from the GestureType enumeration and then provide the result to the TouchPanel.EnabledGestures property. For example, the code in Listing 4-4 enables the tap, hold, and free drag gestures.

Listing 4-4. Enabling gestures required for the game

```
// Enable the gestures that we want to be able to respond to
TouchPanel.EnabledGestures = GestureType.Tap | GestureType. Hold |
                                               GestureType.FreeDrag;
```

The enabled gestures can be set or changed at any stage in your game. If you find that you are moving from the main game into a different area of functionality (such as an options screen or a high score table) and you need to change the gestures that are to be processed, simply reassign the EnabledGestures property as needed. To disable gesture recognition, set the property to GestureType.None.

Processing Gestures

Once the required gestures have been enabled, you can begin waiting for them to occur in your game's Update function. Unlike reading the raw touch data, gesture information is fed via a queue. It is important that this queue is fully processed and emptied each update. Without this it is possible for old events to be picked up and processed some time after they actually took place, giving your game a slow and laggy sensation.

To check to see whether there are any gestures in the queue, query the TouchPanel.IsGestureAvailable property. This can be used as part of a while loop to ensure that all waiting gesture objects within the queue are processed.

If IsGestureAvailable returns true, the next gesture can be read (and removed) from the queue by calling the TouchPanel.ReadGesture function. This returns a GestureSample object containing all the required details about the gesture. Some useful properties of this object include the following:

- GestureType: This property indicates which of the enabled gestures has been recognized. It will contain a value from the same GestureType enumeration that was used to enable the gestures, and it can be checked with a switch statement or similar construct to process each gesture in the appropriate way.

- Position: A Vector2 that contains the location on the screen at which the gesture occurred.

- Position2: For the Pinch gesture, this property contains the position of the second touch point.

- Delta: A Vector2 containing the distance that the touch point has moved since the gesture was last measured. (*Delta* is a standard term used to represent the difference between two measurements, in this case between the two touch positions.)

- Delta2: For the Pinch gesture, this property contains the delta of the second touch point.

A typical loop to process the gesture queue might look something like the code shown in Listing 4-5.

Listing 4-5. Processing and clearing the gestures queue

```
while (TouchPanel.IsGestureAvailable)
{
    // Read the next gesture
    GestureSample gesture = TouchPanel.ReadGesture();

    switch (gesture.GestureType)
    {
        case GestureType.Tap: Shoot(gesture.Position); break;
        case GestureType.FreeDrag: Move(gesture.Position); break;
    }
}
```

Tap and DoubleTap

The Tap gesture fires when you briefly touch and release the screen without moving the touch point. The DoubleTap gesture fires when you quickly touch, release, and then touch the screen again without any movement taking place. If both of these gestures are enabled, a Tap and DoubleTap gesture will be reported in quick succession.

Note that repeat rapid taps of the screen are not quite as responsive through the Gestures API as they are by reading the raw touch information. If you need to be very responsive to lots of individual screen taps, you might find raw touch data more appropriate.

Hold

The Hold gesture fires after stationary contact has been maintained for a brief period of time (about a second).

If the touch point moves too far from the initial contact position, the hold gesture will not fire. This means that although it is quite possible for a Hold to fire after a Tap or DoubleTap, it is less likely after one of the drag gestures.

VerticalDrag, HorizontalDrag, and FreeDrag

The three drag gestures can be used independently or together, though using FreeDrag at the same time as one of the axis-aligned drags can be awkward because once MonoGame has decided the direction of movement, it doesn't change. Beginning a horizontal drag and then moving vertically will continue to be reported as a horizontal drag. For this reason, it is generally better to stick to either axis-aligned drags or free drags, but not mix the two.

In addition to reporting the position within the returned GestureSample object, MonoGame also returns the Delta of the movement—the distance that the touch point has moved on the x and y axes since the last measurement. This can be useful if you want to scroll objects on the screen because it is generally more useful than the actual touch position itself. For VerticalDrag and HorizontalDrag, only the relevant axis value of the Delta structure will be populated; the other axis value will always contain 0.

Once a drag has started, it will continually report the touch position each time it moves. Unlike when reading raw input, no gesture data will be added to the queue if the touch point is stationary. When the touch point is released and the drag terminates, a DragComplete gesture type will be reported.

Flick

Flick gestures are triggered when the user releases contact with the screen while still moving the touch point. This tends to be useful for initiating *kinetic scrolling*, in which objects continue moving after touch is released in the direction that the user had been moving. We will look at how you can implement this in your games in the "Initiating Object Motion" section later in this chapter.

To tell how fast and in which direction the flick occurred, read the GestureSample.Delta property. Unlike drag gestures, however, this property contains the movement distance for each axis measured in pixels per second, rather than pixels since the previous position measurement.

To scale this to pixels per update to retain the existing motion, we can multiply the Delta vector by the length of time of each update, which we can retrieve from the TargetElapsedTime property. The scaled delta value calculation is shown in Listing 4-6.

Listing 4-6. Scaling the Flick delta to represent pixels-per-update rather than pixels-per-second

```
Vector2 deltaPerUpdate = gesture.Delta * (float)TargetElapsedTime.TotalSeconds;
```

One piece of information that we unfortunately do not get from the Flick gesture is the position from which it is being flicked, which is instead always returned as the coordinate (0, 0). To determine where the flick originated, we therefore need to remember the position of a previous gesture, and the only gestures that will reliably provide this information are the drag gestures. It is therefore likely that you will need to have a drag gesture enabled for this purpose as well.

Pinch

When the user makes contact with the screen with two fingers at once, a Pinch gesture will be initiated and will report on the position of both touch points for the duration of the contact with the screen. As with the drag gestures, updates will be provided only if one or both of the touch points has actually moved.

MonoGame will ensure that the same point is reported in each of its position and delta properties (Position, Position2, Delta, and Delta2), so you don't need to worry about them swapping over unexpectedly.

Once either of the contacts with the screen ends, a PinchComplete gesture is added to the queue to indicate that no further updates from this gesture will be sent. If the remaining touch point continues to be held, it will initiate a new gesture once it begins to move.

Using the Windows 8 simulator, testing of pinch gestures can be achieved by using the "pinch" input button in the simulator toolbar. On the Windows Phone emulator, there is no way to simulate pinch input with the mouse. This gesture is best tested on a real device.

Working with Rotated Screens

Just as with the raw touch data coordinates, positions from the Gestures API are automatically updated to match the portrait or landscape orientation that is active on the screen, so no special processing is required if this feature is being used.

Experimenting with the Gestures API

The GesturesDemo_Win8 and GesturesDemo_WP8 example projects will help you experiment with all the gestures we have discussed in this section. It is similar to the TouchPanelDemo from the previous section, but it uses different icons for each of the recognized gestures. The icons are shown in Figure 4-2.

Figure 4-2. *The icons used for the different gesture types in the GesturesDemo project*

■ **Note**   This project deliberately displays the icons a little above and to the left of the actual touch point so that they can be seen when touching the screen. Otherwise on touch devices they appear directly beneath your fingers and are impossible to see. This looks a little odd when using a mouse in the simulator or emulator, however, as their positions don't directly correspond to the mouse cursor position, so don't be surprised by this.

By default, the example projects are set to recognize the Tap, DoubleTap, FreeDrag, Flick, and Hold gestures. Try enabling and disabling each of the gesture types and experiment with the movement patterns needed to initiate each. You can also use this as a simple way to see how the gestures relate to one another (for example, try enabling all three of the drag gestures and see how MonoGame decides which one to use).

Sprite Hit Testing

A very common requirement for games will be the requirement to tell whether the player has touched one of the objects onscreen. We know where the objects all are and we know the point that the user has touched, so how can we tell if they coincide?

There are several approaches that we can use, each with different characteristics. Some of the different mechanisms that can be used are the following:

- Checking against the sprite bounding box. This is very simple and quick, but, as we saw in the last chapter, it doesn't take rotation into account and is therefore not very accurate. For sprites that have not been rotated and are approximately rectangular in shape, this is the easiest and quickest approach to use.

- Rectangular hit tests are similar to the bounding box test but properly take the sprite rotation into account. This test requires a little more calculation, but can accurately reflect whether the point falls within the rendered sprite rectangle.

- Elliptical hit tests are good for sprites whose shape is essentially round. They perform a test by finding the distance from the touch point to the center of the sprite and checking whether this is within the area of the ellipse.

Let's see how each of these approaches can be implemented.

Bounding Box Hit Tests

The easiest but least flexible mechanism for detecting whether a sprite has been touched is to see whether the sprite's bounding box contains the touch point. This can be achieved as shown in Listing 4-7.

Listing 4-7. A simple hit test using the bounding box

```
bool IsPointInObject (Vector2 point)
{
    Rectangle bbox;

    // Retrieve the bounding box
    bbox = BoundingBox;

    // See whether the box contains the point
    return bbox.Contains((int)point.X, (int)point.Y);
}
```

The Rectangle structure conveniently performs this check for us, though it is really just a simple matter of checking that the x coordinate falls between the rectangle's left and right edges, and that the y coordinate falls between the top and bottom edges.

As the sprite's BoundingBox property already takes notice of any scaling and custom sprite origins that may have been applied, this is all that we need to do for this simple check. If we need to be able to work with rotated rectangles, though, we need something a little more sophisticated.

Rectangular Hit Tests

There are various ways that we could test a point within a rotated rectangle. The easiest to conceptualize is taking the four corners of the rectangle and seeing whether the point falls inside them. However, there are simpler and more efficient ways to achieve this in code.

A more efficient way to achieve this is to imagine that we have rotated the rectangle back around its origin until its angle is zero, and correspondingly rotate the test point by the same angle around the same origin. Once we have done this, we can simply perform a simple bounding box check, just as we did in Listing 4-7.

In Figure 4-3, two images are shown of some test points and a rectangle. The rectangle has been scaled so that it is longer along its x axis and rotated by about 15 degrees. Looking at Figure 4-3(a), it is obvious visually that test point 1 is within the rectangle, and test point 2 is not. In order for our code to determine this, we imagine rotating the sprite back until its angle is 0, and we rotate the two points by exactly the same amount. Of course, we don't actually draw it like this or even update the sprite's properties; we just perform the calculations that would be required for this rotation. If we *were* to draw the rotation, we would end up with the arrangement shown in Figure 4-3(b).

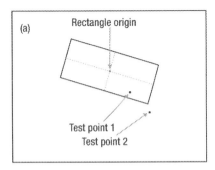 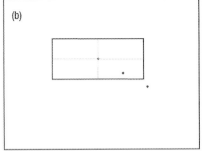

Figure 4-3. *Testing hit points against a rotated scaled sprite*

Having arranged the points as shown in Figure 4-3(b), we can now perform a simple check to see whether each point is within the left-right and top-bottom boundaries, just as we did with the bounding box test. This is a very simple calculation and gives us exactly the results we are looking for.

The code to perform this check is fairly straightforward. The main focus of the calculation is to perform the rotation of the test point around the rectangle's origin. We don't need to actually perform any calculation on the rectangle at all; we just need to rotate the points and then check them against the rectangle's unrotated width and height, which is already returned to us from the BoundingBox property.

When we rotate a point in space, it always rotates around the coordinate (0, 0). If we want to rotate around the rectangle's origin instead, we therefore need to find the distance from the rectangle origin to the test point. The calculation can then be performed in coordinates relative to the rectangle.

We can do this simply by subtracting the rectangle's origin position from the test point position, as shown in Figure 4-4. In Figure 4-4(a), we see the coordinates specified as screen coordinates—the actual pixel position on the screen that forms the origin of the rectangle and the user's touch points. In Figure 4-4(b), these coordinates are specified relative to the rectangle origin. As you can see, this has simply subtracted 200 from the x values and 100 from the y values because they are the rectangle's origin coordinate.

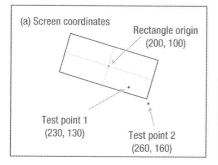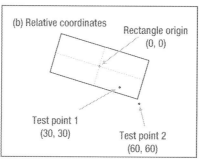

Figure 4-4. *Finding the touch coordinates relative to the rectangle's origin*

These modified coordinates are considered as being in *object space* rather than in the normal *screen space* as they are now measured against the object (the rectangle) rather than the screen. We can now rotate these points around the origin, and, as long as we remember that we are measuring their position in object space rather than screen space, we will find the new positions that we saw in Figure 4-3(b).

▓ **Note**   If at any time we want to map the coordinates back into screen space, all we need to do it re-add the rectangle's origin that we have subtracted. If we move a point to object space (by subtracting the object's origin coordinate), rotate it, and then move it back to screen space (by re-adding the object's origin coordinate), we will have calculated a new screen location for the point rotated around the object's origin, even though that origin is not at the screen's origin coordinate.

Having obtained the coordinate in object space, we now need to rotate it to match the rectangle's angle. The rectangle in the figures we have been looking at is rotated 15 degrees in a clockwise direction. As you can see in Figure 4-3(b), to reset the rectangle back to its original angle, we therefore need to rotate it *back* by the same angle—in other words 15 degrees counterclockwise. We can achieve this by negating the rotation angle.

The calculation to rotate a point around the origin is as follows:

$$x' = x \cos\theta - y \sin\theta$$

$$y' = x \sin\theta + y \cos\theta$$

The code to perform this calculation is shown in Listing 4-8.

Listing 4-8. Rotating the point variable to calculate the new rotatedPoint variable

```
// Rotate the point by the negative angle sprite angle to cancel out the sprite rotation
rotatedPoint.X = (float)(Math.Cos(-Angle) * point.X - Math.Sin(-Angle) * point.Y);
rotatedPoint.Y = (float)(Math.Sin(-Angle) * point.X + Math.Cos(-Angle) * point.Y);
```

Now we have the coordinate relative to the unrotated object's origin. We can therefore simply move the bounding box into object space (by once again subtracting the rectangle position) and then see whether the point is contained within the bounding box. If so, the point is a hit; if not, it is a miss.

Table 4-1 shows the calculations that we have described for each of the touch points shown in Figure 4-3. The sprite in question is 64 x 64 pixels and has been scaled to be double its normal width, resulting in a rectangle of 128 x 64 pixels.

Table 4-1. *Calculation Steps to Determine Whether a Test Point Is within a Rotated Scaled Rectangle*

	Test Point 1	Test Point 2
Screen coordinate	(230, 130)	(260, 160)
Object-space coordinate	(30, 30)	(60, 60)
Rotated coordinate	(36.7, 21.2)	(73.5, 42.4)
Rectangle top-left/bottom-right in object coordinates	(-64, -32) / (64, 32)	
Point contained within rectangle	Yes	No

As this table shows, the rotated test point 1 coordinate is inside the rectangle's object coordinates (its x coordinate of 36.7 is between the rectangle x extent of –64 to 64, and its y coordinate of 21.2 is within the rectangle y extent of –32 to 32), and the rotated test point 2 coordinate is not.

The complete function to perform this calculation is shown in Listing 4-9. This code is taken from the SpriteObject class, so it has direct access to the sprite's properties.

Listing 4-9. Checking a test point to see whether it is within a rotated and scaled sprite rectangle

```
protected bool IsPointInObject_RectangleTest(Vector2 point)
{
    Rectangle bbox;
    float width;
    float height;
    Vector2 rotatedPoint = Vector2.Zero;

    // Retrieve the sprite's bounding box
    bbox = BoundingBox;
```

```
    // If no rotation is applied, we can simply check against the bounding box
    if (Angle == 0) return bbox.Contains((int)point.X, (int)point.Y);

    // Get the sprite width and height
    width = bbox.Width;
    height = bbox.Height;

    // Subtract the sprite position to retrieve the test point in
    // object space rather than in screen space
    point -= Position;

    // Rotate the point by the negative angle of the sprite to cancel out the sprite
    // rotation
    rotatedPoint.X = (float)(Math.Cos(-Angle) * point.X - Math.Sin(-Angle) * point.Y);
    rotatedPoint.Y = (float)(Math.Sin(-Angle) * point.X + Math.Cos(-Angle) * point.Y);

    // Move the bounding box to object space too
    bbox.Offset((int)-PositionX, (int)-PositionY);

    // Does the bounding box contain the rotated sprite?
    return bbox.Contains((int)rotatedPoint.X, (int)rotatedPoint.Y);
}
```

Elliptical Hit Tests

Although rectangular hit tests are appropriate in some cases, in others it might be useful to test against a round sprite shape. To facilitate this, we can perform an elliptical hit test.

The ellipse that will be tested will completely fill the rectangular region occupied by the sprite, as shown in Figure 4-5.

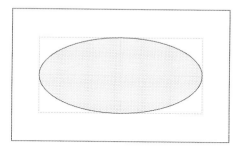

Figure 4-5. *The elliptical test region contained within a rectangular sprite*

Of course, ellipses, unlike circles, are affected by rotation, so we need to take this into account when working out whether a test point falls inside the ellipse. In Figure 4-6(a), we can see a rotated ellipse whose scale is such that its width is twice its height. Also marked in the figure are two test points, the first of which is within the ellipse, whereas the second is not (though it is within the bounds of the sprite rectangle).

The approach that we take to determine whether the points are within the ellipse starts off the same as that used for the rectangle: performing the calculation to rotate the points and the ellipse back to an angle of zero. Once that has been done, we can ignore the rotation and concentrate just on the elliptical shape. Again, we don't actually draw the sprite with the angle reset to zero or update the sprite's properties; we just perform the calculations that would be required for this rotation. If we were to draw the rotation, we would end up with the arrangement shown in Figure 4-6(b).

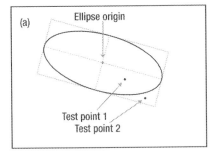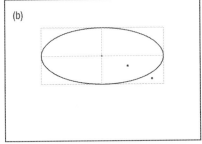

Figure 4-6. *Elliptical hit tests against a rotated scaled sprite*

Having obtained the coordinates relative to an unrotated ellipse, we can now determine whether the points are within the ellipse or not. For a circle, this would be easy—we would find the radius of the circle and we would find the distance from the test point to the center of the circle. If the point distance is less than the radius, the point is inside the circle.

For an ellipse, this process is more complex, however. An ellipse doesn't have a radius because the distance from its center to its edge varies as the edge is traversed.

Fortunately, there is a very easy way to resolve this. We know how the sprite has been scaled, so we can divide the width of the ellipse by the scaled sprite width, and divide the height of the ellipse by the scaled sprite height. This will result in a new ellipse that is exactly one unit wide and one unit high. The size is less important than the fact that this resulting size is now that of a circle (with a radius of 0.5) rather than an ellipse, meaning that we can perform calculations against it very easily. Instead of scaling the sprite in this way, we can scale the test point and then see whether its distance from the circle center is less than 0.5. If so, the point is a hit; otherwise, it's a miss.

The steps required for the whole procedure are as follows; they are just like the steps for the rectangular hit test:

- Move the touch point to be in object space rather than in screen space.

- Rotate the point back by the sprite rotation angle.

- Divide the point's x position by the ellipse width and its y position by the ellipse height to scale down relative to a unit-width circle.

- Test the point distance from the circle center to see whether it is within that circle's radius of 0.5.

Table 4-2 shows each of these calculations for each of the touch points shown in Figure 4-6. The sprite in question is 64 x 64 pixels and has been scaled to be double its normal width, resulting in an ellipse with a width of 128 pixels and a height of 64 pixels. Its center (and origin) is at the coordinate (200, 100).

Table 4-2. *Calculation Steps to Determine Whether a Test Point Is within a Rotated Scaled Ellipse*

	Test Point 1	Test Point 2
Screen coordinate	(224, 117)	(248, 134)
Object-space coordinate	(24, 17)	(48, 34)
Rotated coordinate	(27.6, 10.2)	(55.2, 20.4)
Ellipse width/height	128 pixels by 64 pixels	
Rotated coordinate scaled by width and height	(0.216, 0.159)	(0.432, 0.318)
Distance from circle center at (0, 0)	0.268	0.536
Point contained within rectangle (distance <= 0.5)	Yes	No

As Table 4-2 shows, the test point 1 coordinate is inside the ellipse (its calculated distance is less than 0.5), and the test point 2 coordinate is not.

The complete function to perform this calculation is shown in Listing 4-10. This code is taken from the SpriteObject class, so it has direct access to the sprite's properties.

Listing 4-10. Checking a test point to see if it is within a rotated and scaled sprite ellipse

```
protected bool IsPointInObject_EllipseTest(Microsoft.Xna.Framework.Vector2 point)
{
    Rectangle bbox;
    Vector2 rotatedPoint = Vector2.Zero;

    // Retrieve the basic sprite bounding box
    bbox = BoundingBox;

    // Subtract the ellipse's top-left position from the test point so that the test
    // point is relative to the origin position rather than relative to the screen
    point -= Position;

    // Rotate the point by the negative angle of the sprite to cancel out the sprite
    // rotation
    rotatedPoint.X = (float)(Math.Cos(-Angle) * point.X - Math.Sin(-Angle) * point.Y);
    rotatedPoint.Y = (float)(Math.Sin(-Angle) * point.X + Math.Cos(-Angle) * point.Y);

    // Add back the origin point multiplied by the scale.
    // This will put us in the top-left corner of the bounding box.
    rotatedPoint += Origin * Scale;
    // Subtract the bounding box midpoint from each axis.
    // This will put us in the center of the ellipse.
    rotatedPoint -= new Vector2(bbox.Width / 2, bbox.Height / 2);

    // Divide the point by the width and height of the bounding box.
    // This will result in values between -0.5 and +0.5 on each axis for
    // positions within the bounding box. As both axes are then on the same
    // scale we can check the distance from the center point as a circle,
    // without having to worry about elliptical shapes.
    rotatedPoint /= new Vector2(bbox.Width, bbox.Height);
```

```
// See if the distance from the origin to the point is <= 0.5
// (the radius of a unit-size circle). If so, we are within the ellipse.
return (rotatedPoint.Length() <= 0.5f);
}
```

Building the Hit Tests into the Game Framework

Checking touch points against game objects to see whether they have been selected is an operation that will be common to many games. To save each game from having to reimplement this logic, we will build these checks into the game framework.

This procedure starts off as an abstract function in GameObjectBase called IsPointInObject, as shown in Listing 4-11. It expects a Vector2 parameter to identify the position on the screen to test and returns a boolean value indicating whether that point is contained within the object.

Listing 4-11. The abstract declaration for IsPointInObject contined inside GameObjectBase

```
/// <summary>
/// Determine whether the specified position is contained within the object
/// </summary>
public abstract bool IsPointInObject(Vector2 point);
```

To implement the IsPointInObject function for sprites, it is overridden within SpriteObject. We will enable our sprites to support testing against both the rectangular and elliptical tests that we have described, and to allow the game to specify which type of test to use a new property is added to the class, named AutoHitTestMode. The property is given the AutoHitTestModes enumeration as its type, allowing either Rectangle or Ellipse to be selected.

The SpriteObject implementation of IsPointInObject checks to see which of these hit modes is selected and then calls into either IsPointInObject_RectangleTest (as shown in Listing 4-9) or IsPointInObject_EllipseTest (as shown in Listing 4-10). Any game object can thus have its AutoHitTestMode property set at initialization and can then simply test points by calling the IsPointInObject function.

For sprites that need to perform some alternative or more complex processing when checking for hit points (perhaps just as simple as only allowing a hit to take place under certain conditions or perhaps implementing entirely new region calculations), the IsPointInObject can be further overridden in derived game object classes.

Retrieving the Objects at a Hit Location

Another common function will be to identify the sprites that are contained in a specific location or the frontmost sprite at a specific location. Once again, we can add functions for both of these operations to the GameHost class.

The first, GetSpritesAtPoint, loops through all the game objects looking for those that can be found at the specified position. These are added to an array and returned back to the calling procedure. The code for this function is shown in Listing 4-12.

Listing 4-12. Finding all the objects at a specified position

```
public SpriteObject[] GetSpritesAtPoint(Vector2 testPosition)
{
    SpriteObject spriteObj;
    SpriteObject[] hits = new SpriteObject[GameObjects.Count];
    int hitCount = 0;
```

```
    // Loop for all of the SelectableSpriteObjects
    foreach (GameObjectBase obj in GameObjects)
    {
        // Is this a SpriteObject?
        if (obj is SpriteObject)
        {
            // Yes... Cast it to a SelectableSpriteObject
            spriteObj = (SpriteObject)obj;
            // Is the point in the object?
            if (spriteObj.IsPointInObject(testPosition))
            {
                // Add to the array
                hits[hitCount] = spriteObj;
                hitCount += 1;
            }
        }
    }

    // Trim the empty space from the end of the array
    Array.Resize(ref hits, hitCount);

    return hits;
}
```

The second function, GetSpriteAtPoint, returns just a single sprite and attempts to find the frontmost sprite at the specified location. It does this by keeping track of the LayerDepth value for each matching sprite. When subsequent sprites are ready to be checked, they are compared against the LayerDepth of the previous matching sprite and ignored if the value is higher (remember that lower values appear in front of higher values).

If LayerDepth values are found to be equal, the check is still made, and the later sprite will supersede the earlier sprite if it also matches the hit point. Because MonoGame will normally draw sprites in the order requested when LayerDepth values match, later objects in the GameObjects collection will appear in front of earlier objects with a matching depth. This check therefore allows us to find the frontmost object even if LayerDepths are not being used.

The GetSpriteAtPoint function is shown in Listing 4-13.

Listing 4-13. Finding the frontmost sprite at a specified position

```
public SpriteObject GetSpriteAtPoint(Vector2 testPosition)
{
    SpriteObject spriteObj;
    SpriteObject ret = null;
    float lowestLayerDepth = float.MaxValue;

    // Loop for all of the SelectableSpriteObjects
    foreach (GameObjectBase obj in GameObjects)
    {
        // Is this a SpriteObject?
        if (obj is SpriteObject)
        {
            // Yes... Cast it to a SelectableSpriteObject
            spriteObj = (SpriteObject)obj;
            // Is its layerdepth the same or lower than the lowest we have seen so far?
            // If not, previously encountered objects are in front of this one
```

```
                // and so we have no need to check it.
                if (spriteObj.LayerDepth <= lowestLayerDepth)
                {
                    // Is the point in the object?
                    if (spriteObj.IsPointInObject(testPosition))
                    {
                        // Mark this as the current frontmost object
                        // and remember its layerdepth for future checks
                        ret = spriteObj;
                        lowestLayerDepth = spriteObj.LayerDepth;
                    }
                }
            }
        }
    }

    return ret;
}
```

Hit Testing Example Projects

Two example projects for each platform demonstrating the hit test functionality can be found in the downloads for this chapter. The first, `HitTesting_Win8` and `HitTesting_WP8`, provides a demonstration of the accuracy of the hit testing functions that we have added to the `SpriteObject` class. A screenshot from this project can be seen in Figure 4-7.

Figure 4-7. *A sample image from the HitTesting project*

This example project creates a number of randomly positioned sprites, some of which have a square texture, whereas others have a circular texture. The sprites are rotated and scaled such that they form rectangles and ellipses. The objects can be touched to select them; all the objects that fall under the touch position will be selected and highlighted in red.

The image in Figure 4-7 is taken from the Windows Phone emulator, and the mouse cursor can be seen selecting some of the shapes that are displayed. Using a mouse for selection under any of the supported platforms is a great way to accurately explore the edges of the shapes because the mouse cursor is much more precise than a finger on a touch screen. You will see that the object really is selected only when it is touched inside its displayed shape and that the algorithms we are using for hit testing work exactly as required.

Inside the HitTestingGame.Update method you will find that there are actually two possible calls to object selection functions, one of which is in use (calling SelectAllMatches); the other is commented out (calling SelectFrontmost). SelectAllMatches finds all the objects at the touch point using the GetSpritesAtPoint function and selects all of them, whereas SelectFrontmost uses GetSpriteAtPoint and selects just the one sprite returned (if there is one).

Try swapping these over so that SelectFrontmost is called instead. You will find now that it is always the object in front that is selected when multiple objects overlap, as described in the previous section.

The project defines a new game object class called SelectableSpriteObject and adds to the basic SpriteObject functionality a new boolean property called Selected. It also overrides the SpriteColor property and returns a violet color when the sprite is selected or the underlying sprite color if it is not. This simple class provides a useful mechanism for selecting sprites and visually indicating which are selected. We will use this same approach in the upcoming "Initiating Object Motion" section.

The second pair of example projects, Balloons_Win8 and Balloons_WP8, turn the hit testing into a simple interactive game. Colored balloons gently float up the screen, and the player must pop them by touching them. This can be quite relaxing until too many balloons start to reach the top of the screen, at which point trying to pop them all becomes somewhat more frantic! A screenshot from the project is shown in Figure 4-8.

Figure 4-8. *A sample image from the Balloons project*

These projects bring together a number of the things that you have learned during this and the previous chapters—they use tinting to display the balloons in different colors, layer depths to render the balloons so that the smaller (more distant) balloons appear behind the larger (closer) balloons, raw TouchPanel input to determine when and where the user has touched the screen, and the GetSpriteAtPoint function to determine the frontmost balloon each time the screen is touched (this time using the layer depth to ensure that the frontmost balloon is selected).

This project has very little code and was very quick to put together, but it forms the basis of what could be an enjoyable game with a little more work.

Initiating Object Motion

You should now feel comfortable with reading user input from the touch screen. Before we finish examining screen input, let's discuss a couple of common movement patterns that you might want to include in your games: dragging and flicking.

Dragging Objects

The code required to drag objects is very straightforward. If a touch point is held, we simply need to find the movement distance between its current and previous locations and add it to the position of the objects that are being dragged.

The first part of dragging some objects is to allow them to be selected. Sometimes the selection will be a separate input from the drag (where the objects are tapped and then dragged afterward), but in most cases a drag will include object selection when contact with the screen is first established.

This is easy to do when using raw input as we can look for a `TouchLocation.State` value of `Pressed`. When it is detected, the object selection can be established ready for the objects to be dragged.

If we are using gestures, though, we have a problem: there is no gesture that is triggered when contact is first established with the screen. The tap gesture fires only when contact is released, and the drag gestures fire only once the touch point has moved far enough to be considered as actually dragging. So, how do we perform the object selection?

The answer is to once again use raw input. Raw input and gestures can be mixed together so that the initial screen contact for object selection comes from raw input, and the dragging comes from a gesture.

Once the objects are selected, we can update them in response to the touch point moving around the screen. When using gestures, we simply look for one of the drag gestures and read out the `Delta` property of the `GestureSample` object. This contains the distance that the touch point has moved on each axis, which is exactly what we need.

■ **Tip** Don't forget that the `HorizontalDrag` and `VerticalDrag` gestures will provide only delta values for the appropriate axis. There is no need to cancel out or ignore the other movement axis because MonoGame takes care of this automatically.

To calculate the delta using raw input, we obtain the previous touch position using the `TryGetPreviousLocation` function and subtract that position from the current position. The result is the movement distance. The code for this is shown in Listing 4-14.

Listing 4-14. Calculating the drag delta when using raw touch input

```
if (touches[0].State == TouchLocationState.Moved)
{
    // Drag the objects. Make sure we have a previous position
    TouchLocation previousPosition;
    if (touches[0].TryGetPreviousLocation(out previousPosition))
    {
        // Calculate the movement delta
        Vector2 delta = touches[0].Position - previousPosition.Position;
        ProcessDrag(delta);
    }
}
```

Whichever method we used to calculate the delta, we now simply add the delta value to the position of all the selected sprites. They will then follow the touch location as it is moved around the screen.

Two pairs of example projects are provided to demonstrate this: DragAndFlick_Win8 and DragAndFlick_WP8 use a gesture-based implementation, whereas DragAndFlickRaw_WP8 and DragAndFlickRaw_WP8 achieve the same effect using raw touch data. Both projects contain a SelectableSpriteObject class based on the one from the HitTesting projects, and they all contain identical functions for selecting the sprites at a point (SelectAllMatches), deselecting the sprites (DeselectAllObjects), and dragging the selected objects (ProcessDrag). There are some additional properties present, but we will look at them in the next section.

Try running both of the examples and see how they work. You'll notice that they don't feel exactly the same even though they do essentially the same thing. In the gesture-based project, you will notice a delay between when you begin to move the touch point and when the objects actually respond to the movement—you may frequently find that the shape is no longer actually under your finger once it starts moving. The reason for this is that the gesture system waits for the touch point to move a small distance before it considers a drag gesture to have started. As a result, it feels a little less responsive.

The raw touch input assumes that all movement is part of a drag, so there is no delay at all. As a result, it feels a lot more responsive. Bear this difference in mind when considering the input options that are available when you are coding your games.

Flicking Objects

With the object movement under our control, it is sometimes useful to allow the user to *flick* or *throw* them across the screen. This is often known as *kinetic* movement, and it consists of retaining the velocity at which the object is moving when the touch point is released and continuing to move the object in the same direction, gradually decreasing the speed to simulate friction.

To control the movement of the object, some new code has been added to the SelectableSpriteObject class. This code consists of a new Vector2 property called KineticVelocity, which tracks the direction and speed of movement; a float property called KineticFriction, which controls how strong the friction effect is (as a value between 0 and 1), and an Update override that applies the movement and the friction.

The Update code simply adds the velocity to the position and then multiplies the velocity by the friction value. This function is shown in Listing 4-15. Notice how it uses the MathHelper.Clamp function to ensure that the friction is always kept between 0 and 1. (Values outside of this range would cause the object to accelerate, which is probably undesirable, though perhaps it might be useful in one of your games!)

Listing 4-15. Updating the SelectableSpriteObject to allow it to observe kinetic movement

```
public override void Update(GameTime gameTime)
{
    base.Update(gameTime);

    // Is the movement vector non-zero?
    if (KineticVelocity != Vector2.Zero)
    {
        // Yes, so add the vector to the position
        Position += KineticVelocity;
        // Ensure that the friction value is within range
        KineticFriction = MathHelper.Clamp(KineticFriction, 0, 1);
        // Apply 'friction' to the vector so that movement slows and stops
        KineticVelocity *= KineticFriction;
    }
}
```

With the help of this code, the objects can respond to being flicked, so now we need to establish how to provide them with an initial KineticVelocity in response to the user flicking them. The example projects contain a function called ProcessFlick, which accepts a delta vector as a parameter and provides it to all the selected objects.

To calculate this flick delta using the gesture input system is very easy. We have already looked at the Flick gesture and seen how to translate its pixels-per-second Delta value into pixels-per-update. We can do this now and provide the resulting Vector2 value to the ProcessFlick function, as shown in Listing 4-16.

Listing 4-16. Initiating object flicking using gesture inputs

```
while (TouchPanel.IsGestureAvailable)
{
    GestureSample gesture = TouchPanel.ReadGesture();
    switch (gesture.GestureType)
    {
        case GestureType.Flick:
            // The object has been flicked
            ProcessFlick(gesture.Delta * (float)TargetElapsedTime.TotalSeconds);
            break;
        [... handle other gestures here ...]
    }
}
```

Unfortunately, using raw input is a little more work. If we calculate the delta of just the final movement, we end up with a fairly unpredictable delta value because people tend to involuntarily alter their movement speed as they release contact with the screen or mouse. This is coupled with the fact that the Released state always reports the same position as the final Moved state, meaning that it alone doesn't provide us with any delta information at all.

To more accurately monitor the movement delta, we will build an array containing a small number of delta vectors (five is sufficient), and will add to the end of this array each time we process a Moved touch state. At the point of touch release, we can then calculate the average across the whole array and use it as our final movement delta.

This is implemented using three functions: ClearMovementQueue, AddDeltaToMovementQueue, and GetAverageMovementDelta. The first of these clears the array by setting all its elements to have coordinates of float.MinValue. We can look for this value when later processing the array and ignore any elements that have not been updated. ClearMovementQueue is called each time a new touch point is established with the screen.

AddDeltaToMovementQueue shifts all existing array elements down by one position and adds the provided delta to the end, as shown in Listing 4-17. This ensures that we always have the most recent delta values contained within the array, with older values being discarded. AddDeltaToMovementQueue is called each time we receive a touch point update with a state of Moved, with the delta vector calculated as described in the previous section.

Listing 4-17. Adding new delta values to the movement queue

```
private void AddDeltaToMovementQueue(Vector2 delta)
{
    // Move everything one place up the queue
    for (int i = 0; i < _movementQueue.Length - 1; i++)
    {
        _movementQueue[i] = _movementQueue[i + 1];
    }
    // Add the new delta value to the end
    _movementQueue[_movementQueue.Length - 1] = delta;
}
```

Finally, the GetAverageMovementDelta calculates the average of the values stored within the array, as shown in Listing 4-18. Any items whose values are still set to float.MinValue are ignored. The returned vector is ready to be passed into the ProcessFlick function. Of course, the movement array is storing deltas in distance-per-update format, so we have no need to divide by the update interval as we did for gestures. GetAverageMovementDelta is called (along with ProcessFlick) when a touch point is detected with a state of Released.

Listing 4-18. Calculating the average of the last five delta values

```
private Vector2 GetAverageMovementDelta()
{
    Vector2 totalDelta = Vector2.Zero;
    int totalDeltaPoints = 0;

    for (int i = 0; i < _movementQueue.Length; i++)
    {
        // Is there something in the queue at this index?
        if (_movementQueue[i].X > float.MinValue)
        {
            // Add to the totalMovement
            totalDelta += _movementQueue[i];
            // Increment to the number of points added
            totalDeltaPoints += 1;
        }
    }
    // Divide the accumulated vector by the number of elements
    // to retrieve the average
    return (totalDelta / totalDeltaPoints);
}
```

The main Update loop for the raw input example is shown in Listing 4-19. You will see here the situations that cause it to deselect objects, select objects, and reset the movement queue (when a new touch point is made), drag the objects and add their deltas to the movement queue (when an existing touch point is moved), and calculate the average and process the object flick (when a touch point is released).

Listing 4-19. The update code for selecting, dragging, and flicking objects using raw touch data

```
// Get the raw touch input
TouchCollection touches = TouchPanel.GetState();
// Is there a touch?
if (touches.Count > 0)
{
    // What is the state of the first touch point?
    switch (touches[0].State)
    {
        case TouchLocationState.Pressed:
            // New touch so select the objects at this position.
            // First clear all existing selections
            DeselectAllObjects();
            // The select all touched sprites
            SelectAllMatches(touches[0].Position);
```

```
            // Clear the movement queue
            ClearMovementQueue();
            break;
        case TouchLocationState.Moved:
            // Drag the objects. Make sure we have a previous position
            TouchLocation previousPosition;
            if (touches[0].TryGetPreviousLocation(out previousPosition))
            {
                // Calculate the movement delta
                Vector2 delta = touches[0].Position - previousPosition.Position;
                ProcessDrag(delta);
                // Add the delta to the movement queue
                AddDeltaToMovementQueue(delta);
            }
            break;
        case TouchLocationState.Released:
            // Flick the objects by the average queue delta
            ProcessFlick(GetAverageMovementDelta());
            break;
    }
}
```

Try flicking the objects in the DragAndFlick and DragAndFlickRaw projects. The behavior of this operation is much more consistent between the two than it was for dragging. Also try experimenting with different friction values and see how this affects the motion of the objects when they are flicked.

Finger-Friendly Gaming

When designing touch input mechanisms for your game, always be aware that people are using their fingers to control things. Unlike stylus input that was commonly used on earlier generations of mobile devices (but are much less common with today's device), fingers are inherently inaccurate when it comes to selecting from small areas on the screen, and they also tend to obscure the area of the screen that the user most needs to be able to see.

With a little planning, you can help the user to have a comfortable experience despite this limitation; without such planning, you can turn your game into an exercise in frustration! If you have lots of objects that can be selected in a small area, give some thought to how you can help the users to select the object they actually desire rather than having them continually miss their target.

One option is to allow users to hold their finger on the screen and slide around to select an object rather than simply tapping an object. As they slide their finger, a representation of the selected object can be displayed nearby to highlight the current selection. Once users have reached the correct place, they can release contact, happy that they have picked the object they desired.

Another possibility is to magnify the area of the screen surrounding the touch point, making all the objects appear larger. Users can then easily select the object they want, at which point the magnified area disappears.

Finger-friendly input options don't need to involve a lot of additional work, especially if they are planned and implemented early in a game's development. It is definitely a good idea to avoid irritating your target audience with fiddly and unpredictable input mechanisms wherever possible.

Reading Mouse Input

As we have already seen, it is very easy to get MonoGame to treat mouse input in your Windows 8 games as if it were touch input. This is extremely useful as it allows you to write one set of input processing functions that handle both touch and mouse input without needing to distinguish between the two. You can see this in action by running any of the touch input example projects on a desktop PC and interacting with them using the mouse.

The TouchPanel functionality is unable to return data on a whole series of other mouse events; however, it cannot tell you where the mouse is unless the left button is pressed, it cannot process other mouse buttons, nor can it respond to the mouse wheel. These can, of course, be very useful devices for desktop PC users.

You should carefully consider whether your game *needs* to use any of these mouse input features, however. Unless you are designing your game to only work with a mouse, it is in your interest to be as inclusive as possible to touch-screen users so as to avoid eliminating a section of your potential audience. Ideally, treat mouse functionality as "value added" functionality rather than making it an essential part of the input mechanism of your game.

Also, be aware that the mouse data will only ever return readings from the mouse itself and never from the touch screen. For that reason, all input for which you want to support both touch and mouse input must be processed from the TouchPanel instead of by reading the mouse directly.

Reading Mouse State Data

Just as we read touch data by using the TouchPanel.GetState function, we read mouse data by calling the Mouse.GetState function and interrogating the returned MouseState structure. This structure contains values indicating the position of the mouse, the state of the mouse wheel, and details about whether each of the buttons are pressed.

A simple example showing how to read the mouse is included in the MouseDemo_Win8 project that accompanies this chapter. It displays a crosshair at the current mouse position, and it also shows text indicating which of the mouse buttons are currently pressed. Rolling the mouse wheel will increase or decrease the size of the crosshair image.

The code required to interact with the mouse is very straightforward, and it can be found inside the CrosshairObject class's Update function.

The position of the mouse is simply read from the X and Y properties of the MouseState structure. These use the same coordinate system as MonoGame, so setting a sprite to match the mouse cursor position is simply a matter of transferring these two values into a sprite's Position vector.

The state of each of the mouse buttons can be interrogated by reading the LeftButton, MiddleButton, RightButton, XButton1, and XButton2 properties. Each of these returns a ButtonState value, which will be either Pressed or Released as appropriate.

The mouse wheel can be queried using the ScrollWheelValue property. This maintains a "position" for the mouse wheel, indicating how far it has been scrolled since the game launched. The default value for this property will be zero. Each time the mouse wheel is rolled up the value will be increased by 120; each time it rolls down it will be decreased by 120. For mice that use smooth scrolling on their mouse wheels, this will increase in smaller intervals.

The demonstration project shows how each of these values can be read and processed, so please refer to its code for more specific examples of using each of the available mouse properties. Also, if you have a touch-screen device available, try running the project on that. You will notice that touching the screen elicits no response from the mouse input code whatsoever.

Reading from a Compatible Gamepad

If your game's control mechanism is such that it could be controlled via a gamepad, it is very easy to allow the player to use one, providing that you're running in Windows 8. (Windows Phone has no gamepad support.) MonoGame is able to work with Xbox 360 controllers, though they will need to be Windows-compatible versions of the controller—http://tinyurl.com/gamepadforwin8 shows one such compatible controller.

■ **Note** These gamepads work fine with Windows RT tablets, too, such as the Surface RT, providing that they have full-sized USB ports. Just plug the controller or the wireless receiver into the USB port, and Windows will take care of everything. Don't forget to point out to your users that they can use gamepads with your game on all Windows 8 devices!

Once again, we can poll the state of any connected gamepad by calling a GetState function, this time on MonoGame's Input.GamePad object. This returns yet another data structure detailing the states of all the directional pads and the buttons, ready for your game to interrogate.

There is one additional detail to consider with the gamepad, however: MonoGame and Windows actually support up to four connected gamepads at once. This makes it very easy to support multiplayer games should you wish to. When calling the GetState function, you simply indicate which of the players' gamepads you wish to read the state for.

Detecting Gamepad Connections and Capabilities

You may recall from the GameHelper.GetInputCapabilities function that we discussed at the beginning of this chapter that the returned data structure returns a simple boolean value to indicate whether a gamepad is connected. That function actually takes a bit of a shortcut and simply checks whether player 1's gamepad is connected. If you wish to support multiple gamepads at once, you will need to check each gamepad individually to find which ones are connected.

This is achieved by calling the Input.GamePad.GetCapabilities function, passing the gamepad number as a parameter from one of the available PlayerIndex enumeration values. From the returned data structure, query the IsConnected property to check whether a gamepad is connected for that player number. Listing 4-20 shows how to check each of the four possible gamepad connections. (Note that the GamePad class is contained within the Microsoft.Xna.Framework.Input namespace so you will need to reference this via a using statement, or include the full namespace in the commands—they are omitted here for brevity.)

Listing 4-20. Checking to see which gamepads are connected

```
bool gamepad1 = GamePad.GetCapabilities(PlayerIndex.One).IsConnected;
bool gamepad2 = GamePad.GetCapabilities(PlayerIndex.Two).IsConnected;
bool gamepad3 = GamePad.GetCapabilities(PlayerIndex.Three).IsConnected;
bool gamepad4 = GamePad.GetCapabilities(PlayerIndex.Four).IsConnected;
```

The GetCapabilities function actually returns a GamePadCapabilities structure that contains a long list of possible buttons and features that a gamepad may support. If you need to check that a gamepad supports a particular feature before you offer support for it to the player, this is where you can verify the capabilities of the gamepad against your requirements.

Reading Gamepad State Data

Once you're ready to read data from the gamepad, call the GamePad.GetState function, passing in the player index once again to identify which gamepad's state should be retrieved.

The function returns a `GamePadState` structure, which contains all of the available information about the state of the gamepad. The relevant properties of the structure are as follows:

- `Buttons` is a `GamePadButtons` structure, inside which is a `ButtonState` property for each of the "simple" buttons on the controller. `ButtonState` is an enumeration containing values for `Released` (the button is not pressed) and `Pressed` (the button is pressed). The button properties available are `A`, `B`, `Back`, `BigButton`, `LeftShoulder`, `LeftStick`, `RightShoulder`, `RightStick`, `Start`, `X`, and `Y`. All of these buttons are usable on a standard Xbox 360 controller apart from `BigButton`, which is not used by this controller type. None, any, or all of these may indicate that their buttons are pressed at any given time.

- `DPad` is a `GamePadDPad` structure, inside which are four further `ButtonState` properties named `Down`, `Left`, `Right`, and `Up`. These indicate which of the directional pad ("d-pad") buttons are being pressed. It is possible for more than one of these buttons to be pressed at once, but, due to the design of the controller, it is not possible for two opposing directions to be pressed at the same time.

- `ThumbSticks` contains a `GamePadThumbSticks` structure, inside which are two properties named `Left` and `Right`, to indicate the positions of each of the two thumbsticks. The `Left` and `Right` properties each contain a `Vector2` structure to indicate the stick position. The vector values you can expect to find within range from -1 when the stick is left or down to +1 when the stick is right or up. When the stick is moved diagonally, the values will indicate an approximate circle, so you won't find that both the `X` and `Y` properties contain these extreme values at the same time.

- `Triggers` is a `GamePadTriggers` structure that contains two `float` properties named `Left` and `Right`. Each of these provides a value for the corresponding trigger button from 0 (not pressed at all) through to 1 (fully depressed).

In addition to these properties, the `GamePadState` structure also offers two functions that allow the gamepad state to be queried: `IsButtonDown` and `IsButtonUp`. These can be called with any single input passed as a parameter, and a boolean value will be returned indicating the state of the button. This makes sense for all of the simple on/off buttons, but it is possibly less useful for the analog controls such as the thumbsticks and trigger buttons. Each of the analog controls will switch to consider being down at a pre-defined state, but, generally, it is better to query the more detailed properties if you wish to work with any of these controls.

As this shows, there are lots of options for controlling input through gamepads! The `GamePadDemo_Win8` example project demonstrates reading all of the possible inputs, and it displays what it finds on the screen. An example of the display from this project can be seen in Figure 4-9.

Figure 4-9. *Reading the state of a connected gamepad*

Reading the Keyboard and Text Input

There are two different areas where we might consider reading some form of keyboard input from the user: for controlling a game (by using the cursor keys, for example) and for text input (perhaps to enter a name in a high score table).

The first of these requires a hardware keyboard. This is an obvious input mechanism for Windows 8 desktop PCs and laptops, and it is also available on some tablet devices such as Microsoft's Surface with a "touch cover" or "type cover" keyboard present.

Theoretically, this is a valid option for Windows Phone devices as well. At the time of writing, no Windows Phone 8 devices with hardware keyboards have been made available, but several such devices were produced to run Windows Phone 7 so there is a chance that we'll see more devices with keyboards in the future. MonoGame does not currently support keyboard input in Windows Phone. The API exists and can be used without error, but it doesn't return any data, even when running in the emulator. Should devices with hardware keyboards become available in the future, you can expect MonoGame to be upgraded to support these, but until then this is not an option for games on Windows Phone.

For Windows 8 apps however, as always, providing support for the keyboard as another optional input mechanism makes a lot of sense. Let's take a look at how to interact with the keyboard and find out how to allow the player to use it to control your game.

For text input, users can type on a hardware keyboard if they have one, or use the onscreen keyboard known as the Soft Input Panel (SIP) if they do not. The methods both produce the same end result from the perspective of your game—it can ask for some text input, which it receives from the user. How the user physically enters it is not something that your game needs to worry about.

Let's take a look at how to interact with hardware keyboards and how to get the user to enter some text into your game.

Reading a Hardware Keyboard

Just as MonoGame provides the TouchPanel, Mouse, and GamePad objects, it also provides the Keyboard object to allow keyboard input to be read. This object offers a single method, GetState, which provides a snapshot of the current keyboard activity. Just as with the other input objects, Keyboard allows us to poll the keyboard state rather than use an event-based model such as the one you might be familiar with if you have spent time in WinForms development.

GetState returns a KeyboardState object from which we can read whatever information we need to control a game. There are three methods that can be called on the KeyboardState object:

- GetPressedKeys returns an array of Keys values from which the complete set of current pressed keys can be read. If you want to allow a large range of keys to be used (such as to read the user typing, for example), this is probably the best method for querying the keyboard. Note that the array contains simple keycodes and nothing more—no information about pressed or released states is contained within this data.

- IsKeyDown returns a boolean indicating whether a specific key (provided as a parameter) is currently pressed down.

- IsKeyUp is the reverse of IsKeyDown, checking to see whether a specific key is not currently pressed.

All these functions operate using the MonoGame-provided Keys enumeration. This enumeration includes a huge range of keys that might potentially be pressed, even though some of them won't exist on any given target device. The alphabetical characters have values in the enumeration with names from A to Z; because the enumeration deals only with pressed keys rather than typed characters, there is no provision for lowercase letters. The numeric digits are represented by the names D0 to D9 (enumerations do not allow names starting with digits, so a prefix had to be applied to these items to make their names valid). The cursor keys are represented by the values named Up, Down, Left, and Right.

░ **Tip**   If you are unsure about which enumeration item corresponds to a key on the keyboard, add some code to
your Update function that waits for GetPressedKeys to return one or more items and then set a breakpoint when this
condition is met. You can then interrogate the contents of the Keys array to see which keycode has been returned.

Direct Keyboard Polling

The example project KeyboardDemo_Win8 provides a very simple implementation of moving a sprite around the screen
using the cursor keys. The code to perform this, taken from the Update function, is shown in Listing 4-21.

Listing 4-21. Using the keyboard to move a sprite

```
// Move the sprite?
if (Keyboard.GetState().IsKeyDown(Keys.Up)) sprite.PositionY -= 2;
if (Keyboard.GetState().IsKeyDown(Keys.Down)) sprite.PositionY += 2;
if (Keyboard.GetState().IsKeyDown(Keys.Left)) sprite.PositionX -= 2;
if (Keyboard.GetState().IsKeyDown(Keys.Right)) sprite.PositionX += 2;
```

If you are running on a device with a hardware keyboard, you can try the example and see how it responds.

Polling for input in this way is ideal for games. There is no *keyboard repeat delay* between the first report of a key
being pressed and subsequent reports for the same key, and no *repeat speed* to worry about that would cause delays
between reports of a held key even after the initial delay had expired. Polling gives us a true and accurate picture of
each key state every time we ask for it.

It also allows us to easily check for multiple keys pressed together. If you try pressing multiple cursor keys,
you will see that the sprite is happy to move diagonally. This is perfect for gaming, in which pressing multiple keys
together is a common requirement. Many keyboards are only able to report a fixed number of keys at once however,
so be sure not to become over-reliant on multiple key presses.

Checking for Key Pressed and Key Released States

If you need to monitor for the point in time where the user has just pressed or released a key, MonoGame's Keyboard
object doesn't provide any information to this effect for you to use. It is easy to work this out with a little extra code,
however.

Once the keyboard state has been read, the returned KeyboardState structure retains its values even after the
keyboard state has moved on. By keeping a copy of the previous state and comparing it with the current state, we can
tell when a key has been pressed or released: if it was up last time but is down now, the key has just been pressed; if it
was down last time but is up now, it has just been released.

We can easily use this approach to look for individual keys or can loop through the array returned from
GetPressedKeys in order to look for all keys that were pressed or released since the last update. Listing 4-22 shows
how details of all pressed and released keys can be printed to the Debug window. It uses a class-level KeyboardState
variable named _lastKeyState to track the previous key states. This code can also be found within the KeyboardInput
example projects.

Listing 4-22. Checking for pressed and released keys

```
// Read the current keyboard state
currentKeyState = Keyboard.GetState();

// Check for pressed/released keys.
// Loop for each possible pressed key (those that are pressed this update)
```

```
Keys[] keys = currentKeyState.GetPressedKeys();
for (int i = 0; i < keys.Length; i++)
{
    // Was this key up during the last update?
    if (_lastKeyState.IsKeyUp(keys[i]))
    {
        // Yes, so this key has been pressed
        System.Diagnostics.Debug.WriteLine("Pressed: " + keys[i].ToString());
    }
}
// Loop for each possible released key (those that were pressed last update)
keys = _lastKeyState.GetPressedKeys();
for (int i = 0; i < keys.Length; i++)
{
    // Is this key now up?
    if (currentKeyState.IsKeyUp(keys[i]))
    {
        // Yes, so this key has been released
        System.Diagnostics.Debug.WriteLine("Released: " + keys[i].ToString());
    }
}

// Store the state for the next loop
_lastKeyState = currentKeyState;
```

There are two important things to remember when monitoring for pressed and released keys. First, you must check them during every single update if you want to avoid missing key state updates. Second, you should query the keyboard state only once per update and should store this retrieved state data away for use during the next update. Without following this approach, the state might change between the individual calls to GetState resulting in key state changes being overwritten and lost.

Prompting the User to Enter Text

The Keyboard object provides a simple way to read the keyboard for controlling a game, but if you want your user to enter text, it is generally not the best approach. One reason for this is that users without hardware keyboards will be completely unable to enter any text at all.

The solution is to allow Windows or Windows Phone to take control of the text entry. This will allow the SIP to be displayed if required or the hardware keyboard to be used if it is available. It also results in a familiar and consistent user experience without any requirement to re-implement onscreen keyboards.

This sounds very simple, but it turns out to be a little more complex than it might have been. First of all, let's look at how this can be made to work on Windows Phone.

XNA provided a function named BeginShowKeyboardInput, which could be called in order to display a "text entry" input panel, exactly meeting our requirements. MonoGame retains this function, and it works exactly as it did in XNA, providing a quick and simple solution to the question of text entry on the phone. Figure 4-10 shows how this looks.

Figure 4-10. *Entering text using the SIP in Windows Phone*

This sounds like the ideal solution, and if you're only developing for Windows Phone, then it probably is. The problem arises when the same functions are used in Windows 8—MonoGame doesn't offer the same functionality on this platform, and instead of a nice input panel we run into an exception. This leaves the only option for Windows 8 being for us to implement a solution ourselves.

Windows 8 is very possessive over the SIP—it doesn't offer any way to explicitly display or hide it via program code. Instead, Windows automatically shows it (assuming no hardware keyboard is available) only when an input field has focus. In order to allow text entry on touch devices, we therefore need to display and focus upon a text field.

We'll cover all of the details of exactly how we can do this when we look at XAML user interfaces starting in Chapter 11, but suffice it to say that with a little effort we can programmatically display a panel over the screen that consists of some informational text for the user, a textbox into which the user can type, and OK and Cancel buttons. This can then be used both with a hardware keyboard or a touch screen without us having to worry too much about how the user is entering text. The results of this can be seen in Figure 4-11.

High score achieved

Please enter your name!

| My name   ✕ |

OK   Cancel

Figure 4-11. *Entering text in Windows 8*

You can try out these input panels by running the TextEntry_Win8 and TextEntry_WP8 projects that accompany this chapter.

Of course, the code required to present the Windows 8 version of the panel is entirely different from that used by Windows Phone, but we can hide all of that complexity in the GameFramework project and expose a simple API that is consistent regardless of the platform being used. This is implemented by a function in the GameHelper class named BeginShowKeyboardInput. This function is called with the following parameters:

- The graphics parameter is the game's GraphicsDeviceManager instance. This is stored in the game class's class-level _graphics variable.

- The callbackfnc parameter is the name of a function to which the keyboard input panel will call back once the user has finished with the panel. We'll look at this in more detail in a moment.

- The title and body parameters control the informational text that will be shown to the user. In Figures 4-10 and 4-11, these were set to "High score achieved" and "Please enter your name!" respectively.

- The initialValue parameter provides some text to initially display within the textbox.

These are all fairly self-explanatory apart from the callbackfnc parameter. We use this to pass the name of a function within the game class that will be called once the OK or Cancel buttons have been clicked. The function will be called with a boolean value indicating which of the two buttons was used, and, providing the user clicked OK, the text that was entered.

Listing 4-23 shows a section of code from the TextEntry example projects that deals with invoking and responding to the input panel. Note that this code is identical in both the Windows 8 and Windows Phone versions of the project.

Listing 4-23. Invoking and processing the keyboard input panel

```
protected override void Update(GameTime gameTime)
{
    UpdateAll(gameTime);

    // Has the user touched the screen?
    TouchCollection touches = TouchPanel.GetState();
    if (touches.Count == 1 && touches[0].State == TouchLocationState.Pressed)
    {
        // Make sure the input dialog is not already visible
        if (!(GameHelper.KeyboardInputIsVisible))
        {
            // Show the input dialog to get text from the user
            GameHelper.BeginShowKeyboardInput(_graphics, KeyboardInputComplete,
                    "High score achieved", "Please enter your name!", "My name");
        }
    }

    base.Update(gameTime);
}

/// <summary>
/// Callback function that will be called when the keyboard input panel is closed
/// </summary>
/// <param name="result">true if the OK button was clicked, false if Cancel</param>
```

```
/// <param name="text">If OK was clicked, contains the entered text</param>
private void KeyboardInputComplete(bool result, string text)
{
    if (result)
    {
        // Store it in the text object
        ((TextObject)GameObjects[0]).Text = "Your name is " + text;
    }
    else
    {
        // The input panel was cancelled
        ((TextObject)GameObjects[0]).Text = "Name entry was canceled.";
    }
}
```

Any function may be used as the callback function, providing it has exactly the same signature as the KeyboardInputComplete function shown here.

One thing to be aware of when using the input dialog is that it is not synchronous. You might expect that your game will stop running while the dialog box is open, but this is not the case. The game continues to run in the background the whole time.

There might be some useful aspects to this—for example, it will allow you to keep your music and sound effects generating (a subject we will be covering in the next chapter). In terms of the game, however, you might want to have this pause while the dialog box is open.

We can achieve this very easily by checking the GameHelper.KeyboardInputIsVisible property (which you already saw in Listing 4-23). If this returns true, skip updating the game objects or any other game logic during that call to Update. Once the function returns false, the dialog box has closed and updates can be resumed once again.

Reading the Accelerometer

An *accelerometer* is a piece of hardware contained within a device (usually a phone or tablet, but occasionally this will extend to laptops as well) that can report the device's current orientation or position. In other words, it can tell if the device is lying flat on a desk, being held upright, being rotated onto its side, or is being held in any position in between. Accelerometers have become common in mobile devices over the last couple of years. They are a required component of all Windows Phone 8 devices and will be present in the majority of Windows 8 tablets, too, so they can be used in games as another interesting input device. Once again, be careful not to exclude players by *requiring* an accelerometer unless your game fundamentally depends on one.

The accelerometer information presents all sorts of opportunities for games. If we can tell the angle of the device, we can use it as a control mechanism. Instead of touching the screen or pressing a button to move objects on the screen, the player can simply tilt the device in whatever direction is needed to affect the gameplay.

In this section, we will investigate how to read and interpret the data from the accelerometer. The code presented here can be found in the AccelerometerDemo_Win8 and AccelerometerDemo_WP8 example projects, an image from which is shown in Figure 4-12.

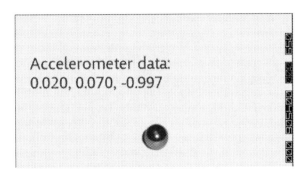

Figure 4-12. *Rolling a ball around the screen using the accelerometer*

The accelerometer data is not provided to us from MonoGame, but it is instead read through the Windows and Windows Phone APIs. Fortunately, the accelerometer is one of the good classes that provide an identical API across both of the platforms, making life easier. It also returns data in a fashion that is consistent with the "get state" calls that we've been making for the MonoGame input classes.

Accessing the Accelerometer

The accelerometer object lives inside the Windows.Devices.Sensors namespace, so we can add a using directive, as shown in Listing 4-24, to save having to fully qualify the namespace each time we want to refer to it.

Listing 4-24. Adding a using directive for the Windows.Devices.Sensors namespace

```
using Windows.Devices.Sensors;
```

Next, we declare a class level variable to hold an instance of the Accelerometer object, as shown in Listing 4-25. This will be populated during initialization and will remain for the duration of the game.

Listing 4-25. Declaring a class variable to hold the accelerometer object instance

```
private Accelerometer _accelerometer;
```

With these code sections in place, we can now instantiate and initialize the Accelerometer object inside the game's Initialize method. The code required for this is shown in Listing 4-26. If the current system doesn't support an accelerometer, the GetDefault method will return null.

Listing 4-26. Getting a reference to the accelerometer object

```
// Instantiate the accelerometer
_accelerometer = Accelerometer.GetDefault();
```

Reading the Accelerometer Data

With the accelerometer ready and waiting, we can now read its values whenever we need to by calling the Accelerometer object's GetCurrentReading method. This returns back an AccelerometerReading class, which provides three values, consisting of a reading for the X, Y, and Z axes. To keep these in a format that is compatible with MonoGame, we can extract the axis readings and copy them into a Vector3 structure, stored in this example in the class-level variable _accelerometerData. Listing 4-27 shows the code to achieve this.

Listing 4-27. Reading the data from the accelerometer and storing it for later use

```
void GetAccelerometerReading()
{
    // Check we have an accelerometer to read...
    if (_accelerometer == null)
    {
        // No accelerometer is available
        AccelerometerData = Vector3.Zero;
    }
    else
    {
        // Get the current accelerometer reading
        AccelerometerReading accData = _accelerometer.GetCurrentReading();
        // Translate it into a Vector3 structure
        AccelerometerData = new Vector3((float)accData.AccelerationX,
                                        (float)accData.AccelerationY,
                                        (float)accData.AccelerationZ);
    }
}
```

▒ **Note** The Vector3 structure is very similar to the Vector2 structure that we've been using in the last few chapters, except that it stores an additional Z component to represent the third dimension. We will be using Vector3 structures a lot more in later chapters once we start working with 3-D graphics.

Now we have readings for the x, y, and z axes from the accelerometer. Together they provide a reading of the acceleration of the device relative to freefall. What exactly does that mean?

First, let's look at the vector itself. It contains three properties that can be used to interrogate the device orientation: X, Y, and Z. Each of them is a float value that represents the movement of the device in the real world in the appropriate axis. If the device is lying flat and face up on a table, the values returned for the vector will be approximately as follows:

```
X = 0, Y = 0, Z = -1
```

The value -1 represents the full force of gravity applied along the appropriate axis. The x axis represents the direction between the left and right edges of the device, the y axis the direction between the top and bottom of the device, and the z axis the direction between the front and back of the device. As gravity is pulling the device toward its back while it lies flat on the table, the accelerometer shows a value of –1 on the z axis. (–1 on this axis represents the back of the device, whereas +1 represents the front of the device, and this is what would appear if the device were put face down on the table.)

This z value reading is very useful because it means we always get a movement reading relative to the force of gravity, even when the device is not in motion. By working out which of the x, y, and z axes the reading applies to, we can therefore work out which way up the device is.

As you've seen, with the device face up, we get a negative reading on the z axis. With the device upright, the accelerometer returns a value of –1 on the y axis (and upright but upside down, it returns the opposite value, 1). Turn the device on its side, and you'll get a value between –1 and 1 on the x axis, depending on which way the device has rotated. All orientations between these extremes return values spread across the three axes.

Because our screen is only two-dimensional, we can for the most part ignore the value on the z axis. We can instead read out the x and y values and apply them as acceleration to objects in the game. When the device is flat on the desk, x and y are 0, so our objects don't move at all. Tip the device up, and the x and y values change based on the tilt angle, providing acceleration for our objects—the steeper the tilt, the faster the acceleration.

The AccelerometerDemo projects in the accompanying downloads for this chapter include all the code required to move a ball around on the screen under control of the accelerometer. They also display the vector values on the screen, so you can easily see the data coming back from the accelerometer as you change the orientation of your device.

The project contains a single game object, BallObject, which is mostly the same as the sprite objects we have looked at in earlier projects. The ball offers a Velocity vector, and in its Update method it adds this to the ball position, bouncing if the edges of the screen are hit.

The one new addition is the use of the accelerometer data within the Update code. It retrieves the data from the game class, adds the accelerometer's x axis reading to its horizontal velocity, and subtracts its y axis reading from its vertical velocity, as shown in Listing 4-28. This is what makes the ball move in response to the device being rotated. As you can see, we observe only the x and y axis readings because the z axis doesn't do anything useful in this 2-D environment.

Listing 4-28. Applying the accelerometer data to the ball velocity

```
// Add the accelerometer vector to the velocity
Velocity += new Vector2(_game.AccelerometerData.X, -_game.AccelerometerData.Y);
```

You now have all the code that is required to simulate a ball rolling around a virtual desktop. Try running the project on a device and see how the ball reacts to the device being tilted. Observe the way the ball moves faster when the devices is tilted at a steeper angle.

There are a couple of additional things to be aware of when using the accelerometer. First, unlike touch input, the returned vector is not automatically rotated to match the orientation of the screen. The values will be completely unaffected by rotating the device, so you will have to compensate for this in your game code if your game plays in a non-default orientation: for Windows 8 devices, the accelerometer will always work relative to the device in landscape orientation, and for Windows Phone it will work relative to the device in portrait orientation.

Second, if your game has been configured to allow multiple orientations (as we discussed back in Chapter 2), MonoGame will automatically rotate your display whenever it detects that the device has been rotated to a different orientation. This might be useful for non-accelerometer-based games, but if the screen flips upside down every time the player tries to roll a ball toward the top of the screen, it will quickly become very annoying. To cure this, you should ensure that you explicitly specify a single supported orientation when working with the accelerometer.

Using the Accelerometer in the Simulator and Emulator

If you want to work with an accelerometer but you don't have a physical device that contains an accelerometer, this clearly presents a bit of a problem.

First, the bad news. The Windows 8 Simulator doesn't offer any simulation of an accelerometer. If your main device doesn't have one, the simulated device won't either. Perhaps this is something that Microsoft will revise in a future version of the simulator, but for now it's not an option.

If you find yourself in this position, the best you can do is to mock up your own simulation of an accelerometer. You could do this by maintaining the accelerometer data Vector3 structure as in the example project and use the cursor keys to update the X and Y values within it. This will give a crude but workable simulation of the accelerometer. It would be an extremely good idea to check the functionality on a real device before releasing to the public, however!

If you are developing for Windows Phone, there is much better news: the emulator does provide a fully controllable artificial accelerometer that you can use to test with, without needing to run on an actual phone. This is accessed via the "Additional Tools" window, accessed by one of the emulator toolbar buttons, as highlighted in Figure 4-13.

Figure 4-13. *Opening the emulator's additional tools window*

Once the button has been clicked, the Additional Tools window will appear and the Accelerometer tab will be displayed, as shown in Figure 4-14. The main area of the window shows a 3-D model of a phone, with a red dot displayed in the center of it. This dot indicates the phone's rotation position; drag it around to simulate rotating the phone. Displayed beneath this are the accelerometer reading values for the current device orientation.

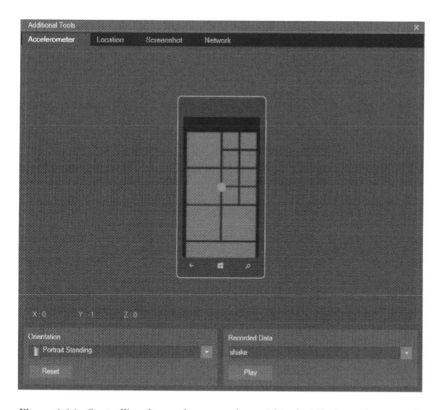

Figure 4-14. *Controlling the accelerometer data within the Windows Phone emulator*

If you try running the AccelerometerDemo_WP8 demo in the emulator, you'll see that the ball immediately drops to the bottom of the screen and that it's impossible to get it to move back upward again. This is because the emulator defaults to having the accelerometer simulation with the phone in an upright position, whereas the demo expects the default position to be flat, with the screen pointing straight upward.

We can switch the accelerometer simulation among a number of different positions in the Orientation panel at the bottom of the window. If you change this from Portrait Standing to Portrait Flat, you will see that the reading values change from (0, –1, 0) to (0, 0, –1). This now has the simulated accelerometer facing directly upward, just as we need.

With this done, you can now drag the red dot around within the accelerometer window to simulate moving the phone and you'll see that the ball rolls around in a much more controlled fashion. If at any point you wish to set the accelerometer exactly back to its home position, just click the Reset button.

Once again, there's no way to truly test accelerometer input except on a device with a real accelerometer, but the emulator does make it easier to test and debug along the way.

Handling the Windows Phone Back Button

One final user input mechanism that we've yet to address is that of the Back button on Windows Phone devices. This is the only one of the three buttons at the bottom of the display that you are able to respond to. In fact, it's important that you do respond or your game may fail certification when you ultimately submit it to the Windows Phone Store.

MonoGame treats the Back button as if it were a button on a game controller. To read it, we therefore use code that is the same as for Windows 8 gamepads. Listing 4-29 shows a few lines of code that check for the Back button in the game class's Update method and close the game down if it has been pressed.

Listing 4-29. Detecting and responding to the Back button

```
protected override void Update(GameTime gameTime)
{
    // Allows the game to exit
    if (GamePad.GetState(PlayerIndex.One).Buttons.Back == ButtonState.Pressed)
    {
        this.Exit();
    }

    [... other update processing goes here ...]

    base.Update(gameTime);
}
```

There are some specific expectations for the handling of the Back button in Windows Phone apps and games. These can be found in the Windows Phone Store certification requirements, which we'll look at in more detail in Chapter 14.

An Example Game: Cosmic Rocks (Part II)

Now that we are comfortable with all the options for reading input from the user, let's use them to add to the *Cosmic Rocks* game that we started building in the last chapter. The rest of this chapter will focus on using input techniques to turn the project into an actual playable game.

There are three actions that we need to be able to support: shooting in a specified direction, firing the ship thrusters to move the spaceship forward, and hitting the hyperspace button to randomly transport the player to another location on the screen.

For maximum flexibility, we'll support a variety of different input methods. The obvious choices for Windows 8 systems are the keyboard and gamepad, but we need to be able to support touch input both for Windows 8 tablet devices and for Windows Phones. This also doubles up for allowing mouse control on a desktop PC.

There are various touch-based mechanisms that we could use to implement these actions. It would seem sensible to make tapping the screen the instruction for the spaceship to shoot. Thrusting has various options, including dragging the ship or holding at the point to fly toward. Hyperspace needs to be easily accessible, but not interfere with either of the other controls.

After some experimentation, the following controls were found to be the most natural-feeling:

- *Shoot*: Tap the screen. The spaceship will rotate toward the touch point and shoot.

- *Thrust*: Hold contact with the screen. The spaceship will rotate toward the touch point and thrust forward.

- *Hyperspace*: Pinch the screen. Using multitouch allows a clear indication of the player's intention without having to worry about distinguishing hyperspace requests from moving or shooting.

Let's see how each of these controls is implemented and then build the rest of the game. There's quite a lot of new code involved, and not all of it is featured here for space reasons. The full project can be found in the CosmicRocksPartII_Win8 and CosmicRocksPartII_WP8 example projects from the accompanying downloads for this chapter.

Making the Player's Ship Shoot

Getting the ship to shoot is one of the easier pieces of game functionality that we need to add, so this is a good place to start our tour of how the new game code has been put together. Simply put, if the player presses the fire button on the gamepad (for which the "A" button has been designated), presses space on the keyboard, or taps the screen, the spaceship will shoot.

In common with all input processing in the Windows 8 version of the game, we first check to see whether a gamepad or keyboard is available. If so, the appropriate input processing functions are called—in this case, they are named Update_ProcessGamepadInput and Update_ProcessKeyboardInput. You'll find these functions in the CosmicRocksPartII_Win8 project's SpaceshipObject class.

▓ **Note**   We are reading input values in the SpaceshipObject class because this is where we need to actually process it. You can process input wherever you like, but if you are working with the TouchPanel class, you need to ensure that all TouchPanel inputs are retrieved just once per update and all gestures are processed exactly once per update as well. Reading either of these more than once per update will result in inputs being retrieved in one place but not the other, which can be very confusing to track down and debug.

In both of the functions, we want to respond only to *new* presses—holding the button down should not result in a stream of bullets. This is achieved by comparing the current button or key state against the state that was present during the previous update. If the button or key is now pressed, but the last update was not, this must be a new press; if it was pressed last time too, we ignore it.

A section of the Update_ProcessGamepadInput function that deals with this is shown in Listing 4-30. The _lastGamePadState variable referenced on the final line of code shown here is a class-level GamePadState structure, and it is the way in which we are able to compare the current input state against the previous input state. The keyboard input function does exactly the same thing, but with a KeyboardState variable named _lastKeyboardState.

Listing 4-30. Checking for new gamepad button presses

```
// If the player is pressing the A button, fire a bullet
if (gamepadState.IsButtonDown(Buttons.A))
{
    // Was the first button pressed during the last update too?
    // If so, ignore this button press
    if (!_lastGamePadState.IsButtonDown(Buttons.A))
    {
        // Fire a bullet
        FireBullet();
    }
}

// Remember the gamepad state for next time so that we can detect
// button down/up events
_lastGamePadState = gamepadState;
```

Once the new button press is detected, the FireBullet function is called to fire a new bullet. We'll look at the FireBullet function itself in a moment.

For touch-screen devices, we shoot by simply tapping the screen. We've already covered how to do this earlier in the chapter: the code simply waits for a touch point to appear with a State of Pressed. The Windows 8 version of the game checks for the presence of a touch screen before working with this area of input, whereas the Windows Phone version only supports touch-screen input.

So, what happens when we detect that the player wants to shoot? This is fairly simple to implement. We need a sprite that will initially appear at the same position and angle as the spaceship and will travel in the direction that the spaceship is facing.

The bullets are implemented in a new game object class, BulletObject. In addition to the standard SpriteObject properties, it also stores a movement vector that will be added to the position each update, and it keeps track of the number of times the bullet has moved so that it can expire after it has traveled a certain distance.

To avoid having to create and destroy bullet objects each time one is fired or expired, we use the same approach as described for the ParticleObject in the previous chapter: we keep all the bullet objects that we create and mark them as inactive when they are no longer required. When a new object is required, we first look for an existing inactive object and create a new one only if no existing object can be found.

For this reason, all the volatile properties of the bullet are initialized in a function named InitializeBullet rather than in the class constructor because the constructor cannot be used when a bullet object is recycled.

InitializeBullet expects the bullet position and angle to be passed as its parameters. They are placed directly into its Position and Angle properties. It then needs to calculate its movement vector so that the bullet travels forward each update. This is easily calculated from the bullet angle using a little trigonometry—the Sine of the angle will provide the distance to move horizontally, whereas the Cosine will return the vertical distance. The code to perform this initialization is shown in Listing 4-31.

Listing 4-31. Initializing a bullet object

```
internal void InitializeBullet(Vector2 Position, float Angle)
{
    // Initialize the bullet properties
    this.Position = Position;
    this.Angle = Angle;

    // Calculate the velocity vector for the bullet
    _velocity = new Vector2((float)Math.Sin(Angle), -(float)Math.Cos(Angle));
```

```
    // Mark the bullet as active
    IsActive = true;
    // Reset its update count
    _updates = 0;
}
```

Updating the bullet requires a few simple tasks. First, the _velocity vector is added to the sprite position (it is actually multiplied by 10 to make the bullet move faster). Then the position is checked against the edge of the window and moved to the opposite edge if it goes off the screen. The _updates count is incremented, and if it reaches the lifetime of the bullet (defined as 40 updates), it is expired by setting its IsActive property to false.

Finally, the bullet position is checked against each of the rocks. This is similar to the spaceship collision detection described in the last chapter, but it is actually a little easier. Because the bullet is very small, we can consider it as being just a single point rather than a rectangle. The collision check is therefore simply a matter of seeing whether the distance from the rock position to the bullet position is less than the rock size. The CheckForCollision function is shown in Listing 4-32.

Listing 4-32. Checking to see if the bullet object has collided with a rock

```
private void CheckForCollision()
{
    int objectCount;
    GameObjectBase gameObj;
    RockObject rockObj;
    float rockSize;
    float rockDistance;

    // Loop backwards through the rocks as we may modify the collection when a rock is
    // destroyed
    objectCount = _game.GameObjects.Count;
    for (int i = objectCount - 1; i >= 0;  i--)
    {
        // Get a reference to the object at this position
        gameObj = _game.GameObjects[i];
        // Is this a space rock?
        if (gameObj is RockObject)
        {
            // It is... Does its bounding rectangle contain the bullet position?
            rockObj = (RockObject)gameObj;
            if (rockObj.BoundingBox.Contains((int)Position.X, (int)Position.Y))
            {
                // It does.. See if the distance is small enough for them to collide.
                // First calculate the size of the object
                rockSize = rockObj.SpriteTexture.Width / 2.0f * rockObj.ScaleX;
                // Find the distance between the two points
                rockDistance = Vector2.Distance(Position, rockObj.Position);
                // Is the distance less than the rock size?
                if (rockDistance < rockSize)
                {
                    // Yes, so we have hit the rock
                    rockObj.DamageRock();
```

```
                        // Destroy the bullet
                        IsActive = false;
                }
            }
        }
    }
}
```

Note how the loop across the game objects runs backward; this is because we can remove rock objects from the collection when they are destroyed. This modifies the collection size, which means that accessing the elements at the end would result in an out-of-bounds index. Looping backward ensures that the rocks we remove will always affect the indexes of only the objects that we have already processed, removing the need to worry about this situation.

The BulletObject class now contains all the code it needs to be initialized, to move, to collide with rocks, and to expire when it has traveled a set distance. All that is left is the code to create the bullet in response to the player's input.

This is handled in the SpaceshipObject.FireBullet function, shown in Listing 4-33. It tries to retrieve a bullet object using the GetBulletObject function (which we will examine in a moment). If one is obtained, it calls its InitializeBullet function as already detailed in Listing 4-31.

Listing 4-33. Firing a bullet from the player's ship

```
private void FireBullet()
{
    BulletObject bulletObj;

    // Try to obtain a bullet object to shoot
    bulletObj = GetBulletObject();
    // Did we find one?
    if (bulletObj == null)
    {
        // No, so we can't shoot at the moment
        return;
    }

    // Initialize the bullet with our own position and angle
    bulletObj.InitializeBullet(Position, Angle);
}
```

GetBulletObject uses exactly the same approach that we saw for obtaining ParticleObject instances in the previous chapter. It looks for an existing bullet object whose IsActive value is false. If one is found, it is returned. If no such object is found, it creates a new object. However, to make the game a little more challenging, we allow the player to have only four bullets active at any time. If these bullets are already present, GetBulletObject returns null to prevent any further bullets from being fired. The code for this function is shown in Listing 4-34.

Listing 4-34. Finding or creating a bullet object for the player to fire

```
private BulletObject GetBulletObject()
{
    int objectCount;
    int bulletCount = 0;
    GameObjectBase gameObj;
    BulletObject bulletObj = null;
```

```
    // Look for an inactive bullet
    objectCount = _game.GameObjects.Count;
    for (int i = 0; i < objectCount; i++)
    {
        // Get a reference to the object at this position
        gameObj = _game.GameObjects[i];
        // Is this object a bullet?
        if (gameObj is BulletObject)
        {
            // Count the number of bullets found
            bulletCount += 1;
            // Is it inactive?
            if (((BulletObject)gameObj).IsActive == false)
            {
                // Yes, so re-use this bullet
                return (BulletObject)gameObj;
            }
        }
    }

    // Did we find a bullet?
    if (bulletObj == null)
    {
        // No, do we have capacity to add a new bullet?
        if (bulletCount < MaxBullets)
        {
            // Yes, so create a new bullet
            bulletObj = new BulletObject(_game, _game.Textures["Bullet"]);
            _game.GameObjects.Add(bulletObj);
            return bulletObj;
        }
    }

    // No more bullets available
    return null;
}
```

Rotating the Ship

The method used for allowing the player to rotate the ship is quite different between the touch and non-touch input methods. When the player is using a gamepad or the keyboard, we simply offer "rotate left" and "rotate right" controls. With a touch screen, each time the player touches the screen we will rotate the ship to face the point that has been touched. The touch-screen method is rather more complex to implement, so let's deal with the gamepad and keyboard approach first.

For keyboard input, we'll use the cursor left and right keys to control the rotation. With the gamepad, we'll offer both the d-pad left/right controls, but also the left thumbstick. The thumbstick provides analog readings depending on how far the control has been moved. Gentle movements will therefore allow the ship to be rotated more gradually than the d-pad or keyboard allow. The code to process the gamepad is shown in Listing 4-35; the keyboard input is very similar to that of the d-pad code. The RotationSpeed value referenced here is a class-level constant that controls how fast the ship rotates.

Listing 4-35. Rotating the player's ship using a gamepad

```
// If the dpad left/right has been pressed, rotate the ship at a fixed speed.
// The value here can be varied to change how quickly the ship rotates.
if (gamepadState.DPad.Left == ButtonState.Pressed)
                        _targetAngle -= MathHelper.ToRadians(RotationSpeed);
if (gamepadState.DPad.Right == ButtonState.Pressed)
                        _targetAngle -= MathHelper.ToRadians(-RotationSpeed);

// If the left thumbstick has been moved left or right, rotate the ship according
// to the distance the stick has moved. Once again we scale the input amount by
// a speed to control how quickly the ship rotates.
if (gamepadState.ThumbSticks.Left.X != 0)
    _targetAngle += MathHelper.ToRadians(
                        gamepadState.ThumbSticks.Left.X * RotationSpeed);
```

Regardless of the input mechanism used, the code updates a class-level variable named _targetAngle. The spaceship sprite's Angle property itself, however, isn't modified at all here and so the spaceship doesn't actually rotate as a result of this code. The rotation is instead performed in the SpaceshipObject.Update function, as shown in Listing 4-36. It rotates by 20 percent of the difference between the current angle and the target angle, with the result that it rotates quickly at first and then more slowly as it approaches the desired angle. This gives a pleasingly smooth movement without too much delay getting to the target angle, even if the rotation is large.

Listing 4-36. Rotating the spaceship toward the target angle

```
// Rotate towards the target angle
if (Angle != _targetAngle)
{
    Angle += (_targetAngle - Angle) * 0.2f;
}
```

That covers input from the gamepad and keyboard, but what about the touch screen? The processing for this is unfortunately a little more involved, but it's not too bad. Let's look at it in more detail.

Tapping the screen actually causes two things to happen: the ship will begin to rotate to face the tapped position and it will shoot a bullet. It will shoot in whichever direction it is facing at the time the screen is tapped, which might not be toward the touch point, but repeated taps of the screen will ultimately get the bullets going in the direction the player wants.

As we observed back in the gestures discussion, using the Tap gesture is not quite as responsive as using raw touch data because it misses some of the user's touches. Because it is important for our game to feel as responsive as possible, we will bypass gestures in this instance and use raw touch data instead. We can easily tell that the user has touched the screen by waiting for a touch point with a state of Pressed.

The code that takes care of this can be found within the SpaceshipObject.Update_ProcessTouchInput method, and the relevant portion of it is shown in Listing 4-37.

Listing 4-37. Detecting and handling taps on the screen

```
// Is the player tapping the screen?
TouchCollection tc = TouchPanel.GetState();
if (tc.Count == 1)
{
    // Has the first touch point just been touched?
    if (tc[0].State == TouchLocationState.Pressed)
```

```
    {
        // Yes, so rotate to this position and fire
        RotateToFacePoint(tc[0].Position);
        // Shoot a bullet in the current direction
        FireBullet();
        // Note the time so we can detect held contact
        _holdTime = DateTime.Now;
    }
}
```

On detection of a new touch, it calls two functions: RotateToFacePoint and FireBullet. It also puts the time into a class variable called _holdTime, but we'll look at that in more detail when we discuss ship movement in the next section.

We've already looked at the FireBullet function, but let's see how RotateToFacePoint works. To rotate to face a particular point, we need to use more trigonometry. For those of you not of a mathematical persuasion, don't panic! This really isn't too complicated, thanks in part to some of the functionality provided by MonoGame.

In order to rotate to a point, we first need to find the distance of the point from the spaceship's own position. We have a Vector2 for the spaceship and another for the touch point, so to find the distance we can simply subtract the spaceship position from the touch point. This is the first thing that the RotateToFacePoint function does, the beginning of which is shown in Listing 4-38. If it finds that the touch point is exactly the same as the spaceship position, it returns without doing anything because there is no real way to know which direction we should turn toward in order to look exactly at ourselves.

Listing 4-38. Finding the direction of the touch point relative to the spaceship position

```
private void RotateToFacePoint(Vector2 point)
{
    // Find the angle between the spaceship and the specified point.
    // First find the position of the point relative to the position of the spaceship
    point -= Position;

    // Is the point is exactly on the spaceship, ignore the touch
    if (point == Vector2.Zero) return;
```

Now we are ready to find the angle toward which we need to face. Before doing this, the code ensures that the current sprite Angle property is greater or equal to 0 radians and less than 2 PI radians (360 degrees). The reason is that we can actually end up rotating outside of this range, as you will see shortly.

Once this has been established, the sprite angle is converted to degrees. Personally, I find working in radians quite uncomfortable and I much prefer degrees, so this makes the code much easier to understand. There is, of course, a small performance hit for performing this conversion, so if you can work in radians (or convert your code back to using radians once you have it working), it will run a little faster as a result.

Now for the trigonometry. MonoGame provides a Math class function called Atan2, which returns the angle through which we need to rotate in order to go from 0 radians to face the specified point—exactly what we need. Because we are now storing the touch point in object space, we can simply find the angle needed to face the touch point and we are there—well, nearly, anyway. To keep things using the same measurements, we convert the return value from Atan2 into degrees. The code is shown in Listing 4-39.

Listing 4-39. Finding the angle required to face the touch point

```
// Ensure that the current angle is between 0 and 2 PI
while (Angle < 0) { Angle += MathHelper.TwoPi; }
while (Angle > MathHelper.TwoPi) { Angle -= MathHelper.TwoPi; }
```

```
// Get the current angle in degrees
float angleDegrees;
angleDegrees = MathHelper.ToDegrees(Angle);

// Calculate the angle between the ship and the touch point, convert to degrees
float targetAngleDegrees;
targetAngleDegrees = MathHelper.ToDegrees((float)Math.Atan2(point.Y, point.X));
```

We have a little more work to do, however. MonoGame drawing system considers 0 degrees to point straight upward, and we generally expect it to range from 0 to 360 degrees. Atan2 returns an angle in the range of –180 to 180 degrees, however, with 0 degrees pointing to the left instead of up.

To map this angle into the same space that MonoGame uses, we can first add 90 to the angle we have calculated. This puts the 0 degree angle pointing up again, and it results in a range of -90 to 270 degrees. To get back to the positive degree range, we check to see whether the value is less than 0 and add 360 if it is. This finally results in a MonoGame-aligned angle in the range of 0 to 360. Listing 4-40 contains the calculations for this.

Listing 4-40. Aligning the Atan2 angle with the angle system used by MonoGame

```
// MonoGame puts 0 degrees upwards, whereas Atan2 returns it facing left, so add 90
// degrees to rotate the Atan2 value into alignment with MonoGame
targetAngleDegrees += 90;
// Atan2 returns values between -180 and +180, so having added 90 degrees we now
// have a value in the range -90 to +270. In case we are less than zero, add
// 360 to get an angle in the range 0 to 360.
if (targetAngleDegrees < 0) targetAngleDegrees += 360;
```

So, do we now have an angle that we can turn to face? Well, yes we do, but making the spaceship jump immediately toward the touch point feels very unnatural. It is much nicer to get it to rotate toward the touch point, so let's transition from the current angle to the target angle. We've already looked at how the _targetAngle variable is used for this, so can't we just set that to point to the angle we've calculated?

Well, we could, but there is one final complication here. If the current spaceship angle is at 350 degrees and the calculated target angle is at 10 degrees, the approach that we have just discussed will cause the spaceship to rotate all the way around through 340 degrees in a counterclockwise direction, whereas it would be much more efficient for it to rotate just 20 degrees clockwise. This is illustrated in Figure 4-15. In practice, having the ship rotate like this is very jarring and will be very frustrating for the player who asked for only a minor rotation!

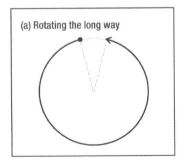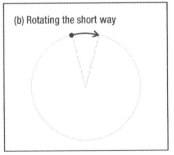

Figure 4-15. *The long and the short way to rotate across the 0-degree boundary*

To prevent this from happening, we will check to see whether the target angle is more than 180 degrees away from the current spaceship angle. If it is more than 180 degrees above the spaceship angle, we subtract 360 from the target angle so that the spaceship rotates the other way (which will be less than 180 degrees and is thus the shorter angle). If it is more than 180 degrees below the spaceship angle, we do the reverse and add 360 degrees to the target angle.

These will ensure that we always take the shorter route to the desired angle. It might also result in a target angle that is above 360 degrees or below 0 degrees, however. This in itself doesn't cause any problems, but it is the reason we ensure that the Angle value is between 0 and 2 PI back in Listing 4-39.

Listing 4-40 shows the remainder of the RotateToFacePoint function. Once the target angle has been calculated as described, it is converted back to radians and stored in the class-level _targetAngle variable.

Listing 4-40. Ensuring that the rotation always takes the shorter route and storing the target angle ready for use

```
// Is the target angle over 180 degrees less than the current angle?
if (targetAngleDegrees < angleDegrees - 180)
{
    // Yes, so instead of rotating the whole way around to the left,
    // rotate the smaller distance to the right instead.
    targetAngleDegrees += 360;
}
// Is the target angle over 180 degrees more than the current angle?
if (targetAngleDegrees > angleDegrees + 180)
{
    // Yes, so instead of rotating the whole way around to the right,
    // rotate the smaller distance to the left instead.
    targetAngleDegrees -= 360;
}

// Store the calculated angle, converted back to radians
_targetAngle = MathHelper.ToRadians(targetAngleDegrees);
}
```

Making the Player's Ship Move

The spaceship is a bit of a sitting duck in the middle of the screen and a collision with a rock is pretty much inevitable if the ship can't move. Fortunately, the ship is fitted out with powerful plasma thrusters that it can use to move around the screen.

For gamepad and keyboard input, we provide a button and keypress that can be used to control the thruster. These have been set to use either of the trigger buttons on the gamepad (ignoring the analog input and just treating them as either pressed or released), and the cursor up key on the keyboard. When the game detects that one of these is pressed, it calls a function named Thrust, which we'll look at in a moment.

A slightly different approach is provided for touch-screen input. When the player holds a point on the screen for a brief period, we will use that as the signal that the ship should fire its thrusters and move toward the point the user is touching. This gives a simple and intuitive mechanism for moving the ship around the screen.

We could have used the Hold gesture to initiate this, but it has a drawback in this situation: the time between initiating the hold and the Hold gesture triggering is too long—about a second, which is just too slow for a fast-moving game such as this one. There is no way to control this trigger time, so the gesture is not suitable for our needs in this instance.

Instead, *Cosmic Rocks* uses the raw touch API to implement its own version of the hold gesture. The process is actually very simple:

- When a touch point with a state of Pressed is received, it stores the current time in a class-level variable.

- Each time the touch point returns a state of Moved, the current time is compared to the stored time. If sufficient time has elapsed between the two, the touch point is considered as being held and the thrust processing is executed.

The code from SpaceshipObject.Update_ProcessTouchInput required to perform this (which also includes the bullet firing check from the previous section) is shown in Listing 4-41. The code waits for 300 milliseconds (0.3 seconds) before it starts thrusting the ship. This figure seems to work well; increasing it makes the thrust control unresponsive, whereas lowering it makes it possible for the users to accidentally thrust when they were intending only to shoot.

Listing 4-41. Detecting a held touch point using raw touch data

```
// Is the player tapping the screen?
TouchCollection tc = TouchPanel.GetState();
if (tc.Count == 1)
{
    // Has the first touch point just been touched?
    if (tc[0].State == TouchLocationState.Pressed)
    {
        // Yes, so rotate to this position and fire
        RotateToFacePoint(tc[0].Position);
        // Shoot a bullet in the current direction
        FireBullet();
        // Note the time so we can detect held contact
        _holdTime = DateTime.Now;
    }
    if (tc[0].State == TouchLocationState.Moved)
    {
        // Has sufficient time passed to start thrusting?
        if (DateTime.Now.Subtract(_holdTime).TotalMilliseconds > 300)
        {
            // Yes, so thrust towards this position
            RotateToFacePoint(tc[0].Position);
            Thrust();
        }
    }
}
```

Once the hold is established, the touch-screen code also calls into the Thrust function to initiate the movement of the spaceship.

Moving the ship is achieved in a similar way as when we initializing the bullet object—the ship's Angle is used to determine a movement vector. This vector is then added to the ship's existing velocity so that its existing movement is taken into account, too. This means that continuing to thrust in the same direction will cause the ship to accelerate, whereas thrusting in the opposite direction to movement will cause it to slow down and eventually stop.

One final check is performed with the ship's speed. The code calculates the length of the velocity vector, which tells us how fast the ship is moving. If this exceeds a maximum speed limit (which has been set at 25 in this case), we stop the ship from moving any faster. This stops the ship from reaching ridiculous speeds, which is easy to do with the gamepad or keyboard by simply holding down the thrust button.

The way in which the speed is limited is interesting and worth a little explanation. First, the velocity vector is *normalized*. This is an operation that can be performed on a vector that keeps it facing in exactly the same direction, but that reduces its length to 1. This alone would cause the ship's speed to drop from 25 to 1, which isn't what we want, but we can now simply multiple the normalized vector by 25 to return it back to our maximum permitted speed. If ever the speed exceeds 25, this puts it back to 25 again, preventing the ship from moving any more quickly.

The Thrust code is shown in Listing 4-42. In the game, it also adds some particle objects to represent the thruster exhaust, but this is omitted from the listing here for brevity.

Listing 4-42. Thrusting—adding to the ship's velocity

```
private void Thrust()
{
    Vector2 shipFacing;

    // Calculate the vector towards which the ship is facing
    shipFacing = new Vector2((float)Math.Sin(Angle), -(float)Math.Cos(Angle));
    // Scale down and add to the velocity
    _velocity += shipFacing / 10;
    // Stop the ship from traveling too fast
    if (_velocity.Length() > 25)
    {
        _velocity.Normalize();
        _velocity *= 25;
    }

    [...]
```

The _velocity is applied in the SpaceshipObject.Update code, just as it has been for the bullets and rocks. Note that we don't apply any kind of friction to the spaceship; it is floating in a vacuum after all, so once the player has started moving, it is quite a challenge to stop again!

Implementing Hyperspace

The final input control left to handle is for hyperspace. Hyperspace can be used as a last-resort emergency measure when the player cannot escape from the approaching rocks. It makes the player's ship disappear for a few seconds before reappearing at a random location somewhere on the screen. This can be a lifesaver, but it can also cause the ship to reappear right on top of a rock, so it needs to be used with caution.

For gamepad and keyboard input, another button and key is provided. The B button on the gamepad will act as hyperspace, as will either of the Ctrl keys on the keyboard. When one of these is detected, the game calls a function named Hyperspace.

For touch input, we need another way for the player to signal that is obviously a request to hyperspace and that is unlikely to be accidentally triggered. In this case, we can use the Pinch gesture as a trigger for hyperspace. This is easily accessed by the player, but it is not something that is likely to be triggered unintentionally.

The touch-screen input processing code relating to hyperspace is shown in Listing 4-43, taken from SpaceshipObject.Update_ProcessTouchInput.

Listing 4-43. Checking the user input for hyperspace

```
// Is the player pinching?
while (TouchPanel.IsGestureAvailable)
{
    GestureSample gesture = TouchPanel.ReadGesture();
    switch (gesture.GestureType)
    {
        case GestureType.Pinch:
            Hyperspace();
            break;
    }
}
```

Hyperspacing is implemented using two class-level variables: _hyperspaceZoom and _hyperspaceZoomAdd. Normally, these are both set to zero, but when hyperspace is active the _hyperspaceZoomAdd variable is set to a value that is added to _hyperspaceZoom each update. While _hyperspaceZoom is greater than zero, the ship is in hyperspace.

Once _hyperspaceZoom reaches a certain level, _hyperspaceZoomAdd is negated so that it starts reducing the value of _hyperspaceZoom back toward zero. Once it reaches zero, the hyperspace is finished—both variables are set back to zero, and the spaceship update process returns to its normal state.

The Hyperspace function, shown in Listing 4-44, therefore simply sets the _hyperspaceZoomAdd variable to have a value of 5.

Listing 4-44. Initiating hyperspace

```
private void Hyperspace()
{
    // Initiate the hyperspace by setting the zoom add
    _hyperspaceZoomAdd = 5;
}
```

In Update, the code checks to see whether the _hyperspaceZoomAdd value is non-zero. If so, it is applied to the _hyperspaceZoom variable as has been described. When _hyperspaceZoom reaches its maximum level (defined in the code as 150), the spaceship is put into a random new position and _hyperspaceZoomAdd is negated. When _hyperspaceZoom reaches zero, the hyperspace variables are set to zero. The spaceship velocity is also cancelled as part of a hyperspace transition, meaning that hyperspace is the one thing that can completely stop the ship from moving.

Note that the hyperspace processing code returns out of the Update function at the end. This stops all other processing of the spaceship (movement, input controls, and so on) while hyperspacing is active.

Also note that all touch gestures are read and discarded before returning; this is important because without this they will queue up and all be processed together when the hyperspace has finished. If the gesture system reports a number of Pinch gestures in response to the user's initial input, it would result in the ship going into hyperspace over and over again until the whole queue is empty. Discarding the queued gestures ensures that these extra gesture reports will have no effect.

The relevant Update code is shown in Listing 4-45.

Listing 4-45. Updating the hyperspace variables

```
// Are we hyperspacing?
if (_hyperspaceZoomAdd != 0)
{
    // Add to the zoom
    _hyperspaceZoom += _hyperspaceZoomAdd;
```

```
    // Have we reached maximum zoom?
    if (_hyperspaceZoom >= 150)
    {
        // Yes, so move to the new location
        // Start to zoom back out
        _hyperspaceZoomAdd = -_hyperspaceZoomAdd;
        // Set a random new position
        PositionX = GameHelper.RandomNext(0,
                _game.GraphicsDevice.Viewport.Bounds.Width - SpriteTexture.Width)
                        + SpriteTexture.Width / 2;

        PositionY = GameHelper.RandomNext(0,
                _game.GraphicsDevice.Viewport.Bounds.Height - SpriteTexture.Height)
                        + SpriteTexture.Height / 2;
    }
    // Have we finished hyperspacing?
    if (_hyperspaceZoom <= 0)
    {
        // Yes, so cancel the hyperspace variables
        _hyperspaceZoom = 0;
        _hyperspaceZoomAdd = 0;
        // Stop movement
        _velocity = Vector2.Zero;
    }
    // Discard any queued gestures and then return
    while (TouchPanel.IsGestureAvailable) { TouchPanel.ReadGesture(); }
    // Don't allow any other updates while hyperspacing
    return;
}
```

Finally, to indicate visually that hyperspace is in effect, we increase the scale of the ship and fade out its alpha across the duration of the hyperspace processing. This is achieved by overriding the ScaleX, ScaleY, and SpriteColor properties. The scale properties increase the return value based on the contents of the _hyperspaceZoom variable, whereas SpriteColor reduces the alpha level toward zero. Because the _hyperspaceZoom value is 0 when not hyperspacing, these property overrides will have no effect unless the hyperspace is active. The overrides are shown in Listing 4-46.

Listing 4-46. Overriding the scale and color properties to indicate the progress through hyperspace

```
// If the player is hyperspacing, zoom the spaceship to indicate this
public override float ScaleX
{
    get { return base.ScaleX + (_hyperspaceZoom * 0.02f); }
}
// If the player is hyperspacing, zoom the spaceship to indicate this
public override float ScaleY
{
    get { return base.ScaleX + (_hyperspaceZoom * 0.02f); }
}

// If the player is hyperspacing, fade out the spaceship to indicate this
public override Color SpriteColor
```

```
{
    Get
    {
        Color ret = base.SpriteColor;
        ret.A = (byte)MathHelper.Clamp(255 - _hyperspaceZoom * 2.5f, 0, 255);
        return ret;
    }
}
```

Considering Input Design

In this chapter, we have looked at all the different mechanisms that you have at your disposal when dealing with user interaction with your game.

The limited standard control mechanisms available to Windows Phone and tablet devices mean that some thought might be needed to set up the input approach for your game. With no buttons or directional pad, some types of game can be a challenge to implement, whereas other game types will hugely benefit from the presence of the touch screen. The accelerometer is also useful as an input and can be used either in isolation or alongside the touch screen.

For devices that do have keyboards and gamepads, an almost bewildering array of input options is available, providing plenty of options for game controls.

Before you start working on a game, you should have a clear idea of how you expect the user to interact with it. Your ideas might change during development, of course, but it is important to consider them before starting to try to avoid unexpected input problems once you have invested time in your game.

Cosmic Rocks is now looking and playing like a real game and, hopefully, you are already finding it fun to play. It is, of course, still missing some important elements, such as moving to new levels, a score, and player lives. We could implement them with a little effort, but there is one other thing that it is missing that we haven't explored at all yet: sound. It will be the subject of the next chapter.

Summary

- Windows 8 and Windows Phone devices offer lots of different input mechanisms: touch screens, keyboards, gamepads, mice, and accelerometers. All of these mechanisms are supported by MonoGame on the relevant platforms. It is important to consider how the player will interact with your game on each possible hardware configuration and to ensure that no players are excluded because they don't have the particular input hardware that your game wants to use.

- The available input mechanisms can be determined by calling the GameHelper.GetInputCapabilities function.

- Touch-screen data can be obtained in two ways: by reading the raw touch data or by using gestures.

- Raw touch-screen data is obtained by calling the TouchPanel.GetState function. This allows multiple touch points to be read, and it easily allows each one to identify whether it is a newly pressed point, an existing point, or a point that has just been released. The previous position of each point can be determined, too.

- A series of predefined gestures are available. To use these, you must first declare which of them you want to listen for and then regularly query the `TouchPanel.IsGestureAvailable` property and call the `TouchPanel.ReadGesture` function if it indicates that gestures are waiting to be processed. The gesture queue must be emptied in this way during every update to avoid gestures being processed later than intended, a problem that can be very difficult to track down.

- Both raw touch data and gestures can also be read for the mouse if desired by setting the `TouchPanel.EnableMouseTouchPoint` and/or the `TouchPanel.EnableMouseGestures` properties to `true`.

- The `GameFramework` project's sprites offer various simple "hit testing" functionality via the `IsPointInObject` function to identify whether a given point is contained within the sprite. This can be set to automatically detect points using a rectangular or elliptical hit test, or it can be overridden if a more complex test is required.

- The GameHost class also offers functions named `GetSpritesAtPoint` and `GetSpriteAtPoint`, which will use the sprite's hit testing functions to identify all sprites at a given point, or the frontmost sprite at a given point.

- Both raw touch input and gestures can be easily used to allow objects to be dragged and flicked around the screen.

- In addition to passing mouse events through to the `TouchPanel` functions, the `Mouse.GetState` function can be used to retrieve more detailed information about the mouse. This includes its position (available at all times, unlike via the `TouchPanel` when the position is only available when the mouse button is pressed), the state of all buttons, and the position of the mouse wheel.

- Compatible gamepads can be used to control the game, with full access to the values from all buttons and other gamepad controls, both digital and analog. The gamepad data is obtained by calling the `GamePad.GetState` function, passing the index of the player whose controller is to be read. Multiple gamepads may be interrogated in this way and read independently for multiplayer gaming.

- Hardware keyboards can be accessed by calling the `Keyboard.GetState` function.

- The user can be prompted to enter some text by calling the GameFramework's `GameHelper.BeginShowKeyboardInput` function. This will display an input dialog box on both Windows 8 and Windows Phone, and it will call back into a provided function once the user is finished, indicating the results of the dialog.

- For mobile devices (tablets, phones, and some laptops), the accelerometer can be used to provide another way for the user to interact with your game. For debugging, the Windows Phone emulator has a tool that allows the values of the accelerometer to be simulated.

- You can read input in any area of code within your game, but it is strongly advised to focus all input processing into a single section of code, and to ensure that the various `GetState` functions are called only once per update.

CHAPTER 5

Sounding Out with Game Audio

Our worlds have been very quiet so far. Apart from the occasional sound of keys being pressed or a screen being tapped, everything has moved in complete silence. That's no way for a game to be so, in this chapter, we'll make some noise by adding sound effects and music to our games.

Game audio plays a significant role in the experience that a player has when playing a game. A game with little or no sound feels hollow and empty, whereas distinctive and characteristic sound effects and music can really draw a player into the game and make it a much more absorbing event.

Mobile devices typically have less opportunity to impress regarding sound effects and music than desktop PCs or game consoles because they are usually limited to smaller speakers. On the other hand, PCs or consoles might well be hooked up to powerful surround sound systems. Headphones are likely to be commonly used with mobile devices, however, and they can provide very effective sound to your players.

Regardless of the way that the device is producing sound, you should still ensure that your games sound as good as possible. In this chapter, we'll explore just how you can go about achieving that goal.

Sound Effects and Music

MonoGame makes a distinction between two types of sound that it can play: sound effects and music. Sound effects are ideal for sounds that correspond to the actions taking place within your game, while music can be played on a loop in the background to accompany your game the whole time it is playing.

Both of these have certain requirements that must be taken into account as well as various options that can affect the sound playback.

Let's start by looking at sound effects.

Playing Sound Effects

MonoGame provides a fair amount of flexibility for playing sound effects inside your games. It can play multiple sounds simultaneously (including multiple instances of the same sound), and it offers control over volume levels, stereo panning, and pitch shifting. It can loop sounds or play them just once, and it also offers controls to allow sounds to be paused and resumed.

▧ **Caution**   Sound effects are really intended just for sounds that take place as your game is playing, not for playing background music. When you are ready to distribute your game in the Windows or Windows Phone Stores (as we will discuss in Chapter 14), you may find that your game fails the certification process if you use sound effects to play long music clips.

Adding Sound Effects to Your Project

Sound effects are added as part of the Content project, as has been the case with all the other resource data (textures and sprite fonts) that we used in previous chapters. They are added in just the same way: by creating an XNA Content project, right-clicking the main Content project node inside Solution Explorer, and then selecting Add / Existing Item. The sound file can then be located and added to the project.

You will see after adding a sound file that the content item's `Content Importer` is set to `WAV Audio File` and the `Content Processor` is set to `Sound Effect`, as shown in Figure 5-1.

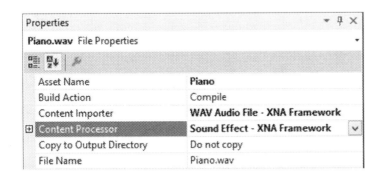

Figure 5-1. *The properties for a WAV file added to an XNA Content project*

All sound effects must be created from *WAV* (short for *Waveform Audio File Format*) files. WAV files are one of the oldest sound formats used by Microsoft. They usually store sound in an uncompressed format, making them easy to read and write, but resulting in large file sizes.

On desktop PCs, WAV files have largely been replaced by formats offering higher levels of compression such as MP3, but MonoGame unfortunately cannot use MP3 files for sound effects (though it can use them for background music, as you will see later in this chapter). As a result, we find ourselves with no choice but to use WAV files for our sounds.

▓ **Note** It is possible to use MP3 or WMA files as sound effects by adding them and then changing the `Content Processor` from the initial value of `Song` back to `Sound Effect` (refer to Figure 5-1). This change will provide access to the sound from within your game. Unfortunately, however, during compilation the `Sound Effect` content processor will silently convert your MP3 or WMA file into a WAV file for the compiled game, resulting in the same large file that would have resulted from adding a WAV file in the first place.

Once the file has been added, we are ready to load it into our game. Once again, this is handled in the same way as with other resources that we have loaded from the Content project: using the `Content.Load` method. Listing 5-1 shows a piece of code that declares a `SoundEffect` object and loads it from the Content folder. Just as before, we provide the `Load` method with the type of object that is being loaded.

Listing 5-1. Loading a sound effect from the Content project

```
SoundEffect mySound;
mySound = Content.Load<SoundEffect>("Piano");
```

Playing the Sound Effects

With a sound effect loaded, we are now ready to play it by simply calling the Play method of the SoundEffect object.

Two overloads of this method are available. The first one takes no parameters and simply plays the sound at full volume. The second overload provides some additional control, allowing us to provide values for the volume level, the pitch, and the stereo panning of the sample:

- Volume is a float that specifies the playback volume level from 0 (silent) to 1 (full volume).

- Pitch is a float that controls the frequency of the sound playback. The specified value indicates how many octaves the playback should be offset from the default sample pitch. For example, passing 0 plays at the default pitch, –1 plays an octave lower, and 1 plays an octave higher. Larger values may be passed to shift through further octaves, and fractional values can be used to shift through a fraction of an octave.

- Pan is a float that controls the stereo position of the played sound. Values range from –1 (fully to the left) through 0 (centered) to 1 (fully right).

■ **Note**   Sound effect volume is always played relative to the volume setting of the device, so a volume level of 1 actually means to play at the configured device volume level. When using the Windows Phone emulator, you can press F9 to increase the device volume level or press F10 to decrease it. Press the key repeatedly to reach full volume or to silence the emulated device.

Play is asynchronous and returns back to your game immediately, leaving the sound playing in the background. If you call Play again before an earlier call has completed, the new sound will play alongside the older sound. Options to stop the earlier sound are provided via the SoundEffectInstance object, which we'll discuss in a moment.

Integrating Sound Effects into the Game Framework

Just as we have added GameFramework support for textures and fonts, we will add support for sound effects, too. This support is implemented using another Dictionary within the GameHost class, this time named SoundEffects. The declaration of the dictionary is shown in Listing 5-2.

Listing 5-2. The SoundEffects dictionary present within the GameFramework.GameHost class

```
// A dictionary of loaded sound effects.
public Dictionary<string, SoundEffect> SoundEffects { get; set; }
```

We can then use the dictionary to load sound effects in the same way as we do for textures and fonts, and we can access the dictionary items anywhere within the game.

The SoundEffects_Win8 and SoundEffects_WP8 example projects that accompany this chapter show how sound effects can be loaded into the game engine and then played back. They load four different samples (named EnergySound, Piano, MagicSpell, and Motorbike) and divide the screen into four regions to allow each to be played. Experiment with the projects and with playing multiple sounds together.

The example projects also set the sound effect's panning based on the horizontal position of the screen tap. Tapping the left side of the screen will pan to the left; tapping the right will pan to the right.

Try experimenting with changing the source code to produce different volume levels and different pitches, too.

Sound Effect Instances

Calling the Play method on a SoundEffect object provides a very easy way to get a sound playing, and, in many cases, this will be sufficient. For gunfire, explosions, player achievement sounds and all sorts of other one-off effects, this is likely to be all that you need.

In other places, however, you might find that a greater level of control is needed over the sounds that you play. The ability to loop a sound, for example, can be very useful, but the functions provided by the SoundEffect class alone cannot offer this ability. The main reason is that we would have no way to stop the sound; we don't obtain a sound ID value or anything similar, so once several sounds were active we would be unable to tell the class which one it should stop.

This problem is resolved by the inclusion of the SoundEffectInstance class. Instances of this class are created by calling the CreateInstance method of a SoundEffect object.

SoundEffectInstance objects are very similar to SoundEffect objects, with the following key differences:

- Each instance can play only one sound at a time. Calling Play multiple times will have no effect. To play multiple sounds simultaneously using sound effect instances, multiple instance objects would need to be created from the underlying SoundEffect.

- The Volume, Pitch, and Pan of an instance are specified using class properties rather than as parameters to the Play method. This allows the properties to be easily altered after the sound has started playing.

- SoundEffectInstance objects contain a property named IsLooped that can be set to true to instruct the sound to loop.

- In addition to the Play method, effect instances also have methods to Pause and Stop the sound. They don't need to be used at all if the sound is not looping, but if it is looping, one or the other will likely be useful to stop the sound from playing. Pause will remember how much of the sound has been played and will resume from this point the next time Play is called. Stop will reset the sound so that it plays from the beginning when Play is next called. To find out whether a sound effect instance is stopped, paused, or playing, query its State property.

The SoundEffectInstances_Win8 and SoundEffectInstances_WP8 example projects demonstrate the use of this class. The running project looks just the same as the SoundEffects example, but works in a different way. When you press and hold your finger on one of the sound panels, the sound will play and will loop endlessly. When you release your finger, the sound will pause. When the panel is touched again, playback resumes from where it left off (this is most noticeable with the Piano and Motorbike sounds). This behavior couldn't have been accomplished with just the SoundEffect class.

Additionally, if you slide your finger to the left and right as the sound is playing, the pitch of the sound will change in response. Once again, only the SoundEffectInstance allows this change to be made because the SoundEffect class allows the pitch (as well as the volume and panning) to be set only when the sound playback is first initiated.

The code that plays, repitches, and pauses the sounds, taken from the example project's Update method, is shown in Listing 5-3.

Listing 5-3. Playing, setting the pitch, and pausing SoundEffectInstances

```
TouchCollection tc = TouchPanel.GetState();
if (tc.Count > 0)
{
    // Find the region of the screen that has been touched
    screenRegion = (int)(tc[0].Position.Y * 4 / Window.ClientBounds.Height);
    // Ensure we have a region between 0 and 3
    if (screenRegion >= 0 && screenRegion <= 3)
```

```
    {
        // What type of touch event do we have?
        switch (tc[0].State)
        {
            case TouchLocationState.Pressed:
                // Set the pitch based on the horizontal touch position
                _soundInstances[screenRegion].Pitch =
                        (tc[0].Position.X / this.Window.ClientBounds.Width) * 2 - 1;
                // Start the sound for this region
                _soundInstances[screenRegion].Play();
                break;
            case TouchLocationState.Moved:
                // Is the sound for this region currently playing?
                if (_soundInstances[screenRegion].State == SoundState.Playing)
                {
                    // Yes, so set the pitch based on the horizontal touch position
                    _soundInstances[screenRegion].Pitch =
                        (tc[0].Position.X / this.Window.ClientBounds.Width) * 2 - 1;
                }
                    break;
                case TouchLocationState.Released:
                    // Pause all of the sounds
                    for (int i = 0; i < _soundInstances.Length; i++)
                    {
                        _soundInstances[i].Pause();
                    }
                    break;
        }
    }
}
```

Try changing the code when the touch point is released so that it calls the Stop method of the SoundEffectInstance objects rather than Pause. You will then see that each time the sound is played, it restarts from the beginning rather than resuming from where it was interrupted.

Other Sound Effect Properties

Among the other properties exposed by the SoundEffect class are two that we will briefly look at.

The first is the Duration property, which returns a TimeSpan indicating exactly how long the sample will take to play at its default pitch. This property can be useful for queuing up sounds to play one after another.

The second is the MasterVolume property, which is actually a static property called against the SoundEffect class rather than on an instance. It controls the overall volume of all sound effects, subsequently played or already playing, so it is a great way to fade up or down the sound from or to silence. It's also a particularly easy way to offer a "volume control" setting in your game so that the user can change the overall volume level (or indeed, switch the sound off entirely). By changing the master volume, the volume of all your other game sound effects will change automatically, without your having to cater for the volume setting on each individual call to play one of the sounds.

Just like the volume of individual sounds, MasterVolume is set in the range of 0 (silence) to 1 (full volume, based on the current device volume level). It defaults to 1.

Obtaining Sound Effects for Your Game

Although you might want to create your own sound effects, there are also many thousands available on the Internet that you can use in your game instead. It is generally much easier to get hold of quality sounds this way because you can search through the libraries, playing each sound you find until you locate one that will fit into your game.

The main issue to be aware of with downloaded sounds is licensing. Just as with everything else in life, it is hard to find good things for free—particularly if you intend to sell your game. Fortunately, an organization called Creative Commons has made this particular area easier to deal with. This is extremely helpful for getting good sound effects.

A number of different Creative Commons licenses are available, many of which permit the material that they cover to be used in free or commercial products, and some of which also allow modifications to be made to the licensed items. The only general requirement is that you include attribution for the source of the material in your game. So if you include the details of the sound author and a link to the site from which it was downloaded, all such licensed sounds can be freely used within your games. Make sure you check the license of each individual sound that you want to use, however, because some licenses forbid commercial use.

A couple of great sites for finding Creative Commons licensed sound effects are the following:

- `http://www.freesound.org`
- `http://www.soundbible.com`

Both of these sites clearly describe the license applied to each sound and have search facilities and online previews of each sound in their database. Many other sound sites exist, too, and can be found via your favorite search engine.

Selecting a sound can be time-consuming, and finding just the right one can be tricky. It is essential to try out each sound that you like and see how it fits in with the game environment. Sometimes sounds that initially seem ideal just don't work well inside a game, so spend some time experimenting to get things sounding just right. Don't forget that altering the volume or pitch can help with getting your sounds to fit in, too.

To manipulate sounds that you have downloaded or to convert them between different formats, a sound editing application is essential. This application will let you cut out or exclude sections of a sound, fade its volume up or down, add echo and distortion, and do dozens of other useful things.

Lots of commercial applications are available for this task, but if you are looking to keep your costs down, a free application called Audacity is well worth a look. It has a large range of sound processing effects, has flexible editing features, and supports saving to numerous file formats (including WAV and MP3). Visit `http://audacity.sourceforge.net` to download a copy.

An Interactive Example

Recall the `Balloons_Win8` and `Balloons_WP8` projects that we created in Chapter 4 to illustrate mapping input coordinates to objects on the screen. To bring a little more life to the example, updated versions of the projects are included with this chapter with some sound effects added.

Three different popping sounds are included to make the sound a little more varied and, as each sound is played, it is also given a slightly randomized pitch as well as being panned to match the balloon position on the screen. This makes for an entirely more satisfying balloon-popping experience! If you have an opportunity to try this with a touch-screen, then do so—it's much more satisfying than using the mouse.

Playing Music

We have already discussed the fact that the `SoundEffect` class is not to be used for playing music, but that doesn't mean that we can't provide backing tracks for our games. MonoGame provides separate functionality for playing music, but, in the context of Windows Phone, there are some things that we need to be aware of in order for our game to meet Microsoft's certification requirements.

Let's look at how (and when) you can play music within your games.

To Play or Not to Play

The certification requirement complication for Windows Phone games revolves around the fact that one of the other primary uses for the device is as a media player. The operating system has a flexible media library that allows music and other audio content to be played on the device, even when the media library has been moved to the background.

As a result, it is entirely possible that when the user launches your game, music is already playing in the background. Microsoft has decided that this existing music should take priority over your game music and that you must not stop it from playing without either directly asking the user for permission (by displaying a dialog box, for example, asking if the user wants to play the game music instead of the current audio track) or by providing a configuration option that allows it to be configured on a more permanent basis (in which case the option must default to not interrupting the existing media playback). Without observing this requirement, your game will be rejected when you submit it to the Windows Phone Store.

We will look at how to perform this check (and how to pause the background music if appropriate) in a moment, but for now please bear in mind the need to do this.

Note that this check applies only to playing music with the `MediaPlayer` class, which is the class that provides access to the music player functionality. Sound effect playback is permitted even if the device is already playing music, so no special checking needs to be performed for sound effects. The certification requirements state that sound effect objects should not be used for playing background music, however, so this isn't a way to bypass the requirement.

There is no such similar certification requirement for Windows 8 games—this only applies when developing for Windows Phone.

Adding Music to Your Project

Music is also added via an XNA Content project. Unlike sound effects, music is expected to be in either MP3 or WMA format. This is a good thing because such formats produce much smaller files than WAV files due to the way they are compressed. Because music is likely to be much longer in duration than a sound effect, having compression applied is essential for keeping the size of your finished game under control.

MP3 files have taken over the world during the last decade and must surely form one of the most widely known file formats in existence. Sound files encoded using MP3 are compressed using a lossy compression algorithm. Although this means that there is some degradation of the audio when it is played back (just as there is a loss of image quality with JPG images), in most cases the quality loss is virtually or completely unnoticeable.

MP3 can compress audio data to different degrees and the higher the compression, the greater the quality loss on playback. The compression level is set when the MP3 is created by specifying a bit rate, which controls how many kilobits of data can be used to store each second of compressed audio. Compressing files at a bit rate of 128 kilobits per second will typically reduce CD quality audio to about 9 percent of its original file size—a massive saving.

Windows Media Audio (WMA) files are similar in approach to MP3s, also using a proprietary Microsoft compression format to provide lossy compression (although a lossless variation is available). Microsoft claims that WMA files can be created that have the same quality level as an MP3 while using only half the storage space, though there are those who dispute this claim. Nevertheless, it is still a capable format and certainly usable for your game music.

▧ **Note**   Audacity is capable of exporting sounds in both MP3 and WMA format.

When you add a music file to the content, the properties show the `Content Processor` as `Song`, as shown in Figure 5-2.

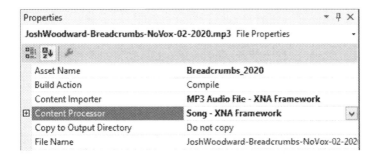

Figure 5-2. *The properties for an MP3 file added to an XNA Content project*

When you compile your Content project, you will find that instead of just a single `.xnb` file being produced for your music file, you will actually have two files: the `.xnb` file and also a `.wma` file. Both of these are required in order for your audio file to play, so copy them both into your game project's Content folder, include both of them in your project, and set both of them to have `Build Action` set to Content and Copy to Output `Directory` set to Copy if newer.

"Song" is in fact the term that MonoGame uses to refer to a piece of music, and its class names reflect this. To load a song, we use the Song class along with the usual `Content.Load` call. In the game framework, we store a collection of songs within the GameHost class inside a `Dictionary` named Songs. Listing 5-4 shows the instruction within a project's `LoadContent` function that loads a song into the framework.

Listing 5-4. Loading a song into the game framework from the Content project

```
// Load our song
Songs.Add("2020", Content.Load<Song>("Breadcrumbs_2020"));
```

Playing the Music

Playing a song is very easy—just call the static `MediaPlayer.Play` function, passing in the Song object that you have loaded. Only one song can play at a time; trying to play a second song will stop the first song from playing.

However, as already mentioned, for Windows Phone we have the tricky issue of whether we are allowed to play music or not because if the device is already playing background music, we must leave it alone.

This is determined using the `MediaPlayer.GameHasControl` property. If it returns true, we have full access to playing music; if it returns false, there is music already playing. Unless the user has explicitly confirmed that they want for our game to take control, we must allow the existing music to continue. Listing 5-5 shows some code from the `LoadContent` function of the `BackgroundMusic` example project that accompanies this chapter. If it detects that media is already playing, it doesn't even attempt to load the song; otherwise, the song is loaded and played.

Listing 5-5. Checking whether the game is allowed to play music and then loading and starting playback

```
// Load songs
if (MediaPlayer.GameHasControl)
{
    // Load our song
    Songs.Add("2020", Content.Load<Song>("Breadcrumbs_2020"));

    // Play the song, repeating
    MediaPlayer.IsRepeating = true;
    MediaPlayer.Play(Songs["2020"]);
}
```

░ **Note**   The GameHasControl function can be called in Windows 8, too, and it always returns true. If you are sharing code between the two platforms, there is no need to make an exception here for Windows 8—the same code will work on both platforms.

Assuming that we can play our music, a number of other methods and properties can be accessed from the MediaPlayer class to affect the way in which the music plays:

- Pause and Stop can be used to halt playback. Just as with sound effects, Pause will remember the position at which the song was paused, allowing it to be later resumed, whereas Stop will discard the position. Either way, you can call the Resume method to start the song playing again.

- IsMuted and Volume provide control over the playback volume. IsMuted is a boolean property that will completely silence the song without pausing it, while Volume allows the playback volume to be faded between silence (0.0) and the current device volume (1.0).

- IsRepeating allows you to set the song to loop endlessly. This looping is often very useful for games because they tend to have background music that plays repeatedly the whole time the game is running.

There is also a property named PlayPosition that is intended to return a TimeSpan object detailing the current playback time through the song. At the time of writing, this property is not working in Windows 8 or Windows Phone and so cannot be used. This will hopefully be fixed in a future release of MonoGame. Until then, you will need to implement your own timing mechanism to keep track of how much of the song has played should you need this information.

Each loaded Song object also has a series of interesting-looking properties that might be interrogated. Unfortunately, it turns out that they aren't too useful after all. Properties are available to provide information on the song's Album, Artist, and Genre, among other things, but when songs are read from a MonoGame project, none of them are populated even if the information is present inside the original MP3 file. One useful property that we can read from the Song is its Duration, which also returns a TimeSpan containing the length of the song.

An Example Game: *Cosmic Rocks* Part III

We could certainly enhance *Cosmic Rocks* by adding some sound effects, so let's do so now.

After giving some thought to the aspects of the game that could use sound effects, we came up with the following list:

- A laser gun sound for when the player fires. It needs to avoid being overpowering because it will be played a lot of times

- A white noise sound for when the player is thrusting

- A sound for hyperspace

- A substantial explosion for when the player's ship is destroyed

- A smaller explosion for when a rock is damaged. Once again, this is a very frequent sound, so it needs to be much quieter than the player explosion.

I spent some time searching through the Creative Commons sound effect sites. After a little hunting, I managed to find a set of samples that I think work very well. All the sounds and the attribution information can be found within the Content project of the CosmicRocksPartIII_Win8 and CosmicRocksPartIII_WP8 projects that accompany this chapter. The attribution information is contained within the `Attribution.txt` file, also included in the Content project. In a finished game, this information would need to be included somewhere inside the game itself (perhaps in an "About" or "Credits" screen, but we've not developed one of those yet, so this will suffice for the time being).

For the most part, the integration of the sound is very straightforward: At the appropriate trigger points (the spaceship's `FireBullet`, `Hyperspace`, and `Explode` functions and the rocks' `DamageRock` function), the game simply needs to call the `Play` method of the appropriate sound effect.

The only sound that is a little more complex is that of the thruster. It is implemented using a looping sound effect, so a `SoundEffectInstance` object is used. This is declared as a class-level variable within the `SpaceshipObject` class and is named `_thrusterSound`.

Two simple functions are present within the spaceship code to support this: `StartThrusterSound` and `StopThrusterSound`. When the game detects that the screen has been touched long enough for thrusting to begin, it calls the first of these functions to start the sound. When contact is released, it calls the second function to stop it again.

The only minor complication is that when the spaceship explodes or enters hyperspace, the thrust is cancelled immediately, without waiting for the player to release contact with the screen. To stop the thruster sound from continuing to play when these events occur, the `Explode` and `Hyperspace` functions both call into `StopThrusterSound`. Remember when you are writing your own games to keep track of looping sounds so that they can be carefully controlled.

One final feature worth noting is the sound of the player's ship exploding. The sound effect used for this is already quite a deep bassy sound, but when the ship explodes, the game actually starts two instances of the sound. The first is played at the default pitch, but the second has a very small random variation to its pitch. These two sounds interfere with one another in a pleasing way when they are played, giving the impression of even more depth to the produced sound. This combination provides a satisfying auditory output for an event as significant as the player losing a life.

Make Some Noise

Sound and music form an important part of a game experience. Carefully crafted sound effects and background music can really bring the game to life and help the player to connect with the action that is taking place on the screen. It is well worth investing some time and effort into choosing the sounds that you include with your game.

Don't overlook the possibility that your player will want to completely disable all of the game sound, however. There are many environments (such as in an office or a public space) where someone might want to have a quick play of your game, but doesn't want to have sound unexpectedly blasting from their device. Be considerate and provide players with an option to switch the sound off quickly and easily should they want to do so.

Summary

- Sound is an important part of any game, a part that will help immerse your players into your game world.

- MonoGame offers sound effects (via the `SoundEffect` class) and music (via the `Song` class). Background music should always be played using the `Song` class, not `SoundEffect`.

- All sound effects are added to the game via the Content project, supplied as `.wav` files.

- The `GameFramework` project offers a `Dictionary` of `SoundEffect` objects, named `SoundEffects`. Sounds can be added to it using the `Content.Load<SoundEffect>` function.

- Sound effects can be played with control over their volume, stereo panning, and pitch.

- For finer control, the `SoundEffectInstance` class can be used. This allows sounds to be started, stopped, and paused, and it also provides control over the volume, stereo panning, and pitch of each sound at all times while it is playing.

- The SoundEffect.MasterVolume property can be used to control the overall volume of all sound effects in your game via one single value.

- The GameFramework project offers a Dictionary of Song objects, named Songs. Music files can be added to it using the Content.Load<Song> function.

- All songs are added to the Content project, usually as either an .mp3 or a .wma file.

- In Windows Phone games, the code must use the GameHasControl property before starting music playback. If the function returns false, the game either withholds playback of its music, or it must first prompt the users to confirm that they wish to switch from their existing music playback to that of your game.

CHAPTER 6

■ ■ ■

Drawing with Vertices and Matrices

For the next few chapters, we will begin to move away from the two-dimensional graphics that we have been using so far and enter the brave new world of the third dimension. Before we get too far, however, there are some new concepts and approaches that you need to become familiar with.

A New Approach to Drawing

Three-dimensional rendering introduces a variety of new challenges: 3-D graphics are rendered as models rather than as simple bitmaps—our brains need to shift into a different gear to keep track of movement in and out of the screen, and we have an entirely different way of telling MonoGame where we want to draw things on the screen.

We will examine some of these changes in this chapter so that you can fully understand the environment in which you need to work in order to draw 3-D graphics. This chapter doesn't get too involved in the actual 3-D rendering—we'll cover that in Chapter 7—but everything contained here is essential to know in order to be able to effectively use MonoGame's 3-D rendering technology.

Let's start by discussing some of the fundamental features of the 3-D rendering environment.

Matrix-Based Positioning

All the graphics that we have rendered in the chapters up to this point have been based around sprites. The graphics were configured by using a series of simple properties to define their position, rotation, scaling, and coloring. This gave us a simple mechanism for putting sprites wherever we needed them, perfect for 2-D games.

As we prepare to render 3-D graphics, we leave this approach behind for the time being (though don't forget about it because we can use sprites and 3-D graphics together, as we'll discuss in Chapter 8). Instead, we use a system based around *matrices*.

Matrices allow us to encode a series of movements and transformations into a compact structure that can then be applied to the graphics that we want to draw. Most of the calculations required to do this are all conveniently wrapped up in handy MonoGame functions, so we don't need to get too involved in their inner workings.

Just like anything else, it might take a little time to become accustomed to thinking with matrix transformations, but, once you do, you will find them a very useful tool. In fact, you might ultimately decide that you prefer them to MonoGame's sprite rendering approach.

Abstract Coordinate System

When we render in 3-D, MonoGame generally uses an *abstract coordinate system* rather than a pixel-based coordinate system like the one used for sprite rendering, meaning that we are not concerned with pixels. Although this might sound like a disadvantage at first, freeing ourselves from pixel coordinates actually turns out to be rather useful.

When we initialize MonoGame for rendering with matrices, we can tell it the dimensions of the screen and the coordinate system will scale to match. Moving a graphic object a certain distance to the right, therefore, moves the same distance regardless of the screen resolution. As a result, when you need to switch between different screen sizes (such as we encounter when switching between Windows 8 and Windows Phone, or even just between different devices on the same platform with differing screen resolutions), none of the rendering code needs to change (as it did when we were rendering sprites).

▓ **Note**   3-D rendering with a pixel-based coordinate system is also an option if you want. This will be discussed in the "Orthographic Projection" section in Chapter 7.

After all the time we have spent with sprites, coming to grips with the 3-D coordinate system requires a slight twist of the brain. First of all, the coordinate (0, 0) is generally right in the center of the screen rather than in the top-left corner. Second, movement along the positive y axis will travel up the screen, as opposed to down for sprites. It can be a nuisance having to keep these two conflicting coordinate systems in your brain, but once you are in the frame of mind for one system over the other, it should be easy to remember which way is up.

Because we are now using a 3-D graphical environment, we actually need to add a third element to our coordinates. The coordinate values we have looked at in the past have been in the form of (x, y), representing the specified distances along the x and y axes. 3-D coordinates are in the form (x, y, z), providing values in the z axis as well as the x and y axes. The z axis represents movement into or out of the screen—literally the third dimension. Positive values on the z axis result in movement toward the player, negative values result in movement into the screen.

Drawing Primitives

When it comes to drawing graphics, MonoGame is actually not able to draw anything more complex than triangles. This might at first seem very restrictive, but, in fact, it is not as you will see when we start to use it in some example projects.

The reason we can create more complex scenes is partly because much more complex shapes can be created by putting lots of triangles together (for example, a rectangle is just two right-angled triangles joined along their long edge) and partly because we can put graphic images onto the triangles. As a simple example, we can display graphics that work along very similar lines to the sprites from earlier chapters by simply rendering rectangles with graphics displayed across them.

When we are drawing, we refer to each triangle as a *surface*. The points that form the triangle are called *vertices*. Figure 6-1 shows two triangular surfaces created using four vertices. Two of the vertices are shared between the triangles.

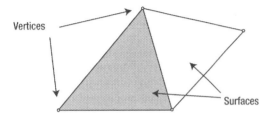

Figure 6-1. *Vertices and surfaces used in MonoGame rendering*

The vertices themselves are not actually displayed by MonoGame, just the surfaces that they define. The vertices are shown in Figure 6-1 just to clarify what they are.

The only drawing primitive available other than the triangle is a straight line.

Textures

Just as we used `Texture2D` objects to provide graphics for our sprites, we can use them to fill the triangles that we are rendering. We have a lot of flexibility to use textures within our applications—in fact, much more so than we had with sprites. We can take small rectangular sections just as we did with sprites, or we can stretch textures in a variety of different ways across the shapes that we draw. We'll look at some of the tricks and techniques that we can use when texturing in the "Applying Textures" section later in this chapter.

MonoGame Is a State Engine

With sprite rendering, each individual call to draw graphics provided all the information needed for drawing to take place, whereas the approach for 3-D rendering is slightly different. MonoGame maintains lots of *state* values for things such as which texture is currently being used for rendering, whether transparency is enabled, whether lighting is switched on, and so on.

In order for our rendering to appear as we expect, each of these states must be set prior to the rendering call. Once a state has been set, it will stay with its value until we decide to change it again.

▓ **Note**   All this actually applies to sprite rendering, too, except that the sprite engine always sets the state values according to the parameters passed to the `SpriteBatch.Draw` and `DrawString` methods. Under the covers, the rendering of sprites is using exactly the same approach as described in this chapter.

Creating Our First Vertex Rendering Project

Before we get into too much more detail, let's see what is involved in setting up a simple project that uses the new rendering approach. Some of the code that we will work through here will be unfamiliar, and we will gloss over some of it for the time being just so that we can get some code running. All this will be explained in much more detail during the rest of this chapter and the following chapters.

The full source code for this project can be found in the `ColoredSquare_Win8` and `ColoredSquare_WP8` examples accompanying this chapter.

Setting Up the Environment

We start off by creating a new MonoGame project, exactly as we have always done. For simplicity, in this example we will work in isolation of the game framework, so don't worry about adding a reference to it or changing the game class derivation; it can continue to derive from MonoGame's `Microsoft.Xna.Framework.Game` class for this example.

We need to add some class-level variables to the game class to manage the scene that we wish to render. The required declarations are shown in Listing 6-1.

Listing 6-1. Variables required for the scene to be rendered

```
private BasicEffect _effect;
private VertexPositionColor[] _vertices = new VertexPositionColor[4];
```

Next, we need to set up these variables ready for them to be used by MonoGame. The code required for this is added to the Initialize function.

The first thing we do here is set up the *projection matrix*. This is something that we will discuss in more detail in the next chapter, but for the moment we can consider its main task as being to set up the abstract coordinate system. As you can see in Listing 6-2, the screen's aspect ratio is determined by dividing the viewport width by its height. This ratio is one of the values used to initialize the matrix. This ensures that objects remain square when drawn on the screen.

Listing 6-2. The beginning of the Initialize function, creating the projection matrix

```
protected override void Initialize()
{
    // Calculate the screen aspect ratio
    float aspectRatio =
            (float)GraphicsDevice.Viewport.Bounds.Width
                                        / GraphicsDevice.Viewport.Bounds.Height;
    // Create a projection matrix
    Matrix projection = Matrix.CreatePerspectiveFieldOfView(MathHelper.ToRadians(45),
                                            aspectRatio, 0.1f, 1000.0f);
```

Note how the projection matrix is being initialized by calling one of the shared methods of the Matrix structure. There are dozens of such methods that allow us to create all kinds of matrices, as you will see as we progress. In this instance, we are using the CreatePerspectiveFieldOfView function to build a matrix. You can see the aspect ratio being passed as a parameter, along with various other values. Don't worry too much about these at the moment. We'll revisit this function in the "Perspective Projection" section in Chapter 7, where we examine everything in much more detail.

The next step is to create the *view matrix*. This can be likened to a camera within the scene, and it controls which objects rendered are visible and where they appear on the screen. Our example project's view matrix is created as shown in Listing 6-3. Once again, this will be discussed in more detail later. The particular matrix function used here, CreateLookAt, is another one that we will look at later on—this time in the "Camera Position and Orientation" section of Chapter 8—so once again don't worry about the detail of what this is doing for now.

Listing 6-3. Initializing the view matrix

```
// Calculate a view matrix (where we are looking from and to)
Matrix view = Matrix.CreateLookAt(new Vector3(0, 0, 10), Vector3.Zero, Vector3.Up);
```

Now we need to create an *effect* object to tell MonoGame how it should render our graphics to the screen. All rendering needs an effect of some kind and several are provided by MonoGame. We'll look at some of the interesting things that they can achieve in Chapter 8, but for the time being we will use the BasicEffect to allow us to render without doing anything fancy.

The effect object is passed a reference to our graphics device when it is instantiated, and we then set a series of properties to control how it will behave. These are some of the state values that were discussed at the beginning of this chapter. Listing 6-4 shows the creation and initialization of the effect object. Note that among the values passed are the projection and view matrices that we have just constructed.

Listing 6-4. Creating and initializing the effect object

```
_effect = new BasicEffect(GraphicsDevice);
_effect.LightingEnabled = false;
_effect.TextureEnabled = false;
_effect.VertexColorEnabled = true;
_effect.Projection = projection;
_effect.View = view;
_effect.World = Matrix.Identity;
```

The environment is now fully initialized. We don't yet have anything to draw, however, so we need to take care of this before we can render anything.

As mentioned earlier, MonoGame expects us to define our objects using vertices. It can then use them to construct the solid triangles that form the graphics we see on the screen.

Vertices can hold various pieces of information. They will always hold a position, but in addition to that they might contain color information, texture information, and other data that affects the way they are drawn. MonoGame provides some built-in configurations for common vertex structures, and the one we will use here is called VertexPositionColor. As its name implies, it stores position and color information, and nothing more.

We will get our example to draw a simple square on the screen. To tell MonoGame about the square, we must set up an array of vertex objects, telling it the position and color of each. Figure 6-2 shows the vertices that we will be using to form this square. The coordinate (0, 0, 0) is right in the middle of the square, and the square extends 2 units across the x and y axes (from -1 to 1 on each axis). Note that the z coordinate is left at 0 for all the vertices so that the square remains flat.

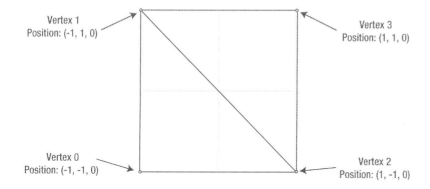

Figure 6-2. *The vertices for the square that we will be rendering*

The vertices are constructed within the program code by setting their coordinates into the _vertices array that we declared back in Listing 6-1. The code for this is shown in Listing 6-5.

Listing 6-5. Setting the vertex positions to form a square

```
_vertices[0].Position = new Vector3(-1, -1, 0);
_vertices[1].Position = new Vector3(-1, 1, 0);
_vertices[2].Position = new Vector3(1, -1, 0);
_vertices[3].Position = new Vector3(1, 1, 0);
```

Just as we used Vector2 structures for providing positions for sprites, we now use Vector3 structures to declare positions in three-dimensional space.

The final part of our initialization is to provide a color for each vertex. For our example, we will give each vertex a different color; MonoGame will provide a smooth color blend between each of the vertices when it renders the triangles. This will produce an attractive effect when it is rendered—and also one that we could not easily achieve using sprites without having to generate a texture containing the different colors. The remaining vertex initialization and the conclusion of the Initialize function are shown in Listing 6-6.

Listing 6-6. Setting the vertex colors

```
_vertices[0].Color = Color.Red;
_vertices[1].Color = Color.White;
_vertices[2].Color = Color.Blue;
_vertices[3].Color = Color.Green;

base.Initialize();
}
```

Rendering the Object

Everything is fully initialized now and we're ready to draw the square to the screen. Because we are only using vertex colors without textures, there is nothing to read in the LoadContent function, so we can leave this alone. We have nothing to update at the moment, either, so let's move straight on to the Draw function.

The screen is cleared (to CornflowerBlue once again) as it was for sprites, but the approach we take to drawing now is very different. Instead of the SpriteBatch object, we use the BasicEffect that we created earlier to manage the drawing for us.

Each effect can contain one or more *techniques*. These are the specific rendering operations that are contained within the effect—the effect acting as a container for one or more techniques. Each of the MonoGame effects we'll be working with contains just a single technique, so we don't need to pay much attention to this. We will just use the default technique that the effect provides for us.

Finally, each technique contains one or more *passes* that perform the actual rendering to the screen. If the rendering of an effect needs to perform multiple updates to the content of the screen in order to render, there will be multiple passes returned from the technique, each of which will need to be drawn. BasicEffect uses only one pass, but, just for good form, we will set our code to loop for all passes that might be returned from the effect in order to save confusion later on when we do encounter multiple-pass effects.

Bearing all that in mind, the code required to render the square is shown in Listing 6-7. Once the pass has been determined, its Apply method is called to tell MonoGame to activate it. The code then calls DrawUserPrimitives in order for our triangles to be drawn, telling it the type of primitive that it is rendering and passing various details about what to draw. The parameters for the DrawUserPrimitives function are as follows:

- primitiveType contains the type of primitive that we wish to draw. In this case, we draw a TriangleStrip. The available primitives will be discussed in the next section.

- vertexData allows us to pass the array of vertices that we have defined.

- vertexOffset is a value that allows us to start considering the vertices at a position within the array other than its start. We are not using this, so we just pass 0.

- primitiveCount is the number of primitives that we are drawing. As we specified that we are drawing triangles, setting this to 2 means to draw 2 triangles. Remember that this is counting primitives, not vertices.

The code for the Draw function is shown in Listing 6-7.

Listing 6-7. Drawing the colored square

```
protected override void Draw(GameTime gameTime)
{
    GraphicsDevice.Clear(Color.CornflowerBlue);

    foreach (EffectPass pass in _effect.CurrentTechnique.Passes)
    {
        // Apply the pass
        pass.Apply();
        // Draw the square
        GraphicsDevice.DrawUserPrimitives(PrimitiveType.TriangleStrip, _vertices, 0, 2);
    }

    base.Draw(gameTime);
}
```

The resulting graphic can be seen in Figure 6-3.

Figure 6-3. *The rendered output from the ColoredSquare example*

Notice how MonoGame has handled the colors within the rendered square. Each vertex is colored exactly as we had requested, but between them the renderer performs a smooth fade between the colors. This is known as *color interpolation* and is something that you will see again in the future. Any vertex parameters such as colors that differ from one vertex to the next will result in a smooth fade as MonoGame renders between them. This can be very useful and attractive, as this example demonstrates.

Moving the Object

The section titled "Understanding Matrix Transformations" later in this chapter will full cover the approach to moving our objects, but to make things a little more interesting than a static square, let's take a quick preview and get our square to spin around on the screen.

To achieve this, we first need to track the rotation angle. We will do this by adding a class-level float variable named _angle, and we will update it by 1 degree each update, as shown in Listing 6-8.

Listing 6-8. Updating the angle of the square

```
protected override void Update(GameTime gameTime)
{
    _angle += MathHelper.ToRadians(1);

    base.Update(gameTime);
}
```

To apply the angle to the square, we need to update the world matrix (full details of which will also be provided in the "Understanding Matrix Transformations" section). Because we want to rotate the square, we need to give it a rotation matrix. MonoGame's Matrix class provides various methods for creating such a matrix and the one we will select for our example is the CreateRotationZ function. This function accepts a single parameter (the rotation angle) and returns a matrix ready for us to use.

The updated code to draw the square with rotation is shown in Listing 6-9.

Listing 6-9. Rotating and drawing the colored square

```
protected override void Draw(GameTime gameTime)
{
    GraphicsDevice.Clear(Color.CornflowerBlue);

    // Set the world matrix so that the square rotates
    _effect.World = Matrix.CreateRotationZ(_angle);

    foreach (EffectPass pass in _effect.CurrentTechnique.Passes)
    {
        // Apply the pass
        pass.Apply();
        // Draw the square
        GraphicsDevice.DrawUserPrimitives(PrimitiveType.TriangleStrip, _vertices, 0, 2);
    }

    base.Draw(gameTime);
}
```

Note that the call to DrawUserPrimitives that is actually drawing the square is completely unchanged; it is the state of the effect that is causing the object to rotate, not the instruction to draw. This is clearly different from the approach we used with sprite-based rendering.

Adding Some Sparkle

Of course, this rotating square only scratches the surface of what we can achieve with MonoGame. Let's make a simple change to the project that results in a dramatic and attractive enhancement to the displayed graphics.

If we modify the Draw code so that it is as shown in Listing 6-10, we will see that it has a significant effect on the graphics that are drawn to the screen, as shown in Figure 6-4. The code for this can be found in the NestedSquares_Win8 and NestedSquares_WP8 example projects.

Listing 6-10. Rendering the square in the NestedSquares example project

```
protected override void Draw(GameTime gameTime)
{
    GraphicsDevice.Clear(Color.CornflowerBlue);

    // Reset the world matrix
    _effect.World = Matrix.Identity;

    // Loop for each square
    for (int i = 0; i < 20; i++)
    {
        foreach (EffectPass pass in _effect.CurrentTechnique.Passes)
        {
            // Apply a further rotation
            _effect.World = Matrix.CreateRotationZ(_angle) * _effect.World;
            // Scale the object so that it is shown slightly smaller
            _effect.World = Matrix.CreateScale(0.85f) * _effect.World;

            // Apply the pass
            pass.Apply();
            // Draw the square
            GraphicsDevice.DrawUserPrimitives
                            (PrimitiveType.TriangleStrip, _vertices, 0, 2);
        }
    }

    base.Draw(gameTime);
}
```

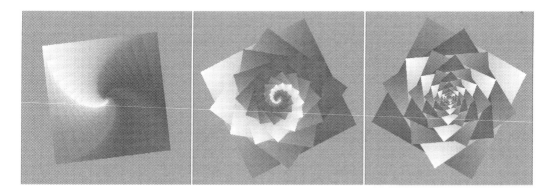

Figure 6-4. *The rendered output from the NestedSquares example*

The screen shots in Figure 6-4 sadly don't do justice to the effect of the project in operation; it is much better in motion than in still images, but this gives an idea of the patterns that this tiny piece of code is able to generate.

All that the loop is doing is drawing 20 shapes instead of one, each of which is slightly smaller than the last and rotated to a different angle. The scale and rotate operations are cumulative, meaning that although the first (largest) square is rotated by the angle specified in _angle, the second square is rotated by double this angle, the third by three times the angle, and so on.

Tinting Objects

One of the useful features we explored when using sprites is the ability to tint the sprite into a different color. The same facility is available when rendering objects using vertices, too.

The effect object has a property named DiffuseColor, which allows the tint color to be set. This property defaults to white, which leaves the colors of our objects unchanged, but can be modified to any color that we desire. The color is applied to our vertex colors just as it was for sprites: It takes the red, green, and blue values of each vertex color and represents them as a value between 0 and 1. Each of them is then multiplied by the corresponding color element within DiffuseColor and the resulting values used for the final vertex color.

Setting DiffuseColor to black will therefore result in all vertex colors becoming black, too. Setting DiffuseColor to red will remove all green and blue color information from the vertices, resulting in just the red color elements surviving.

Unlike the color properties we have seen so far, however, DiffuseColor is implemented as a Vector3 structure rather than as a Color. Each of the three elements within the Vector3 relates to one of the color elements in a color—the x element stores the amount of red, the y element stores the amount of green, and the z element stores the amount of blue. All three of these measure color using a float value in the range of 0 to 1, rather than an integer from 0 to 255.

To make our lives easier, MonoGame has taken into account the need to translate color values between the Color structure and the Vector3 structure and it has provided built-in functions to accomplish this.

To convert a Color into a Vector3, simply call its ToVector3 method. The resulting vector values will match those of the color. A simple example of this can be seen in Listing 6-11.

Listing 6-11. Converting a Color structure into a Vector3

```
Vector3 myColorVector;
myColorVector = Color.PeachPuff.ToVector3();
```

To convert a Vector3 into a Color, create a new Color and pass the Vector3 as a parameter to its constructor. This will produce a color whose values match that of the vector. A simple example of this is shown in Listing 6-12.

Listing 6-12. Converting a Vector3 structure into a Color

```
Vector3 myColorVector = new Vector3(1.0f, 0.8f, 0.2f);
Color myColor;
myColor = new Color(myColorVector);
```

Try modifying the NestedSquares example project so that the _effect.DiffuseColor is set prior to rendering the squares in the Draw method and see the effect that it has on the generated graphics.

Being a Vector3, however, gives no opportunity to set an alpha value. When we tinted sprites, alpha values were also available and allowed us to control the transparency of the sprites that were being rendered. In the vertex-rendering approach, it is still possible to change the alpha of rendered objects, but this is controlled using a separate property. This will be discussed in the Object Transparency section later in this chapter.

Understanding Matrix Transformations

Let's take a closer look at what is happening when we move the shape that we are drawing.

Within MonoGame, the position at which we will draw objects is tracked using the *world matrix*. A matrix is a set of values, arranged in rows and columns, which can be applied to the coordinates of our vertices in order to move them around on the screen.

By combining multiple matrices, movement operations can be grouped together. For example, we might want to move an object 1 unit to the right and then rotate it by 45 degrees. To do this, we start with an empty matrix, apply the movement matrix, and then the rotation matrix. The resulting matrix can be used to transform any vertex coordinate so that it moves 1 unit to the right and rotates by 45 degrees. There is no need to separately apply the movement and rotation to each vertex because the transformation matrix will perform both steps in one calculation.

This allows for transformations to be built up into greater and greater levels of complexity, but it doesn't make calculating the point onscreen at which each vertex will be drawn any more difficult or processor-intensive.

Exactly how these matrices are created, manipulated, and applied is not something that we will cover in any detail in this book. There are plenty of online references that will explain this subject in further detail; for example, see http://en.wikipedia.org/wiki/Matrix_(mathematics) for information on what a matrix is, how matrices are constructed, and how arithmetic operations are performed. See http://tinyurl.com/matrixtransform to read about how matrix transformations work at a mathematical level.

We will discuss how matrix transformations are actually used in practical terms. Though the numerical representations of transformations might be somewhat abstract, visualizing what each transformation will do is a bit easier.

Setting the Identity Matrix

We have already discussed the fact that MonoGame maintains state for lots of properties that affect how it will render to the screen and that one of these is the world matrix. Each time we begin drawing, a world matrix of some description will already be set, usually from a previous call to Draw, and we won't necessarily have any idea what it contains. We should therefore always ensure that the world matrix is properly set prior to performing any drawing.

In order to reset this matrix to its initial state, we set the matrix to a preset set of values called the *identity matrix*. This ensures that any rendering that takes place will initially be centered at the origin—at coordinate (0, 0, 0)—and will not be rotated or scaled at all.

We can obtain an identity matrix at any time from the static Matrix.Identity property. To render objects without any transformation, set the identify matrix as the effect's world matrix prior to applying the effect passes. You can see this being used at the beginning of Listing 6-10.

A square with a width and height of one unit can be seen in Figure 6-5 after the identity matrix has been applied. It is directly centered on the origin of the coordinate system.

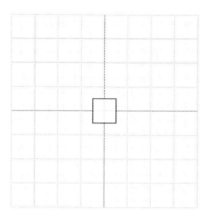

Figure 6-5. *A unit square rendered after a call to LoadIdentity*

Applying Translation Transformations

In the terminology of matrix transformations, moving an object along one or more of the axes is called a *translation*. The shape, size, and angle of the object are entirely unchanged; the object is just moved left or right, up or down, and in or out of the world to a new position.

Figure 6-6 shows the effect of a translation matrix. The image on the left shows the unit square in position after the identity matrix has been loaded; the image on the right shows the same square after it has been translated 3 units in the x axis and –2 units in the y axis. (For simplicity, we will ignore the z axis for the moment, but transformation along the z axis is achieved in exactly the same way as for the x and y axes.)

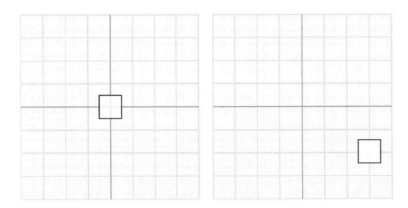

Figure 6-6. *Translation of a square along the x and y axes*

To obtain a translation matrix, call the static `Matrix.CreateTranslation` function. This function has a couple of overloads. The first overload requires three parameters (the translation distance for the x, y, and z axes, respectively); the second accepts a single `Vector3` parameter.

Both overloads have their uses depending on the way you want to specify your movement. The `Vector3` approach is very handy because it allows a movement path to be stored as a vector (just as we did in two dimensions for the rocks in the *Cosmic Rocks* examples from the previous chapters) and easily transformed into a translation matrix.

▓ **Note**   In addition to the overloads, `Matrix.CreateTranslation` function has two different calling styles: one that returns its generated matrix as a return value from the function, and another that returns the matrix in an output parameter. All the other matrix generation functions share these two approaches. Feel free to use whichever you are more comfortable with, but in the text of this book we will use the versions that return matrices as their return values.

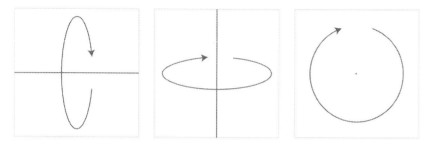

Figure 6-7. *Rotations around the x, y, and z axes*

Applying Rotation Transformations

We can also rotate the objects that we draw. Objects can be rotated around any of the three axes, as shown in Figure 6-7.

Rotation around the x axis rotates around a horizontal line drawn across the screen. If you held a sheet of paper in front of you so that you were looking directly at the flat face of the paper, rotation on the x axis would rotate the paper so that the bottom edge was brought toward you and the top edge away, resulting in you looking at the paper's front edge.

Rotation on the y axis is exactly the same, but rotating around a vertical line.

Z axis rotation rotates around a line that traces a path into and out of the screen. This is the axis of rotation that we have used in the ColoredSquare and NestedSquares example projects.

To obtain a matrix to rotate around one of these axes, call one of the following static functions:

- `Matrix.CreateRotationX` to rotate around the x axis

- `Matrix.CreateRotationY` to rotate around the y axis

- `Matrix.CreateRotationZ` to rotate around the z axis

All three functions require the rotation angle to be passed as a parameter (in radians).

▓ **Note** A positive rotation around the z axis will result in counterclockwise rotation. To rotate clockwise, simply negate the rotation angle.

Rotation around other axes can also be achieved by using the `Matrix.CreateFromAxisAngle` function. It requires two parameters: an *axis vector* defining the line around which the rotation is to take place and the rotation angle.

To calculate the axis vector, imagine the rotation axis as a line that passes through the origin point at (0, 0, 0). Then determine a point that is on that line and provide its coordinate as the values for the vector.

For example, if we want to rotate around a line that slopes upward at a 45-degree angle, we can visualize it passing through the origin point, as shown in Figure 6-8. The figure shows a point that has been selected on the line at coordinate (2, 2, 0), though any point on the line would be fine. This coordinate forms the values for the axis vector.

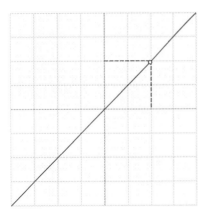

Figure 6-8. *Calculating a rotation vector*

One important detail must be taken into account for the axis vector, however: It must be normalized. If it is not, the objects will warp and distort as they rotate around it. Listing 6-13 provides an example of using the CreateFromAxisAngle function to rotate around the line from Figure 6-8.

Listing 6-13. Rotating around an arbitrary axis

```
Vector3 axisVector = new Vector3(2, 2, 0);
axisVector.Normalize();
_effect.World = Matrix.CreateFromAxisAngle(axisVector, _angle);
```

Applying Scaling Transformations

The last of the transformations that we will be working with for the time being is for scaling the objects that we render. Scaling matrices can be either *uniform*, in which case the object scales by the same amount on all three axes; or *nonuniform*, in which case each axis scales by a different amount.

Figure 6-9 shows an object in its identity location on the left with a uniform scale of 2.0 in the middle, and then on the right with a scale of 4.0 on the x axis and 0.5 on the y axis.

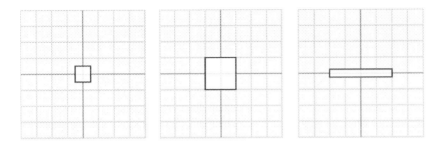

Figure 6-9. *Scaling transformations*

To obtain a scaling matrix, call the static `Matrix.CreateScale` function. It has three calling methods: It can be passed a single `float` to perform a uniform scale; it can be passed three `floats` to perform a nonuniform scale with the values provided for the x, y, and z axes; or it can be passed a `Vector3` containing the values for nonuniform scaling.

Passing a scale value of 0 for any of the axes will squash the shape on that axis so that it is completely flat. It can be easy to accidentally pass this when you had intended to leave the scaling unchanged for an axis. For any axis that you want to leave unchanged when scaling, pass a value of 1.

Negative scale values are also permitted. These will cause the object to flip over so that the vertices appear on the opposite side of the negatively scaled axis.

Applying Multiple Transformations

To apply a single transformation to our objects, we can simply obtain the required matrix and set it into the effect's `World` matrix property. We have already seen several examples of this.

Any practical application of matrix transformations will quickly find that setting the matrix for just a single transformation is insufficient, however. If we need to perform multiple transformations at once (for example, perhaps we need to move the object to another point within the world and then rotate it), we need some way to combine these transformations together.

Fortunately, matrix transformations are perfectly suited to this task. We can combine two or more transformations by simply multiplying the matrices together. The resulting matrix will contain the effects of both of the input matrices.

The different types of translation can have an effect on each other that might not at first be obvious, so let's first look at the effects of applying multiple transformations. We will then come back and look at how they are implemented in code.

Rotating Objects

When we rotate an object, we actually rotate its entire coordinate system because we are transforming the entire world, not just the object itself. If the identity matrix is loaded, the world coordinates are reset so that the origin point (0, 0, 0) is in the center and no scaling or rotation is applied. Once we begin to transform this matrix, the coordinate system moves around accordingly.

Objects always move relative to the transformed coordinate system, not to the identity coordinate system. This means that if we rotate an object by 45 degrees around the z axis and then translate it along the y axis, it will actually move diagonally onscreen rather than vertically. The rotation has changed the direction of the axes within the world coordinate system.

The effects of this rotation can be seen in Figure 6-10. On the left is the usual unit square at the identity position. In the middle, we rotate it by 45 degrees around the z axis (counterclockwise). The pale lines show the x and y axes in the identity coordinate system, whereas the darker diagonal lines show the x and y axes for the transformed world coordinate system. On the right, we translate it along its y axis. Observe that it has moved diagonally relative to the identity coordinates, though it has followed the transformed world y axis. Also note that the world coordinate system follows the translation, too. The coordinate (0, 0, 0) moves along with the translations that are applied to the world matrix.

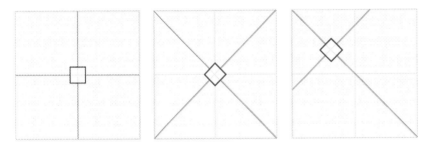

Figure 6-10. *Rotation and translation in the world coordinate system*

This sequence of updates brings us to another important feature of matrix transformations: The order in which they are applied is significant. In Figure 6-10, we first rotated and then translated our object. If we instead swap over the order in which we apply these so that we translate and then rotate it, the coordinate system for the translation would still be aligned with the identity coordinate system, so the movement on the screen would be vertical. This is shown in Figure 6-11, which contains exactly the same transformations but performed with the translation before the rotation.

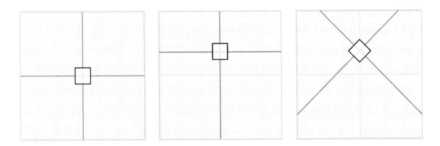

Figure 6-11. *Translation before rotation*

As you can see, the object ends up in a different place if we translate it first.

This is actually very easy to visualize. Imagine that you are standing in place of the square object in these diagrams. You are initially standing at the origin of the identity coordinate system, looking along the positive y axis (up the screen).

You then decide to rotate 45 degrees counterclockwise, just as in Figure 6-10. You are still facing straight ahead of your body, but relative to the identity coordinates, you are now looking diagonally. If you now take a few paces forward, you are walking diagonally in terms of the identity coordinates but straight ahead in terms of your own position within the world.

If you hold your arms out to the sides, they will be pointing along the x axis relative to your position but are once again at a diagonal angle relative to the identity coordinates.

Any time you want to visualize the transformations that you are applying, think of this same scenario and apply each transformation in sequence relative to yourself in the world. It should then be easy to see the sequence of transformations that you need to apply to get from one place to another. (It gets slightly harder to visualize in three dimensions, but just imagine you have wings or a jet pack.)

Hopefully, this makes the effects of cumulative transformations clear. Always remember that when you transform an object, the transformation will be relative to the existing transformed coordinates, not to those of the identity coordinate system.

Scaling Objects

When we scale an object, the transformation once again has an effect on the world coordinate system. If we scale an object so that its size doubles, a movement of one unit in the x axis in the transformed world coordinate system will correspond to a movement of two units relative to the identity coordinate system.

If you simply want to draw an object at a different size but without affecting its position, remember to perform the scale transformation after all the translations have been completed to avoid affecting the movement distances.

Applying Multiple Transformations in MonoGame

We know that multiple transformations can be combined by multiplying them together, so let's see some sample code to achieve this in MonoGame.

The first transformation that we want to use can be obtained directly by calling the appropriate static `Matrix` function. From that point on, subsequent transformations must be obtained and multiplied with the existing calculated matrix.

To translate an object two units along the y axis and then rotate it by a specified angle, we would use the code shown in Listing 6-14. It causes the object to rotate on the spot a short distance away from the center of the screen.

Listing 6-14. Multiple transformations: translation and then rotation

```
// First translate...
_effect.World = Matrix.CreateTranslation(0, 2, 0);
// ...then rotate
_effect.World = Matrix.CreateRotationZ(_angle) * _effect.World;
```

Notice the order of multiplication: The new transformation is on the left of the multiplication symbol, and the existing matrix is on the right. Unlike multiplication of simple numbers, matrix multiplication is not commutative, which is why the order of transformations is significant. If we multiply matrix A by matrix B, we will get results different from multiplying matrix B by matrix A.

Alternatively, we can swap the order of these transformations so that we first rotate and then translate along the (rotated) y axis, as shown in Listing 6-15.

Listing 6-15. Multiple transformations: rotation and then translation

```
// First rotate...
_effect.World = Matrix.CreateRotationZ(_angle);
// ...then rotate
_effect.World = Matrix.CreateTranslation(0, 2, 0) * _effect.World;
```

Even though we are generating the same matrices with the same parameter, the resulting behavior is different. Instead of spinning on the spot, the object now rotates around a circular path, centered at the identity origin and with a radius of two units (because this is the distance that the object was translated).

Try plugging each of them into the `ColoredSquare` project in place of the existing matrix code to see their effects.

We are not limited to using transformation types just once within a transformation sequence, of course, and some movement paths will require the same transformation to be applied repeatedly at different stages of the calculation.

For example, let's get the object to trace a circle as in Listing 6-15, but this time the circle will be away from the identity origin and the object itself will remain "upright" without rotating at all. This is achieved using the transformations shown in Listing 6-16.

Listing 6-16. Repeatedly transforming to achieve a more complex movement path

```
// First translate to the center of the circular path
_effect.World = Matrix.CreateTranslation(0, 3, 0);
// Rotate the object towards the current position on the circular path
_effect.World = Matrix.CreateRotationZ(_angle) * _effect.World;
// Translate to the edge of the circle
_effect.World = Matrix.CreateTranslation(0, 2, 0) * _effect.World;
// ...then rotate back to an upright position
_effect.World = Matrix.CreateRotationZ(-_angle) * _effect.World;
```

This time the circular path is centered at (0, 3, 0) because we translate to here before rotating. Then the object is rotated toward the point on the circle at which it will be rendered. The object is then translated to the edge of the circle; as the translation is two units along the (rotated) y axis, this will be the radius of the circle. Finally, to keep the object upright, it is rotated back by its angle. This cancels out the rotation that was applied in the original rotation. The original rotation, therefore, results in having an effect on the position of the object but not its final angle.

As you can see, this entire series of events is eventually contained in the single _effect.World matrix. There is no limit to the number of calculations that can be accumulated into a single matrix in this way.

Specifying Vertex Positions

You might recall that when we looked at the ColoredSquare example back in Listing 6-5, the code defined the square's vertices by specifying four vertices with coordinates at (–1, –1, 0), (1, –1, 0), (–1, 1, 0), and (1, 1, 0). These coordinates are, as you may well now be able to guess, interpreted relative to the world matrix, not the identity coordinate system.

When we use transformations to manipulate the world matrix, this resulting matrix is applied to each individual vertex when rendering, which causes the object to actually move onscreen. Because the coordinate system has been moved, rotated, and scaled relative to the world, all the vertex positions are transformed in exactly the same way. We can, therefore, define any shape we like using these vertex coordinates and it will move around the screen as specified by our matrix transformations.

Drawing Multiple Objects at Different Positions

The example code in the projects we have looked at has always set the world matrix before looping through the effect passes and calling the Apply method on each. This is important because it is the world matrix that is present at the point of calling Apply that will be used for the subsequently rendered objects.

If you want to draw multiple objects within the same call to Draw (as you will undoubtedly want to!), you need to ensure that the calls to the EffectPass.Apply function are made after each object's world matrix is set into the effect. Any changes made to the world matrix after this will be ignored.

There are two sequences with which this can be implemented. The first is to loop for the effect passes for each object, repeating the loop for each subsequent object. The second is to loop through the passes just once, applying each one multiple times and drawing each object after its matrix has been applied.

The first of these approaches can be seen in Listing 6-17. The effect loop is present twice, once for each of the objects being rendered. Each effect pass is applied once per loop.

Listing 6-17. Drawing multiple objects with an effect pass loop per object

```
// Draw the first object
foreach (EffectPass pass in _effect.CurrentTechnique.Passes)
{
    // Set the world matrix
    _effect.World = Matrix.CreateRotationZ(_angle);
```

```
    // Apply the pass and draw
    pass.Apply();
    GraphicsDevice.DrawUserPrimitives
                            (PrimitiveType.TriangleStrip, _vertices, 0, 2);
}

// Draw the second object
foreach (EffectPass pass in _effect.CurrentTechnique.Passes)
{
    // Set the world matrix
    _effect.World = Matrix.CreateRotationZ(_angle * 2);
    // Apply and draw
    pass.Apply();
    GraphicsDevice.DrawUserPrimitives
                            (PrimitiveType.TriangleStrip, _vertices, 0, 2);
}
```

The second approach is shown in Listing 6-18. It loops through the effect passes just once, but it applies each one multiple times (once per object being rendered).

Listing 6-18. Drawing multiple objects with a single effect pass loop

```
// Draw the objects
foreach (EffectPass pass in _effect.CurrentTechnique.Passes)
{
    // Set the world matrix for the first object
    _effect.World = Matrix.CreateRotationZ(_angle);
    // Apply the pass and draw
    pass.Apply();
    GraphicsDevice.DrawUserPrimitives
                            (PrimitiveType.TriangleStrip, _vertices, 0, 2);

    // Set the world matrix for the second object
    _effect.World = Matrix.CreateRotationZ(_angle * 2);
    // Apply the pass and draw
    pass.Apply();
    GraphicsDevice.DrawUserPrimitives
                            (PrimitiveType.TriangleStrip, _vertices, 0, 2);
}
```

These code samples produce exactly the same visual results. The one you use is entirely up to you; you might find that one approach or another better fits in with the object structure that you are rendering. The important thing to remember is that the pass.Apply method needs to be called each time an updated world matrix needs to be observed.

There is one area where the two approaches will result in a performance difference, however. When we begin to apply textures to our objects (which we will examine in the "Applying Textures" section later in this chapter), we will need to pass the texture graphics to the graphics hardware each time we draw an object, just as we did in earlier chapters when working with textured 2-D objects. As we saw then, moving the graphic around in memory is a relatively expensive process because graphic files can be quite large.

We can, therefore, optimize our rendering by loading each texture into the graphics hardware just once and then drawing all objects that use that texture together. The next texture can then be loaded and all of its objects drawn. This way, we load each texture only once per draw, rather than potentially once per object.

The second rendering approach, shown in Listing 6-18, is, therefore, potentially less efficient for textured objects. If we have multiple passes in our effect and each of the objects rendered has a different texture, we will end up alternating between the two textures. The first approach in Listing 6-17 deals with the object in its entirety before moving on to the next object, allowing its texture to be used by all the passes without needing it to be reloaded.

Drawing Primitives

All the drawing in our examples has been handled by making a call to the GraphicsDevice.DrawUserPrimitives function. The first parameter passed to this function, the primitiveType parameter, has always been PrimitiveType.TriangleStrip. There are several values that we can pass here, so let's take a look at each one and discuss what it does and how it is used.

Drawing Lines

There are two different mechanisms provided for drawing lines on the screen: PrimitiveType.LineList and PrimitiveType.LineStrip.

LineList will work through the supplied vertices, taking each pair as the beginning and end coordinate of a line. The lines do not need to be connected (and, indeed, if they are, it might be more efficient to use the LineStrip drawing mode). The DrawUserPrimitive primitiveCount parameter specifies how many lines are to be drawn. Because each line requires two vertices, the vertex array must contain at least twice the number of entries as the specified primitive count.

Figure 6-12 shows the lines drawn between four vertices using the LineList mode primitive type and a primitive count of 2.

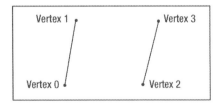

Figure 6-12. *Drawing lines with the LineList primitive type*

LineStrip is similar, but instead of working through pairs of vertices, it takes each new vertex and draws a line between it and the previous vertex. The result is a line drawn between all the specified vertices, as shown in Figure 6-13. The first line requires two vertices, but each subsequent line requires just one more. As a result, the vertex array must contain at least primitiveCount + 1 elements.

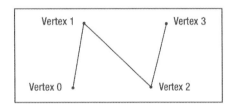

Figure 6-13. *Drawing lines with the LineStrip primitive type*

MonoGame does not offer a line drawing mode that automatically reconnects the final vertex back to the first vertex (to create a *line loop*). If such rendering is required, a final additional vertex will need to be added to the end of the LineStrip with a position that matches that of the first vertex.

You can easily see the effects of drawing lines by modifying the ColoredSquare project to use the line primitive types instead of its existing TriangleStrip type. Notice how the vertex colors are still observed when drawing lines and the line color fades between the colors of each connected vertex.

There is no facility for setting the width of the line—all lines will be drawn with single-pixel thickness. If you need to draw lines thicker than this, you will need to simulate lines by drawing long, thin rectangles formed from a pair of triangles instead.

Drawing Triangles

The remaining drawing primitives provide two different methods for creating triangles. Triangles are by far the most common type of object drawn in MonoGame, so these primitive types will become very familiar. The available triangle primitive modes are PrimitiveType.TriangleList and PrimitiveType.TriangleStrip.

The TriangleList primitive takes each set of three vertices as an individual triangle, allowing multiple isolated triangles to be drawn. Figure 6-14 shows how six vertices are used to build two triangles using this mode. Because each triangle requires three vertices, the vertex array must contain at least three times the number of entries as the specified primitive count.

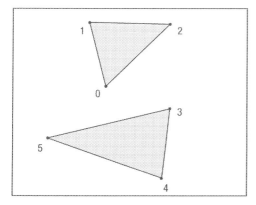

Figure 6-14. *Drawing triangles with the TriangleList primitive type*

The TriangleStrip primitive reuses vertices within the vertex array to create multiple triangles, each of which shares an edge with the previous triangle. The first three vertices are used to create the first triangle; after that, the next triangle is formed by removing the earliest vertex in the triangle and replacing it with the next vertex in the array. The first triangle is, therefore, formed from vertices 0, 1, and 2; the second triangle from vertices 1, 2, and 3; the third triangle from vertices 2, 3, and 4; and so on.

As long as you can arrange your triangles so that they share their edges in this way, the triangle strip is a very efficient way of drawing because the shared vertices need to be transformed only once even though they are used by as many as three different triangles.

Figure 6-15 shows an example using the TriangleStrip to join a series of vertices. The first triangle requires three vertices, but each subsequent triangle requires just one more. As a result, the vertex array must contain at least primitiveCount + 2 elements.

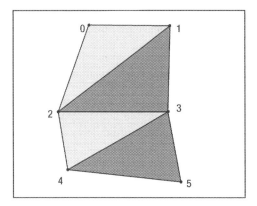

Figure 6-15. *Drawing triangles with the TriangleStrip primitive type*

The `TriangleStrip` mode is perfectly suited for drawing squares and rectangles because they are formed from two triangles that share an edge. As more complex objects are encountered, however, the ability to model them using triangle strips soon becomes difficult or impossible, and for them a triangle list will be required instead.

If you have used earlier versions of XNA prior to using MonoGame or if you are familiar with DirectX or OpenGL, you might be expecting to find a further primitive type known as a *triangle fan*. It defines a series of triangles that all share a single vertex, allowing that vertex to be calculated just once for the entire object. Support for triangle fans was removed in XNA version 4.0 (on which MonoGame is based), so this primitive type is no longer available for use.

When you are defining your triangles, you will need to be aware of MonoGame's *hidden surface culling*. This is a feature that prevents it from having to draw unnecessary triangles, particularly in 3-D graphic objects. We'll discuss this in more detail in the "Hidden Surface Culling" section in the next chapter, but, for now, just be aware that you need to ensure that the vertices of your triangle are defined so that they are in clockwise order when you look at the triangle front on. You will observe that both of the triangles shown in Figure 6-14 are defined in this way.

For triangle strips, however, this would appear to present a problem: As each triangle shares its vertices with the previous triangle, the points alternate between clockwise and counterclockwise order. This can be seen in Figure 6-15: The first triangle (consisting of vertices 0, 1, and 2) is defined in clockwise order, but the second (vertices 1, 2, and 3) is counterclockwise. MonoGame realizes this and takes it into account automatically; the important thing is to ensure that the *first* triangle in a triangle strip is defined in a clockwise direction.

Drawing Points

Just like the triangle fan, support for drawing points (individual pixels) to the screen using vertices was removed in XNA version 4.0, so there is no support for this in MonoGame either. To simulate drawing points, you will need to instead draw very small triangles, rectangles, or lines.

Point drawing is generally of limited use anyway, particularly with the extremely high resolution displays on some tablet and desktop devices these days, so this will hopefully not present too much of a problem for your games.

Applying Textures

Colored shapes are all very nice, but they're not generally what we need when we are creating a game. For our games, we want to be able to display graphics onscreen. How do we do this with MonoGame when rendering with vertices?

Fortunately, it is very easy to do so. First, we need to load a texture and then we tell MonoGame to display that texture on the triangles that it draws. The following sections show how this is done. The `TexturedSquare_Win8` and `TexturedSquare_WP8` example projects that accompany this chapter contain code that uses the techniques detailed here.

Loading Graphics

Even though we can render 3-D objects when we render with vertices, the graphics that we apply to them are still 2-D bitmap graphics. The graphics are wrapped around the 3-D objects as if they were stickers that we are applying to a solid object.

Textures are therefore added to the XNA Content project and loaded, ready for use by our 3-D objects using the exact same code as we used when loading textures for sprites.

Alpha channels and color keys can still be used with textures just as they were with sprites, but there is a wide range of different ways that we can process them. These will be discussed in the "Using Transparency and Alpha Blending" section later in this chapter.

Setting the Active Texture

When we are ready to render with our texture, we first need to instruct MonoGame to use the texture. Just as with the other state properties inside MonoGame, it will remember the specified texture until we tell it to use a different texture. The code in Listing 6-19 tells MonoGame to use our loaded texture for subsequent textured objects.

Listing 6-19. Loading and activating a texture

```
// Load our texture
_texture = Content.Load<Texture2D>("Grapes");
// Set it as the active texture within our effect
_effect.Texture = _texture;
```

Applying the Texture to an Object

When we rendered triangles using colored vertices, we specified a color for each vertex. Now that we are rendering with textures, we instead tell each vertex to map to a point within the texture instead.

You will recall that sprite rendering allowed us to render either the entire texture across the surface of the sprite or a subsection of the texture. When we render using vertex buffers, we can also render subsections of the texture, although we achieve this in a different way. We can also distort or stretch the texture in a variety of ways that were not available to sprites.

Just as coordinates on the screen are measured using axes called x and y, textures have axes called u and v. The u axis covers the distance across the width of a texture, whereas the v axis covers the distance across its height.

▓ **Note** If you are familiar with OpenGL, you might expect the texture axes to be called *s* and *t*. Although MonoGame uses the letters *u* and *v* instead, the function and purpose of these axes are identical to the *s* and *t* axes in OpenGL.

Regardless of the resolution of the graphic that has been loaded, the u and v coordinates will scale from 0 to 1, where 0 represents the left edge of the u axis and the top edge of the v axis, and 1 represents the right edge of the u axis and the bottom edge of the v axis, as shown in Figure 6-16. This is a very useful feature because it lets you switch between high- and low-resolution textures without needing to modify your code in any way.

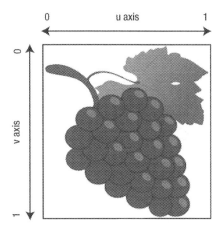

Figure 6-16. *The u and v axes for texture coordinates*

When we want to draw using texture mapping, we provide a (u, v) coordinate for each vertex that tells it the position within the texture that should be applied at that vertex. Just as colors are interpolated between the vertices of rendered objects, so too are texture coordinates. The area inside the triangle formed by the texture coordinates will be stretched to fill the triangle formed onscreen by the vertex coordinates. This can be seen in Figure 6-17, which shows a triangle along with its vertex coordinates, the positions of those coordinates on a texture, and the resulting textured triangle.

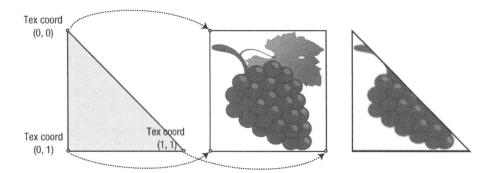

Figure 6-17. *A triangle and its texture coordinates, their positions on a texture, and the resulting textured triangle*

Although the vertices are specified in three dimensions and, therefore, contain three values per vertex, texture coordinates are reading from a 2-D image. So, we provide just two values per vertex: the u and v coordinates for that vertex to use. They are provided to each vertex in a Vector2 structure. Because the Vector2 uses X and Y for its property names, we will use the X property to store the texture's u value and the Y property to store the texture's v value. The value is stored in the TextureCoordinate property of each vertex.

But hold on—the vertex structure that we have been using doesn't have a TextureCoordinate property! This is because we have been using the VertexPositionColor vertex structure, which (as its name suggests) can only store a position and a color for each vertex. To store texture coordinates, we need to switch to a different structure that supports texture information. We will use the VertexPositionTexture structure, which stores position and texture information.

▦ **Note** You could alternatively use the `VertexPositionColorTexture` structure, which has properties for both colors and texture coordinates. This will allow a texture and per-vertex colors to be used together.

In the TexturedSquare example projects, you will see that the _vertices array has been modified to use this new structure, as shown in Listing 6-20.

Listing 6-20. The _vertices array using the VertexPositionTexture structure

```
private VertexPositionTexture[] _vertices = new VertexPositionTexture[4];
```

To draw a square so that it displays the entire texture mapped on it, we specify u and v coordinates of (0, 1) for the bottom-left corner; (1, 1) for the bottom-right corner; (0, 0) for the top-left corner; and (1, 0) for the top-right corner. Each of these coordinates is specified for the vertex's TextureCoordinate property. Listing 6-21 contains the code required to initialize the vertex positions and texture coordinates for such a texture mapped square object.

Listing 6-21. Creating a square from two triangles and displaying an entire texture on its surface

```
_vertices[0].Position = new Vector3(-1, -1, 0);
_vertices[1].Position = new Vector3(-1, 1, 0);
_vertices[2].Position = new Vector3(1, -1, 0);
_vertices[3].Position = new Vector3(1, 1, 0);

_vertices[0].TextureCoordinate = new Vector2(0, 1);
_vertices[1].TextureCoordinate = new Vector2(0, 0);
_vertices[2].TextureCoordinate = new Vector2(1, 1);
_vertices[3].TextureCoordinate = new Vector2(1, 0);
```

Alternatively, we can specify just a section of the texture that we want to map. Remember that the physical vertex coordinates are completely unaffected by this; all we are doing is specifying the area of the texture that will be applied to the object. If we provide texture coordinates that cover only a smaller portion of the texture image, this portion will be stretched to fit the shape being drawn.

Figure 6-18 shows an example of using a subsection of the texture in this way. The texture coordinates span from 0 to 0.5 along both the u and v axes.

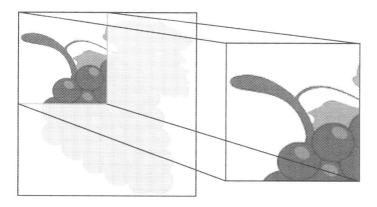

Figure 6-18. *Mapping a section of the source texture into a rendered square*

Another feature of the texture coordinates is that they are not restricted to staying within the range of 0 to 1. If we specify coordinates outside of this range, we can get the texture to repeat within our rendered graphics. Figure 6-19 shows a square object rendered with values from 0 to 3 on the u axis and 0 to 2 on the v axis. This might not be so useful when our texture is a bunch of grapes, but if you use a texture that tiles seamlessly (maybe a pattern of bricks or a stone texture), this can be a very handy way of filling the entire body of the object with a relatively small source image repeated over and over again.

Figure 6-19. *Wrapping the texture*

Preparing the Effect for Texture Mapping

The final thing we need to do is tell the MonoGame effect that we want it to use texture mapping. In the earlier examples, we told the effect to observe the vertex coloring by setting its VertexColorEnabled property to true. This time we will set that to false and instead set its TextureEnabled property to true. The complete effect initialization code for texturing is shown in Listing 6-22.

Listing 6-22. Configuring the effect for texture mapping

```
_effect = new BasicEffect(GraphicsDevice);
_effect.LightingEnabled = false;
_effect.VertexColorEnabled = false;
_effect.TextureEnabled = true;
_effect.Projection = projection;
_effect.View = view;
_effect.World = Matrix.Identity;
```

___

■ **Note** If you want to use the VertexPositionColorTexture structure to combine texturing and coloring, you will, of course, need to set both the VertexColorEnabled and TextureEnabled properties to true.

___

Our Draw code remains entirely unchanged. Because we have set the state of the effect object to use textures and provided a reference to a texture we have loaded, and we have provided texture coordinates for each vertex, MonoGame will automatically apply the texture to the object when it draws.

The `TexturedSquare` example projects contain all the code needed to get this up and running. An image from the running example is shown in Figure 6-20. Try experimenting with the texture coordinates to get a feel for how they work. Some things that you can try to achieve with these are the following:

- Provide a texture coordinate range that spans only part of the texture (for example, ranging from 0 to 0.5 instead of from 0 to 1) and observe how the texture is stretched across the square.

- Provide texture coordinates outside of the range of 0 to 1 (for example, 0 to 3) and observe how the texture is repeated across the square.

- Provide coordinates that don't correlate with the position of the vertex and observe how the texture is distorted and stretched to fit within the rendered object.

Figure 6-20. *The output from the TexturedSquare example projects*

Configuring the Sampler State

When MonoGame renders your texture, it queries a set of values known as the *sampler state* in order to fine-tune the resulting graphics. There are a couple of properties that we might want to change within the sampler state to alter the way in which the textures are processed.

Updating the Sampler State

The sampler state data can be read from the `SamplerStates` property of the `GraphicsDevice` object. This actually returns a collection of `SamplerState` objects, but the object at index 0 is that one that MonoGame will use for rendering.

However, the properties of this object are all read-only once the object has been attached to a `GraphicsDevice` (which it has by the time we can query it), and attempting to set one will result in an exception being thrown.

To change the sampler state properties, we must instead create a new `SamplerState` object, set its properties, and then set it into the `SamplerStates` collection. Listing 6-23 shows how this is achieved.

Listing 6-23. Providing a new SamplerState object for MonoGame

```
// Create a new SamplerState object
SamplerState samplerstate = new SamplerState();
// Set its properties as required...
// (set properties here)
// Give the object to MonoGame
GraphicsDevice.SamplerStates[0] = samplerstate;
```

The `SamplerState` class also provides a series of static properties that return pre-initialized `SamplerState` objects in various configurations. If one of them matches your needs, you can set it directly into the `SamplerState` collection without having to instantiate and configure it yourself. The available preconfigured sampler states are `AnisotropicClamp`, `AnisotropicWrap`, `LinearClamp`, `LinearWrap`, `PointClamp`, and `PointWrap`. The purpose of each of these will become clear once you have read through the following sections.

It is important to remember not to create new `SamplerState` objects during each `Update` or `Draw` because this will quickly cause garbage collection problems as we discussed earlier. (`SamplerState` is a class, not a structure.) If you need to use multiple sampler states within your drawing code, create them all once during initialization and just reuse these existing objects when drawing.

Texture Addressing Modes

The first `SamplerState` properties that we might want to set are the *texture address mode* properties. Back in Figure 6-19, we saw a texture with a coordinate range that causes the texture to be repeated across the object when the texture coordinates exceed the range of 0 to 1. This is known as `Wrap` mode.

There are two other modes available, however: `Clamp` and `Mirror`. The `Clamp` mode tells MonoGame to observe texture coordinates only in the range 0 to 1. Any texture coordinate that falls outside of that range will be *clamped* back into the range (in other words, all values greater than 1 will be treated as if they were 1, and values less than 0 will be treated as if they were 0). This is the default mode used by MonoGame.

The primary effect is that the texture will not wrap within the rendered object. The secondary effect is that any texture coordinate that does fall outside of the 0 to 1 range will stretch out the pixel at that texture boundary for the whole of the clamped area. In other words, setting a horizontal texture coordinate range of 0 to 2 with clamping would display the texture as normal in the left half of the rendered object, and it would then stretch the pixels from the right edge of the texture image across the whole of the right half of the rendered object.

The same texture coordinates shown in Figure 6-19 are shown again in Figure 6-21 with a `Clamp` address mode active.

Figure 6-21. *Drawing a texture with Clamp addressing*

The final mode, `Mirror`, works very much like `Wrap`, except that every alternate repeat will be flipped back to front (on the u axis) or upside down (on the v axis). The same texture can once again be seen in Figure 6-22 with `Mirror` addressing active.

Figure 6-22. *Drawing a texture with Mirror addressing*

The addressing modes can be set independently for each axis, so, if you want, you can mirror horizontally and wrap vertically. The horizontal address mode is set using the `RenderState.AddressU` property, and the vertical address mode is set using the `RenderState.AddressV` property.

Texture Filtering

The other sampler state property that we might want to set is the `Filter` property. This specifies the mechanism with which MonoGame will enlarge and shrink textures as it renders them to the screen. Three options are available: `Linear`, `Point`, and `Anisotropic`.

The `Point` filter is primarily noticeable when enlarging textures so that they are rendered at greater than their native size. When MonoGame uses a point filter, it determines for each pixel rendered on the screen which of the underlying texture pixels most closely matches in position. This texture pixel color is then directly displayed on the screen. The result is that the displayed graphic becomes very pixelated and blocky, reminiscent of early 3-D games before dedicated graphics hardware became commonplace. Often, this is not desirable, but sometimes you may wish to take advantage of this (games with "retro" graphics might work will in this mode).

The `Linear` filter (which is active by default) is a little clever when it comes to enlarging textures. Instead of directly mapping texture pixels onto the screen, it blends together the surrounding pixels to approximate a smooth blend of the underlying texture pixels. This is not magic, of course, and the image will quickly become blurry, but it generally provides a substantially better result than the `Point` filter.

Figure 6-23 shows the textured square from in the earlier example projects, but greatly zoomed in. On the left it, is rendered with a point filter and, on the right, with a linear filter.

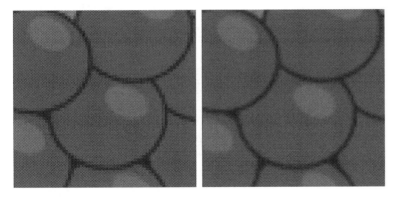

Figure 6-23. *The SamplerState's Point filter on the left and its Linear filter on the right*

The final filter, `Anisotropic`, comes into play when textures are being rendered so they stretch off into the distance of the screen. The perspective transformation (which we will examine in the next chapter) will result in the texture in the distance appearing much smaller than the texture in the foreground.

Linear filtering can cause noticeable visual artifacts to appear on textures that are rotated in this way. They are particularly noticeable when the texture is moving toward the player as it would be on the road in a racing game, for example. Using an anisotropic filter in this environment would provide the same general results as the linear filter, but with these texturing artifacts lessened so as to be much less apparent.

Supported Texture Image Formats

MonoGame is happy to apply any of its supported image types to your objects, so textures can be provided in PNG and JPG formats, as with sprites. However, due to the way that the graphics hardware handles textures, you will find under some conditions that your texture pixel width and height must exactly match a power of 2 (1, 2, 4, 8, 16, 32, 64, 128, 256, and so on).

The images do not need to be square, so you can, for example, use a texture that is 32 x 256 pixels, but, for maximum flexibility, they must observe these restrictions.

Images with sizes that are not powers of 2 can still be used in MonoGame provided that the texture address mode on the appropriate axes is set to `Clamp`, as described in the previous section. This will allow the texture to be displayed, but it means that wrapping and mirroring the texture cannot be supported on that axis.

If you want to use other texture address modes and your texture dimensions are not powers of 2, you have a couple of options available.

First, you can enlarge or shrink your texture using a graphics editing application so that its dimensions are powers of 2. The easiest way to handle this is to stretch (or shrink) the graphic to fit the new dimensions. This gives you the greatest degree of control over the final image size and the way in which your graphic is manipulated to fit within its new space.

The second option is to get Visual Studio to automatically resize your image when compiling. This is, by far, the easiest approach, but it does reduce the amount of control you have over the process. In many cases, this will be quite sufficient, however.

To instruct Visual Studio to resize the image for you, edit the properties of the image within the Content project. Inside the `Content Processor` section, you will find a property called `Resize to Power of Two`, as can be seen in Figure 6-24. Simply set this to `True`, and the image will be expanded to the next power of 2 on each axis when the content project is compiled.

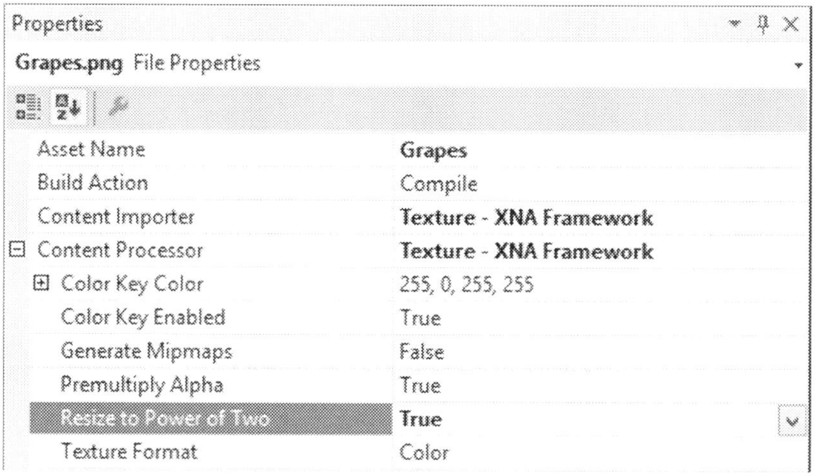

Properties	▾ ⌐ ✕
Grapes.png File Properties	▾

Asset Name	Grapes
Build Action	Compile
Content Importer	**Texture - XNA Framework**
⊟ Content Processor	**Texture - XNA Framework**
⊞ Color Key Color	255, 0, 255, 255
Color Key Enabled	True
Generate Mipmaps	False
Premultiply Alpha	True
Resize to Power of Two	True
Texture Format	Color

Figure 6-24. *Setting an image to be automatically resized to a power of 2*

Using Different Textures within the Same Draw Call

In the TexturedSquare project, the single texture is set into the effect's Texture property as soon as it is loaded. This stays active for the entire duration of the project.

In any real game, it is highly likely that you will need multiple textures so that different objects can be drawn with different appearances on the screen.

This is easy to achieve. Once all the textures have been loaded, each one can be activated as needed within the Draw function by setting the effect's Texture property before applying the passes of the effect.

As mentioned earlier, setting the active texture is one of the most expensive things you can do in terms of performance. Consequently, you should try to batch up your drawing so that all objects for each texture are drawn together. Avoiding setting the texture unnecessarily within each draw will help to ensure that your game performs the best it can.

▓ **Note** Just as we used the GameFramework project to ensure that sprites were drawn texture-by-texture, we can use it to ensure that our matrix-based objects are drawn texture-by-texture as well, helping to ensure that unnecessary texture changes are avoided. You will see this in more detail once we add the GameFramework into our projects in the "Integration into the Game Framework" section near the end of this chapter.

The MultipleTextures_Win8 and MultipleTextures_WP8 example projects demonstrate drawing two objects together, each with a different texture. The code from their Draw function is shown in Listing 6-24.

Listing 6-24. Drawing multiple objects, each using different textures

```
// Activate the first texture
_effect.Texture = _texture1;
// Apply a transformation to move and rotate the object
_effect.World = Matrix.CreateRotationZ(_angle);
_effect.World = Matrix.CreateTranslation(0, 1.2f, 0) * _effect.World;
foreach (EffectPass pass in _effect.CurrentTechnique.Passes)
```

```
{
    // Apply the pass
    pass.Apply();
    // Draw the square
    GraphicsDevice.DrawUserPrimitives(PrimitiveType.TriangleStrip, _vertices, 0, 2);
}

// Activate the second texture
_effect.Texture = _texture2;
// Apply a transformation to move and rotate the object
_effect.World = Matrix.CreateRotationZ(_angle);
_effect.World = Matrix.CreateTranslation(0, -1.2f, 0) * _effect.World;
foreach (EffectPass pass in _effect.CurrentTechnique.Passes)
{
    // Apply the pass
    pass.Apply();
    // Draw the square
    GraphicsDevice.DrawUserPrimitives(PrimitiveType.TriangleStrip, _vertices, 0, 2);
}
```

Using Transparency and Alpha Blending

MonoGame offers us support for dealing with transparency when we render our graphics. We can achieve various effects with this, such as removing transparent parts of an image or drawing an image so that it is semitransparent, allowing the graphics behind to show through. This is known as *alpha blending*.

The examples we have looked at so far in this chapter have rendered images with solid black backgrounds. As you will see, alpha blending allows us to remove this and observe the alpha channel within the texture, just as we did for sprites in earlier chapters.

In this section, we'll look at the available alpha blending options and learn how you can customize them for your games.

Enabling and Disabling Alpha Blending

In order to take advantage of alpha blending, we need to instruct MonoGame to use a *blend state* object. This contains information that MonoGame will use to determine exactly how to mix the pixels of the objects that it is drawing with the pixels that are already present on the screen.

This might be as simple as determining whether to completely replace an existing pixel or leave it with its current color, or it might involve a blend of the existing pixel and the pixel from the rendered object.

The active BlendState object can be found in the GraphicsDevice.BlendState property. The object can be interrogated, but its properties cannot be updated—just like the SamplerState objects we saw in the last section, a BlendState object's properties all become read-only once it has been set into the GraphicsDevice.

To alter the active BlendState, we must create a new BlendState object, configure its properties, and only then pass it to the GraphicsDevice, as can be seen in Listing 6-25. Once again, it is important to avoid doing this inside your Update or Draw functions. Any required BlendState objects should, instead, be created just once during initialization and then reused as and when needed.

Listing 6-25. Creating and activating a new BlendState object

```
// Create a new BlendState object
BlendState blendState = new BlendState();
// Set blend state object properties
// ...
// Set the object into the GraphicsDevice
GraphicsDevice.BlendState = blendState;
```

To disable alpha blending, the `BlendState` property should be set to `BlendState.Opaque`, as shown in Listing 6-26. You should always use this to disable alpha blending as soon as you have finished with it. There are two reasons why this is important. First, alpha blending has a higher processing overhead on the graphics hardware than opaque rendering because it needs to consider the pixels already on the screen as well as those being rendered. Second, having blending active when you are not expecting it to be can produce very confusing results in your game, causing objects to become transparent or even disappear.

Listing 6-26. Disabling alpha blending

```
// Switch to the Opaque blend state
GraphicsDevice.BlendState = BlendState.Opaque;
```

MonoGame's Built-In Blend States

Some transparency effects are more frequently used within games than others. To simplify using these effects, MonoGame provides a series of static `BlendState` objects whose properties reflect this. Before we get into the complexities of how alpha blending actually works, let's take a look at some of these predefined states and describe the purpose and use of each. We will look at how the blend states work under the covers later in this section.

Throughout this section, we will describe colors and alpha values as float values rather than as integers. This means that they will always be in the range of 0 to 1, rather than 0 to 255. The reason for this will become apparent later in the section.

You can experiment with these blend states by opening one of the `AlphaBlending_Win8` or `AlphaBlending_WP8` example projects and changing the state that is set at the end of the `Initialize` function.

Opaque

The `BlendState.Opaque` reference that we saw in Listing 6-26 is not an enumeration as it might at first appear, but it is, in fact, one of the built-in blend state objects. Opaque is a static property on the `BlendState` class that returns a `BlendState` object configured with alpha blending disabled.

This is the default blend state that is active when your MonoGame game launches and is, therefore, the state that we have been using so far in this chapter.

With opaque blending active, every pixel rendered from the source texture will be written to the screen so that it entirely replaces the content that is already present. Any alpha values within the source image, or any areas of the image that would normally be made transparent via the color key, are treated as being fully opaque.

Figure 6-25 shows the Grapes texture rendered using the opaque blend mode.

Figure 6-25. *Overlapping textures rendered with the Opaque blend state*

AlphaBlend

A particularly useful blend state is `AlphaBlend`, which is actually the mode that we were using with sprites when an alpha channel or a color key was present. This mode reads the alpha value from the source texture and uses it to determine how opaque the pixel should be when rendered on top of the existing graphics.

Pixels whose alpha values are 0.0 within the texture will be rendered entirely transparent (invisible). Pixels whose alpha values are 1.0 are rendered entirely opaque. Alpha values between them will result in varying levels of semitransparency. This is, therefore, ideal for textures that contain an alpha channel or color key because it allows them to be rendered with sections that are partially or completely transparent.

Figure 6-26 shows the Grapes textures once again, this time rendered with the `AlphaBlend` blend state.

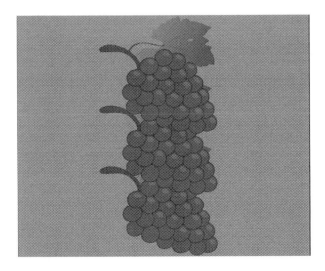

Figure 6-26. *Overlapping textures rendered with the AlphaBlend blend state*

Additive

Setting the blend state to BlendState.Additive applies another blend that takes into account the existing graphics that have already been displayed on the screen. It also takes into account the alpha information contained within the texture being rendered.

This time, however, the colors of the pixels being rendered are added to the colors on the screen, rather than replacing them. Colors are added by taking their individual red, green, and blue color elements, multiplying them by the texture's alpha value to make them observe the texture transparency information, and then finally adding them to the existing red, green, and blue color values already present on the screen. This might well result in some of the elements exceeding their maximum level of 1.0. When this happens, they are clamped to 1.0.

If, for example, the screen were filled with a dark green color whose RGB values are (0.0, 0.5, 0.0) and we render a solid red texture with RGB values (1.0, 0.0, 0.0) and full alpha (1.0), the resulting calculation would be as follows:

$$\text{Red}_{new} = (\text{Red}_{source} \times \text{Alpha}) + \text{Red}_{dest} = (1.0 \times 1.0) + 0.0 = 1.0$$

$$\text{Green}_{new} = (\text{Green}_{source} \times \text{Alpha}) + \text{Green}_{dest} = (0.0 \times 1.0) + 0.5 = 0.5$$

$$\text{Blue}_{new} = (\text{Blue}_{source} \times \text{Alpha}) + \text{Blue}_{dest} = (0.0 \times 1.0) + 0.0 = 0.0$$

The resulting color will have RGB values (1.0, 0.5, 0.0)—an orange color. If we had a yellow color already on the screen (1.0, 1.0, 0.0) and we rendered a purple texture (1.0, 0.0, 1.0) with an alpha value of 0.5, the final color would be calculated as follows:

$$\text{Red}_{new} = (\text{Red}_{source} \times \text{Alpha}) + \text{Red}_{dest} = (1.0 \times 0.5) + 1.0 = 1.5$$

$$\text{Green}_{new} = (\text{Green}_{source} \times \text{Alpha}) + \text{Green}_{dest} = (0.0 \times 0.5) + 1.0 = 1.0$$

$$\text{Blue}_{new} = (\text{Blue}_{source} \times \text{Alpha}) + \text{Blue}_{dest} = (1.0 \times 0.5) + 0.0 = 0.5$$

The resulting color would be (1.0, 1.0, 0.5) as the red value would be clamped at 1.0. This is a pale yellow color.

Because additive blending is adding two colors together, repeated rendering of the same area on the screen pushes the color toward full red, green, and blue intensity. If the colors being mixed contain elements of all three color components, the color will tend toward white.

▦ **Tip** Additive blending is ideally suited for making explosion effects. The explosion of the spaceship in the *Cosmic Rocks* examples we saw in earlier chapters uses additive blending for just such a purpose.

Figure 6-27 shows the grape textures rendered with additive blending. The color of the background is being retained and mixed with the texture as it is drawn, resulting in a blue tinge across everything, and cyan leaves on the grapes as the texture's green color and the screen's blue color are mixed together.

Figure 6-27. *Overlapping textures rendered with the Additive blend state*

Creating Custom Blend States

Although the built-in blend states will be appropriate in many situations, sometimes it is useful to further customize the blend state that MonoGame uses. There is an enormous number of combinations of blend states that can be created. They are defined using three properties of the `BlendState` object: `ColorBlendFunction`, `ColorSourceBlend`, and `ColorDestinationBlend`. They are matched by three similar properties that refer to the alpha channel: `AlphaBlendFunction`, `AlphaSourceBlend`, and `AlphaDestinationBlend`.

The way in which blending is performed using these properties is consistent and understandable on a mathematical level, but it can sometimes require a little experimentation to achieve the desired effect. As we saw with the Additive blend, a calculation is performed against the individual red, green, and blue components of the source and destination colors in order to obtain the final color that will appear on the screen.

The calculation is as follows:

(source color x `ColorSourceBlend`) `ColorBlendFunction` (destination color x `ColorDestinationBlend`)

For each pixel that MonoGame renders to the screen, it first takes the red, green, blue, and alpha elements of the source color (the color of the pixel being rendered from the texture) and multiplies them by the corresponding elements from the `ColorSourceBlend` value. It then repeats this with the color of the pixel already present on the screen, multiplying it by the `ColorDestinationBlend` elements.

With these two colors calculated, they are combined using the appropriate `ColorBlendFunction`.

We will look at all the available options for them in a moment, but before we do that, let's pick a simple example to demonstrate this calculation.

One of the available blend types is `Blend.One`, which provides the value 1.0 for each of the red, green, blue, and alpha color elements. Another factor is `Blend.Zero`, which provides the value 0.0 for each color component. Finally, we have a blend function named `BlendFunction.Add`, which simply adds the source and the destination color element values together.

If we use `Blend.One` as the source blend, `Blend.Zero` as the destination blend, and `BlendFunction.Add` as the blend function, the color for each pixel is calculated as follows:

$$\text{Red}_{new} = (\text{Red}_{source} \times 1.0) + (\text{Red}_{dest} \times 0.0)$$

$$\text{Green}_{new} = (\text{Green}_{source} \times 1.0) + (\text{Green}_{dest} \times 0.0)$$

$$\text{Blue}_{new} = (\text{Blue}_{source} \times 1.0) + (\text{Blue}_{dest} \times 0.0)$$

As you can see, if these blending parameters are used, the end result is that the object is rendered absolutely opaque; no blending takes place at all. The output colors calculated are exactly the same as the source colors, with the existing destination color completely ignored. This is, in fact, the configuration that is provided by the BlendState.Opaque object. The code to configure this blend state is shown in Listing 6-27.

Listing 6-27. Manually configuring a BlendState object for opaque blending

```
// Create a new BlendState object
BlendState blendState = new BlendState();

// Set the color blend properties
blendState.ColorBlendFunction = BlendFunction.Add;
blendState.ColorSourceBlend = Blend.One;
blendState.ColorDestinationBlend = Blend.Zero;

// Copy the color blend properties to the alpha blend properties
blendState.AlphaBlendFunction = blendState.ColorBlendFunction;
blendState.AlphaSourceBlend = blendState.ColorSourceBlend;
blendState.AlphaDestinationBlend = blendState.ColorDestinationBlend;

// Set the object into the GraphicsDevice
GraphicsDevice.BlendState = blendState;
```

▦ **Note** The initial configuration of a newly instantiated BlendState object is exactly the same as that of the built-in BlendState.Opaque object.

Let's take a look at a different pair of blend types. We will use Blend.SourceAlpha for the source blend and combine it with Blend.InverseSourceAlpha for the destination. SourceAlpha provides the source color's alpha value, whereas InverseSourceAlpha provides the source color's alpha subtracted from 1 (so a source alpha of 1 becomes 0, a source of 0 becomes 1, a source of 0.2 becomes 0.8, and so on). Using BlendFunction.Add once again, the output color of each pixel is therefore calculated as follows:

$$\text{Red}_{new} = (\text{Red}_{source} \times \text{Alpha}_{source}) + (\text{Red}_{dest} \times (1 - \text{Alpha}_{source}))$$

$$\text{Green}_{new} = (\text{Green}_{source} \times \text{Alpha}_{source}) + (\text{Green}_{dest} \times (1 - \text{Alpha}_{source}))$$

$$\text{Blue}_{new} = (\text{Blue}_{source} \times \text{Alpha}_{source}) + (\text{Blue}_{dest} \times (1 - \text{Alpha}_{source}))$$

Think for a moment about the results of this calculation. If the source alpha is 1 (opaque), the calculation will take the entire source color (because it is being multiplied by 1) and none of the destination color (because it is being multiplied by 0). The result will be that the pixel is rendered opaque.

If, on the other hand, the source alpha is 0 (transparent), the calculation will take none of the source color (as this is being multiplied by 0) and all of the destination color (because it is being multiplied by 1). The result will be that the pixel is rendered entirely transparent.

Alpha values that fall between 0 and 1 will provide a gradual transition between transparent and opaque. This is exactly the effect that we need for rendering textures onto the screen so that they observe the image's alpha channel.

The available Blend enumeration values are shown in Table 6-1. The Values column uses the characters R, G, B, and A to refer to the red, green, blue, and alpha color components and adds a subscript of s or d to identify whether this relates to the source or destination color. Some of these values also use a subscript of blendfactor. This blendfactor is another property of the BlendState object into which any color at all may be placed (including an alpha component) such that it can be involved in the blending calculations.

Table 6-1. *Blend Types*

Blend	Description	Values
One	All color elements are set to 1	$(1, 1, 1, 1)$
Zero	All color elements are set to 0	$(0, 0, 0, 0)$
SourceColor	The color elements of the pixel in the source texture	(R_s, G_s, B_s, A_s)
InverseSourceColor	The inverse color elements of the pixel in the source texture (each subtracted from 1)	$(1 - R_s, 1 - G_s, 1 - B_s, 1 - A_s)$
SourceAlpha	The alpha value of the pixel in the source texture	(A_s, A_s, A_s, A_s)
InverseSourceAlpha	The inverse alpha value of the pixel in the source texture	$(1 - A_s, 1 - A_s, 1 - A_s, 1 - A_s)$
DestinationColor	The color elements of the pixel already present on the screen	(R_d, G_d, B_d, A_d)
InverseDestinationColor	The inverse color elements of the pixel already present on the screen	$(1 - R_d, 1 - G_d, 1 - B_d, 1 - A_d)$
DestinationAlpha	The alpha value of the pixel already present on the screen	(A_d, A_d, A_d, A_d)
InverseDestinationAlpha	The inverse alpha value of the pixel already present on the screen	$(1 - A_d, 1 - A_d, 1 - A_d, 1 - A_d)$
BlendFactor	The color elements of the graphic device's BlendFactor color	$(R_{blendfactor}, G_{blendfactor}, B_{blendfactor}, A_{blendfactor})$
InverseBlendFactor	The inverse color elements of the blend factor color	$(1 - R_{blendfactor}, 1 - G_{blendfactor}, 1 - B_{blendfactor}, 1 - A_{blendfactor})$
SourceAlphaSaturation	Either the source alpha or the inverse of the destination alpha, whichever is less	$(f, f, f, 1)$, where f is the calculation $\max(A_s, 1 - A_d)$

The ColorBlendFunction can set to any of the values shown in Table 6-2. Remember that each of them operates on the red, green, blue, and alpha values independently to calculate the final color.

Table 6-2. *Blending Functions*

BlendFunction	Description
Add	The color is calculated by adding the source and destination colors: `Output = (source color * source blend) + (dest color * dest blend)`
Subtract	The color is calculated by subtracting the destination color from the source: `Output = (source color * source blend) - (dest color * dest blend)`
ReverseSubtract	The color is calculated by subtracting the source color from the destination: `Output = (dest color * dest blend) - (source color * source blend)`
Min	The color is calculated by finding the lesser value from the source and destination colors: `Output = Min( (source color * source blend), (dest color * dest blend) )`
Max	The color is calculated by finding the greater value from the source and destination colors: `Output = Max( (source color * source blend), (dest color * dest blend) )`

A huge range of effects can be obtained using different combinations of these functions and blendtypes. Try experimenting with them inside the AlphaBlending example projects to see some of the results that you can obtain.

▓ **Note** You might recall that we passed BlendState objects into the BlendState parameter SpriteBatch.Begin function in our 2-D examples in earlier chapters. These are exactly the same BlendState objects that we are using here. Now that you have a greater understanding of how they work, you can apply that knowledge to your sprite rendering, too.

Object Transparency

One very useful rendering feature that we've not yet seen support for in this section is the ability to fade an entire object between opaque and transparent. With sprite rendering, this could be controlled using the alpha component of the sprite tint, but as you saw in the "Tinting Objects" section earlier in this chapter, no such element is available for tinting when rendering vertices.

The reason is simply because the alpha value is stored in a separate property. Each Effect object (including BasicEffect) has an Alpha property that can be given a value between 0 (invisible) and 1 (opaque). All the source alpha values within the object will be multiplied by the Alpha property value to generate the value for the SourceAlpha blend. Providing your blend state observes the source alpha, you can use the Alpha property to fade your objects between opaque and transparent and still observe the alpha information stored in your textures.

Handling Orientations

We discussed support for different orientations back in Chapter 2. Everything we looked at before still applies when rendering with vertices and matrices. However, there is an additional step that we need to take to make things work properly.

The OrientationSupport_Win8 example project demonstrates the problem that we need to address as well as its solution. If you start the project running with the device or simulator in landscape mode, you will see that it displays three textured squares just as it did in the alpha blending example. The exception is that this time the squares rotate back and forth so that they stay essentially upright. This will allow us to ensure that the graphics are being kept the right way up, not sideways.

The initial landscape display from the project is just as we would expect, with the squares arranged vertically above one another. The project is configured to support both landscape and portrait orientations, however. So, now, rotate the device or the simulator so that it is in a portrait orientation.

MonoGame correctly rotates the screen so that the graphics remain upright (the grapes are still the right way up, and the objects are still arranged vertically within the new orientation). However, the objects are no longer square: They are instead very squashed, as shown in Figure 6-28.

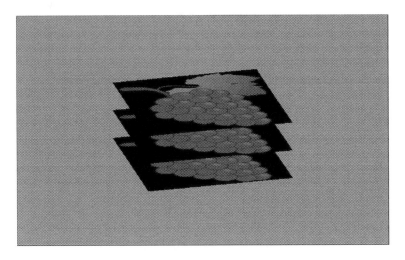

Figure 6-28. Distorted objects after switching between landscape and portrait orientations

To find the reason for this, we need to look back at Listing 6-2. This is where we calculated the aspect ratio for the screen by dividing the back buffer width by its height. For a landscape screen, this calculation is (for example) 1920 / 1080, which equals approximately 1.77. For a portrait screen, however, the calculation is switched around to be 1080 / 1920, which results in 0.5625. Because MonoGame is still rendering with the original landscape aspect ratio, it continues after rotation to render with the belief that the screen width is 1.77 times its height, which is no longer the case.

To address the problem, we simply need to recalculate the aspect ratio when the orientation changes. We can add a handler for the `Window.ClientSizeChanged` event in the game class's constructor, as shown in Listing 6-28.

Listing 6-28. Handling the window's ClientSizeChanged event

```
// Add a handler to update projection matrix if the window size changes
Window.ClientSizeChanged += Window_ClientSizeChanged;
```

The implementation of the `Window_ClientSizeChanged` event handler function is shown in Listing 6-29. This results in a small amount of code duplication as the `Initialize` function also sets the projection matrix. Consequently, you might want to separate this out into a separate function that can be called from each of these two locations. For simplicity, we will duplicate the code in this example.

Listing 6-29. Updating the projection matrix when the screen size (or orientation) changes

```
void Window_ClientSizeChanged(object sender, EventArgs e)
{
    // Calculate the new screen aspect ratio
    float aspectRatio =
            (float)GraphicsDevice.Viewport.Width / GraphicsDevice.Viewport.Height;
    // Create a projection matrix
    Matrix projection = Matrix.CreatePerspectiveFieldOfView(MathHelper.ToRadians(45),
                                                    aspectRatio, 0.1f, 1000.0f);
    // Set the matrix into the effect
    _effect.Projection = projection;
}
```

This block of code is initially commented out in the `OrientationSupport_Win8` example project, which is why the graphics appeared distorted after the orientation was changed. Uncomment the code and then run the project again. This time you will see that the behavior after rotation from portrait to landscape is quite different: The objects are no longer distorted, and the scene "zooms in" so that the amount of vertical space that is displayed on the screen is the same in landscape orientation as it was in portrait. This can be seen in Figure 6-29.

Figure 6-29. *Portrait orientation with the aspect ratio correctly recalculated*

Although the objects appear larger than they were, the code to render them and the transformations that are applied are completely unchanged; it is just the projection matrix that has caused the change in appearance.

Integration into the Game Framework

Just as we added support for sprite and text rendering into the game framework project, we will add support for matrix-based rendering. This allows us to continue the simple object-based approach that we have used in the previous chapters and apply it to the new rendering techniques that we have learned in this chapter. All the code in this section can be found inside the `GameFrameworkExample_Win8` and `GameFrameworkExample_WP8` projects that accompany this chapter.

Sprites have a fairly limited set of operations that can be performed, so it was easy to wrap up a significant amount of their functionality in the game framework's SpriteObject class. When we render with matrices, there are many more variables to take into account, such as the flexibility of specifying the object's transformation matrix, the different primitives that can be rendered, and the different types of effect. (BasicEffect is just one of several effects that are available, as you will see in Chapter 8.)

As a result, the game framework's support for matrix rendering is a little less comprehensive than it was for sprite rendering. It provides the features that are most likely to be useful and then allows the individual object classes to use or ignore them as they see fit. They are present in a new class within the GameFramework project, named MatrixObjectBase.

The MatrixObjectBase Class

MatrixObjectBase is an abstract class that derives from GameObjectBase (see Figure 6-30). It provides useful properties and functions that we might want to use within our derived game object classes (though, in many cases, they will be insufficient in isolation and will require additional object-specific properties to be added to the derived classes).

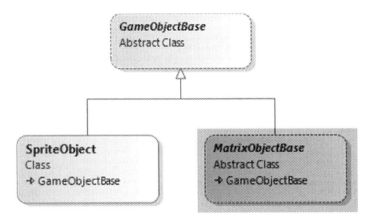

Figure 6-30. The MatrixObjectBase class's position within the framework project

The first content that is present in the class is a range of properties that can be used to control how instances of derived classes will be rendered. The properties contained within the class are as follows:

- ObjectTexture: a reference to a texture that will be used when rendering the object (or null if no texture is required). Defaults to null.

- Transformation: a matrix that defines the transformation to use when rendering the object. This will normally be set during the object's Update call and then used as the world matrix when rendering from the Draw call.

- Position, PositionX, PositionY, and PositionZ: a 3-D position for the object, represented both as a Vector3 and a series of floats (though they share the same underlying storage, so modifying the vector will affect the float values, and vice versa). Defaults to (0, 0, 0).

- Angle, AngleX, AngleY, and AngleZ: three angles that can be used to track rotation of the object around each axis. The Angle property sets or returns the same values as a Vector3. Defaults to (0, 0, 0).

- Scale, ScaleX, ScaleY, and ScaleZ: the scaling factors for each axis, available as a Vector3 or as three float values. Defaults to (1, 1, 1).

- ObjectColor: just as with sprites, this allows the color and alpha for the object to be specified. The red, green, and blue components will be passed into the effect object's DiffuseColor property. Its alpha component will be used to determine a value for the effect's Alpha property.

Object Transformation

The general approach when rendering objects is to calculate their transformation matrix during the call to each object's Update method, and then use that calculated matrix in its Draw method. Let's take a look at how the transformation is calculated.

There is clearly some overlap between the class's position properties: Transformation is used to store the calculated transformation for the object. whereas the Position, Angle, and Scale properties each make up a part of that transformation. Transformations can be much more complex than simply applying a translation, rotate, and scale matrix, however, because many transformations might need to be applied in an appropriate sequence to achieve the final matrix to use for rendering.

To allow us to achieve a balance between simplicity and flexibility, the class offers a few different approaches for calculating the Transformation matrix.

The first approach is to fully calculate the transformation matrix within the derived class. Essentially, this requires the derived Update code to simply place the required matrix into the Transformation property ready to be read back during rendering.

It can do this by multiplying matrices together as we saw in earlier examples in this chapter. It can also take advantage of two simple functions within MatrixObjectBase: SetIdentity and ApplyTransformation.

SetIdentity simply loads the identity matrix into the Transformation property, as shown in Listing 6-30.

Listing 6-30. The SetIdentity function implementation

```
protected void SetIdentity()
{
    Transformation = Matrix.Identity;
}
```

ApplyTransformation takes a transformation matrix as a parameter and multiplies it with the existing Transformation matrix, as shown in Listing 6-31.

Listing 6-31. The ApplyTransformation function implementation

```
protected void ApplyTransformation(Matrix newTransformation)
{
    Transformation = newTransformation * Transformation;
}
```

These are clearly very simple and are almost unnecessary, but they allow step-by-step transformations to be applied in an Update function. Listing 6-32 shows an example of such an Update function from a derived class in a game project. (It can actually be found in the GameFrameworkExample project's TexturedSquareObject class.) This code resets the object transformation to the identity matrix, rotates by the angle stored in the AngleZ property, scales the matrix as per the object's Scale vector, and then translates according to the object's Position. At each stage, the resulting matrix is updated in the Transformation property.

Listing 6-32. Applying a series of transformations using the ApplyTransformation function

```
// Calculate the transformation matrix
SetIdentity();
ApplyTransformation(Matrix.CreateRotationZ(AngleZ));
ApplyTransformation(Matrix.CreateScale(Scale));
ApplyTransformation(Matrix.CreateTranslation(Position));
```

Alternatively, the code shown in Listing 6-33 achieves the exact same result using direct matrix multiplications instead of the SetIdentity and ApplyTransformation functions.

Listing 6-33. Applying a series of transformations using direct matrix multiplication

```
Transformation = Matrix.CreateRotationZ(AngleZ);
Transformation = Matrix.CreateScale(Scale) * Transformation;
Transformation = Matrix.CreateTranslation(Position) * Transformation;
```

▓ **Note**   If you have experience of programming using OpenGL, the approach that specifies a sequence of transformations shown in Listing 6-32 will probably feel more comfortable because it approximates the approach used by OpenGL to specify its world transformation. Both approaches are functionally identical, though, so use whichever you prefer.

Note that although these code samples have used some of the standard properties (AngleZ, Scale, and Position), nothing else within the class is taking any notice of them. In this example, they are being used simply as handy places to store information about the location of the object, but they have no further meaning to the class.

The second approach that we can use is to get MatrixObjectBase to apply all the transformation properties automatically. When we do this, it will perform the following steps, in this order:

1. Translate the object according to its Position vector.

2. Rotate the object around the x axis according to its AngleX value.

3. Rotate the object around the y axis according to its AngleY value.

4. Rotate the object around the z axis according to its AngleZ value.

5. Scale the object according to its Scale vector.

The code that performs these transformations, taken from the MatrixObjectBase class, is shown in Listing 6-34.

Listing 6-34. The MatrixObjectBase.ApplyStandardTransformations function

```
protected void ApplyStandardTransformations()
{
    Matrix result;

    // First obtain the object's underlying transformation
    result = Transformation;
```

```
    // Apply the object position if any of the coordinates are non-zero
    if (PositionX != 0 || PositionY != 0 || PositionZ != 0)
    {
        // Yes, so apply the position to the current transformation
        result = Matrix.CreateTranslation(Position) * result;
    }

    // Rotate the object if any of the angles are non-zero
    if (AngleX != 0) result = Matrix.CreateRotationX(AngleX) * result;
    if (AngleY != 0) result = Matrix.CreateRotationY(AngleY) * result;
    if (AngleZ != 0) result = Matrix.CreateRotationZ(AngleZ) * result;

    // Scale the object if any of the scale values are set to a value other than 1
    if (ScaleX != 1 || ScaleY != 1 || ScaleZ != 1)
    {
        // Yes, so apply the Scale to the current transformation
        result = Matrix.CreateScale(Scale) * result;
    }

    // Store the final calculated matrix
    Transformation = result;
}
```

Sometimes this set of steps will be quite sufficient for a game object, in which case no further processing is required. Listing 6-35 shows how to apply these steps to the object to calculate its transformation matrix. Note that these steps are applied in addition to the existing transformation. As a result, it is important to remember to call SetIdentity first so that they are applied to an identity matrix rather than to any matrix left over from a previous update.

Listing 6-35. Applying the standard transformations to an object

```
// Calculate the transformation matrix
SetIdentity();
ApplyStandardTransformations();
```

Finally, a combination of these two approaches can be used, mixing both custom transformations and the standard transformations. The transformation matrix can be set both before and after the standard transformations are applied so that customized behavior can be achieved. Listing 6-36 first offsets the object position to the left by one unit and then applies the standard transformations and translates one unit along the (potentially rotated) y axis.

Listing 6-36. Mixing custom and standard transformations

```
SetIdentity();
ApplyTransformation(Matrix.CreateTranslation(-1, 0, 0));
ApplyStandardTransformations();
ApplyTransformation(Matrix.CreateTranslation(0, 1, 0));
```

Generally, however, it is best to stick to simple transformations prior to calling ApplyStandardTransformations and no further transformations afterward. Because the standard transformations are not listed step-by-step within the code as all the other transformations are, it can be confusing to visualize exactly what happens during the ApplyStandardTransformations function call; mix the two approaches with caution.

Object Rendering

With the transformation matrix for the object calculated, the object can now be drawn. As with sprite rendering, this is achieved using a method named Draw, but this time it is passed an Effect object instead of a SpriteBatch. The function is declared as an abstract function, as shown in Listing 6-37, because it has no default implementation, but must be overridden in each derived class.

Listing 6-37. The declaration of the MatrixObjectBase.Draw function

```
public abstract void Draw(GameTime gameTime, Effect effect);
```

When a class overrides this, it is its responsibility to perform the required steps to draw the object to the screen. Some of this will vary from one class to another, but there are some properties of the effect that can be looked after by MatrixObjectBase. They are handled within a function called PrepareEffect.

The PrepareEffect function ensures that the appropriate texture is set into the effect, that the texturing is enabled or disabled as required, that the DiffuseColor and Alpha properties are set according to the ObjectColor value, and that the calculated Transformation is set. Once all these are in place, the object is ready for rendering. Listing 6-38 shows the implementation of the PrepareEffect function.

Listing 6-38. Preparing an effect ready for rendering

```
protected void PrepareEffect(BasicEffect effect)
{
    // Do we have a texture? Set the effect as required
    if (ObjectTexture == null)
    {
        // No testure so disable texturing
        effect.TextureEnabled = false;
    }
    else
    {
        // Enable texturing and set the texture into the effect
        effect.TextureEnabled = true;
        if (ObjectTexture != effect.Texture) effect.Texture = ObjectTexture;
    }

    // Set the color and alpha
    effect.DiffuseColor = ObjectColor.ToVector3();
    effect.Alpha = (float)ObjectColor.A / 255.0f;

    // Apply the transformation matrix
    effect.World = Transformation;

    // Now the effect is ready for the derived class to actually draw the object
}
```

This can then be easily used within a derived class to set the required effect properties before rendering. Listing 6-39 shows another piece of code from the TexturedSquareObject example class, this time for the Draw function.

Listing 6-39. Drawing an object in a derived class

```
public override void Draw(Microsoft.Xna.Framework.GameTime gameTime, Effect effect)
{
    // Prepare the effect for drawing
    PrepareEffect(effect);

    // Draw the object
    foreach (EffectPass pass in effect.CurrentTechnique.Passes)
    {
        // Apply the pass
        pass.Apply();
        // Draw the square
        effect.GraphicsDevice.DrawUserPrimitives(PrimitiveType.TriangleStrip, _vertices, 0, 2);
    }
}
```

This should all be looking very familiar. If you examine the TexturedSquareObject class as a whole, you will see that it has very little code present, but it still manages to render our textured object to the screen.

There is, of course, no actual requirement to call PrepareEffect. If necessary, this work could be carried out directly within the derived class.

Updates to the GameHost Class

The game framework's GameHost class needs a small enhancement to support rendering matrix objects. This takes the form of the DrawObjects function.

DrawObjects performs the same task for matrix-based objects as DrawSprites performs for sprites: It draws all the objects in the game, potentially filtering them by a specified texture for performance reasons. However, we have a slight additional complexity for objects: Sometimes not all of them will actually *have* a texture. We need to be able to distinguish between drawing all the objects (without caring about which textures they are using) and drawing the objects for which the texture is null.

We achieve this by creating two public overloads, one that takes a texture as a parameter and draws only objects that use that texture, and one that doesn't take a texture parameter and draws all the objects. Internally, each of these calls into a third (private) overload that expects to be explicitly told whether to filter on textures or not. This allows it to look for objects whose ObjectTexture value is null and draw them alone, should this be required.

The code for these functions is shown in Listing 6-40.

Listing 6-40. The DrawObjects function overloads in the GameHost class

```
/// <summary>
/// Call the Draw method on all matrix objects in the game
/// </summary>
public virtual void DrawObjects(GameTime gameTime, Effect effect)
{
    DrawObjects(gameTime, effect, false, null);
}


/// <summary>
/// Call the Draw method on all matrix objects in the game that use
/// the specified texture. Pass as null to draw only objects that do
/// not have a texture specified at all.
```

```
/// </summary>
public virtual void DrawObjects(GameTime gameTime, Effect effect,
                                            Texture2D restrictToTexture)
{
    DrawObjects(gameTime, effect, true, restrictToTexture);
}

/// <summary>
/// Draw the specified objects
/// </summary>
private void DrawObjects(GameTime gameTime, Effect effect, bool specifiedTextureOnly,
                                            Texture2D restrictToTexture)
{
    GameObjectBase obj;
    int objectCount;

    // Draw each matrix-based object
    objectCount = _objectArray.Length;
    for (int i = 0; i < objectCount; i++)
    {
        obj = _objectArray[i];
        // Is this a matrix object?
        if (obj is MatrixObjectBase)
        {
            // Does this object use the required texture?
            if (specifiedTextureOnly == false ||
                        ((MatrixObjectBase)obj).ObjectTexture == restrictToTexture)
            {
                ((MatrixObjectBase)obj).Draw(gameTime, effect);
            }
        }
    }
}
```

Using the Game Framework for Matrix Rendering

The game framework is now all ready to use for rendering our objects, so how is it used in a game project?

This is very easy, as can be seen in the GameFrameworkExampleGame class in the example project. All the class-level variables have been removed except for the BasicEffect variable, and the Initialize function has been reduced in size so that it simply creates and initializes this effect object.

LoadContent now once again loads its textures into the Textures collection that we've used throughout all the sprite examples. At the end, it calls ResetGame to create the game's objects. ResetGame, shown in Listing 6-41, simply adds some instances of the game project's TexturedSquareObject class to the GameObjects collection and initializes each of their properties as required.

Listing 6-41. Resetting the example project

```
private void ResetGame()
{
    // Clear any existing objects
    GameObjects.Clear();
```

```
  // Add some new game objects
  GameObjects.Add(new TexturedSquareObject(this, new Vector3(0, 0.6f, 0),
                                       Textures["Grapes"], 2.0f));
  GameObjects.Add(new TexturedSquareObject(this, new Vector3(0, -0.6f, 0),
                                       Textures["Strawberry"], 2.0f));
}
```

Finally, we call `UpdateAll` from the game's `Update` function and `DrawObjects` from the game's `Draw` function. That's all that is needed.

Enter the Matrix

This chapter has provided a tour through a whole new way of rendering in MonoGame, using matrix transformations and vertices. If you haven't encountered this approach before, it might seem like a lot of extra work to achieve similar results to those that were already accessible just using sprites.

The real power of this new approach is still ahead of us, however. The examples in this chapter have remained mainly in two dimensions, but matrix transformations and vertex declarations are the gateway into the third dimension, opening up an enormous number of new opportunities for gaming on Windows 8 and Windows Phone 8.

All the techniques that we have learned here operate in 3-D, too. Once you feel comfortable with the material that we have covered, prepare yourself for the next chapter, in which you will step into a new world of graphical rendering.

Summary

- Matrix-based rendering provides an alternative to the sprite-based rendering used in earlier chapters. For 2-D graphics, some tasks are easier with sprites and others are easier with matrix rendering. Matrix rendering is essential for 3-D graphics, however. It is often best adopted for combined 2-D and 3-D rendering to help keep a consistent approach to both styles of graphics.

- Matrix rendering uses an abstract coordinate system rather than a strictly pixel-based system as used for sprite rendering. Typically, the point (0, 0) is in the very center of the screen, with positive x and y values heading right and upwards.

- When rendering using matrices, we define *objects* that contain the shape of the areas to be drawn. These objects are formed from *vertices* that are joined together to make triangular *surfaces*.

- Only triangles and lines may be used to form objects, but in general everything is usually built just using triangles. Triangles may be rendered as lists of independent triangles or as *strips* of adjoining triangles with shared vertices.

- Vertex positions are always specified using `Vector3` structures. These are similar to the `Vector2` structure that we used for sprite rendering, but we add an additional Z property to control the distance into or out of the screen. For 2-D rendering, the Z property is simply left with the value 0.

- Vertices can store more detail than just their position. Other properties that can be stored include the vertex color and texture coordinates. Different vertex structures (such as `VertexPositionColor` and `VertexPositionTexture`) allow the appropriate data for each vertex to be defined and stored.

- MonoGame will *interpolate* color values and texture coordinates between each defined vertex. This is the method with which textures are displayed across the internal area of each surface. It also allows for smooth color or alpha fades to be applied to an object.

- Textures may be enlarged by using texture coordinates that cover only a portion of the original texture image. They may also be wrapped or mirrored by using texture coordinates that extend outside the range of 0..1 on each texture axis. MonoGame's SamplerState class is used to control how these extended coordinate ranges are handled when rendering.

- The SamplerState can also be used to specify the texture *filtering* that MonoGame should use, which controls how texture graphics are enlarged or reduced for display on the screen.

- When preparing textures for use with matrix rendering, they should ideally have a pixel width and height that is a power of 2, though they do not need to be square.

- Control over how MonoGame will draw its objects is managed via an *effect* object, such as the BasicEffect that we have used throughout this chapter. The effect object contains all of the *state* of the rendering engine, including properties to specify the camera position, the current object render position, flags to identify whether to use vertex colors or textures, and many others.

- Multiple objects can be drawn by setting the texture and object (world) transformation for the first object, then drawing that object, and then repeating these two steps for each subsequent object. As with sprite rendering, unnecessary changes to the active texture should be avoided for performance reasons.

- Object transformations are calculated by multiplying matrices together in order to apply the different types of supported transformation (such as a translation, rotation, or scaling matrix). The order in which the matrices are multiplied is important as the same matrices multiplied in different orders can result in significantly different output values.

- The MonoGame Matrix structure contains numerous functions for creating various matrices, which can then be incorporated into your object transformations.

- MonoGame has a flexible set of functionality around transparency and alpha blending, allowing lots of different rendering effects to be achieved. These are controlled using BlendState objects. Such objects can be manually configured, or one of a set of pre-defined objects can be used.

- Switching between portrait and landscape orientation works just as expected, except that we need to remember to tell MonoGame about the new screen aspect ratio in its new orientation. This can be achieved using the Window.ClientSizeChanged event. It requires us to update the current Effect object's Projection matrix based on the new aspect ratio.

- The GameFramework project wraps much of the required functionality for working with matrix-based rendering into its MatrixObjectBase class. This class is abstract and must therefore be implemented in derived classes. However, the base class provides a series of useful properties for storing transformation data for each object and various functions to help with the manipulation of these properties and with rendering objects to the screen.

- All object transformation calculations should be performed in the Update method, with just drawing functionality in the Draw method.

- The GameFramework is instructed to draw its known objects by calling the GameHost.DrawObjects method. This can be instructed to draw either all objects or just those using a specific texture in order to avoid unnecessary texture switching.

CHAPTER 7

■ ■ ■

The World of 3-D Graphics

Three-dimensional graphics have completely revolutionized computer games over the last couple of decades. From the start, it became obvious that 3-D games were going to be big, with games such as *DOOM* creating moving images the likes of which had never been seen before.

When dedicated 3-D graphics hardware began to appear back in the late 1990s, graphics were transformed even more, moving away from the blocky and grainy images that players had become accustomed to and replacing them with smooth textures, dynamic lighting, and enormous levels of detail. Game worlds really started to look like real worlds.

Mobile graphics hardware, even in dedicated devices such as Sony's PlayStation Vita, are trailing a fair distance behind the power of modern PC graphics hardware. This applies in many cases to the hardware within Windows RT and Windows Phone devices, too. The capabilities of these devices are still quite sufficient to create very impressive 3-D scenes and games, and the platform is perfectly capable of providing dynamic and complex 3-D gaming opportunities for your audience. Running your game on a desktop PC will provide even greater levels of graphical rendering power.

This chapter examines how to bring the third dimension to life.

Perspective Projection

The vast majority of 3-D games use a *perspective projection* to display their graphics. This projection simulates the application of perspective to objects rendered within the game so that objects that are farther away appear smaller than objects that are closer, just like in the real world.

In addition to this obvious size effect, the more subtle effects of perspective are picked up intuitively by the brain and add a substantial feeling of depth to the rendered scene. The sides of a cube will very slightly narrow due to the effects of perspective as they increase in distance from the viewer, allowing the brain to automatically determine the exact position in which the cube is situated.

The Viewing Frustum

When we use a perspective projection in MonoGame, we create as part of the Effect object initialization a three-dimensional volume known as a *viewing frustum*. The shape of the frustum is that of a rectangular cone with its tip cut off. A demonstration of such a frustum is shown in Figure 7-1.

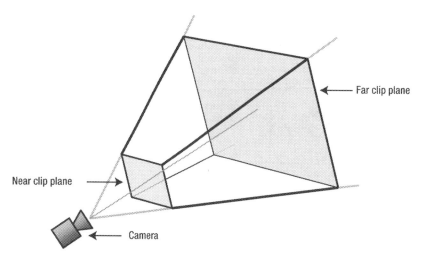

Far clip plane

Near clip plane

Camera

Figure 7-1. *A diagram showing a 3-D viewing frustum*

The frustum can be visualized in the real world by imagining that you are looking through a window. Outside the window, you can see the ground and various objects. The farther away into the distance you look, the wider the area that you can see. Objects that are too far to the side, above, or below will be hidden by the window frame.

Objects that fall inside the volume described by the frustum are visible to the camera (and would be visible through the window). Objects that fall outside the frustum volumes are hidden from the camera (and would not be able to be seen through the window).

The near and far clip planes are also taken into account when deciding whether objects are visible. Objects nearer to the camera than the near clip plane are deemed to be too close and are excluded from rendering. Similarly, objects farther than the far clip plane are too far away to be seen and are also excluded.

▓ **Note** When we specify an object's z position (its distance into the screen), the negative z axis represents movement away from the player and into the screen: as an object's z coordinate decreases, it moves farther away. When we specify the distance of the near and far clip planes, however, they are specified purely as distances from the camera and are, therefore, positive values.

When MonoGame transforms the objects that fall inside the frustum from the 3-D space in which we have defined our world into the 2-D space that is actually presented on the screen, it takes into account how much of the width and height of the frustum is filled by any particular object. An object will occupy a greater proportion of the frustum when it is positioned toward the near clip plane than it will at the far clip plane (see Figures 7-2 and 7-3). Figure 7-2 shows two identically sized objects within the viewing frustum. Figure 7-3 shows the same scene after the perspective projection has taken place to transform the scene into two dimensions for display on the screen. Note that the object at the near clip plane appears substantially larger than the one at the far clip plane.

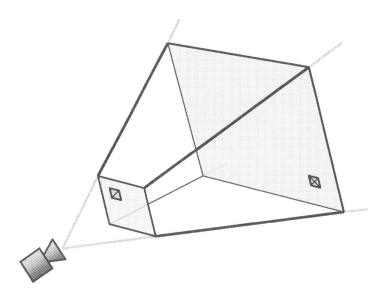

Figure 7-2. *Two identically sized objects in the viewing frustum shown in 3-D space*

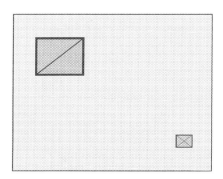

Figure 7-3. *The same two objects after perspective projection into 2-D*

In addition to the clip planes, the frustum is defined by two more pieces of information: the viewing angle and the aspect ratio.

The *viewing angle* defines the angle, in degrees, between the camera and the upper edge of the frustum (the angle on the y axis). Changing this angle will make the overall shape of the frustum expand or compress, causing the apparent reduction in size of objects farther away to be increased or decreased.

Figure 7-4 shows two viewing frustums from the side: the first with a viewing angle of 45 degrees, the second with 22.5 degrees. The distance of the near and far clip planes is the same in both cases.

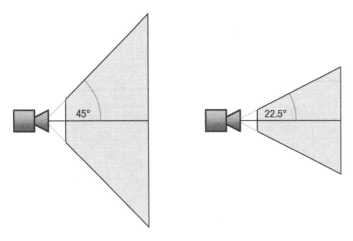

Figure 7-4. *Two viewing frustums, one with a 45-degree viewing angle (left) and one with a 22.5-degree angle (right)*

Consider how objects that fall into these two frustums will be projected. In the frustum with the 45-degree viewing angle, objects can deviate further from the center of the frustum and still be seen by the camera. Objects that are farther away will become rapidly smaller as their size relative to the extent of the frustum becomes less and less. With the 22.5-degree viewing angle, objects farther from the center will leave the frustum more quickly and, consequently, will disappear off the edge of the screen. Distant objects will appear larger than with the first frustum as they occupy a greater proportion of the frustum's area.

Exactly what you should specify for the viewing angle will potentially vary from one game to the next. An angle of 45 degrees is usually a safe value. Setting the angle too low can make it appear that everything is closer to the player than it really is, which can result in the game feeling uncomfortable to play.

■ **Tip**   Some interesting effects can be achieved by varying the viewing angle at strategic times within the game. For example, you could provide a transition between two scenes by rapidly decreasing the viewing angle down to zero, switching the scene, and then increasing the angle back to its original value. This process will cause everything in the center of the screen to appear to zoom toward the player and then zoom back again after the scene change. "Slow-motion" effects can often be accentuated by slightly reducing the viewing angle while they are active.

The second piece of information that the viewing frustum requires is the *aspect ratio*, which is calculated by dividing the display width by its height. The aspect ratio allows the viewing angle on the x axis to be calculated by MonoGame in response to the explicit angle that we provided for the y axis. The aspect ratio, together with the viewing angle and the distance of the clip planes, provides everything that is needed to fully describe the frustum.

Defining the Viewing Frustum in MonoGame

MonoGame actually performs the perspective transformation with the use of another matrix. You might recall that in the `Initialize` function of the example classes from Chapter 6, the code shown in Listing 7-1 is present to set up the default projection matrix.

Listing 7-1. Creating the viewing frustum matrix

```
// Calculate the screen aspect ratio
float aspectRatio = (float)GraphicsDevice.Viewport.Width / GraphicsDevice.Viewport.Height;
// Create a projection matrix
Matrix projection = Matrix.CreatePerspectiveFieldOfView(MathHelper.ToRadians(45),
                                                        aspectRatio, 0.1f, 1000.0f);
```

You should be able to spot all the information that we have discussed as being required for the viewing frustum. The work of generating the projection matrix is performed by the static `Matrix.CreatePerspectiveFieldOfView` function. The parameters that it expects to be passed are as follows, in the following order:

- `fieldOfView`: the viewing angle for the projection (in radians)

- `aspectRatio`: the aspect ratio of the display width/height

- `nearPlaneDistance`: the near clipping plane distance

- `farPlaneDistance`: the far clipping plane distance

In Listing 7-1, a viewing angle of 45 degrees is specified, along with the aspect ratio calculated from the game's `ViewPort`, and near and far clipping planes of 0.1 and 1000, respectively.

When rendering, MonoGame first calculates the positions of all the object vertices in 3-D space and then uses the projection matrix to transform them into 2-D coordinates to display on the screen.

If you want to change the viewing angle (or any of the other properties of the frustum), you can simply set a new projection matrix into the effect's `Projection` property before rendering your objects.

The `Perspective_Win8` and `Perspective_WP8` example projects in this chapter's accompanying download show how objects move when a perspective projection is applied. The code is very simple; it creates a number of objects with random x, y, and z coordinates. Each time the objects update, they add to their `PositionZ` value, moving them closer to the screen. When they get to a value of 0, they add 100 to move them back into the distance. A screenshot from the demo can be seen in Figure 7-5.

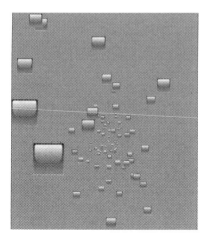

Figure 7-5. *The perspective project showing same-sized objects at different distances*

Rendering 3-D Objects

Moving objects around our 3-D game world is great, but we need to be able to create 3-D objects, too. So far, we've worked just with flat rectangles. This section discusses how solid objects can be created.

The objects that we have been drawing up to this point have defined four vertices, all with a z value of zero, and used a triangle strip to combine them into the rendered shape. When we move into three-dimensional objects, we will very often find that we run into objects that cannot be defined using triangle strips. Every triangle of a triangle strip shares an edge with the previous triangle, and with 3-D objects we will quickly find that we can't draw objects in this way. Instead, we will use a list of individual triangles, which gives us the flexibility to draw whatever triangle we need wherever we need it.

Defining a 3-D Object

To get us started, we will define our 3-D object by manually providing all its vertex coordinates. This is fairly straightforward for simple shapes, but it quickly becomes impractical once we want to move on to more complicated objects. We'll use a simple cube for the time being, however, and we will look at how complicated geometry can be constructed in the "Importing Geometry" section in the next chapter.

A cube consists of six square faces and eight vertices. As each square needs to be rendered as two triangles, we end up with a total of 12 triangles to draw, as shown in Figure 7-6.

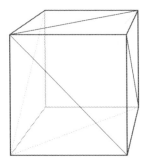

Figure 7-6. *The triangles required to build a 3-D cube*

Because we will draw individual triangles rather than use a triangle strip, we need to specify each triangle coordinate individually. This means that when two triangles share a single coordinate, we actually need to specify the coordinate twice, once for each of the triangles. As a result, we have to provide a total of 36 vertices, three for each triangle. Because there are only eight distinct vertices forming the cube, this respecification of vertices is quite wasteful and requires MonoGame to perform the same calculations over and over again. We will look at a more efficient rendering method in the "Vertex and Index Buffers" section coming up shortly.

To build the vertices of the cube, we simply declare an array of vertices and add to it sets of three values, representing the vertices of each of the triangles. The coordinates for the front face of a unit-size cube can be seen in Listing 7-2. Note that the z coordinate in each coordinate is 0.5, meaning that it extends half a unit toward the viewpoint.

Listing 7-2. Defining the front face of a cube

```
// Create and initialize the vertices
_vertices = new VertexPositionColor[6];

// Set the vertex positions for a unit size cube.
int i = 0;
```

```
// Front face...
_vertices[i++].Position = new Vector3(-0.5f, -0.5f, 0.5f);
_vertices[i++].Position = new Vector3(-0.5f, 0.5f, 0.5f);
_vertices[i++].Position = new Vector3(0.5f, -0.5f, 0.5f);
_vertices[i++].Position = new Vector3(0.5f, -0.5f, 0.5f);
_vertices[i++].Position = new Vector3(-0.5f, 0.5f, 0.5f);
_vertices[i++].Position = new Vector3(0.5f, 0.5f, 0.5f);
```

Plotting out these coordinates shows that we have indeed formed a square that will form the front face of the cube, as shown in Figure 7-7.

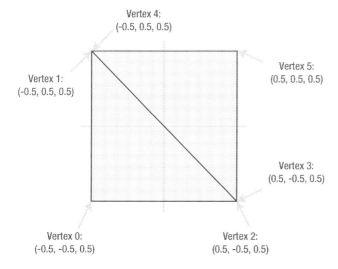

Figure 7-7. *The vertices forming the front face of the cube*

The array is extended to cover all the faces of the cube, extending into the 3-D space by using positive and negative values for the z positions. The full array is not included here because it is fairly large and not particularly interesting, but it can be seen in full inside the CubeObject.BuildVertices function in the ColoredCubes_Win8 and ColoredCubes_WP8 example projects. The code in this function also sets the vertices for each face to be a different color to make the cube look nicer.

■ **Tip** The CubeObject class declares its array of vertices as static, so only a single instance of the array exists and is shared by all instances of the CubeObject class. Because the contents of this array are identical for every class instance, declaring the array in this way means that .NET allocates memory for the vertices only once for the whole application instead of once per cube object, saving some precious memory.

With all the vertices defined, the object can be rendered using exactly the same code used for flat objects. The result is shown in Figure 7-8. Notice how the subtle effects of the perspective transformation can be seen here: the cube appears larger at its front and smaller behind.

Figure 7-8. *The cube resulting from the set of 3-D vertices*

Fundamentally, that is all there is to it! If you run the ColoredCubes example project, you will see how this basic object can be easily reused within the game engine to create a much more visually exciting scene, as shown in Figure 7-9. This example creates 100 cubes, gives each a random angle and position, and then rotates them around the y axis, resulting in a swirling tornado of colored blocks.

Figure 7-9. *The ColoredCubes example project*

The Depth Buffer

Something you might have observed in both the Perspective and ColoredCubes examples is that the objects nearer the camera all appear in front of the objects farther away, just as they should. When we displayed our graphics using sprites, we had to put in some effort to provide a LayerDepth value for each sprite in order to facilitate depth sorting like this. There is no equivalent functionality in these 3-D projects, though, and yet the objects still all appear in the right places. Why does this happen?

The answer is that MonoGame has a built-in mechanism for ensuring that objects in the front of the scene automatically hide any objects that fall behind them. This happens regardless of the order in which objects are drawn: objects drawn behind existing objects can still be partially (or totally) obscured even though they might be rendered after the object in front.

MonoGame achieves this effect by using a feature known as the *depth buffer*. It can be enabled or disabled, and it is enabled by default. When rendering simple 2-D graphics, the depth buffer might be unnecessary, but in 3-D scenes it is almost certain to be required.

Just as the color of each rendered pixel is written into a graphical buffer for display on the screen, so the distance into the screen of each rendered pixel is written into a corresponding depth buffer when the buffer is enabled. For each individual pixel that it is about to render, MonoGame checks the depth of the pixel against the depth already stored in the buffer. If it finds that the new pixel is farther away than the pixel already in the buffer, the new pixel is not rendered to the screen; otherwise, the pixel is rendered and the depth buffer updated to remember the new depth of the pixel.

This per-pixel depth checking can be clearly seen in the `DepthBuffer_Win8` and `DepthBuffer_WP8` example projects, an image from which is shown in Figure 7-10. This figure displays two rotating cubes, positioned so that they intersect one another; and below them a third cube, squashed to form a "floor." Observe the behavior when the cubes intersect one another: at every single pixel position, the frontmost cube surface is always displayed.

Figure 7-10. *The effect of the depth buffer on intersecting objects*

The way that intersecting objects are handled can be very useful. For example, if you want to draw a landscape scene with water such as lakes or an ocean, the ground can be drawn in its entirety (the parts that are above the water level and also those that are below) and then a single semitransparent flat plane can be drawn at the water level across the entire scene. Only those parts of the scene that are below the water level will be affected by the water plane, providing a reasonably convincing approximation of water with very little complexity or processor cost.

Enabling and Disabling the Depth Buffer

Most of the time when you are rendering objects in your game, you will want the depth buffer to be available and active. Without it, distant objects will appear in front of nearer objects that were drawn earlier during the frame, destroying the illusion of the 3-D world that you are trying to render.

On some occasions, however, you might want to render without updating the depth buffer. Examples include rendering background scenery that should never obscure any of the other graphics rendered and objects that are rendered in front of a scene to provide overlay content such as status bars or health displays.

The depth buffer can be temporarily disabled by setting the `GraphicsDevice.DepthStencilState` property to `DepthStencilState.None`. After this property has been set, graphics that are rendered will entirely ignore the depth buffer, neither observing values that are stored in it nor updating the values when new objects are rendered. To restore the normal behavior of the depth buffer, set the property back to its default value: `DepthStencilState.Default`.

You can see the effect of disabling the depth buffer by inserting the code from Listing 7-3 at the end of the `LoadContent` function into one of the `Perspective` example projects.

Listing 7-3. *Disabling the depth buffer*

```
// Disable the depth buffer
GraphicsDevice.DepthStencilState = DepthStencilState.None;
```

Once the depth buffer has been disabled, you will find that the objects appear in the order that they are rendered rather than being sorted by their depth. This can be seen in Figure 7-11, in which some of the smaller, more distant shapes are clearly being displayed in front of the larger closer objects.

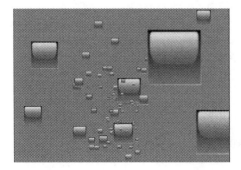

Figure 7-11. *The Perspective project with the depth buffer disabled*

■ **Note**   If you want to *entirely* disable the depth buffer, you can set the _graphics.PreferredDepthStencilFormat property to DepthFormat.None in your game class constructor, directly after creating the _graphics object. This setting will initialize the graphics device without creating a depth buffer, which can save you some memory and processing overhead if you have no need for it.

There is another mode that can be set for the depth buffer: read-only mode. In this mode, MonoGame will observe the values in the depth buffer when rendering objects and will use it to prevent objects from being drawn if they are behind existing objects. However, the depth buffer will not be updated in response to rendered objects.

This mode might seem like an unlikely feature to need, but it has various uses. One such use is for drawing *particles* in a 3-D scene. We'll discuss particles in more detail in the next chapter, but they can be used for creating effects such as sparks, fire, and smoke. Although it is important that these correctly appear behind objects in the scene, we need to ensure that they don't obscure one another or else they won't display correctly.

MonoGame can be set to use a read-only depth buffer by setting the GraphicsDevice.DepthStencilState property to DepthStencilState.DepthRead. Don't forget to set it back to DepthStencilState.Default once you are finished with this mode.

Clearing the Depth Buffer

In some situations, you might want to clear the values stored in the depth buffer. This might be the case if you are drawing two scenes, one in front of the other, and want to prevent each one from interfering with the other. The first scene can be drawn (with the depth buffer active and working), the depth buffer then cleared, and the second scene then drawn. The depth data from the first scene will not interfere with the second scene at all.

To clear the depth buffer, we can call the GraphicsDevice.Clear method, just as we do at the start of the game's Draw function, but instead of simply passing a color we pass some additional parameters that tell it to clear only the depth buffer, not the graphics that have been rendered. The code for clearing the depth buffer can be seen in Listing 7-4.

Listing 7-4. Clearing the depth buffer

```
GraphicsDevice.Clear(ClearOptions.DepthBuffer, Color.White, 1, 0);
```

Because the Clear method's first parameter is set to ClearOptions.DepthBuffer, only the depth buffer will be affected. We still have to pass a color (which will be ignored) and a stencil value (which we are not using), but the value 1 passed for the depth buffer tells MonoGame to set the buffer so that the depths are all considered as being at the very back of the viewing frustum. Subsequently, drawn objects will therefore appear in front of this far depth and will not be obscured by previously drawn objects.

Rendering Transparent Objects with the Depth Buffer

The depth buffer might not work exactly as you expect when it comes to drawing semitransparent objects. Although MonoGame's alpha blending feature can merge together objects that are being drawn with those already on the screen, the depth buffer can store only a single depth for each pixel. This means that if you draw a semitransparent object and then draw an object behind it, the object behind will be completely eliminated by the depth buffer, even though the first object was transparent.

There are several approaches that can be employed to handle this. The first is to draw all your transparent objects so that those in the back of your scene are rendered first. This will ensure that objects in the front do not obscure those behind due to the depth buffer.

The second approach is to draw all your opaque objects first and then switch the depth buffer into DepthRead mode before drawing the transparent objects. This way the transparent objects will not obscure anything subsequently drawn behind them.

The final option is to use the AlphaTest effect (instead of the BasicEffect that we have been using so far), which can update the depth buffer only for pixels that match certain conditions in terms of their calculated alpha values. We will examine this effect in more detail in the next chapter.

Exactly which of these approaches is best will depend on what your game is drawing. Bear this limitation in mind when creating transparent objects in 3-D space.

Hidden Surface Culling

When we draw solid opaque objects such as cubes, the inside of the cube is completely obscured from view. MonoGame is unaware of this, however, and would potentially continue drawing the inside faces of the cube. This is a waste of processing power because it would unnecessarily compare and update the inside faces with the depth buffer. If the faces at the back are processed before those at the front, it would also actually render them, only to subsequently draw over them completely with the outer faces of the cube.

You probably won't be surprised to hear that MonoGame has a solution for this problem—and it's nice and easy to use, too.

MonoGame can work out whether each triangle is facing toward us (as the front face of the cube is) or away from us (as the back face of the cube is). It does this based on how the triangle is actually rendered, not just how its vertices were defined so that as a triangle rotates, the direction in which it is facing will change. Those triangles that are found to be facing away from us are *culled* and are not considered for inclusion in the depth or color buffers, saving all the work that would otherwise have been involved in checking and updating them.

In order for MonoGame to be able to determine the direction in which the triangles are facing, we need to give our triangle vertices to it in a particular way. When we define the triangles, we ensure that when the front of the triangle is facing toward us, the vertices are provided such that they appear in a clockwise direction. Figure 7-12 shows two triangles, one whose vertices are defined in clockwise order (on the left) and the other in counterclockwise order.

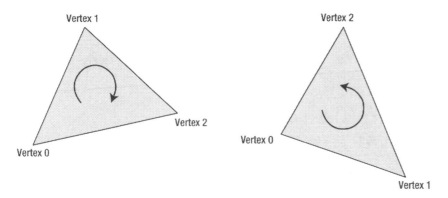

Figure 7-12. Triangles with vertices defined in clockwise (left) and counterclockwise (right) order

Given these two triangles to render, MonoGame will, by default, display the one on the left and not the one on the right. If we rotate them around so that their backs are toward us, the triangle on the left would not display and the triangle on the right would appear.

■ **Note**   Remember that the vertices must appear in clockwise order *when the triangle is facing you.* When we define a cube, the rear face is initially facing away from us, so the triangles would appear to be in counterclockwise order instead. If the cube were rotated around so that the back face was oriented toward us, the vertices would then appear to be clockwise, as we need them to be.

If you look back at the vertices defined for the front face of the cube in Figure 7-7, you will see that both of the triangles have their vertices defined in clockwise order. This is by design, of course. With our triangles specified correctly, MonoGame will automatically ignore those triangles that face away from us.

The HiddenSurfaceCulling_Win8 and HiddenSurfaceCulling_WP8 projects draw yet another cube, but this time they omit the final triangle from the cube (telling DrawUserPrimitives to draw 11 triangles instead of 12), resulting in a triangular hole. We can look through this hole to the interior of the cube to see exactly what MonoGame is drawing for the reverse sides of the cube triangles.

If you run this project, you will see that the orange side of the cube that contains the missing triangle shows nothing behind it whatsoever (see Figure 7-13). This demonstrates that MonoGame really is rendering the triangles only when they are actually facing toward us.

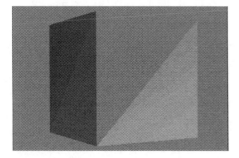

Figure 7-13. The rear faces of the cube's triangles have been culled

Sometimes it is useful to draw the rear surfaces of triangles, too. If you have objects that are completely flat and need to be viewed from in front or behind, or if you have objects that are hollow and whose interior can be seen, we can configure MonoGame to render both surfaces of each triangle.

To instruct MonoGame to render in this way, we need to disable surface culling. Culling is controlled by the `GraphicsDevice.RasterizerState.CullMode` property, which accepts one of these values: `CullCounterClockwiseFace` (the default), `CullClockwiseFace` (the reverse; culls faces that are defined in clockwise order), or `None` (the value we need here; none of the faces are culled).

Just as with the `BlendState` and `SamplerState` objects we saw in the last chapter, the `RasterizerState` object's properties all become read-only once the object has been set into the `GraphicsDevice`. We, therefore, can't update the properties of the existing object. Instead, we create a new object, configure it as required and then set the whole object into the `GraphicsDevice`, as shown in Listing 7-5.

Listing 7-5. Disabling hidden surface culling

```
// Create and activate a new RasterizerState with a different cull mode.
RasterizerState rs = new RasterizerState();
rs.CullMode = CullMode.None;
GraphicsDevice.RasterizerState = rs;
```

You will find this code present but commented out within the `HiddenSurfaceCulling` project's `Initialize` function. Uncomment it so that it becomes active and then run the project again. Now you will find when the orange face is toward you that you can see through the missing triangle into the fully rendered interior of the cube, as shown in Figure 7-14.

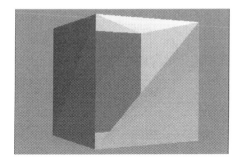

Figure 7-14. *The rear faces of the cube's triangles have not been culled*

The important thing to remember with hidden surface culling disabled is that the interior faces are being calculated and compared against the depth buffer even when they are completely hidden from view. When hidden surface culling was enabled, the interior faces were discarded immediately as MonoGame knew that they faced away and therefore didn't need to be checked against the depth buffer at all.

The final culling mode, culling clockwise faces, can be useful if you are importing model files (as we will learn to do in the next chapter) that have been defined with their faces counterclockwise instead of clockwise. Some modeling applications will define triangles in this way and this is, in fact, the default culling mechanism used by OpenGL. The easiest way to deal with such objects is to swap the culling mode.

When the culling mode doesn't match the order with which the vertices have been defined, MonoGame will render just the inside of the object, hiding all the triangles that face toward you. This can result in potentially useful effects, though they can be visually disorientating. Try modifying the example project code so that it culls clockwise faces and running it again. You will now see the inside of the cube, as shown in Figure 7-15.

Figure 7-15. *The front faces of the cube's triangles have been culled*

Vertex and Index Buffers

We're making good progress in our journey into 3-D rendering, but there are some inefficiencies in the approach that we have used so far that it would be wise to address before we go any further. These can be addressed by using two new constructs: *vertex buffers* and *index buffers*. Let's take a look and see what they can do for us and how they are used.

All the techniques discussed in this section can be seen in the VertexAndIndexBuffers_Win8 and VertexAndIndexBuffers_WP8 example projects. These projects add three cubes to the scene, each using a different one of the techniques that we are about to explore.

Using Vertex Buffers

In all the examples we have used so far, we have called the DrawUserPrimitives function to render our objects, passing it an array of vertices containing the object geometry. This works just fine, but it is not the most efficient way of rendering. In order for the graphics hardware to use the vertex data, all the vertices must be transferred into the graphics memory. Just as we saw with repeated texture copying in earlier chapters, this data transfer can have a negative impact on performance.

We can address this performance issue by using a *vertex buffer*, which allows the vertex data to reside permanently within the graphics hardware. The advantage of this approach is that we can switch between vertex buffers with much less overhead than copying vertex data arrays.

A cube defined using a vertex buffer can be found in the VertexBufferCubeObject class. There are only a couple of differences between this class and the cube classes that we have looked at previously. First of all, a new static class-level variable has been defined of type VertexBuffer and with the name _vertexBuffer. When the class finds that the vertices have not been initialized, it creates them as before, but it then also uses them to initialize the vertex buffer, as shown in Listing 7-6.

Listing 7-6. Creating and initializing a VertexBuffer object

```
// Have we already built the cube vertex array in a previous instance?
if (_vertices == null)
{
    // No, so build them now
    BuildVertices();
    // Create a vertex buffer
    _vertexBuffer = new VertexBuffer(game.GraphicsDevice,
            typeof(VertexPositionColor), _vertices.Length, BufferUsage.WriteOnly);
    _vertexBuffer.SetData(_vertices);
}
```

The parameters passed to the VertexBuffer constructor are as follows, in this order:

- graphicsDevice: the graphics device to which this vertex buffer will be rendered

- vertexType: the type of vertex being added to the buffer

- vertexCount: the number of vertices to be added to the buffer

- usage: special usage flags

Most of these parameters should be self-explanatory. We know the vertex count because we've already built an array of vertices, so we can simply read the array size for the vertexCount parameter. The usage parameter needs a little additional explanation, however. It can be passed as either None or WriteOnly. The first of these options allows the vertex data to be retrieved at a later time (using the VertexBuffer.GetData function), but it results in less efficient usage of the buffer in the graphics hardware. The WriteOnly option optimizes the buffer memory usage, but makes it impossible to read the vertex data back. It is unusual to need to read the data back (in this example, we have it in a separate array, anyway), so unless you need to read the data from the buffer, you should always specify WriteOnly.

This object creation results in an initialized but empty vertex buffer. The vertex data is copied into it by calling the SetData function, passing the vertex array as a parameter.

The buffer is now ready for use. To render it, we need to make some small changes to the object's Draw function. Prior to drawing, we must tell the graphics device which vertex buffer it should render. Only a single vertex buffer can be set at any time, so it must be specified before the drawing instruction is executed. The buffer is set into the device, as shown in Listing 7-7.

Listing 7-7. Setting a vertex buffer into the graphics device

```
// Set the active vertex buffer
effect.GraphicsDevice.SetVertexBuffer(_vertexBuffer);
```

To render with the active vertex buffer, we use a different drawing method. Previously, we had been calling DrawUserPrimitives and passing in the vertex array as a parameter. To render using a vertex buffer, we instead call DrawPrimitives. No vertex data needs to be passed because the vertex buffer from the graphics device will be used. We just need to tell MonoGame the primitive type, the start vertex, and the primitive count, just as we did before. The code to render the vertex buffer is shown in Listing 7-8.

Listing 7-8. Drawing the active vertex buffer

```
// Draw the object
foreach (EffectPass pass in effect.CurrentTechnique.Passes)
{
    // Apply the pass
    pass.Apply();
    // Draw the object using the active vertex buffer
    effect.GraphicsDevice.DrawPrimitives(PrimitiveType.TriangleList, 0, 12);
}
```

Other than these changes, the code and approach are identical to the examples we have already used. When running the example project, the cube implemented in this way is the one that appears at the top of the screen.

Using Indexed Vertices

In order to draw the cube shown in the previous examples, we have had to provide the same vertex coordinates to MonoGame multiple times. As we discussed earlier, a cube has 8 vertices, and yet, in our examples, we are creating our vertex array with 36 vertices in it, 6 for each face (consisting of 3 vertices for each of the 2 triangles used to draw the face).

This configuration of vertices is, of course, quite wasteful in terms of processing resources because we are calculating the exact same vertex position many times.

MonoGame provides an alternative mechanism for providing the list of vertices that allows the number of repeated identical coordinates to be reduced. Instead of creating each vertex independently of the others, we can instead provide a list of just the unique vertices and then separately tell MonoGame how to join them together to make the triangles that it is to render. The list of vertex numbers that specifies how to join the vertices is simply stored as an array of numbers.

Consider again the front face of the cube that we saw in Figure 7-7. If we were to specify just the unique vertices, the vertex count would be reduced from the previous six to four. The four vertices are shown in Figure 7-16.

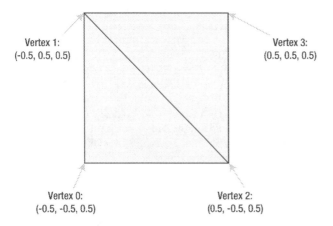

Figure 7-16. *Specifying just the unique coordinates for the front face of the cube*

Although this new set of coordinates allows the vertices to be defined, we no longer have the information required to join them together to form the rendered triangles. At this point, the index array comes to the rescue. To draw the front face, we need two triangles and the vertex indices for each are as follows:

- First triangle: 0, 1, 2

- Second triangle: 2, 1, 3

Just as before, the triangle is formed by specifying its vertices in clockwise order so that hidden surface culling can hide the triangles when they are facing away from the viewer.

The only additional complexity with this approach is that vertices do not only store a position; they also store colors, texture coordinates, and other information (as we will see in the next chapter). Just because two vertices share the same location, it doesn't necessarily mean that they are identical.

Each vertex position in our cube will be part of three different faces (because each corner of the cube has three squares attached to it), and each face in our example is a different color. We will, therefore, need to repeat the vertices for each face, even though they are in the same position, because they have different colors.

This still allows us to reduce the vertex count from the original 36 (6 vertices per face x 6 faces) to a much more efficient 24 (4 vertices per face x 6 faces). The two redundant vertices within each square face are eliminated, reducing the vertex count by one-third.

As a result, the code required to build the vertex array now needs only to specify the unique indexes. The beginning of the code to generate these vertices, from the IndexedCubeObject class, can be seen in Listing 7-9. Compare this code to that in Listing 7-2 and you will see that the repeated vertices are no longer present.

Listing 7-9. Specifying vertex data for indexed rendering

```
// Set the vertex positions for a unit size cube.
i = 0;
// Front face...
_vertices[i++].Position = new Vector3(-0.5f, -0.5f, 0.5f);
_vertices[i++].Position = new Vector3(-0.5f, 0.5f, 0.5f);
_vertices[i++].Position = new Vector3(0.5f, -0.5f, 0.5f);
_vertices[i++].Position = new Vector3(0.5f, 0.5f, 0.5f);
```

In order to join the vertices together, we need to build the array of indices. MonoGame provides functions that allow them to be stored either as an array of short values (permitting a maximum of 32767 vertices), or as an array of int values (with a maximum vertex count exceeding 2 billion), but only the short implementation of the functions are actually supported. This vertex limit still allows for very complex objects and is unlikely to present any practical limitation; it also saves memory by requiring two bytes per index instead of four.

For rendering a triangle list as we are, the array needs to be given sets of three indices in order to identify the three vertices for each triangle. The BuildIndices function sets them all up, and a small section of this can be seen in Listing 7-10. The resulting data is stored in the static class-level _indices array.

Listing 7-10. The start of the index array creation

```
private void BuildIndices()
{
    int i;

    // Create and initialize the indices
    _indices = new short[36];

    // Set the indices for the cube
    i = 0;
    // Front face...
    _indices[i++] = 0;
    _indices[i++] = 1;
    _indices[i++] = 2;
    _indices[i++] = 2;
    _indices[i++] = 1;
    _indices[i++] = 3;
    // Back face...
    _indices[i++] = 4;
    _indices[i++] = 5;
    _indices[i++] = 6;
    _indices[i++] = 5;
    _indices[i++] = 7;
    _indices[i++] = 6;
```

Note that we store 36 elements in the array: 6 faces x 2 triangles x 3 vertices = 36 elements in total. The first triangle is formed from the vertices at positions 0, 1, and 2; and the second triangle from the vertices at positions 2, 1, and 3—exactly as described in Figure 7-16. The array then continues to form another triangle from vertices 4, 5, 6; and another from vertices 5, 7, 6; and so on for all the triangles in the cube.

This is clearly quite a lot more work to set up than simply providing the stand-alone list of vertices, and in many cases the benefit of this approach will be negligible. In more complex objects, it can provide a noticeable performance boost, however. This indexed rendering approach can be taken advantage of without having to enter pages and pages of index numbers when geometry is read from external model files (as we will see in the next chapter) and also if you should write code that programmatically generates vertex coordinates and indices.

To render the cube using the index data, we call the DrawUserIndexedPrimitives function in the Draw function rather than DrawUserPrimitives. In addition to the DrawUserPrimitives parameters, this call also expects the index array to be provided and an offset through the index array from which it should start processing (which we will pass as 0 to specify that it should be processed from the beginning). The code for this call is shown in Listing 7-11.

Listing 7-11. Rendering the cube using the index array

```
// Draw the object
foreach (EffectPass pass in effect.CurrentTechnique.Passes)
{
    // Apply the pass
    pass.Apply();
    // Draw the object using the active vertex buffer
    effect.GraphicsDevice.DrawUserIndexedPrimitives(PrimitiveType.TriangleList,
                             _vertices, 0, _vertices.Length, _indices, 0, 12);
}
```

This approach results in the elimination of unnecessary processing of identical vertices in the rendered object. When running the example project, the code rendered with this technique is the one displayed in the middle of the screen.

Using Vertex Buffers and Indexing Together

Vertex buffers and indexing each provide optimizations to the way in which our objects are calculated. To get the best of both worlds, we can use them both at the same time. When we render an indexed vertex buffer, the vertex buffer itself is created exactly as we have already seen, but the indexes are specified in a slightly different way. Instead of storing them just as an array, we instead place the array data into an IndexBuffer object.

This combined approach can be seen in the VertexAndIndexBufferCubeObject class. The vertex and index data is created exactly as it was for indexed rendering, with the reduced number of vertices (24 instead of 36) and the index array joining them together into the finished object. In the class constructor, both of these arrays are set into buffer objects, as shown in Listing 7-12.

Listing 7-12. Creating a vertex buffer and an index buffer

```
// Have we already built the cube vertex array in a previous instance?
if (_vertices == null)
{
    // No, so build them now
    BuildVertices();
    // Create a vertex buffer
    _vertexBuffer = new VertexBuffer(game.GraphicsDevice,
                typeof(VertexPositionColor), _vertices.Length, BufferUsage.WriteOnly);
    _vertexBuffer.SetData(_vertices);

    // Create the index array
    BuildIndices();
    // Create an index buffer
    _indexBuffer = new IndexBuffer(game.GraphicsDevice, typeof(short),
                                    _indices.Length, BufferUsage.WriteOnly);
    _indexBuffer.SetData(_indices);
}
```

The constructor parameters required when creating the IndexBuffer object are as follows:

- graphicsDevice: the graphics device to which this index buffer will be rendered

- type: the type used for each index array element (short or int)

- indexCount: the number of indices to be added to the buffer

- usage: special usage flags (None or WriteOnly, just as with the vertex buffer)

This object creation sets up everything that is required to render the indexed vertex buffer. To actually draw it, we need to tweak the Draw function again.

Just as with the vertex buffer example, we need to provide the vertex buffer to the graphics device using the SetVertexBuffer function. Additionally, we now need to provide the index buffer into the graphics device's Indices property.

With these objects set in place, we render this time by calling the DrawIndexedPrimitive function. No vertex or index data needs to be passed because the function reads both of these from the objects set into the graphics device. Listing 7-13 shows the complete code to draw the cube using this approach.

Listing 7-13. Drawing indexed vertices from a vertex buffer

```
public override void Draw(Microsoft.Xna.Framework.GameTime gameTime, Effect effect)
{
    // Prepare the effect for drawing
    PrepareEffect(effect);

    // Set the active vertex and index buffer
    effect.GraphicsDevice.SetVertexBuffer(_vertexBuffer);
    effect.GraphicsDevice.Indices = _indexBuffer;

    // Draw the object
    foreach (EffectPass pass in effect.CurrentTechnique.Passes)
    {
        // Apply the pass
        pass.Apply();
        // Draw the object using the active vertex buffer
        effect.GraphicsDevice.DrawIndexedPrimitives(PrimitiveType.TriangleList, 0, 0,
                                          _vertices.Length, 0, 12);
    }
}
```

This approach provides the greatest efficiency for rendering in MonoGame because it reduces the calculation of redundant vertices and prevents unnecessary copying of vertex data within the device memory. When running the example project, the cube rendered with this technique is the one at the bottom of the screen.

Lighting

Up to this point, all the colors used in our examples have been directly specified within our program code. This gives us a high level of control over the appearance of the graphics, but it leads to a flat and cartoony look to the graphics. To add a further degree of realism to the objects that we render, we can use MonoGame's lighting features.

This section examines the lighting capabilities and explores how they can be used within our games.

Lights and Materials

MonoGame offers the facility to place up to three different lights into the game world and use these to illuminate the objects that are rendered. When lighting is switched on, the way in which objects are colored is altered from the behavior we have seen so far. MonoGame applies lighting to our objects by calculating the amount and color of light that falls onto each vertex and actually adjusts the rendered vertex colors based on the result of this.

The outcome is that we can generate highly dynamic and realistic-looking shading on our objects. The minor downside is that because MonoGame implements lighting by taking control of coloring the object vertices, we can't specify vertex colors ourselves. We can still apply textures to our objects just as before, but vertex colors cannot be used.

Although we are no longer able to directly color vertices, we can still use different colors within a texture to provide coloring to different sections of our objects. As a result, this is not necessarily as big a problem as it might at first sound.

Additionally, the DiffuseColor property can still be used to change the overall color of the objects being rendered. This is also known as the *material color* as it defines the color of the object. This works alongside the colors of lights that we place within the scene, allowing colors of lights and objects to be set independently. This provides a fair degree of flexibility with regard to how our objects are lit.

The following sections will discuss how lights and materials can be used within our game worlds.

Types of Illumination

A number of different types of illumination are available to shine onto our objects. Any or all of the illumination types can be applied to MonoGame's lighting model and the color of each type of illumination can be specified independently.

Let's take a look at each of the illumination types that a light can use.

Ambient Light

The simplest type of light is *ambient light*, which is light that comes from all directions at once and falls equally on to all parts of each object rendered. It is completely flat in intensity, leaving no bright or dark areas on the objects that it illuminates.

In the real world, the closest analogy to ambient light is the light that is reflected from all the objects in the environment. If you are in a room with a single light source, those areas of the room that are not in direct line of sight from the bulb still receive some light from their surroundings. This is the illumination that ambient light seeks to simulate.

When an ambient light is present, all vertices will be equally lit by the appropriate ambient light level.

An example object illuminated with ambient light can be seen in Figure 7-17. The figure shows a 3-D cylinder with a medium-intensity ambient light applied and no other lighting. Note how the object appears just as a silhouette: no variation of light intensity can be seen anywhere within the object.

Figure 7-17. *A cylinder illuminated with an ambient light source*

MonoGame's default ambient light is black, meaning that no ambient light appears within the rendered scene at all.

Diffuse Light

Diffuse light is reflected by an object based on how the object is angled toward the light source. If an object is rotated so that its faces are directly toward the light source, the faces will radiate the light with a high intensity. As they rotate away from the light, the intensity fades away.

The light is radiated equally in all directions, so the viewpoint from which the object is seen has no effect on the intensity of the lit surfaces. This is how an object with a matte surface would behave in the real world, as opposed to a reflective surface that would reflect more or less light depending upon the observation viewpoint.

An example object illuminated with diffuse light can be seen in Figure 7-18. The figure shows the same cylinder with a bright diffuse light situated directly to its right. Note that the object illumination increases as the object surface becomes more directly angled toward the light source.

Figure 7-18. *A cylinder illuminated with a diffuse light source*

Specular Light

Specular light is also reflected by an object based upon its angle with regard to the light source, but this type of illumination radiates light more like a mirror: light is reflected from the surface based on the angle of the surface relative to the viewer and light source.

If the light source is in the same location as the viewpoint and a surface also faces directly toward the viewpoint, the specular light will radiate intensely. As soon as the surface rotates away from the viewpoint, the specular light will rapidly fall away. If the viewpoint and light source are in different locations, those faces that are angled directly between the two will radiate light most brightly, just as a mirror would.

This behavior allows objects to be given a "shine" or "highlight" that can make for very realistic looking objects.

An example object illuminated with specular light can be seen in Figure 7-19. The image shows the same cylinder with a bright specular light situated directly to its right. Note that the object illumination increases as the angle of the cylinder reflects our viewpoint toward the light, where the surface of the cylinder is at about a 45-degree angle from the viewpoint. As the surface deviates from this angle, the light intensity rapidly drops away.

Figure 7-19. *A cylinder illuminated with a specular light source*

Material Properties

Just as lights emit different types and intensities of light, so can objects reflect different types of light in different colors. For example, a red object in the real world is red because it reflects any red light that falls upon it, and it absorbs the green and blue light.

In MonoGame, we can set the color and intensity of light reflected from each individual object by setting the object *material*. Just as each light can have different colors for ambient, diffuse, and specular light, we can define the intensity and color that objects reflect for each different type of light.

Let's take a look at the different material properties and then we will examine exactly how lights and materials interact with each other.

Diffuse Material

As the material's ambient property controls the amount of ambient light reflected, so its diffuse property controls the amount of diffuse light reflected. This can be set to white to reflect all the light that reaches the object, or it can be changed in order to absorb and reflect different elements of the color instead.

We have already discussed the diffuse material in the "Tinting Objects" section in the last chapter.

Specular Material

The material's specular color controls the amount of specular light that is reflected from the object. Setting the material's specular color to white will reflect all specular light that arrives at the object, whereas setting it to black will absorb and, therefore, completely disable the specular element of the light, preventing any shine effects from displaying on the object.

In addition to controlling how much of the specular light is reflected, MonoGame also offers control over the focus of the specular highlight. Low specular power values (values up to around 4 or 5) will result in a very soft specular component, reflecting lots of light back. As the value increases, the specular light becomes more and more focused, requiring faces to be angled more directly toward the light source before any reflection is made. There is no specific upper limit for the specular power value, but as it begins to reach into the hundreds, its effect becomes so slight that the specular light effects begin to disappear.

Emissive Material

The final material property allows us to set an *emissive color*. This property is used to specify a color that is then simulated as originating from the object, allowing it to have its own illumination independently of that of the lights around it.

Normally, if an object has no light shining on it, it will appear completely black. However, emissive colors allow the basic object color to be set even when it is not illuminated by any light at all.

It should be noted, however, that rendering an object with an emissive color set does not make the object into a light source itself. It will not add any light to the rest of the scene or cause any other objects to be illuminated in any way.

Light and Material Interaction

Now that you understand the role of light in a 3-D scene and how it affects game objects, how do these lights and materials actually interact together?

A fairly simple calculation is used to determine the level of light for each vertex that is rendered. The engine first calculates the amount of diffuse light to apply to the object by multiplying each of the red, green, and blue diffuse values for the light (which range from 0 to 1) by the corresponding red, green, and blue diffuse values for the material (also ranging from 0 to 1). The resulting values are used to form the final diffuse color level for the object.

Let's look at an example. If we have a midlevel gray diffuse light with (red, green, blue) values of (0.5, 0.5, 0.5) and an object that has a blue diffuse material with color (0.7, 0.2, 0.2), the color components are multiplied as follows:

- *Red*: 0.5 x 0.7 = 0.35
- *Green*: 0.5 x 0.2 = 0.1
- *Blue*: 0.5 x 0.2 = 0.1

The resulting diffuse color for the object is therefore (0.35, 0.1, 0.1).

Consider another example in which we have a pure red diffuse light with color (1, 0, 0) and a pure green diffuse material with color (0, 1, 0). The calculation for this would be the following:

- *Red*: 1 x 0 = 0
- *Green*: 0 x 1 = 0
- *Blue*: 0 x 0 = 0

The resulting color is therefore (0, 0, 0): black. Shining a green light onto a red object results in all the green light being absorbed, so the object is not illuminated at all.

Once the final diffuse light has been calculated as shown, the same calculation is repeated for the specular light. The ambient light is then multiplied by the diffuse material to create a third calculated color. A fourth and final color is derived from the emissive material color.

The red, green, and blue components of these four colors are then simply added together to produce the final color of light that will be applied to the object. If any of the color components exceed their upper limit of 1, they are clamped at this value and treated as being equal to 1.

Using Multiple Lights

We are not limited to having a single light active within our rendered scene. Up to a maximum of three available lights can be switched on when an object is rendered to provide light of different color and in different directions.

If an object is rendered with more than one light active, the final color for the object is calculated as explained a moment ago in the "Light and Material Interaction" section for each individual light. The color components for the individual lights are then all added together to provide a final color for the object being rendered.

This behavior means that it is possible for colors to become oversaturated if lots of different lights are present at once. Some thought and attention might be required to ensure that light sources don't cause objects to be flooded with so much light that they are overwhelmed by it.

Reusing Lights

An important feature to remember when using lights is that they are observed only at the moment at which an object is rendered. After an object render has been called, the lights that were active can be reconfigured, moved, enabled, or disabled in whatever way you want for the next object, and these changes will have no effect at all on those objects already rendered.

Lights do not, therefore, need to affect all objects in the game world as lights in the real world would; they can be configured to apply only to specific game objects if needed.

■ **Tip**   Also remember that you can switch the entire lighting feature on and off partway through rendering if you want. It is quite acceptable to draw a series of objects with lighting enabled, then disable the lighting features, and subsequently draw further objects without any lighting effects at all so that vertex colors can be used instead.

Types of Light Source

Many 3-D graphics APIs support multiple different types of light; they normally include directional lights, point lights, and spotlights. Each of these changes the way that the reflection of the light is calculated on each object that it illuminates. MonoGame does not provide all of these, instead implementing just one type of light: directional lights.

Directional lights shine light in a single direction equally across an entire scene. They do not have a position, but rather they are treated as being infinitely far away from the scene. The rays of light are parallel to each other.

The closest analogy in the real world is sunlight. Although the sun clearly does actually have a position, it is so far away that the light it emits is, for all intents and purposes, coming from the entire sky rather than from a single point.

Figure 7-20 shows the way in which a directional light shines on objects rendered within a 3-D scene. Note that the light has direction but does not have a position: the rays shown are all parallel and do not converge on or originate from any specific location.

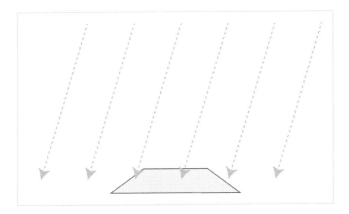

Figure 7-20. *Light rays from a directional light source*

How MonoGame Calculates Light Reflections

The explanations we have looked at for each light revolve to a significant degree around determining whether each triangle in a rendered object is facing toward or away from a light. Triangles that are at the appropriate angle relative to the light will be illuminated brightly, whereas triangles facing away from the light will become darker or not be illuminated at all.

How does MonoGame tell whether a triangle is facing toward a light or not? There's nothing magical about this. In fact, the answer is rather basic: we have to tell MonoGame the direction in which each triangle is facing.

We do this just once when we create our object. When the object is rotating or moving in the game world, MonoGame will use this information and apply all the object transformations to the direction in which the triangle is facing, just as it does to the position of the vertices. The object lighting will therefore be automatically and dynamically calculated as each object or light moves within the scene.

Describing a Triangle's Face Direction

To tell MonoGame the direction in which each triangle is facing, we provide a Vector3 value known as a *normal*. A normal describes a line that is pointing in a direction perpendicular to the front of the triangle. Figure 7-21 shows a single triangle with its normal. The triangle itself is completely flat with its surface pointing directly upward. The normal, which is represented by a dashed arrow, therefore points upward, too.

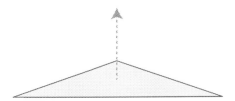

Figure 7-21. *A triangle and its normal*

In Figure 7-22, a solid shape is shown with its normals. Each side of the cube faces in a different direction, and once again dashed arrows are used to indicate the direction of the normal from each side.

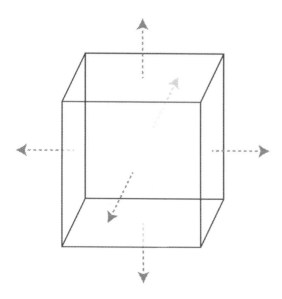

Figure 7-22. *A cube and the normals of each of its faces*

To describe each normal, we use a different type of vertex object: VertexPositionNormalTexture. In addition to the Position and TextureCoordinate vectors that we explored already, this object contains an additional vector called Normal. This vector allows the three different values (for the x, y, and z axes) to describe the distance along each axis that would need to be traveled to move along the line of the normal.

For the triangles on top of the cube whose faces point directly upward, the normal vector would be (0, 1, 0). This vector shows that to travel along the line of the normal, we would move zero units along the x and z axes, and one unit along the positive y axis. In other words, we would move directly upward. The opposite face that points downward would have a normal vector of (0, -1, 0). Moving in the direction of this vector would move us along the negative y axis.

Similarly, the triangles on the right edge of the cube have a normal vector of (1, 0, 0), and the triangles at the back of the cube (facing away from us) have a normal vector of (0, 0, -1).

We need to provide these normal vectors to MonoGame for it to use when our object is being rendered. We only need to provide the vectors for when the object is in its default untransformed position. As the object is rotated within the scene, MonoGame will recalculate its resulting normal vectors automatically.

Notice that the normals we have discussed all have a length of one unit. This is important because MonoGame takes the normal length into account when performing its lighting calculations, and normal vectors that are longer or shorter than this might cause the reflected light to become unexpectedly brighter or darker. Vectors with a length of one unit are known as *normalized* vectors, whereas those with longer or shorter lengths are *unnormalized* vectors.

Once MonoGame knows the direction each triangle is facing, it can work out whether they face toward or away from the scene's lights and hence determine how much light to provide for the triangle.

Calculating Normals

Although working out normal vectors is easy when they are aligned directly along the x, y, or z axis, they can be much more difficult to work out in your head when the triangle faces in a direction away from these axes. Calculating the normals manually for these triangles would be both tedious and prone to errors.

Fortunately, we are writing computer software, so we can get it to calculate the normals for us automatically.

There are all sorts of mathematical operations that can be calculated on vectors (and there are lots of books and online references that will cover this subject in immense detail if you want to investigate it further), and we can use one of these called a *cross product* to calculate the normal for us.

We will now briefly look at the calculation performed by the cross product in order to understand what it does. Don't worry if you find the arithmetic complex or off-putting, however. As you will see in a moment, MonoGame has support for doing all this built in to its Vector3 structure, so we don't have to calculate any of this manually. The explanation here simply describes what is going on under the covers.

To perform a cross product calculation, we need to find two vectors that lie along the surface of our triangle. They are easy to calculate because we can simply find the difference in position between the vertices of the triangle. For the purposes of this example, we will call these vectors a and b.

Consider the triangle shown in Figure 7-23. It is oriented so that its surface points directly upward (to keep the example simple!) and has vertex coordinates as shown.

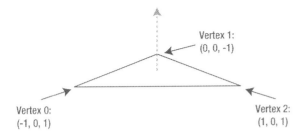

Figure 7-23. *The vertices of a triangle ready for normal calculation*

Note that the triangle vertices are, as always, defined in clockwise order. This is important to our calculation. If they were defined in counterclockwise order, the normal we calculate would be facing in the opposite direction (downward in this case).

To calculate the two vectors that we need, we subtract the coordinates of vertex 1 from vertex 2 for the first vector, and subtract the coordinates of vertex 0 from vertex 1 for the second vector, as follows:

- Vector a: Vertex 2 – Vertex 1 = $(1 - 0, 0 - 0, 1 - -1) = (1, 0, 2)$

- Vector b: Vertex 1 – Vertex 0 = $(0 - -1, 0 - 0, -1 - 1) = (1, 0, -2)$

As you can see, these do indeed represent the distances from each vertex to the next. To move from vertex 1 to vertex 2, we would need to move 1 unit along the x axis, 0 units on the y axis, and 2 units on the z axis. To move from vertex 0 to vertex 1, we would need to move 1 unit on the x axis, 0 units on the y axis and -2 units along the z axis.

To perform the cross product operation, we need to perform the following calculations on vectors a and b. These will produce the normal vector n:

- $n.x = (a.y \times b.z) - (a.z \times b.y)$

- $n.y = (a.z \times b.x) - (a.x \times b.z)$

- $n.z = (a.x \times b.y) - (a.y \times b.x)$

Let's substitute in the values for our vectors and see the results:

- $n.x = (0 \times -2) - (2 \times 0) = 0 - 0 = 0$

- $n.y = (2 \times 1) - (1 \times -2) = 2 - -2 = 4$

- $n.z = (1 \times 0) - (0 \times 1) = 0 - 0 = 0$

The resulting vector n is therefore calculated as (0, 4, 0). This does indeed describe a line in the positive y axis, directly upward, exactly as we had hoped. The same calculation can be performed for any triangle regardless of its vertex locations.

So, having seen what the cross product calculation actually does, let's make things a little simpler and take a look at how MonoGame can do this work for us. We still need to calculate the vectors a and b, but MonoGame will allow us to simply subtract one vertex position from another to calculate these. With the a and b vectors prepared, we can pass them to the static `Vector3.Cross` function, and it will return the normal. The code required to perform all of this is shown in Listing 7-14, which uses the same triangle as we used for our manual calculations.

Listing 7-14. Calculating the normal for a triangle

```
// Create three  vertices for our triangle
Vector3 vertex0 = new Vector3(-1, 0, 1);
Vector3 vertex1 = new Vector3(0, 0, -1);
Vector3 vertex2 = new Vector3(1, 0, 1);

// Calculate the a and b vectors by subtracting the vertices from one another
Vector3 vectora = vertex2 - vertex1;
Vector3 vectorb = vertex1 - vertex0;

// Calculate the normal as the cross product of the two vectors
Vector3 normal = Vector3.Cross(vectora, vectorb);

// Display the normal to the debug window
System.Diagnostics.Debug.WriteLine(normal.ToString());
```

Hopefully, that should be a bit easier to understand! The output that is displayed by the code is the vector (0, 4, 0), exactly as with our manual calculations.

The normal vector we have calculated is not normalized, however—its length is 4 rather than 1. MonoGame's `Vector3` structure has a `Normalize` method that we can call to easily normalize the value, so we can just let MonoGame do it for us. The code shown in Listing 7-15 can be added after the call to `Vector3.Cross` from Listing 7-14 to normalize the vector.

Listing 7-15. Normalizing the normal vector

```
normal.Normalize();
```

The resulting normalized vector is (0, 1, 0)—a unit-length vector pointing directly upward. Perfect.

We will look at implementing all this in our program code in the section entitled "Programmatic Calculation of Normals," coming up shortly.

Surface Normals and Vertex Normals

We have so far considered normals as applying to each face in our 3-D object. In actual fact, it is not the faces that we apply normals to but the individual vertices that form the face. MonoGame uses the vertices to calculate the color based on its lighting equations, and it then applies this to the whole triangle by interpolating the colors between the vertices just as we have previously manually interpolated colors ourselves by providing explicit vertex colors.

This gives us an opportunity to perform a very useful lighting trick. We can provide different normals for the vertices of a single triangle. MonoGame will then consider each vertex of the triangle to be facing in a different direction and will interpolate the light directions across the surface of the triangle.

Consider the object shown in Figure 7-24. Its surfaces are shown as thick lines, representing the surfaces viewed edge-on. The long dashed arrows show the normals that have been applied for each of the vertices within the surfaces. Note that for each surface, the normals are pointing in different directions (they point slightly away from one another).

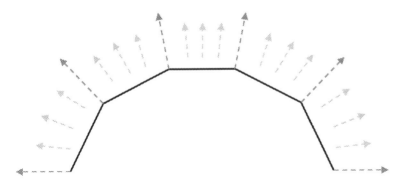

Figure 7-24. *Interpolated vertex normals*

The shorter dashed arrows show the effective normals within the interior of the surfaces due to interpolation. They smoothly transition from one normal to the next, giving the impression that the surface of the object when viewed face on is perfectly smoothly curved, whereas in fact it is created from just five flat faces.

An example of normal interpolation in practice can be seen in Figure 7-25. The two images shown are both of the same cylinder, rendered using a number of flat surfaces. The individual surfaces can be clearly seen in the image on the left, which uses the same normals for all vertices within each face. On the right, the vertex normals are modified so that they differ from one side of the face to the other (exactly as we did in Figure 12-20). Note that the appearance of this cylinder is entirely smooth, even though it is formed from the exact same faces as the image on the left.

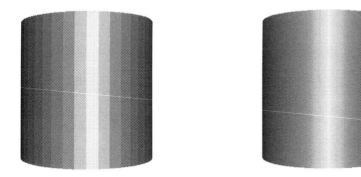

Figure 7-25. *A cylinder with normals applied to each whole face (left) and to individual vertices (right)*

Adding Lighting to Games

So, that's the theory; now let's take a look at how we implement lighting in our game code. All the code in this section can be found in the Lighting_Win8 and Lighting_WP8 example projects that accompany this chapter. A screenshot from the project is shown in Figure 7-26.

Figure 7-26. *An illuminated cube and a cylinder rendered by the Lighting example project*

Enabling and Disabling Lighting

The first thing that is needed is to tell the BasicEffect object that we want to use lighting. Without this, all light features will be disabled and ignored, as has been the case in our example projects up until now.

Lighting is enabled by simply setting the LightingEnabled property to true when initializing the effect, as shown in Listing 7-16.

Listing 7-16. Enabling MonoGame's lighting feature

```
_effect.LightingEnabled = true;
```

Lighting can, of course, be disabled by setting this back to false. This property can be updated anywhere within your game; it isn't restricted just to the Initialize function.

Light Configuration

Once the lighting system has been switched on, the next step is to configure the lights. We have three directional lights at our disposal, exposed via the DirectionalLight0, DirectionalLight1, and DirectionalLight2 properties of the BasicEffect object. Each of these lights has the following properties that can be used to configure its behavior:

- DiffuseColor: the diffuse color of the light. Defaults to black to disable diffuse lighting.

- Direction: a Vector3 structure indicating the direction in which the light is pointing. Defaults to (0, 0, 0), effectively disabling the light.

- Enabled: a bool indicating whether this light is switched on or off.

- SpecularColor: the specular color of the light. Defaults to black to disable specular lighting.

░ **Note**　All the light colors are represented as Vector3 structures. Remember that you can convert a Color to a Vector3 by calling its ToVector3 method.

Updating the light settings is very easy because the parameters can be freely updated. To change a light's direction or its colors, or to switch it on and off, simply set the properties as required before rendering your objects.

The code in Listing 7-17 configures light 0 so that it is directed along the negative z axis. As the user's viewpoint is also looking along the negative z axis in our examples so far, this configuration results in the light illuminating the objects from the camera position.

Listing 7-17. Configuring a white light to shine along the negative z axis

```
_effect.DirectionalLight0.Enabled = true;
_effect.DirectionalLight0.Direction = new Vector3(0, 0, -1);
_effect.DirectionalLight0.DiffuseColor = Color.White.ToVector3();
```

For the light itself, this code is all that is required to light up the objects within our scene. However, we haven't done anything to set the normals for our objects yet. Continuing to use the cube from our previous examples, we first modify the class to use the VertexPositionNormalTexture structure for its vertices. After setting the vertex positions as we always have, we now need to set the normal for each vertex. For a cube, the normals all point directly along the x, y, or z axis so it is easy to set these up manually. Listing 7-18 shows the beginning of the code to perform this task, taken from the Lighting project's CubeObject class.

Listing 7-18. Setting the cube's vertex normals

```
// Set the vertex normals
i = 0;
// Front face...
_vertices[i++].Normal = new Vector3(0, 0, 1);
_vertices[i++].Normal = new Vector3(0, 0, 1);
_vertices[i++].Normal = new Vector3(0, 0, 1);
_vertices[i++].Normal = new Vector3(0, 0, 1);
_vertices[i++].Normal = new Vector3(0, 0, 1);
_vertices[i++].Normal = new Vector3(0, 0, 1);
// Back face...
_vertices[i++].Normal = new Vector3(0, 0, -1);
_vertices[i++].Normal = new Vector3(0, 0, -1);
```

```
_vertices[i++].Normal = new Vector3(0, 0, -1);
_vertices[i++].Normal = new Vector3(0, 0, -1);
_vertices[i++].Normal = new Vector3(0, 0, -1);
_vertices[i++].Normal = new Vector3(0, 0, -1);
// ... and so on for the remaining faces ...
```

The cube's class is otherwise unchanged. Running the project displays a cube as shown in Figure 7-27. You can see that each face of the cube has its own color, determined by the light calculation that we have already explored.

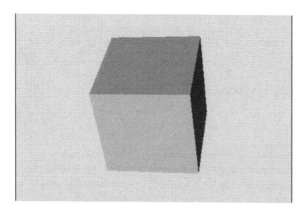

Figure 7-27. *A cube lit using a directional light*

The cylinder class defines its vertices and normals a little differently. The way in which this works is left as an exercise for the reader, but the vertices and normals are all calculated programmatically using some basic trigonometry rather than relying on manual entry of the required coordinates and normal vectors. The code that builds this data, inside the CylinderObject.BuildVertices function, is well commented to explain the calculations that are being performed.

Try experimenting with the light and material colors to see how they interact. The light color is set in the project's Initialize function (refer to Listing 7-17), whereas the object materials are set against each individual object in its ObjectColor property. The cube and cylinder in the example project are added by the ResetGame function, and their colors can be modified there.

As additional lights are enabled, MonoGame has additional work to do to calculate the light for each vertex within the rendered objects. For this reason, it is important to disable lights when they are not required. Lighting is a relatively inexpensive calculation, so feel free to get your lights set up exactly how you need them for your game.

Ambient Light

To use an ambient light, simply set the BasicEffect.AmbientLight property to the required color. All the objects rendered will take the ambient light into account.

Specular Light

Specular lighting is calculated both from the specular color of the active lights and from the specular material color. As the material colors are specific to each object, we will create new properties in the game framework's MatrixObjectBase class to support specular color for each individual object.

The new properties, SpecularColor (of type Color) and SpecularPower (of type float), mirror the properties within the BasicEffect that control the specular material. These can then be set within each object to control its specular lighting settings.

To apply the specular lighting, the MatrixObjectBase.PrepareEffect is modified to pass the object's values into the BasicEffect object's SpecularColor and SpecularPower properties.

Specular light generally looks at its best when it is white. By all means, experiment with colored specular light, but the effects might not always be natural-looking.

Figure 7-28 shows another cube with a white specular light and a specular power of 10. You can enable this for the objects in the example project by uncommenting the lines in ResetGame that set the two new specular lighting properties. Notice how shiny the objects look compared to when they were rendered without specular lighting. One of the reasons for this shininess is that specular light affects each vertex differently, even if all the vertices of a face point in exactly the same direction. This effect results in a much more dynamic appearance on the rendered objects.

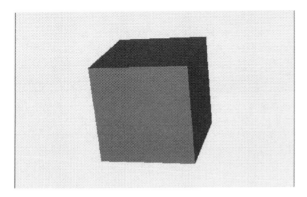

Figure 7-28. *A cube lit using a directional light and specular lighting*

Try experimenting with the specular power and see the results. As the power value increases into the tens and hundreds, the objects start to reflect specular light only when their faces get closer and closer toward the light source as the specular effect becomes more and more tightly focused.

There is one additional BasicEffect property that has an effect on specular lighting: PreferPerPixelLighting. This property defaults to false, which results in the specular component of the lighting model being calculated for each vertex, as we have already discussed. On objects that have large triangles (and therefore have areas of the object where there are no vertices nearby to be illuminated), this can result in some visual artifacts that can detract from the otherwise very attractive-looking specular lighting.

The first of these problems can be seen in the left image of Figure 7-29. The image shows a cube that is facing nearly directly toward the camera and the light source, but it is slightly rotated so that the rightmost corner is the only one that is reflecting the specular light. As you can see, the light has a very angular look caused by the fact that only four vertices are being used to display the entire face of the cube. The interpolation is inaccurate due to this small number of color points.

Figure 7-29. *Two cubes, without (left) and with (right) per pixel lighting enabled*

The image on the right is of the exact same object and lighting configuration, except that `PreferPerPixelLighting` has been switched on. This property instructs MonoGame to calculate the specular lighting for each individual pixel that it renders, rather than just for the vertices. As will be clearly seen, the reflection looks much better: the angular lines have all disappeared, leaving a perfect round highlight in its place.

The second problem with specular lighting also occurs on objects with large triangles, but primarily affects specular light that is very tightly focused. Figure 7-30 shows two images of a cube that is directly facing toward the camera and the light source. The specular power has been set to 1000 for a very focused effect. Because the effect is so small, it doesn't reach any of the vertices at all. As a result, the specular light has no impact on the face. On the right is the same scene with per pixel lighting enabled. As each pixel then has its specular light individually calculated, the specular light effect clearly appears within the face.

Figure 7-30. *Two cubes, without and with per pixel lighting enabled with a high specular focus*

Of course, as you might expect, there is a downside to per pixel lighting. Because the specular component needs to be calculated for each individual pixel as opposed to each vertex, it has a much higher processing requirement. Consider the cubes in Figure 7-30: the visible face consists of more than 30,000 pixels, as compared with only 6 vertices.

■ **Caution** Due to the additional processing overhead of per pixel lighting, it should be used sparingly, particularly if you are targeting tablets or phones. If you have an object that is not using specular light, has no large faces, has a low specular power, or doesn't exhibit either of the problems discussed in this section, you will probably find a performance benefit from leaving it disabled for that object. Experiment and find which setting provides the best balance between appearance and performance for your game.

Emissive Light

The emissive light for rendered objects is also most usefully set for each individual object, so we will add a new property for this to the `MatrixObjectBase` class just as we did for the specular material color.

The `EmissiveColor` property (of type `Color`) can then be set within each object to control its emissive lighting settings and is applied in the `MatrixObjectBase.PrepareEffect`, which passes its value into the `BasicEffect` object's `EmissiveColor` property.

The Standard Lighting Rig

The lighting properties of the `BasicEffect` object give you a great deal of freedom to set up your lighting system in whatever way you want, but MonoGame has one more lighting feature that you might find useful in your games: the *standard lighting rig*.

I will allow Shawn Hargreaves, one of the Microsoft developers that worked on XNA v4.0 prior to its release for Windows Phone 7, to explain with the following text from his blog (the full text of which can be found at `http://tinyurl.com/standardlightingrig`):

> *Many years ago photographers discovered that a single light was not enough to make their subjects look good. Instead, they use three.*
>
> *The* key light *is the brightest, and provides the main illumination and shadows. This will typically be positioned to match a real light source such as an overhead lamp, a window, or the sun for an outdoor scene.*
>
> *The* fill light *is dimmer, and usually angled at 90 degrees to the key. This is used to soften the shadows, adding shading and definition to areas that would otherwise be solid black.*
>
> *Finally, the* back light *is positioned behind the character, facing toward the camera. This illuminates only the silhouette edges, helping the character stand out against the background.*

Because this is potentially a very useful light configuration, it can be applied to your 3-D game world by simply calling the `BasicEffect.EnableDefaultLighting` function. In practice, it might provide a useful set of lights, it might provide a useful basis but require a little subsequent modification, or it might not be suitable for your game at all. Give it a try and see what kind of results it provides; you might just like it.

Programmatic Calculation of Normals

Earlier in this section, we explored the calculations required to automatically compute the normals for a triangle within a 3-D object. As a final lighting-related addition to the game framework, let's add a function that will calculate normals for our objects automatically.

This will be relatively basic and will operate within the following restrictions:

- It will only generate normals that are the same for all vertices of a triangle, so no smoothing using normal interpolation will be supported.

- It will assume that each vertex will be either used only once or that all of its uses will have the same vertex normal. The code could potentially be enhanced to average out multiple uses of the same vertex, but this enhancement is left as an exercise for the reader. When we begin importing geometry in the next chapter, you will see that this might not be as valuable an enhancement as it currently appears.

- It will support only triangle lists.

As we have two different ways of rendering triangles (a simple list of triangles or using vertex indices), we will create two corresponding functions that process data in these two formats. To reduce the amount of code, we will set the two functions up so that one simply calls into the other, allowing all the calculation to be put into just a single function.

The easiest way to implement this efficient code approach is to get the version that takes a simple list of triangles (without vertex indices) to build a corresponding index array. Once this is done, the vertices and the fabricated indices can be passed into the other function to calculate on its behalf.

Generating indices for an unindexed triangle list is very simple: each triangle is formed from the next three vertices in the list, so the indices are just a sequence of incremental numbers. The first triangle is formed from indices 0, 1, and 2; the second triangle from indices 3, 4, and 5; the third from indices 6, 7, and 8; and so on.

The code for the function that handles unindexed vertices, named CalculateVertexNormals and added to the MatrixObjectBase class, can be seen in Listing 7-19. It creates an array for the indices whose length is equal to the number of vertices. The array is then filled with sequential numbers starting from 0, and the vertices and constructed indices array are passed into a second overload of the same function to actually generate the normals, which we will examine in a moment.

Listing 7-19. Generating indices for an unindexed triangle list

```
public void CalculateVertexNormals(VertexPositionNormalTexture[] vertices)
{
    short[] indices;
    short i;

    // Build an array that allows us to treat the vertices as if they were indexed.
    // As the triangles are drawn sequentially, the indexes are actually just
    // an increasing sequence of numbers: the first triangle is formed from
    // vertices 0, 1 and 2, the second triangle from vertices 3, 4 and 5, etc.

    // First create the array with an element for each vertex
    indices = new short[vertices.Length];

    // Then set the elements within the array so that each contains
    // the next sequential vertex index
    for (i = 0; i < indices.Length; i++)
    {
        indices[i] = i;
    }

    // Finally delegate to the other overload to do the work
    CalculateVertexNormals(vertices, indices);
}
```

The second overload of the function accepts two parameters: the vertex array and the index array. This version of the function would be used directly if you are working with indexed vertices, or it will otherwise be called from the code in Listing 7-19 if the vertices are unindexed.

The second overload works through the vertices in the array, using the indices to determine which vertices are used to form each triangle within the object. Once the vertices of each triangle have been determined, their vectors are calculated and stored in the va and vb variables. Their cross product is then calculated in order to determine the triangle's normal, and the resulting vector is normalized. The normal vector is then written into all three of the vertices that formed the triangle. This is all exactly as per the processes we discussed in the "Calculating Normals" section earlier in this chapter.

Note that as we are updating the vertex array that was passed in as a parameter, there is no need to return anything from this function. The normals will be written "in place" into the existing vertices.

The code to calculate the normals is shown in Listing 7-20.

Listing 7-20. Calculating the normals for an indexed triangle list

```
public void CalculateVertexNormals(VertexPositionNormalTexture[] vertices,
                                                            short[] indices)
{
    // Vectors to describe the relationships between the vertices of the triangle
    // being processed
    Vector3 vectora;
    Vector3 vectorb;
    // The resulting normal vector
    Vector3 normal;

    // Loop for each triangle (each triangle uses three indices)
    for (int index = 0; index < indices.Length; index += 3)
    {
        // Create the a and b vectors from the vertex positions
        // First the a vector from vertices 2 and 1
        vectora = vertices[index + 2].Position - vertices[index + 1].Position;
        // Next the b vector from vertices 1 and 0
        vectorb = vertices[index + 1].Position - vertices[index + 0].Position;

        // Calculate the normal as the cross product of the two vectors
        normal = Vector3.Cross(vectora, vectorb);

        // Normalize the normal
        normal.Normalize();

        // Write the normal back into all three of the triangle vertices
        vertices[index].Normal = normal;
        vertices[index+1].Normal = normal;
        vertices[index+2].Normal = normal;
    }
}
```

This function can simply be called after the vertex positions for an object have been calculated. If you look at the CubeObject class in the Lighting example project, you will find that this can be used in place of the code that manually provides the normals. Try commenting out all the BuildVertices code that sets the vertex normals (from the "Set the vertex normals" comment on to the end of the function) and instead enable the call to CalculateVertexNormals. The end result is identical, but with a lot less code and a lot less effort.

Orthographic Projection

Right at the start of this chapter, we looked at the perspective projection matrix, and we have used this for all the subsequent exploration of 3-D graphics. MonoGame offers another projection matrix that can be useful in certain game environments, however, called an *orthographic projection*.

Whereas the perspective projection causes objects farther away from the camera to become smaller, an orthographic projection does not: distant objects appear at exactly the same size as near objects. This is clearly an unrealistic representation of the real world and unsuitable for any game that tries to present a lifelike approximation of a 3-D environment, but it does have two specific uses.

The first of these uses is for isometric 3-D games. They are generally tile-based games viewed such that the camera is rotated around and elevated from its default position. Isometric viewpoints were common in pseudo-3-D games before hardware acceleration become popular. Some famous games that have used this style of 3-D graphics include *Q*bert*, *Zaxxon*, *Knight Lore*, *Marble Madness*, *Populous*, and (more recently) *Civilization III* and *Diablo II*. Isometric games are less common these days, but they do still make occasional appearances, particularly as role-playing and strategy games.

The second thing that orthographic projections are useful for is creating a pixel-aligned coordinate system. Clearly with perspective projections, moving an object one unit along the x or y axis might cause it to move a different number of physical pixels along that axis, depending on how near or far the object is from the camera. Because distance makes no difference in orthographic projections, a coordinate system can be set up that exactly matches the pixels on the screen, making precise pixel-based movement much easier.

Despite their different appearance, all other aspects of 3-D rendering that we have explored still hold true with orthographic projection: hidden surfaces will still be removed, objects will still be lit, and transformations and rotations will still operate exactly as with perspective projection (though rotations can look a little strange without perspective—the brain thinks they are distorting and stretching because no equivalent transformation exists in the real world).

The Viewing Frustum

The shape of an orthographic viewing frustum is simply a cuboid area, such as the one shown in Figure 7-31.

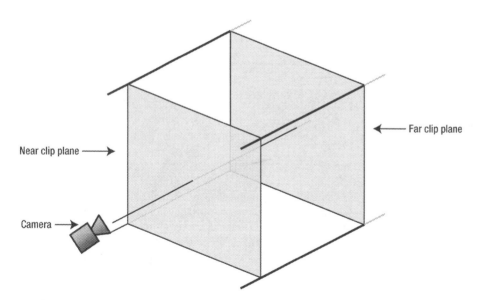

Figure 7-31. *A diagram showing a 3-D orthographic viewing frustum*

Just as with a perspective projection, we still have a near and far clip plane, and objects that are rendered will still be checked to ensure that they fall within this region. Despite objects not growing or shrinking as their depth changes within a scene, the depth buffer is still used and will ensure that objects with a higher z value will appear in front objects with a lower z value.

The reason why depth has no effect on the object size is that objects at the far clip plane occupy exactly the same proportion of the plane as objects on the near clip plane. If you look back at Figure 7-2, you will see two objects, one near and one far, contained within a perspective viewing frustum, and then in Figure 7-3 the projected outcome on the screen of those two shapes. Let's repeat these with an orthographic viewing frustum. Figure 7-32 shows the objects within the frustum, one at the near clip plane and one at the far clip plane just as before.

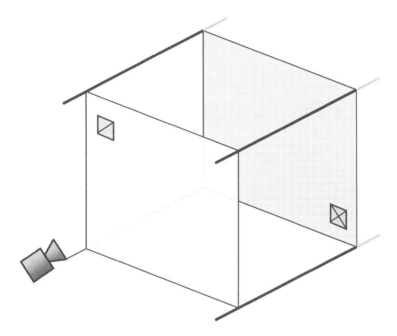

Figure 7-32. *Two identically sized objects in the viewing frustum shown in 3-D space*

When these objects are transformed by the orthographic projection, they continue to appear at the same size, as can be seen in Figure 7-33. The proportion of the clip plane filled by the shapes is the same in both cases, so they are not enlarged or shrunk at all.

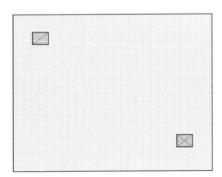

Figure 7-33. *The same two objects after orthographic projection into 2-D*

When we set up an orthographic projection, we simply tell it how many units we want it to use across the x and y axis. It will automatically stretch the rendered objects to fit within this defined set of coordinates. If the ratio of the axes does not match that of the screen, we can end up with objects becoming distorted as they are rendered. For example, if we used a range of -1 to +1 for both the x and y axes and displayed it on a 1920 x 1080 pixel screen, a 1-unit-square object would appear with a width of 960 pixels and a height of 540 pixels. It is clearly not square! For this reason, we generally still use the aspect ratio in our own calculations when setting the orthographic scale.

There is no need for a viewing angle to be specified for this projection because the angle is always parallel.

Defining the Orthographic Viewing Frustum in MonoGame

Just as MonoGame provided a useful function for creating perspective projection matrices, so it provides another for orthographic projections—two, in fact, as you will see.

The first of these functions is the static `Matrix.CreateOrthographic` function. This expects the following four parameters:

- `width`: the number of units to display across the projection. The center point will always be 0, so providing a width of 4 will result in a frustum that extends from -2 to +2 across the x axis.

- `height`: the number of units to display vertically for the projection. Just as with the `width`, the center point will always be 0.

- `zNearPlane`: the near clipping plane distance.

- `zFarPlane`: the far clipping plane distance.

■ **Tip** Because distance has no effect on the sizing of objects, it is quite acceptable to set a near clipping plane with a negative distance, allowing objects that are effectively behind the camera to still be rendered. This configuration allows a coordinate system to be created where the value 0 is the center of all the 3-D axes, which can simplify the object positional calculations.

Listing 7-21 shows an example orthographic projection matrix being created. Its vertical size is set at 16 units, and the horizontal size is calculated from the aspect ratio to display the appropriate amount to keep the coordinate system square.

Listing 7-21. Calculating the normals for an indexed triangle list

```
// Calculate the screen aspect ratio
float aspectRatio =
            (float)GraphicsDevice.Viewport.Width / GraphicsDevice.Viewport.Height;
// Create a projection matrix
Matrix projection = Matrix.CreateOrthographic(16 * aspectRatio, 16, 0, 100.0f);
```

Let's take a look at a couple of applications of orthographic projection.

Isometric Projection

To obtain an isometric projection, we simply need to set the orthographic projection up as described and then rotate the camera so that it looks upon the scene from an angle, instead of straight on.

The effects of this camera rotation can be seen in Figure 7-34. The two images both display a unit-size cube with an orthographic projection. On the left, the camera is looking directly along the negative z axis, so only the front face of the cube can be seen. On the right, the camera has been moved so that it looks from the point (1, 1, 1) toward the origin point (0, 0, 0). As a result, the cube is now seen with its corner facing toward the camera. Note that the cube's front face (lit in medium gray) is now appearing at the bottom left of the cube; this should help you to visualize how the camera position has moved.

Figure 7-34. *Direct orthographic projection and rotated orthographic projection*

The code required to set the camera into this position is shown in Listing 7-22. This replaces the previous calculation of the view matrix in the game's Initialize function.

Listing 7-22. Setting the camera position for an isometric projection

```
// Calculate a view matrix (where we are looking from and to) for isometric projection
Matrix view = Matrix.CreateLookAt(new Vector3(1, 1, 1), Vector3.Zero, Vector3.Up);
```

With the camera so positioned, the world axes are shifted so that they are no longer aligned with the screen axis. Moving an object along the positive x axis will now cause it to move to the right and down on the screen. Moving an object along the positive z axis will cause it to move left and down on the screen, and the positive y axis will move up on the screen.

These positional effects can be seen in Figure 7-35. The cube labeled A is at position (0, 0, 0), the cube labeled B is at position (0, 1, 0), the cube labeled C is at position (0, 0, 1), and the cube labeled D is at position (2, 0, 0).

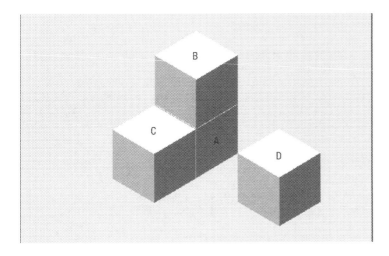

Figure 7-35. *Objects in different positions with an isometric projection*

An example of using an isometric projection can be seen in the `Isometric_Win8` and `Isometric_WP8` projects accompanying this chapter. They set up a grid of unit-size cubes along the x and z planes, and then scale them along the y axis to make them increase and decrease in height. An image from the project can be seen in Figure 7-36.

Figure 7-36. *The Isometric example project*

Using an isometric view of an orthographic projection will be useful in only a minority of games, but for those that need it, MonoGame's rich 3-D features create a powerful environment for displaying such graphical environments.

Pixel-Aligned Projection

We can also use orthographic projections to align the coordinate system exactly to the pixels on the screen. This is generally useful only for 2-D rendering and, in many cases, will be more easily achieved by simply using MonoGame's sprite technology instead. As you have seen by now, however, there are features that the 3-D rendering environment offers that sprites cannot achieve, such as powerful matrix-based positioning and flexible lighting.

To set up a pixel-aligned projection, we simply need to provide the actual viewport width and height when creating the matrix, as shown in Listing 7-23. Given a width of 1920 and a height of 1080, this configuration will create a coordinate system ranging from position (-960, -540) in the screen's bottom-left corner to position (960, 540) in its top-right corner.

Listing 7-23. Creating a pixel-aligned orthographic projection matrix

```
// Create a pixel-aligned orthographic projection
Matrix projection = Matrix.CreateOrthographic(GraphicsDevice.Viewport.Width,
                                 GraphicsDevice.Viewport.Height, 0, 100);
```

This works fine, but it has put the origin (0, 0) coordinate in the center of the screen. Normally when working with 2-D coordinate systems (such as the one used by MonoGame's sprites), the origin is in the top-left corner, and the positive y axis points toward the bottom of the screen. We can replicate this same coordinate system by using a different projection matrix creation function: `CreateOrthographicOffCenter`.

This function expects six parameters to be passed, as follows and in this order:

- `left`: the coordinate to use to represent the left edge of the screen

- `right`: the coordinate for the right edge of the screen

- `bottom`: the coordinate for the bottom edge of the screen

- `top`: the coordinate for the top edge of the screen

- `zNearPlane`: the near clipping plane distance

- `zFarPlane`: the far clipping plane distance

Any values can be passed for the `left`, `right`, `bottom`, and `top` coordinates, so we can set the left and top values to be zero, and the right and bottom to be the viewport width and height, respectively. Listing 7-24 shows an example of setting the projection up in this way.

Listing 7-24. Creating an off-center pixel-aligned orthographic projection matrix

```
// Create a pixel-aligned orthographic projection with its origin in the top-left
// of the screen.
Matrix projection = Matrix.CreateOrthographicOffCenter
                                (0, GraphicsDevice.Viewport.Width,
                                 GraphicsDevice.Viewport.Height, 0,
                                 -100, 100);
```

If you wanted to put the origin (0, 0) coordinate to the bottom left instead, simply swap the `bottom` and `top` parameters and the whole display will flip vertically to achieve this.

Mastering the 3-D World

Moving out of the realm of flat 2-D graphics and into the depths of 3-D is undeniably a big step. All sorts of additional challenges appear both in terms of code complexity and graphical modeling. MonoGame does provide a sound and flexible technology base to build on, and the rewards of 3-D game programming can be great for players and developers alike.

Once you are happy and comfortable with the concepts and the code that we have discussed in this chapter, the next chapter will introduce you to a number of additional techniques that you can use in MonoGame to help bring your games to life.

Summary

- 3-D rendering is initialized by setting up a "viewing volume" called a *frustum*. Normally, 3-D games will use a frustum that simulates a *perspective* projection so that objects within the scene get smaller as they move away from the camera, but *orthographic* projection can also be used for isometric displays.

- The viewing frustum has near and far *clip planes*, and any objects that fall outside of these planes will not be drawn.

- MonoGame provides functions within the Matrix structure to allow the frustum projection matrices to be easily constructed.

- When rendering in 3-D, MonoGame provides a *depth buffer*, which keeps track of how far into the scene each rendered pixel lies. Any pixel that would be drawn behind existing content in the scene is discarded. This means that objects will correctly appear in front of one another, regardless of the order they are rendered in.

- The depth buffer can be switched on or off if required, which is useful for rendering multiple scenes together or for overlay graphics.

- Special care needs to be taken with regard to the depth buffer when rendering transparent objects so that the objects in front do not completely obscure the objects behind.

- 3-D objects are constructed using triangles. For efficiency reasons, *vertex buffers* and *index buffers* may be used to reduce redundant calculation of the points that form these triangles.

- By default, MonoGame will *cull* triangles that are facing away from the camera to eliminate unnecessary calculation and rendering. This culling may be switched off to enable double-sided surfaces to be displayed.

- MonoGame provides a number of flexible and useful lighting features. These include ambient lighting, three directional lights, and emissive object light. The directional lights have diffuse and specular components to allow objects to reflect as "flat" or "shiny" surfaces.

- Objects also have *material* properties that control the object colors and how those colors interact with any lights that have been defined.

- MonoGame can calculate lighting either just at each vertex (which is fast but sometimes inaccurate) or can calculate *per pixel* (which is much more accurate but can be a lot slower).

- In order for objects to reflect light properly, each triangle within the object must have *normals* defined for each of its vertices. These allow MonoGame to calculate the direction in which the triangle is facing and from that determine how the light interacts with the triangle.

- These normals are defined for each vertex rather than for the triangle as a whole. This means that the normals can be interpolated across the triangle, allowing the impression of smoothly curved surface to be given.

- Normals can be programmatically computed for any given triangle by performing a *cross product* calculation. The GameFramework project provides a function to automatically compute normals for a provided object.

■ ■ ■

CHAPTER 8

Further 3-D Features and Techniques

In this chapter, you will extend your knowledge of MonoGame and take the features and capabilities of your code up to the next level. When you finish working through this chapter, you will be able to import 3-D models from an external modeling application. You will also be able to use a number of additional MonoGame features to add life to your games.

Importing Geometry

In Chapter 7, we used two different methods for defining 3-D objects in our projects. The first method required us to manually define a big array of vertex coordinates. This might be workable for simple objects such as cubes (though it is fairly tedious even for that!), but when we move on to more complex objects, such as treasure chests or spaceships, it quickly becomes unrealistic. The second approach used mathematical formulae to create shapes for us (the cylinder from the Lighting example project). This is useful for regular geometric shapes, but once again it is unlikely to be of value for real-world game objects.

The solution is to use a 3-D modeling application. Modeling applications are third-party software products that provide a rich (and often rather complex) user interface that is specifically designed to allow 3-D models to be constructed.

In addition to creating the geometry, most modeling applications also allow textures to be mapped on to the objects that they build and will provide the resulting texture coordinates. They might also allow vertex normals to be calculated and stored as part of the object.

All this sounds wonderful, but, unfortunately, there is a bewildering array of formats into which 3-D object definitions can be saved, and not all are easy to read.

Many such products can be used to create geometry files for our MonoGame projects. These range from free products—such as the open source Blender (visit www.blender.org for details)—to costly commercial applications—such as Autodesk's 3ds Max (see www.autodesk.com for more information)—and many others in between. Wikipedia has a large list of 3-D modeling applications at http://en.wikipedia.org/wiki/3D_computer_graphics_software, where you might be able to find other packages that suit your requirements.

The good news is that there is a modeling application available that is free to download, is relatively easy to use, and (with a bit of creative tweaking) can save to a file format that you can easily read. This application is SketchUp, published by Trimble.

SketchUp

SketchUp was originally created by a company called @Last Software, with the design goal of creating a 3-D modeling application that was just as easy to use as a pen and paper. As such, its user interface was considerably easier to learn than that of many other competing applications.

Some years later, @Last Software enhanced SketchUp so it could create 3-D building models for Google Earth. Shortly after this, Google acquired the company and rebranded SketchUp as one of its own applications. Then, in April 2012, Google sold the application to Trimble, a company with a background in GPS technology.

SketchUp is available in two different versions: SketchUp and SketchUp Pro. The basic SketchUp version is freely available and contains a huge amount of functionality. The Pro version adds even more features, including support for reading and writing a larger range of 3-D file formats. You can visit www.sketchup.com to download a copy of either of these versions for yourself. At the time of writing, the current version is SketchUp 8.

Unfortunately, the free version doesn't export to a file format that we can easily use within our MonoGame applications. There is a clever workaround, however, which we will look at shortly. If you are using SketchUp Pro, you can save to the .fbx file format, which can be directly added into a game's Content project without any further processing.

Creating 3-D Objects in SketchUp

Even the easiest 3-D modeling applications can be complex to use. The challenge of interactively describing a 3-D world using 2-D input and output devices that we have available to use (the mouse, keyboard, and monitor) is always going to make this requirement difficult to fulfill.

Despite SketchUp's relative ease of use, there is still a lot to learn to become proficient in using it—a full guide to how to use it is beyond the scope of this book. Don't let this discourage you, though, because SketchUp also has an immense amount of help and guidance available online, including manuals, tutorials, walkthroughs, and video guides. All of these resources can be accessed from the links presented when SketchUp is first launched.

In order to work with imported geometry in this chapter, we will create a simple object in SketchUp that will be subsequently read into an example project by the game framework. The following paragraphs explain how a very simple model of a house was created. They are not intended as a step-by-step guide to using SketchUp. Rather, they merely provide information about the sequence of operations that could be used to create such a model. The model itself is included with the example projects, so you don't need to re-create it for yourself.

When SketchUp is launched, it initially displays a Welcome window with two panels within it. The top panel, "Learn," contains links to various online resources to help get started with using the program. Below this is a second, collapsed panel named "Template." Click this to see the templates that are available for starting a new, empty design space.

Within the Template panel, select one of the two Simple Template options (Meters or Feet and Inches, as you prefer) and then click Start using SketchUp to launch its main user interface. By default, SketchUp adds an image of a person to the empty scene to help put the scene's scale into perspective. The figure can be deleted to make way for the 3-D object.

Our object can now be constructed in the empty scene. The first few steps toward this are shown in Figure 8-1. A rectangle is first drawn along the x/z plane to form the base of the house, as shown in Figure 8-1(a). The rectangle is then extruded using the Push/Pull tool to form a box, as shown in Figure 8-1(b). The Line tool is then used to create a line across the center of the top face of the box, as shown in Figure 8-1(c).

Once the top face has been divided in two, the line that was drawn can be moved around and all the faces connected to it will move accordingly. Moving the line directly upward, therefore, creates a rudimentary but satisfactory roof shape, as shown in Figure 8-1(d). The basic geometry of the house is complete at this point.

Of course, we will almost certainly want to apply textures to our objects to complement the structure that we have created, and we will do just that now to make the house look more realistic. SketchUp has a set of tools for adding textures to objects, and its online help will provide everything you need to know to become familiar with them.

In Figure 8-1(e), a texture has been applied to the front face of the house. Figure 8-1(f) shows the finished house object, with textures applied to all the faces in the object.

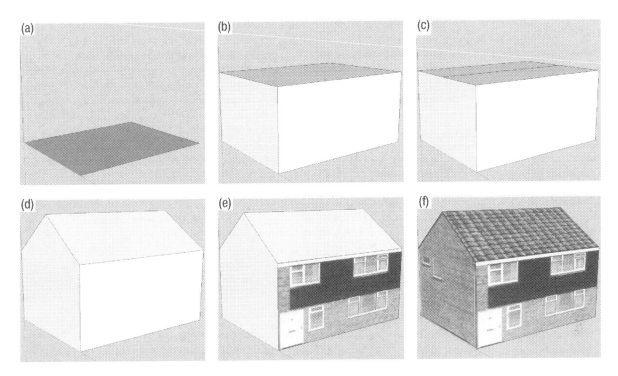

Figure 8-1. *The steps required to build a simple 3-D house object in SketchUp*

As you might be able to tell, 3-D modeling abilities are not among my strengths! Rest assured that SketchUp and MonoGame can both handle much more complex objects than the simple example object presented here.

SketchUp and MonoGame are both capable of using multiple textures within a single object, so you can import multiple graphic files into the workspace and apply them all as needed. Don't forget, though, that textures can use significant resources in a game. Wherever possible, try to keep the texture count as low as you can.

One simple approach that reduces the number of textures as far as possible is to place all the graphics for your object into a single texture image and apply subsections of the image to the model's faces rather than applying the entire image. This is the approach that has been taken with the house shown here: The front, sides, and roof are all contained within a single texture image, as shown in Figure 8-2.

Figure 8-2. *The texture graphic used for the 3-D house object*

As the graphic shows, the house texture has been divided into three sections. The left third of the texture contains the graphic for the roof, while the remaining area is split into a graphic for the side of the house and another graphic for the front. Putting all the required texture information into a single graphic file in this way simplifies both the design of the object and the rendering. Using a single graphic makes rendering more efficient because the graphics hardware can process the whole object in a single step without needing to move as many textures around inside the device's memory.

With the object completed, it can be saved to a SketchUp .skp file in case it needs to be retrieved later on.

Exporting 3-D Geometry

Unfortunately, the free version of SketchUp has very limited options when it comes to exporting its objects. The two formats natively supported are Collada (.dae) files and Google Earth (.kmz) files.

We could potentially write code to import either of these formats into our MonoGame games, but a far preferable solution is to find a way to create .x geometry files.

The .x geometry file format was introduced as part of Microsoft's DirectX many years ago. It continues to be supported within both DirectX and MonoGame today. MonoGame has native support for reading .x files by adding them into a Content project, just as it does for images and sound files. In fact, MonoGame provides a very easy-to-use programming interface that saves a huge amount of work in terms of reading and processing the geometry file.

So, how do we get SketchUp to save its models in .x format? Unfortunately, neither the free nor Pro versions of SketchUp support this file format.

The good news is that enterprising programmers on the Internet have managed to persuade both of these versions of SketchUp to export objects in a variety of other geometry file formats, including .x format. SketchUp provides a programming interface, accessed using the Ruby programming language and able to query all the information about the object currently being worked on. A Ruby script, created by a developer named Fernando Zanini, uses this interface to create .x files from the free version of SketchUp. You can visit http://tinyurl.com/skp2x to download the script or find it in the downloadable content for this chapter in the Resources/3DRadExporter.rbs file. The script works with older versions of SketchUp, too, from version 6 onward.

To install the exporter into SketchUp, close its application and then copy 3DRadExported.rbs into SketchUp's PlugIns directory (which can be found by default at C:\Program Files (x86)\Google\Google SketchUp 8\Plugins). Restart SketchUp. A new 3-D Rad menu item should appear under its PlugIns menu, under which is a long list of different export options, as shown in Figure 8-3.

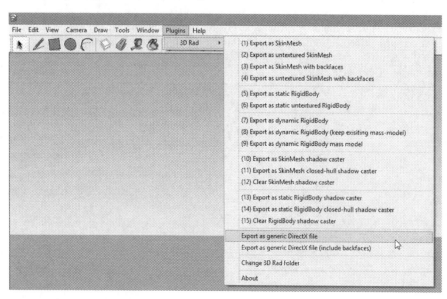

Figure 8-3. *The 3-D Rad Plugins options inside SketchUp*

The option that we are primarily interested in is the "Export as generic DirectX file" option. When this option is selected, it will prompt you to select a location and file name for your .x file. You can save it directly into your Content product directory if you want. The exporter will automatically save all the required textures into the same location.

■ **Caution**   Don't forget to save your objects into SketchUp's native .skp file format, too. An exported .x file is ideal for loading into your game, but SketchUp can't read data back from it.

Importing Saved Geometry into MonoGame Projects

Adding the saved object into a project for use within a game is very easy: Simply add the .x file to a Content project just as you would for any other content resource. Just add the .x file; there is no need to add any of the textures that it uses. The ImportingGeometry_Win8 and ImportingGeometry_WP8 example projects have been created using the house model described in the previous section.

■ **Tip**   If you want to add the textures into the Content project so that you can see them in Solution Explorer, add them and set their Build Action property to None in the Properties window. This will instruct the compilation process to ignore them, but they can still be manipulated or added to source code control via the Visual Studio IDE. The textures have been added in this way to the example XNA Content projects supplied with this chapter.

The Properties for the .x model's Content Processor contain several useful options that you might want to configure before using your object, as shown in Figure 8-4. When the project is being compiled, Visual Studio converts the .x file into a format that it can more easily use for rendering (stored as yet another .xnb file). At this stage, it can perform some basic transformations on the object geometry.

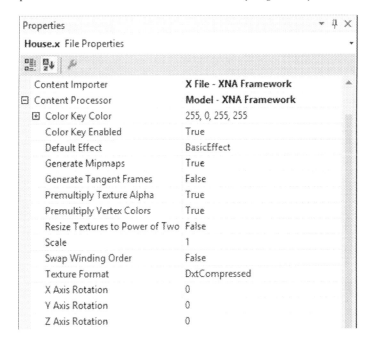

Figure 8-4. Properties for the Model Content Processor

The first of these properties is Scale. It is not uncommon for objects to be created with wildly different geometry scales, which can end up with objects that are entirely the wrong sizes. This could, of course, be adjusted for by scaling the object within the game, but it adds additional complexity to the game's matrix transformations.

This scaling requirement can be simplified by setting the Scale property, allowing the vertices to be scaled during compilation. The value entered is a numeric value and, as such, only uniform scaling is supported through this property. If you need to scale nonuniformly, you will still need to use a scaling transformation matrix to achieve it.

It is also fairly common when importing an object to find that the coordinate system used for the model is different from that used by MonoGame. This results in models that are upside down or otherwise rotated from the way you want them to be. The three Axis Rotation properties can be used to rotate them back to the desired angle. Positive or negative values can be entered, but note that they are entered here in degrees, not radians, as normally used by MonoGame.

We discussed hidden surface culling in Chapter 7. We also mentioned that some other graphics APIs such as OpenGL display counterclockwise triangles instead of the clockwise triangles used by MonoGame by default. If you find that one of your models appears to be rendering inside out, showing you the internal surfaces instead of the external surfaces, you can set the Swap Winding Order property to True. This will instruct the content compiler to rearrange the vertices of each triangle so that they are in the opposite direction to that defined within the model.

The final properties that we'll touch on here are the Resize Textures to Power of Two property and the two Color Key properties. They are applied to the textures that are used by the model and are identical in function to the properties of the Texture Content Processor with the same names.

When you compile the content project, you will find that the compiled model file appears in the output Content directory (named House.xnb in this case) and so do the images that the model uses, also as .xnb files. These are, in fact, just standard texture files. The content compiler will slightly change the names of the compiled texture files. In the example project, this gets the name Building3_0.xnb.

All of the resulting files (the model and all textures that it uses) need to be added to your MonoGame project. They can be added to the Content directory exactly as we have in all of the earlier examples we have looked at. Note that all of the files in the MonoGame project need to have their Build Action set to Content and Copy to Output Directory set to Copy if newer, just as with all other content files we have used (but not the same as the XNA Content project, for which the textures were either excluded from the project altogether, or had their Build Action set to None).

With the model content added into the project, we are now ready to load the model into your game. This is achieved simply by calling the Content.Load method, just as we have for all the other types of content data we have used. The object type to specify for the call is Model. A simple example of loading the house model is shown in Listing 8-1.

Listing 8-1. Loading a model into a MonoGame project

```
myModel = Content.Load<Model>("House");
```

Loading a model automatically handles loading all the textures required by the model, so there is no need to load them separately.

Listing 8-1 shows the model being loaded into a local variable named myModel. In the "Adding Support into the Game Framework" section, we will see that the GameFramework project provides yet another dictionary for models to be stored in, saving the need to declare lots of variables to store them.

Final Preparation Prior to Rendering

In an XNA project, having loaded the model, we would then be ready to begin rendering. In an equivalent MonoGame project, there is one other detail to be aware of first. Due to two small bugs present in MonoGame 3.0, the loaded object will initially render as an untextured jet-black silhouette.

In order to fix this, we need to do two things: We need to reset the diffuse and specular light color for DirectionalLight0, and we need to initialize the GraphicsDevice's SamplerStates collection, which incorrectly starts in an unconfigured state. The code to achieve these is shown in Listing 8-2. It can be found in the ImportingGeometry example projects at the end of the LoadContent method. It is important to execute this code *after* the models have been loaded.

Listing 8-2. Preparing MonoGame for rendering

```
// ** Debug, reset the light to undo Content.Load<Model> switching them off...
_effect.DirectionalLight0.DiffuseColor = _effect.DirectionalLight0.DiffuseColor;
_effect.DirectionalLight0.SpecularColor = _effect.DirectionalLight0.SpecularColor;
// ** Debug, set the initial samplerstate to LinearWrap
GraphicsDevice.SamplerStates[0] = SamplerState.LinearWrap;
```

Hopefully, the MonoGame bugs that make this necessary will be fixed in a future release, but until then, the section of code required here will be necessary for things to render properly.

Rendering Imported Geometry

How do we render the geometry that we have loaded in our games? The answer, as you might hope, is fairly straightforward, though there are some complexities that we will have to deal with.

The MonoGame Model object ultimately contains a series of VertexBuffer and IndexBuffer objects. These are what we will be using to draw the object to the screen. Unlike the simple cube example from the last chapter, however, it is very possible that the model will consist of multiple sets of triangles that all need to be drawn together to form the complete object. For this reason, the model object contains a hierarchy of collections, as shown in Figure 8-5, which must be navigated in order to obtain the vertex data to be drawn.

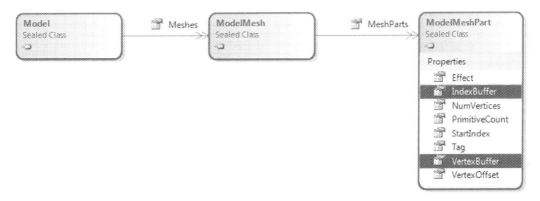

Figure 8-5. The Model, ModelMesh, and ModelMeshPart class hierarchy

Contained within the model object is a property named Meshes, which provides a collection of ModelMesh objects. Each ModelMesh represents a group of triangles that are to be rendered in a single position within the object.

The reason for having multiple model mesh objects is that Model objects are able to store geometry that contains complex hierarchies of parts. Imagine, for example, that you wanted to render a model of a helicopter. There are three primary parts to a helicopter model: the main body, the rotor above the body, and the tail rotor. Both of the rotors must move, relative to the helicopter, in order for them to be able to rotate. They are clearly part of the helicopter, but they cannot be rendered purely using the helicopter's transformation matrix.

MonoGame allows each of these separate pieces of the model, called *bones* in MonoGame's terminology, to be individually transformed. This is the reason why the model is stored and rendered in multiple pieces. We won't be going into any further detail about bones and how to use them in this book, but there are plenty of references on the Internet about using bones in XNA. These resources should all apply equally to MonoGame projects, too.

Contained within the ModelMesh object is yet another collection, this time of ModelMeshPart objects obtained from the property named MeshParts. Model mesh parts are subsections of the model mesh that, collected together, contain the geometry of the whole part. The reason for dividing model meshes into separate parts in this way is that each part might have parameters that differ from the other parts, such as the texture. If multiple textures are used within a model, this is the way different textures can be activated and individually rendered.

Within the ModelMeshPart class, we finally find where the IndexBuffer and VertexBuffer have been hiding away. Alongside them are several other properties that are essential for rendering the mesh part: VertexOffset, NumVertices, StartIndex, and PrimitiveCount are all required by the DrawIndexedPrimitives function.

There are two different methods that we can use to draw the model. The first requires us to loop through each of the mesh parts, telling each one to draw itself using its own Effect object.

These Effect objects are provided by the model so we do not have to create them, but, of course, they don't know anything about the environment that we have set up. In order for the mesh part to render correctly to the screen, we need to give it the world, view, and projection matrices that it is to use. The easiest way to obtain them is from our own class-level BasicEffect, as defined within our main game class.

A sample piece of code that performs this task is shown in Listing 8-3. In this code, the ObjectModel variable contains the Model being rendered, the effect variable is the class-level BasicEffect, preconfigured with all the matrices required for rendering, and the mesheffect object is used to iterate through each of the Effect objects provided by the model.

Listing 8-3. Drawing a model using its component ModelMesh objects

```
// Build an array of the absolute bone transformation matrices
Matrix[] boneTransforms = new Matrix[ObjectModel.Bones.Count];
ObjectModel.CopyAbsoluteBoneTransformsTo(boneTransforms);

// Loop for each of the meshes within the model
foreach (ModelMesh mesh in ObjectModel.Meshes)
{
    // Initialize each of the effects within the mesh
    foreach (BasicEffect mesheffect in mesh.Effects)
    {
        mesheffect.World = boneTransforms[mesh.ParentBone.Index] * effect.World;
        mesheffect.View = effect.View;
        mesheffect.Projection = effect.Projection;
    }
    // Draw the mesh (including all of its meshparts)
    mesh.Draw();
}
```

░ **Note**   Besides drawing the model, this code also handles the positions of the bones within the model. The call to CopyAbsoluteBoneTransformsTo populates an array with all the final positions for each bone, taking the bone hierarchy into account. These transformations are then combined with the active World matrix to determine the final position for each bone. Because our model does not include bones, the transformations will have no effect at all, but the code is present for compatibility with more complex models.

The code does everything that is needed to get the object to appear on the screen, but it has a drawback. Because the Effect objects being used for rendering the model are not the Effect that we have created and configured in our main game class, none of our Effect property values are present in the model's effect objects. As the code in Listing 8-3 shows, the Effect transformation matrices need to be individually copied from our effect into the model's effect objects.

While setting these matrices gets the model appearing in the correct place onscreen, there are lots of other properties that are not being copied here. As a result, they will be ignored by the rendered object. These properties include the lighting properties, diffuse and emissive colors, the alpha value, and more.

The alternative, therefore, is for us to render the model using our own Effect object. This already contains all the properties that we need the model to observe, so we don't need to worry about processing any of them within the rendering code. We can simply loop through the mesh parts, rendering each directly.

There is one critical piece of information that the model's Effect objects contain that our own Effect object does not: the texture to use for each mesh part. The code from Listing 8-3 draws the object fully textured, even though there is no mention of texturing anywhere within the code. We can read the texture out of the model's effects and use it in our own Effect to ensure that the correct texture is applied for each part of the model.

Having done this, the code can then use the information provided by the ModelMeshPart objects to set up the vertex and index buffers, and then draw them. The code to render in this way is shown in Listing 8-4.

Listing 8-4. Drawing a model using our Effect object

```
Matrix initialWorld;
Matrix[] boneTransforms;

// Store the initial world matrix
initialWorld = effect.World;

// Build an array of the absolute bone transformation matrices
boneTransforms = new Matrix[ObjectModel.Bones.Count];
ObjectModel.CopyAbsoluteBoneTransformsTo(boneTransforms);

// Loop for each mesh
foreach (ModelMesh mesh in ObjectModel.Meshes)
{
    // Update the world matrix to account for the position of this bone
    effect.World = boneTransforms[mesh.ParentBone.Index] * initialWorld;

    // Loop for each mesh part
    foreach (ModelMeshPart meshpart in mesh.MeshParts)
    {
        // Set the texture for this meshpart
        SetEffectTexture(effect, ((BasicEffect)meshpart.Effect).Texture);
        // Set the vertex and index buffers
        effect.GraphicsDevice.SetVertexBuffer(meshpart.VertexBuffer);
        effect.GraphicsDevice.Indices = meshpart.IndexBuffer;

        // Draw the mesh part
        foreach (EffectPass pass in effect.CurrentTechnique.Passes)
        {
            // Apply the pass
            pass.Apply();
            // Draw this meshpart
            effect.GraphicsDevice.DrawIndexedPrimitives(PrimitiveType.TriangleList,
                            meshpart.VertexOffset, 0, meshpart.NumVertices,
                            meshpart.StartIndex, meshpart.PrimitiveCount);
        }
    }
}

// Restore the initial world matrix
effect.World = initialWorld;
```

There are several points of interest in this code. Some of the processing is the same as in Listing 8-3: We retrieve the array of absolute bone transforms and then we loop through the model's Meshes collection. Within each mesh, we no longer have to update the effect properties because we are using our own Effect this time. It is already configured with all the required matrices and its other properties such as lighting, material, and so on. The one thing we do need to do, however, is observe the bone position. We do this by taking a copy of the original World matrix prior to the loop and multiplying this by the bone position for each mesh.

The effect is now ready to render the mesh, so we begin to process each of its parts. The first thing we do for each part is to interrogate its own Effect object to read out the texture that it needs. We pass this, along with our own Effect object, into a procedure called SetEffectTexture. This is a simple function that places the provided Texture2D into the supplied Effect, provided that it is not already present.

With the texture set as needed, the code then sets the mesh part's VertexBuffer and IndexBuffer into the graphics device. This prepares it for indexed rendering as described in the previous chapter.

At last, the mesh part is ready to render. Just as we always have, we then loop for each EffectPass, rendering the indexed triangle list into each pass. Note that all the details that DrawIndexedPrimitive needs to render are provided by the mesh part, making this process very straightforward.

Finally, having completed all the loops, the initial World matrix is restored back into our Effect, overwriting any bone transformations that might have been left in place. This stops unexpected transformations from creeping into the rendering process.

Although the code shown in Listing 8-4 isn't especially complicated, it is a little bulky. It would be ideal if we could avoid having to repeat it for each object in our game. Fortunately, the game framework will help us out with this once again, so let's see how we can integrate model rendering into the functionality that we have already added.

Adding Support into the Game Framework

Just as we have with the other content resource that we have worked with, we will simplify the task of working with models by allowing them to be loaded into the game framework. These models are added into the GameHost class as a Dictionary of Model objects. All the models that we need can therefore be loaded into the dictionary in the game's LoadContent method, ready to be accessed when they are needed for drawing to the screen.

We could leave it at that as far as the game framework is concerned, but we can also add another abstract base class set up for the purpose of rendering models. This class is named MatrixModelObject and is derived from the MatrixObjectBase class, as shown in Figure 8-6.

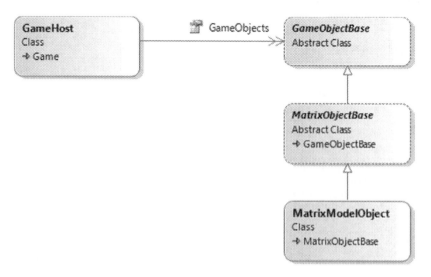

Figure 8-6. *The MatrixModelObject's position within the game framework class hierarchy*

Inheriting from `MatrixObjectBase` means that we immediately pick up all the matrix-based rendering properties. On top of these, we can add some further properties and methods specifically meant for dealing with models. The class is a concrete (nonabstract) class, however. It can be either directly instantiated and added into the `GameObjects` collection or inherited from to create customized classes with additional game-specific functionality.

The derived class's new properties are as follows:

- `ObjectModel`: a reference to a `Model` object that will be rendered by this class.

- `ObjectTexture`: this property is actually declared by the `MatrixObjectBase` class. However, it is overridden by `MatrixModelObject` in the case that it is queried without a texture ever having been explicitly provided. If this is the case, it will attempt to read from the model's textures instead. Once a texture has been set into this property, it will take precedence and be returned in place of the model texture. It will also cause the model to be rendered using the provided texture.

The following methods are present in the class:

- `DrawModel`: this is essentially the same code as shown in Listing 8-4, and it will draw the loaded model using the provided `Effect` object. It first ensures that an `ObjectModel` has been provided, and it returns without doing anything if no such object is present. Additionally, if a texture has been explicitly provided for the object using the `ObjectTexture` property, this will be used instead of the textures from the model, allowing for simple customization of the model textures.

- `Update`: the standard `Update` method is overloaded so that the `Effect` properties can be applied prior to drawing the object. This can be overridden in classes deriving from `MatrixModelObject` as normal so that the object properties can be updated as required.

- `Draw`: the standard `Draw` method is overloaded and set by default to first call `PrepareEffect` to load all the object settings and then call `DrawModel` to render the loaded model. As this will be the exact behavior required for many objects, implementing this in the `MatrixModelObject` class removes the need for any derived classes to have to implement their own `Draw` override.

The new class can be seen working in the `ImportingGeometry` example projects, which include the updated `GameFramework` project for this chapter. Once again, the code contained here is very straightforward, taking advantage of the game framework to manage all the more complex aspects of updating and presenting the game. In this project, a derived class named `ImportedObject` is created solely for the purpose of changing its rotation angles during each call to `Update`.

The SketchUp 3-D Warehouse

Alongside the SketchUp application, Trimble also offers a huge database of SketchUp models, known as the 3-D Warehouse. This service allows other users to upload 3-D models that they have created and share them with the rest of the world.

All of the models are in `.skp` format, ready for immediate download into SketchUp. Visit `http://sketchup.google.com/3dwarehouse/` to find the front page of the 3-D Warehouse. A page of search results can be seen in Figure 8-7.

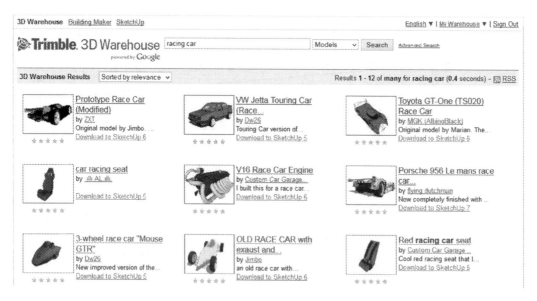

Figure 8-7. *Search results from the 3-D Warehouse*

SketchUp isn't designed just for creating game models, however. It can also create extremely intricate 3-D scenes and objects that would be far too complex to calculate and display in real time. If you decide to search the 3-D Warehouse for objects to include within a game, it is important to try to find *low polygon* objects (that is, objects that have been designed with fast rendering in mind by reducing the number of triangles that are needed).

Objects that use small numbers of textures (preferably just one) are desirable, too. Some complex geometry will cause problems for the .x exporter, so you'll need to try the models out in your code and see how they look before you get too attached to them.

The other important aspect of the 3-D Warehouse is that the license terms of the objects are not made very clear by Trimble. This means it is not necessarily safe to use the objects within projects that you distribute. If you find a good object, you should contact the author to get permission to use it in your game.

Importing Other File Formats

In addition to .x files, XNA's content compiler is also capable of natively working with Autodesk .fbx files. Other file formats, such as 3D Studio's .3ds format and the popular .obj format, are not supported.

There are several ways that model definitions in other formats might be used by MonoGame projects. The first is to import them into SketchUp (or another modeling application that is able to save geometry to .x or .fbx files) and then save them for use within MonoGame.

Another option that may be worth considering is to create your own geometry import code. If you can read the file format, you can open the file and work through its content, building vertex and index buffers along the way. However, depending on the complexity of the file format and the capabilities that you need to support, this process might be a very labor-intensive solution to the problem.

Working with the Camera

If you have ever used a video camera, you know that the most dynamic scenes will have movement from the camera as well as from the actors within the scene. In many games, the ability to manipulate the camera is just as important.

Moving the camera changes the position from which the player looks into the 3-D world. The camera is implemented using the View property of the Effect. In fact, we have been using it, albeit without moving it, in all our 3-D example projects.

In some ways, having a camera might seem unnecessary. After all, there wouldn't seem to be any visual difference between moving the camera toward an object and moving the object toward the camera. As soon as we start to build up complex multi-object scenes with lights, however, it becomes much more convenient to be able to calculate the object and light positions without having to worry about moving them all to simulate camera movement.

Let's look at the way in which the position of the camera can be changed in MonoGame.

Camera Position and Orientation

To move the camera, we need to figure out exactly how to set the View matrix for the required camera position. Fortunately, MonoGame takes care of this for us and provides a very useful Matrix function called CreateLookAt. This builds a view matrix such that the objects subsequently rendered will be positioned as if the camera had moved to the requested location.

The CreateLookAt function requires three pieces of information to be provided, all of which are Vector3 structures. The parameters, in the order required by the function, are as follows:

- cameraPosition: the current position of the camera as a coordinate in the 3-D world

- cameraTarget: a coordinate at which the camera is looking

- cameraUpVector: a vector that tells MonoGame which way is up

The first two values are easy to understand. The view will be generated as it would be seen when looking from the camera position directly toward the target position. The specified target position will appear directly in the center of the rendered scene.

The up vector requires a little more explanation. In simple terms, it tells MonoGame which way is up (toward the top of the screen) relative to the camera position. In most cases, you can provide a vector that simply points along the positive y axis: (0, 1, 0). The up vector does not need to be perpendicular to the camera's direction of view.

There are two situations when a different value for the up vector might need to be used. The first is if we want to be able to *roll* the camera. Rolling the camera rotates it around its z axis so that its own view of which way is up deviates from the world's view of up. (Rolling the camera by 180 degrees would result in everything appearing upside down.)

Figure 8-8 shows three views of the house object we imported earlier. In each of these, the house is identically positioned; it is only the camera's up vector that has changed. On the left is the view with the camera's up vector set (0, 1, 0), the default up vector. The middle image shows the view from a camera with an up vector of (0.5, 0.5, 0). The camera has rolled to the right so that its up vector is pointing between up and to the right (similar to tilting your head to the right). As a result, the house appears to have tilted to the left. In the final image, the camera's up vector is (1, 0, 0) so that up is along the positive x axis. The house now appears to have rotated 90 degrees to the left.

Figure 8-8. *Three views of a house displayed with different camera up vectors*

Rolling the camera might not be useful in all games, but for some it is extremely handy. Any game that simulates the movement of an aircraft or spaceship, for example, will probably want to use it to allow the craft to bank to the sides as it flies.

The second situation when a different up vector is required is when the camera is looking directly along the y axis. If the camera were looking directly upward, we would be telling it that *forward* and *up* were both in exactly the same direction. This can't possibly be true, so MonoGame's transformation matrix results in nothing displaying at all.

In all other cases, MonoGame is very tolerant of the values provided for the up vector, and it will cope fine with unnormalized vectors and vectors that are not perpendicular to the camera viewing angle.

Listing 8-5 shows a simple call to CreateLookAt that sets the camera so that it is located at position (0, 5, 5), is focused on position (0, 0, 0), and has an up vector of (0, 1, 0).

Listing 8-5. Creating a view matrix using CreateLookAt

```
Matrix view = Matrix.CreateLookAt(new Vector3(0, 5, 5),
                        new Vector3(0, 0, 0),
                        new Vector3(0, 1, 0));
```

This code can be made slightly more readable by using some of the static Vector3 properties, as shown in Listing 8-6.

Listing 8-6. Creating a view matrix using CreateLookAt and some of the static Vector3 properties

```
Matrix view = Matrix.CreateLookAt(new Vector3(0, 5, 5), Vector3.Zero, Vector3.Up);
```

▓ **Note** Don't forget the near and far clip planes that have been defined for the viewing frustum. If you move the camera near enough to or far enough away from an object that falls outside these clip planes, it will disappear from view.

It is also possible to set the camera position using matrix manipulation (rotation, translation, and son on), just as we do for the objects within our scenes. We will look at how to do this in the "Camera Positioning with Matrix Transformations" section.

Integrating Camera Support into the Game Framework

Once again, we can simplify the management of the camera by integrating it into the game framework. Let's take a look at how it is implemented and how we can use it in our game projects.

The Camera Class

In some ways, the camera is similar to the general game objects that we are using in our scenes: It has a transformation matrix and a position, and it can be transformed using the matrix transformation functions. For this reason, we will implement a camera class, derived from the MatrixObjectBase and named MatrixCameraObject. The class is concrete (nonabstract) so it can be used directly without needing to inherit a further class from it. The position of the camera class in the inheritance hierarchy can be seen in Figure 8-9.

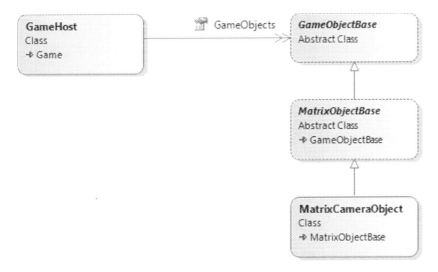

Figure 8-9. The MatrixCameraObject class within the game framework class diagram

However, there are some distinct differences between the camera and a standard game object:

- There can only be one camera active within the game at any time.

- Cameras don't have anything to draw, though they can still update their position like any other normal game object.

- The order that the camera position is updated and applied is significant within the 3-D scene. If its position is altered halfway through a set of objects, some of the objects will appear relative to the old camera position and others relative to the new camera position, which could produce very odd-looking results.

- We need to know the location at which the camera is looking. MatrixObjectBase class has no property to define this.

The first of these points is addressed by adding a specific provision for a camera object directly into the GameHost class. Instead of adding the camera object to the GameObjects collection, the camera is set into the GameHost.Camera property. If a camera has been set, it will be processed during each call to Update and Draw. If no camera has been set, no camera-related processing will take place.

Although the second of the points is true (cameras don't have anything to draw), we will still take advantage of both the Update and Draw methods of the MatrixCameraObject class. In the Update method, we can set the camera position, just as we set the position for normal objects. In the Draw method, we will apply the camera position into the Effect object so that it is active for all subsequently rendered objects.

The third point is easily addressed by the game framework. It ensures that the camera is the very last object to be updated (in the GameHost.UpdateAll function) and the first to be drawn (in its DrawObjects function). Updating last ensures that if the camera position is to be set relative to other objects in the scene (as we will demonstrate shortly), the target objects are always positioned before the camera so that the camera gets up-to-date information. Drawing first ensures that the camera position is active before any of the objects are rendered.

The fourth point is addressed by adding a new Vector3 property to the MatrixCameraObject class named LookAtTarget. This property can be used to specify the location toward which the camera is focused.

The default behavior for the camera class is to position itself at the location specified by its Position matrix and to look toward the location specified in its LookAtTarget vector. If additional positioning logic or a different implementation of the call to Matrix.CreateLookAt is required, the Update and/or Draw methods can be overridden in a derived class as required.

Camera Positioning with Matrix Transformations

Although we clearly have a good deal of control over the camera simply by setting its Position and LookAtTarget, there is another camera position mechanism that we can take advantage of that will, in some situations, provide an easier way to put the camera where we want it. This mechanism is to use the matrix transformation approach that we are already using for our game objects.

If we use matrix transformations, we can once again provide a series of operations that the camera will follow through to determine its final position. For example, we might decide to translate the camera to a different position within the scene, rotate the camera's matrix around the y axis by a preset angle, and finally translate a little way along the camera's local z axis. As the rotation angle changes, the camera will orbit around the position defined within the first translation. This is much simpler to calculate than having to use trigonometry to figure out the circular path of the camera if we were simply setting its position vector.

Listing 8-7 shows an example of positioning the camera using this technique, taken from a derived camera class's Update method. It first rotates the camera, and then it translates along its new z axis and also along its y axis. The end result is that the camera gradually orbits around the scene.

Listing 8-7. Positioning a camera using matrix transformations

```
// Reset the position using the identity matrix
SetIdentity();
// Rotate the camera
ApplyTransformation(Matrix.CreateRotationY(AngleY));
// Translate the camera away from the origin
ApplyTransformation(Matrix.CreateTranslation(0, 5, -14));
```

Compare this approach with the approach shown in Listing 8-8, which generates exactly the same camera movement, but uses trigonometry instead of matrix transformations. Assuming that you are comfortable with using matrix transformations, you will probably find Listing 8-7 much easier to read and understand. The difference between the two would be emphasized further if more complex camera position transformations were required.

Listing 8-8. Positioning a camera using the Position vector

```
// Reset the position using the identity matrix
SetIdentity();
// Calculate the camera position
Position = new Vector3((float)Math.Sin(AngleY) * 14, 5, (float)Math.Cos(AngleY) * 14);
// Apply the standard transformations to the object
ApplyStandardTransformations();
```

The Camera Object in Action

Accompanying this chapter are example projects named CameraMovement_Win8 and CameraMovement_WP8, which provide a simple example of using the camera within a game.

These two projects create a simple scene consisting of a square of ground on top of which a number of houses have been placed. The camera then rotates around the scene, allowing it to be seen from different angles. All the objects within the scene are completely stationary except for the camera. An image from the project can be seen in Figure 8-10.

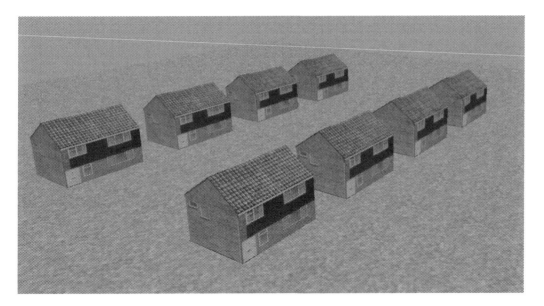

Figure 8-10. *The CameraMovement project*

The projects' `ResetGame` function adds the objects for the ground and the houses into the `GameObjects` collection. It then creates a camera object and sets this into the `Camera` property.

The camera object is implemented using a custom-derived class named `CameraObject` in order to move the camera around the scene. Within its `Update` function, you will see two different blocks of code for positioning the camera: one using matrix transformations and the other directly setting the `Position` property. One of these is initially commented out. Try swapping out the two approaches and experiment with each one to see how they work.

You can also try experimenting with the `LookAtTarget` property so that the camera looks in different directions as it moves around the scene.

Creating a Chase Cam

One type of camera that is very commonly used within computer games is the *chase cam*, a camera that follows along behind a key object (usually the player) to provide a first- or third-person view of what the object is able to see within the game world.

We already have many of the pieces in place needed to implement such a camera in our own games. With a little enhancement to the game framework's camera class, we can make this absolutely simple to implement within a game.

This section works through these changes and builds up a scene with a paper plane flying through the scene that we created in the last project. Once we have the plane moving (which will be an interesting task in itself), you will see how to attach the camera so that it automatically chases the plane and how to configure some different chase cam views.

All the code for this process can be found in the `ChaseCam_Win8` and `ChaseCam_WP8` example projects.

Adding the Paper Plane

The paper plane is a very simple 3-D model created in SketchUp. It consists of just four triangles arranged to give the basic shape of a paper airplane. The model can be seen inside the SketchUp editor in Figure 8-11.

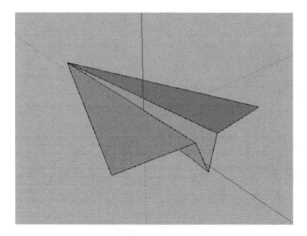

Figure 8-11. *The paper plane model*

The plane is positioned so that its center point is approximately on the origin point (0, 0, 0). This positioning will ensure that when we rotate it, it rotates around its center point.

The object consists only of flat triangles, so, in this case, we need to make sure that it is exported so that the back faces of each triangle are included, too. Without this, the plane would be visible only from the top side of each triangle, disappearing entirely when viewed from underneath. The .x exporter has an option to export the back faces, too, so this option was used to create the model file.

The SketchUp model file can be found in the Resources folder along with the source code for this chapter.

As it happens, the plane object has been created with a size that is not proportional to that of the houses. In fact, the initial size of the plane makes it a little bigger than each house. To give it a more realistic proportion, it has been scaled down as part of the Content project compilation process. You will see this inside the ChaseCam_XNA project, by expanding the Content Processor section in the Properties window for the PaperPlane.x content file. The Scale property has been given a value of 0.2 to reduce the plane size by 80 percent.

Finally, the plane is added to the game project as a standard MatrixModelObject-derived class, named PaperPlaneObject. Our goal for the plane is to make it fly smoothly between the houses, however, so we need to add some additional functionality to the class to achieve this.

Animating the Plane

Several of our previous projects have created objects that move smoothly around the screen in a variety of ways. They have all been based upon velocities that are applied to the objects' positions. In this case, we would get a much better flight path for the plane by allowing it to follow a series of movement points that are distributed throughout the 3-D scene.

This works well for an example, but it is probably not the kind of control mechanism that you would use in a game, which would more likely rely on user input to control the player's movement. Following a movement path is, nevertheless, a useful technique to know. It has a variety of applications in games, from *on rails* shooters (where the player controls aiming and firing a weapon but has no direct control over his or her movement) to computer-controlled characters in games.

The first thing that we will do is define a series of points along the movement path that the plane is to follow. They are declared as a static array of Vector3 structures at the beginning of the PaperPlaneObject class. We also store the array size to avoid having to re-query it later. The point declaration is shown in Listing 8-9.

Listing 8-9. Movement points that define the path along which the plane will travel

```
// Points on the spline movement path
static Vector3[] _movementPath =
{
    new Vector3(-1, 1.5f, -2),
    new Vector3(-1.5f, 2.5f, 2),
    new Vector3(0, 1, 6),
    new Vector3(3, 0.5f, 6),
    new Vector3(4, 1, 2),
    new Vector3(0, 0.4f, 2),
    new Vector3(-4, 0.8f, 1),
    new Vector3(-5, 1.5f, 1),
    new Vector3(-4, 2.5f, -2),
    new Vector3(2, 2.0f, -4),
    new Vector3(4, 1.5f, -7),
    new Vector3(2, 1.0f, -7.2f),
    new Vector3(0, 0.5f, -6),
};
static int _movementPathLength = _movementPath.Length;
```

■ **Tip**   These points were determined through a simple process of trial and error. In a game where lots of these points need to be defined with a reasonable degree of accuracy, it would be worthwhile creating a simple designer utility that allows them to be positioned on the screen rather than entered by hand.

We could now move the plane between these positions, but the paths between them are undefined. The plane cannot simply jump from one position to another. If we calculated a straight line between each pair of points and moved the plane along that line, its movement would look very angular and unnatural.

MonoGame provides another very useful tool that we can use to solve this problem: a function to calculate *splines*. A spline is a curved line that passes through a series of points such as those that we have defined. As well as asking for positions directly on the movement path points, we can also ask for points in between. The spline will calculate a smooth curved transition from one point to the next. This calculated path is ideal for the movement of our plane.

The movement path generated from the spline for the set of movement path positions is shown in Figure 8-12, with a camera looking directly down on the scene. The images of the plane show the positions of the defined movement path points. The lines between show the approximate spline paths.

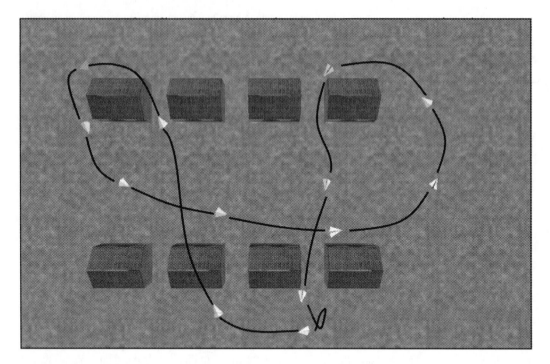

Figure 8-12. *The paper plane's flight path*

There are various spline calculation functions, but the one we will call upon in MonoGame is a *Catmull-Rom spline* (named after its creators, Edwin Catmull and Raphael Rom). It is very useful and simple to use, and it ensures that the spline path passes exactly through all the defined positions (which not all splines do).

To generate the spline, the function needs to be passed four consecutive positions on the path along with a *weight* value between 0 and 1. As the weight increases between these two extremes, the spline returns positions further along the path.

When a weight value of 0 is provided, the spline will return a position exactly on the second input position. When a weight value of 1 is provided, the spline will return a position exactly on the third input position. All four of the values are used in these calculations, however, to ensure a smooth path both between the second and third positions, and also onward into the next set of movement points.

This is illustrated using the diagram in Figure 8-13. If the spline is calculated using points 0, 1, 2, and 3 and a weight of 0.0, the resulting position will be exactly on point 1. As the weight increases to 1.0, the spline positions travel along the line between points 1 and 2, reaching point 2 as the weight reaches 1.0. Note that from this set of points, the spline positions never return values on the line toward point 0 or point 3, even though they are being passed to the spline function. These outside points are used just to calculate the angle of the curve between the central two points.

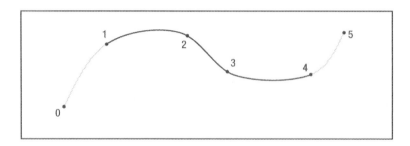

Figure 8-13. *A series of points and the resulting spline path*

Once the weight has reached 1.0, the spline can move on to the next set of points, passing in points 1, 2, 3, and 4. The weight is then once again increased from 0.0 to 1.0, causing the calculated positions to travel along the line between points 2 and 3.

From this set of points, it is impossible to return spline positions between points 0 and 1, or between points 4 and 5 (shown in gray in the diagram) as there are insufficient outer points for these parts of the path to be processed.

By moving point-by-point through the movement path, a smooth curved line can be produced that passes through all the defined locations. This all works perfectly well in three-dimensional space, too.

▦ **Tip**   When defining a path, don't forget that it will take exactly the same amount of time to move between each consecutive pair of points along the path. You should therefore try to make sure that the points are equally spaced. Points that have a larger gap than others will result in faster movement to traverse the increased distance within the fixed time interval. Points that are closer together will result in slower movements because less distance needs to be traveled.

In order to create a closed path that allows the plane to loop seamlessly back to the beginning of its journey and start again, we need to ensure that the final three points of the spline are identical to the first three points. As the weight of these points reaches 1.0, the spline position will eventually land exactly back at the position of point 1 within the movement path, allowing the whole path to be traced from the beginning once again.

We implement the spline calculations in the PaperPlaneObject code by storing two class-level variables—an int called _splineIndex, which defines the index of the first of the four points to use for spline calculation, and a float called _splineWeight, which allows us to traverse the path along the spline between the defined points.

In the Update function, we add a small amount to the _splineWeight variable. If it reaches or exceeds 1.0, we subtract 1.0 from it and increment the _splineIndex. If _splineIndex passes the end of the movement path point array, it is reset back to the start. These updates move the plane along the spline and reset it back to the start when it reaches the end of its movement path.

With these updates made, we call a function named GetPlanePosition to perform the spline calculation and return the final plane coordinate. The function, which expects the spline index and spline weight values to be passed as parameters, is shown in Listing 8-10.

Listing 8-10. Calculating the position on the spline for a given spline index and spline weight

```
private Vector3 GetPlanePosition(int splineIndex, float splineWeight)
{
    Vector3 ret;

    // If the weight exceeds 1, reduce by 1 and move to the next index
    if (splineWeight > 1)
    {
        splineWeight -= 1;
        splineIndex += 1;
    }
    // Keep the spline index within the array bounds
    splineIndex = splineIndex % _movementPath.Length;

    // Calculate the spline position
    ret = Vector3.CatmullRom(_movementPath[splineIndex],
                    _movementPath[(splineIndex + 1) % _movementPathLength],
                    _movementPath[(splineIndex + 2) % _movementPathLength],
                    _movementPath[(splineIndex + 3) % _movementPathLength],
                    splineWeight);

    return ret;
}
```

The code first checks that the spline weight is not greater than 1. If it is, it subtracts 1 and shifts on to the next spline index (we'll see the reason for this in a moment). This is followed by a check that loops the spline index if it exceeds the bounds of the _movementPath array items.

The spline position is then calculated simply by passing in the four vertex positions and the spline weight to the Vector3.CatmullRom function. Note, however, that we are using the modulus operator on the spline index values because, if they exceed the array length, they loop back to the beginning. This operation allows us to implement our closed loop (requiring the first three points to be repeated) without actually having to repeat them in the array. They are simply reused from the beginning when the end of the array is reached.

With the ability to calculate the plane position in hand, we can now set the plane's position and smoothly move it along the path. This is a good start, but there is a very obvious visual problem when it is put in motion—the plane is always facing the same direction. It should, of course, always be facing in the direction that it is moving. (Paper planes, as a rule, don't fly sideways very well.)

Fortunately, it is very easy to make the plane look in the direction that it is flying. The first thing we need to do is calculate another position for the plane just a little farther along the path. We do this by calling GetPlanePosition a second time, this time adding 0.1 to the spline weight. This addition is the reason that GetPlanePosition checks whether the weight has exceeded 1.0 because this second call might cause this overflow to occur.

The two calls allow us to see where the plane is now and where it will be in a moment. The direction of the plane must be from the first of these points to the second because it is its path of movement. Consequently, we need a way to rotate the plane so that it is facing from the first position toward the second.

This rotation can be achieved using another of the very handy static Matrix functions: CreateWorld. The CreateWorld function creates a world matrix (which is ultimately what we are trying to do in each object's Update method) so that it is positioned at a particular location and facing in a particular direction. This is just what we need: The position is the first spline point we have calculated, and the direction is from there toward the second spline point.

The direction itself is calculated simply by subtracting the current position from the next position. The resulting vector is ready to be passed to CreateWorld.

Only one minor problem remains: The plane is now continuously flying sideways because it has been defined sideways within the SketchUp model. To correct this, we simply rotate it by 90 degrees after the matrix has been calculated.

The full code to calculate the position and orientation of the plane is shown in Listing 8-11.

Listing 8-11. Positioning the plane and ensuring that it faces in the direction of flight

```
// Calculate the current position and store in the Position property
Vector3 Position = GetPlanePosition(_splineIndex, _splineWeight);

// Calculate the next position too so we know which way we are moving
Vector3 nextPosition = GetPlanePosition(_splineIndex, _splineWeight + 0.1f);

// Find the movement direction
Vector3 delta = nextPosition - Position;

// Create the world matrix for the plane
Transformation = Matrix.CreateWorld(Position, delta, Vector3.Up);
// The plane needs to be rotated 90 degrees  so that it points
// forward, so apply a rotation
ApplyTransformation(Matrix.CreateRotationY(MathHelper.ToRadians(-90)));
```

The end result is that we have a plane that smoothly and realistically flies around the scene between the houses. You can see this in action by running one of the ChaseCam projects. The initial view uses a camera that doesn't chase the plane but instead slowly circles the scene, allowing the flight path to be easily seen.

Now that we have the plane moving, we are ready to set the camera to follow it.

Implementing the Chase Cam

To allow a game to easily use a chase cam, we will add a new property to the `MatrixCameraObject` class into which a reference to the target object can be placed. If this property, named `ChaseObject`, is left at its default (`null`) value, the camera will act exactly as it did before and position itself according to its `Position` and `LookAtTarget` coordinates. If a game object is placed into `ChaseObject`, however, the behavior of the camera will change so that it follows the object around the scene.

When operating in chase cam mode, the camera has two responsibilities that it must fulfill with each of its updates: It must position itself a little way behind the target object, and it must look directly at the target object. Let's see how this can be implemented.

First, the `Update` code checks to see whether a `ChaseObject` has been provided. If not, it applies the default object transformation and returns without doing anything more, as shown in Listing 8-12.

Listing 8-12. Part of the camera's Update code: Behavior for when no ChaseObject has been provided

```
base.Update(gameTime);

// Do we have a chase object?
if (ChaseObject == null)
{
    // No, so simply apply the identity matrix
    // Calculate and apply the standard camera transformations
    SetIdentity();
    ApplyStandardTransformations();
    return;
}
```

If a chase object *has* been provided, we need to first calculate the camera position. We do this by finding the distance between the current camera position and the object position. Initially, the camera position might be nowhere near the object itself, but within a couple of frames, it will be positioned behind it, ready to chase.

The distance between the camera and the object is found by subtracting the object position from the camera position. The resulting value, named `delta`, is then normalized to provide a unit-length vector. This vector can then be scaled by the distance at which the camera is to chase in order to locate the camera position.

But what if the camera and the object are in exactly the same place? To deal with this circumstance, we always store the most recent of the distance vectors in a class-level variable, `_lastChaseCamDelta`. We will reuse this in case of a zero vector. This part of the `Update` code can be seen in Listing 8-13.

Listing 8-13. Part of the camera's Update code: Finding the distance between the camera and the target object

```
// Find the vector between the current position and the chase object position
delta = Position - ChaseObject.Position;
// Normalize the delta vector
delta.Normalize();
// If the delta is zero (the camera position is already directly on the chase
// object, which will happen if the object stops moving) retain the last used delta
if (delta == Vector3.Zero)
{
    delta = _lastChaseCamDelta;
}
else
{
    // Store the delta for later use
    _lastChaseCamDelta = delta;
}
```

Having calculated the direction between the camera and the object, the code is now ready to build the camera's transformation matrix. It begins by translating exactly on top of the object. From here, it translates a little way back from the object so that we can see it from behind. The direction in which this translation is performed is the direction that we have calculated into the delta variable. This direction vector is scaled by the distance we want to keep between the camera and the plane.

The distance is defined in a public property named ChaseDistance. Setting it to positive values will position the camera behind the target object. It can also be set to negative values, however, which will put it in front of the object looking back at it (and generally traveling backward). This camera position can be useful in some situations, but it does mean that if the players are in control of the object, they cannot see where they are going!

We also support a special value for ChaseDistance. If it is set to 0, we treat it as being in "first person" mode, which means we are looking directly from the point of view of the object rather than looking over its shoulder. Unfortunately, if we tell MonoGame to look at the same position as the camera location, it gets confused because it doesn't know in which direction to actually point the camera. To work around this problem, we still subtract a small distance from the object position by multiplying delta by 0.01.

We also allow an elevation to be specified for the camera to raise it up a little from the object's location. Typically, you will provide a small elevation so that the camera is looking very slightly downward toward the object. This elevation is set into the ChaseElevation property.

Listing 8-14 shows all the transformations for the camera position.

Listing 8-14. Part of the camera's Update code: Transforming the camera into position

```
// Transform the camera position to position it relative to the chase object
SetIdentity();
// Translate to the chase object's position
ApplyTransformation(Matrix.CreateTranslation(ChaseObject.Position));
// Apply the chase distance. Are we in first- or third-person view?
if (ChaseDistance != 0)
{
    // Third person view
    // Translate towards or away from the object based on the ChaseDistance
    ApplyTransformation(Matrix.CreateTranslation(delta * ChaseDistance));
    // Apply the vertical offset
    ApplyTransformation(Matrix.CreateTranslation(0, ChaseElevation, 0));
}
else
{
    // First person view
    // Translate a tiny distance back from the view point
    ApplyTransformation(Matrix.CreateTranslation(delta * 0.01f));
}
```

The camera is now positioned relative to the object as defined by the distance and elevation. The final couple of steps are to ensure that the camera is actually looking toward the object and then to update the camera position ready for the next update.

To set the direction that the camera is looking, we simply set the LookAtTarget property to contain the position of the chase object. When the camera's Draw method executes, it will use this value for its CreateLookAt matrix, ensuring that the chase object remains in the center of the screen.

The camera position is then updated by simply setting it to be exactly on top of the chase object. The next time Update is called, assuming that the object has moved, the camera will once again be able to determine the direction of movement of the object by comparing the new object position with the current camera position.

These last lines of the Update code are shown in Listing 8-15.

Listing 8-15. Part of the camera's Update code: Setting the camera's direction and position

```
// Ensure that we are looking at the chase object
LookAtTarget = ChaseObject.Position;

// Set the camera position to exactly match the chase object position
// so that we can continue to follow it in the next update
Position = ChaseObject.Position;
```

Using the Chase Cam

You're ready to fly now, so let's make the last few small changes to the game and see how it looks.

The ResetGame function creates the paper plane object and stores it in a class-level variable called _plane for easy access later on. The camera is created, but it is initially left without a chase object. As a result, the camera position obeys the transformation that is manually provided rather than following the plane.

This initial configuration appears when the project is run. The houses and plane are visible, but the camera slowly circles the scene. This camera movement path is handled using simple rotation and translation matrices in the game's CameraObject.Update function.

When the player clicks or taps the screen, however, we then activate the chase cam. The game class's Update method checks for touches. Each time one is found, it increments to the next of four camera configurations. The code required to activate the chase cam is shown in Listing 8-16.

Listing 8-16. Activating the chase cam

```
// Follow the plane from behind
Camera.ChaseObject = _plane;
Camera.ChaseDistance = 1;
Camera.ChaseElevation = 0.3f;
```

This is virtually all that is required to set the camera on its way. The only other change needed is to our CameraObject.Update function: If it detects that a chase cam is active (the camera's ChaseObject is not equal to null), it simply calls into the base class and then returns. Any further transformations that the camera code made would either interfere with or entirely replace the camera's own chase cam transformations.

If you run the project and click or tap the screen once, you will see the chase cam in full effect. An image from the project running in this mode is shown in Figure 8-14.

Figure 8-14. *In flight behind the paper plane*

Click or tap a second time and the camera is repositioned in front of the plane, looking back. This is achieved simply by setting the camera's `ChaseDistance` to a negative value (–1 in this case). Remember that although the plane knows its flight path and can calculate positions in its future, the camera knows nothing of its future positions. Yet, it still positions itself correctly in front of the plane. Being able to set its position without knowledge of the future is important because if the object were to be player-controlled, it would be impossible to predict its future movements.

Click or tap a third time to activate the final mode, which displays a first-person camera, activated by setting `ChaseDistance` to 0. There is one further minor change we need to make in order for this to work well: Putting the camera directly on the position of the plane results in a clipped image of the front half of the plane being rendered, which looks rather odd. For a first-person camera, we don't want to render the plane at all.

To resolve this first-person rendering problem, we make a small change to the `PaperPlaneObject.Draw` method. If it detects that it is the camera's `ChaseObject` and the camera's `ChaseDistance` is zero, it returns without drawing itself.

Just for fun, we can add some other planes into the scene, too. You will find a small block of code inside `ResetGame` that does this, but it is initially commented out. Uncomment it and you will find a trail of planes happily circling around within the game world.

Adding Fog

A useful facility provided by MonoGame is the ability to add *fog* to a rendered scene. This provides a simple simulation of real-world fog, making objects that are further away from the camera gradually fade away until they are no longer visible.

Clearly, there are limits to the amount of content that can be rendered to the screen, particularly on mobile devices. If you have open environments that stretch off into the distance, you need to draw a line at some stage and tell MonoGame not to draw things that are too far away. This distance limit is generally achieved by setting an appropriate value for the far clip plane when setting up the projection matrix, as we discussed in Chapter 7.

The downside is that as objects reach the far clip plane, they very visibly vanish. They often leave parts of themselves still visible as they edge past the clip plane, which can result in some very unnatural-looking scenes.

You can use fog to help reduce the impact of the vanishing objects by allowing them to fade away before they disappear. This fading results in a much less jarring effect that will often go completely unnoticed by the player.

Fog is also useful as a game feature in its own right. It can make an environment feel much more enclosed and claustrophobic. It can also add atmosphere to a scene, taking away some of the clinical cleanliness that rendered graphics can often suffer from.

Figure 8-15 shows some examples of the scene from the earlier example projects rendered in MonoGame using fog. The image on the left has fog disabled, while the remaining two images show increasing levels of fog. The distant buildings in the image on the right have completely vanished into the background.

Figure 8-15. *A scene rendered with increasing levels of fog*

MonoGame implements fog by using a simple but effective trick. As it calculates the color and lighting for each vertex that it is going to render, it determines how far away the vertex is from the viewpoint. As the vertex becomes more distant and is therefore affected to a greater degree by the fog, MonoGame gradually fades the vertex color toward the defined fog color. If the object is sufficiently distant, its vertex colors will be fully set to the defined fog color, causing the object to fade completely away into the background. Just as with other vertex properties, the fog effect interpolates between the vertices of the triangles, causing them all to be appropriately affected by the fog.

Fog is very easy to use, requiring just a small number of parameters to be set. All these parameters are provided by the BasicEffect object, so we can set them up alongside the rest of the Effect properties when our class-level Effect object is being initialized. The fog properties can, of course, be modified at any stage within the game (even between individual object renders), as required.

There are four properties available to set the behavior and appearance of fog:

- FogEnabled: this boolean value switches the fog feature on and off. It defaults to false.

- FogStart: sets the distance (in MonoGame units, from the camera viewpoint) at which the effects of the fog will begin to be applied. Vertices in front of this distance will not be affected by the fog at all.

- FogEnd: sets the distance at which the effects of the fog will end. At the end point, the fog is completely opaque. All vertices at or beyond this distance will be colored entirely in the fog color.

- FogColor: the color of the fog. Generally when rendering with fog, a solid background color is used and the fog color is set to match it.

An example of MonoGame's fog in action can be found in the Fog_Win8 and Fog_WP8 example projects. The fog parameters are set in the FogGame.Initialize function. Feel free to play around with these parameters and experiment with the effect they have on the generated graphics.

A little care is required to produce a good foggy scene. Fog affects only rendered triangles, so the background is not altered by the presence of fog at all. It is therefore important to ensure that the fog color and background color are pretty much the same; otherwise, solid, fog-colored structures appear in sharp contrast with the background color.

Using different fog and background colors can be useful, however. If the fog is configured so that the start and end values are both 0 (the whole scene is entirely full of fog), this configuration will produce a silhouette against the scene background in whatever fog color has been defined. The silhouette can be faded back into view by increasing the fog end and start values off into the distance.

It is also important to remember that fog within each triangle is calculated only by interpolation between its vertices. If very large triangles are used (such as the ground in our example), the fog might not always be applied in the way you expect, sometimes resulting in closer objects being affected more by the fog than those farther away.

Adding a Skybox

Our 3-D worlds are gradually beginning to look and feel more sophisticated, but they currently all suffer from one obvious visible shortcoming—they are all being presented against a blank background.

We created a background image for our sprite projects in Chapter 2 by simply drawing an image with the dimensions of the screen prior to rendering the sprites. This works well in 2-D, but it falls apart in 3-D. As the camera moves, the background needs to move, too, and we cannot make this happen with a static image.

There are various approaches that we can take to implement a working 3-D background. The one we will look at here is called a *skybox*. It is called this because it is implemented as a box (a cube) inside which the camera is placed. The camera is centralized within the box. As its angle changes to look around the scene, it also looks around inside the skybox. The result is a realistic-looking background with movement that is consistent with the camera and with the objects within the scene.

An example of a skybox working within our house scene, taken from the SkyBox_Win8 and SkyBox_WP8 example projects, is shown in Figure 8-16.

Figure 8-16. *Rendering a scene with a cloudy sky implemented using a skybox*

Although this example uses a cloudy sky, the skybox technique can be used for all sorts of background effects, from city skylines to interstellar star fields.

The skybox is drawn before any other rendering takes place and switches off writing to the depth buffer. This ensures that the box is always present in the background and that it has no effect on or interference with the objects drawn in the foreground of the scene. The box is actually fairly small, much smaller than the objects in the main scene, in fact. However, the rendering order ensures that this is not at all apparent to the end user.

To make the skybox look realistic, we need to move it in a particular way, or, rather, we need to prevent it from moving from the point of view of the camera. As the camera moves forward through the world, all the objects in the scene should get closer and larger, but the sky remains at a constant distance. This gives the impression that the sky is much larger and farther away than it really is.

We achieve this movement behavior for the sky by always setting the position of the skybox to exactly match that of the camera. As the camera moves around the scene, so does the skybox. Relative to the camera, therefore, the skybox is not moving at all, resulting in its apparent constant position.

Only the camera's position is copied into the skybox—the skybox rotation and up vector are left unchanged. As a result, when the camera looks around in the world, it will look around inside the skybox, too.

Creating Skyboxes

In our example, the skybox is actually implemented as a square tube; it has no top or bottom face. This greatly simplifies the task of creating graphics for the skybox.

The effects of using a tube in this way have been hidden at the top of the skybox by ensuring that the top edge of the sky texture is the same color as the scene's background color. This makes it hard to see where they skybox ends and the background begins unless it is being directly looked at. At the bottom edge, we make sure that sufficient ground is drawn to hide away the lower edge of the texture. Instead, it simply disappears behind the contents of the scene.

If you are creating a game that needs to be able to look all around the skybox, including up and down, you need to enhance it to create a full cube instead of the tube shape that it is using at present. This is simply a matter of adding two additional faces at the top and bottom of the skybox, both pointing inward.

Generating skybox images can be something of a challenge, depending on what kind of environment you need. One option is to create the background texture yourself. This is how the texture in the example was created: I simply took a photo with a digital camera and then cropped it so that its width was four times its height. You can find the image in the SkyBox_XNA Content project folder.

After being cropped, the image just needed a little manual manipulation so that the left and right edges of the image link up properly without leaving a strip where the texture doesn't join together. This tiling effect was achieved using the "Seamless Tiling" effect in Corel's Paint Shop Pro application. If you don't have this or a similar application available, you can copy a strip from one side of the image, flip it around, and then blend it into the opposite side of the image. This will make it opaque where it touches the edge of the image and then fade to transparent after a short distance across the image.

The skybox image needs to be four times wider than it is tall because it wraps around the four sides of the cube horizontally. Many digital cameras have a *panorama* feature that allows a number of pictures to be taken and digitally stitched together to create an extra-wide image. This feature can be very handy for creating the required images.

Another option is to use a computer application to create the skybox image. One application that can help with this is Planetside Software's Terragen application (see `http://www.planetside.co.uk` for details), which allows a variety of realistic-looking earth scenes to be created, including skies, terrain, and water. These scenes can then be rendered into images with the camera looking north, south, east, and west. When they are combined, they make an artificially generated skybox image. A good tutorial that explains how this can be achieved can be found at `http://tinyurl.com/terragenskybox`. After the images have been saved, they can be manually stitched together to create the sky scene.

Terragen has a number of editions, including the Classic edition, which is free for noncommercial use. Any commercial application of any edition of the software will require a license to be purchased. (The price of this varies between editions.) Details of how to buy this application are available on the Planetside Software web site.

Implementing the Skybox into the Game Framework

To make it as easy as possible to use skyboxes, we will integrate a special skybox class into the game framework, allowing us to ensure that it is rendered prior to any other content in the scene.

The skybox is created in a new game framework class: `MatrixSkyboxObject`. The class is derived from `MatrixObjectBase` and fits into the inheritance hierarchy, as shown in Figure 8-17.

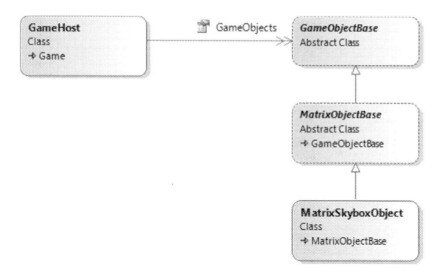

Figure 8-17. *The MatrixSkyboxObject class within the game framework class diagram*

Inside the class, the code creates a vertex buffer for the skybox consisting of the four side faces of a cube (excluding the top and bottom faces), all facing toward their interior. They are configured with texture coordinates that wrap the supplied texture around the inside of the box.

In the skybox class's Update method, the position of the camera is retrieved by reading its Transformation. Translation property and is set as the skybox's own position. Doing this ensures that they skybox always appears the same distance from the camera, regardless of where the camera is positioned within the scene. Reading the position from the camera's transformation matrix ensures that an accurate reading is retrieved regardless of how the camera has been positioned. (The camera's Position property might not reflect its final position, depending on how the camera is being transformed.) The Update function is shown in Listing 8-17.

Listing 8-17. Setting the position of the skybox

```
public override void Update(GameTime gameTime)
{
    base.Update(gameTime);

    // Calculate the transformation matrix
    SetIdentity();

    // Observe the camera's position if one is active
    if (Game.Camera != null)
    {
        // Read the camera's calculated position
        ApplyTransformation(
                    Matrix.CreateTranslation(Game.Camera.Transformation.Translation));
    }

    // Now apply the standard transformations
    ApplyStandardTransformations();
}
```

When the skybox is drawn, it first switches off any lighting that might be active and then disables the depth buffer. The lighting is important because we don't want light calculations to be applied to the sky—that's not how the real sky works. Disabling the depth buffer ensures that subsequently rendered objects will never appear behind the sky, an effect that would also look somewhat unrealistic.

With the rendering configured, the skybox is drawn. Once the drawing is complete, lighting and the depth buffer are set back to their previous states.

The code for the Draw function is shown in Listing 8-18.

Listing 8-18. Drawing the skybox

```
public override void Draw(Microsoft.Xna.Framework.GameTime gameTime, Effect effect)
{
    // Prepare the effect for drawing
    PrepareEffect(effect);

    // Disable lighting but remember whether it was switched on…
    bool lightingEnabled = ((BasicEffect)effect).LightingEnabled;
    ((BasicEffect)effect).LightingEnabled = false;
    // Disable the depth buffer
    DepthStencilState depthState = effect.GraphicsDevice.DepthStencilState;
    effect.GraphicsDevice.DepthStencilState = DepthStencilState.None;

    // Set the active vertex buffer
    effect.GraphicsDevice.SetVertexBuffer(_vertexBuffer);

    // Draw the object
    foreach (EffectPass pass in effect.CurrentTechnique.Passes)
    {
        // Apply the pass
        pass.Apply();
        // Draw the sky box
        effect.GraphicsDevice.DrawPrimitives(PrimitiveType.TriangleList,
                                               0, _vertices.Length / 3);
    }

    // Re-enable lighting and the depth buffer if required
    if (lightingEnabled) ((BasicEffect)effect).LightingEnabled = true;
    effect.GraphicsDevice.DepthStencilState = depthState;
}
```

For the skybox to draw correctly, it needs to be the very first thing that is drawn within the scene. To make sure that this is the case, we treat the skybox as a special case within the GameHost object. In the same way that we added a Camera property to allow the camera to be processed at the appropriate points, we will add a Skybox property, too. This new property can be set to an instance of the MatrixSkyboxObject class or any class that derives from it.

The GameHost.UpdateAll function updates the skybox object directly after the camera so that the camera position can be retrieved by the skybox. The GameHost.DrawObjects function draws the skybox after the camera, but before any further objects are rendered. To make sure that the skybox is rendered only once per draw (even if DrawObjects is called multiple times), an internal class variable is used to track the drawing operation, preventing repeat draw operations from taking place.

Overall, this implementation provides a simple but effective skybox that will suffice for many games, particularly those that keep the camera so that it is primarily horizontally oriented. The class can be easily extended as a derived class to provide full cube geometry, if needed, or to change the cube into a cylinder if the corners of the skybox cube become noticeable.

Particles

Another very useful technique that many games will benefit from is the use of *particles*. Particles are small, flat, textured rectangles that are drawn into the scene using transparency to create a variety of effects that can add a great deal of atmosphere to your game worlds.

In this section, we will look at how to use particles in a game and then discuss some specific examples.

How Particles Are Implemented

Particles are added to the game just as any other objects would be, but with the following characteristics:

- They frequently use a technique known as *billboarding* to orient them so that they directly face the camera.

- They usually switch off writing to the depth buffer so that they do not occlude one another.

- They are often the last things to be rendered into the scene each update. Because they do not update the depth buffer, this rendering order prevents objects that are behind them from appearing in front.

- They are often added in groups rather than individually.

You should already be familiar with everything here except for the billboarding technique, so let's look at that in a little more detail.

Billboarding

Billboards are simple quads (flat, square, or rectangular textured objects) rendered in the game world so they face directly toward the camera. As the camera moves around the world, the billboard objects rotate so that they continue to face directly toward it.

Billboards have a number of potential uses other than for particles, including for rendering lens flares around bright points of light and rendering basic trees using a 2-D image such that they always appear face-on to the camera.

For many types of rendered objects, applying a billboard in this way will give the appearance of depth, even though the object is actually completely flat. For example, imagine that you want to render an untextured and unlit spherical object in your game. Such a sphere looks exactly the same from all angles. If we can simply render a flat drawing of a sphere and keep it angled directly toward the camera, it will be indistinguishable from an actual sphere but with considerably less computational power required to display it.

Billboard quads are very useful for particle systems. If we want to render a firework, we need to ensure that all the points of light that are rendered are actually visible. If we do not use billboarding, the quads that make up the firework could be drawn edge-on to the camera, causing them to become virtually invisible.

Quads rendered as billboards are still placed within the 3-D scene, however. They will still retain their position within the game world, they will observe the perspective transformation, and they will be affected by the z-buffer just as any normal object would.

Figure 8-18 demonstrates the way in which quads are oriented in order for them to appear as billboards. The arrows show the direction in which they are facing. Notice that all the arrows are aligned directly toward the camera. As the camera moves, the quads rotate so that they are always facing toward it.

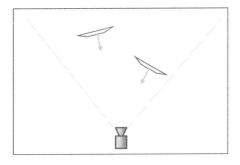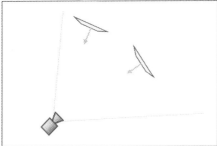

Figure 8-18. *A scene viewed from above with billboard quads rotated toward two different camera locations*

Getting quads to rotate in this way is actually fairly straightforward. Once again, we can call another extremely useful static `Matrix` function, this time called `CreateBillboard`. When we call this function, passing it the position of the billboard object and details of the camera position and orientation, it will return a matrix that translates the object to the specified position and rotates the object directly toward the camera.

`CreateBillboard` expects the following parameters to be passed:

- `objectPosition`: the position of the billboard object

- `cameraPosition`: the position of the camera, which can most easily be obtained by querying the `Camera.Transformation.Translation` property

- `cameraUpVector`: the camera's up vector, obtained from the `Camera.Transformation.Up` property.

- `cameraForwardVector`: a vector indicating the direction in which the camera is looking, obtained from the `Camera.Transformation.Forward` property

With the help of this matrix, we ensure that the particles are always aligned to face directly toward the camera. Listing 8-19 shows a section of a particle class's `Update` code that uses this new function to transform itself ready for display. Notice that it rotates on the z axis after applying the billboard transformation. Because the rotation is relative to the object's position, it rotates on the axis that is aligned toward the camera, regardless of how the camera is positioned within the world.

Listing 8-19. Billboard transformations for a particle object

```
// Calculate the transformation matrix
SetIdentity();
// Apply the billboard transformation
ApplyTransformation(Matrix.CreateBillboard(Position,
                                    Game.Camera.Transformation.Translation,
                                    Game.Camera.Transformation.Up,
                                    Game.Camera.Transformation.Forward));
// Rotate and scale
ApplyTransformation(Matrix.CreateRotationZ(AngleZ));
ApplyTransformation(Matrix.CreateScale(Scale));
```

At the time of writing, however, there is a bug in MonoGame's `Matrix.CreateBillboard` function that causes it to return incorrect results. Fortunately, there are two different versions of this function, one that passes back its matrix as the function return value, and the other that returns the matrix via an `out` parameter. While the first of these (which is the version shown in Listing 8-19) is broken, the second is working correctly.

To work around this problem while keeping the convenient syntax of the first overload, a new `CreateBillboard` function has been added to the game framework project, as mentioned in the next section. The game framework wraps around the working MonoGame version of the function. Until the MonoGame bug is fixed, this new function should be used instead of directly calling `Matrix.CreateBillboard`.

Adding Particle Support to the Game Framework

The game framework provides some minor changes to more easily support the rendering of particles. It defines a new abstract base class, `MatrixParticleObjectBase`, from which particle object classes can be derived. The class is abstract, so it cannot be directly instantiated. Instead, it just provides support for derived classes. Its position within the inheritance class hierarchy can be seen in Figure 8-19.

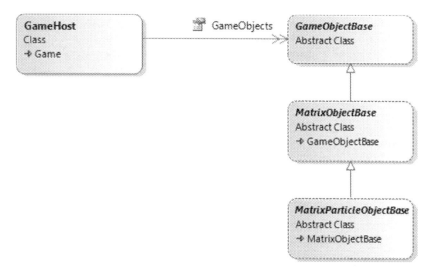

Figure 8-19. *The MatrixParticleObjectBase class within the game framework inheritance hierarchy*

The reason for having this class is that normally particles will be generated after all other objects within the scene, as we have already discussed. Making it possible to identify particle objects through the inheritance hierarchy in this way allows us to ignore them during the normal calls to `GameHost.DrawObjects`. To allow them to be rendered, the `GameHost` class provides a new function, `DrawParticles`, which can be called after all regular object rendering is complete. Just as with `DrawObjects`, two overloads are provided for `DrawParticles`: One draws all particles in the whole system, while the other only draws particles using a specified texture. This, once again, allows you to avoid unnecessary texture changes within the graphics hardware.

The class also contains the `CreateBillboard` matrix function needed to work around the MonoGame `CreateBillboard` bug, as described in the previous section.

The only other functionality added to the particle base class is a public boolean property named `IsActive`. As particles are frequently created in large volumes and often have short lifespans, they can be put into a dormant state when no longer required rather than being destroyed. This saves unnecessary object instantiation, reducing the frequency of garbage collection. This property can be seen being put to work in the first of the particle example projects, so let's see some particles in action.

Creating Fire and Smoke

The example projects `FireAndSmoke_Win8` and `FireAndSmoke_WP8` use two different particle classes to create a fire within the scene with smoke drifting away from it, as shown in Figure 8-20. Much of the code will be very familiar by now, so we will just focus on the areas that relate to the particle effect.

Figure 8-20. *Particle effects being used to create fire and smoke*

The fire is managed through a class called `FireParticleObject`. Each instance manages a single particle within the fire. The particles are textured using a simple gray blob with an alpha channel applied so that the white areas of the texture are transparent and the darker areas are opaque. The texture is shown in Figure 8-21.

Figure 8-21. *The texture used for the fire particles*

When each particle is created, it generates a position that is randomized within the area of the fire, sets a random vertical velocity, and assigns a random color that is either somewhere between orange and yellow, or between yellow and white. The game creates 75 of these particles, all positioned within the same area.

The particles update themselves by adding their velocity to their `PositionY` value and then slowly increasing the velocity so that the particles accelerate upward. If they reach a preset maximum height, they reset themselves back to the base of the fire so that the particles are continuously reused to keep the fire burning.

The particles also subtract a small amount from their `ObjectColor` alpha value, which causes the particles to fade away as they move upward, leaving the fire thinner nearer the top than at the bottom.

Finally, the transformation matrix is calculated, using the code shown back in Listing 8-19.

One further step is performed at the end of the Update function: initializing smoke particles. We'll look at this in more detail in a moment.

When it comes to drawing the particle, the code has a few preparatory steps to perform. First, it switches off the lighting because it is unlikely to be useful when the objects are orientated toward the camera (and fire isn't affected by surrounding light, anyway). It then disables writing to the depth buffer and switches on alpha blending. The blend that we use for the fire is the built-in BlendState.Additive blending. As discussed in Chapter 6, this blend mode adds the colors being rendered to those already on the screen, pushing the colors toward white. This results in a bright, glowing effect that is perfect for the fire particles.

The particle is then rendered with a simple call to DrawPrimitives and then the lighting, depth buffer processing, and blend state are all restored to their original states. Restoring these values ensures that the particle rendering leaves the environment in a predictable state for subsequent rendering.

These steps are all that is required to render the fire.

The smoke is implemented by using a second particle class, SmokeParticleObject, which is very similar to the fire particle. Its movement behavior is a little different, but its largest visual difference is that it uses the BlendState.AlphaBlend blending mode instead. It blends the existing screen content directly toward the texture graphics, resulting in a darker effect that works well for smoke.

The smoke particles are managed in a different way from the fire particles. Instead of resetting themselves to their original position after they have expired, they set a property called IsActive to false. Each time the FireParticleObject code wants to add a new smoke particle to the game, it first scans the GameObjects list looking for existing smoke particles that have become inactive. If one is found, it is reset and reactivated, saving the need to create new objects. If no inactive objects are found, a new one is created. This is exactly the same approach that we used for the explosion particles in *Cosmic Rocks* in Chapter 3.

When the main FireAndSmokeGame class renders the scene's graphics, it draws the smoke particles first and then draws the fire particles. Rendering in this order displays the fire in front of the smoke, which produces a more natural-looking interaction between the two elements of the scene.

The resulting effect might not be exactly photorealistic, but it is pleasing enough and sufficiently convincing for use within games. It is ideal for campfires, flaming torches, or (with a few tweaks to the particle movement) explosions.

Vapor and Smoke Trails

Another attractive effect, implemented along very similar lines to the smoke in the previous section, is the vapor or smoke trail. This effect can be applied to all sorts of vehicles, from cars to airplanes. It simulates the exhaust fumes, vapor trails, or dust plumes that the vehicles leave behind as they travel along.

The effect can be seen in the VaporTrails_Win8 and VaporTrails_WP8 example projects, an image from which is shown in Figure 8-22. These are based on the paper plane scene set up in the ChaseCam project, but with the addition of a simple smoke particle class.

Figure 8-22. *Particles used to create vapor trails*

During every second update, a smoke particle is added to the scene at the end of the `PaperPlaneObject.Update` function. The function uses exactly the same particle-recycling technique used for the smoke in the `FireAndSmoke` example, but this time passes the plane's position into the particle's constructor and `ResetParticle` function. Each smoke particle is therefore positioned directly on top of the plane.

The smoke particles do very little: They gradually increase in size and fade their alpha away toward zero. When the alpha value hits zero, the object is made inactive. Because a new particle is added every second update and they take 255 updates to fade away, this gives approximately 128 smoke particles active in the scene at any time. Try changing the rate at which they are added by altering the modulus operator at the end of the `Update` code. The trail looks even nicer with more objects, but, of course, it becomes more and more processor-intensive as a result. On most phones, adding a particle every frame will cause the frame rate to drop below 60 frames per second.

The smoke particles in this example are rendered using additive blending rather than alpha blending. Once again, this pushes the rendered graphics toward white (particularly as the particles are themselves rendered in white), resulting in a dense smoke trail.

Vapor trails can add a huge amount of energy to a rendered scene. If processing power permits, they are well worth considering if you have a use for them.

Fairy Dust

By now, you are probably getting the hang of particles, so this will be the final example. This example shows another style of particle that once again can enhance the atmosphere of an otherwise simple scene. The `FairyDust_Win8` and `FairyDust_WP8` example projects, shown in Figure 8-23, create a "fairy" particle that moves around the scene, showering multicolored sparkling dust behind it.

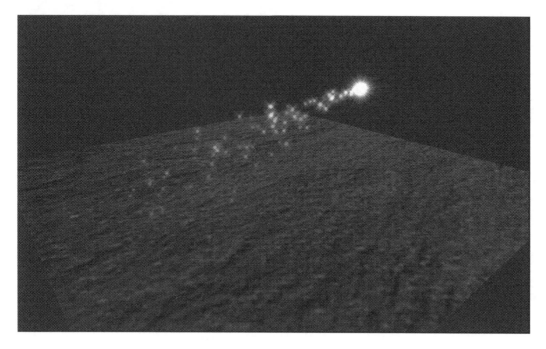

Figure 8-23. *Fairy dust particles*

Much of the code in this project is just the same as in the earlier particle projects, so we'll just take a look at the specifics that create this effect. First, there is the fairy. If you look carefully at it as it moves around the screen, you will see that it has a shimmering radiance around it formed from beams of light emanating from the center of the object. These moving light beams are created by overlaying two different particle objects in exactly the same location and rotating them in opposite directions. The texture contains the light beams. As they rotate around one another, they produce this shimmering effect. It is a lot less computationally expensive than it looks!

The dust particles are simply star-shaped textures created in random colors. They are positioned on top of the fairy when they are initialized. They move in a random direction and gradually apply gravity by increasing the y axis velocity with each update.

Simple, but, once again, an effective tool for many types of games.

Using Effect Objects

Throughout all the matrix-based rendering, we have been using a MonoGame class called BasicEffect as the gateway into rendering to the screen. We have defined this in a class-level variable named _effect at the top of each of our game classes. There are several other effects that can be used, however. The complete list is as follows:

- BasicEffect is a general-purpose effect with a large number of different configuration options.

- AlphaTestEffect is an effect that allows flexible depth buffer updates in response to alpha transparency.

- DualTextureEffect allows two textures to be rendered to geometry at the same time.

- EnvironmentMapEffect provides a simple way of simulation reflection of the surrounding environment on to an object.

- SkinnedEffect is a specialized effect that allows for animation of bones within a MonoGame model.

This section examines the properties and usage of some of these effects.

Effect Capabilities

Not all effects can use all the features that you have learned about up to this point. In fact, `BasicEffect` is the only effect that can use many of the features at all. Table 8-1 summarizes the effects and the features that are available for use within each. The features flagged as *Always* are always available and enabled ready for use. The features marked *Optional* are available but must be specifically enabled before they have any effect. Features marked *Not available* cannot be used by that effect at all.

Table 8-1. *Effect Types and Capabilities*

Feature	Basic	AlphaTest	EnvironmentMap	DualTexture	Skinned
Projection, view, and world matrix	Always	Always	Always	Always	Always
Diffuse color	Always	Always	Always	Always	Always
Alpha blending	Always	Always	Always	Always	Always
Fog	Optional	Optional	Optional	Optional	Optional
Vertex coloring	Optional	Optional	Not available	Optional	Not available
Texture mapping	Optional	Always	Always	Always	Always
Ambient lighting	Optional	Not available	Always	Not available	Always
Directional lighting	Optional	Not available	Always	Not available	Always
Specular lighting	Optional	Not available	Not available	Not available	Always
Per-pixel lighting	Optional	Not available	Not available	Not available	Optional
Emissive lighting	Optional	Not available	Always	Not available	Always
Special features	None	Alpha comparison function	Environment map control properties	Second texture property	Properties to set the transforms of the model's bones

Let's look at the rest of these effects in more detail.

AlphaTestEffect

The depth buffer is essential for proper rendering in 3-D environments, but you can run into problems when you begin rendering transparent objects.

This is because the depth buffer can track only a simple, single depth value for each pixel on the screen—it doesn't have any concept of transparency. If a semitransparent object is drawn on the screen, and then another opaque object is drawn behind it, how should MonoGame handle this? Should the object behind be rendered where it overlaps the transparent object (in which case it would incorrectly appear in front of it) or not (in which case the semitransparent object would in effect become opaque)?

The only solution for semitransparent objects is to change the order in which they are rendered to the screen. Objects should be rendered from those in the background first to those in the foreground last. This way, objects will always render on top of other objects that are behind them, allowing the alpha blending to work as required.

There is a special case exception, however, which MonoGame helps us handle more easily. When we render objects that are opaque in some parts and fully transparent in other parts, MonoGame offers us an *alpha test* feature that we can use to change the interaction with the depth buffer. Pixels within the texture that pass the alpha test will be rendered both to the screen and the depth buffer as opaque pixels. Pixels that fail the alpha test will be considered as transparent. The screen and depth buffer for that pixel will be left unchanged. Subsequent objects rendered behind the alpha-tested object will therefore show through the transparent areas while still being hidden by the opaque areas.

Just to restate the limitation with the alpha test, the comparison is a binary operation: Pixels from the object will either be considered fully transparent or fully opaque. Semitransparent rendering is not supported by this effect.

Figure 8-24 shows an image in which three cubes have been rendered one in front of another using a `BasicEffect`. The cube is textured with an image that contains a lattice of opaque bars with fully transparent regions in between. To allow the inner faces of the box to be seen, culling has been switched off for this example. The background color is showing through the transparent areas of the texture, as would be expected.

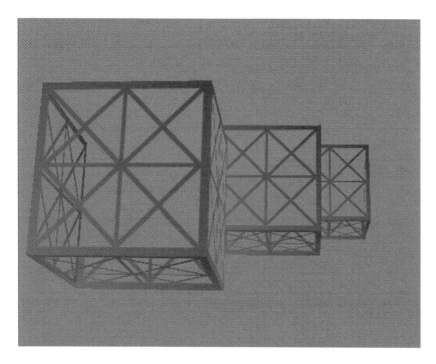

Figure 8-24. *Rendering transparent objects using BasicEffect*

Unwanted interactions between the alpha blending and the depth buffer are visible in two different areas. First, the distant cubes are being completely hidden by those in front, even though they are supposed to be transparent. Second, the inner surfaces of each cube are only partly displayed. On the left side of the front most box, the inner surface can be seen. The top and back surfaces are hidden because the front face was drawn before the top and back faces. As a result, the depth buffer thinks they are hidden.

Both of these problems can be cured by switching to use `AlphaTestEffect` instead of `BasicEffect`. The same scene is rendered again using `AlphaTestEffect` in Figure 8-25. You can see that all areas of the boxes that are supposed to be transparent now really are showing through both to their internal surfaces and also to the objects behind.

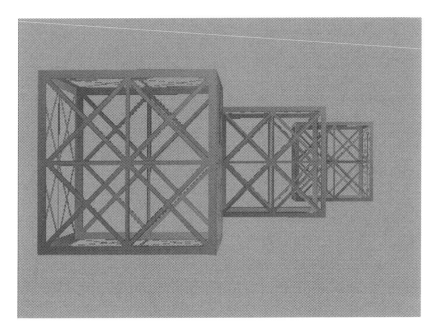

Figure 8-25. *Rendering transparent objects using AlphaTestEffect*

Switching over to use the `AlphaTestEffect` is easy, and all the code can be found in the `AlphaTest_Win8` and `AlphaTest_WP8` example projects. First of all, the `_effect` variable is changed to be of type `AlphaTestEffect` instead of `BasicEffect`, and it is instantiated accordingly within the `Initialize` function.

Next, the effect properties are set. Some of the properties are identical to those used by `BasicEffect` (including the three matrix properties `Projection`, `View`, and `World`; the `VertexColorEnabled` property; fog; diffuse color; and alpha). Other properties are forced on by this effect. (It always uses texturing and alpha blending, so there is no need to explicitly set them.)

As shown in Table 8-1, however, some of the properties of `BasicEffect` do not exist within this new class. The most awkward of these are probably the lighting properties. Without lighting, it can be difficult to mix alpha-tested objects in with other objects that are rendered using `BasicEffect` with lighting enabled. You will instead need to fall back to specifying vertex colors to provide a rough approximation of lighting.

Finally, we get to the good stuff: the new properties offered by this effect. There are two such properties: `AlphaFunction` and `ReferenceAlpha`. Between them, these properties provide the mechanism whereby MonoGame determines whether each calculated pixel should be rendered or not.

Transparency is determined by comparing the alpha value of each pixel in the texture to a *reference alpha* value that we provide to the effect. The type of comparison performed depends upon the *alpha function* that we tell the effect to use. If we were to specify an alpha function of `GreaterEqual` and a reference alpha of 128, all pixels whose alpha value is 128 or more will be rendered as opaque, whereas all those with alpha less than 128 will be rendered transparent.

A number of different alpha functions are available, provided by the `CompareFunction` enumeration. These functions are `Always` (the pixel is always rendered as opaque regardless of its alpha value), `Never` (always rendered transparent, which makes the object entirely invisible), `Less`, `LessEqual`, `Equal`, `GreaterEqual`, `Greater`, and `NotEqual`. All these functions work just as you would expect.

The alpha reference is specified as an integer between 0 (pixels that are fully transparent) and 255 (pixels that are fully opaque).

The code required to instantiate and initialize the `AlphaTestEffect` is shown in Listing 8-20.

Listing 8-20. Creating and initializing an AlphaTestEffect

```
// Create and initialize the effect
_effect = new AlphaTestEffect(GraphicsDevice);
_effect.VertexColorEnabled = false;
_effect.Projection = projection;
_effect.View = view;
_effect.World = Matrix.Identity;
// Set the effect's alpha test parameters
_effect.AlphaFunction = CompareFunction.GreaterEqual;
_effect.ReferenceAlpha = 250;
```

The GameFramework project also provides a modified version of MatrixObjectBase.PrepareEffect, which expects an AlphaTestEffect as its parameter. It sets only those properties that are relevant for this type of effect.

AlphaTestEffect and BasicEffect objects (and indeed, any of the effect objects) can be used together within the same rendered scene. This is achieved by creating two or more separate effect objects of the required types and passing the appropriate object into the DrawObjects function from the game class's Draw method.

DualTextureEffect

Another useful rendering feature provided by MonoGame is the ability to combine two textures together when rendering each triangle.

So far, all our textured objects have been given a texture coordinate for each vertex. This coordinate has been used by MonoGame to stretch the texture across the surface of the rendered object. When we use DualTextureEffect, we need to provide two texture coordinates for each vertex as well as two textures to blend together when displaying the object.

This additional texture presents a couple of initial problems to overcome. The first is easy to solve: Our game framework objects have been storing a reference to only a single texture. We'll address this by simply adding a second texture property, ObjectTexture2, to the MatrixObjectBase class.

Then we come to the second problem, whose solution is a little less obvious. The vertex definition structures that we used for textured objects (one of either VertexPositionTexture, VertexPositionNormalTexture, or VertexPositionColorTexture) all contain only a single property for specifying a texture. How, therefore, are we able to tell MonoGame the vertex coordinates of the second texture?

The answer lies in MonoGame's capability to work with *custom vertex formats*. Lots of different pieces of information can be encoded into a vertex format, and we have worked with positions, texture coordinates, colors, and normals throughout this and previous chapters. In order to support additional vertex information such as that required here, it is possible for customized structures to be used in place of these in-built structures.

We can thus create such a structure containing a position and two texture coordinates, one for each of the dual textures. We will give the new structure a name of VertexPositionDualTexture to match MonoGame's naming scheme. To make it easily accessible to our games, it has been added to the GameFramework project inside the VertexDeclarations.cs source file. The code for the structure is not included here because it doesn't provide anything that we will build on. It can simply be treated as a closed source structure, but if you are curious about its implementation, you can take a look in the game framework source code.

How then does MonoGame combine the two textures together when it is rendering? The calculation is very simple, but it deserves a little exploration to understand its implications.

Each final rendered pixel color is calculated using the following formula (treating all red, green, and blue values as floats in the range of 0 to 1):

$$Red_{new} = (Red_1 \times Red_2) \times 2$$
$$Green_{new} = (Green_1 \times Green_2) \times 2$$
$$Blue_{new} = (Blue_1 \times Blue_2) \times 2$$
$$Alpha_{new} = (Alpha_1 \times Alpha_2) \times 2$$

In many cases, the easiest way to visualize this calculation in action is to consider the first texture as being the actual texture that is displayed upon the object and to consider the second texture as *modulating* it by increasing or decreasing its brightness in each of the color components based upon its own color value.

Because each output pixel calculation multiplies the final value by 2, a color component value of 0.5 within one of the textures will have no effect at all on the color from the other texture (it will be multiplied by 0.5, halving it, and then multiplied by 2, restoring it to its original value). On the other hand, a value of 0.0 will remove all color from the other texture, and 1.0 will double the value from the other texture. As always, the colors are clamped, and resulting values above 1.0 will be treated as if they were 1.0.

The DualTexture example project shows two applications of this effect. The one that appears when the project is first launched has its first texture as a piece of rocky ground and its second texture as three white circles on a dark-gray background, as shown in Figure 8-26. The code changes the texture coordinates with each update, causing the two textures to gradually move across the face of the rendered square.

Figure 8-26. *The ground and lights textures used by the DualTexture example project*

The circles form an effective-looking spotlight effect on the ground. Their background color is darker than mid-gray, causing them to darken the ground texture, but the circles themselves are obviously very bright, illuminating the texture. The resulting image is shown in Figure 8-27. Once again, it looks better in motion than in a still image.

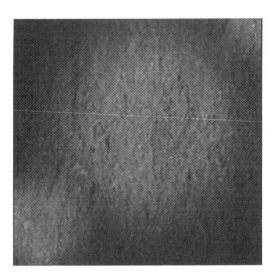

Figure 8-27. *The ground and lights textures combined by DualTextureEffect*

The example project contains a second, much more colorful example, too. Edit the code and swap over the commenting of the two calls to GameObjects.Add in the DualTextureGame.ResetGame function so that the two moiré textures are passed instead of the ground and lights textures. These two new textures contain a series of concentric circles, as shown in Figure 8-28. Both textures contain the same pattern but in different colors.

Figure 8-28. *The moiré pattern texture*

These textures are combined using exactly the same code as before, but this time the concentrated patterns of bright and dark color interact with each other to create a fantastic-looking interference pattern, which can be seen in Figure 8-29. And yes, this one looks better in motion, too!

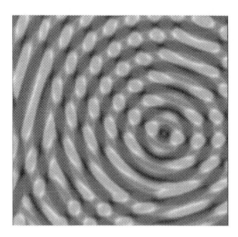

Figure 8-29. *The effects of dual texturing the two moiré textures*

Using DualTextureEffect is very simple. Create an instance of it in your game class and configure its properties as necessary. Once again, it has a limited set of properties compared to BasicEffect, with no support for lighting.

When setting up your vertex buffers, declare them to be of type VertexPositionDualTexture and set their texture coordinates using the two properties TexCoord0 and TexCoord1. The two textures are provided to the game objects in their ObjectTexture and ObjectTexture2 properties.

EnvironmentMapEffect

The next of the MonoGame effects is the `EnvironmentMapEffect`. We already saw some fairly shiny objects when we were experimenting with specular lighting in the previous chapter, but environment mapping allows us to take shiny surfaces to a whole new level.

Environment mapping is a technique that simulates the reflections of an object's surroundings onto the object itself. If your game is set in a forest, for example, you might want to reflect a forest image onto some of the objects in your game. Objects that use environment mapping in this way look like they are highly polished. (This suits some objects more than others. For example, objects made of metal, glass, or polished wood will benefit from environment mapping, but objects with matte surfaces such as brick or plastic will probably look very strange.)

It usually isn't important that the reflections being used for the environment map actually be accurate. As long as they fit in with the scene, users will be fooled into thinking they are seeing the real environment rather than a static image. Showing a reflection of a forest when the player is exploring a cave will, of course, be a little more jarring, so make sure the scene and the environment map match up.

In addition to allowing objects to reflect the environment, MonoGame's environment mapping also allows objects to have their own static textures just like those used by the other effects, which are blended with the effect's environmental texture. The combination of the object's own texture and its reflected environment leads to a very convincing illusion of reflectivity.

There are some minor challenges involved in setting up an environment map, but, fortunately, once you know how to do it, the process is very easy. And you will know exactly how to do it very soon! The code that we will look at in this section can be found in the `EnvironmentMap_Win8` and `EnvironmentMap_WP8` projects. Some images from it can be seen in Figure 8-30 (and yes, once again, this example also looks better in motion).

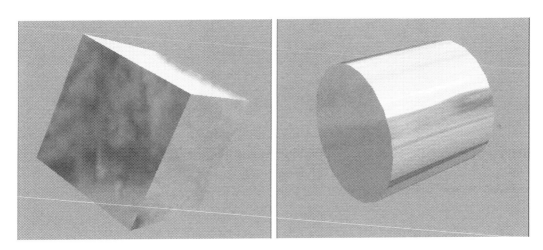

Figure 8-30. *A cube and a cylinder reflecting a landscape environment*

The `EnvironmentMapEffect` object is, in many ways, very similar to `BasicEffect` because it offers most of the same lighting properties and other effects. The only features that are absent, as compared with `BasicEffect`, are specular lighting and vertex coloring.

The effect needs a texture so that it can texture the object. In the `GameFramework` project, the `MatrixObjectBase.PrepareEffect` function will once again take care of providing this texture from each object's `ObjectTexture` property. A valid texture is a requirement of the `EnvironmentMapEffect`. Setting its texture to `null` will result in a black silhouette of the object appearing. It is possible to render without applying a texture to the object, however, and we will look at how this can be achieved in a moment.

Preparing the Environment Map

The reflection functionality offered by this new effect is implemented by a new feature called an *environment map*. This map contains the texture that will be used for reflections on the rendered objects. However, we have a problem with setting the effect's EnvironmentMap property: Its type is TextureCube rather than Texture2D, and this is a new type of object that we have not encountered before. How can we generate a TextureCube object?

A texture cube is similar in function to the skybox that we looked at earlier on. It is a set of six textures that can be applied to the front, back, left, right, top, and bottom faces of a cube such that when viewed from the inside they form a consistent, seamless environment in all directions. Neither MonoGame nor the XNA Content projects provide a built-in way to create texture cubes from an image, but one of the XNA sample projects that Microsoft released separately provides everything that is needed to very easily create a texture cube.

The sample project can be found at http://tinyurl.com/xnaenvironmentmap. The relevant project from it is also included in this chapter's source code in the CustomModelEffectPipeline folder. It has been copied directly from the sample project without any modification.

The project contains an XNA game library, but it is one that we will use only as part of the compilation process; it doesn't get distributed along with your finished game. Instead, it adds a custom content processor that the Content project can use to transform a simple PNG or JPG image into a texture cube.

To use the content processor, add the CustomModelEffectPipeline project to your XNA Content project's solution. Then open the References branch of the Content project within Solution Explorer, right-click Add Reference, and select the CustomModelEffectPipeline item from the Add Reference window's Projects tab. When this is done, the project will appear as a reference alongside the other content processors provided by XNA, as shown in Figure 8-31. You can find the project so configured in the EnvironmentMap_XNA example project.

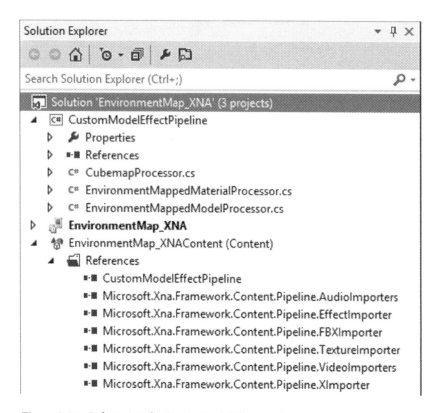

Figure 8-31. *Referencing the CustomModelEffectPipeline from the game's Content project*

Now that the Content project is aware of the custom content processor, it can be used to transform a graphic file into a TextureCube instead of a Texture2D object. To do this, add the image that you want to use for the environment map (Landscape.jpg in the example project) and edit its properties. The initial setting for the Content Processor property is Texture - XNA Framework. If you open the drop-down list for this property, you will find that some new processors have appeared, all of which are provided by the CustomModelEffectPipeline code. Select CubemapProcessor as the processor to use, as shown in Figure 8-32. When the project is compiled, this texture will now be created as a texture cube.

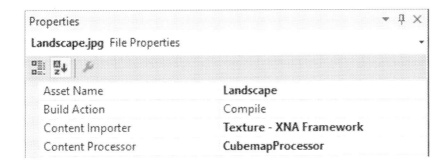

Figure 8-32. *A graphic file configured to be processed by the CubemapProcessor*

▒ **Note**   There is no need to worry about making seamless wrapping graphic files before providing them to the CubemapProcessor. It will cleverly distort the image in a way that automatically wraps the image seamlessly around all the faces of the texture cube.

This configuration change is everything we need to prepare the TextureCube; now we simply need to activate it within the game. After instantiating and initializing the EnvironmentMapEffect, the TextureCube can be read from the Content object and set into the EnvironmentMap property. The code to do this, taken from the example project's LoadContent function, is shown in Listing 8-21.

Listing 8-21.   Loading a TextureCube into the EnvironmentMapEffect object

```
// Load the environment cube map
_effect.EnvironmentMap = Content.Load<TextureCube>("Landscape");
```

▒ **Note**   We could easily add a new collection of TextureCube objects into the GameFramework project, but because it is likely that only one will be used at a time, it is more straightforward to simply load it directly into the effect. Feel free to extend the game framework yourself to support a collection of texture cubes if you would find it useful.

Once the effect's environment map is set, all that is left is to simply render some objects. It is important that the objects have vertex normals configured correctly because the effect uses them (along with the vertex position) to determine which part of the environment map should reflect on each part of the object, but no further object configuration is required.

In the example project, the cube is set with a marble texture, so this is blended with the environment map reflection. The cylinder, on the other hand, is given a null texture, so it displays only the environment with no static texture of its own.

▓ **Tip** Don't forget to configure the scene's lighting. Without it, your objects will be entirely unlit but will still reflect their environment, which is probably not what you are expecting to see.

Environment Map Properties

Several additional effect properties are available to control the way in which the environment mapping is applied to your rendered objects.

First is the EnvironmentMapAmount property, which controls the strength of the blending effect between the environment texture and the object's own texture, in the range of 0 to 1. When set to 1 (its default value), the environment map will completely replace the object's texture; when set to 0, the environment map will be completely switched off. Values in between will provide varying levels of subtlety to the strength of reflections.

Next is the EnvironmentMapSpecular property. If you encode additional data into your image's alpha channel, this property can be used to implement a cheap simulation of specular lighting on your objects. The EnvironmentMapSpecular property allows a color to be specified with which the alpha channel data will be tinted. It defaults to black, which disables this effect. This effects works better when the object is highly curvy because large flat surfaces tend to break the illusion of the specular lighting.

▓ **Tip** Don't forget that JPG graphic files can't store alpha channel information, so this feature can be used only with PNG image files. Due to the way that the cubemap processor transforms the image into its texture cube, the resulting image sizes will not be hugely different because the images are recompressed in the same way regardless of the source image format.

The final property is the FresnelFactor. Another float property that ranges from 0 to 1, this property controls how the reflectivity of an object changes relative to the viewing angle. With a FresnelFactor value of 1 (the default), object surfaces will stop reflecting the environment entirely when they are facing directly toward the camera, though they will increasingly reflect as they rotate away. A FresnelFactor of 0 disables this effect completely so that the object reflectivity takes no account of the viewing angle. Values in between make this effect more or less pronounced.

It is very useful to be able to experiment with these properties when setting up your environment-mapped objects. Highly reflective objects look very pretty, but they are not necessarily all that realistic. Great results can be had from applying subtle environment mapping to your objects that the user is perhaps only subconsciously aware of.

To allow each of the objects within our games to have independent control over their environmental mapping settings when running in the GameFramework, corresponding properties named EnvironmentMapAmount, EnvironmentMapSpecular, and FresnelFactor have been added to MatrixObjectBase in the game framework. They default to the values 1, Black, and 1, respectively, to match the defaults provided by MonoGame.

Rendering Untextured Objects with Environment Maps

It will sometimes be useful to draw objects that are entirely reflective and that have no texture of their own visible at all. This can be achieved by setting the EnvironmentMapAmount to 1, but it is still necessary to have a texture applied to the object itself, or else the object will appear completely black.

There are two things we can do to address this problem. The first is to create a 1-x-1-pixel white dummy texture and apply it to the objects in question. They will therefore be textured (in white), so the environment mapping will apply as required.

The only real downside is that the dummy texture needs to be loaded into the graphics hardware, replacing any other texture that might already be there. That other texture might then need to be subsequently reloaded, causing a performance hit.

The other alternative is to leave whatever texture is already in the graphics hardware active so that it will apply to the object being rendered. This texture might, of course, be entirely unsuitable for the new object, which probably hasn't been set up with any texture coordinates at all. To prevent it from causing unpredictable results, we can configure the environment mapping settings for the object to have an `EnvironmentMapAmount` of 1 and a `FresnelFactor` of 0. This will cause the environment map to completely overpower the object texture so that it has no visible effect whatsoever.

The game framework will set the environment map properties in this way if it detects that no texture has been set for the object being rendered. It is essential that there are other objects within the scene that do activate a texture within the `EnvironmentMapEffect`, however, so that a texture is set prior to the object being rendered. If this is not the case, a dummy texture will need to be applied as described previously.

SkinnedEffect

The final effect is the `SkinnedEffect`. This effect doesn't provide graphical effects in the way that the other effects have, but rather it allows models that contain multiple bones to be controlled such that each bone can be moved around its joints to position complex models into different poses.

Creating models such as these is beyond the scope of this book, so we will not be going into any further detail about this particular effect. If you want to learn more and see the effect in action, take a look at the XNA Reach Graphics Demo, which can be found by pointing your web browser at `http://tinyurl.com/xnareach` and downloading the source code at the bottom of the page. This is, of course, an XNA project, but the ideas and code should port across to MonoGame with very little effort.

Mixing Sprite and Matrix Rendering

We have nearly finished our journey through MonoGame's matrix-based rendering, but there is one final topic to cover: mixing rendering from sprites and from matrix-based graphics together at the same time.

There are obvious uses to rendering sprites and matrices together: 3-D games will frequently need to display text, for example, and it is likely that 2-D status overlays (energy bars, number of lives left, and so on) might be useful, too. MonoGame allows us to achieve this by rendering sprites and 3-D objects together into the same scene.

Simply draw the 3-D objects first and then draw the sprites afterward. Both will render exactly as you would expect, with the sprites appearing on top of any 3-D objects that have already been rendered onscreen.

MonoGame's sprite renderer does, however, make some changes to the state of the rendering engine, and they will most likely need some minor additional changes to your code to compensate for. When MonoGame begins rendering sprites, it reconfigures the environment as follows:

- `GraphicsDevice.BlendState` is set to `BlendState.AlphaBlend`. You will probably want to set it back to `BlendState.Opaque`, or whatever other blend state you require.

- `GraphicsDevice.DepthStencilState` is set to `DepthStencilState.None`, disabling the depth buffer. (Remember that sprites handle depth purely through the `LayerDepth` value on each rendered sprite.) You will almost certainly need to set this back to `DepthStencilState.Default`.

- `GraphicsDevice.RasterizerState` is set to `RasterizerState.CullCounterClockwise`. This is its default value anyway, so it might not have any impact on your code.

- `GraphicsDevice.SamplerState[0]` is set to `SamplerState.LinearClamp`. This will prevent tiling of textures on your 3-D objects, so you might want to revert this back to `SamplerState.LinearWrap`.

To simplify the management of these render states, two new functions have been added to the game framework's GameHost class: StoreStateBeforeSprites and RestoreStateAfterSprites. The StoreStateBeforeSprites function reads the current value for all four of these state properties and stores them away into private class variables within GameHost. This function should be called prior to calling the SpriteBatch.Begin method. The RestoreStateAfterSprites function retrieves these stored values and makes them current once again. It should be called after SpriteBatch.End. Storing and restoring the state in this way hides the state changes that the SpriteBatch makes, allowing the rest of the rendering code to continue unaffected.

Listing 8-22 shows the source code for these two functions, taken from the GameHost class.

Listing 8-22. Storing and restoring the graphics device state for before and after rendering sprites

```
protected void StoreStateBeforeSprites()
{
    _preSpriteBlendState = GraphicsDevice.BlendState;
    _preSpriteDepthStencilState = GraphicsDevice.DepthStencilState;
    _preSpriteRasterizerState = GraphicsDevice.RasterizerState;
    _preSpriteSamplerState = GraphicsDevice.SamplerStates[0];
}

protected void RestoreStateAfterSprites()
{
    GraphicsDevice.BlendState = _preSpriteBlendState;
    GraphicsDevice.DepthStencilState = _preSpriteDepthStencilState;
    GraphicsDevice.RasterizerState = _preSpriteRasterizerState;
    GraphicsDevice.SamplerStates[0] = _preSpriteSamplerState;
}
```

Listing 8-23 shows a Draw function that renders both 3-D objects and sprites together, using the StoreStateBeforeSprites and RestoreStateAfterSprites functions to ensure that the rendering state is not modified by the sprites.

Listing 8-23. Drawing 3-D objects and sprites together, storing and restoring the rendering state

```
protected override void Draw(GameTime gameTime)
{
    GraphicsDevice.Clear(Color.CornflowerBlue);

    // Draw all 3D objects
    DrawObjects(gameTime, _effect);

    // Draw all sprites and text…
    // First store the graphics device state
    StoreStateBeforeSprites();
    // Draw the sprites
    _spriteBatch.Begin(SpriteSortMode.BackToFront, BlendState.AlphaBlend);
    DrawSprites(gameTime, _spriteBatch);
    DrawText(gameTime, _spriteBatch);
    _spriteBatch.End();
    // Now restore the graphics device state
    RestoreStateAfterSprites();

    base.Draw(gameTime);
}
```

An example of using this technique can be found in the SpritesAndSolids_Win8 and SpritesAndSolids_WP8 examples, from which Listing 8-23 was copied and from which an image is shown in Figure 8-33. You will see that it displays solid 3-D objects, sprites, and text all on the screen at once. The two cubes intersect and can be clearly seen to still be observing and updating the depth buffer despite the SpriteBatch having disabled it. The semi-transparent balloons show through to the 3-D rendered content behind them.

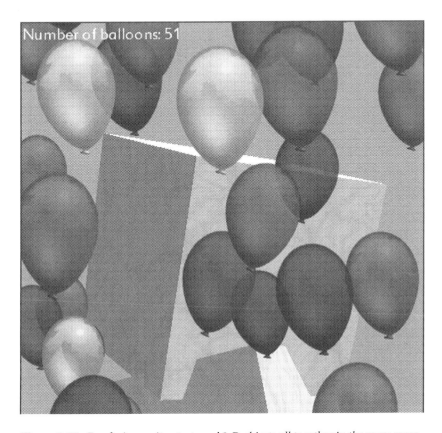

Figure 8-33. Rendering sprites, text, and 3-D objects all together in the same scene

Because the sprites disable the depth buffer, they have no impact at all on any subsequent 3-D objects that are rendered. It is, therefore, very easy to display sprites behind 3-D objects, too: Just render the sprites first and the 3-D objects second. If you want to create scenes that have some sprites behind the 3-D objects and others in front, draw the background sprites first, then the 3-D objects, and finally the foreground sprites. Listing 8-24 demonstrates a simple example code snippet showing how this can be achieved.

Listing 8-24. Drawing background and foreground sprites

```
// Draw background sprites
StoreStateBeforeSprites();
_spriteBatch.Begin(SpriteSortMode.BackToFront, BlendState.AlphaBlend);
DrawSprites(gameTime, _spriteBatch, Textures["BackgroundTexture"]);
_spriteBatch.End();
RestoreStateAfterSprites();
```

```
// Draw all 3D objects
DrawObjects(gameTime, _effect);

// Draw foreground sprites
StoreStateBeforeSprites();
_spriteBatch.Begin(SpriteSortMode.BackToFront, BlendState.AlphaBlend);
DrawSprites(gameTime, _spriteBatch, Textures["ForegroundTexture"]);
_spriteBatch.End();
RestoreStateAfterSprites();
```

A Universe of Possibilities

The gaming opportunities with 3-D graphics are immense, and I hope that you now feel prepared to conquer them. It is a complex environment to work with, and sometimes things won't work or look exactly the way you expect them to. Experimentation is key, however, so use the knowledge that you have gained to create test projects and try things out. With a little practice, you should find that things start to feel much more natural and manageable.

The next chapter takes a step back from 3-D rendering and looks at some useful functions that you can add to your games to enhance their features.

Summary

- 3-D objects can be imported into a MonoGame project as a Model object. The XNA Content compiler can build such models from .x or .fbx files. Model files hold several different types of information: the physical representation of the model's shape, vertex normals, and texture coordinate data.

- A number of 3-D modeling software packages are available to produce such files. One such package is Trimble's SketchUp, which can be extended with a simple plug-in script to produce .x files that are compatible with MonoGame.

- Loading a model will also automatically load any required textures. Models can use multiple textures if required, but to keep performance high by reducing unnecessary texture transfers into the graphics hardware, it is advisable to stick to a single texture per model if possible.

- Each Model object contains one or more ModelMesh objects, inside which are one or more ModelMeshPart objects. Each ModelMeshPart contains an IndexBuffer and a VertexBuffer that can be passed to the DrawIndexedPrimitives function when rendering.

- To simplify the task of managing and rendering models, a new abstract MatrixModelObject class is present in the GameFramework project.

- As well as moving 3-D objects around a scene, it is also possible to move the camera. The camera is controlled by giving it a position (where the camera is looking from), a "look at" location (where the camera is pointing), and an "up vector" to control which way up the camera is orientated. These can be combined into the required matrix format by using the Matrix.CreateLookAt function.

- The camera position is placed into the effect object's View property prior to rendering the objects within the scene.

- The GameFramework project provides simple camera support by defining a MatrixCameraObject class. An instance of this class (or a derived class) can be passed to the GameHost.Camera property in order for the game framework to automatically position the camera as defined by the class properties.

- The `MatrixCameraObject` also makes it simple to position and orient the camera using matrix transformations (translations, rotations, and so on).

- The `MatrixCameraObject.ChaseObject` property can also be set in order to turn the camera into a chase cam, which will follow along behind the target object as it moves through the scene. The `ChaseDistance` and `ChaseElevation` properties can be used to further control the camera positioning in this configuration.

- Fog can be used as a quick way to add atmosphere to scenes or to hide the effects of the far clip plane. By tweaking the fog parameters, fades and silhouettes can also be achieved.

- In order to present a realistic-looking background to a 3-D scene, a skybox can be created. This is a box rendered prior to the rest of the scene, which follows the camera movement so as to simulate being a great distance away from the camera.

- The `GameFramework` project provides the `MatrixSkyboxObject` to simplify creating and management of skyboxes. An instance of this class (or a derived class) can be placed into the `GameHost.Skybox` property to activate the skybox.

- Particles can be used to add flat, textured quads into a scene as a way to simulate a variety of effects including smoke, fire, lens-flare, gravel, sparks, and other similar details within a scene. Particles are always rotated to face directly toward the camera, giving the illusion of depth.

- The `GameFramework` project caters for particles with a new abstract class, `MatrixParticleObjectBase`. This allows particle objects to be rendered after the rest of the scene is finished, ensuring that they correctly observe the depth buffer for other objects while not interfering with the rendering of other particles.

- In addition to the `BasicEffect` that has been used for most of the examples provided, several other effects are made available by MonoGame: `AlphaTestEffect`, `DualTextureEffect`, `EnvironmentMapEffect`, and `SkinnedEffect`. Each of these has slightly different capabilities when used for rendering.

- `AlphaTestEffect` is used to allow "masking" of the rendered content based upon the alpha values in the rendered textures. Areas of the texture that pass the effect's alpha test will be rendered and will affect the depth buffer, while the remaining areas will effectively become invisible by not being rendered or updating the depth buffer.

- `DualTextureEffect` allows two texture to be blended together across the object when rendering. This can be used to provide complex-looking interference patterns or to mask out sections of the texture.

- `EnvironmentMapEffect` provides a mechanism for simulating a reflection of the scene upon each rendered object. This can lead to incredibly shiny-looking objects, or it can be toned down to provide much more subtle shading in order to increase the apparent realism of the rendered objects.

- `SkinnedEffect` can be used to control animation of subsections of a model.

- It is simple to include a mix of sprites and 3-D objects in the same scene by simply drawing one and then the other. Using sprites will reset a number of game state properties, so the `GameFramework`'s `StoreStateBeforeSprites`, and `RestoreStateAfterSprites` functions can be used to store and recall the relevant state values before and after sprite rendering is performed.

CHAPTER 9

Enhancing Your Game

There are many different styles and varieties of games, and they can be diverse in the ways that they play and function. Some game features are useful in many different games, though, and, in this chapter, we'll examine some useful pieces of functionality that fall into this category. These game enhancements will be created to be easily reusable so that they can be quickly and easily dropped into any game that would benefit from them.

The enhancements that we will create are as follows:

- A framework for supporting multiple "modes" of operation. Examples of modes might include actually playing the game, viewing a menu, setting game options, viewing the credits, and so on.

- A settings class, allowing us to easily set and retrieve configuration values and to save them to files so that they can be retrieved the next time the game is executed.

- A high-score table, providing a very easy mechanism for adding and displaying scores that the player has achieved.

These features will be created within the game framework and can be easily accessed by calling into the methods of the appropriate class.

Along the way, we will also examine some other mechanisms that will be very useful within your games, such as handling the Back button, reading and writing data from and to isolated storage, and working with multiple sets of game objects.

Let's take a look at what each of these enhancements does in more detail, how each one is used, and how each one works internally. The internal workings are only discussed fairly briefly here as they are intended as end user components, but they are described in case you want to make any changes to how they work or to lift any of the code out for use in other projects. The full source code is, of course, available in the GameFramework project for this chapter in the accompanying download.

Managing Multiple Game Modes

All of the examples that we have covered so far have stuck rigidly to performing one single task. That's great for demonstrations of the techniques that we have been working through, but not so good in real-world game examples. Pretty much any game will need to support multiple "modes" of operation—to cover things like the game menu, playing the game, showing a high-score table, and so on.

Each of these game modes needs to do just the things that we have already set our simple projects to do: they need to maintain a collection of game objects, to allow those objects to be updated, and to allow those objects to be drawn. These are three fairly simple requirements.

With a little help in the GameFramework project, we can simplify the task of managing multiple modes so that each one can exist pretty much independently of the others, just concentrating on their own requirements. This has some great advantages, allowing each mode to be self-contained and encapsulated without a sprawl of unrelated functions and variables. With some simple code, we can switch between the different game modes, keeping the state of each mode persisted in memory so that we can return to it exactly where we left it later on, should we wish to.

■ **Tip** One important thing to bear in mind with regard to multiple modes is that it can be quite a nuisance to add them after you have already built the main bulk of your game project. If you make plans for supporting multiple modes from the beginning, even if you only have one mode implemented to start with, you may save yourself a lot of tedious refactoring later on.

A simple example of managing multiple game modes can be found in the MultipleModes_Win8 and MultipleModes_WP8 example projects in the downloads that accompany this chapter. When they are first launched, they display a "menu" screen, allowing various other parts of the game to be accessed. From here, you can click or tap the "Start new game" item to launch the "game play" part of the game (which is just a simple graphical effect of tumbling playing card graphics, used for illustration purposes).

Touching or clicking while the "game play" mode is active will return back to the menu. From here, the "new game" link may be used again to start another game (resetting the graphics so that they start from stationary positions once again), or the "resume game" link may be used to return to the game that was previously interrupted.

Other options on the main menu allow separate screens for high scores, settings, and game credits to be displayed. These modes are all placeholders at the moment, but they already demonstrate how we can easily switch between as many modes as we need to and how each mode class can support its own independent collections of game objects.

Let's take a look at how the multiple modes are being supported in the GameFramework project and how they are being used in the example code.

Multiple Mode Support in the Game Framework

To allow the game to create each game mode that it wants to support, the GameFramework project defines a new abstract base class, GameModeBase. Each mode that the game needs to support will be implemented as a class derived from this base class.

The base class provides a number of different methods, as follows:

- Reset can be used to set the initial state of the class. This must be called by the game itself, it is not called directly by the GameFramework.

- Activate is called automatically by the GameFramework each time this particular game mode class becomes the current mode, and it can be used to set any state information required for the mode to function.

- Deactivate is called as the game mode ends its run as the current mode, allowing the class to tidy up any resources that it has been using.

- Update is called by the framework each time a game update takes place while the mode class is the current mode. It should perform just the same tasks as would be performed by the Update function in the main game class.

- Draw is called by the framework each time the game needs to draw itself while the mode class is the current mode. It should perform just the same tasks as would be performed by the Draw function in the main game class.

As you can see, the core functionality expected of the game mode is very similar to that of the main game class, with the added abilities for the mode to be informed when it becomes current (is activated) or passes control over to another mode (is deactivated).

GameModeBase fits into the framework as shown in Figure 9-1. The GameHost class maintains a private dictionary of all known mode classes such that it can switch between any of them whenever it needs to.

Figure 9-1. *GameModeBase's position in the game framework object hierarchy*

The dictionary of game modes is private because GameHost needs to maintain control over how its items are populated. In order for your game to interact control the way in which the modes are used, a number of new functions are provided. Let's take a look at how each of them is used to control a game with multiple modes.

Defining Game Mode Classes

Each game mode class is created and set to inherit from GameFramework.GameModeBase. The game mode class code can perform whatever tasks it needs in its constructor, but be aware that the content (textures, models, and so on) may not have been loaded at the time the constructor executes.

The Reset, Activate, and Deactivate methods can be overridden to provide a way of responding to the events described for these methods in the previous section.

When it comes to manipulating game objects, the game mode classes each have their own local GameObjects collection. This is structured identically to the GameHost.GameObjects collection that we have been using in all of the previous example projects, and, in fact, when each game mode is activated, its local GameObjects collection is actually set as the GameHost.GameObjects collection, so the rest of the game runs against the game mode's objects as if they are the entire game's objects.

Game mode classes should usually manipulate their own GameObjects collection, however, and not the GameHost's collection. This ensures that the code will continue to work as expected even if it executes while another game mode class is active.

In the MultipleModes example projects, five separate game mode classes have been created—for the main menu, the game itself, the high scores, settings, and credits. Each of these has been named with a prefix of Mode_ in order to keep them grouped together inside Solution Explorer and to make them easier to identify. This is a convention that you may wish to observe or customize, but it is not a requirement of the framework.

Don't forget that the game mode classes are not derived from the GameHost class itself, so any access to properties or methods within that class will need to be performed using an instance of the game that is passed to the game mode constructor. The GameModeBase class automatically stores this reference in a protected property named Game, but it may make things easier to store this as a properly typed class-level variable within the derived class, too. An example of this technique can be seen in the MultipleModes project's Mode_Menu class. The class defines a class-level field named _game of type MultipleModesGame, and it sets this during the constructor.

Registering the Game Modes

Before any of the game mode classes can be used, the game needs to tell the game framework that the classes exist by passing it an instance of each class. These instances are passed to the framework by calling the GameHost.AddGameModeHandler function for each of the game mode classes. Listing 9-1 shows the code that performs this task within the MultipleModes, which can be found in the MultipleModesGame.Initialize function.

Listing 9-1. Adding an instance of each known game mode handler to the GameFramework

```
// Add the game mode handlers
AddGameModeHandler(new Mode_Menu(this));
AddGameModeHandler(new Mode_Game(this));
AddGameModeHandler(new Mode_Settings(this));
AddGameModeHandler(new Mode_HighScores(this));
AddGameModeHandler(new Mode_Credits(this));
```

The GameHost class will store each of the handler objects that have been passed to it for later use, and it will use the appropriate object instance each time the game mode changes. These instances are reused throughout the lifetime of the game.

Activating and Interrogating the Game Mode Handlers

Once all of the game mode handlers have been set into the GameHost, the game is ready to activate one of them. This is achieved by calling the GameHost.SetGameMode function and specifying the type of the game mode class that is to be activated. The class type is specified using C#'s generics feature, and it is specified in angled brackets along with the function call. This is a handy way to identify the class that doesn't rely upon passing the class name as a string, and it also ensures that the specified class is of the appropriate type.

Listing 9-2 shows how the MultipleGameModes example project uses this function to activate the game's "menu" mode at the end of its LoadContent function.

Listing 9-2. Activating a game mode handler

```
// Activate the initial handler
SetGameMode<Mode_Menu>();
```

When the current game mode is changed with the SetGameMode function, the game framework will automatically call the Deactivate method of whichever mode class was previously being used, and it will then call the Activate method of the newly activated game mode class.

It is easy to obtain the current game mode handler instance by querying the GameHost.CurrentGameModeHandler function. This will return an object of type GameModeBase, which will be the handler object that is currently active. If you need to be able to check the type of the returned handler object, the is operator can be used to check this, as shown in Listing 9-3.

Listing 9-3. Checking the type of the current game mode handler

```
if (CurrentGameModeHandler is Mode_Game)
{
    // Perform whatever tasks are necessary
}
```

Sometimes it is useful to be able to access other game modes than the one that is currently active. For example, a "game over" mode may wish to read out the score that was achieved by the player, which might be stored in a "game playing" mode.

Other game mode classes may be easily obtained by calling the GameHost.GetGameModeHandler method, once again passing the type of the handler using generics. Listing 9-4 shows a section of code from the Mode_Menu class in the example project, which interrogates the "game" mode to identify whether or not a game is currently active.

Listing 9-4. Obtaining an instance of a different game mode handler

```
// Is the game already active?
if (Game.GetGameModeHandler<Mode_Game>().GameIsActive)
{
    // Yes, so switch back to the existing game
    Game.SetGameMode<Mode_Game>();
}
```

Using the Game Mode Classes

So the classes are defined, the GameHost class knows about this, and the appropriate class has been activated. What needs to be done to get the game framework to actually use the classes and call their Update and Draw methods?

The simple answer is that virtually nothing needs to be done; GameHost will take care of this itself. In your main game class's own Update and Draw methods, make sure you leave just the default calls to the base class methods in place. When these base class calls are made, the game framework will identify the fact that a game mode class has been activated, and it will automatically call its methods. In fact, you could remove these two methods from your game class entirely if you wish.

You can see this in place by looking at these two methods in the MultipleModesGame class code. They are both empty other than their call to the base class.

▨ **Caution** Don't forget to remove the call to GraphicsDevice.Clear from your game class's Draw method. You should allow your game mode classes to clear the graphics device themselves so that they have control over the clear color. Including the call in the game class as well will result in the screen being cleared twice, which is an unnecessary extra operation that could reduce the performance of your game.

By organizing your project around multiple game modes from the outset, you will be able to easily extend your game project later on to support all the other functions that you need to implement.

Managing Game Settings

Most games and applications will want to have control over some of the settings of the program. In a game, these settings will include things such as user options (difficulty level, different game types), settings for the game environment (sound effect and music volume levels, graphic options), or settings that are controlled by the application itself (such as remembering the date the game was last played or the name that the player last entered into a high-score table).

There is nothing particularly difficult about managing this information, but, as with everything else we have done with the game framework, our objective is to make this as simple to manage as possible. To look after all of this for us, we will add a new class, SettingsManager, to the GameFramework project. This class will allow us to easily set and query game settings and to save them to the device and retrieve them later on.

There are a number of parts to this class and also some things to consider when it comes to actually using it, so let's take a look at how it all fits together.

All the code for this section is present in the Settings_Win8 and Settings_WP8 example projects that accompany this chapter. These simple example projects contain two game modes (building on the game mode implementation from earlier in this chapter)—one for a "game" mode that shows a number of bounding balls and another for a "settings" mode. Most of these settings are provided just for the sake of example, but the Speed setting does actually work and controls the animation speed of the balls.

Clicking or tapping the screen while the game is playing will display a (not particularly attractive—hopefully you can do better!) settings screen. Each of the displayed settings can be clicked or tapped to cycle through the available options, and then the Continue text can be used to store the updated settings and return back to the game. On a Windows Phone device, the Back button can be used for this purpose, too (though in order to meet with Microsoft's certification guidelines, it is important that the Back button returns the users to the prior screen rather than taking them anywhere else within your game).

Note that if you close and restart the game after changing the settings, all of the modified values will have been retained.

▦ **Note**　When running in Windows Phone, you need to exit the game "properly" for the settings to be saved—either by pressing the Back button or the Start button to navigate away from the running project. If instead you use the Stop Debugging button in Visual Studio to terminate the game, the settings will not be saved. This is not the case for Windows 8 projects, where the settings are saved regardless of how the project is terminated.

Class Structure

The SettingsManager class is declared as a public static class. It is therefore accessible from anywhere in your game at any time simply by accessing it as GameFramework.SettingsManager.

Setting and Retrieving Values

The main purpose of the SettingsManager class is to store values that we give to it and to allow those values to later be retrieved. These two actions can be accomplished by calling the SetValue and GetValue methods.

A number of different overloads of these two functions are provided for different data types, with versions available for string, int, float, bool, and DateTime types. Internally they are all stored as strings, but the overloads ensure that the values are encoded and decoded properly so this internal storage mechanism is transparent to the calling code.

▦ **Note**　When passing a setting name to SetValue or GetValue, the name is treated as being case-insensitive.

Whenever a value is retrieved using one of the GetValue methods, a defaultValue parameter is provided. This parameter serves two purposes. First, it allows for a sensible value to be returned if the requested setting is unknown and doesn't exist within the object. This simplifies the use of the class, as shown in Listing 9-5. If we try to retrieve the sound-effects volume level and it hasn't already been set, we default it to 100 so that its initial setting is at full volume, even though no setting value actually exists within the object.

Listing 9-5. Retrieving a setting value from the SettingsManager Object

```
int volumeLevel;

// Retrieve the volume level from the game settings
volumeLevel = SettingsManager.GetValue("SoundEffectsVolume", 100);
```

The second role that the defaultValue parameter performs is identifying the expected return type of the GetValue function. If the defaultValue is passed as an int, the return value will be an int, too. This provides a convenient variable data-typing mechanism, avoiding the need to cast and convert values to the appropriate types.

In addition to setting and getting values, the class also allows existing settings to be deleted. The DeleteValue function will remove a stored setting, causing any subsequent calls to GetValue to return the provided default once again. To remove *all* the stored settings, the ClearValues function can be called. All the settings that have been previously written will be erased.

Inside the SettingsManager class, the values that are passed in to be set are routed into a single version of the SetValue function, which expects its value to be of type string. Within this function, the exact processing performed depends on the platform being used.

For Windows 8 games, the value is written away into an ApplicationDataContainer object, provided by the .NET Framework's Windows.Storage namespace. This object will hold on to the value even after the application is closed.

For Windows Phone games, the setting value is written into a special collection provided by the phone called ApplicationSettings, contained within the System.IO.IsolatedStorage namespace. ApplicationSettings is a dictionary collection, and every item added to the dictionary is written away into *isolated storage*, a special data storage system used within the phone. We will look at the implications of isolated storage in more detail in the "Reading and Writing Files in Isolated Storage" section later in this chapter.

▓ **Note** When running Windows Phone applications on the emulator, the isolated storage is reset every time the emulator is closed. This can sometimes be frustrating because stored data does not persist from one emulator session to the next, but it can also be useful as it presents an opportunity to test your game in a fresh environment that has no previously written files or settings.

We can now set, update, and interrogate the settings for our game, but then we come to the next question: How do we allow the player to view and change the settings?

Creating the Settings User Interface

MonoGame has no built-in graphical user interface components, so we can either implement our own or use the XAML capabilities of Windows 8 or Windows Phone 8. We will look at how to add XAML functionality to your game projects starting in Chapter 11, but, for the moment, we will instead look at how a simple MonoGame-based settings user interface can be constructed.

For the settings screen, we can keep things fairly simple and implement our own primitive user interface using TextObject instance. Each object instance will be configured with a position, a value, and a set of available values. Each time the object is tapped on the screen, it will cycle to the next available value, looping past the final value back to the beginning.

Clearly this is not particularly sophisticated and it could be enhanced to support all sorts of other features, but this is left as an exercise for the reader. These simple classes will suffice for this example and also for many games.

So that the game framework can identify settings objects (which will be useful, as we will see in a moment), they are implemented as a new class in the game framework. SettingsItemObject inherits from TextObject, as shown in Figure 9-2.

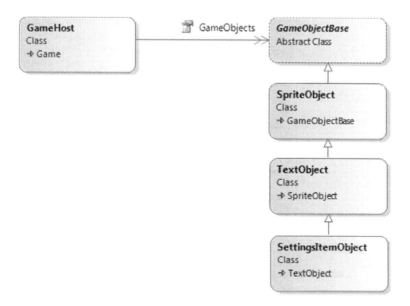

***Figure 9-2.** SettingsItemObject's position in the game framework object hierarchy*

SettingsItemObject adds the following four public properties to those provided by the base TextObject:

- Name is the name of the setting as it will be stored in SettingsManager.
- Title is the display name for the setting.
- Values is an array of strings that form the permitted list of values for the setting.
- SelectedValue is the currently selected value.

Values for each of these properties are also required to be passed as parameters to the class constructor.

The class also exposes a new public method: SelectNextValue. Each time it is called, the object cycles to the next value within the Values array, looping back to the start once the final item is passed.

To use the settings screen, we need to add three new pieces of functionality to the game mode class: one to initialize the SettingsItemObject instances (and any other game objects) required for the setting screen, another to allow the user to click or tap the settings items to update them, and a final piece to save the settings and return to the game. Let's look at how they are implemented.

Opening the Settings Screen

For our example we will simply tap the screen to open the settings screen. This won't be good enough for a real game, but it will suffice for this example. In a real game, you might instead choose to implement a menu system similar to the one from the MultipleModes example earlier in this chapter.

When the game detects a tap on the screen (in the Mode_Game.Update function), it activates the Mode_Settings game mode. This mode class has been set to include a number of SettingsItemObject instances in its GameObjects collection, all of which are added in its Reset method. Some of the code that performs this initialization is shown in Listing 9-6 (though the code shown here omits some of the content for brevity—the full function can be seen in the example project's code).

Listing 9-6. Entering Settings mode

```
public override void Reset()
{
    SpriteObject spriteObject;

    base.Activate();

    // Add some settings items...

    // Game speed
    spriteObject = new SettingsItemObject(_game, _game.Fonts["WascoSans"],
            new Vector2(60, 100), 0.9f,
            "Speed", "Speed", "1",
            new string[] { "1", "2", "3" });
    spriteObject.SpriteColor = Color.Yellow;
    GameObjects.Add(spriteObject);

    // Difficulty
    spriteObject = new SettingsItemObject(_game, _game.Fonts["WascoSans"],
            new Vector2(60, 170), 0.9f,
            "Difficulty", "Difficulty", "Medium",
            new string[] { "Easy", "Medium", "Hard" });
    spriteObject.SpriteColor = Color.Yellow;
    GameObjects.Add(spriteObject);

    // Music volume
    spriteObject = new SettingsItemObject(_game, _game.Fonts["WascoSans"],
            new Vector2(60, 240), 0.9f,
            "MusicVolume", "Music volume", "Medium",
            new string[] { "Off", "Quiet", "Medium", "Loud" });
    spriteObject.SpriteColor = Color.Yellow;
    GameObjects.Add(spriteObject);

    // Add the "continue" text
    spriteObject = new TextObject(_game, _game.Fonts["WascoSans"],
            new Vector2(20, 400), "Continue...");
    spriteObject.Tag = "Continue";
    GameObjects.Add(spriteObject);
}
```

As this code shows, there are several new SettingsItemObject instances created, and a number of parameters are passed into the class constructor each time. These parameters are as follows:

- game is the game's GameHost instance.
- font is the font to use to display the text.
- position is the display position for the settings item.
- scale is a scaling value to apply to the text.
- name is the name of the setting within the SettingsManager.

- • `title` is the name for the item to display onscreen. (Note the difference between this and the item's `name` for the music volume setting.)

- • `defaultValue` is used if no existing setting value can be found in the `SettingsManager` object; this value will be used as an initial value for the setting.

- • `values` is an array of string values that will be cycled through when the user taps the settings item.

The result of this function is that a new set of objects is created to display the settings screen. All the actual settings items are created as `SettingsItemObject` instances. With the game mode activated and the standard update and draw code in place, the screen appears as shown in Figure 9-3.

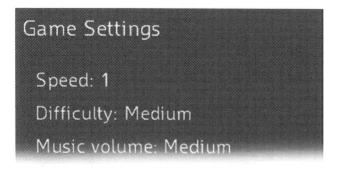

Figure 9-3. *The settings screen*

One other detail about the code in Listing 9-6 is worthy of a quick mention. Note that when the `Continue` text object is being added, a new object property named `Tag` is being set. `Tag` is added to the `GameFramework.GameObjectBase` class in the update for this chapter, and it simply allows a string value to be associated with each object. If you take a look in the `Mode_Settings.Update` function, you'll see that the code determines whether this piece of text has been clicked by checking the `Tag` of the clicked game object. This is a convenient method for finding the identity of an item.

Items can also be retrieved based upon their tag by calling the `GameHost.GetObjectByTag` function. This will scan the object collection and return the first object it finds whose tag matches the supplied search string. Note, however, that it is a lot less efficient to find objects in this way than by simply storing a reference to the required object, so you should avoid making frequent calls to this function in your main game code if at all possible.

Updating the Settings Values

The user can change the value of any of the settings by simply clicking or tapping on its text onscreen. This is easily implemented by asking the `GameHost` to identify the selected object for each screen tap. If an object is found and is a `SettingsItemObject`, we can simply call its `SelectNextValue` method to move to the next available value.

The code to achieve this is performed in the `Mode_Settings.Update` function, shown in Listing 9-7.

Listing 9-7. Part of the Update function, allowing object values to be updated

```
GameObjectBase obj;
TouchCollection tc;

// Has the user touched the screen?
tc = TouchPanel.GetState();
if (tc.Count == 1 && tc[0].State == TouchLocationState.Pressed)
{
    // Find the object at the touch point
    obj = GetSpriteAtPoint(tc[0].Position);
    // Did we get a settings option object?
    if (obj is GameFramework.SettingsItemObject)
    {
    // Yes, so toggle it to the next value
    (obj as SettingsItemObject).SelectNextValue();
    }
}
```

Nothing more is required to allow the objects to update themselves.

Leaving the Settings Screen

Once the settings screen is up and running, the player can change the settings as required and can then click or tap the Continue link (or, on Windows Phone, press the hardware Back button, providing you return the user directly back to the prior screen) to leave the settings screen and return to the game. This is handled by simply calling GameHost.SetGameMode and asking it to switch back to using the Mode_Game class.

One of the effects of this call is that the game framework will call the Mode_Settings.Deactivate method. This is the trigger that we will use to apply the updated settings to the game and to ensure that they are stored away for use in future invocations of the game.

To store the values, all that is required is to call the SettingsManager.StoreSettingsItemValues function. This function will scan through all of the current game objects to identify any that are of type SettingsItemObject, and it will then automatically write their value away into the stored settings.

The other thing that we need to do is to make sure that the current game observes the updated settings values. For this example, the code simply queries the Mode_Game's GameObjects collection and directly inserts the updated speed value into each BallObject that it finds. Listing 9-8 shows the full code of the Deactivate function.

Listing 9-8. Deactivating the Settings screen and returning to the game

```
/// <summary>
/// This mode is deactivating, store and apply any settings that the user has selected
/// </summary>
public override void Deactivate()
{
    int newSpeed;

    base.Deactivate();

    // Store all of the values that the user has configured
    SettingsManager.StoreSettingsItemValues();
```

```
    // Update the speed of each ball to match the modified settings
    newSpeed = SettingsManager.GetValue("Speed", 1);
    // Loop through the "Game" mode's game objects
    foreach (GameObjectBase obj in _game.GetGameModeHandler<Mode_Game>().GameObjects)
    {
        if (obj is BallObject)
        {
        (obj as BallObject).Speed = newSpeed;
        }
    }
}
```

▧ **Note**   Because this is just an example, the Speed setting is the only one that is actually observed by the project. In a real game, all the values would be considered and put into action as the settings page is deactivated.

If you give the example project a try, you will see that the balls all observe whatever speed is selected in the settings screen. The settings are saved to storage when the game closes and restored when it starts again.

Adding a High-Score Table

Another common requirement across many games is the ability to keep track of the highest scores that players have achieved. .NET provides some useful features to implement high scores (such as sortable collections into which we can place all our scores), but actually implementing the feature into a game requires a little effort, most of which is fairly unexciting—not what we want to be spending time addressing when we could be being creative instead.

To reduce the amount of work required, we can build support for high scores into the game framework. We won't make things too complicated, but our implementation will have the facility for keeping track of multiple tables at once if the game requires such a feature (for different difficulty levels, for example) and a very simple API so that the game doesn't require very much code to interact with the high scores.

The final feature that we will add is the ability to save the score tables to storage each time they are updated and load them back in each time the game is launched. Scores can therefore be stored indefinitely, providing a constant challenge to the player to better his or her earlier efforts.

All the code for maintaining and manipulating the high-score table can be found in the GameFramework project for this chapter. The functionality is demonstrated in the example projects named HighScores_Win8 and HighScores_WP8. These projects show some simple user interaction with the high-score table. A screenshot showing a populated score table from the example is shown in Figure 9-4.

Figure 9-4. *An example high-score table display*

Implementing the High-Score Table

The high scores are implemented using three new classes in the game framework: HighScores, HighScoreTable, and HighScoreEntry.

The first of these classes, HighScores, provides the top-level API for working with high scores. Its functions include loading and saving scores to and from storage, creating and obtaining individual high-score tables, and a simple mechanism for displaying the scores from a table on the screen.

The HighScoreTable class represents a single table of scores (of which we may maintain several, as already mentioned). Its responsibilities are around maintaining the individual tables, allowing scores to be added and interrogated.

The final class, HighScoreEntry, represents a single score item within a high-score table. It keeps track of the score and the player's name as well as the date the score was achieved (the reason for which we will discuss shortly).

All three of these classes are declared with internal class constructors, preventing code outside the game framework from instantiating them. Instead, a single instance of HighScores can be accessed from the GameHost.HighScores property, and functions within this class and the HighScoreTable class allow instances of the other two objects to be created and manipulated. The relationships of the classes within the rest of the game framework can be seen in Figure 9-5.

Figure 9-5. *The high-score classes within the game framework*

Defining Tables

Before the high-score classes can be used for storing game scores, the tables within the high-score environment must first be defined. This has to be done before any scores are added and also before scores are loaded from storage.

The tables are added by calling the HighScores.InitializeTable function. There are two overloads for this function—the first overload expects a table name to be supplied along with the number of score entries that it is to hold; the second overload also expects a description of the table.

If you decide to implement multiple high-score tables for your game, each one must be given a different name. You may want to base these on your game's difficulty levels (for example, Easy, Normal, and Difficult) or on some other factor that is significant to the game. These values will be used as a key into a dictionary of HighScoreTable objects, so they will need to be provided again later when you want to update or read one of the tables.

If you provide a description, it will be stored alongside the table for later retrieval.

Each table can store an arbitrary number of score entries, depending on the needs of your game. Many games will only store ten entries per table, but there is nothing stopping you from storing hundreds if you want.

References to the individual tables can be obtained by calling the HighScores.GetTable function, passing in the name of the table to be returned. This returns a HighScoreTable object, with which the scores inside the named table can be manipulated.

Working with High-Score Tables

Having created a table and retrieved a reference to its object, the next set of functions is within the HighScoreTable class.

New scores can be added by calling the AddEntry function, passing in the name and the score. Providing the score is high enough to make it into the table, a new HighScoreEntry object will be added into the class's private _scoreEntries list, and the entry object returned back to the calling procedure. If the score is not good enough to qualify, the entry list is left alone and the function returns null. The table will always be sorted by score, so there is no need for your game code to sort the entries.

All high scores are date stamped, so if there is a collision between the new score and an existing score, the existing score will be given precedence and will appear higher in the list than the later entry.

Accompanying this function is another useful function, ScoreQualifies, which returns a boolean value that indicates whether the supplied score is good enough to make it on to the table. The return value from this function can be used to determine whether users should be prompted to enter their name or not.

A collection of all the scores can be retrieved by querying the Entries property. The description of the table (if one was set when it was initialized) can be retrieved from the Description property.

High-Score Entries

Each entry into the high-score table is represented as an instance of the HighScoreEntry class. This class stores the name, score, and date for each entry, allowing the contents of the table to be read and displayed.

In addition to storing these properties, the class also implements the .NET IComparer interface. This interface is used to provide a simple mechanism for the HighScoreTable class to sort the entries in its table. The Compare method first sorts the items by score and then by date, ensuring that higher scores appear first, and for matching scores, older entries appear first.

Clearing Existing High Scores

If you decide that you want to clear the high scores (preferably at the user's request), you can call the Clear method of either the HighScores object (which will clear all entries from all tables) or an individual HighScoreTable object (which will clear that table alone).

Working with Asynchronous Functions

The final part of the HighScores data API is the ability to load and save the scores to and from the device so that they persist from one game session to the next.

As we reach this section, it is necessary to introduce a feature of the .NET 4.5 Framework that we have largely ignored so far: the async and await keywords. This may sound like a bit of a diversion, but bear with us as it's important to the high-score code.

The two new keywords are used when calling some functions within the .NET Framework to simplify the task of working with asynchronous operations—those that return from the called procedure immediately and then, at some later stage, invoke a "callback" function with the results of the requested task.

These asynchronous methods are written to execute in this way because they may be time-consuming to complete (for example, retrieving a web page from the Internet, which could be nearly instantaneous or could take many seconds). Running them asynchronously puts them into a separate background execution thread, allowing the main thread to keep working. Operating in this way allows the application to keep working on the main app thread, preventing the app from pausing or stuttering as the requested task performs its work.

The await keyword can be provided prior to a call to one of the asynchronous functions to effectively hide away the fact that any kind of asynchronous processing is taking place. The called function does still execute in a background thread, but, as far as your code is concerned, this fact can be ignored. The compiler automatically wires up your code so that when the background thread completes its task, your function seamlessly resumes from where it was left off. You can therefore code as if the calls were actually synchronous, taking away all the pain of executing tasks in this way.

In order to avoid breaking old code that may have used the keyword await for other purposes, .NET will only observe the keyword in procedures that are marked with the async keyword in their procedure declarations. You will see examples of using with await and async in a moment.

There is one final implication of the asynchronous functions: in order to make it obvious which functions are asynchronous and which are not, by convention all asynchronous functions have a suffix of Async on their name.

▧ **Note**   Asynchronous functions are a much bigger topic than we have the space to cover here. If you wish, you can just take them at face value as described above. Alternatively, if you would like to know more about them, the MSDN article at `http://tinyurl.com/asyncawait` provides substantially more information about what is actually going on when these keywords are used.

The reason that all of this is relevant here is that in Windows 8, the file storage functions are asynchronous. This has several implications: the functions in the game framework that interact with stored files must also be asynchronous; these function names are suffixed with Async as per the .NET convention; and your functions that call the high-score load and save functions must therefore also be asynchronous functions.

This only applies to Windows 8, however. For Windows Phone, the storage functions are *not* asynchronous. As a result, we end up with slightly different method names across the two platforms: LoadScoresAsync and SaveScoresAsync for Windows 8, which are both called with the await keyword, as opposed to LoadScores and SaveScores for Windows Phone for which the await keyword is not used. This is one of the few instances we have encountered so far where the code will differ in your own game code between the two platforms—don't forget that you can use conditional compilation to work around this if you are trying to maintain the same code base across the two platforms.

Loading and Saving Scores

Now that we understand some of the details of file interaction, let's take a look at how the load and save functions actually work. These functions for loading and saving are accessed using the appropriate methods of the HighScores class.

Prior to calling either of these functions, however, your game can choose to set the file name within which the scores will be loaded and saved via the FileName property. If no file name is specified, the class defaults to using a name of Scores.dat. Being able to store high scores in different files allows for different sets of scores to be written should this be of benefit.

The high-score data is written as an XML document, the structure of which is demonstrated in Listing 9-9. A new <table> element is created for each defined table, and inside is an <entries> element containing an <entry> for each score within the table.

Listing 9-9.   The content of a stored high-scores file

```
<?xml version="1.0" encoding="utf-16"?>
<highscores>
    <table>
        <name>Normal</name>
        <entries>
            <entry>
                <score>9781</score>
                <name>Rick</name>
                <date>2013-03-21T21:27:46</date>
            </entry>
            <entry>
                <score>4302</score>
                <name>Glenn</name>
                <date>2013-03-21T20:46:03</date>
            </entry>
```

```
        <entry>
            <score>583</score>
            <name>Hershel</name>
            <date>2013-03-21T08:33:04</date>
        </entry>
        <entry>
            <score>60</score>
            <name>Maggie</name>
            <date>2013-03-21T23:14:51</date>
        </entry>
    </entries>
  </table>
  <table>
      <name>Difficult</name>
      <entries />
  </table>
</highscores>
```

The code within SaveScores required to generate this XML is fairly straightforward, looping through the tables and the score entries, and adding the details of each into the XML output. The output is constructed with an XmlWriter object by the code shown in Listing 9-10.

Listing 9-10. Building the XML for the high-score file

```
StringBuilder sb = new StringBuilder();
XmlWriter xmlWriter = XmlWriter.Create(sb);
HighScoreTable table;

// Begin the document
xmlWriter.WriteStartDocument();
// Write the HighScores root element
xmlWriter.WriteStartElement("highscores");

// Loop for each table
foreach (string tableName in _highscoreTables.Keys)
{
    // Retrieve the table object for this table name
    table = _highscoreTables[tableName];

    // Write the Table element
    xmlWriter.WriteStartElement("table");
    // Write the table Name element
    xmlWriter.WriteStartElement("name");
    xmlWriter.WriteString(tableName);
    xmlWriter.WriteEndElement();     // name

    // Create the Entries element
    xmlWriter.WriteStartElement("entries");
```

```
    // Loop for each entry
    foreach (HighScoreEntry entry in table.Entries)
    {
        // Make sure the entry is not blank
        if (entry.Date != DateTime.MinValue)
        {
            // Write the Entry element
            xmlWriter.WriteStartElement("entry");
            // Write the score, name and date
            xmlWriter.WriteStartElement("score");
            xmlWriter.WriteString(entry.Score.ToString());
            xmlWriter.WriteEndElement();     // score
            xmlWriter.WriteStartElement("name");
            xmlWriter.WriteString(entry.Name);
            xmlWriter.WriteEndElement();     // name
            xmlWriter.WriteStartElement("date");
            xmlWriter.WriteString(entry.Date.ToString("yyyy-MM-ddTHH:mm:ss"));
            xmlWriter.WriteEndElement();     // date
            // End the Entry element
            xmlWriter.WriteEndElement();     // entry
        }
    }

    // End the Entries element
    xmlWriter.WriteEndElement();     // entries

    // End the Table element
    xmlWriter.WriteEndElement();     // table
}

// End the root element
xmlWriter.WriteEndElement();     // highscores
xmlWriter.WriteEndDocument();

// Close the xml writer, which will put the finished document into the stringbuilder
xmlWriter.Close();
```

▨ **Tip** The comments present on each call to `WriteEndElement` help to clarify exactly which element is ending. Reading the code later on becomes much easier.

We will look at where the data is actually written to in a moment, but first let's take a quick look at the code that processes the XML after reading it back in. It uses the LINQ to XML functions to quickly and easily parse the content. LINQ to XML (LINQ being short for *Language INtegrated Query* and pronounced as *link*) allows the XML elements to be interrogated using a syntax similar in many ways to a database SQL statement, and it provides a simple mechanism for us to loop through each setting element and read out the name and value contained within.

The LINQ to XML code for loading the scores is shown in Listing 9-11. This code loops through all the entry elements so that we obtain an item in the result collection for each entry in the file. Besides reading out the details of the entry itself (from the name, score, and date elements), it also reads the entry's table name. This is achieved by looking at the parent node of the entry (the entries node), then looking at its parent (the table node), and then finally retrieving the value of that node's name element. Once these four values have been identified, the foreach loop that follows can easily add each score into the appropriate high-score table.

Listing 9-11. Loading saved high-score data from the stored XML document

```
// Parse the content XML that was loaded
XDocument xDoc = XDocument.Parse(fileContent);
// Create a query to read the score details from the xml
var result = from c in xDoc.Root.Descendants("entry")
                  select new
                  {
                      TableName = c.Parent.Parent.Element("name").Value,
                      Name = c.Element("name").Value,
                      Score = c.Element("score").Value,
                      Date = c.Element("date").Value
                  };
// Loop through the resulting elements
foreach (var el in result)
{
    // Add the entry to the table.
    table = GetTable(el.TableName);
    if (table != null)
    {
        table.AddEntry(el.Name, int.Parse(el.Score), DateTime.Parse(el.Date));
    }
}
```

Reading and Writing Files to Storage

Everything is now present to save the high-score file, parse the file, and retrieve its contents, but there is still the issue of actually reading from and writing to files. Let's address that now.

Applications running under Windows Phone have a *closed storage system*. Apps have access to multiple files and directories just like on a desktop PC, but they can access only files that were created within their own application—there is no access to files from other applications or from the operating system whatsoever.

On Windows 8, things are slightly different in that it is possible to gain access to the main desktop filing system, but each application also has its own local private storage that is not accessible from outside the app itself.

In most cases, this storage mechanism won't present any problems for your games, but one significant implication is that the System.IO.File namespace that you might be familiar with using from programming .NET on the desktop cannot be used from apps on either platform.

For Windows 8 apps, files are accessed using the ApplicationData class. This has a static property named Current from which various storage folders can be obtained. We will use one named LocalFolder to store our content—this is a file storage area local to the current PC into which we can read and write anything we need.

When loading the high scores, we first need to check whether the required high-score data file actually exists. Sadly, there is no Exists-type method with which to accomplish this, so we have two options: just try to open the file blindly and see if an exception is thrown, or scan the files within the folder looking for one with a matching name. Personally, I dislike the exception approach, so I have included an *extension* method for the folder class named FileExistsAsync, which performs this file scan and returns an appropriate value. The code for this can be found in the GameFramework.Win8FileExtensions class should you wish to take a closer look.

Having found that the file exists, we can then get a reference to it via a StorageFile object and call the ReadTextAsync method to read the contents as a string. The code required for this is shown in Listing 9-12.

Listing 9-12. Reading the contents of the high-scores data file in Windows 8

```
// Does the file exist?
if (!await ApplicationData.Current.LocalFolder.FileExistsAsync(FileName))
{
    // It doesn't exist
    return;
}
// Read the contents of the file
StorageFile file = await ApplicationData.Current.LocalFolder.GetFileAsync(FileName);
fileContent = await FileIO.ReadTextAsync(file);
```

The equivalent code for Windows Phone is a little different. File access is performed using another class within the System.IO.IsolatedStorage namespace. The class is called IsolatedStorageFile, instances of which are obtained by calling the class's static GetUserStoreForApplication method.

Once an instance has been obtained, it can be used to perform the file-based operations that you would expect to be able to use: creating files, reading and writing files, checking whether files exist, creating directories, reading lists of file and directory names, and so on. The MSDN documentation contains plenty of information on this class if you want to learn more about it.

We will, therefore, call on this class to read and write our high-score XML data. Listing 9-13 shows the code from the LoadScores function that executes on Windows Phone. This performs the exact same task as in Listing 9-12 for Windows 8, with the end result being that the function exits if the file doesn't exist, or it leaves the data from within the file in the fileContent variable if the file is successfully loaded.

Listing 9-13. Reading the contents of the high-scores data file in Windows Phone

```
// Get access to the isolated storage
using (IsolatedStorageFile store = IsolatedStorageFile.GetUserStoreForApplication())
{
    if (!store.FileExists(FileName))
    {
        // The score file doesn't exist
        return;
    }
    // Read the contents of the file
    using (StreamReader sr = new StreamReader(
                                  store.OpenFile(FileName, FileMode.Open)))
    {
        fileContent = sr.ReadToEnd();
    }
}
```

The code for saving data back to these files is similarly different between the two platforms. For Windows 8, the data is written by simply creating a StorageFile in the appropriate folder and then calling the WriteTextAsync method upon it, as shown in Listing 9-14. Note that the XML to be written has already been constructed at this point and is stored in a StringBuilder object named sb.

Listing 9-14. Writing the high-score file in Windows 8

```
StorageFile file = await ApplicationData.Current.LocalFolder.CreateFileAsync
                               (FileName, CreationCollisionOption.ReplaceExisting);
await FileIO.WriteTextAsync(file, sb.ToString());
```

The equivalent code for Windows Phone is a little more long-winded, but it essentially does the same thing. Having obtained a reference to isolated storage, the code calls the CreateFile method to create an IsolatedStorageFileStream object. This is then written to with a StreamWriter in order to transfer the data from the StringBuilder into the file itself. Listing 9-15 shows the code required for this.

Listing 9-15. Writing the high-score file in Windows Phone

```
// Get access to the isolated storage
using (IsolatedStorageFile store = IsolatedStorageFile.GetUserStoreForApplication())
{
    // Create a file and attach a streamwriter
    using (StreamWriter sw = new StreamWriter(store.CreateFile(FileName)))
    {
        // Write the XML string to the streamwriter
        sw.Write(sb.ToString());
    }
}
```

We can now update, load, and save the high scores for our game. All we need to do now is actually use them, and this is what we will look into next.

Using the HighScore Classes in a Game

All the data structures are present and correct, but they still need to be actually wired up into a game. Refer to the two HighScores example projects for a working example of how you can do this.

The projects begin by initializing the high-score tables and loading any existing scores in the main game class's Initialize method, as shown in Listing 9-16.

Listing 9-16. Initializing the high-score table

```
// Initialize and load the high scores
HighScores.InitializeTable("Normal", 20);
HighScores.InitializeTable("Difficult", 20);
HighScores.LoadScores();
```

Next, the game begins. The game supports two mode classes: Mode_Game (which actually just simulates the game finishing and presents you with your final score, a random number for the purposes of demonstration) and Mode_HighScores (which deals with getting a name from the player, if needed, and displays the high-score table on the screen).

Inside Mode_Game.Reset, after creating the random score, the code adds some TextObject instances to the game to tell the player that the game is over and to provide some information about the score. It calls into the HighScoreTable.ScoreQualifies function to determine whether the player's score is good enough and displays an appropriate message onscreen.

The update loop then waits for the user to click or tap the screen before continuing. When Update detects that this has happened, it calls SetGameMode to switch to the high-score mode of the game.

In the Mode_HighScores.Activate function, shown in Listing 9-17, the code checks again to see whether the score qualifies for a new high-score entry. If it does, it calls the GameHelper.BeginShowKeyboardInput function (which we first looked at back in Chapter 4) to prompt the user to enter his or her name. The dialog is given some suitable captions and also reads the default input text value from the game settings. We'll look at this again in a moment.

Listing 9-17. Preparing the game to display or update the high-score table

```
public override void Activate()
    {
        base.Activate();

        // Clear any existing game objects
        GameObjects.Clear();

        // Did the player's score qualify?
        if (_game.HighScores.GetTable("Normal").ScoreQualifies(GetLatestScore()))
        {
            // Yes, so display the input dialog
            GameHelper.BeginShowKeyboardInput(_game._graphics, KeyboardInputCallback,
                                "High score achieved", "Please enter your name",
                                SettingsManager.GetValue("PlayerName", ""));
        }
        else
        {
            // Show the highscores now. No score added so nothing to highlight
            ResetHighscoreTableDisplay(null);
        }
    }
```

Alternatively, if the score isn't good enough, it calls into the ResetHighscoreTableDisplay function, which initializes the scores for display onscreen. You will see the code for this function shortly.

If the text entry dialog were displayed, it would call into the KeyboardInputCallback function after text entry is complete, as shown in Listing 9-18. (The code here is the Windows 8 version. The Windows Phone version is slightly different when it comes to calling SaveScores, as we have already discussed.) Assuming that a name was entered, the callback function adds the name to the high-score table and retains the HighScoreEntry object that is returned before saving the updated scores. Once this is done, the ResetHighscoreTableDisplay function is called to show the high scores, passing the newly added entry as its parameter.

Listing 9-18. Responding to the completion of the text entry dialog

```
private async void KeyboardInputCallback(bool result, string text)
    {
        HighScoreEntry newEntry = null;

        // Did we get a name from the player?
        if (result && !string.IsNullOrEmpty(text))
        {
            // Add the name to the highscore
            newEntry = _game.HighScores.GetTable("Normal").AddEntry(text, GetLatestScore());
            // Save the scores
            await _game.HighScores.SaveScoresAsync();
            // Store the name so that we can recall it  next time a high score is achieved
            SettingsManager.SetValue("PlayerName", text);
        }

        // Show the highscores now and highlight the new entry if we have one
        ResetHighscoreTableDisplay(newEntry);
    }
```

Notice that the name that was entered is stored into SettingsManager for later use. This is a nice little feature that allows the player's name to be remembered between gaming sessions, saving it from having to be typed in again the next time the game is played. This is also an example of using SettingsManager for system settings that aren't directly configured by the player via a settings screen.

Finally, there is the ResetHighscoreTableDisplay function that was called twice in the previous listings. It sets up the GameObjects collection to show all the scores for the high-score table. It uses a function named CreateTextObjectsForTable inside the HighScores class to assist with this. This function simply adds a series of text objects containing the score details, but it accepts among its parameters a start and end color (used for the first and last score items, with the items in between fading in color between the two); a highlight entry (when the player has just added a new score, pass its HighScoreEntry object here to highlight the entry within the table); and a highlight color. There is no requirement to use this function, and the high-score classes can be used purely as a data manipulation structure if desired, but it can be a time saver if its functionality is sufficient for your game. (See Listing 9-19.)

Listing 9-19. Responding to the completion of the text entry dialog

```
private void ResetHighscoreTableDisplay(HighScoreEntry highlightEntry)
{
    // Add the title
    GameObjects.Add(new TextObject(_game, _game.Fonts["WascoSans"], new Vector2(10, 10),
                                                                "High Scores"));

    // Add the score objects
    _game.HighScores.CreateTextObjectsForTable("Normal", _game.Fonts["WascoSans"], 0.7f,
                    80, 45, Color.White, Color.Blue, highlightEntry, Color.Yellow);
}
```

Creating Reusable Game Components

It is very easy to find yourself rewriting sections of code over and over again as you develop games, and each time you write things slightly differently or change how things work. Creating reusable components such as those in this chapter can save you the effort of reinventing these same concepts in each new project that you create.

Even though writing reusable components such as these may require a little extra work, you'll be pleased that you made the effort when you plug them into your future projects because the overall amount of development time will be decreased (plus you'll have consistency in the appearance and functionality of your games).

Summary

- In this chapter, we looked at some reusable functions in the GameFramework project that can be used to simplify the flow and functionality of your games.

- The GameModeBase class provides a simple way to create multiple "modes" for your game to cover areas such as menus, the game itself, a game over sequence, a high-score screen, settings, credits, and anything else that you may need. Creating modes like this can be thought of as being analogous to creating multiple Forms in a WinForms desktop application.

- Each mode is created as a class derived from GameModeBase, is registered within the game framework by calling GameHost.AddGameModeHandler, and is activated by calling GameHost.SetGameMode. The current mode can be retrieved by querying the GameHost.CurrentGameModeHandler property, and any registered mode handler can be retrieved at any time by calling the GetGameModeHandler function.

- Each game mode will have its `Activated` method called when it is set as the activate mode, and it will have its `Deactivated` method called when another game mode takes control. While a game mode is active, its `Update` and `Draw` methods will be called continuously, just as in all of the other single-mode projects we have looked at.

- Each game mode has its own independent `GameObjects` collection, which it may manipulate in any way required. The game framework will automatically switch to the object collection for each mode when the mode is activated.

- Values within the application that are to be persisted between sessions can be stored away using the `static SettingsManager` class. Methods are present to read and write values of a variety of data types, keyed by a "setting name" for each.

- The game framework also provides a simple user interface for cycling between various valid settings values, via the `SettingsItemObject` class.

- A simple high-score table implementation is provided by the game framework. This supports multiple score tables, a definable number of entries within each table, and simple functionality to allow scores to be added, retrieved, loaded, and saved.

- The `HighScore` class also offers a method that will create a series of `TextObject` objects to the game objects collection to display the values currently stored within one of the high-score tables.

■ ■ ■

CHAPTER 10

Application Management

This chapter covers a subject area that may be a little less exciting than some of the other game-related areas we have worked through, but it is still important to understand: application management. Specifically, it is important to understand how to deal with the application life cycle (launching, moving to the background, and closing) and how to handle the screen resizing (either due to an orientation change or, in Windows 8, due to the application being "snapped" to the edge of the screen).

Managing the Application Life Cycle

If you are used to developing desktop Windows applications, you are, no doubt, very aware that Windows is a fully multitasking operating system. You can put any desktop application into the background and it essentially carries on running, oblivious to the fact that it no longer has the focus.

When creating Windows 8 Store apps (such as the ones we are building in this book) or apps for Windows Phone, things operate a little differently, however. With the exception of some specific application types of such as music players, these apps are put to sleep when they lose focus. On Windows Phone, they are actually terminated. They are, therefore, not able to perform any further processing until the user returns the focus back to them.

The reason for this is to reduce the amount of resources required by applications that have been moved into the background. Terminating them in this way frees up memory and processing resources. For mobile devices (both tablets and phones), this reduced resource consumption can be significant, and it is this behavior that helps contribute to the impressive battery life that many of these devices are able to offer.

In the first versions of Windows Phone 7, apps terminating in this way were a particular nuisance due to the manner in which such sleeping application instances were reawakened. Instead of just springing back to life at the point they had been left, they were entirely reset. This process was known as *tombstoning* because a marker (a *tombstone*) was left for the terminated application and that marker was all the app had to work with when it restarted in order to know what it had been doing.

This behavior resulted in a large volume of applications that completely lost track of what they were doing should they be closed and then resumed, which can be an extremely frustrating experience for the user—particularly in a game where progress through the level could be lost.

With the arrival of Windows Phone 7.1 (also known as *Mango*), a new feature arrived called *fast application switching*. This provided the functionality that everyone had been wishing for: the ability to instantly and seamlessly resume the application at the exact point it was left. Only a fixed number of applications could be stored in memory in readiness to be continued in this way, but those that were could be resumed by holding down the phone's Back button to show a list of the frozen applications and then selecting the one to resume.

With Windows Phone 8, this same behavior has been retained, so you can easily take advantage of it in your games. It is, in fact, the standard behavior of all Windows Phone apps now, so you don't need to do anything special to use fast app switching.

For Windows 8 applications, the functionality is very similar. When an app loses focus, it continues running in the background for a few seconds, and then it is frozen and no longer receives any attention from the processor.

By swiping in from the left of the screen (or moving the mouse cursor to the top-left corner of the screen), a panel appears showing all the background apps that are currently open. Selecting one will bring it back into the foreground so that it can continue to work at the same point that it was previously suspended.

In this section, we will look at the processes involved here in Windows 8 and Windows Phone 8 in more detail. As each platform handles the process slightly differently, this is divided into two parts, one for each.

The Application Life Cycle in Windows 8 Apps

When your app first launches, its entry point is the constructor of the App class, which is present in all of your games and applications. When your game is closing, its Suspending event it invoked—although not always, as we will see. Let's take a look at these entry and exit points in more detail.

The Application Launch Process

By default, the application's App class constructor does two things: it calls its internal InitializeComponent method, which prepares the object for execution, and it sets an event handler for the Suspending event, which we'll look at in just a moment.

Once the App class finishes initializing itself, the .NET Framework then calls into its OnLaunched method, which the class overrides in order to carry out any further initialization that is needed. This is the point at which our game itself is prepared for execution.

The default code checks to see whether a *game page* is already available, and, if not, one is created. The game page is actually implemented by a class within the game project itself named GamePage. The GamePage class simply initializes an instance of the game's main Game class and passes it to MonoGame to process, after which the game's own initialization functions are called (Initialize, LoadContent, and so on) and the Update/Draw game loop commences. These steps are all that take place when a game is first launched.

If you take a look at the ApplicationLifeCycle_Win8 project (or indeed, any of the MonoGame example projects that we've worked with along the way), you will find the code for the App and GamePage classes and you can take a closer look at what the functions within are actually doing.

There is a little extra information available at launch time, however. If you look in the example project's App.OnLaunched functions, you will see that the code makes reference to the args.PreviousExecutionState property. This value can be used to identify whether your app has previously been executed. It will be one of the following enumerated values:

- ApplicationExecutionState.NotRunning indicates that this is the first time the app has launched during the user session. This is the value you can expect to find when the app is run for the very first time, but also after the user launches for the first time after logging on to Windows.

- ApplicationExecutionState.Running will be present if the application is in fact already running. There are several things that can trigger this, including the use of a secondary tile on the Start screen (these are not scenarios that we will be covering in this book). All application state data will already be present in memory when the game launches in this way so you can simply carry on execution as if nothing had happened.

- ApplicationExecutionState.Suspended is the value that will be used if the operating system has placed the game into a suspended state so that it is no longer running, but has not yet removed it from memory. Resuming in this state will also have retained the application state so there is no need to restore anything.

- ApplicationExecutionState.Terminated indicates that the application had previously been running but was terminated by the operating system (and not by the user), often due to being inactive and the system running low on resources.

- ApplicationExecutionState.ClosedByUser will be present if the previous instance of the application was closed by the user.

The `ApplicationLifeCycle_Win8` project will allow you to explore these state values in a little more detail. The project contains a simple MonoGame project with a series of bouncing balls, but each time the project launches, the `ApplicationExecutionState` is displayed in a dialog box on the screen. It also writes the date and time into persisted storage each time the `Suspending` event fires and displays this value each time the application restarts.

The first time you launch this project, you will see that it displays `NotRunning` as its state value, with no previous suspension date stored.

Switch back to Visual Studio using the Alt-Tab keys so that the example project is left running in the background. Then move the mouse cursor up to the top-left corner of the screen to reveal the running Windows Store applications. You will see a thumbnail version of the project still running happily away in the background, as shown in Figure 10-1. If you wait for about ten seconds, the project will suddenly freeze. After this period of inactivity, Windows decides that the application is no longer being used and stops allocating any processing resources to it.

Figure 10-1. *The thumbnail image of the running example application*

Now if you click the application thumbnail, it springs directly back into life as if nothing had ever happened. Note that no further dialog box is triggered (so the application did not pass through the `OnLaunched` code when it resumed) and that exactly the same set of animated balls is present as was displayed prior to the app reopening, so the application state has been retained. This is *not* a `Suspended` state—it is simply Windows pausing the application so that it doesn't use as much processing power.

Close the application by pressing Alt+F4 or swiping from the top of the screen to the bottom and then return to Visual Studio. You will find that it is still in "Run" mode. Keep waiting and, after about 10–15 seconds, the running project will terminate and Visual Studio will return to edit mode.

Now relaunch the project and, as expected, you will see the execution state set to `ClosedByUser` and the suspension date set to the point in time at which Visual Studio terminated the previous debugging session. All good so far.

The Suspending Event

The general purpose of the `Suspending` event is to fire when the application is closing down so that you can perform some last-minute processing in response to this happening. There is, however, an oddity lurking in the way Windows 8 handles applications that are closed by the user and then quickly reopened.

Terminate the project in Visual Studio and then launch it again but, this time, by clicking its tile in the Start menu (in other words, don't launch via Visual Studio itself). Once the game is running, make a note of the displayed suspension date/time, then close the game (via Alt+F4 or a downward swipe again), and finally relaunch from the start menu tile once again straight away.

You will notice two things that are not what we are expecting: first, that the previous execution state is set to `NotRunning` (rather than the expected `ClosedByUser`) and, second, that the suspension date was not updated. This reveals that when an application is closed and quickly relaunched, it does not fire its `Suspending` event at all. A small amount of time needs to pass before the application suspends in this way, and this corresponds to the time we had to wait for Visual Studio to return to edit mode when we closed the application earlier.

Because of this behavior, the `Suspending` event is unfortunately not a reliable place to write game state information for when an application is closing—under the circumstances demonstrated here, the game can be closed and restarted without the event ever firing.

A Possible Game State Storage Strategy for Windows 8

Due to the unreliable nature of the Suspending event, an alternative mechanism for storing game state data is recommended for situations where the game actually closes and cannot, therefore, resume from exactly where it left off. The following steps show a strategy for this that you might consider adopting:

- For situations where the game is simply paused by Windows, there is no need to worry about writing game state information at all. The running application state will be preserved when the game is resumed.

- For situations where the game is actually closed, pre-empt the possibility by writing game state at strategic points throughout your game. This may be at the start of a level or at checkpoints throughout the level.

- When the game launches with a previous execution state of NotRunning, Terminated, or ClosedByUser, check to see whether any such saved game state information is available. If so, return the user to this point instead of opening the game to an uninitialized state. The game will not resume from exactly the point at which it had terminated, but the loss of progress will hopefully be minimal.

This allows the user to switch away from the game to perform other tasks and, in most cases, will allow them to seamlessly resume. In the worst-case scenario, they may have to restart from a recent checkpoint, but hopefully this is something that will be encountered infrequently.

The Application Life Cycle in Windows Phone Apps

Let's start by understanding the behavior on Windows Phone. Load up the ApplicationLifeCycle_WP8 example project and start it running (on the emulator or on a real device). Once it has launched, click the phone's Back button and observe what happens. The phone returns to the Start screen, but the Visual Studio IDE stays in run mode.

▨ **Tip**   If you are working in the emulator, you can use its keyboard shortcuts to activate the hardware buttons instead of clicking with the mouse. F1 clicks the Back button, F2 clicks the Windows button, and F3 clicks the Search button.

But hold on. Didn't we just say that Windows Phone applications always close when they lose the focus? This certainly isn't what appears to have just happened. Both the phone and Visual Studio appear to have indicated that the game was suspended and then restarted. What is happening?

The answer is that the game *was* closed, but Visual Studio doesn't reset its debug state. It stays in run mode and immediately reattaches to the application if you should restart it on the phone. This is useful behavior as it allows us to debug the code within a project even if the project has been terminated by the operating system.

Don't let this fool you into thinking that the application was still running the whole time, however. It really was terminated on the phone when focus was switched away. When Visual Studio reconnects to the application on the device, it is connecting to an entirely new instance of the application.

If the application is relaunched by tapping its icon from the Start menu or application list, it will restart afresh with none of the previous state data retained. If, however, it was relaunched by navigating back to it in the application history (by pressing Back repeatedly until the app regains the focus or by holding the Back button and picking the app from the recent application list), the app that appears is still a new instance of the application, but all state from before is retained. The previous instance of the application has effectively been resumed even though in reality this is not quite what happened.

Just as the Windows 8 App class has its OnLaunched and Suspending functions, so too do we have some life-cycle events in Windows Phone that we can hook into. Let's take a look at these in closer detail. The event handlers for each of these events are pre-created in the initial Windows Phone project, and they can all be found in the App class code. The event handlers are all named with an Application_ prefix. In the example project, each one contains a simple System.Diagnostics.Debug.WriteLine call so that you can see exactly when each one fires while interacting with the running project.

The Launching Event

The first of the events is the Launching event. This event will be triggered when a game launches completely from scratch and no existing state data is available. This event can be used as an opportunity to load or initialize any data that is only required when the game is being started without any previous state data being present. This may include loading data that has been persisted into isolated storage (perhaps via the GameFramework.SettingsManager class) in order to recall information about the player's previous position within the game.

▒ **Note**   The Launching event is fired before the game's Initialize and LoadContent methods have been called and before the game class has been initialized. As a result, you are not able to interact with any data within those classes at the time the event code executes.

The Closing Event

At the opposite end of the application life cycle is the Closing event, which fires when your game is closing down.

An app will normally close due to the user pressing the Back button, but the default behavior when the Back button is pressed in a MonoGame event is for nothing to happen. Instead as you have seen in earlier chapters, we detect the Back button as if it were a gamepad button, and call the Game class's Exit method should it be detected. This call actually bypasses the Closing event, and so this event cannot be relied upon in MonoGame games.

The Deactivated Event

The next life-cycle event is the Deactivated event. This event is fired when the user navigates away from your game (or is taken away by an external event, such as an incoming phone call).

The Activated Event

The final life-cycle event is the Activated event, which is triggered when the user returns to a previously deactivated game by pressing the Back button until the game comes back into focus or by picking it from the recent application screen.

When an application restarts with this event, all of its state data will have been retained so there is nothing that you need to do in order to get your game up and running again. If your game is an action game, it might be a good idea to pause the game in response to this event, however.

The Activated and Launching events are mutually exclusive; only one or the other will ever fire when your game is starting up.

A Possible Game State Storage Strategy for Windows Phone

The strategy that you might consider for restoring state in Windows Phone games is essentially identical to that described in the section above entitled "A Possible Game Stage Storage Strategy for Windows 8." Essentially, the strategy is to store checkpoint save data at regular intervals. When the game starts via its Launching event, check to see if any such stored data is available and, if so, restore the game to that point. When the game starts via its Activated event, state data will have been retained within the game so there is no need to restore anything from storage.

If you are developing your game to run on both platforms, with a little effort you will be able to route the appropriate startup states on both platforms through to the appropriate functions within your game, allowing the game state to be stored and restored regardless of which environment your code is running in.

Responding to the Game Window Resizing

Another area of behavior that you may need to consider, particularly on Windows 8, is how to respond to the game window being resized.

In Windows Phone games, the only thing that would cause this to happen is the screen orientation changing between landscape and portrait. In many cases, you probably won't have to worry about this occurring because the game can be locked into just one or other of these orientations. For games that can run in either, however, you will need to know when the orientation switches.

This requirement applies to Windows 8 games, too, but there is another consideration for Windows 8: two applications can be "snapped" side by side so that one occupies three-fourths of the screen and the other the remaining quarter. There is nothing stopping the user from snapping your game in this way, too, and you'll most likely want to be able to respond to this in an appropriate way. Your game may not be affected too much if you still have three-fourths of the screen, but being snapped into just one-fourth will almost certainly require some kind of special processing.

We can make some changes to the game framework to help keep this all under control. You will find examples of this in action in the WindowResize_Win8 and WindowResize_WP8 example projects that accompany this chapter.

Detecting When the Window Size Changes

The GameFramework can easily check whether the window size has changed by keeping track of the size that it expects the window to be and checking during each Update to see whether it is still that size. If it finds that the size has changed, it can notify the game of the size change so that the game can respond in whatever way it needs.

This is mainly implemented in the GameHost class. It begins by declaring a private class-level Vector2 variable named _knownWindowSize, which is initially set to Vector2.Zero to indicate that the size has yet to be determined.

Within the standard GameHost.Update method (which should be being called for every single update), a call is added to a new function named CheckForResize. This function is where all the work of monitoring window-size changes takes place.

The first thing CheckForResize does is determine the current window size, the code for which can be seen in Listing 10-1. The route to achieving this differs across the two platforms. For Windows Phone devices, the size is read from the GraphicsAdapter.DefaultAdapter.CurrentDisplayMode object, which has properties for the window's Width and Height. Windows 8, on the other hand, uses a Windows.UI.Core.CoreWindow object to retrieve the same information. A reference to this object is stored in the class-level variable _window, and it is placed there during the GameHost class constructor.

The size that is read is placed into a Vector2 structure named windowSizeUnscaled. However, there is one additional complication for Windows 8 that we need to pay attention to: on devices with very large screens (such as the simulated 10.6" 2560 x 1440 pixel device in the Windows 8 Simulator), the returned window size is actually adjusted for the physical screen size, and it is not a pixel size.

To map this returned size to the physical pixels, we have to scale it back into pixels by multiplying the size by the display's dots-per-inch value, returned from the LogicalDPI property, and then dividing by the standard pixel-scaled dots-per-inch value, which is 96. This value is placed into the windowSize variable, and this is the final value that we will use as our screen size.

If you would like to see the effects of this pixel scaling, try running the example project in the Windows 8 Simulator with the 10.6" 2560 x 1440 screen resolution selected and examine the values that appear in the windowSizeUnscaled and windowSize variables. The windowSizeUnscaled variable receives the value (1422.22217, 800), whereas windowSize contains the expected (2560, 1440).

Listing 10-1. Determining the size of the game window

```
// The window bounds
Vector2 windowSize;
// The window bounds without scaling
Vector2 windowSizeUnscaled;

#if WINDOWS_PHONE

// Read the raw unscaled window dimensions
windowSizeUnscaled = new Vector2(GraphicsAdapter.DefaultAdapter.CurrentDisplayMode.Width
                           , GraphicsAdapter.DefaultAdapter.CurrentDisplayMode.Height);
// The window on Windows Phone is not scaled so the window size will always match
windowSize = windowSizeUnscaled;

#else

// Read the raw unscaled window dimensions
windowSizeUnscaled = new Vector2((float)_window.Bounds.Width,
                               (float)_window.Bounds.Height);
// Scale the dimensions by the device dpi to get the actual pixel dimension
windowSize = windowSizeUnscaled
                       * Windows.Graphics.Display.DisplayProperties.LogicalDpi / 96;

#endif
```

Now that the code knows the window size, it needs to figure out what to do with it. It checks it against the previous known size, stored in the knownWindowSize variable mentioned earlier, to see if they match. If not, the size has either changed, or this is the very first call into the function and the previous size is not actually yet known. The code remembers which of these it is so that it only notifies the game upon an actual change. The first call where the previous size is not known does not therefore trigger Resize functions to be called.

Next, the code determines the *window view state*. This is how Windows 8 applications can tell whether they are running full screen, have been reduced to three-fourths of the screen width, or have been snapped down to just one-fourth. The state is found by querying the .NET Framework's Windows.UI.ViewManagement.ApplicationView.Value property, which returns an item from the ApplicationViewState enumeration. The items within this enumeration are as follows:

- FullScreenLandscape: the application is in full-screen mode with landscape orientation.

- Filled: the application is running side-by-side with another app and is occupying three-fourths of the screen.

- Snapped: the application is running side-by-side and is occupying just one-fourth of the screen.

- FullScreenPortrait: the application is in full-screen mode with portrait orientation.

The code reads the appropriate value but then uses it to select from another enumeration, WindowStates, which is defined within the GameHost class. Why not just use the ApplicationViewState enumeration rather than inventing a copy of it?

The reason for this is that Windows Phone has no concept of these view states—it only supports full-screen applications, and the ApplicationViewState enumeration does not exist in its flavor of the .NET Framework. In order to allow a consistent GameFramework API, we cannot, therefore, use the .NET enumeration. The GameFramework's own WindowStates enumeration, on the other hand, is available to both platforms, and it is simply set to always contain FullScreen when running on Windows Phone. The WindowStates enumeration is virtually identical to the .NET ApplicationViewState enumeration, except that it combines FullScreenLandscape and FullScreenPortrait into a single FullScreen item instead.

All of the code for determining the window state across both platforms is shown in Listing 10-2. Note that the CurrentWindowState variable in which the calculated value is stored is actually a public class-level property, so the game can query this at any time it needs to.

Listing 10-2. Finding the window state

```
    // Determine the new window state
#if WINDOWS_PHONE
    // Windows Phone doesn't support window states, we will always be FullScreen
    CurrentWindowState = WindowStates.FullScreen;
#else
    // Read the current application view state and use that to derive the
    // appropriate WindowStates enumeration item.
    switch (Windows.UI.ViewManagement.ApplicationView.Value)
    {
        case ApplicationViewState.Filled:
            CurrentWindowState = WindowStates.Filled;
            break;
        case ApplicationViewState.Snapped:
            CurrentWindowState = WindowStates.Snapped;
            break;
        default:
            CurrentWindowState = WindowStates.FullScreen;
            break;
    }
#endif
```

With the window size and state now known, the last thing to do is to notify the game about the size change. Providing that this isn't the initial startup call to CheckForResize, the code notifies the game in two different ways.

First, for games that are not using game mode handlers (as described in the previous chapter), a new virtual function named Resize has been added to the GameHost class, so this is called to notify the game of the size change. The function parameters contain the window state, the new window size, and the old window size.

Then, for games that are using game mode handlers, all registered handlers are processed and a new virtual Resize function within each of those is called, too. All game mode classes are, therefore, instantly notified of the resize and are able to process this as needed. The parameters for the GameModeBase.Resize function are identical to those of the GameHost.Resize function.

Handling Window Size Changes

With the ability to tell exactly when our window size changes, we need to figure out what to do when this actually happens. There are several things that you might want to consider in this area—let's take a look at them.

Size Changes with Sprite-Based Games

The good news for sprite-based games is that there is very little you need to do in terms of MonoGame itself—the game will automatically switch to the new window size and carry on uninterrupted. Any code that you have written that queries the `GraphicsDevice.ViewPort.Bounds.Width` and `.Height` properties will see the new dimensions immediately.

It is entirely possible that you will want to do something in terms of the layout of your game, however. If the player has swapped between portrait and landscape or has snapped the game into one-fourth of the screen, it's very likely that the arrangement of game objects you were previously using will no longer be appropriate.

Your job in the `Resize` method (either of one or more game mode classes or in your main game class) is, therefore, to provide whatever kind of layout reorganization is needed.

There is generally not very much that the `GameFramework` project can do to assist in this task because it doesn't have any understanding of how your game objects are being used, but there is one thing it can help with—positioning of text.

As you may recall from back in Chapter 3, we can add `TextObject` instances to the `GameObjects` collection to display text, and one property of the `TextObject` class is the text's `HorizontalAlignment`, which will be `Near` for left-aligned text, `Center` for centered text, or `Far` for right-aligned text.

The game framework can have a good guess at how to reposition these in response to the window width changing and, if you wish to take advantage of this, you can call the `GameHost.AutoUpdateTextPositions` method in order for it to process the positions for you. This won't always do what you need, but in many cases it will.

For text that is `Near` aligned, the function leaves the text position unchanged so that it maintains its defined distance from the left edge of the window. For text that is `Far` aligned, it adds or subtracts the difference between the old and new width so that the text maintains its defined distance from the right edge of the window. Finally, for text that is `Center` aligned, it adds or subtracts half the difference between the old and new width so that the center point is maintained relative to both edges of the window.

You can see this function being used in the `WindowResize` example. This is set to display two text items at the top of the page: a simple title string on the left and the current window size on the right. Try changing the device orientation or docking another application alongside the example in Windows 8. You will see that the window width changes, but, despite this, the right-aligned text maintains its position relative to the edge of the window.

If you edit the project source code and comment out the call to `AutoUpdateTextPositions` in the `WindowResizeGame.Resize` function, you will see then that the right-aligned text becomes uncontrolled and can end up out of view or incorrectly positioned away from the right edge of the window.

Size Changes with Matrix-Based Games

If your game is using matrices and vectors for its rendering, most of the needs of your game code are the same as for sprite-based games, but there is one additional thing that you need to do: update the aspect ratio used by your `Effect` objects.

You may recall from back in Chapter 6 that we need to provide a projection matrix to the effect and that one element contained within this matrix is the window's aspect ratio. Whenever the window size changes, so does the aspect ratio, and unless we account for this in the projection matrix, the game will continue to render as if it were at the previous window size, but it will then squash or stretch itself to fit in the actual space available. This generally looks awful.

The effect of this incorrect aspect ratio is shown in Figure 10-2. Figure 10-2(a) shows how the cube from the `WindowResize_Win8` project looks when snapped into one-fourth of the screen without updating the projection matrix to match. Figure 10-2(b) shows the same cube in the same window, but this time with the projection matrix updated accordingly. The cube is square once again.

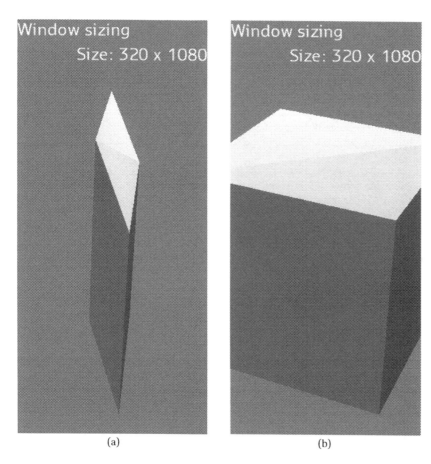

(a)   (b)

Figure 10-2. *A cube rendered into a snapped window both with and without making an adjustment to the projection matrix*

If you take a look at the WindowResizeGame.Resize method in the WindowResize example (which uses matrices and vectors to render a 3-D cube), you will see that the code recalculates the aspect ratio and uses it to rebuild the projection matrix. This matrix is then passed into the _effect variable, just as it was when initializing the game.

▨ **Tip** To eliminate the duplication of code for building the projection matrix, it would be a good idea to take the code out into a separate function that builds and returns the matrix for you. This could then be called from both the Initialize and Resize functions. Building the matrix in one central location means that if you need to change its code in any way (to change the fieldOfView, for example) you don't have to worry about multiple pieces of code becoming unsynchronized.

When the project runs, try changing the device orientation or setting the project window to be filled or snapped. In all cases, the cube retains the correct size and is not stretched or squashed at all. If, on the other hand, you comment out the code in the Resize function that sets the updated matrix into the _effect.Projection property and then try running the project again, you will see that the cube is stretched and distorted when the window size changes and no longer looks square at all.

Working with Snapped Windows

Snapped windows in Windows 8 can sometimes present something of a challenge. If your game is designed to run in landscape orientation, the snapped window size is often simply too small for your game to run. Filled windows are generally OK as they still have a reasonable amount of space left, but snapped windows can be tiny. On a Surface RT device, for example, the snapped window has a width of only 320 pixels, which for a landscape-orientated game can be a problem.

You have two options for dealing with this: rearrange your game objects to fit or simply abandon this window mode and present a placeholder screen instead of the game itself. Clearly if you can support snapped mode, then that is a far superior option because it allows your users to continue to play while doing something else—this may be greatly appreciated! If this is just simply not practical, however, your other option is to display a simple graphic or animation informing the user that the game will resume when the window is expanded. You could set up a new game mode for this if your game is using game modes.

There are lots of inbuilt Windows 8 applications that do not support snapped mode such as the Store application. Lots of games give up with this mode, too. The Xbox Live game *Taptiles* is one such example; when its window is snapped, the game pauses and simply shows a summary of the current game score.

Examples of applications that respond well to being snapped are the inbuilt Mail and People apps, both of which rearrange their content to compensate for the reduced window size. Which approach you adopt will depend to a great extent on the nature of your game.

Summary

- Applications stop executing when they are moved out of focus. Windows 8 and Windows Phone will store the application state and, if possible, will automatically restore the app to exactly where it left off when the user returns to it. Application state will be flushed from memory once too many other applications have been opened, however.

- Windows 8 apps indicate the previous state of execution, providing a way to determine whether to attempt to load a previously saved game state from storage or to continue working with the game state that is already present.

- Windows 8 apps generally fire the Suspending event when the application is put to sleep, but, under certain circumstances, this event does not trigger. This is, therefore, not a reliable place for storing game state data. Instead, store state data at strategic points throughout your game.

- Windows Phone apps have four events that are raised by the application as its running state changes. Launching indicates that the event is starting up afresh, whereas Activated is fired when a previously suspended app is reawakened with its game state still intact. Closing is used when the application is closed by the user (by pressing the Back button, for example), while Deactivated is called when the application is suspended with its game state stored for potential reactivation later on.

- A number of events may lead to the game window resizing. These include a change of screen orientation (if your game supports this) or, for Windows 8 apps, in response to the user "snapping" another application alongside the game window.

- The GameFramework project simplifies the task of working with windows that can change their size by providing abstract Resize methods in the GameHost and GameModeBase classes. The Resize methods are passed parameters to tell them the new and old window sizes as well as the window state (full screen, filled, or snapped).

- Sprite-based games don't need do anything special to respond to the window size changing. They just need to ensure that their game objects are appropriately positioned for the new window size. The GameHost.AutoUpdateTextPositions can help to put TextObjects into the required locations in many cases.

- Matrix-based games need to update any Effect objects that they are using with a new projection matrix that takes the new window size aspect ratio into account.

- Working with windows that are "snapped" to one-fourth of the screen width in Windows 8 can present additional challenges due to the small amount of horizontal space available. Games can either adapt their layout in response to this, or they can simply display a message stating that the game will resume once the window is expanded.

CHAPTER 11

Getting Started with XAML

For the next few chapters, we will head in a different direction as we explore the options for using the main user interface environment provided to Windows 8 and Windows Phone apps: *XAML*. Short for "eXtensible Application Markup Language" and generally pronounced as "zammal," XAML provides an optional mechanism for easily adding powerful and flexible user interface constructs to your games.

So, why would you want to use XAML when you could create your own user interface using MonoGame? It's a good question, and in some cases it will be advantageous to use MonoGame and to ignore XAML. Reasons for this may include portability (XAML differs between Windows 8 and Windows Phone and, should you wish to port your game to other platforms entirely, XAML will not be available at all) and presentational consistency (you may not be able to get the XAML UI elements to have quite the same look and feel as your game elements).

If you can live within those constraints, however, you may find that XAML will save you a lot of tedious work. By overlaying its controls on top of your game, a substantial amount of functionality can be achieved with very little effort.

In this chapter, we will begin to explore the fundamentals of XAML, its capabilities, and its potential in development. If you haven't used XAML before in its current or in any of its historical forms, you will gain a broad understanding of how to use it. This book's focus is on gaming rather than XAML itself, however, so we cannot hope to cover everything that XAML can do. Many other excellent books and online resources are available if you want to further your understanding beyond the information that is presented here.

If you are already familiar with XAML, much of this material may already be familiar to you. It might still be worth skimming the chapter, however, because there are differences that you might not expect in the way XAML operates in its new environments from how its previous versions worked in the past.

A Brief History of XAML

Let's take a quick tour through the past and present of XAML so that we can understand its evolution.

Windows Presentation Foundation

In the beginning, there was Windows Presentation Foundation (WPF). This technology, introduced by Microsoft in 2006 as part of .NET 3.0, was for desktop PC development, and it introduced a new graphics API.

Prior to this, 2-D rendering in Windows was generally performed using the aging *Graphics Device Interface (GDI)*. GDI has its strengths, but rendering games and fast-moving animated graphics are not among them. The majority of operations performed using GDI are driven by the processor rather than by the graphics hardware, limiting the performance of applications that use it.

WPF dramatically improves on these capabilities by offloading the graphics rendering onto the graphics hardware via the DirectX rendering system. As a result of this change, vastly improved levels of performance can be obtained with less load to the CPU itself, allowing the processor instead to focus on tasks such as data processing, game logic, and so on.

The sophisticated rendering abilities of the graphics hardware can also be taken advantage of by WPF, allowing for a much richer visual display. Graphics hardware can easily rotate, scale, perform alpha blending and transparency effects, and perform other visual transformations. All of this functionality becomes immediately available to the WPF user interface. 3-D graphics rendering is also supported.

One of the important features of WPF is a layout engine that allows flexible and complex user interface designs to be specified. This engine first introduced XAML to define the contents of the screens generated by WPF.

Silverlight

A year after the release of the first version of WPF, Microsoft released the first version of Silverlight. Silverlight began as a web browser technology, based on WPF (and in fact was originally codenamed *WPF/E*, short for "Windows Presentation Foundation/Everywhere"). It took the central graphic presentation functionality present in WPF and allowed it to be used to deliver content within web pages using a small and reasonably unobtrusive browser plug-in. The 3-D rendering element of WPF was not included in the transformation to Silverlight.

Silverlight 1.0 was useful and powerful in many ways, but it was not as flexible as it might have been. It exposed a Document Object Model (DOM) that could be used to interact with and manipulate the content that it was presenting within the browser, but all interaction with this object model had to be performed using JavaScript. It also had no user interface controls built in to its runtime.

Silverlight 2, which was released in 2008, contained a large number of changes and enhancements. Possibly the most significant of these was the capability for it to be programmed using the .NET Common Language Runtime (CLR). As a result of this enhancement, code could be created using any of the managed .NET languages such as C# or Visual Basic.NET. This greatly increased the flexibility of the environment and opened it up as a usable platform to millions of existing .NET developers. Code embedded into Silverlight apps is known as *code-behind code* because it sits behind the user-facing presentation layer. This is analogous to the code that is contained within a Form class in WinForms development.

Along with this change were numerous others, including the addition of flexible user interface controls (such as text boxes, combo boxes, check boxes, sliders, and many more), LINQ, data access functionality, and the ability for managed code within a Silverlight application to interact with the HTML on the page outside of the application itself. This resulted in a highly flexible and dynamic environment to work in.

In 2009, Silverlight 3 was released, bringing with it a number of additions such as new user interface controls, better audio and video decoding, and high-definition video streaming. Another very useful change in this new version is its capability to run outside of the browser. Instead of having to live inside a web page, a Silverlight application could now be installed on the PC as a stand-alone application, resulting in a very simple delivery and deployment experience.

Silverlight 4 was released in 2009 and then the latest version, version 5, in 2011. These contain another list of enhancements, including 3-D rendering, abilities to work with printers and the clipboard, support for the right mouse button and mouse wheel, capability for using a web cam and microphone, and 64-bit support.

Despite some success, Silverlight 5 looks to be the final version of the application that will be produced, with Microsoft now concentrating on open standards such as HTML5.

Silverlight on Windows Phone 7

With the introduction of Windows Phone 7, Silverlight was chosen as the user interface-rendering engine that the platform would utilize. Clearly, a Silverlight application running on a Windows Phone 7 device is working in a very different environment from one running in a web browser or on the desktop. Nevertheless, it still offers a huge amount of functionality and a great degree of flexibility for presenting data to and interacting with the user.

A substantial number of applications were built with this technology. Just as with the vast majority of Windows Phone 7 applications, these are compatible with Windows Phone 8, too.

XAML on Windows 8 and Windows Phone 8

Finally, we reach the current platforms, which still use XAML for the construction of their user interfaces. Due to the effective discontinuation of the Silverlight product line, the markup is simply referred to as XAML on these platforms.

The good news with the current implementation of XAML is that the structure and content used for Windows Phone 8 applications is highly compatible with that used in Windows Phone 7, so any experience or existing code that you have will transfer to Windows Phone 8 very easily.

The bad news is that the Windows 8 implementation of XAML used different control libraries. This means that some controls from Windows Phone 8 do not have corresponding equivalents in Windows 8. It also means that all of the control namespaces differ between the two platforms. Unfortunately, building a XAML page on each platform is therefore not simply a question of copy-and-paste (though a lot of content will transfer across in this way if a little care is taken with exactly which parts of the page are copied).

Creating XAML Projects for Windows 8 and Windows Phone 8

To keep things simple, let's create a simple project that doesn't involve MonoGame. To create a Windows 8 project, select the Blank App (XAML) project template from within the Windows Store branch of the template tree, as shown in Figure 11-1. For a Windows Phone 8 project, select the Windows Phone App template from within the Windows Phone section of the tree, as shown in Figure 11-2. After entering the Windows Phone project name and location, be sure to choose to target Windows Phone OS 8.0 in the dialog box that appears.

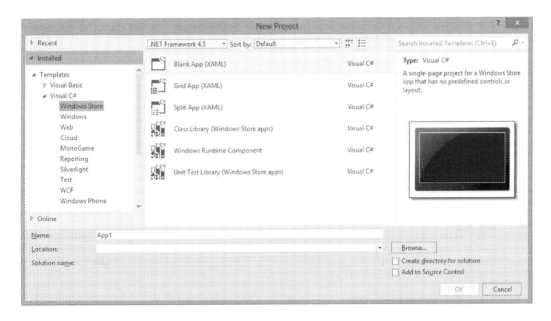

Figure 11-1. *Creating a new Windows 8 XAML project*

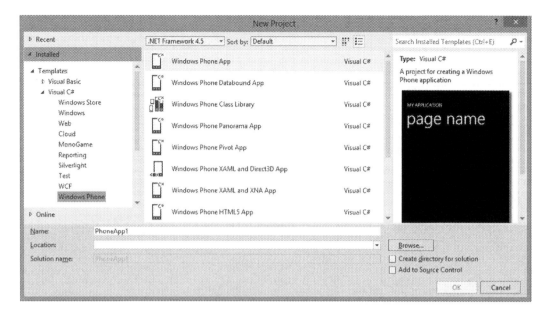

Figure 11-2. *Creating a new Windows Phone 8 XAML project*

Try this now and create an empty XAML project to experiment with based on the platform of your choice. Then run the resulting project and allow it to run on the local machine for a Windows 8 project, or on a device or the emulator for Windows Phone. Whichever platform you choose, the resulting application shows essentially an empty black screen. The Windows 8 empty project shows a completely empty page, whereas the Windows Phone project displays an application name and a title at the top. The title initially displays the value page name. As this name suggests, the top-level design unit within XAML applications is called a *page* (analogous to the *form* in WinForms projects).

Working with XAML Projects

Getting comfortable with the Visual Studio IDE can take a little time when working with XAML projects. The main building blocks of the projects are the pages, which are represented by .xaml files. You will see the default initial page, MainPage.xaml, present in Solution Explorer. Double-click this now to display it in the page designer.

Generally, when working on the design of XAML pages, the IDE will operate using a "split" view, with the actual XAML code on one side of the screen and a preview of the page on the other. As changes are made to the XAML, they are immediately reflected in the preview, allowing the effect of code changes to be quickly and easily understood.

Visual Studio 2012 allows you to build the page visually, just like the WinForms Form designer. Using the preview to visually design pages can be extremely useful and time-saving. Controls can be visually added to and arranged within the preview, and the corresponding XAML code updates in real-time to reflect the changes that have been made. Clicking a control within the preview not only visually selects it within the designer, but it also scrolls to and highlights the corresponding control in the XAML pane. Using these two panes together provides a very rich and powerful user interface design experience—that is, once you've got the hang of it!

▓ **Note**   As an additional or alternative method for editing page designs, Microsoft provides a comprehensive user interface design tool called Blend for Visual Studio 2012. The idea behind this application is that designers, who don't necessarily have any programming experience, can use Blend to create rich and attractive user interface frameworks, behind which the programmers can then slot in the required program code. Blend is well worth investigating if you find that you have large amounts of page design to do. This book will focus only on developing XAML applications within the main Visual Studio IDE, however.

When designing Windows 8 pages, the XAML page designer opens by default with the designer split horizontally, showing the page design at the top of the window and the XAML code below. This orientation is based on the general assumption that pages are more likely to be developed in landscape orientation for Windows 8 systems.

Windows Phone projects, on the other hand, default to opening with a vertical split, on the assumption that Windows Phone projects are more likely to be developed in portrait orientation.

In either case, you can swap the split direction very easily by clicking on the Vertical Split or Horizontal Split buttons that appear at the right or the bottom of the split bar. If you prefer, you can use the Swap Panes button at the left or top edge of the split bar to swap over the page preview and XAML editor locations.

Don't forget that you can zoom in and out the page preview in order to get a larger overview, or perhaps to see it in finer detail if you are making more intricate changes to the page design. The zoom level can be set using the zoom percentage drop-down on the bottom edge of the page preview, or by holding the Ctrl key and rolling the mouse wheel while the page preview has focus and is under the mouse cursor.

Associated with each .xaml page file is a corresponding .cs code file, containing the "code behind" the page. This code file can be accessed either by clicking the View Code button in the Solution Explorer toolbar or by expanding the .xaml file within Solution Explorer's tree and double-clicking the .cs file that is revealed, as shown in Figure 11-3.

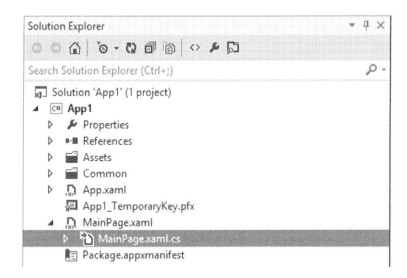

Figure 11-3. *Accessing the code behind a XAML page*

All these areas of the IDE are important for designing XAML applications. As we will see in the next chapter, XAML interfaces and MonoGame graphics can be combined into one single window. The user interface will be created in the page and XAML designer. The rest of the game functionality will be created exactly as we have seen in the preceding chapters.

The Hidden Source Files

Although not initially visible within Solution Explorer, there are some additional files included in the project. They can be found by expanding the `Properties` node in the project tree.

Inside, you will find `AssemblyInfo.cs`, which provides all the details of the assembly (title, author, copyright details, and so on) that will be built into the binary when it is compiled.

For Windows Phone projects, two further files are present. The first of these is `AppManifest.xml`, which is essentially an empty XML document. The second is `WMAppManifest.xml`, which contains various application parameters that will be used to control how the application is deployed and launched. Double-click this file to open it and you will find that instead of displaying its content within a text editor window, a graphical editor window appears. We will look at the options presented in this window in more detail in Chapter 14 when we prepare an application for submission to the Windows Phone Store.

There is no file such as this one in the `Properties` node of the solution for Windows 8 applications. However, there is a very similar configuration file present, but placed in the root project node instead. The file is named `Package.appxmanifest` for Windows 8 apps, and it also displays an equivalent graphical editor when opened.

Exploring XAML

Let's continue our journey into XAML pages by spending some time looking at the actual markup code itself.

XAML is both intricate and complex. Although it is not a full-fledged programming language in its own right, it nonetheless contains all sorts of tricks and features that will take time to master. In this section, you will take a crash course in XAML and learn just the basics you need in order to set up a simple user interface.

While you will get a good idea of what XAML can do and a high-level understanding of how it works, providing a full and in-depth description of all its features is beyond the scope of this book. If and when you want to further your knowledge, there are many good books and online resources about XAML. Much of the content presented here may be of use in your gaming projects, but hopefully you will find information here that will be useful if you decide to create any non-gaming applications, too.

What Is XAML For?

XAML's primary purpose is to define the user interface layout of pages displayed within an application.

Visual development environments have internally used text-based representations of form designs for a very long time. Starting back with the original pre-.NET versions of Visual Basic, forms were designed using a visual layout tool. Those designs were stored using a special syntax built purely around the need to define user interface elements and to set the values of their properties. These designs were system-generated and only designed to be system-readable. They could be modified by hand, but to do so required the designer to explore the data files outside of the IDE and "hack" them. Such editing was not supported or recommended.

Things improved somewhat with the introduction of the .NET environment. The visual form designer continued to result in system-generated code, and it was, by default, still hidden away. The code it created was no longer in a special structure, however. It was plain C# or VB.NET, and it could be viewed and edited directly within the IDE if the developer wanted to do so. Generally, it was still easier to simply use the form designer, not least of which because it generated reams and reams of verbose code.

The approach taken with WPF, Silverlight, and now XAML applications is somewhat different. The UI is marked up in XAML code. This code is not only in plain view and editable, but also editing is encouraged and recommended. In fact, in earlier versions of Visual Studio, manual editing of XAML was the only way to build it at all.

This open and structured approach to layout provides a number of benefits. It allows you to see exactly, without any ambiguity, what the structure and content of your user interface actually is. It lets you interact at a detailed level with its objects and properties without having to navigate through a complex visual interface. And, with a little practice and experience, it also allows you to create your user interface more quickly than using the visual designer.

One of the things that made this approach less usable in the pre-XAML approach to form design was the verbosity of the UI construction code. Adding a text box to a form and setting its properties could require a dozen or more lines of code. XAML removes this problem by using a concise and targeted notation for specifying its content. User interface controls (or elements) are defined by simple XML elements, whose names correspond to the classes that they represent. Properties and events are defined by XML attributes (though support for complex properties that cannot be represented by a simple attribute value is present, too).

When you compile your project, the compiler processes all the XAML that has been defined and actually turns it into C# code. This code is then compiled as part of your project, just as any other C# code would be. Because of this, virtually everything that you can do in XAML, you could also do by writing code, should you need to do so.

In addition to all of this, the XAML editor has a degree of predictive intelligence. While you are using it, the editor will do its best to insert the markup that you will need next (quotes around attribute values, closing elements, and so on), and Visual Studio's IntelliSense feature will provide suggestions for available attributes and property values. It can take a little time to learn to work with this feature rather than fight against it, but once you come to terms with it, you will find that it saves you a lot of time.

To begin with, feel free to use the visual designer to create your XAML for you. You can easily create and modify elements and their properties and, more or less, leave the XAML code itself alone. But keep an eye on what is happening behind your page design and don't be afraid to make any changes to the markup directly in the XAML editor. Before long, you might find editing the XAML more comfortable than using the designer.

The Page Structure

XAML pages are structured in a conceptually similar way to pages in HTML. They are set up in a hierarchical system whereby elements are contained within other elements. If you add a panel and then want to add a text box inside that panel, the text box must be defined inside the panel's element within the XAML definition.

XAML pages and elements can even have styles applied to them in a similar way to the way cascading style sheets (CSS) can be used for HTML documents. XAML styles are not as sophisticated as CSS, but they can still provide a method for updating elements within pages in a consistent manner.

Other comparisons with the HTML world exist, too. We have already seen that each XAML design is stored within a page. When we want to take the user from one page to another, we do this by navigating to a page using a URI, just as we would in a web browser. The URIs are formed in a way that references content within the application rather than actually looking on the Internet.

Parameter values can be passed between these pages by specifying them within the URI's *query string*, just as parameters are passed between pages within a web browser.

If you create an empty project based on the Windows Phone Databound App template, you can see this application page navigation feature in use. Inside the `MainPage.xaml.cs` file is the code shown in Listing 11-1. The `NavigationService.Navigate` call is provided with the target page URI including the query string, which in this case indicates the index of the item within the list that has been touched by the user.

Listing 11-1. Navigating to the DetailsPage and passing it a parameter value

```
// Handle selection changed on LongListSelector
private void MainLongListSelector_SelectionChanged(object sender,
                                                    SelectionChangedEventArgs e)
{
    // If selected item is null (no selection) do nothing
    if (MainLongListSelector.SelectedItem == null)
        return;

    // Navigate to the new page
    NavigationService.Navigate(new Uri("/DetailsPage.xaml?selectedItem=" +
        (MainLongListSelector.SelectedItem as ItemViewModel).ID, UriKind.Relative));
```

```
    // Reset selected item to null (no selection)
    MainLongListSelector.SelectedItem = null;
}
```

XAML's Syntax

Let's take a more detailed look at some XAML code and break it down so that we can understand what it is doing. We'll examine this by taking a tour through some of the classes within a XAML project, and then we will summarize everything at the end.

Starting Off with App.xaml

The first example that we will look at is the App.xaml file from the default Windows Phone 8 Application template, the beginning of which is reproduced in Listing 11-2.

Listing 11-2. The start of the App.xaml file

```
<Application
    x:Class="PhoneApp1.App"
    xmlns="http://schemas.microsoft.com/winfx/2006/xaml/presentation"
    xmlns:x="http://schemas.microsoft.com/winfx/2006/xaml"
    xmlns:phone="clr-namespace:Microsoft.Phone.Controls;assembly=Microsoft.Phone"
    xmlns:shell="clr-namespace:Microsoft.Phone.Shell;assembly=Microsoft.Phone">
```

You might notice that this particular file doesn't display the visual editor when it is opened in Visual Studio; you will see the reason for that in a moment.

The very first line declares an XML element named Application. The name of the element defines the class from which this particular class inherits. The first line after this sets the x:Class attribute to have the value PhoneApp1.App. It specifies the namespace inside which the class resides (PhoneApp1) and the name of the class (App).

If you open the code behind the XAML, you will find that the class declaration begins with the code shown in Listing 11-3. This is exactly the same information in terms of the namespace, class name, and class derivation, but written using the C# syntax.

Listing 11-3. The App class declaration in the C# code behind

```
namespace PhoneApp1
{
    public partial class App : Application
    {
```

■ **Note** The XAML and the code for a class definition must agree on the details specified here; if the base class, namespace, or class name are inconsistent between the two, a compilation error will occur.

The next block of content within App.xaml in Listing 11-2 defines four XML namespaces. These namespaces allow us to map elements within the following XAML back to specific DLLs or areas of functionality.

The first namespace that is defined references the URL http://schemas.microsoft.com/winfx/2006/xaml/presentation, which is the namespace used for XAML page layouts. No namespace prefix is specified for this, so all following elements within the document will default to this namespace unless another is explicitly specified.

Following this is the x namespace, referencing `http://schemas.microsoft.com/winfx/2006/xaml`. This namespace provides additional content specific to XAML, such as the `x:Class` attribute that was already discussed.

The remaining namespaces both reference .NET namespaces `Microsoft.Phone.Controls` and `Microsoft.Phone.Shell`. With these namespaces present, we can refer to items within these .NET namespaces by specifying the appropriate XML namespace (phone or shell). The editor will automatically create further namespace entries if controls from other assemblies are added to the page from the Toolbox.

Moving On to MainPage.xaml

Bearing all this in mind, let's now skip forward to another file: `MainPage.xaml`. The file begins as shown in Listing 11-4.

Listing 11-4. *The beginning of MainPage.xaml*

```
<phone:PhoneApplicationPage
    x:Class="PhoneApp1.MainPage"
    xmlns="http://schemas.microsoft.com/winfx/2006/xaml/presentation"
    xmlns:x="http://schemas.microsoft.com/winfx/2006/xaml"
    xmlns:phone="clr-namespace:Microsoft.Phone.Controls;assembly=Microsoft.Phone"
    xmlns:shell="clr-namespace:Microsoft.Phone.Shell;assembly=Microsoft.Phone"
    xmlns:d="http://schemas.microsoft.com/expression/blend/2008"
    xmlns:mc="http://schemas.openxmlformats.org/markup-compatibility/2006"
```

This time, the root element is of type `PhoneApplicationPage` from the phone namespace. We already know that the phone namespace maps into the `Microsoft.Phone.Controls` .NET namespace, so this tells us that the type of class represented by this XAML is derived from `Microsoft.Phone.Controls.PhoneApplicationPage`. The second line names the class as `MainPage` within the `PhoneApp1` namespace. Once again, we can confirm this by viewing the code behind for the class and seeing that it reveals exactly the same information, as shown in Listing 11-5.

Listing 11-5. *The code behind for the MainPage class declaration*

```
namespace PhoneApp1
{
    public partial class MainPage : PhoneApplicationPage
    {
```

Following the class name in the XAML listing is another slightly larger list of XML namespaces. They are the same as in `App.xaml`, except for the addition of the d and mc namespaces. These namespaces are present primarily for the benefit of the visual designer (and for external designers such as Expression Blend). We can safely ignore them from the perspective of managing our page designs.

A few lines farther down within the file you will see an element of type `Grid` being defined. The complete declaration for this and its content is shown in Listing 11-6 (a couple of page comments have been omitted for brevity).

Listing 11-6. *The code behind for the MainPage class declaration*

```
<!--LayoutRoot is the root grid where all page content is placed-->
<Grid x:Name="LayoutRoot" Background="Transparent">
    <Grid.RowDefinitions>
        <RowDefinition Height="Auto"/>
        <RowDefinition Height="*"/>
    </Grid.RowDefinitions>
```

```
    <!--TitlePanel contains the name of the application and page title-->
    <StackPanel x:Name="TitlePanel" Grid.Row="0" Margin="12,17,0,28">
        <TextBlock Text="MY APPLICATION" Style="{StaticResource PhoneTextNormalStyle}"
                                                        Margin="12,0"/>
        <TextBlock Text="page name" Margin="9,-7,0,0"
                                    Style="{StaticResource PhoneTextTitle1Style}"/>
    </StackPanel>

    <!--ContentPanel - place additional content here-->
    <Grid x:Name="ContentPanel" Grid.Row="1" Margin="12,0,12,0">

    </Grid>
  </Grid>

</phone:PhoneApplicationPage>
```

This code declares a series of controls that are present within the page. Before we look in more detail at what the controls are for and how the XAML syntax is used to declare them, let's look at a visual representation of the controls within the page. Figure 11-4 shows the same controls within MainPage inside a Windows Phone application. Other pages can be contained within the application, too, represented conceptually as Page2 and Page3 in this diagram.

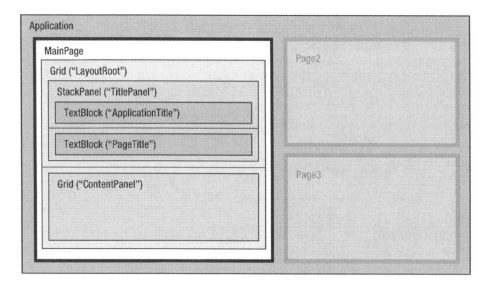

Figure 11-4. *The hierarchy of pages and controls within an application*

Let's focus on the outermost Grid element first. Elements defined within the body of the XAML document represent objects that are being created. The name of the element specifies the name of the class to be used to create the object. Because the element's name is Grid, this element will create an instance of the Grid class. No namespace has been specified, so the default namespace will be used; as we know, this is the XAML namespace, so the control will be taken from XAML's built-in classes, of which Grid is one.

The element declaration also specifies two attributes: x:Name and Background. When attributes are provided for an element, these attributes are used to set properties of the object that has been created. In other words, this XML element creates a Grid object, sets its Name to be LayoutRoot, and sets its Background to be Transparent. In addition, the grid is not simply floating within the page class; it is added as part of the collection of controls within the page.

This tiny piece of XAML creates an internal class variable, assigns to it a new instance of the Grid class, sets the grid's Background property, and adds the grid into the page's control collection. Clearly, the corresponding C# required to do this would be a lot longer. Although XAML definitely needs an investment of time to learn, its capability to create content in a concise way is second to none.

More examples of creating and configuring objects can be seen in the TextBlock definitions inside the grid. TextBlock elements are similar to WinForms Label controls in many ways, and they can be used to simply place text onto the page. The "MY APPLICATION" and "page name" text items displayed at the top of the page are both implemented using the TextBlock element.

For each of the TextBlocks defined, three attributes are specified to set the element's Text, Margin, and Style properties. The text can be set to whatever is required; the style is configured to apply the standard presentation being used by the application; margins are used to provide fine-control over the padding on each edge of the control.

░ **Note**   The Grid and StackPanel elements we have seen both provided an x:Name attribute, but as these two Textbox controls demonstrate, there is no need for elements to specify this. If such an attribute is provided, an internal variable with the specified name will be created so that the defined object can be referenced from within the page's C# code. If the name is omitted, the object will be created as normal but without this internal variable, making it impossible to directly access the created object. You should therefore set the x:Name attribute on any objects that you need to refer to in your code.

There is an alternative syntax for specifying properties of the elements created within the XAML. Instead of specifying an attribute, we can create a child element and set its name to be the name of the class whose property it is to set, followed by a period, and then the property name. The XAML shown in Listing 11-7 is functionally identical to the first TextBlock declaration from Listing 11-6. Setting properties in this way is known as the *property-element syntax*.

Listing 11-7. Setting an element property using a child element

```
<TextBlock Style="{StaticResource PhoneTextNormalStyle}" Margin="12,0">
    <TextBlock.Text>MY APPLICATION</TextBlock.Text>
</TextBlock>
```

This new syntax for setting properties is useful because we can use it to set more complex values than we can provide in a simple attribute string value. Many properties need to set other objects as their values, and we need a way to initialize those objects, too. The property-element syntax allows for those objects to be defined and have all their properties initialized in just the same way that the main elements are.

░ **Note**   Property elements, such as the TextBlock.Text attribute shown in Listing 11-7, cannot have attributes of their own. They cannot duplicate properties set by the parent element's attributes. Configuring the XAML in either of these ways will result in a compilation error.

We can see an example that uses property-element syntax to create a more complex property value in Listing 11-8. The XAML here defines a Border element within the page. This new element provides a way of drawing a rectangular border around an object inside it, and we will examine it in more detail later in the next chapter. The object it contains is stored in a property named Child. In this example, the property is given another TextBlock object. Clearly, we could not specify this child object just in an attribute string.

Listing 11-8. Setting an element property to be a complex object rather than a simple value

```
<Border BorderBrush="Yellow" BorderThickness="3">
    <Border.Child>
        <TextBlock Text="Bordered text" Margin="10" />
    </Border.Child>
</Border>
```

There are two simplifications that we can apply to the XAML in order to reduce the amount of code that is present—though they do also result in a degree of behavior that might appear to be "magic" at first glance, performing tasks that are not explicitly spelled out in the code.

First of all, each element provided by or for XAML can be defined with a ContentProperty attribute. This provides the compiler with a default property to use if a child element is specified without first specifying a property of the parent.

As an example, look again at the XAML present in Listing 11-8. The Border object's Child property is set to contain a TextBlock object by explicitly providing the Border.Child element using property-element syntax. If we take a look at the definition for the Border class inside the IDE, we will find that it is declared, as shown in Listing 11-9. The presence of the ContentProperty attribute tells us that by default, objects created for the Border will be assigned to its Child property if no explicit property assignment is made.

Listing 11-9. The declaration of the XAML Border class

```
// Summary:
//      Draws a border, background, or both around another object.
[ContentProperty("Child", true)]
public sealed class Border : FrameworkElement
{
    [...]
}
```

As a result, we can simplify the code from Listing 11-8 to that in Listing 11-10.

Listing 11-10. Setting the Border.Child property based on its ContentProperty attribute

```
<Border BorderBrush="Yellow" BorderThickness="3">
    <TextBlock Text="Bordered text" Margin="10" />
</Border>
```

This cut-down XAML can be a little harder to understand if you don't understand the way in which the objects have been configured in terms of their ContentProperty attributes. Generally, however, these are set to the most obvious and sensible property, which can result in simpler and more readable code overall.

The second simplification in the XAML is with regard to collections. If the class to which child elements are being added is a list or dictionary class (in other words, it implements one of the generic IList or IDictionary interfaces), those elements will be added to the list or dictionary if they do not specify an explicit property name. This collection behavior takes precedence over the ContentProperty attribute.

Returning to App.xaml

Before we wrap up and summarize everything we've seen about XAML, let's quickly return back to App.xaml where we started and look at the rest of the file. All the remaining content should make sense now.

After the opening of the Application XML element, the code shown in Listing 11-11 is present.

Listing 11-11. The remainder of App.xaml

```
<!--Application Resources-->
<Application.Resources>
</Application.Resources>

<Application.ApplicationLifetimeObjects>
    <!--Required object that handles lifetime events for the application-->
    <shell:PhoneApplicationService
        Launching="Application_Launching" Closing="Application_Closing"
        Activated="Application_Activated" Deactivated="Application_Deactivated"/>
</Application.ApplicationLifetimeObjects>
</Application>
```

The first element here sets the `Resources` property of the `Application` class. This contains one single default element, which we aren't using, but its presence within the markup creates a placeholder into which resources can be added later on.

The next element sets the `ApplicationLifetimeObjects` property of the `Application` class. This time, the element does contain some content, and it creates an instance of the `Microsoft.Phone.Shell.PhoneApplicationService` class. Four attributes are specified for this new object for the `Launching`, `Closing`, `Activated`, and `Deactivated` properties.

These are, of course, the application life-cycle events that were discussed for Windows Phone projects in the previous chapter. The values being provided for these attributes are the names of the event handlers within the code behind that will be used to handle the events. If you view the code behind, you will see the four event handlers. You can also access the code behind the page by right-clicking the function name inside the XAML and selecting Navigate to Event Handler.

So, as this demonstrates, event handlers can be hooked into the XAML just as if they were property values. .NET will automatically wire the event and the handler together.

The final question to answer is one that we asked earlier: Why doesn't the page designer appear for this XAML file? The reason is because the class derives from `Application`, which is not recognized by Visual Studio as a class that requires a designer. If the class were instead deriving from a designable class such as `PhoneApplicationPage` (as `MainPage.xaml` does), the designer would appear.

XAML Syntax Summary

Here is a summary of the rules that we have explored for creating XAML code:

- The root element of the XAML specifies the class from which we are inheriting.

- The `x:Class` attribute defines the .NET Namespace and class name for the class being created.

- XML namespaces define names for .NET namespaces from which classes can be retrieved.

- Elements within the XAML document specify instances of objects, the class of which is defined by the element name.

- Element objects can be made accessible as internal fields by using the `x:Name` attribute, though there is no requirement to do so if access to the object through code is not necessary.

- Element attributes set properties of the object being created.

- Property-element syntax allows nested elements to set properties of their parent by specifying `[ParentClass].[PropertyName]` as their element name.

- If no parent property is specified for content contained within a parent element, it will either be added to a list or dictionary within the parent element, or it will apply to the property specified as the parent's ContentProperty.

- Object event handlers can be set with attributes that contain the C# event handler function names.

This is not a complete list of XAML syntax rules. We have glossed over certain areas of internal complexity, but this list should be sufficient to keep moving forward into XAML page design.

Working with the Page Designer

Regardless of how dirty you want to get your hands in terms of manually crafting XAML, you will spend a lot of time working with the visual page designer displayed alongside the XAML window. Until you are comfortable crafting XAML directly, this designer is a great way to get started with adding new page elements. It can often provide a way of updating the XAML that is more efficient than manual editing.

In this section, we will look at some of the options available for using the designer.

Adding and Positioning Elements

Controls can be added to the page designer in a very similar way to how controls are added to forms using the WinForms form designer. A control can be selected from the Toolbox and then drawn on to the page. Alternatively, a control can be double-clicked in the Toolbox to add a new instance with a default size to the page.

An important thing to remember about the page is that it follows a hierarchical design, much more so than a WinForms form generally does. WinForms might place some controls inside panels or tabpanels, but the hierarchy inside a XAML page tends to be much deeper than this. For example the default MainPage provided when an empty Windows Phone project is created already contains the page itself, inside which is a Grid control that handles the separation of the headings and the main content, inside which is a further Grid handling the layout of the main page content.

When controls are added by being drawn onto the page, their container will be set based on the point at which the draw operation first begins. As the mouse cursor moves across the page design, the page designer highlights the container that is effective at each position by putting a border around it. This makes it much easier to see where the control will be added before actually creating it.

When a control is added by double-clicking it in the Toolbox, it will be added to whichever container is currently selected within the designer. If the currently selected control is not a container, it will be added to that control's container.

Figure 11-5 shows a capture of the page designer with a new Rectangle control added and currently selected within the designer for a Windows Phone page. (The designer for Windows 8 is identical—Windows Phone is used for illustration simply because its default page already contains some content to work alongside.) The Rectangle is a very simple control that is easy to see on the page, so it is handy for us to experiment with. It has had its Fill property set so that the region occupied by the rectangle is clearly visible. (It would be a good idea at this stage for you to create a blank Windows Phone App project so that you can experiment with the XAML features described in the rest of this section.)

Figure 11-5. *A Rectangle control selected within the Windows Phone page designer*

Controls can be repositioned simply by dragging them. The designer will automatically snap the control's position to match the positions of other nearby controls within the page. Controls can also be moved with finer control by selecting them and then using the cursor keys. Holding the Shift key while using the cursor keys will increase the distance the control is moved with each keypress.

Resizing controls is achieved by dragging one of the eight handles around the perimeter of the control until they reach the required dimensions. The designer will show a very handy measurement indicator alongside the control as it is resized. This indicator shows the control's new size. To force a proportional resize, hold the Shift key while resizing.

It is also possible to drag a control into a new container. If the point under the mouse cursor passes into another container as the control is dragged around, a message will appear stating that you can press the Alt key to place the control into that container, as shown in Figure 11-6. This highlights which container it will be moved into. If the Alt key is not pressed, the control's container will not be changed.

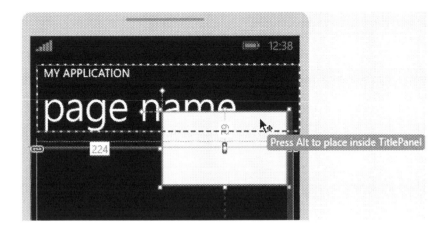

Figure 11-6. *Dragging a control over the top of another container*

░ **Tip** When you select controls within the page designer, the corresponding XAML element within the code window will be highlighted. Similarly, when you click a XAML element, the page designer will highlight the corresponding control. This can be a very useful way of understanding the relationship between the two views of the page and of quickly reaching a relevant part of the code or the page design.

The Document Outline Window

Optionally displayed alongside the page designer is a window called Document Outline. This displays a constantly updated map of the element hierarchy of the current page. This is synchronized with the page designer and the XAML view. It provides both a useful way of visualizing the structure of the elements within your page and a quick way of selecting one of the controls.

The Document Outline window is shown in Figure 11-7. If it is not open within your development environment, it can be opened from the View/Other Windows/Document Outline menu item. This window provides a simple view of the control structure similar in concept to the diagram that we used to visualize the page contents in Figure 11-4, but it is interactive and always up-to-date. Controls that have names will be listed by their names within the window. Controls that have not been named will be listed by their control type instead—for example, [TextBlock].

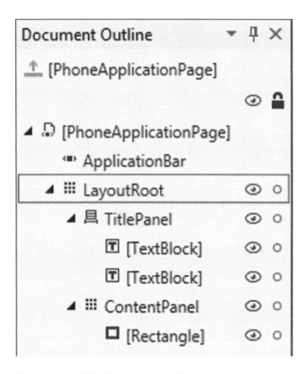

Figure 11-7. *The Document Outline window*

In addition to allowing you to visualize and navigate around the control hierarchy, there are some useful page design control functions available from the Document Outline window. Each of the controls can be hidden from the designer by clicking the *eye* icon. For container controls, this will also hide all of the controls within the container. This action only affects the design-time view of the control—it will still be displayed when the project is run.

To the right of this icon is a *lock* icon. Activating this for a control will lock its position and size so that it can no longer be manipulated in the page designer. This can be extremely useful if you have lots of controls overlapping one another: You can lock some of the controls to avoid accidentally repositioning them.

Using the Properties Window

Just as in the WinForms designer, the XAML page designer provides a Properties window inside which all available properties of the selected control can be configured. As you would expect, it also supports multiple selections of controls, allowing many property values to be updated together. It can be a great time saver compared with manually editing a series of properties in the XAML editor.

The Properties window has a number of useful enhancements compared with the WinForms designer. One of these is the capability to filter the displayed properties to just those containing a specific search string. Enter some text into the Search box above the property values, and the property list will be filtered as required, as shown in Figure 11-8.

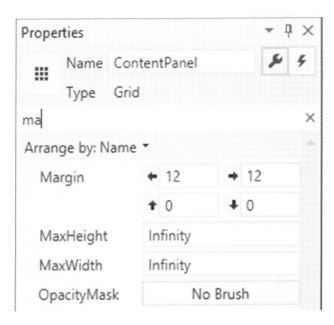

Figure 11-8. *Filtering the property list*

The control name display works a little differently than in the WinForms designer. Because controls are not required to have a name, there is no drop-down list at the top of the Properties window to allow named controls to be selected. (The Document Outline window is the closest approximation.) Instead, the control type is provided, along with the control's name if it has one, or the text `<No Name>` if it does not. The name is editable here. It can be modified, added, or removed by clicking into the name box.

While many properties require simple values to be entered (numbers, strings, and so on), many others do not and, instead, require more complex objects to be specified. The Properties window displays custom input fields for these, as appropriate, so that the required values can either be entered directly into the Properties window itself or a pop-up window can be opened for data that needs more space than the Properties window can provide. One of these editors—in this case, for the `Margin` property—can be seen in Figure 11-8.

While many of these property editors are very useful, one worthy of particular note is the color editor. This editor is used by many control properties (the `Fill` property of the `Rectangle` control, for example), and it can be seen with its editor window open in Figure 11-9.

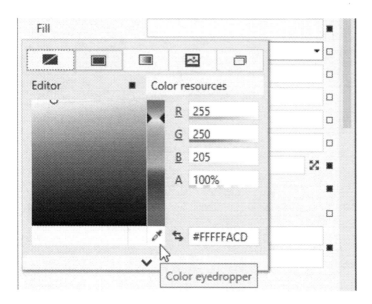

Figure 11-9. *The color picker property editor*

In addition to allowing colors to be entered by RGBA value or selected from the color patch, the property panel also allows selection using the *eyedropper*. After activating the eyedropper, any pixel on the entire screen can be clicked, and its color will be pulled into the property editor.

The color editor can also work with color gradients and images. It offers control over alpha levels so that objects can be made semitransparent. The small downward-pointing arrow at the bottom of the panel can be clicked to reveal additional advanced properties for the color selector.

Configured values can be removed from properties by clicking the square icon to the right of the property value and selecting Reset from the pop-up menu, as shown in Figure 11-10. This will remove the property value from the XAML, resetting it back to its default value. The square icon will be solid to indicate that a value has been set for that property, or hollow to indicate that no value has been set.

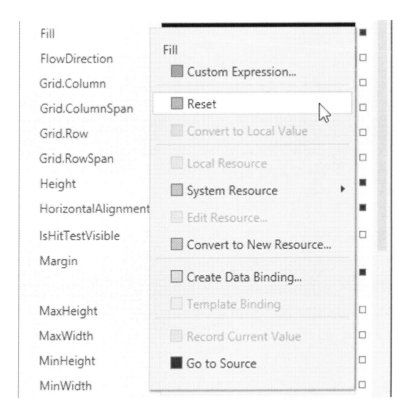

Figure 11-10. *Resetting a property to its default value*

The Properties window has another purpose, too: allowing event handlers for controls to be created. If you click the Events bottom at the top-right of the window (it has an image of a small lightning bolt displayed upon it), the Properties window will display all possible events for the selected control. To create a handler for one of the events, simply double-click its value in the list and Visual Studio will take care of the rest.

Double-clicking the blank value for the Rectangle control's Tap event (which fires each time the user taps the rectangle) will modify the Rectangle's XAML, as shown in Listing 11-12.

Listing 11-12. The Rectangle's XAML after the addition of an event handler

```
<Rectangle Fill="#FFF4F4F5" HorizontalAlignment="Left" VerticalAlignment="Top"
    Height="127" Width="222" Margin="40,50,0,0" Stroke="Black"
    Tap="Rectangle_Tap_1"/>
```

■ **Note**   The Tap event seen in Windows Phone is instead called Tapped in Windows 8. You may notice that there is quite a discrepancy between the available events across the two platforms.

Visual Studio has created a handler function for the event named Rectangle_Tap_1, and it can be found in the code behind the page. The empty handler is shown in Listing 11-13.

Listing 11-13. The Rectangle's event handler function

```
private void Rectangle_Tap_1(object sender,
                                    System.Windows.Input.MouseButtonEventArgs e)
{

}
```

▓ **Note**   If Visual Studio is adding an event handler to a control with a name, it will name the handler as
controlname_eventname (for example, `MyControl_Tap`). If the control does not have a name, it will prefix the handler
with the control's class name instead and suffix it with a unique number for that pairing of control and event type (for
example, `Rectangle_Tap_1`). It is a good idea, therefore, to name your controls if you intend to before you begin adding
event handlers in order to provide a more comprehensible set of event handler function names.

Understanding Control Alignment

As Figure 11-5 shows, solid connector lines and measurements are displayed to the top and left edges of the rectangle
in the page designer, pointing toward the inner edges of its container (which have also been highlighted). These arrows
help you to visualize the position of the control, the position of its container, and the way in which the control is *anchored*
to the container.

   Because the connector lines are shown as solid above and to the left, the control is anchored to the top and left
edges of its container. If its container moves or changes size, the rectangle will always maintain the same distance from
the top and left of its container.

   The XAML for the control is shown in Listing 11-14. Notice that among its properties are HorizontalAlignment
(set to Left) and VerticalAlignment (set to Top). These are the properties that control the anchoring of the element.

Listing 11-14. The XAML for the Rectangle control

```
<Rectangle Fill="#FFF4F4F5" HorizontalAlignment="Left" VerticalAlignment="Top"
    Height="127" Width="222" Margin="40,50,0,0" Stroke="Black"/>
```

   The position of the rectangle is not set using Left and Top coordinates, as it would be in a WinForms form, but
instead by specifying a margin between itself and its container. The margin here specifies that it should be set 40 pixels
away from its container's left edge and 50 pixels from the container's top. (The four elements within the margin represent
the left, top, right, and bottom margin sizes, respectively.) Because the control has been given an explicit Width and
Height, the right and bottom elements of the margin are ignored.

   If we modify the HorizontalAlignment so that it is set to Right, the rectangle jumps all the way across so it is
touching the right edge of its container. Now the margin's left distance is being ignored because the rectangle is no
longer left-aligned. If we increase the right element of the margin (the third element), the rectangle sets itself to be this
distance from the right edge of its container, moving back toward the left of the page. The designer now shows solid
connector lines from the rectangle to the top and right of its container, indicating that they are the edges to which it is
now anchored, as shown in Figure 11-11.

Figure 11-11. *A Rectangle right-aligned within its container*

You can see the right alignment working by resizing the Grid control inside which the rectangle is contained. This is most easily achieved by selecting the grid control and then dragging the sizing handle on its right edge, as shown in Figure 11-12. You will see that as the grid is resized, the rectangle maintains a constant distance from its right edge.

Figure 11-12. *Resizing the Rectangle's containing Grid*

Another available alignment mode is Stretch, which anchors to both sides of the container and displays solid connector lines on either side to indicate it. However, there is a sizing conflict within the control at this stage: We are specifying both a width and also a left and right margin. When the control is so configured, the width takes precedence, so the stretch mode is actually ignored. Try editing the XAML and removing the Width attribute; the control will calculate its width based on its left and right margins. Set up like this, the control does indeed stretch and shrink when its container resizes.

The final alignment value is Center. Just as with Stretch, we have another sizing conflict: If the Margin is specified, the control position cannot be automatically calculate, so, for centering to work, the margin must be removed. In this mode, both solid connector lines disappear from the rectangle to indicate that it is not anchored to either side of its container. Try setting this alignment mode and then resize the grid; the rectangle stays proportionally in the same position. (Don't forget to add back in the Width attribute if you removed it, as it is needed for this alignment mode.)

This automatic sizing is another example of how XAML's layout behaves in many ways along the same lines of that of HTML. Whereas in a WinForms project you would have to put specific design effort into making the user interface resize (using the controls' Anchor properties), in XAML this behavior is pretty much automatic and requires a minimum of design effort.

Colors and Brushes

Before we move on to look at the available XAML controls in the next chapter, let's discuss how we specify colors and brushes in XAML pages.

Color Specifications

XAML colors can be specified in several different formats. The first is via the standard set of named colors (as we have already used in XNA). An example of this approach can be seen in Listing 11-15. Any known color name can be specified for one of the XAML color properties.

Listing 11-15. Specifying a named color

```
<Rectangle Fill="Tomato" />
```

Alongside the normal list of named colors, there is also the special color value Transparent. Setting this value causes the color to become completely invisible, showing through whatever is behind.

Alternatively, colors can be specified numerically as a hexadecimal number. The number is formed with a hash character followed by three sets of two-digit hex values: The first two digits are the red intensity, the following two digits are the green intensity, and the final two digits are the blue intensity. The value #8000F0 therefore represents a color with half-intensity red (80), no green (00), and nearly full blue (F0). An example of using a color in this way is shown in Listing 11-16.

Listing 11-16. Specifying a color using hexadecimal notation

```
<Rectangle Fill="#8000F0" />
```

The hex notation can be extended to include an alpha component, too. The alpha component in XAML colors controls transparency just as it did in XNA. A control whose color is set to have full alpha will appear opaque, whereas those with their alpha value set to zero will be entirely invisible. Values in between will result in semitransparency. Transparency can be used all over the place in XAML, and it can allow for some very rich-looking graphical displays.

To specify an alpha component, add an additional two digits to the front of the hex value. If we want to specify the color in Listing 11-16 with a 25 percent alpha component, we can modify the color value to be #408000F0. If the alpha component is not included within the color specification, it is assumed to be set to its maximum value (FF).

Brushes

Although these color examples make it look like the Rectangle's Fill property is a simple color property, it is, in fact, storing a *brush* rather than a color. In XAML, a brush allows us to specify how a solid region of the screen should be filled. Filling with a single color is clearly one of the brush options available, but there are several others. Let's take a look at how all of these fit together.

SolidColorBrush

When a color is specified for a control's property without any further brush information being provided, XAML defaults to creating an instance of the SolidColorBrush class. If we were to write the code from Listing 11-15 in full instead of relying on the ContentProperty attributes, it would actually look like Listing 11-17.

Listing 11-17. Specifying a named color using the SolidColorBrush

```
<Rectangle>
    <Rectangle.Fill>
        <SolidColorBrush>
            <SolidColorBrush.Color>
                <Color>Red</Color>
            </SolidColorBrush.Color>
        </SolidColorBrush>
    </Rectangle.Fill>
</Rectangle>
```

While this code is clearly much more verbose than it needs to be, it does clarify what is actually happening within the XAML objects' properties. The Fill property of the rectangle isn't being given just a color, but rather a SolidColorBrush, and it is this brush that is receiving the color.

The Color structure is being set here using a named color, but the hex notation can be used, too. When colors are set directly into their structure, they also support a third notation, in which we set the alpha, red, green, and blue intensity levels individually as properties of the color. Listing 11-18 shows how this notation can be used to set an opaque orange color. It also omits the SolidColorBrush.Color property specification because this is the defined content property for SolidColorBrush.

Listing 11-18. Specifying a color using the Color structure's properties

```
<Rectangle>
    <Rectangle.Fill>
        <SolidColorBrush>
            <Color A="255" R="255" G="127" B="0" />
        </SolidColorBrush>
    </Rectangle.Fill>
</Rectangle>
```

LinearGradientBrush

XAML can provide more sophisticated color fills than just solid color. It has two *gradient brushes* that provide color fades within the area being filled. The first of these is the LinearGradientBrush.

The first thing that this brush needs to know is a start point and end point within the area that it is filling. Each of these points is specified as a coordinate in the range of 0 to 1 along each axis (similar to the way we specified texture coordinates in XNA). The coordinate (0, 0) is the top left of the area, while (1, 1) is the bottom right of the area.

The brush draws an imaginary line between these two points and places its first gradient fade color at the start point and the last gradient color at the end point. It then fades between these two points, extending the color out perpendicular to the imaginary line to fill the whole area.

For example, if we specify a start coordinate of (0, 0) (top left) and an end coordinate of (0, 1) (bottom left), the imaginary line will stretch down the entire left edge of the fill region. Because the line is vertical, the gradient fade will extend horizontally across the region. This fill effect is shown in Figure 11-13, which uses white as its start color and gray as its end color. The two coordinates and the imaginary line are shown to help clarify the effect, although they are not displayed by the brush itself.

Figure 11-13. *A linear gradient brush with a vertical linear path*

If the coordinates were changed to start at (0, 0) (top left) and end at (1, 0) (top right), the imaginary line would extend across the width of the area, so the gradient would fade across the area instead.

The coordinates need not be restricted to forming horizontal or vertical lines, of course. Figure 11-14 shows a linear gradient brush with coordinates (0,0) to (1,1) (top left to bottom right). The brush fades diagonally across the area of the fill.

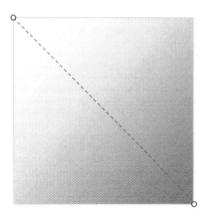

Figure 11-14. *Fading the linear gradient brush diagonally*

The XAML required to set up these gradient fades is really very simple. Listing 11-19 configures a Rectangle to use the gradient fill shown in Figure 11-14.

Listing 11-19. Specifying a diagonal linear gradient fill

```
<Rectangle>
    <Rectangle.Fill>
        <LinearGradientBrush StartPoint="0,0" EndPoint="1,1">
            <GradientStop Color="White" Offset="0" />
            <GradientStop Color="Gray" Offset="1" />
        </LinearGradientBrush>
    </Rectangle.Fill>
</Rectangle>
```

Tip If you would rather set the StartPoint and EndPoint coordinates in pixels rather than as a proportion of the fill area, you can do it by setting the LinearGradientBrush's MappingMode property to Absolute. Both coordinates will then operate as pixel offsets from the top left corner.

You will see in the XAML code that the two fade colors are specified by providing GradientStop structures and that each one also contains an Offset property as well as a color. This offset specifies the proportion across the imaginary gradient line at which this particular color should appear. Gradient fills are not limited to just two GradientStop items; we can use as many as we like, allowing more complex color fades to be achieved.

Tip You can also use the alpha component of the colors in your GradientStop items, which can result in gradients that fade between being transparent and opaque in addition to or instead of fading colors.

Listing 11-20 shows another piece of XAML, this time containing four GradientStop items. The gradient fill begins in white and fades to black 25 percent of the way along. At 50 percent, it fades to white again, finally fading to gray at the end of the line.

Listing 11-20. Multiple GradientStop items within a gradient fill

```
<Rectangle>
    <Rectangle.Fill>
        <LinearGradientBrush EndPoint="0,1" StartPoint="0,0">
            <GradientStop Color="White" Offset="0" />
            <GradientStop Color="Black" Offset="0.25" />
            <GradientStop Color="White" Offset="0.5" />
            <GradientStop Color="Gray" Offset="1" />
        </LinearGradientBrush>
    </Rectangle.Fill>
</Rectangle>
```

The end result of this fill is shown in Figure 11-15. The four gradient stop points are displayed on the left edge of the figure for illustrative purposes.

Figure 11-15. *Multiple GradientStop items within a gradient fill*

▪ **Tip** If you don't fancy creating the GradientStop items by hand, the color property editor contains comprehensive support for editing them. Stops can be easily added, colored, and positioned by moving colored sliders within the editor window. The editor can be accessed by selecting the property whose color is to be set—for example, the Fill property of the Rectangle control.

Another feature that the LinearGradientBrush can offer is the ability to place its start and end points so they do not completely cover the whole of the fill area. For example, if the start and end points were (0.333, 0) and (0.666, 0), respectively, the line would only cover the middle third of the fill area.

The brush has three different ways of handling such coordinate ranges, specified by the SpreadMethod property. If set to Pad (the default), the line will be extended in each direction until it fills the entire area. All the additional area will be filled with the color specified nearest to that end of the line. (In simple terms, the line extension at its beginning will be filled with the color at offset 0, and the extension at its end will be filled with the color at offset 1.)

If SpreadMethod is set to Repeat, it will extend the line and repeat the original color range across the extension area at both ends. If it is set to Reflect, it will repeat the original color range once again, but it will reverse it so that it mirrors the defined gradient stop colors.

These color-spread methods can provide a useful and simple way of providing more complex fills than could be practically achieved by adding large numbers of repeating gradient stop items.

Figure 11-16 shows a horizontal white-to-gray gradient fill from coordinates (0.333, 0) to (0.666, 0), using each of the different SpreadMethod modes. On the left is Pad mode, in the middle is Repeat, and on the right is Reflect.

Figure 11-16. *The three different SpreadMethod modes for the LinearGradientBrush*

With very little effort, some very pleasing effects can be obtained from this brush.

RadialGradientBrush

The second gradient brush is the RadialGradientBrush, which provides similar functionality to the LinearGradientBrush but works with gradients that radiate out from an origin point. An example of this brush is shown in Figure 11-17, fading from white at its start point to gray at its end point.

Figure 11-17. *A Rectangle filled with a RadialGradientBrush*

■ **Note**   Unfortunately the RadialGradientBrush is not supported for Windows 8 projects, only for Windows Phone 8. Hopefully, this will be revised in a future update to .NET for Windows 8.

The XAML required to achieve this fill is shown in Listing 11-21.

Listing 11-21. Filling an area with a RadialGradientBrush

```
<Rectangle>
    <Rectangle.Fill>
        <RadialGradientBrush>
            <GradientStop Color="White" Offset="0" />
            <GradientStop Color="Gray" Offset="1" />
        </RadialGradientBrush>
    </Rectangle.Fill>
</Rectangle>
```

Just like the linear brush, RadialGradientBrush allows multiple GradientStop items to be added to provide additional color points within the filled area. The Offset of each of these stops still ranges between 0 and 1, but now refers to the distance between the origin of the radial fill (with an offset of 0) and its outer edge (with an offset of 1).

The radial fill does not use start and end points as the linear fill does, but. instead, it has two similar points called Center and GradientOrigin. Center specifies a point that will be the center of the outermost circle formed by the radial fill. GradientOrigin specifies a second point that is the focal point of the fill. Both of these points are specified with values in the range of 0 to 1 on each axis, where 0 is the left or top edge, and 1 is the right or bottom edge. Once again, the MappingMode property can be set to Absolute to change them to be interpreted as pixel offsets instead.

Alongside these properties are two values that define the size of the outermost circle. RadiusX and RadiusY both default to 0.5 to specify that the circle should be the same width and height as the area it fills. They can be decreased to focus the fill more tightly or increased to allow the circular area to expand so that it is greater than the fill area. Increasing the radius will allow the gradient to extend right into the corners of the area, which would otherwise be a solid color (as can be seen in Figure 11-17).

The RadialGradientBrush also supports the SpreadMethod property that we saw in the LinearGradientBrush. Setting it to Repeat or Reflect will cause the area outside of the defined circular region to be filled using this same behavior.

ImageBrush

The final type of brush we can use for filling areas is the ImageBrush. As its name suggests, this brush fills the area with an image.

The image that you are going to use for the brush will first need to be added into your project with a Build Action of Content. Once this has been added, you can provide a path to the image relative to your project root to the ImageBrush element, as shown in Listing 11-22. In this example, an image file named Mouse.png has been placed into a project folder named Resources.

Listing 11-22. Filling an area with an ImageBrush

```
<Rectangle>
    <Rectangle.Fill>
        <ImageBrush Stretch="Fill" ImageSource="/Resources/Mouse.png"/>
    </Rectangle.Fill>
</Rectangle>
```

■ **Note** Just as in XNA, XAML's ImageBrush supports BMP, JPG, and PNG images. GIF images are not supported, and BMP images are not recommended!

By default, the selected image will appear stretched completely across the area that it is filling. There are four values available for the Stretch property that can be used to affect the size of the image within the brush.

Setting it to None will display the image at its actual size, without any stretching taking place at all. The default stretch mode is Fill, which results in the behavior you have already seen. If the aspect ratio of the area does not match that of the image, the image will be distorted. We can avoid this by using either of the remaining modes: Uniform will stretch (or shrink) the image so that it is as large as it can possibly be while still fitting entirely inside the fill area without distorting. UniformFill will entirely fill the area without distorting (possibly resulting in some of the image being clipped).

Examples of each of these modes can be seen in Figure 11-18. From left to right, the modes are None, Fill, Uniform, and UniformFill.

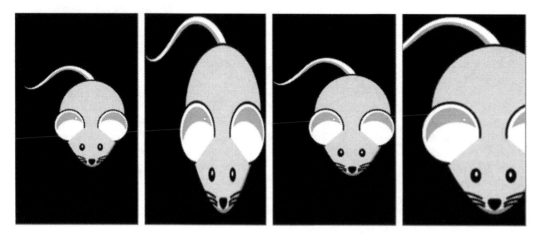

Figure 11-18. *The four ImageBrush Stretch modes*

The image can also be positioned within the fill area by setting the `AlignmentX` and `AlignmentY` properties. These properties allow the image to be aligned to the left or right, top or bottom, or remain vertically or horizontally centered as required.

Setting Colors in Code

It is very likely that you will want to set colors in C# code, too, and this can be easily accomplished. XAML's capability to hide the object structure away doesn't apply in C# code, however, so it is not possible to simply assign a color to a `Fill` property, for example. Listing 11-23 shows the code that is needed to create a new `SolidColorBrush` and put it into place inside the `Fill` property of a `Rectangle`. Of course, if the `Rectangle` were already configured with a brush at design time and we simply wanted to change its color, we could update the existing brush rather than creating a new one.

Listing 11-23. Creating a SolidColorBrush for a Rectangle's Fill property

```
MyRectangle.Fill = new SolidColorBrush(Color.FromArgb(255, 255, 127, 0));
```

The `ColorFade_Win8` and `ColorFade_WP8` example projects that accompany this chapter provide a simple demonstration of updating the gradient stops in a `LinearGradientBrush`. The design time configuration for the page puts a linear brush into the large `Rectangle` occupying the main area of the page. Each time the rectangle is tapped, it removes the existing gradient stops and adds three new ones. The first two stops will have offset 0 and 1, respectively, while the last stop will have a randomized position between the two. All the stops are given a random color.

The XAML for the `Rectangle` is shown in Listing 11-24 (taken from the Windows 8 version of the project). Note that it is the brush that has been given a name instead of the `Rectangle` in this example because we don't need to access any of the `Rectangle`'s other properties.

Listing 11-24. The Rectangle's XAML from the ColorFade example project

```
<Rectangle Tapped="Rectangle_Tapped_1">
    <Rectangle.Fill>
        <LinearGradientBrush x:Name="FadeBrush" StartPoint="0,0" EndPoint="1,1">
            <GradientStop Color="Black" Offset="0" />
            <GradientStop Color="White" Offset="1" />
        </LinearGradientBrush>
    </Rectangle.Fill>
</Rectangle>
```

The code that updates the brush is implemented in the `Rectangle_Tapped_1` event handler, shown in Listing 11-25. You can also see from this listing that the gradient stops do not need to be sorted into the order of their `Offset` values; the brush will take care of this automatically.

Listing 11-25. Randomizing the gradient stops within the LinearGradientBrush

```
private void Rectangle_Tapped_1(object sender, TappedRoutedEventArgs e)
{
    GradientStop gradStop;
    Random rand = new Random();

    // Clear the existing gradient stops
    FadeBrush.GradientStops.Clear();

    // Add a new stop with offset 0 (leading edge)
    gradStop = new GradientStop();
```

```
    gradStop.Color = Color.FromArgb(255, (byte)rand.Next(256), (byte)rand.Next(256),
                                                (byte)rand.Next(256));
    gradStop.Offset = 0;
    FadeBrush.GradientStops.Add(gradStop);

    // Add a new stop with offset 1 (trailing edge)
    gradStop = new GradientStop();
    gradStop.Color = Color.FromArgb(255, (byte)rand.Next(256), (byte)rand.Next(256),
                                                (byte)rand.Next(256));
    gradStop.Offset = 1;
    FadeBrush.GradientStops.Add(gradStop);

    // Add a new stop with a random offset
    gradStop = new GradientStop();
    gradStop.Color = Color.FromArgb(255, (byte)rand.Next(256), (byte)rand.Next(256),
                                                (byte)rand.Next(256));
    gradStop.Offset = rand.Next(100) / 100.0f;
    FadeBrush.GradientStops.Add(gradStop);
}
```

Using Brushes Together

More complex effects can be achieved by placing multiple objects together, each with different brushes. A simple (and rather garish) example of this can be seen in the MultipleGradientBrushes_Win8 and MultipleGradientBrushes_WP8 example projects, an image from which is shown in Figure 11-19.

Figure 11-19. *A Border and a TextBlock control with various brushes applied*

These example projects create a TextBlock control contained within a Border control. The Border has been filled with a linear red-white gradient background and also a linear gradient border, while the text has been given another linear gradient for its foreground color. You will find that these brushes can be used in a large variety of places throughout all the available XAML controls.

The thing that this example probably demonstrates best is that it is very easy to overuse these brushes. Used with a little more subtlety than they have been here, however, they can be a very effective way of adding interest to areas of the user interface that would otherwise be dull and unexciting.

Exploring XAML

XAML provides a rich and complex environment with many features and functions, lots of which will not be obvious the first time you encounter them or find a need to call on them. This chapter has given you a rapid tour through some of the areas of functionality that XAML has to offer. Hopefully, it has given you an understanding of the fundamentals of the page structure and XAML markup.

Please spend some time experimenting and familiarizing yourself with XAML. In the next chapter, we will turn our attention to the various controls that can be used in the XAML environment.

Summary

- XAML (eXtensible Application Markup Language) is an XML-based representation of controls within a user interface. All aspects of the controls can be set using XAML. Manual editing of the XAML is encouraged.

- In addition to the underlying XAML, Visual Studio also provides a capable page designer that can also be used for making changes to the layout of controls within a page.

- The XAML support provided for Windows 8 and Windows Phone 8 projects has evolved from the Silverlight project. It retains many features that were offered by Silverlight. The Windows 8 and Windows Phone 8 implementations are not actually part of Silverlight, however; they simply build on the same foundations.

- While there are many similarities in XAML controls across the Windows 8 and Windows Phone platforms, they are far from identical. Each platform has its own subtle differences in available features, properties, and events. Any cross-platform project that uses XAML for its user interface will need to take in account all these differences.

- The Document Outline window provides a very useful hierarchical view of the controls within a page. This window also allows specific controls to be locked or hidden from the page designer.

- Controls are arranged with a flexible alignment system, allowing them to easily adapt to changes in the size of their container controls. This helps to aid with portability of the user interface across multiple resolutions and screen sizes.

- Colors are specified using *brushes*, a number of which are available to use. Among these brushes are gradient fill brushes that allow flexible color fades to be achieved.

CHAPTER 12

■ ■ ■

XAML Controls and Pages

Now that you feel comfortable with the page design environment and with using XAML, it's time to get more familiar with the controls that are available to use in your game projects, with ways to visually transform those controls, and with ways the pages in your projects can be managed and manipulated.

The XAML Controls

Let's take a tour through some of the controls that are available for use within your XAML pages. We won't cover them all, but we will look at those that are most likely to be useful for the user interface in your games.

The controls can be broadly divided into three different groups: those that *display* information to the user, those that are *interactive* UI elements that the user can update as well as look at, and *layout* controls that help organize the presentation of the controls on the screen.

As you read through this section, please spend some time in Visual Studio and experiment with each of the controls—add and configure instances to a page in a test project. Then then run the project to see how they look and how they can be interacted with on Windows 8 and Windows Phone. Having some basic experience with using the controls will be very beneficial when it comes to using them in your games because you will already have a feel for what each one can achieve.

Display Controls

The controls that we will look at for the purposes of displaying information and content to the user are the TextBlock, Image, ProgressBar, Ellipse, Rectangle, Line, Polyline, and Polygon controls.

TextBlock Controls

One of the most frequently used controls is the TextBlock, whose responsibility is simply to display a piece of text within the page.

A number of properties are present to control the appearance and position of the text. Its font can be set using the FontFamily property. Its size can be set using the FontSize property. XAML renders vector fonts rather than using bitmaps, so specifying a larger font size does not result in additional resource data as it did with MonoGame's SpriteFont objects. As a result, all text rendered by XAML will appear sharp and focused regardless of how large it gets. These controls, therefore, represent a good way of presenting scores, status displays, and all sorts of other textual information in your game.

■ **Note** XAML pages, unlike MonoGame, render the actual underlying font to the screen rather than building a bitmap representation of the font. You should try, therefore, to select a font that will exist on the target user's device rather than one that is only available on your PC. If your selected font doesn't exist when the application executes, it will default back to a standard system font instead.

The font can also be italicized using the FontStyle property and set to be bold using the FontWeight property. Windows Phone also offers a TextDecorations property that can be set to Underline, though this property is currently missing from Windows 8.

The rendered text can be padded away from the boundaries of the TextBlock by setting the Padding property. It may be horizontally aligned using the TextAlignment property to one of Left, Center, Right, or Justify. (However, please note that the Justify option only works in Windows 8, and it will result in left-aligned text in Windows Phone.) The text can be configured to word-wrap inside the TextBlock area by setting the TextWrapping property appropriately.

What is less obvious is that the control can display much more complex text formatting than the simple Text property would suggest. The Properties window does not offer any support for it, but the TextBlock has an alternative method for setting its text: the Inlines property. This new property is, in fact, the ContentProperty for the TextBlock. Consequently, any content entered directly inside the TextBlock's element will be assigned to it.

Besides simple text, a child element named Run can be added to the text. This can be used somewhat like a span in HTML, allowing custom formatting to be applied to a section of the text. Listing 12-1 shows how this can be used in XAML to highlight a word in a different color.

Listing 12-1. Using the Inlines property in a TextBlock

```
<TextBlock Height="147" FontSize="28" FontFamily="Arial" TextWrapping="Wrap">
    This is an example of using <Run Foreground="Blue">Inlines</Run> in a
    XAML TextBlock.
</TextBlock>
```

The text-formatting properties available for the Run element are FontFamily, FontSize, FontStretch, FontStyle, FontWeight, Foreground, and (on Windows Phone only) TextDecorations; any of them can be customized for the piece of text contained within the element. Note that Run elements cannot be nested, however.

Although the TextDecoration property is missing from Windows 8, it is possible to underline text using a similar approach to the Run element. An Underline element can be added into the TextBlock content in order to mark out certain sections as being underlined. Listing 12-2 shows an example of this being used. While Underline elements cannot be placed within Run elements, it is possible to place Run elements inside Underline elements, so the effects of both can be used together. The Underline element works on Windows Phone, too, so this is an approach that can be used consistently on both platforms.

Listing 12-2. Using the Underline elements to mark out sections of underlined text

```
<TextBlock Height="147" FontSize="28" FontFamily="Arial" TextWrapping="Wrap">
    This is an example of using <Underline>underlined text</Underline> in a
    XAML TextBlock.
</TextBlock>
```

Image Controls

To display a static image within the page, use an Image control. The image to be displayed is selected using its Source property. It can be added and addressed in exactly the same way as we saw with the ImageBrush in the previous chapter.

The selected image can be stretched or shrunk using the Stretch property, which again behaves in the same way for each option as in the ImageBrush. If the displayed image is smaller than the control, it will always appear in the control's top-left corner.

ProgressBar and ProgressRing Controls

Just as in the desktop world, the ProgressBar allows us to provide the user of our application with an indication of how far through a long-running process our code has progressed. This can be useful in gaming, whether it be for initializing a level, loading resources, or downloading content from the Internet.

In Windows Phone apps, the ProgressBar is space-optimized, allowing it to occupy very little vertical space within the page, which can be particularly important as screen space is often at a premium. In Windows 8, the height of the bar can be set to any size that you wish. The bar will stretch vertically to accommodate this.

Figure 12-1. *A ProgressBar showing 25 percent completion*

The displayed progress level is set using three properties: Minimum, Maximum, and Value. The progress indication will be calculated by finding the proportion of the value between the minimum and maximum extents. By default, Minimum and Maximum have the values of 0 and 100, allowing Value to provide a percentage-based display. Figure 12-1 shows a ProgressBar using this default value range and with an actual Value setting of 25.

There is an alternative way in which the control can be used, however, which is useful if you do not know how long your task will actually take to complete. If the IsIndeterminate property is set to be true, the Minimum, Maximum, and Value properties will be ignored. Instead, a series of animated dots will appear (which will probably look very familiar to you!). These dots can be displayed while the task is running and then hidden once the task is complete.

▓ **Tip**　In the Windows Phone page designer, indeterminate ProgressBar controls are animated within the page designer at design time, too, which can be very distracting! It is, therefore, a good idea to leave IsIndeterminate set to false at design time and then switch it to true when your game is running and you are ready to display it. Additionally, an indeterminate ProgressBar can consumes processor resources even if it is invisible or off screen. You should always, therefore, make sure that IsIndeterminate is set to false at runtime, too, unless you actually need it to be displayed onscreen.

For Windows 8 applications, another alternative to the indeterminate ProgressBar is available: the ProgressRing, shown in Figure 12-2. This is another visual cue that will be familiar to all Windows 8 users as the operating system and its standard applications use this control fairly extensively.

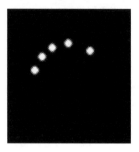

Figure 12-2. *A ProgressRing control*

ProgressRing controls are only able to operate in this indeterminate mode, They do not display an actual completeness proportion in the way that ProgressBar controls do. In order for them to begin animation, the controls' IsActive property must be set to true. Just as with indeterminate ProgressBar controls, it is a good idea to set this property back to false once the control is no longer required.

Ellipse and Rectangle Controls

As you might expect, these controls allow ellipses, circles, rectangles, and squares to be placed inside your page. They can be filled (using all the available brushes) or transparent, and they can have a border around them.

To create a circle or square, simply make sure that the ellipse or rectangle control's Width and Height are set to the same value.

The interior of the shapes are filled using their Fill property, whereas their border is controlled using a series of properties whose names all begin with Stroke. The Stroke property itself sets the color, whereas the StrokeThickness sets the border width.

The border offers up an extra feature that might be useful, however: It doesn't need to be a continuous line. One of the properties, StrokeDashArray, allows a dashed pattern to be configured for the border. This property cannot be edited via the Properties window, but it can be directly entered into the XAML. Its value should be a list of numbers (separated by spaces) that define alternating length of filled and empty areas of the border.

For example, if this were set to a value of "1 1", the border would display dashes that were 1 unit long, followed by a gap that was also 1 unit long. Setting it to "3 1" would result in dashes 3 units long and gaps 1 unit long. More complex patterns can be formed by providing a larger pattern; "1 1 3 5" would result in a 1-unit dash, a 1-unit space, a 3-unit dash, and then a 5-unit space. Fractional numbers can be provided for any of these array elements, too.

The measurement unit that the border is using is the StrokeThickness. As the value for this property increases or decreases, so, too, do the lengths of the dashes.

Listing 12-3 shows how these properties can be used to create a filled ellipse with a dashed border.

Listing 12-3. Creating a filled ellipse with a dashed border

```
<Ellipse Height="250" Width="250" Stroke="SkyBlue" StrokeThickness="15"
                                  StrokeDashArray="3 3" Fill="Gray" />
```

The resulting ellipse is shown in Figure 12-3.

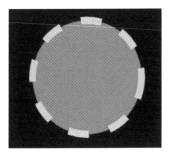

Figure 12-3. *The resulting ellipse*

Some additional options are available for the dashed border, too. The StrokeDashCap can be used to control the transition between the dashes and the empty space between. The default value for this property is Flat, but it can also be set to one of Square, Round, or Triangle. This difference can be seen in Figure 12-4, which uses the same ellipse as in Figure 12-3, but with each of the new dash cap values. Note that all these except for Flat will eat into the space allocated for the gaps. If you want to use a dash cap while also retaining equal sizes of the dashes and gaps, you will need to manipulate the StrokeDashArray to accommodate the dash caps.

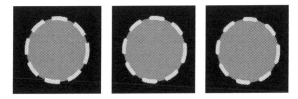

Figure 12-4. *Dashed ellipses with Square, Round, and Triangle stroke dash caps*

It is also possible to rotate the dashes around the ellipse by applying a StrokeDashOffset. This is measured in the same units as the StrokeDashArray is measured in. If the total length of the stroke dashes is 6 units, the offset will produce identical results with a value of 0 or 6, but other values in between will change the positioning of the dashes. The StrokeDashOffset could be animated within a game to provide a simple implementation of a spinning outline box or disc—useful for highlighting selected game objects, for example.

The Rectangle offers a final pair of properties that might come in very handy: RadiusX and RadiusY. They allow rounded corners to be applied to the rectangle, and the elliptical rounding area will have its width and height defined by these two properties. Figure 12-5 shows a rectangle using a value of 15 for both of the corner radius properties.

Figure 12-5. *A rectangle with rounded corners*

Line, Polyline, and Polygon Controls

While we are discussing the Ellipse and Rectangle shape controls, it seems an appropriate time to also look at three additional shape-based controls. The Line control allows a simple straight line to be drawn within a page. Polyline controls allow a series of lines to be joined together. Finally, Polygon extends this further to create a solid shape from a number of lines and optionally fill its interior.

None of these controls is available from the Toolbox; instead, they must be manually created within the XAML editor. Once the control has been declared, all its properties can be viewed and modified in the Properties window as usual.

The Line requires two coordinates to be specified, one for the start and one for the end of the line. They are specified in pixels, relative to the top-left corner of their container. They also provide all the Stroke properties that we looked at for the Ellipse and Rectangle controls, allowing the line color, thickness, dashes, and so on to be configured.

Listing 12-4 shows the XAML required to create a line from coordinate (50, 50) to (200, 200).

Listing 12-4. Creating a Line

```
<Line Stroke="SkyBlue" StrokeThickness="15" X1="50" Y1="50" X2="200" Y2="200" />
```

Lines that have sufficient thickness will, by default, appear with flat ends. They can be changed by *capping* the line ends so that they have a different shape. This is controlled by the StrokeStartLineCap and StrokeEndLineCap properties, each of which can be set to one of Flat (the default), Square, Round, or Triangle.

The next shape is the Polyline, which allows a series of coordinates to be joined together using a chain of joined lines. The coordinates this time are specified as X,Y pairs using the control's Points property. Listing 12-5 shows a Polyline that creates a zigzag shape within its container.

Listing 12-5. Creating a Polyline

```
<Polyline Stroke="SkyBlue" StrokeThickness="15"
                          Points="100,50 200,100 100,150 200,200 100,250 " />
```

Besides simply joining between the points, the Polyline can provide additional flexibility around the corner points of the rendered lines. They are controlled using the StrokeLineJoin property, which can be set to one of Miter (the corners are extended into points), Bevel (the corners are flattened), or Round (the corners are rounded). Figure 12-6 shows the Polyline defined in Listing 12-5, but with each of the available StrokeLineJoin styles applied: Miter on the left, Bevel in the middle, and Round on the right.

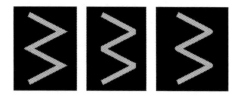

Figure 12-6. *Polylines using each of the available StrokeLineJoin properties*

Just like Lines, Polylines also allow their start and end to be capped if needed.

The final shape is the Polygon, which is configured in exactly the same way as the Polyline, but it creates an enclosed region. (The end point is automatically joined back to the start point.) It supports all the same features as the Polyline, except for the stroke start and end line caps because the Polygon doesn't have any start or end point.

What it provides instead is the ability to set its Fill property, resulting in a solid interior to the rendered shape. Any of the available brushes can be used for this purpose.

Listing 12-6 shows the XAML for a filled Polygon.

Listing 12-6. Creating a Polygon

```
<Polygon Stroke="SkyBlue" StrokeThickness="15" Fill="Gold"
                          Points="100,50 200,100 150,150 200,200 100,250 " />
```

The resulting shape is shown in Figure 12-7.

Figure 12-7. *The result of creating the filled Polygon*

Interactive Controls

The controls that we will look at for the purposes of allowing user interaction and data entry are the TextBox, ListBox, ComboBox, CheckBox, RadioButton, Button, and ApplicationBar.

TextBox Controls

XAML's TextBox control provides a field within which the user can enter text, just like the TextBox control used in WinForms projects.

When the TextBox receives focus in a running application, Windows 8 and Windows Phone will both automatically display the onscreen keyboard unless a hardware keyboard is currently available, in which case it will expect that to be used instead. If the onscreen keyboard would normally obscure the text box, the page will scroll to bring the text box back into view. Once focus is lost, the onscreen keyboard will disappear again.

Several properties are available to control the behavior of the control. Its font can be set using the same properties as for the TextBlock. The control can be locked to prevent text edits by setting the IsReadOnly property. The maximum number of characters that can be entered is controlled by the MaxLength property, defaulting to 0 for unlimited text.

The control can also support multiline text. If the AcceptsReturn property is set to True, pressing Enter on the keyboard will insert a line break. This can also be used with the TextWrapping property that will wrap text that is too long to fit on one line. In the Windows Phone page designer, you will see that the TextBox also offers properties named HorizontalScrollbar and VerticalScrollbar, which, on the earlier desktop implementation of Silverlight, allow the displays of the field's scrollbars to be controlled, but unfortunately they have no effect on Windows Phone. The properties don't exist at all for Windows 8 pages.

Useful events include GotFocus and LostFocus, KeyDown and KeyUp, and TextChanged.

ListBox Controls

ListBox controls in XAML pages are also fairly similar to their WinForms equivalent. They contain an Items collection into which any type of object can be added; the text displayed within the list will be obtained by calling the ToString method on each object. If the number of items exceeds the space available for them to be displayed, the user can scroll the items by dragging them up and down.

Additional functionality can be obtained, however, by adding ListBoxItem objects to the list instead of other objects. Each ListBoxItem offers a Content property (into which a text string can be placed or any other type of object just as if the object were being added directly to the ListBox). In addition, ListBoxItem also offers properties to allow the Background and Foreground colors to be changed, a selection of font properties, the IsEnabled property to allow individual items to be enabled or disabled, and HorizontalAlignment and Visible properties, among others. These properties allow for very flexible control over the items within the list.

ListBoxItem objects can be added to the list either by entering them manually into the XAML as the content for the list or by clicking the ellipsis button against the ListBox's Items property in the Properties window.

Listing 12-7 shows a simple ListBox with some configuration applied to a few of the items.

Listing 12-7. *Setting up a ListBox and its items*

```
<ListBox Height="300" Width="300" BorderBrush="Gray" BorderThickness="1">
    <ListBoxItem Content="Item1" />
    <ListBoxItem Content="Item2" />
    <ListBoxItem Background="Navy" Content="Item3" />
    <ListBoxItem Content="Item4" />
    <ListBoxItem Content="Item5" IsEnabled="False" />
</ListBox>
```

The resulting ListBox is shown running in a Windows Phone project in Figure 12-8.

Figure 12-8. *The resulting ListBox control*

List items need not be limited just to displaying text strings, however. Other UI elements can be placed inside the list in order to create a very rich display of information. List items can, therefore, be formed from images, text boxes, and even other list boxes! Only a single control element can be placed inside each list item, but by using a Grid or StackPanel control (both of which we'll look at shortly), it is possible to nest multiple controls inside. By crafting your UI carefully, you can create all sorts of ListBox display configurations such as those used to display messages in the Windows Phone e-mail application.

It is also possible to select multiple items within a ListBox. This feature can be activated by setting the SelectionMode property to Multiple. Once this has been done, tapping an item will toggle its selected state rather than deselecting the other items.

To track changes to the ListBox selection in your code, add a handler for the SelectionChanged event. Your event handler can use the ListBox's SelectedItem, SelectedItems (for multiselection), and SelectedIndex properties to query the items that are selected, but it can also use the handy AddedItems and RemovedItems collections provided by the event's SelectionChangedEventArgs property. This will contain the details of all items that were added to or removed from the SelectedItems collection as part of that event.

ComboBox Controls

If you are looking through the available controls in the Windows Phone Toolbox, you might have noticed the conspicuous absence of one of the most useful controls: the ComboBox control. Unfortunately, this control is not supported for Windows Phone. The control does exist and can be manually added to the XAML, but it is broken and does not work at all.

If you need a ComboBox control for Windows Phone, it is worth investigating the *Windows Phone Toolkit*, an open source project that adds a number of high quality controls to the Windows Phone Toolbox. The controls include one named ListPicker, which provides functionality that is equivalent to a ComboBox. Take a look at http://phone.codeplex.com if you wish to find out more about the toolkit.

In Windows 8, however, the ComboBox is supported and works very well. It is set up along the exact same lines as the ListBox, except that instead of adding ListBoxItems, you should add ComboBoxItems to its Items collection. Once again, these item objects can be given a simple text value for their Content, or other UI elements can be used.

Listing 12-8 shows a simple ComboBox containing several items.

Listing 12-8. Setting up a ComboBox and its items

```
<ComboBox Width="200" Height="40">
    <ComboBoxItem Content="Easy" />
    <ComboBoxItem Content="Medium" IsSelected="True" />
    <ComboBoxItem Content="Hard" />
</ComboBox>
```

The ComboBox created from this XAML can be seen in Figure 12-9. The image on the left shows the combo in its closed state; on the right, it is dropped open.

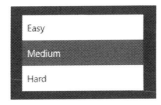

Figure 12-9. *The resulting ComboBox control in a Windows 8 project*

Useful events for the ComboBox include the DropDownClosed and DropDownOpen events as well as the SelectionChanged event. This latter event offers the AddedItems and RemovedItems collections just as they are provided to the ListBox, but because there is no multiselection option in the ComboBox, these collections will always simply identify the previously selected item (if there was one) and the newly selected item. The ComboBox's SelectedItem and SelectedIndex properties are also available for interrogating the selection within the control.

CheckBox Controls

A simple but useful control, the CheckBox allows simple boolean values to be gathered from the user. When the control's value is true, it displays a check mark within the control; when it is false, the box is shown empty.

The caption displayed next to the CheckBox is part of the control itself rather than its being implemented as a separate control. As a result, tapping on either the actual displayed box or its caption will cause the state of the box to be toggled.

The caption is provided using the CheckBox control's Content property. It is not limited to being just a simple string—other controls can be placed into the content to provide additional formatting options.

The control offers a few useful properties that we might want to use. Among them are the IsChecked property, which allows the initial state of the CheckBox to be set (and which can, of course, also be set or queried in code to update or read the state of the control).

Another potentially useful property is the IsThreeState property. When this property is set to true, the CheckBox will cycle through three different states when it is used: checked, unchecked, and indeterminate. This final state can be used when the CheckBox is at an unknown state or when its value cannot currently be represented as a simple boolean value. When the control's value is indeterminate, the IsChecked property in code will return null. To set this in XAML, the special value {x:Null} must be provided for the property (though this can be picked from the Properties window).

Listing 12-9 shows the XAML for three CheckBox controls, each with a different initial state.

Listing 12-9. Several CheckBox controls

```
<CheckBox Height="70" Width="215" Margin="50,100" VerticalAlignment="Top"
          Content="Unchecked" />
<CheckBox Height="70" Width="215" Margin="50,160" VerticalAlignment="Top"
          Content="Checked" IsChecked="True" />
<CheckBox Height="70" Width="215" Margin="50,220" VerticalAlignment="Top"
          Content="Indeterminate" IsThreeState="True" IsChecked="{x:Null}" />
```

The resulting controls are shown in Figure 12-10.

Figure 12-10. *The resulting CheckBox controls*

The CheckBox offers two different ways of responding to its state changing. The first is to add a handler for its Click event that will fire every time the control is tapped by the user. This allows the IsChecked property to be queried to determine the control's new value.

Alternatively, you might add handlers to any or all of the Checked, Unchecked, or Indeterminate events. These handlers will fire when the CheckBox is updated to the corresponding state.

■ **Note**　A useful feature of the Checked, Unchecked, and Indeterminate events is that they fire when the page first loads, allowing for any initial processing that is required based on the CheckBox state to be performed. The Click event only fires when the user actually interacts with the control.

RadioButton Controls

RadioButton controls offer similar functionality to the CheckBox, except that they are formed into mutually exclusive groups from which only a single RadioButton at a time can be selected. The properties and events used by the RadioButton are virtually identical to those of the CheckBox.

An additional property, called GroupName, is available. It is not set by default, and leaving it in this state will result in the radio buttons being set as a group according to the container that they are placed in (only one of the radio buttons in the container can be selected). In many cases, this will be the desirable behavior. However, if you want to have radio buttons that span across multiple containers or if you want to create separate groups of radio buttons within the same container, set the GroupName to a consistent value for all the controls within each group.

Button Controls

The last of the interactive controls that we will look at in this section is also one of the simplest. Button controls simply display some content within a rectangular frame on the screen and respond to being clicked by raising their Click event.

The Button's text is specified within its Content property, but, once again, the property is not limited only to strings. Other UI elements can be placed within the button to facilitate buttons with images or other content.

In Windows 8 projects, however, a large number of standard button icons are available that can be easily applied to any of your buttons. These icons all use imagery from the Segoe UI Symbol font, which is used throughout Windows. You will have seen many of the icons in Windows itself and its standard applications. Their primary purpose is for being placed on an *application bar* control (which we will look at in the Layout Controls section next), but they can be placed anywhere within your application where they are needed.

If you wish to use one of these icons on a button, you use the button's Style property to identify which icon to use, as shown in Listing 12-10, which displays a "refresh" button.

Listing 12-10. Using button styles to display a refresh button.

```
<Button Style="{StaticResource RefreshAppBarButtonStyle}"
                         HorizontalAlignment="Left" VerticalAlignment="Top" />
```

The button that results from this is shown in Figure 12-11.

Figure 12-11. *The resulting Button control*

However, if you try adding this XAML into a test project, you will find that Visual Studio displays a warning message against the Style attribute in the XAML markup, "The resource "RefreshAppBarButtonStyle" could not be resolved." This is because, by default, all of these button styles are commented out within your initial project. The reason for this is because there are hundreds of them. Including them all would increase the compilation time and the size of the resulting executable unnecessarily. Instead, you will need to uncomment them one-by-one as you need them.

The definition of the styles can be found in the Common/StandardStyles.xaml file within your project. If you search for RefreshAppBarButtonStyle within this file, you will find the commented Style element that defines it. To uncomment it, place the XML "end comment" sequence --> on the line prior to the required element. Then the "begin comment" sequence `<!--` on the line following the element. The single Style element should now be part of the source code again. A fragment of the StandardStyles.xaml XML with the RefreshAppBarButtonStyle uncommented is shown in Listing 12-11. Note the comment sequences around this element.

Listing 12-11. Uncommenting the RefreshAppBarButtonStyle Style element

```
[...]
<Style x:Key="VideoAppBarButtonStyle" TargetType="ButtonBase"
                                      BasedOn="{StaticResource AppBarButtonStyle}">
    <Setter Property="AutomationProperties.AutomationId" Value="VideoAppBarButton"/>
    <Setter Property="AutomationProperties.Name" Value="Video"/>
    <Setter Property="Content" Value="&#xE116;"/>
</Style>
-->
<Style x:Key="RefreshAppBarButtonStyle" TargetType="ButtonBase"
                                        BasedOn="{StaticResource AppBarButtonStyle}">
    <Setter Property="AutomationProperties.AutomationId" Value="RefreshAppBarButton"/>
    <Setter Property="AutomationProperties.Name" Value="Refresh"/>
    <Setter Property="Content" Value="&#xE117;"/>
</Style>
<!--
<Style x:Key="DownloadAppBarButtonStyle" TargetType="ButtonBase"
                                         BasedOn="{StaticResource AppBarButtonStyle}">
    <Setter Property="AutomationProperties.AutomationId" Value="DownloadAppBarButton"/>
    <Setter Property="AutomationProperties.Name" Value="Download"/>
    <Setter Property="Content" Value="&#xE118;"/>
</Style>
[...]
```

There are many hundreds of available symbols, many of which are not actually included within the StandardStyles.xaml document at all. To help locate those that may be of use, I have created a Segoe UI Symbol Reference page on my web site. Visit http://tinyurl.com/segoesymbol to see the full list of symbols that are available for use.

If you wish to use a symbol from the table that doesn't have an entry in StandardStyles.xaml, you have two options available. The first is to create your own new element within StandardStyles.xaml, which references the symbol that you wish to use. For example, to use the pizza symbol with code 🍕, you might add the code shown in Listing 12-12.

Listing 12-12. Adding new button styles to StandardStyles.xaml

```
<Style x:Key="PizzaAppBarButtonStyle" TargetType="ButtonBase"
                                      BasedOn="{StaticResource AppBarButtonStyle}">
    <Setter Property="AutomationProperties.AutomationId" Value="PizzaAppBarButton"/>
    <Setter Property="AutomationProperties.Name" Value="Pizza"/>
    <Setter Property="Content" Value="&#x1f355;"/>
</Style>
```

Once this has been added, the button can be created in your page with the XAML shown in Listing 12-10, only with RefreshAppBarButtonStyle replaced with PizzaAppBarButtonStyle.

Alternatively, you can leave StandardStyles.xaml alone and reference the button icon and caption directly from within the button itself. This is achieved as shown in Listing 12-13.

Listing 12-13. Specifying Segoe UI Symbol details within a button's XAML

```
<Button Style="{StaticResource AppBarButtonStyle}" Content="&#x1f355;"
                AutomationProperties.Name="Pizza"
                HorizontalAlignment="Left" VerticalAlignment="Top" />
```

Layout Controls

Along with the controls we have seen for the presentation of content and user interaction, a final set of controls exists whose purpose is to facilitate the flexible and predictable layout of control elements on each page. In this section, we will explore some of these controls, covering the Grid, StackPanel, ScrollViewer, Border, Canvas, and ApplicationBar controls.

Grid Controls

One of the most flexible layout controls is the Grid control. This control can seem somewhat puzzling to developers who first encounter it after having worked with grid controls in WinForms development. It is puzzling because developers expect that it will offer functionality along the lines of a data grid, presenting tables of data to the user. That is not the Grid's purpose, however. Instead, it is used to allow the organization of other controls into consistent rows or columns.

A reasonable approximation of the Grid is perhaps the HTML table element, which also defines a layout of rows and columns, and allows content to be placed within them. Just like HTML tables, Grids allow row and column sizes to be set, arbitrary content to appear within each cell, and their content to span across multiple rows or columns.

For an example of a useful application for a grid, imagine that we are creating a Settings page for a game that we are writing. The page can be divided into two columns. For each setting, the first column will contain a TextBlock providing the name of the setting, while the second column will contain a control allowing the value of the setting to be entered or modified. With the columns configured in this way, we can then add as many rows as we need to accommodate each of the available settings.

When a Grid control is first added to the page, it is completely empty and does not define any rows or columns. This empty configuration results in a default row and a default column, providing a single empty cell ready for use. In order to turn the control into an actual grid, we need to tell it how many rows and how many columns we want it to display.

There are two ways to achieve this. The first is through the page designer. If you hover the mouse cursor over the top or left edge of a selected Grid control, you will see that it displays a split point at the cursor position. Clicking the left mouse button will create a new column or row boundary at that position. This process can be repeated for each of the rows and columns that are required, as shown in Figure 12-12.

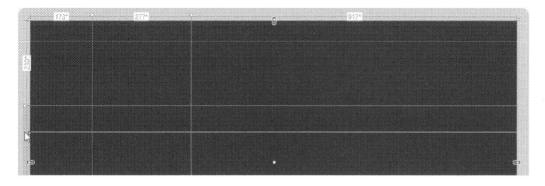

Figure 12-12. *Inserting rows and columns into a Grid control*

The second approach is to create the rows and columns within the XAML. When configuring the grid in this way, we do not necessarily need to specify the size of each of the rows or columns. Instead, we can simply state that there is a row or column and let the page automatically manage the size based on the content that we subsequently provide. This is a great way of dealing with multiple resolutions that the page may need to operate within.

Listing 12-14 shows a Grid defined in XAML with two columns and three rows, with no sizes specified at all.

Listing 12-14. Declaring rows and columns for a Grid in XAML

```
<Grid Name="grid1">
    <Grid.ColumnDefinitions>
        <ColumnDefinition />
        <ColumnDefinition />
    </Grid.ColumnDefinitions>
    <Grid.RowDefinitions>
        <RowDefinition />
        <RowDefinition />
        <RowDefinition />
    </Grid.RowDefinitions>
</Grid>
```

If you declare a grid in this way and then select it in the designer preview, you will see that the row and column headings, which were showing the row or column size in pixels in Figure 12-12, display something that might be unexpected. All the sizes are now displayed as 1* instead of a pixel width. Alongside this displayed value, the rows and columns are evenly distributed across the height and width of the grid.

The reason for this behavior is that we actually have a variety of methods for specifying the sizes of rows and columns:

- *Fixed size*: We specify a size in pixels. The grid uses exactly this size for the row or column.

- *Weighted size*: We specify a proportion of the grid by weighting each column. The grid uses these weights to determine proportional sizes within the overall grid size.

- *Automatic size*: The row or column size will be set to match the largest item that it contains. If there is nothing contained within the row or column at all, it will collapse to have a size of 0.

Fixed-size rows and columns are declared by just giving them a numerical size value. Weighted sizes are specified by providing a numerical weight value followed by an asterisk. The size will be calculated by comparing the weight of each row or column to the total weights of all the rows or columns. For example, if two columns are present with widths of 2* and 1*, the first column will occupy two-thirds of the width, and the second column will occupy the remaining one-third. A weight of 1 can be specified just by using an asterisk character without a numeric prefix. Automatic sizes are specified by providing the keyword Auto as the size.

The grid defined by the code in Listing 12-15 uses all three of these sizing methods for the three columns that it declares.

Listing 12-15. Declaring rows and columns for a Grid in XAML

```
<Grid Name="grid1">
    <Grid.RowDefinitions>
        <RowDefinition Height="50" />
        <RowDefinition Height="2*" />
        <RowDefinition Height="Auto" />
    </Grid.RowDefinitions>
</Grid>
```

Although the page designer clearly shows the lines that separate the grid cells, they are only there as a guide. When the application runs, the grid lines are completely invisible.

So, once we have defined the structure for the grid, how \ do we tell the page which cell to use for each of the controls that we want to place inside the grid? There are two ways to do this.

The first way is to add the new control by selecting a control in the Toolbox and drawing it into the page designer. The control will be added to whichever cell the mouse cursor paints it within.

The second way is to add the control directly via the XAML editor. Controls added in this way should be placed inside the Grid element, but not inside the RowDefinitions or ColumnDefinitions elements. The target cell is then specified by setting a property of the grid as part of the new control's declaration, using the Grid.Row and Grid.Column properties to identify the cell that the control is to occupy. For example, the code in Listing 12-16 places a Button into the third row and the second column of the grid. (Note that the Row and Column properties are zero-based, so these are actually specified as row 2 and column 1.) If either the grid row or column is unspecified, it will be assumed to be the grid's first row or column.

Listing 12-16. Specifying the target Grid cell for a TextBlock

```
<Grid Name="grid1">
    <Grid.ColumnDefinitions>
        <ColumnDefinition />
        <ColumnDefinition />
    </Grid.ColumnDefinitions>
    <Grid.RowDefinitions>
        <RowDefinition />
        <RowDefinition />
        <RowDefinition />
    </Grid.RowDefinitions>
    <Button Content="Button" Grid.Row="2" Grid.Column="1" />
</Grid>
```

The resulting output from this XAML is shown in Figure 12-13.

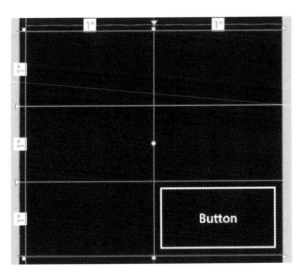

Figure 12-13. *The Button in the page designer, positioned in row 2, column 1*

To span content across multiple rows or columns, the contained control should set the grid's RowSpan and/or ColumnSpan properties. These properties should indicate how many rows or columns should be included in the space (and both default to 1 if not specified).

We can modify the button in the previous listing to span across the second and third rows by changing the XAML, as shown in Listing 12-17.

Listing 12-17. Spanning a contained control across multiple grid rows

```
<Grid Name="grid1" Margin="0,0,0,333" ShowGridLines="True">
    <Grid.ColumnDefinitions>
        <ColumnDefinition />
        <ColumnDefinition />
    </Grid.ColumnDefinitions>
    <Grid.RowDefinitions>
        <RowDefinition />
        <RowDefinition />
        <RowDefinition />
    </Grid.RowDefinitions>
    <Button Content="Button" Grid.Column="1" Grid.Row="1" Grid.RowSpan="2" />
</Grid>
```

The resulting layout from this listing is shown in Figure 12-14.

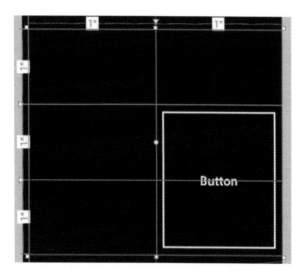

Figure 12-14. The Button in the page designer, spanned across rows 1 and 2

Using the Grid control, you can get a high degree of control over the placement of controls within your page. Another use for the Grid control is to provide a host for complex layouts inside locations that do not directly permit them. For example, inside the ListBoxItem elements that we looked at earlier, we saw that only a single UI element can be placed as the content for each list item. If we were to make that single UI element a Grid, however, we could then place as many controls inside that Grid as we wanted.

StackPanel Controls

While Grid controls provide an open and flexible container inside which controls can be placed in virtually any way required, StackPanel controls take a different approach to organizing their contained controls. Instead of allowing controls to be placed in arbitrary arrangements, they allow an ordered series of controls to be arranged in a single row or column. If a control is added to the middle of this list of controls, all subsequent controls will be pushed out of the way to make space. If a stacked control's visibility is toggled or its size is changed, all the subsequent controls will be pushed or pulled around to fill the available space.

This control can be useful for creating pages or areas that consist of repeating items placed either one above or next to each other. Another useful example is for placement within a ListBoxItem object. If you want to have images displayed as part of each list item, or if you need each item to have an associated check box, you can create a horizontally orientated StackPanel as the Content for each list item and place the Image, CheckBox, and TextBlock controls inside to facilitate the required functionality.

As always, you can add controls to the StackPanel either by drawing them from the Toolbox or by adding them directly in the XAML editor. If you use the Toolbox, the page designer will always add the control at the end of the current control stack, but the controls can be subsequently reordered by simply dragging them into the sequence required.

Alternatively, controls can be added directly to the XAML code. The order in which the controls are present in the XAML dictates the order in which they will be stacked within the panel.

Listing 12-18 shows a simple example of a StackPanel control containing a number of Button elements. Note that the buttons have been given a width and height, but no position data is provided at all. The position is automatically determined by the StackPanel.

Listing 12-18. Stacking multiple buttons within a StackPanel control

```
<StackPanel>
    <Button Content="Button1" Height="80" Width="200"/>
    <Button Content="Button2" Height="80" Width="200"/>
    <Button Content="Button3" Height="80" Width="200"/>
    <Button Content="Button4" Height="80" Width="200"/>
</StackPanel>
```

The resulting layout for this example is shown in Figure 12-15.

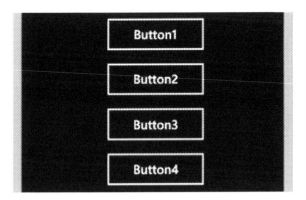

Figure 12-15. *The results of adding Buttons to a StackPanel*

The only significant new property offered by the StackPanel is its Orientation. When set to its default value of Vertical, the controls will be stacked one above another. If the value is changed to Horizontal, the controls will stack from left to right instead.

Canvas Controls

The next layout control that we will look at is the Canvas control. The purpose of this container control is to allow objects placed within it to be positioned absolutely using a simple (x, y) coordinate system. Whereas the other containers we have looked at have taken control alignment and margins into consideration, all controls placed within a Canvas need to know is where they are positioned relative to the top-left corner of the Canvas itself.

Just as controls placed into a Grid can set the Grid.Row and Grid.Column properties as part of their own element declaration, so controls placed into a Canvas can set their Canvas.Left and Canvas.Top properties to specify their positions. They will then appear at exactly the requested location, sized per their own Width and Height properties.

One detail to be aware of with the Canvas control is that, unlike other container controls, objects that do not properly fit into the Canvas will "overflow" outside of the Canvas area. The control acts like this for performance reasons. Because this control is frequently used to contain animated and moving objects, it is quicker for it to simply render all its content rather than have to clip them into its own area.

If this should present an issue, you can work around it by using the Canvas control's Clip property. By applying a rectangular clipping area that exactly matches the size of the Canvas, anything that falls outside of that area will be clipped and obscured from view. Listing 12-19 shows an example. The Canvas contains a Rectangle control that is partly outside of its own area. The Canvas.Clip property is set to prevent the overflowing parts of the Rectangle from being displayed.

Listing 12-19. Clipping the contents of a Canvas

```
<Canvas Width="300" Height="200" Background="LightGray">
    <Canvas.Clip>
        <RectangleGeometry Rect="0 0 300 200" />
    </Canvas.Clip>
    <Rectangle Canvas.Left="250" Canvas.Top="150" Height="100" Width="100"
                                                    Fill="DarkGray" />
</Canvas>
```

Figure 12-16 shows the results both without the clipping region on the left and with it on the right. In both cases, the Canvas itself is shown with a light-gray background, and the rectangle is shown with a dark-gray background.

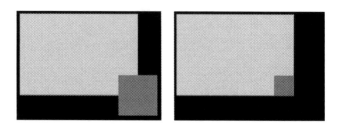

Figure 12-16. *A Canvas control with no clipping on the left and with clipping on the right*

ScrollViewer Controls

ListBox controls provide a very useful way of scrolling up and down through a list of items. Sometimes, you will want a layout that is more flexible than the ListBox, but that is still too large to display all at once and requires the ability to scroll. None of the container controls that we have seen so far has any scrolling capability at all because it is provided instead by the ScrollViewer control.

The ScrollViewer control will take into account the size of the control that is placed inside it. If this content is larger than the ScrollViewer, automatic scrolling facilities will be made available to allow the user to access the parts of the contained control that would otherwise be out of view. Only a single control can be directly contained within a

ScrollViewer, but by using a Grid, StackPanel, or Canvas as that control, we can then place additional child controls indirectly into the ScrollViewer, too.

The ScrollViewer_Win8 and ScrollViewer_WP8 projects that accompany this chapter show an example of this control in action. The ScrollViewer contains a StackPanel whose Width and Height have both been set to Auto so that they automatically expand to match the sizes of the controls contained within. A TextBlock and eight Button controls have then been placed into the StackPanel, causing it to grow much larger than the ScrollViewer that contains it.

When the project is launched, the first few buttons are visible because they fit within the area defined for the ScrollViewer. The remaining buttons are still accessible, however, by scrolling or dragging the area inside the ScrollViewer. On touch-screen devices, it is actually very tolerant of where we initiate the drag. Even if you start dragging within one of the buttons, it will still understand the gesture and begin scrolling its contents.

■ **Note** When running on a non-touch-screen device with a mouse, the only mechanisms for scrolling are to use the scrollbar that appears on the right edge of the ScrollViewer, or the mouse wheel. Dragging the contents by holding the left mouse button and moving the mouse is not supported.

Figure 12-17 shows the ScrollViewer project running in Windows 8 with its StackPanel partly scrolled. The image on the left shows the project on a touch-screen tablet device. Note how the thin scrollbar on the right of the control indicates the position through the overall extent of the StackPanel. The image on the right shows the same project running on a desktop PC with no touch screen. The control now includes a full scrollbar suitable for use with the mouse.

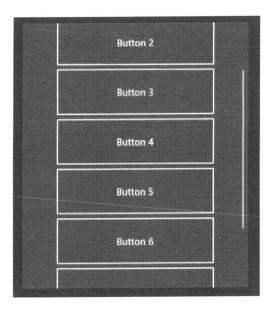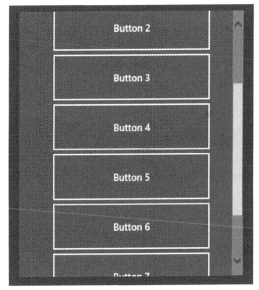

Figure 12-17. *Scrolling through the contents of a ScrollViewer on a touch screen and a desktop PC*

The ScrollViewer can be controlled using its HorizontalScrollMode and VerticalScrollMode properties. Each of these can be set to Disabled, Enabled, or Auto. By default, they are both set to Enabled.

Setting one of these properties to Auto or Enabled will enable scrolling in that particular direction (in the case of Auto, only if there is sufficient content to require scrolling). If the property is set to Disabled, scrolling in that direction will be switched off, even if the content is large enough to allow scrolling.

Border Controls

The next control that we will look at is a simple one. Many of the other controls we have seen support a background color or a border, but these properties are not supported in all instances. The TextBlock, for example, offers neither of these properties. Any time we find a need for a background or border but the control we need to use does not provide for this, we can place that control into a Border.

Border controls allow a single child control to be placed inside them and can then set a background color behind it and a border around it.

The border thickness can be set independently for each of its four edges. The BorderThickness property can be given a single number (which it will use for all edges), two numbers (the first will apply to the left and right edge; the second applies to the top and bottom), or four numbers (for the left, top, right, and bottom edges), separated by spaces or commas.

The control can also display rounded corners using the CornerRadius property.

While the Border can be defined with a Width and Height if you want, it is also possible to omit both of these properties from its definition. When the control is configured in this way, it will exactly match itself to the control that is contained within it. The Padding property also then comes in useful, as it allows you to specify a padding width between the border and the control within it. Padding values can be specified in exactly the same way as for the BorderThickness property.

Windows 8 AppBar Controls

Both Windows 8 and Windows Phone offer "application bar" controls that are used to display command options for use within an application. These are similar in concept across the two platforms, but they are different in the way that they operate and the way that they are constructed. We'll look at the Windows 8 version first.

The Windows 8 version of the control is called an AppBar control. You will no doubt have seen these scattered liberally throughout all of the inbuilt Windows 8 apps. An example of a page using AppBar controls can also be found in the AppBar_Win8 project accompanying this chapter.

AppBar controls can be configured to contain any content that you wish, but their most common use is to display a series of Button controls, each of which is styled as per the example in Listing 12-10 and Figure 12-11. By default, the AppBar is normally hidden, and it is revealed on a touch screen by swiping from the top or bottom edge of the screen, or on non-touch systems by clicking the right mouse button.

Each page can support a maximum of two AppBars, one at the top of the screen and one at the bottom, though you can choose to use just one or other of these if you wish (or indeed, none at all). The bars are set into the page by setting the Page.TopAppBar and/or the Page.BottomAppBar property as needed.

Like many other controls we have seen, the AppBar can only contain a single child control. The easiest way to display a series of buttons is, therefore, to insert a StackPanel control, set it to stack horizontally, and then add the buttons into the stack.

Listing 12-20 shows the top AppBar from the example project, which has been set up to contain a StackPanel and four simple buttons. In addition to the construction of the AppBar's content, its Background property has been set to a color that includes an alpha component. Making it semitransparent in this way allows the page content behind to show through the bar itself, which can be an attractive effect in many environments.

Listing 12-20. The XAML definition for an AppBar at the top of a page

```
<Page.TopAppBar>
    <AppBar x:Name="appbarTop" Background="#f08888ff">
        <StackPanel Orientation="Horizontal">
            <Button Style="{StaticResource RefreshAppBarButtonStyle}" />
            <Button Style="{StaticResource DownloadAppBarButtonStyle}" />
            <Button Style="{StaticResource MailAppBarButtonStyle}" />
            <Button Style="{StaticResource SearchAppBarButtonStyle}" />
```

```
        </StackPanel>
    </AppBar>
</Page.TopAppBar>
```

The result of this AppBar definition is shown in Figure 12-18.

Figure 12-18. *The resulting AppBar, as used at the top of the page in the example project*

Another common configuration for an AppBar is to split the controls into two sections, one on the left and one on the right. The standard use for this approach is to place "global" commands on the right, while "contextual" commands (which will therefore generally change as the user moves around the application) on the left. In practice, you may find that the split AppBar approach lends itself to other configurations, too, so experiment with whatever works best.

Various approaches can be used to implement a split application bar, but generally the approach is to place a Grid into the AppBar and then place two StackPanel controls into the Grid, one of which is right-aligned. Listing 12-21 shows the split application bar from the example project. The resulting bar itself can be seen in Figure 12-19.

Listing 12-21. The XAML definition for a split AppBar at the bottom of a page

```
<Page.BottomAppBar>
    <AppBar x:Name="appbarBottom" Background="#80CCCCCC">
        <Grid>
            <StackPanel Orientation="Horizontal">
                <Button Style="{StaticResource CropAppBarButtonStyle}" />
                <Button Style="{StaticResource RotateCameraAppBarButtonStyle}" />
            </StackPanel>
            <StackPanel Orientation="Horizontal" HorizontalAlignment="Right">
                <Button Style="{StaticResource ClosePaneAppBarButtonStyle}" />
                <Button Style="{StaticResource OpenPaneAppBarButtonStyle}" />
            </StackPanel>
        </Grid>
    </AppBar>
</Page.BottomAppBar>
```

Figure 12-19. *The resulting split AppBar, as used at the bottom of the page in the example project*

It is easy to programmatically open and close an AppBar. This is achieved by setting its IsOpen property as needed. The same property can be used to determine whether or not an application bar is currently open.

Generally, the application bar is expected to close when the user either clicks or taps somewhere else within the screen, or when one of the buttons within the bar is clicked. The former behavior happens automatically, but you will need to programmatically close the bar when a button is clicked. In the example project, the Refresh button in the top application bar is set to close both of the bars when it is clicked.

Sometimes you may wish to have an application bar displayed all of the time. You can prevent the automatic closure of the bar by setting its IsSticky property to true. This doesn't prevent the user closing it by right-clicking or swiping, but it does result in the bar staying open when the user clicks or taps elsewhere within the page.

Finally, the AppBar offers a number of useful events, including the Closed and Opened events, which fire as the bar closes and opens, allowing you to respond if you need to.

Windows Phone ApplicationBar Controls

The Windows Phone version of the application bar is named ApplicationBar. This is the control responsible for displaying the small toolbars that are often seen at the bottom of the screen. It can hold up to a maximum of four image-based application buttons and also a number of menu items. (However, try not to use too many; otherwise, this quickly becomes unwieldy.) The structure of the control is much more rigid than the Windows 8 AppBar, and no further configuration of the content is available. Additionally, it is normal for the Windows Phone ApplicationBar to remain visible at all times rather than being opened and closed as on Windows 8.

An example project named ApplicationBar_WP8 can be found in the download accompanying this chapter. It can be used for experimenting with the ApplicationBar, its buttons, and its menus.

The ApplicationBar is not added to the page from the Toolbox, but manually within the page XAML. To add an ApplicationBar, we need to set the PhoneApplicationPage.ApplicationBar property to a new instance of the ApplicationBar class.

This can be achieved using code along the lines of that shown in Listing 12-22. This should be added to the XAML at the very end of the code, just before the closure of the root phone:PhoneApplicationPage element.

Listing 12-22. A template for an ApplicationBar

```
<phone:PhoneApplicationPage.ApplicationBar>
    <shell:ApplicationBar>
        <shell:ApplicationBarIconButton IconUri="/Images/AppBarButton1.png" Text="Button 1"/>
        <shell:ApplicationBarIconButton IconUri="/Images/AppBarButton2.png" Text="Button 2"/>
        <shell:ApplicationBar.MenuItems>
            <shell:ApplicationBarMenuItem Text="MenuItem 1"/>
            <shell:ApplicationBarMenuItem Text="MenuItem 2"/>
        </shell:ApplicationBar.MenuItems>
    </shell:ApplicationBar>
</phone:PhoneApplicationPage.ApplicationBar>
```

This code produces an ApplicationBar that in its default closed state looks like the one shown in Figure 12-20.

Figure 12-20. *The ApplicationBar in its default closed state*

Tapping the ellipsis button on the right edge of the `ApplicationBar` will cause it to open, revealing the text for each of the buttons and the menu items hidden beneath. (See Figure 12-21.) Note that the application bar has automatically set the text for the buttons and menu items into lowercase; this is the standard behavior across all Windows Phone application bars and cannot be changed.

Figure 12-21. *The ApplicationBar in its open state*

To add more buttons, simply add additional instances if the `ApplicationBarIconButton` class (or, indeed, remove the instances that are already there to show fewer buttons).

Unlike the Windows 8 `AppBar`, which used elements from the Segoe UI Symbol font to provide icons for its buttons, the `ApplicationBar` uses bitmap images for each button. The `IconUri` property of each button is used to identify which image to use. In Listing 12-22, they are shown referencing an image file within the `Images` folder. A small selection of preset images is provided and may be selected from the `IconUri` property in the Properties window. Selecting one of these images will cause it to be automatically added to your project.

Alternatively, you may create your own images and add these to your project. Images should be created at 48 x 48 pixels, and they should be created so that they have a white foreground on a transparent background (using the alpha channel to enforce the transparency). The circle that can be seen displayed around the icons is added automatically and should not be part of the image. To allow for this circular outline, the icon should be restricted to the 26 x 26 pixel region in the center of the provided image.

■ **Tip**   If you can't find a suitable icon and don't feel like creating one yourself, you might want to try visiting `http://modernuiicons.com`, where you will find the Modern UI Icons project. This consists of over 1,000 free icons for Windows Phone apps, covering all sorts of subjects and symbols. The project is based on a Creative Commons license. Some of the icons require acknowledgement in your app's information page if you use them, but many don't even need that. Read the included `license.txt` file for details.

Once you have added your images to the project, their image paths can be entered manually into the XAML or picked from the Properties window editor to help you to select them.

■ **Note**   When adding `ApplicationBar` icon images to your project, it is essential that their `Build Action` be set to `Content`. If they are left with any other `Build Action`, they will simply appear as broken-image icons when your project is run.

Buttons can be enabled or disabled using their IsEnabled property. When the user taps one of the buttons, its Click event will be fired.

Menu items can be added or removed as required by providing an appropriate number of ApplicationBarMenuItem objects. Microsoft recommends a maximum of five menu items to prevent the user having to scroll, but more than this can be added if required. Each menu item also has an IsEnabled property and a Click event.

The ApplicationBar also has several properties that can be used to control its appearance and function. The most useful of these are the IsVisible and Opacity properties.

Setting IsVisible to false will rather predictably cause the bar to disappear.

The Opacity property has some more subtle behavior, however. When set to 1 (its default), it reserves some space from the page for itself, pushing the content up and out of the way. Setting to any lower value than this will cause its background (though not the buttons themselves) to become more and more transparent, but it will also cause it to stop reserving space within the page. The bar will, therefore, appear in front of any other page content that occupies the bottom area of the screen.

■ **Caution**   With an Opacity less than 1, the ApplicationBar will be placed in front of any other content in the bottom of the page, but it will still receive all screen taps in that area, even with an Opacity of 0. Make sure that there is never anything behind the ApplicationBar that the users will want to interact with because they will be unable to do so.

Unlike the Windows 8 AppBar, the ApplicationBar is visible the whole time your application is running. If you find that it takes up too much space, you can collapse it down to a smaller size by setting the ApplicationBar.Mode property to Minimized. The bar will then display itself as an empty horizontal bar just a few pixels tall with the ellipsis button on the right edge. Tapping the ellipsis will open the bar completely, revealing all of the buttons and menu items within.

This is often a useful way to configure the bar, but there is one detail to be aware of: Because the bar is very small in this configuration, actually touching the ellipsis button would be tricky to do. To eliminate this problem, the button has a much larger touch area than it appears to. The width of the button is as you would expect, but the button's height actually extends some way out of the bar. In fact, it is the same height as a normal unminimized ApplicationBar control would be. If you place any other content in your page that your users may want to interact with so that it occupies this area, be aware that they will end up activating the ApplicationBar instead, which may be quite frustrating.

User Interface Design

Clearly, there is an enormous amount of complexity and flexibility in the XAML page designs. Because XAML's original environment (when it existed in its earlier Silverlight guise) was inside a web browser, some of those functions are not appropriate or do not function properly in Windows 8 or Windows Phone environments. The vast majority perform exactly as expected, however, providing enormous potential for flexible UIs and game configurations.

Now that you are familiar with all the controls it uses, you should be able to look again at the default MainPage.xaml file that is created in an empty project (particularly a Windows Phone Application project, which provides some visible content in its empty pages). All the structure of the page should make a lot more sense now than it did when we first began exploring it at the beginning of the previous chapter!

Orientation

XAML pages provide flexible support for multiple orientations within your games and applications just as MonoGame does. Windows 8 application pages default to landscape-only and Windows Phone to portrait-only, but it takes very little effort to support either or both orientations as needed by your game.

Windows 8 XAML pages will automatically rotate between landscape and portrait orientation without anything needing to be added to your pages.

For Windows Phone, however, orientation is explicitly controlled for each individual XAML page, and as such is set using properties provided by the `PhoneApplicationPage` class. You can see these properties in the opening XAML element at the beginning of each page. Listing 12-23 shows the required properties in the initial page.

Listing 12-23. Setting the runtime and design-time page orientation

```
SupportedOrientations="Portrait"
Orientation="Portrait"
```

The first of these properties, `SupportedOrientations`, allows you to specify the orientations that the page can adopt when it is running. The available options are `Portrait`, `Landscape`, and `PortraitOrLandscape`. The `Landscape` option supports both left- and right-landscape mode; `PortraitOrLandscape` support all three orientations.

Because the initial layout of the page is based entirely around containers and controls that automatically expand and contract to fit their surroundings, the page will adjust to changes in orientation without any code being required. As long as you configure your page controls in this way, using margins and alignment rather than absolute widths, they also will behave in this way.

If you are working on a game or application whose primary orientation is landscape, however, it is much easier to set things up if you view the page designer in landscape mode, too. This is achieved using the `Orientation` property. This property can only be set at design time, and its value applies just to the page designer and not to the running application. Figure 12-22 shows the page designer in landscape mode.

Figure 12-22. *Designing a Windows Phone page using landscape orientation*

While the page layout might be able to look after itself in many cases, it is still very likely that you will want to be able to detect when the orientation has changed. This is achieved using the `PhoneApplicationPage`'s `OrientationChanged` event. The `OrientationChangedEventArgs` property provided to the event will indicate the new orientation.

The current orientation can also be queried at any time by reading the page's `Orientation` property.

Multiple Page Projects

If you choose to use XAML pages in your game, there's a chance that you'll want to be able to display more than one page of information. In a game, other such pages may include a title page, game menu, high scores, settings, an About page, and possibly many more.

These pages could be accommodated by placing lots of hidden controls into a single XAML page definition, but there is a much smarter way to implement this requirement. Just as a web site can offer multiple pages that a browser can navigate through, our applications can provide multiple pages that the user can navigate through.

All the XAML projects we have used in the examples so far have been built around a single page: the default MainPage.xaml. We can, however, add as many pages as we need to our projects and then navigate between them.

The MultiplePages_Win8 and MultiplePages_WP8 example projects that accompany this chapter contain the code that we will look at in this section. These projects show a simple main page design, containing a text field into which users can enter their name, and two buttons: Hello (which navigates to another page that says hello to the user) and About (which shows a simple information page).

Unfortunately, page navigation is another area of the API that differs between Windows Phone and Windows 8. The basic concept is the same for both, however, so let's take a look at everything needed to get things working. We'll examine the differences between the two platforms along the way.

Adding New Pages to a Project

To add a new page to your project, right-click the project in Solution Explorer and select Add ➤ New Item. The Add New Item page will appear, allowing you to select the name and type of item to add to the project, as shown for a Windows 8 project in Figure 12-23.

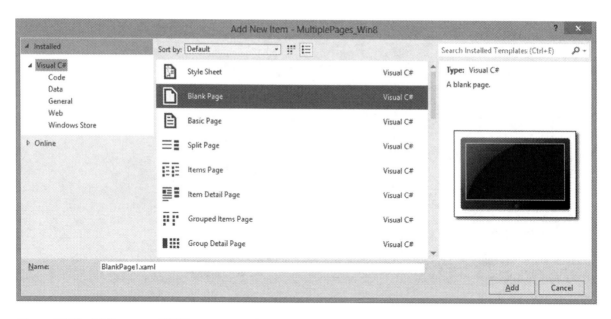

Figure 12-23. *Adding a new XAML page to a project*

In terms of which type of item to add, you will generally want to select Blank Page for a Windows 8 application, or Windows Phone Portrait Page for a Windows Phone app. (The orientation can easily be changed as described in the Orientation section earlier.) Other page types exist, but these generally contain a lot of template layout content that will not usually be useful in game projects.

Give the page a name and click the Add button. The page will be added to your project. It will open, ready for you to modify its design as per your requirements.

Navigating between Pages

Regardless of which platform we are using, moving from one page to another is very easy. Let's take a look at how this is achieved in each environment.

Navigating in Windows Phone Applications

In Windows Phone applications, each page has a property named `NavigationService`, which returns an object that allows us to control page navigation. In Windows Phone, navigation is URI-based. Instead of creating an instance of a page and showing it (as we would in the WinForms world), we simply tell the `NavigationService` the address of the page within our application that we wish to display.

This code required for such navigation can be seen in Listing 12-24, which contains the code from the About button in the example project.

Listing 12-24. Navigating to AboutPage.xaml

```
private void buttonAbout_Click(object sender, RoutedEventArgs e)
{
    // Navigate to the About page
    NavigationService.Navigate(new Uri("/AboutPage.xaml", UriKind.Relative));
}
```

You can see from the code that the way that the code specifies the page to navigate to is by specifying its path. (If you are using subfolders to organize your pages within your project, include the folder names in the path, too.) If you run the project and click the About button, you will find that `AboutPage` is displayed, just as you would expect.

▓ **Note**   Each time you navigate to a page, a new instance of that page is created. Any content that might be present on an existing instance of the page will be retained by the previous instance only.

Having navigated to this page, try pressing the hardware Back button; instead of the application closing down, it navigates back to the main page. This provides an intuitive and consistent navigation experience for the user.

It is possible to programmatically navigate backward (and forward, too). An event handler has been set up in the About page's `MouseLeftButtonDown` event. It contains the code shown in Listing 12-25.

Listing 12-25. Navigating backward using code

```
private void PhoneApplicationPage_MouseLeftButtonDown(object sender, MouseButtonEventArgs e)
{
    // Can we navigate backward?
    if (NavigationService.CanGoBack)
    {
        // Yes, so go there now
        NavigationService.GoBack();
    }
}
```

Tapping the screen when the About page is open triggers this code, which has exactly the same effect as pressing the Back button, navigating back through the page stack. Note that this is different from navigating forward to the main page by using the `Navigate` method, which would add a new entry to the page stack rather than working back to the previous entry. It would also cause a new instance of the page to be created, displaying its default content once again and not the name that the user had previously entered.

Navigating in Windows 8 Applications

Windows 8 page navigation is no more difficult, but it uses a different (and arguably better) approach. The Windows Phone approach relies on text-based URIs. This means that should you rename, relocate, or remove one of your pages after creating your navigation code, the URI would be left pointing to a nonexistent page. This would generate an error, but only at runtime—the compiler would not detect the problem.

Windows 8 uses the `typeof` keyword to identify the navigation target, which relies on the page being valid at compilation time. Renaming or removing the page will not be susceptible to this potential problem.

Listing 12-26 shows the code behind the About button in the Windows 8 example project that navigates to the About page. Instead of using the `NavigationService` object, as used in Windows Phone, the `Navigate` method is called on the page's `Frame` object.

Listing 12-26. Navigating to AboutPage

```
private void buttonAbout_Click(object sender, RoutedEventArgs e)
{
    // Navigate to the About page
    Frame.Navigate(typeof(AboutPage));
}
```

If you run the project and click the About button, you will find that `AboutPage` is displayed just as you would expect. Just as with Windows Phone, a new instance of the page will be created each time you navigate, so no earlier content will be present when the page is displayed.

The next thing we want to be able to do is navigate back to the main page. Unlike Windows Phone, there is no hardware back button, so we need to adopt another approach. The standard solution for this is to place a back button (represented by a left-facing arrow within a circle) into the header section of the page. This can be seen in Figure 12-24.

Figure 12-24. *The page title and its back button*

If you take a look at the XAML markup for `AboutPage`, you will see how this is implemented: A two-column `Grid` is used to space apart the button and the title text, and the button is created as per the code in Listing 12-27. Setting the `Style` property as shown instructs the page to use a standard back button icon.

Listing 12-27. Creating a back button

```
<Button x:Name="backButton" Style="{StaticResource BackButtonStyle}"/>
```

Of course, the button doesn't do anything by default when it is clicked, so we have to programmatically invoke a backward navigation. This is achieved in the button's `Click` event handler, the code for which is shown in Listing 12-28. Just as with the Windows Phone code, we first check that we can actually navigate back (just to be safe) and then call the `Frame.GoBack` method.

Listing 12-28. Navigating back to the previous page

```
private void backButton_Click(object sender, RoutedEventArgs e)
{
    // Go back to the previous page
    if (Frame.CanGoBack)
    {
        Frame.GoBack();
    }
}
```

If you give this a try in the example project, you may notice some behavior that is different to the Windows Phone example. If you enter your name, click the Hello or the About button, and then click the Back button to return to the main page, the name has been lost. Even though you navigated back to a previously used page, its content was reset back to its initial values.

This is the default behavior for Windows 8 pages, but it is easy to override. Adding the code shown in Listing 12-29 to the page constructor will cause the page content to be cached and automatically restored when next navigating to the page.

Listing 12-29. Navigating back to the previous page

```
NavigationCacheMode = NavigationCacheMode.Enabled;
```

You will find this line of code commented out in the example project. Uncomment it and try again. Now you will see that your name is retained.

░ **Note** The NavigationCacheMode can only be set in your page class constructor. Setting it after the constructor has completed will have no effect.

Passing Values When Navigating

Moving between pages is useful, but, chances are, you will need to pass data to the page that you are navigating to, just as we wish to pass the name that has been entered in the example projects. There are various methods that we can use to accomplish this; let's take a look at two of them now.

Adding Navigation Parameters

On both platforms, it is possible to pass additional data to the Navigate method such that the data can be retrieved by the target page when it is activated.

For Windows Phone navigation, we are using URIs to navigate. Because of this, we can take advantage of their *query string* capabilities and pass additional data as part of the URI itself.

These work using exactly the same technique as query strings in a URL in a web browser. The beginning of the query string is indicated by adding a question mark to the URI. It is then followed by any number of name/value pairs formatted as the name, then an equals sign, and then the value. If multiple parameters are being passed, an ampersand is used to separate them. For example, to pass a name and a score to a page named Scores.xaml, we could construct a URI as follows:

```
Scores.xaml?Name=Player name&Score=12345
```

Those of you familiar with using query strings for web navigation will be aware of the need to *encode* values that are passed in query strings. If the user entered the name as "Adam & Joe," the resulting query string would be as follows:

```
Scores.xaml?Name=Adam & Joe&Score=12345
```

In this case, the ampersand in the name will confuse the query string. It will consider the name to be "Adam " (with a trailing space); after the ampersand separator, it will then find an unexpected keyword that it doesn't know how to handle (" Joe", with a leading space), and then finally it will find the score (which it will process correctly). The result of this is that retrieving the name from this query string will return just "Adam "; the rest of the name will be lost.

This is easily solved by using a .NET function that will encode strings for inclusion into URLs and URIs. The HttpUtility.UrlEncode function does this perfectly. The resulting URI, once the name has been encoded, is the following:

```
Scores.xaml?Name=Adam+%26+Joe&Score=12345
```

The + characters will be interpreted by the navigation engine as spaces, and %26 will be decoded to the character whose ASCII value is identified from the hexadecimal number 26 (which results in an ampersand). None of these characters causes any problem when the query string is parsed, however, so the value passes through navigation undamaged.

Listing 12-30 shows how this approach could be used in the example project to pass the entered name to the NamePage page. It passes whatever name the user has entered into the text box as a parameter, encoding it to ensure that it doesn't cause any problems in the query string.

Listing 12-30. Navigating to a new page and passing a parameter in a Windows Phone project

```
private void buttonHello_Click(object sender, RoutedEventArgs e)
{
    // Navigate to the Name page
    NavigationService.Navigate(
            new Uri("/NamePage.xaml?YourName=" + HttpUtility.UrlEncode(textName.Text),
            UriKind.Relative));
}
```

This passes the value into NamePage, but we need to be able to receive and process the value as well. This is also very easily achieved. The target page can override the OnNavigatedTo method in order to locate the data that has been passed to the page. It looks for the data by calling the NavigationContext.QueryString.TryGetValue method. If a value with the specified name exists, it is passed back in an output parameter and the function returns true; if no value can be found, the function returns false.

The good news is that we don't need to do anything at all to decode query string values that have been encoded prior to navigation. The .NET framework will take care of decoding automatically, giving us back the string that we actually need to process.

Listing 12-31 shows an OnNavigatedTo function for NamePage that could be used to read out the provided name and displays it inside a TextBlock for the user to see.

Listing 12-31. Receiving values on navigating to a new page in a Windows Phone project

```
protected override void OnNavigatedTo(NavigationEventArgs e)
{
    base.OnNavigatedTo(e);

    string yourName = "";
    // See if we can retrieve the passed name
    if (NavigationContext.QueryString.TryGetValue("YourName", out yourName))
```

```
    {
        // Display the name
        textblockName.Text = "Hello, " + yourName + "!";
    }
    else
    {
        // Couldn't locate a name
        textblockName.Text = "Couldn't find your name, sorry!";
    }
}
```

When we wish to pass data in Windows 8, the same approach cannot be used as there are no URIs involved in navigation. An alternative is provided, however. If anything, it's easier to use than the Windows Phone option.

When calling the Frame.Navigate method, a second overload of the function is actually available. This second version accepts another parameter that is named parameter. This is defined as type object, allowing absolutely anything to be passed. The parameter may therefore be used to pass a simple string, a dictionary of strings, an instance of some class you define, or anything else you need. Listing 12-32 shows how the name from the main page in the example project might be passed to the NamePage page using this approach. As we just need to pass a single simple value, it is passed in this case just as a string.

Listing 12-32. Passing a parameter to another page when navigating in a Windows 8 project

```
private void buttonHello_Click(object sender, RoutedEventArgs e)
{
    // Navigate to the Name page
    Frame.Navigate(typeof(NamePage), textName.Text);
}
```

When the target page wishes to retrieve the passed parameter value, it does so by once again overriding the OnNavigatedTo method. This time it simply checks the Parameter property of the provided NavigationEventArgs object, as shown in Listing 12-33. Whichever object instance was used when navigating will be returned.

Listing 12-33. Retrieving a parameter value after navigating in a Windows 8 project

```
protected override void OnNavigatedTo(NavigationEventArgs e)
{
    // Do we have a name?
    if (!string.IsNullOrEmpty(e.Parameter as string))
    {
        // Display the name
        textblockName.Text = "Hello, " + (e.Parameter as string) + "!";
    }
    else
    {
        // Couldn't locate a name
        textblockName.Text = "Couldn't find your name, sorry!";
    }
}
```

Passing Values with Static Class Properties

Another approach, which is both simple and consistent across both platforms, is to provide static properties within your pages and set the values of these prior to navigating. Both the source and the target navigation page will have access to these, so values can be passed as appropriate for the form to which navigation is taking place.

This is, in fact, the approach that has been used in the MultiplePages example projects. If you look at the code, you will see that a static property named YourName has been added to NamePage. This is set by MainPage prior to navigation. In NamePage's OnContentLoaded method, the property is queried and its value processed as appropriate.

This generally offers an easy and flexible mechanism for transferring data around your application, and it is well worth considering as part of your app design.

But What about MonoGame?

Over the course of this chapter and the previous chapter, you have taken a crash course in XAML and how it can be used to create user interfaces. The real reason behind covering all of this is, of course, so that you can integrate MonoGame and XAML into the same projects and pages, getting each to play to its particular strengths: MonoGame for game content and XAML for UI content.

In the next chapter, we will take a look at how these two technologies can be brought together. We will work through some of the implications of getting them to communicate with one another.

Summary

- XAML provides a large range of controls for use within user interface designs. Some of the useful controls used to display information and presentational content on the screen include the TextBlock, Image, ProgressBar, ProgressRing (Windows 8 only), Ellipse, Rectangle, Line, Polyline, and Polygon controls.

- Many controls are provided for user interaction. These include the TextBox, ListBox, ComboBox (Windows 8 only), CheckBox, RadioButton, and Button controls.

- XAML also offers a variety of controls for governing the layout of other controls within the page. These are not only very useful for basic presentation, but they are also useful for simplifying the task of adapting to multiple screen resolutions and orientations. In many cases, this allows the page layout to adapt entirely unassisted.

- Grid controls can be used to create tabular layouts of controls within the page. Flexible options are provided for setting the numbers and sizes of grid rows and columns. Cells may also be spanned across multiple rows or columns, if needed.

- StackPanel controls allow a series of child controls to be automatically arranged in a horizontal or vertical line. This can be used for lots of different tasks, including strips of command buttons or simulating the layout of a ListBox.

- ScrollViewer controls may be placed around any content that is too large to fit within the defined space and provides automatic scrolling for the user of its content. Scrolling can be locked to a single axis if required.

- Application bars are used to present commonly used command buttons for the user. In Windows 8 applications, these are normally hidden by default and are displayed when the user clicks the right mouse button or swipes from the top or bottom edge of the screen. The Windows Phone application bar is normally displayed the whole time, and it also provides a set of menu items. The application bars are implemented differently across both platforms, with a different API and feature set.

- XAML pages can be easily configured to display in landscape or portrait orientation, as required by your app.

- Multiple XAML pages may be added to a project. The user can be taken from one page to another using a navigation model similar to that used by a web browser.

- The navigation API differs between Windows 8 and Windows Phone, using strongly typed class references for Windows 8 and text-based URIs for Windows Phone.

- Navigating back to an earlier page will always result in earlier data being persisted in Windows Phone applications, but it will by default return to a page that has reset to its initial values in Windows 8. The `NavigationCacheMode` property can be used in a Windows 8 page's constructor to specify that previously entered data should be cached and restored.

- When navigating to another page, data values can be passed to the new page, if required. Windows 8 projects achieve this by passing an object reference. Windows Phone projects, on the other hand, use the URI query string. Alternatively, values may be set directly into the target page by using `static` class properties.

CHAPTER 13

■ ■ ■

Mixing XAML and MonoGame

In this chapter, we will bring together the two technologies that we have been working with and explore how to add XAML user interfaces to MonoGame projects. In general, everything continues to work in the ways that we have already seen, but there are some special things that we need to do in certain areas in order for everything to play nicely together.

Let's start by taking a look at the most fundamental question: How can XAML content be added to a MonoGame display?

Using MonoGame and XAML Together

In all of the MonoGame projects that we have looked at, we have treated the project as if it contained only the MonoGame content, the Game class (or the GameFramework project's GameHost class), the game objects, the content files, and so on. However, in the background, there has actually been a XAML page of sorts, contained within a file named GamePage.xaml.

Exactly how this page is implemented varies between the two platforms. For Windows 8 projects, GamePage isn't a full page such as those we have looked at in the last two chapters, but rather a SwapChainBackgroundPanel. This class, derived from the XAML Grid control, exists so as to provide a way for XAML and DirectX (on which MonoGame is ultimately built) to interoperate with one another. This is used in place of the Page and offers much of the same functionality and many of the same methods and events. However, there are a few things that differ from standard XAML pages, as you will see as you work through the following sections.

If you take a look at GamePage.xaml in any of the earlier Windows 8 MonoGame example projects, you'll see that its XAML contains nothing more than a few namespace definitions declared against the SwapChainBackgroundPanel itself, and then an empty Grid control within the panel. In fact, even this default grid is unnecessary and can be removed if not required; it is simply provided as a starting point for creating any additional XAML content that is needed for the page.

In the case of the Windows Phone projects, GamePage is implemented as a normal page. It doesn't exist as an implementation of the SwapChainBackgroundPanel. Within the Windows Phone page is a full-page Grid control, inside which is another full-screen control of type DrawingSurface. This is a type of control that DirectX can use to render graphics to a Windows Phone page. Our XAML content can also be placed into the Grid. A MediaElement control is present within the Grid, too. MonoGame uses this for some of its audio playback functionality.

On both platforms, the way that XAML and DirectX have been designed to interact is that the DirectX rendering is processed first. Once this has been completed, the XAML renderer then takes control and adds its content as a second step, prior to presenting the final rendered page to the user. As a result, XAML content will always appear in front of any graphics rendered by MonoGame. This ensures that any XAML controls we use as our user interface (for control buttons, text displays, and so on) will appear unobstructed in front of the game graphics.

The XAML rendering still takes any transparency within the controls into account, so it is quite possible to have controls that are partially transparent or that use alpha shading. These will blend in front of the MonoGame graphics, as you would expect them to.

The effects of mixing MonoGame and XAML can be seen in the example projects MonoGameAndXAML_Win8 and MonoGameAndXAML_WP8, which accompany this chapter. Take a look at the project in operation, a screenshot of which is shown in Figure 13-1. All of the graphical content is being rendered using MonoGame, but the number of lives and the score at the top of the screen as well the two buttons at the bottom are created as XAML controls.

Figure 13-1. *A mixture of MonoGame and XAML content*

▓ **Note**   If you run this example in the Windows Phone emulator, you may find that the XAML content flickers noticeably. This is just a shortcoming of the emulator. When you run the project on a real device, the problem will not appear.

This all sounds great, but there is one drawback that you need to be very aware of: performance. When running on devices with less powerful hardware (tablets and phones), the presence of visible XAML content can have a negative impact on the performance of your game.

This can be seen in the example project if you have access to a Surface RT device. Even with just the biplane and 15 clouds, the performance noticeably stutters on the device. If you switch off the XAML content (which is most easily achieved by editing the GamePage.xaml file and adding Visibility="Collapsed" to the outer Grid control), suddenly, the performance jumps back to a smooth 60 frames per second.

This is a big reason to be cautious with mixing XAML and MonoGame. In many cases, it may be enough to warrant dropping any XAML content from your game page—at least while the main game is running. If your game relies upon a high frame rate, you should test the effects of this in your game projects at all stages of development to ensure that it doesn't cause problems.

Communication between the Game and the Page

Having seen how a game can mix MonoGame and XAML content within the same page, we need to be able to get the two to interact with one another. Specifically, we need to know how to get the game class to update details within the page and how the page can notify the game of events that it needs to know about.

Updating XAML Controls from the Game Class

In the example project, the game simulates having a player score, which is simply a class-level property within the MonoGameAndXAMLGame class that is increased by 10 during each call to Update. The game wants to ensure that an updated copy of this is displayed on the screen each time the Draw method is called.

This sounds like a simple requirement, but, immediately, we run into several problems. The first is that we don't have an instance of the GamePage class in order to access its content.

There are various ways that this could be solved, but a very easy way that also works identically across both platforms is to add a static property to GamePage named Current, which returns a GamePage reference. In the GamePage class constructor, the code simply sets this property to the current object instance, as shown in Listing 13-1. The code shown is taken from the Windows Phone project. In the Windows 8 project, the pre-created call to XamlGame.Create differs, but the relevant code here relating to the Current property is the same.

Listing 13-1. Adding a Current property to the GamePage

```
/// <summary>
/// A static property that returns the current instance of the game page
/// </summary>
public static GamePage Current { get; set; }

/// <summary>
/// Class constructor
/// </summary>
public GamePage()
{
    InitializeComponent();

    // Set the current instance of the page so that the game can access it
    Current = this;

    // Create the game
    _game = XamlGame<MonoGameAndXAMLGame>.Create("", XnaSurface);
}
```

Now, in order to get access to the page from the game class, we can simply query GamePage.Current and use the returned object.

The next problem that we run into is that, by default, all controls within XAML pages are created with private scope, so they cannot be directly accessed from outside the page code itself. This is generally a good thing as it keeps the implementation details of the form away from external code. If you are trying to create a game that runs on both Windows 8 and Windows Phone, it's quite possible that your XAML content will be different across the two platforms anyway, so accessing them directly from the game class will require different code for each platform.

Instead of directly updating the controls, we create public methods within GamePage that can be used to access the controls indirectly. In the example project, the page code contains two methods, SetLives and SetScore, the Windows 8 versions of which are shown in Listing 13-2.

Listing 13-2. The SetLives and SetScore methods inside the Windows 8 GamePage

```
// Last-known values to prevent unnecessary updates of the control text
private int _lives = -1;
private int _score = -1;

/// <summary>
/// Set the displayed number of lives
/// </summary>
public void SetLives(int lives)
{
    if (lives != _lives)
    {
        textLives.Text = "Lives: " + lives.ToString();
        _lives = lives;
    }
}

/// <summary>
/// Set the displayed score
/// </summary>
public void SetScore(int score)
{
    if (score != _score)
    {
        textScore.Text = "Score: " + score.ToString();
        _score = score;
    }
}
```

> ▒ **Note** If, for some reason, you wish to be able to directly access a control's properties from outside the page itself, you can add the property code x:ClassModifier="public" to the control's XAML in order to change the scope to public. Creating your own properties and methods to wrap around the control is generally a better idea, however, as it allows you to keep tighter control over exactly which changes are made to your controls.

As discussed when we first started looking at using .NET in mobile environments, it is important to avoid unnecessarily allocating objects so that the frequency of garbage collection is reduced. Calling the ToString method on a number causes a new string object to be created. The functions keep track of the last known value for the lives and score displays, and they only update the XAML control text if the value has actually changed.

That looks like it should be all we need to update the controls, and indeed on Windows 8 it is. The game class can call these methods and the score and lives text will update as requested. Calling these methods in Windows Phone, however, will result in an exception being thrown. XAML controls may only be updated in one specific application thread, known as the *UI thread*, and in Windows Phone apps the MonoGame code is executed in a different thread. As a result, no updates to the controls are allowed.

Fortunately, there is an easy workaround for this. We can use an object called a *dispatcher* to perform the update for us. When the dispatcher is given a task to perform, it queues it and then executes it within the UI thread as soon as that thread is available.

An instance of the dispatcher can be obtained from the form's `Dispatcher` property. To get it to execute a task, we call its `BeginInvoke` method and pass it the name of a function to call. We can use a delegate to define the function inline, keeping everything much tidier.

As a result, the Windows 8 code from Listing 13-2 changes to that shown in Listing 13-3 for Windows Phone. The basic logic is identical, but the code now wraps the updates to the XAML control within the `Dispatcher.BeginInvoke` call. Note that the detail of the dispatcher is kept hidden away inside `GamePage`, meaning that the code in the main game class is unchanged between the two platforms. This makes it easier to share a code base between the two, if desired.

Listing 13-3. The SetLives and SetScore methods inside the Windows Phone GamePage

```
// Last-known values to prevent unnecessary updates of the control text
private int _lives = -1;
private int _score = -1;
/// <summary>
/// Set the displayed number of lives
/// </summary>
public void SetLives(int lives)
{
    if (lives != _lives)
    {
        Dispatcher.BeginInvoke(delegate()
        {
            textLives.Text = "Lives: " + lives.ToString();
            _lives = lives;
        });
    }
}

/// <summary>
/// Set the displayed score
/// </summary>
public void SetScore(int score)
{
    if (score != _score)
    {
        Dispatcher.BeginInvoke(delegate()
        {
            textScore.Text = "Score: " + score.ToString();
            _score = score;
        });
    }
}
```

Notifying the Game Class from the XAML Page

The techniques we have covered provide a way of allowing the game class to initiate communication with the game page, but what do we do if we want to allow the page to communicate back to the game? There are various scenarios where this may be desirable, including notifying the game that a button has been clicked or that some text has been entered.

An easy way to achieve this is to allow the game to pull such information from the page, rather than trying to get the page to push the information into the game. As an example of how this approach can be used, try clicking the Reset button in the example project. Each time this is clicked, the score resets back to zero. The score is stored within the Score property inside MonoGameAndXAMLGame game class, so how does clicking the button cause the property to be updated?

Because the game is running in a constant loop (unlike the page, which only performs any processing when an event triggers it to do so), the game can constantly check the state of the page. When the button is clicked, the click handler simply sets a flag in a class-level property of the game page. The code for this is shown in Listing 13-4.

Listing 13-4. Handling the Click event of the Reset button

```
/// <summary>
/// Track whether the Reset button has been clicked
/// </summary>
public bool ResetButtonClicked { get; set; }

/// <summary>
/// Respond to the user clicking the Reset button
/// </summary>
private void buttonReset_Click(object sender, RoutedEventArgs e)
{
    // Indicate that the button was clicked
    ResetButtonClicked = true;
}
```

This property is used as a signal to the game that it needs to carry out the action appropriate to the button. Listing 13-5 shows how this is handled in the example project's game class.

Listing 13-5. Checking to see whether the Reset button has been clicked since the last update

```
protected override void Update(GameTime gameTime)
{
    UpdateAll(gameTime);

    // Did the player click the Reset button?
    if (GamePage.Current.ResetButtonClicked)
    {
        // Reset the score
        Score = 0;
        // Clear the 'clicked' property
        GamePage.Current.ResetButtonClicked = false;
    }

    // Increase the player's score
    Score += 10;

    base.Update(gameTime);
}
```

This general approach can be used for all sorts of communication between the page and the game, setting flags and other properties to indicate to the game that it needs to do something and allowing the game to pull the values in as it needs them.

Another alternative would be to add a mechanism into the game class such that it exposed a static Current property, just as we did for the page itself. This would allow the page to obtain a reference to the game. This may be a useful approach in many situations and would be quite sufficient for this simple example, but if you actually need to be able to act on the UI interaction directly within the game's Update method, pulling the data in from the page will probably be the easiest option available.

Using the Application Bar

Even if you don't display any other XAML content on the screen in your game, you may want to consider adding an application bar, particularly for Windows 8 projects as the app bar is, by default, completely hidden. Consequently, it has no impact on performance and doesn't take any screen space away from the game itself.

Adding a Windows Phone ApplicationBar is easy; it can simply be added to the page just as with a plain XAML project. When it comes to Windows 8, however, we have a small problem to overcome. As you hopefully recall from the previous chapter, the Windows 8 AppBar was added to the page by placing it into the Page object's TopAppBar or BottomAppBar property. In MonoGame projects, GamePage doesn't implement a Page, but rather a SwapChainBackgroundPanel, which doesn't provide either of these properties. So, how do we add the AppBar to the UI?

This is actually very easy: Simply add the AppBar as a control directly within the SwapChainBackgroundPanel, set its VerticalAlignment to Top or Bottom as appropriate, and set its Height as appropriate for the content (a height of 90 is about right for standard AppBar buttons). The AppBar will still behave as normal, appearing when the user right-clicks or swipes from the top or bottom edge.

The MonoGameAndXAML_Win8 example project contains a bottom-aligned AppBar (with some placeholder content—just a single, nonfunctional button for the purposes of demonstration). Try right-clicking or swiping to make it appear, and you'll find that it still works exactly as expected.

Page Navigation

The final XAML task we want to address in a MonoGame world is page navigation. We may wish to invoke navigation in either of two different places: from within GamePage (or some other XAML context), or from within the MonoGame game class.

Let's take a look at how these are achieved on each platform.

Page Navigation in Windows 8

As you will recall from the previous chapter, navigation in Windows 8 is initiated by calling the Frame.Navigate method on the object returned by the Page's Frame property. You may by now be able to guess that once again this isn't going to work in a MonoGame GamePage as it isn't an instance of the Page class, but rather it is an instance of the SwapChainBackgroundPanel class. As a result, we need to find a different way to navigate.

The currently active page can be set or retrieved at any time via the Window.Current.Content property. If you take a look at the OnLaunched method in a MonoGame project's App class, you will see that the method that the code uses to activate GamePage in the first place is by setting an instance of it into this property. We can, therefore, navigate to another page directly with this property, bypassing the normal navigation system.

If you click the Menu button at the bottom of the screen in the MonoGameAndXAML_Win8 example project, you are taken to a placeholder page that might be used in a real game to provide an in-game menu. The code behind the button that performs this navigation is shown in Listing 13-6. It simply creates a new instance of the desired page and then sets it to be the current window content.

Listing 13-6. Navigating from GamePage to another XAML page

```
private void buttonMenu_Click(object sender, RoutedEventArgs e)
{
    // Navigate to the Menu page
    Window.Current.Content = new MenuPage();
}
```

This works as expected, but by bypassing the regular Frame navigation approach, we don't have any stack of pages to go back to when the new page is ready to be closed. As a result, we have to always explicitly set the Window.Current.Content property for each and every navigation operation, forward or backward.

So, how do we get back to the game itself? Inside the header section of the example MenuPage is a Back button, which returns back to GamePage. Unlike when we navigated to MenuPage, we can't simply create a new instance of GamePage to use as the window content. If we try to do this, the project gets confused and loses all of its content, resulting in a blank page. What we need to do instead is return back to the existing GamePage instance. As luck would have it, there is a very easy method for us to access that instance: the static GamePage.Current property that we added earlier on.

The code to navigate back to the game page is shown in Listing 13-7.

Listing 13-7. Navigating from another XAML page back to GamePage

```
private void backButton_Click(object sender, RoutedEventArgs e)
{
    // Set the current window back to the game
    Window.Current.Content = GamePage.Current;
}
```

Windows 8 doesn't have any kind of hardware back button, so we don't need to be concerned about any system-provided navigation functions. All navigation is directly under our control and so the above methods for navigating back and forward work acceptably.

If you wish to invoke navigation from within the game class, exactly the same approach can be used. (The Window object is contained within the Windows.UI.Xaml namespace, which isn't included in the class's using statements by default.)

Take a look at the Score value when you navigate to the menu page. Wait a few seconds and then navigate back to the game. You'll see that the score has continued to increase the whole time—navigating away does not cause the game to pause. Your navigation code will therefore need to indicate to the game that it is not currently active in order for any action within your game to stop and wait for the user to return.

Page Navigation in Windows Phone

For Windows Phone page navigation, we continue to use the built-in navigation model. This is convenient because it means that the phone's hardware Back button continues to operate normally without our having to continually intercept it and navigate using alternative means.

Since Windows Phone's GamePage is still a Page object, navigation from the XAML context is simply a matter of calling NavigationService.Navigate, exactly as in a non-MonoGame project. Listing 13-8 shows the code behind the Menu button in the MonoGameAndXAML_WP8 example project.

Listing 13-8. Navigating from GamePage to another XAML page

```
private void buttonMenu_Click(object sender, RoutedEventArgs e)
{
    // Navigate to the Menu page
    NavigationService.Navigate(new Uri("/MenuPage.xaml", UriKind.Relative));
}
```

When the users are ready to navigate back to GamePage, they can press the back button and they are returned back to where they came from. If you wish to programmatically return back from another page, the page can simply call the NavigationService.GoBack method.

If we wish to trigger a page navigation from within the MonoGame game class itself, we need to use a slightly different approach. The game class has no access to the NavigationService object, but it can use another method to access the navigation functions.

The basic approach is to retrieve the application's current *root visual*, which is the element within the page object hierarchy that actually hosts the page itself. The root visual object also exposes the required navigation functions, allowing us to navigate using that object in exactly the same way as with the NavigationService object.

We also have to deal with the same UI thread issue that we encountered with setting XAML properties from the MonoGame game class. Once again, the Dispatcher.BeginInvoke method needs to be used to push the navigation request across into the UI thread itself.

The complete code required to initiate page navigation from within the game class is shown in Listing 13-9.

Listing 13-9. Navigating from GamePage to another XAML page from within the MonoGame game class

```
Deployment.Current.Dispatcher.BeginInvoke(() =>
    {
        (Application.Current.RootVisual as PhoneApplicationFrame).Navigate(
                            new Uri("/MenuPage.xaml", UriKind.Relative));
    });
```

Finally, take a look at the Score value when you navigate to the menu page. Wait a few seconds and then navigate back to the game. Unlike in Windows 8, you'll see that the score did not continue to increase while the menu page was active—navigating away in a Windows Phone project does cause the game to pause.

Summary

- MonoGame and XAML content can be used together within the same screen, with all XAML content appearing in front of the rendered MonoGame graphics.

- While Windows Phone projects continue to use a normal PhoneApplicationPage object for their GamePage classes, Windows 8 projects use a SwapChainBackgroundPanel, which has different properties and methods from that of the more usual Windows 8 Page object. This changes some of the ways that we interact with GamePage.

- The presence of XAML content can cause a drop in performance in your game graphics, noticeable in particular on portable devices. It is recommended to keep testing on real hardware as frequently as possible if a high frame rate is important to your game. XAML content that is present within the page but is hidden does not result in performance degradation.

- Access from the MonoGame game class to the XAML GamePage can be gained by adding a static property to the GamePage class (named Current by convention) and setting this during the GamePage constructor. The property can be queried anywhere else within the project to gain access to the page.

- Code outside of a XAML page does not, by default, have direct access to any of the XAML controls. To work around this, add methods to the page that provide the required access to the control and use these methods from outside the page instead.

- Windows Phone applications cannot interact with the XAML controls from within the game class code as the game code runs in a different thread that is not allowed to access UI components. To deal with this, the `Dispatcher` object is used to queue the updates for processing by the UI thread.

- When the XAML page wishes to notify the game class about an interaction from the user, it can do so by setting properties within the page, which are then interrogated by the game class within its `Update` method.

- Application bars can be added to Windows 8 and Windows Phone projects and used just as in any other project. For Windows 8 projects, any required `AppBar` controls are added directly to the `SwapChainBackgroundPanel` and aligned to the top or bottom edge, rather than being set into the `Page.TopAppBar` or `Page.BottomAppBar` properties.

- Page navigation in Windows 8 requires us to bypass the regular navigation stack model and, instead, implement all navigation directly. This adds a little overhead with regards to navigating backward, but, otherwise, it is perfectly functional. Windows Phone navigation is essentially the same as for a non-MonoGame project.

- Some attention needs to be paid to what happens in the game while the user is navigated away to another page. In Windows 8 projects, the game continues to run in the background, whereas in Windows Phone the game pauses automatically.

CHAPTER 14

■ ■ ■

Distributing Your Game

So, your masterpiece is complete. The graphics are drawn and animating, the game logic is working, everything is sounding great, navigation around the different sections of the game is finished, and you have all sorts of extras such as high scores and information pages. Now, it is time to share your creation with the rest of the world.

The actual process of sharing is conceptually pretty straightforward: You submit your game to the Windows Store for Windows 8 games or to the Windows Phone Store for Windows Phone games. Microsoft will check that the game meets its submission requirements, and, assuming Microsoft is satisfied with the way the game works, it appears in the Store within a few days, ready for others to download.

It is possible (and advisable!) to offer a *trial mode* for your game if you are selling it so that potential customers can download it and try a limited version prior to purchase. This is a great way to win over your audience because it takes the risk out of purchasing.

In this chapter, we will examine the things you need to do in order to release your game to the rest of the world. In theory, this need not be a complex or time-consuming task, but there are a number of things you can do to reduce problems during the submission process.

Trial Mode

On each platform, the Store has integral support for an extremely useful feature: trial mode. This is not mandatory, but I strongly recommend you use it in all applications that you intend to sell. It allows people to download your game free of charge and evaluate it in a restricted form before spending any money purchasing the game.

When you decide to support trial mode, an additional button will appear next to your game in the Store: the Try button. Pressing this button *will install the full application* on the user's device, but it will set a flag within the .NET environment indicating that the game is in trial mode. Your code must check for this and limit the game in some way.

Using trial mode simplifies the development and submission of your games. You do not need to create and submit two versions, one for the user to try for free and the other to buy in full. The user, having discovered your game, does not have to hunt around to determine whether a free trial version exists. Everything is integrated into a single package, quick and easy to use. Better still, it is easy to send users back to the Store from your trial game so that they can quickly and easily purchase the full version.

Exactly how you decide to limit your game is entirely up to you. You might limit the number of levels that are available, restrict or remove certain features of the game, put a limit on the experience levels that the player can gain, disable the game's scoring, put a time limit in place, show advertisements, nag users periodically to upgrade and avoid the reminder messages, or any combination of these. The Store doesn't tell you how to work in trial mode; it simply tells you that the game is running in that mode.

The Windows 8 Store also offers a feature that implements a timed evaluation period. Once this period has elapsed, the application will then refuse to launch. This is an option worth considering, but it can be something of a hindrance. If a user downloads your game but doesn't get around to trying it for a week or two, by which time the evaluation period has expired, he or she won't get any opportunity to try the game at all.

However you decide to limit your game, make sure that a representative sample is offered so that your potential customers can decide whether the game appeals to them.

While you should not hide the trial status from your user, it is often a good idea to prompt the user to purchase at an opportune moment—perhaps at a cliffhanger point in the game or just as an exciting new feature is introduced. When the player is itching for more, the likelihood of buying the game is increased.

The exact mechanism with which the trial mode is managed differs between the two platforms, so let's take a look at each platform individually.

Working with Trial Mode in Windows 8 Apps

In order for our games to work well with trial modes, we need to be able to do several things: detect which mode we are actually in (trial or purchased), respond to the user making a purchase, and guide users to the Store to make the purchase when they are ready to do so.

Detecting Trial Mode

In order for us to check which mode our Windows 8 applications are using, a class is provided by the .NET Framework named `LicenseInformation` from the `Windows.ApplicationModel.Store` namespace. The class contains a small number of properties, but the ones we are particularly interested in are the `IsTrial` and `IsActive` properties. `IsTrial` tells us whether the app is running in trial mode, and `IsActive` confirms the license is still valid and active—this may return `false` if the app has expired or if the license is missing or has been revoked.

▓ **Note**   For performance reasons, you should not query this object directly within your game loop. Instead, the object should be interrogated when needed and the result cached for later reference.

In the simplest possible implementation of using this class, we could obtain an instance of it and check its properties. However, that would deny us the opportunity to test that everything is working during the development cycle. To add support for development checks, we will create a slightly more sophisticated version of this check. All of the code for this can be found in the `TrialMode_Win8` example project that accompanies this chapter.

To obtain an instance of a `LicenseInformation` object, we can query the `Windows.ApplicationModel.Store.CurrentApp.LicenseInformation` property. Calling this in the development environment, however, will always give us back an object that indicates that the app is in trial mode and has an inactive license.

To allow the licensing model to be properly tested, another mechanism can be used to obtain a *simulated* `LicenseInformation` object. This one allows its values to be customized. Such an object can be obtained via the `Windows.ApplicationModel.Store.CurrentAppSimulator.LicenseInformation` property.

▓ **Caution**   The `CurrentAppSimulator` object is *only* permitted for use when developing. If you submit an application to the Windows Store for certification that uses this object, *it will fail certification.* You should always make sure that conditional compilation blocks are wrapped around any code that uses this object, ensuring that nothing accidentally slips through into the Release version of the app that you create for submission.

The simulated license reads its data from a file on disk, specifically a file named `WindowsStoreProxy.xml`, which is found in the `Microsoft\Windows Store\ApiData` folder within the application's local storage folder. To modify the simulated license information object's properties, we need to create and update this file.

You could certainly identify the location of this file and manage it manually if you wanted to, but it is much easier to get the application code and Visual Studio's IDE to manage the file for us. This can be achieved by adding a WindowsStoreProxy.xml file to the IDE and getting the app code to copy it to the required location each time it runs. The file needs to be added with a Build Action of Content and its Copy to Output Directory property set to Copy if newer.

▨ **Note** The WindowsStoreProxy.xml file is only used by the CurrentAppSimulator object. It is ignored by apps that are actually downloaded from the Windows Store. It is, therefore, safe to leave this file present in your submission to the store.

The WindowsStoreProxy.xml file needs to contain certain content, but, for the purposes of debugging, it can be filled with placeholder data. The content of the file from the example project is shown in Listing 14-1.

Listing 14-1. The contents of the WindowsStoreProxy.xml file

```xml
<?xml version="1.0" ?>
<CurrentApp>
  <ListingInformation>
    <App>
      <AppId>00000000-0000-0000-0000-000000000000</AppId>
      <LinkUri>http://apps.microsoft.com/webpdp/app/00000000-0000-0000-0000-000000000000</LinkUri>
      <CurrentMarket>en-US</CurrentMarket>
      <AgeRating>3</AgeRating>
      <MarketData xml:lang="en-us">
        <Name>AppName</Name>
        <Description>AppDescription</Description>
        <Price>1.00</Price>
        <CurrencySymbol>$</CurrencySymbol>
        <CurrencyCode>USD</CurrencyCode>
      </MarketData>
    </App>
  </ListingInformation>
  <LicenseInformation>
    <App>
      <IsActive>true</IsActive>
      <IsTrial>true</IsTrial>
    </App>
  </LicenseInformation>
</CurrentApp>
```

Most of the data here will be unused by our application, but we are interested in the two items within the CurrentApp/LicenseInformation/App node: The IsActive and IsTrial elements here map directly to the corresponding properties in the LicenseInformation object.

Simply adding this file to the project is not sufficient, however. We need to make sure that it gets copied to the folder mentioned above so that the CurrentAppSimulator can read it. A few lines of code can be added into our application to take care of this—it simply needs to be copied from the application's installed location (which will be the bin/Debug folder inside your project folder) to the appropriate target location, which is one of the app's standard data storage folders.

The code to achieve all of this is placed into App.xaml.cs. It can be seen in Listing 14-2. It declares a private class-level LicenseInformation object and a static IsTrial property to allow the rest of the project to identify the current mode. The RefreshLicenseInfoAsync function uses either the simulator or the genuine app data to determine whether the app is in trial mode. If the simulator is being used (in Debug mode), the WindowsStoreProxy.xml file is automatically copied from the project's compilation folder to the required app folder so that it is observed by the simulator.

Listing 14-2. Managing and checking the trial mode value for both debug and release configurations

```
/// <summary>
/// The application's LicenseInformation object
/// </summary>
private LicenseInformation _licenseInfo = null;
/// <summary>
/// Track whether the application is currently running in Trial mode
/// </summary>
internal static bool IsTrial { get; set; }

/// <summary>
/// Refresh the license information for the app
/// </summary>
private async Task RefreshLicenseInfoAsync()
{
    // Do we already have a license information object?
    if (_licenseInfo == null)
    {
        // No, so create one now
#if DEBUG
        // Get a reference to the project's WindowsStoreProxy.xml file
        var sourceFile = await Package.Current.InstalledLocation.GetFileAsync
                                                    ("WindowsStoreProxy.xml");
        // Get the output location for the file
        var destFolder = await ApplicationData.Current.LocalFolder.CreateFolderAsync
                    ("Microsoft\\Windows Store\\ApiData", CreationCollisionOption.OpenIfExists);
        // Create the output file
        var destFile = await destFolder.CreateFileAsync
                        ("WindowsStoreProxy.xml", CreationCollisionOption.ReplaceExisting);
        // Copy the WindowsStoreProxy.xml file to the output file
        await sourceFile.CopyAndReplaceAsync(destFile);
        // Use CurrentAppSimulator to simulate access to the license data
        _licenseInfo = CurrentAppSimulator.LicenseInformation;
#else
        // Use the genuine application license information
        _licenseInfo = CurrentApp.LicenseInformation;
#endif
    }

    // Check if we're in trial mode
    IsTrial = (_licenseInfo.IsTrial == true || _licenseInfo.IsActive == false);
}
```

Due to the use of various asynchronous functions within the code, the RefreshLicenseInfoAsync function has to be declared as asynchronous, too. Its name is also modified to reflect this. Note, however, that in the Release mode path, there are no asynchronous calls made at all. This, unfortunately, generates a compiler warning when in Release mode, but it can be ignored.

The RefreshLicenseInfoAsync function is called from the App class's OnLaunched function. We call it as early as possible so that a valid value for the IsTrial property is available at all times. Due to the use of the await keyword, we also need to mark OnLaunched itself as an async function.

Let's give it a try. Open the WindowsStoreProxy.xml file in the IDE and make sure that the IsTrial element is set to true. When you launch the project, you'll see that it identifies itself as being in trial mode. Now return to the IDE, stop the running project, and edit the XML file again, this time setting IsTrial to false. Now when you launch the app, you'll see that it shows itself as being in full (purchased) mode. Looking good!

Managing Application Purchases

Hopefully, your users will be convinced by what they see and will want to upgrade from the trial to the full version of your game. A few new considerations come into play when this happens, so let's explore the implications of this.

When the user completes the purchase of your game, the existing game instance will continue to run uninterrupted. By default, it will be completely oblivious to the fact that the game has been purchased, so the static IsTrial property will continue to contain the value true. This can lead to confusion and anxiety in your users, not realizing that their purchase will take effect when they close and restart the application. Clearly, we want to be able to detect the purchase straight away so that this situation doesn't occur.

To allow us to deal with this, the LicenseInformation object provides an event named LicenseChanged. Each time the license information is updated in any way, this event will fire so that we can respond appropriately. If you take a look at the code in the example project's RefreshLicenseInfoAsync function, you will see that a handler is added for the event that calls into a function named LicenseInfo_LicenseChanged. All that this latter function does is call back to RefreshLicenseInfoAsync again. This is sufficient to ensure that the IsTrial property is always updated when it needs to be.

When users decide to purchase, you want them to be able to initiate the transaction as quickly and easily as possible. They could do this by navigating their way back through the Store, but it would be very easy for them to get lost or distracted along the way, or to somehow fail to locate your game—possibly resulting in a lost sale.

To eliminate this problem, an API function is present that can be called to initiate the purchase, and using it is simple. Just as we used the CurrentApp object to gain access to the license information, we can use the same object to invoke an app purchase by calling its RequestAppPurchaseAsync method. This method will display a purchase prompt like the one shown in Figure 14-1. Once the user confirms the transaction, control will be returned back to your game with the updated license in place. You won't be able to see this in the test app as this feature only works once the application has been published to the store.

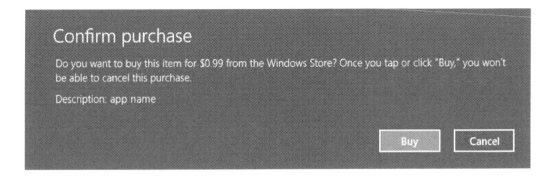

Figure 14-1. Purchasing an application from the Windows Store

Importantly, you cannot assume upon completion of the RequestAppPurchaseAsync function that the transaction was actually made! If the user cancels the purchase, no Internet connection was available, or other problems occur, the function will still complete and return control back to your application. You should always ensure that the LicenseInformation object is used to refresh the trial status after making this call.

This is all fine in theory, but how can we test this prior to submission? Once again, the CurrentAppSimulator object comes to our rescue, as it also provides a RequestAppPurchaseAsync method that simulates the user purchasing the full version of the app. Listing 14-3 shows the code behind the Purchase button in the example project, which allows the simulator to be used for purchasing when in Debug mode, and the real purchase request to be made when in Release mode.

Listing 14-3. Invoking (or simulating) the purchase of the app

```
        private async void buttonPurchase_Click(object sender, RoutedEventArgs e)
        {
            try
            {
#if DEBUG
                await CurrentAppSimulator.RequestAppPurchaseAsync(false);
#else
                await CurrentApp.RequestAppPurchaseAsync(false);
#endif
            }
            catch
            {
                // Failed to complete the purchase
            }
            // The license information will have been updated by this time.
            // Refresh the page content as appropriate for the new trial state.
            ShowTrialState();
        }
```

The button event code uses conditional compilation once again to ensure that the either the real or simulated purchase process is invoked. When the Purchase button is clicked in Debug mode, the simulated purchase process begins and displays a rather ugly-looking dialog box, as shown in Figure 14-2. This dialog box allows you to select the return code for the purchase so that you can simulate both successful and unsuccessful transactions.

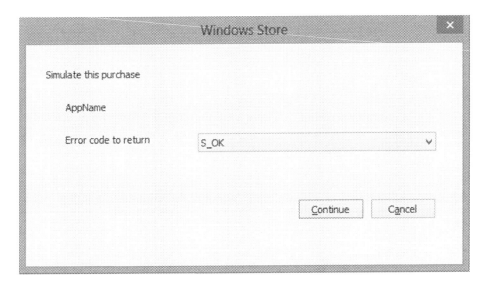

Figure 14-2. *Simulating the purchase of an application*

Once the process completes, the button code calls into the example project's ShowTrialState function, which refreshes the page content once again to respond to the possible new trial mode state. If you give this a try, you will see that the LicenseChanged event triggers as you complete the simulated purchase, and then the page updates to show that the app is no longer in trial mode. You will need to ensure that your application refreshes its feature set as appropriate when the purchase request completes so as to activate the paid-for features if the transaction was successful.

Working with Trial Mode in Windows Phone Apps

All of the same concepts that we have discussed for Windows 8 games apply to Windows Phone games, too, so let's see how they are all implemented for the phone. Unfortunately, the implementation for each task is entirely different.

Detecting Trial Mode

The mechanism for testing trial mode in Windows Phone is broadly similar to that of Windows 8, but it is sadly a little less sophisticated. The fundamental check to determine the mode is performed once again by querying the IsTrial property of a LicenseInformation object, but this time the LicenseInformation object is instantiated directly (it can be found within the Microsoft.Phone.Marketplace namespace).

Unfortunately, there is no equivalent to the CurrentAppSimulator object in Windows Phone, so the features that it offers (such as configuring trial mode via a configuration file and simulating the purchase within the application) are not available for Windows Phone apps. Instead, we have to mock them up ourselves. All of the code required for these tasks can be found in the TrialMode_WP8 project that accompanies this chapter.

The code for checking and simulating trial mode is once again all contained in App.xaml.cs. Just as with the Windows 8 code, we are ultimately updating a static class property named IsTrial from a function named RefreshLicenseInfo.

When in Release mode, the IsTrial property is set directly from the LicenseInformation object, but, in Debug mode, the code reads from a static boolean variable named SimulateTrialMode. By setting the value of SimulateTrialMode as required prior to compilation, you can choose whether the app should initially start in trial or purchased mode. Conditional compilation is used once again to ensure that none of this simulation code gets released into the wild.

445

All of the code responsible for managing the IsTrial property, in both Debug and Release mode, is shown in Listing 14-4. The RefreshLicenseInfo function is called from both the Application_Launching and Application_Activated functions to ensure that no matter how the app starts up, the trial mode value is correctly obtained.

Listing 14-4. Finding and simulating whether the app is running in trial mode

```
    /// <summary>
    /// Track whether the application is currently running in Trial mode
    /// </summary>
    internal static bool IsTrial { get; set; }

#if DEBUG
    // When in debug mode, use this to identify whether to simulate launching in trial
    // mode (true) or purchased mode (false)
    internal static bool SimulateTrialMode = true;
#endif

    /// <summary>
    /// Determine whether the app is running in trial mode and store the result
    /// into the static IsTrial property.
    /// </summary>
    private void RefreshLicenseInfo()
    {
#if DEBUG
        IsTrial = SimulateTrialMode;
#else
        LicenseInformation licenseInfo = new LicenseInformation();
        IsTrial = licenseInfo.IsTrial();
#endif
    }
```

Try launching this project in both Debug and Release modes. In Debug mode, try switching the SimulateTrialMode variable between true and false to see the effect that it has. You'll see that in Release mode, the app always runs in purchased mode.

Managing Application Purchases

In order to make the purchase of your game as easy as possible, we can add functionality for this directly into Windows Phone apps, too. Once again, the approach for this differs from Windows 8.

The way that we initiate app purchase in Windows Phone apps is to take users directly to the application page inside the Windows Phone Store. From there, they can click the Buy button to initiate the purchase transaction.

This is achieved using the MarketplaceDetailTask class, found within the Microsoft.Phone.Tasks namespace. An instance of this can be directly instantiated and its Show method called, and the app page within the Store will appear.

As we discussed when we looked at Application Management in Chapter 10, Windows Phone applications always close when they lose focus. This is no exception—the app will close while the Store page has focus. This means that when the user has finished with the Store and returns to your game (regardless of whether or not the purchase was completed), your game will be relaunched. Due to the fast application switching feature, it will resume exactly where it left off, but the Application_Activated function will execute again so its call back to RefreshLicenseInfo will ensure that the updated trial mode setting is retrieved once more.

It would be extremely useful to be able to simulate all of this for debugging, too, of course. Fortunately, even with our low-tech approach to trial mode simulation, we can still replicate the entire process, including the application closing and reactivating. Let's take a quick look at how.

The Purchase button within MainPage uses the code shown in Listing 14-5 as its Click handler. In Release mode, it simply opens the Store page, but, in Debug mode, it does a little more. First, it displays a MessageBox to see whether we wish to simulate successfully completing the transaction or to simulate the transaction failing or being aborted. If the OK button is clicked, the code sets our SimulateTrialMode variable in the App class to false to indicate that we should no longer be in trial mode. It, too ,then invokes the Store page.

Listing 14-5. Invoking (or simulating) the purchase of the app

```
    private void buttonPurchase_Click(object sender, RoutedEventArgs e)
    {
#if DEBUG
        // In debug mode, prompt the user to switch to full mode
        if (MessageBox.Show("Simulate switching to full (purchased) mode?",
                            "Simulate purchase", MessageBoxButton.OKCancel) == MessageBoxResult.OK)
        {
            // Switch to full mode
            App.SimulateTrialMode = false;
        }
#endif
        MarketplaceDetailTask marketplaceDetailTask = new MarketplaceDetailTask();
        marketplaceDetailTask.Show();
    }
```

When the Store page is opened from an application that has not actually been downloaded from the Store itself, the Store appears but simply displays an error message, as shown in Figure 14-3. As long as you see the error code 805a0194, you can be satisfied that the code is working—this is the expected error code for this scenario.

Figure 14-3. The result of displaying the Windows Phone Store from a non-Store application

Even when this error message is displayed, it still causes your app to close as it moves into the background. When you acknowledge the Store error, the application relaunches, just as it would after a real visit to the Store in a published application. This means that the failed visit to the store actually takes exactly the same path through your game code as will be made once your game has been published. As a result, this simulates the purchase process exactly.

If you run in Debug mode and select to simulate the purchase, you'll find that the app reappears in purchased mode after you close the Store error message. Because the `Application_Activated` function called into `RefreshLicenseInfo` once again when your app re-activated, the updated value of the `SimulateTrialMode` variable was observed. Everything is behaving just as it will once your game is published.

You can now use this process to build in whatever game logic you wish to use around the trial mode feature and test that everything works as expected in all scenarios.

Submission Requirements

Before your game is accepted into the Store, Microsoft will perform a series of tests on it to ensure that it meets all the submission requirements. If any of these tests should fail, the game will fail the submission process and will need to be fixed and resubmitted.

The full list of requirements for Windows 8 apps can be found at `http://tinyurl.com/win8certification` and the requirements for Windows Phone apps at `http://tinyurl.com/wpcertification`. You should review these requirements in detail before submitting. The documents may change in the future and additional requirements might be added or existing requirements relaxed, so don't assume that you know their contents even if you have read through them before. Both documents contain a Change History section at the end to help clarify any areas that have been modified.

In this section, we will briefly review some of the areas that might be relevant to your games.

Content Policies

Your application will fail the submission process if it contains any unlicensed or unpermitted third-party content such as logos, music, sound files, and so on. If this type of content is present, it must be clearly marked as being used with permission.

Any form of illegal, obscene, indecent, threatening, or "adult" content will result in submission failure, as will excessive use of profanity.

The "violence" sections are worth checking carefully if you are creating a game of a violent nature; they list the types of content that will result in submission failure.

Application Requirements

Your game must consist entirely of managed .NET code. Any attempt to use P/Invoke ("API calls") or COM interop will result in the submission failing.

Application Features

For Windows 8 applications, applications must work equally well on both touch devices and keyboard/mouse devices. If an application only works with one or the other of these configurations, it will not pass certification.

For Windows Phone, the submitted application must be able to run on all current Windows Phone 8 devices and must not rely on hardware that is present only in a subset of devices. It needs to correctly adapt to all screen resolutions.

Reliability and Performance

Your game must not cause any unhandled exceptions to be thrown, or it will fail the verification process.

The application should always remain responsive to user input. When a long-running operation is taking place (generating level data or downloading content from the Internet, for example), a progress indicator must be displayed so that users are aware of what is happening and how much longer they will need to wait. A "cancel" option must also be made available to abort the process, and it must be responsive within a reasonable time frame.

Your game must present its first screen within five seconds of being launched. For Windows Phone apps, the time between launching and the game first accepting input must not exceed 20 seconds.

Handling the Windows Phone Back button comes in for some specific attention. The requirements are as follows:

- Pressing Back on the game's first screen must exit the game.

- Pressing Back anywhere else within a game must return the player either to the previous screen or to an in-game pause menu. Pressing Back again while such a menu is open should close the menu and return to the game.

- Whenever Back is pressed while a context menu or dialog box is open, the menu or dialog box should close without any additional navigation taking place.

The handling of the Back button is a common reason for submission failure, so make sure that it behaves appropriately within all game modes and screens.

Technical Information

Your game must include easy access to its name, version number, and contact details for technical support. Using an About screen is an ideal way to present this information. We will look at a simple way to retrieve the version number in the Preparing for Distribution section later in this chapter.

Windows 8 apps can use the *Charms Bar* to host this information. We'll look at how this is achieved in the Considerations Prior to Distribution section later in this chapter.

Music and Sound

As discussed in the earlier sections covering music playback, it is not permitted for Windows Phone applications to stop, pause, resume, or change any music that the user is playing without first asking for consent (including changing the volume level). This restriction does not apply to sound effects, which can play alongside existing background music.

If the game does provide its own background music, the user must also be provided with the ability to disable it. It's a very good idea to allow the same facility for the sound effects, too, so that the game can be played in a quiet environment without disturbing anyone.

Testing Your Game

It might be an obvious assumption, but its importance cannot be overstated: Before you publish your game, you need to test it. Test it until you are sick of looking at it. Get your friends, family, colleagues, and neighbors to test it. Find and fill every hole that anyone can find.

One of the significant reasons for ensuring that you have tested everything as much as possible is that once your game is accepted into the Store, it can take up to a week for new revisions to be submitted and accepted—or even longer if your subsequent submissions fail certification. During this time, your game will potentially be building up poor reviews and low review scores just because of silly bugs; there is nothing you can do to prevent them. Don't let the reputation of your game be ruined before you have even finished working on it!

Testing for Windows 8

As your game is expected to work equally well on touch devices and on devices with mice and keyboards, it's important to try it out in both of these configurations. Testing with a mouse and keyboard is generally easy as you can use your development PC for this, but, if you don't have access to a touch device, this can be harder to achieve.

Such testing can still be performed with the Windows simulator, switching it into one of the touch simulation modes. This doesn't give the same level of interaction with the device that a real tablet would offer, but it's much better than nothing.

Also, don't forget that graphics performance on a desktop PC will generally be much better than on a tablet, which will have much lower hardware specifications.

If you can't test on a tablet device yourself, it's worth trying to find someone that may be able to test it for you. The section later in this chapter entitled "Offering Your Game to Best Testers" describes how you might accomplish this.

Don't forget to test the game on all of the screen resolutions provided by the simulator. Some of the resolutions use different DPI settings, and these can cause your touch input to be processed incorrectly if you haven't accounted for this.

Finally, there is a tool that can be used to perform automated testing of your app. The tool is called the Windows Application Certification Kit. We'll take a look at this in the Automated Application Testing section later in this chapter, once we've looked at how to build your app in order for it to be tested.

Testing for Windows Phone

The first thing to mention is in relation to the emulator. It is a fantastic tool for development, allowing you to quickly and easily access a device environment without needing to actually plug anything in to your PC and to keep everything your program does on your PC screen where your source code is.

Overall, the emulator provides an extremely good representation of how a game or application will work on a real device, but there are certain elements that let it down. Multitouch support is one obvious area in which the emulator cannot satisfactorily stand in for a real device. Accelerometer input is another. While the emulator does provide a simulation of accelerometer input, nothing is as good as really holding and moving a device. Less obvious (but equally significant) is the area of performance.

As we have discussed a couple of times during the course of this book, the emulator is not an accurate representation of how your game will perform on a real phone. You need to make sure that this is not a problem before it hits the Store.

Test on a real device as frequently as you can, and especially before releasing to the public. If possible, test on as many different devices as you can. It's unlikely that you'll have access to many such devices, so you can take advantage of beta testers to help in this area. (See the section entitled "Offering Your Game to Beta Testers" for some advice as to how you can achieve this.) Be aware that devices with higher screen resolutions (such as the Nokia Lumia 920) tend to perform worse with graphically intensive games than the lower-resolution devices—even though they often have higher powered processors—due to the number of pixels they need to refresh.

Use the different versions of the emulator to test your game on all of the available screen resolutions and ensure that everything scales properly in all cases.

Another check to make if your game has been developed using XAML content is to verify that your game appears correctly with both a light- and dark-colored background configured. Real devices and the emulator default to a dark background, but they can be switched to a light background by opening the Settings page, choosing to change the Theme, and then changing the background setting, as shown in Figure 14-4.

Figure 14-4. Setting the dark or light background color

With the background changed, run your game again and check every single page, graphic, and piece of text that it can display. If you have specifically designed anything in a light color and are displaying it on the default background color, it might be hard to see or even be invisible. Also make sure to pay attention to the appearance of ApplicationBar buttons. Windows Phone will automatically invert their colors, but if you have used anything other than simple monochrome buttons with transparency, the inversion might not always produce the result you expect.

Finally, as with Windows 8 apps, Microsoft provides an automated testing tool for Windows Phone apps—the Windows Phone Store Test Kit. You can find more details about this in the Automated Application Testing section later in this chapter.

Considerations Prior to Distribution

Here are a few ideas and suggestions for other things you may want to add to your game before you make your final preparations for submission.

Persuading People to Review Your Game

Even though the Windows and Windows Phone Stores may be lagging behind some of the competing operating systems' app stores in terms of quantity of apps, there are still many, many thousands of apps already published that yours will compete with. One of the things that allows an app to stand out from the crowd is its reviews and its review score.

Many people browsing the Store will make a judgment about your game based purely on its review score, the star rating that is displayed next to all apps. If your game has low ratings, it'll tend to be overlooked. It is, therefore, very important to try to ensure that as many positive ratings are received as possible.

One way that you can do this is simply by asking people to review the game on a periodic basis. Make sure that your users have actually played the game enough to have formed an opinion before asking them—there's no point asking for a review the first time the game launches as the user won't have had an opportunity to see it yet. Allow a certain time period to pass or a number of application launches to occur, and then ask for feedback.

Don't be intrusive when asking. Make sure users have a way of indicating that they don't want to leave a review and that they don't want to be asked again. Continually pestering for a review may end up with one that you would prefer not to receive! Also, offer a choice of being reminded later—users may be receptive to the idea but busy at the particular moment your app chooses to prompt them.

One slightly sneaky trick is to only prompt users who can be fairly well relied upon for a positive review. There are two ways to detect such users: either wait until they have launched your game quite a large number of times (if they keep coming back, then they probably like it), or wait until they buy it (if they paid money, this is a pretty good indication that they're happy!). If you keep your review prompts limited to these groups of users, the chances are that your reviews and their scores will be favorable.

When the users indicate that they are prepared to write a review, take them directly to the review page so that they can do so before they forget or change their mind. This is easy to achieve.

For Windows 8 apps, the app review page is displayed by redirecting the user to a specially formatted web URL. Listing 14-6 shows the code required for this.

Listing 14-6. Taking a user to the app review page in the Windows 8 Store

```
// Open the review page in the store
var uri = new Uri("ms-windows-store:REVIEW?PFN=" + Package.Current.Id.FamilyName);
await Windows.System.Launcher.LaunchUriAsync(uri);
```

This is, unfortunately, another piece of code that you won't be able to test prior to submission—all that will happen when you execute this is that the Store will open, so be careful to enter the URL correctly. The reason for this is, of course, because your app is not present in the Store until after it has been published. The `Package.Current.Id.FamilyName` value referenced within the code will be updated when you publish your app to contain a unique code that applies to your app. This will then be used to ensure that the appropriate Store page is displayed.

For Windows Phone apps, the same thing is achieved using another Task class, similar to the one we used for allowing the user to purchase your trial app earlier in this chapter. The required code for this is shown in Listing 14-7.

Listing 14-7. Taking a user to the app review page in the Windows Phone Store

```
// Open the review page in the store
Microsoft.Phone.Tasks.MarketplaceReviewTask reviewTask;
reviewTask = new Microsoft.Phone.Tasks.MarketplaceReviewTask();
reviewTask.Show();
```

When used in an application that has not been installed from the Store itself, this will once again display an error page with code 805a0194. This is the correct behavior and does not indicate a problem with the code.

Adding Items to the Windows 8 Charms Bar

If you are releasing a Windows 8 game, you may want to consider adding some content to the *Charms Bar*. This is the bar that appears when you hover the mouse cursor in the top- or bottom-right corner of the window, or swipe in from the right edge of the screen. Most of the content of this bar is fixed, but if you click the Settings charm, you can add your own items (known as commands) to the list of headings that subsequently appears and allow these items to perform actions within your game. Typically, these items will be limited to displaying information or configuration windows to the user, though they can potentially do more than that if you want.

▒ **Note** Useful as the Settings item within the Charms Bar is, it is a little obscure, and many users will not notice items that you add to it. For this reason, you should either avoid putting critical areas of functionality into the Charms Bar or make sure that other routes to access the functions are made available from other areas of your game.

The example project CharmsBar_Win8, which accompanies this chapter, contains examples of the functionality that can be added to the Settings charm.

Settings Charm Content

The default empty Settings charm for an unpublished application is shown in Figure 14-5. The application name, author, and Permissions command are automatically added by the application framework and cannot be removed. The application name and author name are read from your application's Package Manifest (which we'll look at in more detail in the Preparing for Distribution section later in this chapter) and are provided by the Application UI/Display Name and Packaging/Publisher display name fields, respectively.

Figure 14-5. *The default items within the Settings charm for an unpublished application*

When the Permissions command is selected, an automatically generated panel appears showing the app details and version number as well as any special system permissions that the application has access to, as shown in Figure 14-6. These details will be discussed in the Preparing for Distribution section, too.

CharmsBar_Win8
By Adam Dawes
Version 1.0.0.0

This app has permission to use:
Your Internet connection

Figure 14-6. *The contents of the Permissions flyout*

Once your application is published to the Store, a second command will be automatically added to the Settings charm, entitled "Rate and review." If this is clicked, the user will be taken directly to the app review page within the windows store. There is, therefore, no need to replicate this functionality in your custom-added Settings charm commands.

Other commands that you may wish to consider include game settings, application information, authorship credits, and contact details. You may also be required to include a privacy statement within the command list, as detailed in the Updating the Application Manifest File section later in this chapter.

Adding Commands to the Settings Charm

Adding your own commands is very straightforward. A class named SettingsPane is available within the Windows.UI.ApplicationSettings namespace, and this is our entry point for working with the charm.

Each time the user opens the Settings charm, the class will raise an event named CommandsRequested. This is our cue to tell the charm which custom items we want it to display. We need to add an event handler for the event, the code for which can be found at the end of the example project's App.OnLaunched function. The code for this and an empty handler function is shown in Listing 14-8.

Listing 14-8. Responding to the CommandsRequested event

```
protected override void OnLaunched(LaunchActivatedEventArgs args)
{
    [... the rest of the code is omitted for brevity ...]

    // Set up an event handler for responding to the charms menu
    SettingsPane.GetForCurrentView().CommandsRequested += App_CommandsRequested;
}


/// <summary>
/// Respond to the charms menu appearing
/// </summary>
void App_CommandsRequested(SettingsPane sender,
                                    SettingsPaneCommandsRequestedEventArgs args)
{
    // Add commands here
}
```

To add each command, we create an instance of the SettingsCommand class, also from the Windows.UI.ApplicationSettings namespace, and populate its properties via its parameterized constructor. These properties are the following:

- settingsCommandId, a string that identifies the command that you may wish to use later to check which command has been selected.

- label, the text to display for the command within the Settings charm. This text doesn't wrap, so if it gets too long it will be truncated. It's a good idea to keep this short and concise.

- handler, a function that will be invoked when the command is activated by the user. This is formed by creating a UICommandInvokedHandler object and providing the function that will handle the command as a parameter to its constructor.

Once this command object has been created, it is added to the settings charm via the `ApplicationCommands` collection contained within the `SettingsPaneCommandsRequestedEventArgs` object passed as a parameter to the `CommandsRequested` event handler.

Listing 14-9 shows an updated version of the `CommandsRequested` event handler from Listing 14-8 that adds a command to the charm. When the user selects the command, the `SettingsAlertCommand` function is called, which displays a simple `MessageDialog` to indicate that it has been executed.

Listing 14-9. Adding and responding to a Settings charm command

```
/// <summary>
/// Respond to the charms menu appearing
/// </summary>
void App_CommandsRequested(SettingsPane sender,
                                    SettingsPaneCommandsRequestedEventArgs args)
{
    // Add an "alert" item and its handler function
    cmd = new SettingsCommand("alert", "Show alert box",
                        new UICommandInvokedHandler(SettingsAlertCommand));
    args.Request.ApplicationCommands.Add(cmd);
}

private async void SettingsAlertCommand(IUICommand command)
{
    MessageDialog msg = new MessageDialog("The charm command was selected.");
    await msg.ShowAsync();
}
```

You can give this a try by running the example project and picking the Show alert box command from the Settings charm. As expected, the message dialog is displayed. This is an example of how you can perform general actions within your game in response to a command in the settings bar.

In many cases, however, it would be good to be able to respond in a similar fashion to the built-in Permissions command and display a slide-out panel at the edge of the screen. These panels are great for information boxes, and sometimes for user settings, too. Such panels are also easy to implement, so let's see they are created.

Implementing Flyout Command Panels

An example of a flyout command panel can be found within the example project, too. Select the About (App Name) command to open it. As you'll see, the panel slides out from the edge of the screen over the top of the Charms bar to display its content. You can then click the arrow button in the panel header to return to the Settings charm command list, or you can click outside of the panel to close it entirely.

The first thing we'll do to create a flyout command panel is to create the panel itself and populate its content. The panels are actually implemented as normal XAML Pages, so we'll start by looking at the Page design. The example project contains a Page named `AboutFlyout.xaml`, which you can use as a template for your own flyouts.

The `AboutFlyout` Page's XAML is just like that for any other page, except that two new attributes have been added to the outermost Page element: `d:DesignHeight` and `d:DesignWidth`, as shown in Listing 14-10. These have no effect on the compiled page, but instead are used to restrict the page designer to the specified size. A width of 346 pixels has been selected as a standard as per Microsoft's UI guidelines, and a height of 768 as this is the minimum screen height that you can expect to have to work with. These dimensions give a good idea of how much content you can fit on the screen.

Listing 14-10. Settings the page design size for a flyout panel

```
<Page
    x:Class="CharmsBar_Win8.AboutFlyout"
    xmlns="http://schemas.microsoft.com/winfx/2006/xaml/presentation"
    xmlns:x="http://schemas.microsoft.com/winfx/2006/xaml"
    xmlns:local="using:CharmsBar_Win8"
    xmlns:d="http://schemas.microsoft.com/expression/blend/2008"
    xmlns:mc="http://schemas.openxmlformats.org/markup-compatibility/2006"
    mc:Ignorable="d"
    d:DesignWidth="346"
    d:DesignHeight="768">
```

▨ **Note**   If you need more space than the 346-pixel wide flyout offers, you can alternatively create a *wide* flyout panel with a width of 646 pixels. You can visit `http://tinyurl.com/settingscommands` to read all of Microsoft's guidelines for using the Settings charm commands.

Within the page, we can now add the required content. This should consist of a colored panel header that includes a back button (a left-facing arrow) and a title that matches the text of the selected command. The remaining space below this can be used for the required flyout content.

The flyout will automatically close if the user clicks in the main app space, but the behavior when the back button is clicked needs to be handled within our own code. The code required to handle this is shown in Listing 14-11. Essentially, the code closes the flyout (by setting its parent Popup object's IsOpen property to false—we'll look at the Popup object next) and then re-displays the Settings charm command list.

Listing 14-11. Responding to the flyout panel's back button

```
private void MySettingsBackClicked(object sender, RoutedEventArgs e)
{
    // First close our Flyout.
    Popup parent = this.Parent as Popup;
    if (parent != null)
    {
        parent.IsOpen = false;
    }
    // Now re-display the Settings charm pane.
    SettingsPane.Show();
}
```

That forms the flyout content, so now we need to be able to display it in response to the charm command being selected. This is a little more work. The complete code to achieve this is shown in Listing 14-12 (and can also be found in the App.SettingsAboutCommand function in the example project).

Listing 14-12. Displaying the flyout in response to the Settings charm command being selected

```
private void SettingsAboutCommand(IUICommand command)
{
    // Check on which side of the screen the SettingsPane is displayed
    bool isRightEdge = (SettingsPane.Edge == SettingsEdgeLocation.Right);
```

```
// Create the flyout and set its size
AboutFlyout flyout = new AboutFlyout();
flyout.Width = 346;
flyout.Height = Window.Current.Bounds.Height;

// Create and initialize a new Popup object for the flyout
_aboutCharmPopup = new Popup();

// Add the proper animation for the panel.
_aboutCharmPopup.ChildTransitions = new TransitionCollection();
_aboutCharmPopup.ChildTransitions.Add(new PaneThemeTransition()
{
        Edge = isRightEdge ? EdgeTransitionLocation.Right :
                            EdgeTransitionLocation.Left
});

// Associate the flyout with the popup and set its position and size
_aboutCharmPopup.Child = flyout;
_aboutCharmPopup.Width = flyout.Width;
_aboutCharmPopup.Height = flyout.Height;
_aboutCharmPopup.SetValue(Canvas.LeftProperty,
                        isRightEdge ? Window.Current.Bounds.Width - flyout.Width : 0);
_aboutCharmPopup.SetValue(Canvas.TopProperty, 0);
_aboutCharmPopup.IsLightDismissEnabled = true;

// Display the flyout
_aboutCharmPopup.IsOpen = true;

// Set a handler for the window's Activated event so that we can automatically close
// the Popup when the window deactivates, and for the Popup's Closed event so that
// we can remove the window Activated event handler when the popup closes.
Window.Current.Activated += OnWindowActivated;
_aboutCharmPopup.Closed += OnPopupClosed;
}
```

The steps performed by this code are as follows:

- The isRightEdge variable is set to check which side of the screen the Charms bar is using in case it has been configured to the left edge of the screen.

- An instance of our AboutFlyout page is created and its size is set as required. The Width is explicitly set to the desired width, and the Height is set to match that of the current window so that it appears the full height of the screen.

- A Popup object is created and stored in the class-level variable named _aboutCharmPopup. The reason for storing this in such a variable is because we may need to programmatically close the popup later on, as we will see in a moment.

- A *transition* object is set into the popup. This is what is responsible for making the flyout *slide* out of the edge of the screen rather than simply appearing in place. The transition type is set as appropriate based on which edge of the screen the settings pane is located on.

- The remaining popup properties are then set. The AboutFlyout instance is placed into the popup's Child property so that our flyout page is used as the popup's content. The popup's Width and Height are set as appropriate. The position is set so that it is at the top of the window, and either offset from the right edge by the flyout width, or directly on the left edge, based on the edge of the screen that is being used. The IsLightDismissEnabled property is set so that touching outside the popup will automatically close it.

- The popup is opened.

- A couple of event handlers are configured. The first, for the current Window, is created so that when the window is deactivated, the popup is automatically closed (and this is why the class-level Popup variable is required). The second, for the popup itself, is set to remove the Window's event handler when the popup closes. The handler functions for both of these can be seen in Listing 14-13.

Listing 14-13. Handling the window deactivating and the popup closing

```
/// <summary>
/// Handle deactivation with a Charm popup open
/// </summary>
void OnWindowActivated(object sender, Windows.UI.Core.WindowActivatedEventArgs e)
{
    if (e.WindowActivationState == Windows.UI.Core.CoreWindowActivationState.Deactivated)
    {
        if (_aboutCharmPopup != null) _aboutCharmPopup.IsOpen = false;
    }
}

/// <summary>
/// When a popup closes, remove the OnWindowActivated event handler
/// </summary>
void OnPopupClosed(object sender, object e)
{
    Window.Current.Activated -= OnWindowActivated;
}
```

If you wish to add more flyout panels, this is easy to do. Duplicate the SettingsAboutCommand function and update it for your new panel, along with a new class-level Popup variable. The same OnWindowActivated and OnPopupClosed event handler functions can be used for all of the flyouts. In the OnWindowActivated function, check for all of the class-level Popup objects (in addition to the _aboutCharmPopup check already present) so that any open popup is closed.

Preparing for Distribution

When you are happy that the game is ready to be distributed, there are just a few final things that you need to attend to prior to submitting it to the Store. These are very straightforward, but they might involve a little graphical work.

This section lists the final steps you need to do to prepare for game release.

- Set your game details inside the application manifest file.

- Set your game's version number.

- Prepare screenshots for the store.

Updating the Application Manifest File

Each application submitted to the Store contains a series of values that provide information about the app such as its title, author, description, copyright information, and so on. The manifest also contains a number of images for icons and tiles. When preparing your game for release, you need to provide appropriate content for each of these fields.

The application manifest is stored in a different location for Windows 8 and Windows Phone projects. While the content of the files is different, it has a significant overlap between the two platforms. The manifest files are actually XML files, but Visual Studio helpfully provides a user interface for editing them, making life much easier.

To open the manifest for a Windows 8 application, double-click the `Package.appxmanifest` in the root of the project. For a Windows Phone 8 app, double-click the `WMAppManifest.xml` file inside the project's Properties node in Solution Explorer.

The manifest UI is divided into four tabs, so let's look at each one. We'll cover the most significant fields—those that are not mentioned can generally be left with their default values. For a more detailed description of all elements of the manifest windows, you can visit `http://tinyurl.com/win8manifest` for Windows 8 or `http://tinyurl.com/wp8manifest` for Windows Phone.

The Application UI Tab

This tab is where the main user-facing details of your application are provided. The fields to pay particular attention to are as follows:

- Display name is the name that will appear on your app's tile in the Windows 8 Start menu and the Windows Phone application list. Make sure that a sensible value is set here that allows your game to be identified.

- Description allows an optional description of your app to be provided.

We'll look at the remaining fields on a platform-by-platform basis.

For Windows 8 apps, everything else on this tab falls into the Visual Assets section. A list of asset categories on the left allows these to be viewed all together or filtered into different categories. We'll look at the most significant fields within this section.

- Supported rotations provides an optional mechanism for you to specify which display orientations your app is able to support. Devices, such as tablets, that support multiple rotations will stay within the specified orientations. Devices that cannot be rotated, such as desktop PCs, will always display in the device's default rotation, so you should ensure that you game always functions correctly with a landscape orientation.

- Short name provides a field where the name of the app can be set as it will appear on the Start menu tile. If not set, this will fall back to using the Display name instead.

- Foreground text and Background color allow you to set the basic Windows Store color scheme for your app. The background color will appear against your app when it is listed in the Store, with the text displayed in either Light or Dark text on top of it. Any transparent areas of your application logos will display this background color. You should ensure that the text is easily readable and ideally uses the background color to help make your app stand out in the Store listings.

- The Logo field allows you to specify the images that will appear on your app's normal square tile in the Start menu. Four separate images may be specified. Windows will pick the one that best fits its requirement based on the user's screen resolution. If you don't wish to create all four of these images, just provide the 150x150 pixel image and Windows will automatically scale it to fit.

- The Wide Logo field allows optional images for the *wide tile* to be specified. There is no requirement to provide any of these, in which case the wide tile will not be available for your app. If you wish to provide only one wide logo image, use the 310x150 pixel image.

- The Small Logo field contains two sets of images, the first four with *Scale* labels, the remaining four with *Target size* labels. The first four of these are used in the Windows Start Menu application list and also in the Alt-Tab window. The last four will appear in the Windows File Explorer should your app be displayed there. If you wish to provide only one of these, use the 30x30 pixel image.

- The Store Logo is used when your app appears in the Windows Store. If you only wish to provide one image, use the 50x50 pixel image.

- The Splash Screen image is displayed on the screen as your app is launching. The image will be displayed centrally within the screen, with the rest of the screen filled with the specified Splash Screen Background color. If you only wish to provide one image, use the 620x300 pixel image.

The options for Windows Phone are thankfully rather more limited, and are as follows:

- App Icon is the icon to use for your app when it is displayed in the full app list, accessed by swiping to the left from the Start menu. It should be a 100x100 pixel PNG file. Any transparent areas of the image will show the user's selected accent color.

- Supported Resolutions allows you to specify which screen resolutions are supported. Phones that use a resolution that you have indicated as being unsupported *will not be able to download your game*. You should ideally keep all of the resolutions checked and make sure that the game works as expected with each resolution.

- The Tile Title is the caption for your app that will be displayed should its tile be pinned to the Start menu. Unless you particularly need this to be different, you should generally set this to be the same as your app's Display name.

- Finally, the three Tile Images are used when your app is pinned to the Start Menu. All apps are required to provide a Small tile at 159x159 pixels and a Medium tile at 336x336 pixels. If you wish, you may also provide a Large tile at 691x336 pixels. Adding the Large tile will enable the option for the user to expand the pinned tile to a double width.

The Capabilities Tab

This tab is used to set specific functional capabilities that your app needs to use. Potential users of your app will be advised of the capabilities prior to downloading, so they may choose not to install your app if they are concerned about possible privacy violations.

You should review the capabilities and ensure that only those that you actually need are selected. The More Information link available in this tab can be used to help gain additional information about the implications of each capability.

Note that in Windows 8 apps, the Internet (Client) capability is checked by default. This is required in order for your app to access the Internet. If you don't need any Internet access at all, you should uncheck this box. If you leave it checked, you are *required* to add a Privacy command item to the Settings charm that details your app's privacy statement, explaining what user information (if any) will be transmitted over the Internet. If the Internet (Client) capability is checked and this Settings command is not found, your app will fail certification.

The Declarations Tab

This tab, present only in Windows 8 applications, is used to provide information about specific tasks that your app is able to perform. Nothing that we have discussed in this book will require any of these, though you may need them for specific applications.

After adding any declaration, a More information link will appear, which can be clicked for full descriptions of each available declaration.

The Requirements Tab

This Windows Phone-only tab allows you to specify hardware requirements that devices running your game must support. Devices that do not support the requirements that you specify will be unable to download your app. You should make sure that these are not checked unless there is a good reason to do so.

The Packaging Tab

The final tab is the Packaging tab, which is present for both platforms, though with mostly different fields.

For Windows 8 apps, most of the editable field values are replaced when you upload to the store so there is no need to configure them. The only exception to this is the Version number. We'll be looking at strategies for managing version numbers in the next section.

The only useful fields in Windows Phone apps are the Author, Publisher, and Version fields, which you should fill in as appropriate.

Managing the Application Version

It is essential to adopt a version numbering scheme for your game so that you and your users know exactly which version of a game they have installed. You will be required to provide the app version number during the upload to the Store, and you must ensure that the version number you provide matches the version number in your game.

As already discussed, the version number is accessed via the Packaging tab of the application manifest.

Version numbers are formed by four numeric values separated by periods. For example, 1.0.0.0 might be the first version of a released executable. The four parts of the version number, from left to right, are the following:

- Major version

- Minor version

- Build number

- Revision

Exactly how you use these version number elements is really up to you, but here is a suggested strategy:

- The major version is incremented each time a whole new version of a product is released (for example, it has been rewritten or is substantially different from a previous version).

- The minor version is incremented each time a new version of an application is released, but the application is still the same basic product as the previous release. This would be incremented when new features have been added to a product, but the product has not been rewritten or substantially modified so that the major version would be increased. The minor version would be reset to 0 if the major version number increases.

- The build number and revision are unlikely to be of any use outside of your own needs, so you could either leave them set to 0 or use them to store an internal build count or something similar.

▓ **Note** It is important to remember that the periods here are just field separators, not decimal separators. Incrementing the revision of a version string set to 1.9.0.0 results in a version string of 1.10.0.0, not 2.0.0.0.

It is a requirement of the Store (and also a very useful thing to have) that the application be able to report its version number from inside the game. You could certainly hard-code the version number into your About page, but then you have to remember to update it with each new release of your game. This could be easily overlooked, resulting in confusion for your users and a potential submission failure.

For Windows 8 apps, this is easy to resolve. We can write a few lines of code to retrieve the project's version number from the application manifest. Listing 14-14 shows how this can be achieved. You can see this in operation within the VersionNumber_Win8 example project.

Listing 14-14. Reading the version number from the application manifest

```
// Get the package Version object
PackageVersion version = Package.Current.Id.Version;
// Build it into a string
string versionText = version.Major.ToString() + "."
                   + version.Minor.ToString() + "."
                   + version.Build.ToString() + "."
                   + version.Revision.ToString();
// Display the string in the page
textVersion.Text = "The version number is " + versionText;
```

In Windows Phone applications, it should, in theory, be just as simple to do this. In practice, unfortunately, it isn't as simple after all. The code used for Windows 8 in Listing 14-14 should have worked too in Windows Phone—the classes are available and their documentation states that they are compatible with Windows Phone—but attempting to use them results in a NotImplementedException being thrown.

Hopefully, this will be addressed in a future version of the Windows Phone development tools, but, until then, there isn't a direct way to access the manifest version number.

Instead, we will take another approach. The version number can also be stored in the AssemblyInfo.cs file, which is also located inside the Properties node in Solution Explorer. At the bottom of the file is a line that stores the assembly version number, as shown in Listing 14-15.

Listing 14-15. The declaration of the assembly version number

```
[assembly: AssemblyVersion("1.0.0.0")]
```

This version number *can* be read by our code. It is completely independent to the manifest version number, however, so you will need to remember to keep both of these version numbers synchronized. Also, be aware that if your game solution uses multiple assemblies, each one will have its own separate assembly version. The version that is returned will depend on which assembly contains the code to read it. You should try to keep all such code in your main game project so that you only need to keep that project's assembly version up-to-date.

With the assembly version number set, it can be read with the code shown in Listing 14-16. This can be seen in operation in the VersionNumber_WP8 project. Try using this project to change the manifest version and the assembly version to different values in order to see how the code responds.

Listing 14-16. Reading the current project's assembly version number

```
// Get the assembly name
string name = Assembly.GetExecutingAssembly().FullName;
// Use this to obtain its version
Version version = new AssemblyName(name).Version;
// Display the string in the page
textVersion.Text = "The version number is " + version;
```

Preparing Screenshots for the Store

When you submit the game to the Store (which we will get to very soon now!), you will need to provide a number of screenshots from your game that will be displayed in the Store page.

These screenshots are one of the main tools that people have when browsing the Store to help them decide whether or not to download your game, so it's important that you provide images that are accurate, enticing, and that show a representative sample of what can be expected from your game. Drab and empty images will be unlikely to persuade anyone to give your game a chance. It is a good idea to spend some time getting really good images to use. The images should be taken directly from your game without subsequent alteration or they may result in your submission being rejected.

For Windows 8 games, you can provide up to eight screenshots, each of which must be at least 1366 x 768 pixels (or 768 x 1366 pixels for portrait-orientated images), and they must not exceed 2 megabytes insize. One easy way to obtain the screenshots is to run your game in the simulator. In the toolbar on the right side of the simulator window, you'll find a button that will capture a screenshot from the current simulator content, and these screenshots are perfect for inclusion with your game.

Windows Phone games also allow up to eight screenshots. The easiest way to capture them is to use the emulator. The Additional Tools window (accessed by clicking the button at the bottom of the emulator's toolbar that displays two right-facing chevrons) has a Screenshot tab. This tab can be used to easily capture and save images from your game.

When you upload your images to the Windows Phone Store, you can choose to either upload separate sets of images for each supported app resolution or upload images at the highest supported resolution and allow the Store to automatically scale them down to lower resolutions for you. Creating images for each resolution may result in slightly clearer images for the lower resolution devices, but also can be substantially more time-consuming!

Make sure you run the emulator at the appropriate resolutions when capturing your images so that you have them at whichever sizes you need for the submission process.

Selling or Giving Your Game for Free

One of the decisions you will need to make is whether your game will be sold or downloaded for free. Free applications can be great promotional tools, or you might simply decide that you want to maximize your audience (many people will give something a try if it's free!).

If you decide to sell your game, you will need to decide on the selling price. This can be set within a defined price range that starts at around US$1.00, or it can be increased to hundreds of dollars. Take a look at other similar apps in the Store to try to find how much your competition costs, and then decide on your price. The price can be changed after publication, so you can move it up or down as needed. You might even try time-limited introductory offers (or even give it away for free for a period of time) to help get your game on the radar before increasing the price.

Microsoft will retain a share of your sales income (typically 30 percent, though this does decrease after certain thresholds have been reached) and you will receive the remaining income, subject to taxes and other applicable deductions.

Payment will be made directly into your bank account once per month after you have accrued enough revenue to meet the minimum payment threshold.

It is also possible to take advantage of some of the other application business models, including using advertising or in-app purchasing. These provide all sorts of new options, but they are beyond the scope of our coverage. You can find out more about these options by visiting http://tinyurl.com/makingmoneywin8 for Windows 8 and http://tinyurl.com/makingmoneywp8 for Windows Phone.

Offering Your Game to Beta Testers

There is, of course, only so much testing that you can do yourself, so you may, at some stage along the route to publishing, decide to enlist the services of others to help with your testing. If so, you can create *beta* copies of your app for people to test.

Windows Phone has the more advanced model for interacting with beta testers in this instance. You can create private beta applications within the Windows Phone Store and provide restricted invitation-only access to these beta copies to whichever specific individuals you choose. The beta will automatically expire after 90 days, or it may be terminated earlier than this if you want.

To create a beta app for Windows Phone, follow the normal store procedure (as detailed in the Submitting Your Game to the Store section below), but make sure to check the "Beta" option on the App info page, under More Options. Beta apps require a little less information that for full Store submissions, so you will find that not all of the steps detailed for the submission are required.

The Windows 8 Store doesn't currently provide a similar beta system. Instead, you are required to package up your app and send it (by e-mail, for example) to your testers. Once you have done this, you have little control as to how they use the app package. Consequently, make sure that you only send to people you trust, or provide sufficient restrictions into your beta app that it wouldn't matter if it is leaked to others.

The package build is initiated by opening your project in Visual Studio, ensuring that you have switched into Release mode, and then selecting Project ➤ Store ➤ Create App Packages from the Visual Studio's main menu. A window will appear asking if you want to build packages for the Windows Store. As we are creating the package for manual distribution this time, select No and click the Next button.

The next page will allow you to choose a location to save your application package. Choose an appropriate folder if the default location is unsuitable. The version number from the application manifest will be displayed and can be modified if needed. You also have the ability to automatically increment the revision part of the version number each time the package is created. Finally, the application architecture can be selected. This should normally be set to have just the Neutral option checked.

With your details entered, click the Create button to build the package. The project will compile and the output package will be created in the specified directory.

If you look at the output files that are produced, you will see that an .appxupload file has been created as well as a subdirectory containing more files. The .appxupload file is the file actually required for submission to the store, but we will ignore it for the moment. The files we're interested in are contained inside the subdirectory.

You will see a file in there with a .ps1 file extension. This is actually a PowerShell script file that contains all the commands required to install your app. The .ps1 file doesn't contain the app itself; these are contained in the other files in the same directory. You can send your app to someone else by zipping up this entire directory and sending it to your testers.

▓ **Tip**   Also within this directory, you will find a file with a .appx extension. This file is actually a .zip file with its extension changed, and it contains the entire contents of your application. If you want to take a look inside it to see exactly what you are sending to the Store, copy and rename it to have a .zip extension and open it with a Zip utility of your choosing. You can then explore this to see the files that are inside.

In order for your testers to install, they will need to unzip the files you have sent them and then right-click on the `.ps1` file. From the menu that appears, they can select Run with PowerShell and then follow the instructions. Once the process is complete, the application icon should appear on their Start screen. This will only work in other copies of Windows 8, of course!

It's a very good idea to test your app via this method yourself prior to distributing to beta testers or submitting to the store. This can be done by finding your application's icon in the Start screen, right-clicking it, and selecting to uninstall it. Then install the app via the `.ps1` file and check that it works. This will run the app in the same configuration as it would be after installing from the store. If you experience any problems here, you will need to fix them prior to Store submission.

Automated Application Testing

There is one final pair of tools at your disposal for testing prior to submission (and indeed at any time during application development). Microsoft provides automated testing tools for each of the platforms. For Windows 8, this is the Application Certification Kit (or *ACK* for short); for Windows Phone, there is the Windows Phone Store Test Kit.

Each of these tools checks your app configuration and runs it to monitor its behavior. It checks for things like manifest misconfigurations, application startup time, responsiveness, and unexpected crashes. At the end of the monitoring process, a report is generated to show you any problems that were encountered.

To launch the ACK for Windows 8 apps, build an application package as described in the previous section. As long as you have Visual Studio configured for Release mode, you will be prompted to run the ACK once the package has been created. It may take a few minutes for the testing to be completed. The app may launch and close multiple times during this process. You should not interact with the app at all while this is taking place. Ideally, you should leave the computer alone entirely until it has finished.

If you find any failure messages in the resulting reporting, you should check these carefully to identify their cause. Such failures are likely to result in your app failing certification when submitted to the store.

To run automated testing for Windows Phone apps, open your app project in Visual Studio, switch to Release mode, and build the project so that its updated `.xap` file is created. Once this is done, select Open Store Test Kit from the Project menu. A new Store Test Kit page will appear to allow you to control the test process.

For full details on using the Store Test Kit, take a look at `http://tinyurl.com/wpstoretestkit`, where Microsoft's online help for the tool can be found.

Submitting Your Game to the Store

So, you are finally ready to submit your game to the Store. The initial submission can take a little time, but should be fairly painless. The process varies between platforms, so once again we'll look at these one by one, but first a quick note regarding rating certificates for games.

Rating Certificates

Due to local laws, games cannot be submitted to some countries without a valid game rating certificate. At the time of writing, the countries affected by this are Korea, Brazil, Russia, and Taiwan. Obtaining such certificates is possible but may be difficult and time-consuming. If you wish to try, you can use Microsoft's documentation at `http://tinyurl.com/storegameratings` as a starting point. It details exactly what is required for each country and provides links to help obtain the required certificates.

If you wish to include these countries in your Store submission, it's a good idea to submit without these countries to begin with. Once your game is accepted into the store and made available to the rest of the world, update it to add the restricted countries. This means that your game is available to the rest of the world during the certification process rather than being entirely absent from the store.

Submitting a Game to the Windows Store

When you are ready to submit to the store, the first thing to do is ensure that Visual Studio is set to build in Release mode. Once you've done this, select `Project > Store > Create App Packages` from the Visual Studio main menu.

A Create App Packages window will appear to guide you through the submission process. The first thing to do is to confirm that you wish to build packages to upload to the Windows Store and click the Sign In button.

Now you will be prompted to sign in to the Store with your Microsoft account details (previously known as a Windows Live account). Enter your account details and click the Sign In button.

Now the window will connect to your Store account and download a list of existing application names that have been reserved. If you have not already reserved a name for your game, click the Reserve Name link to open the Store in your web browser. Names must be reserved within your Store account before applications can be uploaded. When you do upload, you will do so against one of these reserved app names.

▓ **Tip**   You can reserve a name for your application in advance of uploading it. Reserved names will be held for up to one year, after which they will expire and will need to be reserved again. App names must be unique within the Store, so if you have a name in mind, reserve it as soon as you can!

Once your name is reserved, return back to Visual Studio and you should find the name now appears within the list of app names. Select the app name and click the Next button to continue.

The next stage is to build your finished package ready to upload, which is just the same step as you will have gone through if you built a package for the Windows Application Certification Kit. Ensure that your version number is set correctly and that you have the Neutral architecture selected. Then click the Create button to build the package for submission. Upon completion, click the Close button to return to Visual Studio.

At this stage, the application submission has been created within the Store and the app package has been uploaded, but the submission is not yet complete. The remainder of the submission is carried out within the Windows Store Dev Center in your web browser. The easiest way to access this is to select `Project ➤ Store ➤ Open Developer Account...` from the menu in Visual Studio, which will open your app list in the browser.

You will see your app listed as being *in progress*, with a status of *Incomplete*. To continue with the submission process, click the Edit link next to your app. A series of steps will then appear, all of which need to be worked through in order to complete the application submission. These pages include steps for you to upload your game's graphic files, to provide information about the game, and to set how it should be made available.

Most of these pages should be fairly self-explanatory, but, if you need any additional guidance, Microsoft has published a reference guide to everything that is involved. You can take a look at the guide itself at `http://tinyurl.com/winappsubmission`.

Among the steps that you will follow will be one that allows you to specify which markets your game will be available in, how much it will cost (if anything), and whether a trial mode exists within the application. Be sure to enter all the values carefully and remember to exclude those countries that require rating certificates unless you have the required certificates available.

My overriding advice for submitting to the Store is to *take your time*. If you make any mistakes in the process, change your mind about the graphics, decide that the description is wrong, spot glaring spelling mistakes, or find any other fault with the data you have provided, it will take time to fix these and may require you to wait until your submission is certified before any edits can be made. It's much more efficient to get everything right first time.

Once the submission process is complete, the next step is to wait patiently for a few days. Microsoft's stated verification goal is around five days, so the wait won't be too long. The submission status will be updated as it works its way through each of Microsoft's test areas, and it will eventually reach a state of having passed or failed the submission process.

If your application passes verification, congratulations! Your game is now available for download through the Store. If it fails, don't be discouraged; you should receive a detailed failure report that tells you *exactly* what was wrong. If you correct everything that the report identifies, your application should pass verification the next time you submit. Fingers crossed!

Submitting a Game to the Windows Phone Store

The submission process begins for Windows Phone games by first building the app ready for submission. Make sure that you have your project set to build in Release mode and that Visual Studio is configured to target the ARM platform, not the x86 platform. If either of these options is configured incorrectly, your submission will fail certification. Once you're ready, select Build ➤ Build Solution from Visual Studio's main menu.

The compiled application will be found inside your project's directory, in the bin/WindowsPhone/ARM/Release subdirectory. The app will be contained in a file that matches your project name, with a file extension of .xap. This file contains everything your app needs to run. It is the one and only file that we need to upload to the store.

▓ **Tip** The compiled .xap file is actually a .zip file with its extension changed. If you want to take a look inside it to see exactly what you are sending to the store, copy and rename it to have a .zip extension and then you can explore its contents with a Zip utility of your choosing.

Before you can submit to the Store, you will need to have your Microsoft account (previously known as a Windows Live account) set up, have applied to join the Store, and have had your application verified. All these steps were required just to deploy your games to a real phone, however, and we covered them back in Chapter 1. Hopefully, they should all be long taken care of by now.

To begin the submission process, visit http://dev.windowsphone.com in your browser and click the Dashboard link. Within the dashboard, you will find a Submit App link. Click this to get started.

You will now be guided through a series of pages that allow you to upload the game itself and its graphic files, and to provide information about the game and how it should be made available. Most of these should be fairly self-explanatory, but, if you need any additional guidance, Microsoft has published a reference guide to everything that is involved at http://tinyurl.com/wp8appsubmission.

Among the steps that you will follow will be one that allows you to specify which markets your game will be available in, how much it will cost (if anything), and whether a trial mode exists within the application. Be sure to enter all the values carefully and remember to exclude those countries that require rating certificates unless you have the required certificates available.

The final option within the submission allows you to specify whether you want the application to be automatically published to the Store as soon as it passes verification or whether you want to publish it manually. Normally, automatic publication is preferable, but, if you need to time the release to coincide with some external event, you can elect to publish it when you are ready.

Just as with the Windows 8 submission, my overriding advice for submitting to the Store is to *take your time*. Make sure that you don't make any mistakes during the submission as it may be time-consuming to fix these afterwards. Windows Phone submissions should also reach a pass or fail state within around five days. If it fails, a failure report will be provided to help you identify and resolve the problems.

Keeping Track of Your Published Apps

Once your app has passed certification and been released into the Store, there are several things you can do to track its progress. All of these are accessed via the Windows Store Dashboard or the Windows Phone Store Dashboard as appropriate.

One of the most useful things that you can find is the list of reviews and ratings that have been left for your game. The reviews often contain very useful feedback, which you can use to improve future versions of your game. The reviews may also contain unfair and/or negative comments, no matter how good your game is. Be prepared for this and try not to take it to heart! Use the reviews as a way to learn and improve, not as a personal judgment on yourself as a developer.

Unfortunately, there isn't a way to reply or respond to reviewer comments at the moment. Hopefully, this is something that will be addressed in the future.

▓ **Tip** For Windows Phone games, an excellent free app is available for your phone to help you keep track of your app's statistics and reviews. The app is named Dev Center and can be downloaded from the Windows Phone Store.

Other reports are available to show you the number of downloads, the number of purchases, how much money you have made through sales, how many app crashes have been logged, and many other things. Spend some time exploring all the information that is available.

Submitting Revisions

The best apps and games are those that are regularly updated and improved. If you want to build a loyal and appreciative user base, you should consider making updates to your game, whether adding new features or fixing bugs that have been identified.

Making an application update is essentially just the same as for creating a new application, except that the process is initiated in a different way. For a Windows Store app, click the app's Details link from the Store Dashboard, and then click the Create new release button and follow the instructions. For a Windows Phone app, click the Apps link on the Windows Phone Dev Center Dashboard, click your app's name, and then click the Update App link.

Each revision will need to be completely recertified, just as was needed for the original submission. This takes just as long as for the initial submission, so you may need to wait again for up to about five days for this process to complete.

Once your revision passes successfully through the certification process and becomes available in the Store, existing users of the game will be automatically notified so that they can obtain the update. There is no need for you to do anything to initiate this process.

Go Create!

The only thing you need to add to your toolset now is your imagination. There are huge opportunities for gaming on Windows 8 and Windows Phone 8, so let your creativity run free! I look forward to seeing many of your games appearing in the Stores in the future.

This completes our journey through gaming with MonoGame and brings us to the end of this book. I really hope you have enjoyed the ride and that you have found it useful and informative, but, more than anything, I hope that it inspires you to open Visual Studio and get started creating your own games.

Windows 8 and Windows Phone 8 are exciting and powerful environments for gaming, with massive potential for creating original and inventive gaming experiences. Let your imagination run free. Who knows where it will take you? I wish you many happy days of writing games!

Please do let me know about the games that you create. I would also love to hear any feedback that you have about this book. You can contact me by sending e-mail to adam@adamdawes.com or on Twitter @AdamDawes575.

Summary

- The Stores have inbuilt support for trial modes within games and applications. This allows users to download a limited version of your game and give it a try prior to purchasing. It is a very good idea to include a trial mode so that people know what they are going to be buying. Many users will simply ignore your app if it doesn't have a trial mode.

- You should detect whether your game is in trial mode when it launches or activates and cache the value for later use. Querying the .NET API to determine this information can be a slow operation, which will be very noticeable inside an animated game.

- Windows 8 apps will fire a `LicenseChanged` event should the user purchase while your app is active. You should ensure that your code responds to this and updates your game functionality accordingly. Windows Phone apps will always be relaunched when they are reactivated after the user visits the store, so the updated trial state can be detected at this stage.

- For Windows 8 apps, the purchase process can be simulated to ensure that everything is working properly. Windows Phone apps don't support the purchase simulation process, but it is possible to mock the process up fairly accurately.

- Make it as easy as possible for trial users to buy your app, offering direct access to the purchasing function. Don't risk buyers getting side-tracked while making their way back through the Store!

- All apps must pass through a *certification* process when they are submitted to the Store. This checks many aspects of your game including technical suitability (the app doesn't crash, performs acceptably, doesn't consume excessive memory, and so on) and content suitability (doesn't contain excessive violence or other prohibited content). All aspects of testing must pass before your app will make it into the Store.

- Windows 8 apps must work equally well on devices with touch screens, and on devices with mice and keyboards. Ensure that you test thoroughly in both of these hardware profiles. Use the simulator to check that the game works at all of the screen resolutions that the simulator offers. Test on a tablet device (preferably one with an ARM processor running Windows RT) to ensure that performance is acceptable.

- Windows Phone 8 apps should be tested on real hardware to ensure that the game performance is as expected as the emulator's performance is not representative of running on a real device. If you have used XAML controls in your game, ensure that everything appears correctly with both the light and dark themes activated.

- Adopt an approach to persuade users of your app to leave a review. This may be a periodic reminder for all users, or it may just target those that can be identified as regular users or buyers. Ensure that review prompts are not intrusive and can be permanently disabled.

- The Windows 8 Settings charm is a useful place for adding information and content for your game. If your game requires Internet access, you will be required to add a Privacy command to the Settings charm or your app will fail certification.

- Release details for your game are contained in the *application manifest*. These include details such as titles and descriptions, supported resolutions and orientations, icons and colors, and the application version.

- You should adopt a versioning scheme for your game so that both you and your users know exactly which version they are using. Ensure that users can easily find the version of the game when they are running it. For Windows 8 apps, this information is provided automatically via the Permissions command in the Settings charm.

- Before you begin your submission to the Store, you will need to create up to eight screenshots of your game. Ensure that these are enticing and representative of the game and are not modified in any way. Each platform has specific image size requirements that you will need to adhere to. The Windows simulator and the Windows Phone emulator both provide tools to simplify the task of obtaining screenshots.

- If possible, offer your game to others for beta testing. This can be achieved through the Store for Windows Phone games, or by sending a prebuilt package for Windows 8 games. This gives you a great opportunity to find bugs and gather feedback before releasing to the rest of the world.

- Windows 8 apps should be passed through the Windows Application Certification Kit prior to submission to the store. This will help to identify problems that may cause your submission to fail.

- For a small number of countries, games require rating certificates before they can be accepted into the store. It is a good idea to make your initial submission with these countries excluded, and then add them in after the game has been accepted into the store.

- Submission takes place via a series of information pages into which all the details of your game are entered. Once the submission is complete, the certification process begins, which may take up to five days to complete.

- Once your game has been published, you can keep track of it from the Store Dashboard. Various data feeds are available here, including user reviews and ratings, download and purchase counts, information on application crashes, and more.

- Application revisions and updates can be submitted as often as you wish, but these will again need to undergo the certification process prior to appearing in the Store.

Index

■ I, J

▒ T, U

▓ V

■ X, Y, Z